ELEMENTARY READING INSTRUCTION

Sponsored by the
International Reading Association

Elementary Reading Instruction
SELECTED MATERIALS

❖❖❖❖❖❖❖❖❖❖

edited by

Althea Beery

Thomas C. Barrett

William R. Powell

ALLYN AND BACON, INC.
BOSTON

© Copyright 1969 by Allyn and Bacon, Inc., 470 Atlantic Avenue, Boston. All rights reserved. No part of this book may be reproduced in any form, or by any means, without permission in writing from the publishers.

Printed in the United States of America.

Library of Congress Catalog Card Number: 71-76579

Second printing . . . May, 1970

PREFACE

The teacher in the elementary school responsible for developing literacy in children has a rewarding yet tremendous task. Ability to read is almost universally regarded as an essential tool for learning in school, for achieving the power to pursue knowledge independently, and for promoting personal enrichment and fulfillment. Learning to read remains a paramount curricular goal in spite of the emergence of many ways to secure information through media that may seem to be more novel and to make less demands on the young learner. The recognition of the importance of reading power has stimulated widespread comment in the public press, much of it critical of the methods and materials used in the elementary reading program. In addition to public criticism, the teacher is also faced with a bewildering array of programs, systems, practice materials and gadgets, some which purport to guarantee success for every child and others which offer opportunities to diversify and individualize instruction.

This volume of readings is planned to give direct help to the classroom teacher, not as a book of recipes, but as a collection of articles that furnish direction and reliable information on which to base decisions. The point of view of the compilers is that the teacher is a professional person who can read critically and can weigh competing approaches and procedures. Rather than presenting a single point of view, therefore, the volume brings together diverse programs which a school staff and individual teachers can evaluate and from which they can select and adapt content and techniques that fit the local situation and the individual needs of pupils.

This publication also affords a balanced, comprehensive coverage of the problems which classroom teachers encounter. The criteria used to select articles included the following:

1. What does reading involve?
2. What are emerging trends in the teaching of reading?
3. Which approaches to reading offer the best hope for initial and continued success in reading?
4. What implications for practice does current reading research offer?
5. What is relevant to the classroom teacher's task?
6. How can achievement be measured?

The field of reading instruction is a dynamic one with many ideas competing for acceptance: When should children be taught to read? What are the best approaches to reading? What are the pros and cons of programed instruction, ITA, linguistics, phonics, individualized instruction, the language-experience method, the use or modification of basic reading systems, or some other? What is the best way to organize a school or a class to promote progress in reading? What is meant by critical reading? How important is the current impetus to establish a library in every elementary school? These represent some of the questions teachers ask themselves and are frequently asked by parents. The articles included give thoughtful opinion or evidence on these and many other topics to help teachers keep pace with developments in the field.

Educators as well as lay persons are concerned about the number of children who do not have sufficient power in reading to make it an effective learning tool. Teachers who work with children in the inner city often find them lacking in requisite skills. Coming from an environment with limited stimulation for learning to read or for the development of the language skills which underlie reading, these pupils often become slow and reluctant readers. Several articles in this book are devoted to this area. They indicate ways in which more appropriate goals, teaching techniques, and materials may be selected to meet the needs and interests of such pupils, as well as the extra resources that should be provided to ameliorate community and home conditions. Educators and society at large are demanding that, at all costs, every child with the capacity to learn be taught to read.

Elementary Reading Instruction is organized in five parts: *Foundations, The Teacher's Task, Components of Reading, Sequence and Organization,* and *Programs in Today's Schools.* Individual chapters deal with various aspects of each section. For example, under the components of reading there are three chapters: Word Skills—Perceptual Dimensions; Comprehension—Cognitive Dimensions; and Attitudes and Values—Affective Dimensions.

Each chapter contains several articles selected to give, within space limitations, as definitive and comprehensive a coverage of the chapter title as possible. Fortunately, the publications of the International Reading Association offer a rich choice for selection. Preference was given to current materials; most of the articles were published within the last six years. Many of the articles include references for those who wish to explore a topic further.

Elementary Reading Instruction will prove helpful to university and college instructors for use in undergraduate courses in reading, to local school personnel planning in-service workshops or faculty meetings, and to individual teachers wishing to keep abreast of present thinking in the field. While not addressed specifically to parents, administrators, or school board members, it can furnish them with a valuable overview of current problems and practices in the teaching of reading to elementary pupils.

To the authors who graciously gave permission for their articles to be included, the compilers express their deep appreciation. We wish also to acknowledge our debt to the officers of IRA and to the headquarters staff who furnished copies of the selected articles and secured permission for their use. We are grateful to the members of the organization who offered suggestions of articles to include. The responsibility for the final selection, however, rests solely with the three compilers.

Althea Beery
Thomas C. Barrett
William R. Powell

CONTRIBUTORS

ROACH VAN ALLEN—University of Arizona
RICHARD D. ARNOLD—University of Texas
A. STERL ARTLEY—University of Missouri
MARY C. AUSTIN—Western Reserve University
THOMAS C. BARRETT—University of Wisconsin
DOROTHY B. BECKETT—Hiram College
ALTHEA BEERY—Cincinnati, Ohio Public Schools
MILLARD H. BLACK—City Unified School District, Los Angeles, California
JOHN R. BORMUTH—University of Chicago
GERALD W. BREKKE—Gustavus Adolphus College
RICHARD W. BURNETT—University of Missouri at St. Louis
ALVINA TREUT BURROWS—New York University
J. RICHARD CHAMBERS—Boston University
S. ALAN COHEN—Yeshiva University
DAVID W. DARLING—University of New Mexico
WILLIAM Q. DAVIS—State University of New York at Potsdam
EMERALD DECHANT—Fort Hays Kansas State College
KATRINA DE HIRSCH—Columbia University, Presbyterian Medical Center
DOLORES DURKIN—University of Illinois
DONALD D. DURRELL—Boston University
THOMAS J. EDWARDS—Science Research Associates
WILLIAM ELLER—State University of New York at Buffalo
ROBERT EMANS—Ohio State University
CHARLES C. FRIES—Late Professor Emeritus, University of Michigan
MARIANNE FROSTIG—Marianne Frostig Center for Educational Therapy, Los Angeles
EDWARD FRY—Rutgers University
CHRISTINE B. GILBERT—Library School, C. W. Post College
GERALD G. GLASS—Adelphi University
J. P. GUILFORD—University of Southern California
FRANK J. GUSZAK—University of Texas
PRISCILLA HAYWARD—New York State Education Department
ARTHUR W. HEILMAN—Pennsylvania State University
ROBERT L. HILLERICH—Glenview, Illinois Public Schools
CHARLOTTE S. HUCK—Ohio State University
MILDRED H. HUEBNER—Southern Connecticut State College
LYMAN C. HUNT, JR.—University of Vermont

HELEN HUUS—University of Missouri at Kansas City
SARAH M. IRVIN—Portland, Oregon Public Schools
SISTER MARY JULITTA, O.S.F.—Cardinal Stritch College, Milwaukee
JOSEPH P. KENDER—Lehigh University
MARTHA L. KING—Ohio State University
CARL A. LEFEVRE—Temple University
ROGER T. LENNON—Vice President, Test Department, Harcourt, Brace and World
HELENE M. LLOYD—New York City Public Schools
IRVING LORGE—Late Professor, Columbia University
CONSTANCE M. MCCULLOUGH—San Francisco State College
ARTHUR S. MCDONALD—Department of Education, Halifax, Nova Scotia
WALTER J. MCHUGH—California State College at Hayward
JOHN D. MCNEIL—University of California at Los Angeles
AMELIA MELNIK—University of Arizona
QUEENIE B. MILLS—University of Illinois
ROBERT E. MILLS—Mills Center, Fort Lauderdale, Florida
WILLIAM R. POWELL—University of Illinois
ELWOOD L. PRESTWOOD—Lower Merion School District, Pennsylvania
WALLACE RAMSEY—University of Missouri at St. Louis
VIRGINIA M. REID—Oakland, California Public Schools
VICTOR M. RENTEL—University of South Carolina
JEAN R. RICHARDSON—Mills Center, Fort Lauderdale, Florida
CARL SAILER—Jersey City State College
ROGER W. SHUY—Center for Applied Linguistics
NILA BANTON SMITH—San Fernando Valley State College
RUTH STRANG—Sandiford Professor, Ontario Institute for the Study of Education
STANFORD E. TAYLOR—Educational Development Laboratories
MILES A. TINKER—Professor Emeritus, University of Minnesota
SAMUEL WEINTRAUB—Indiana University
CAROL K. WINKLEY—Northern Illinois University
ROBERT C. ZILLER—University of Oregon

CONTENTS

Preface   *v*
Contributors   *viii*
Introduction   *1*

PART ONE
FOUNDATIONS

CHAPTER 1. THE MAJOR ASPECTS OF READING

Introduction   5
(1) The Reading Process and Its Ramifications—*Ruth Strang*   6
(2) Goals of the Reading Program: The Basis for Evaluation—
    Thomas C. Barrett   27
(3) Ends and Means: Developing Specific Objectives for Read-
    ing Instruction—*Victor M. Rentel*   35

CHAPTER 2. LINGUISTIC AND PSYCHOLOGICAL IMPLICATIONS

Introduction   43
(4) Reading Our Language Patterns: A Linguistic View—*Carl
    A. Lefevre*   44
(5) Structural Linguistics: Practical Teaching Suggestions—
    Sarah M. Irvin   52
(6) The Social Psychology of Reading—*Robert C. Ziller*   61
(7) Psychological Correlates of the Reading Process—*Katrina
    de Hirsch*   69

PART TWO
THE TEACHER'S TASK

*CHAPTER 3. CLASSROOM DIAGNOSIS AND CORRECTIONAL
         STRATEGIES*

Introduction   85
(8) The Classroom Teacher as a Diagnostician—*Richard W.
    Burnett*   86
(9) Classroom Methods in Correcting Reading Deficiencies in
    Elementary School—*Sister Mary Julitta*   94

(10) Evaluating Progress in Reading Through Informal Procedures—*Mary C. Austin and Mildred H. Huebner*   100

(11) How Useful Are Informal Reading Tests?—*Joseph P. Kender*   108

(12) Classroom Help for Children with Beginning Reading Problems—*A. Sterl Artley*   113

(13) Corrective Reading in the Classroom—*Marianne Frostig*

CHAPTER 4. CLASSROOM MANAGEMENT AND TEACHING TECHNIQUES

Introduction   128

(14) What Can I Do with the Other Groups While I Am Teaching One Group?—*Millard H. Black*   129

(15) Actual and Recommended Allotments of Time for Reading—*Gerald W. Brekke*   132

(16) Let's Get Variety in the Reading Program—*Virginia M. Reid*   136

(17) Report Cards and Parents—*Mary C. Austin*   141

CHAPTER 5. MATERIALS

Introduction   147

(18) Criteria for Selection of Reading Materials—*Elwood L. Prestwood*   149

(19) Vocabulary Control—*Samuel Weintraub*   153

(20) Phonics Materials: A Big Seller—*Dolores Durkin*   158

(21) What Do Publishers Mean by "Grade Level"?—*Robert E. Mills* and *Jean R. Richardson*   164

(22) New Data on Readability—*John R. Bormuth*   168

(23) Sources of Children's Books or Fitting the Book to the Child—*Christine B. Gilbert*   176

PART THREE
COMPONENTS OF READING

CHAPTER 6. WORD SKILLS—PERCEPTUAL DIMENSIONS

Introduction   183

(24) Extending the Sight Vocabulary—*J. Richard Chambers*   184

(25) Implications of Research on Children's Concepts—*Constance M. McCullough*   187

(26) Context Clues—*Robert Emans*   *197*
(27) When Two Vowels Go Walking and Other Such Things—
      Robert Emans   *208*
(28) Which Accent Generalizations Are Worth Teaching?—
      Carol K. Winkley   *217*

CHAPTER 7. COMPREHENSION—COGNITIVE DIMENSIONS

Introduction   *226*
(29) Frontiers in Thinking That Teachers Should Know About
      —*J. P. Guilford*   *227*
(30) The Teacher's Task in the Development of Thinking—
      Irving Lorge   *235*
(31) Teacher Questioning and Reading—*Frank J. Guszak*   *242*
(32) The Formulation of Questions as an Instructional-
      Diagnostic Tool—*Amelia Melnik*   *251*
(33) Developing Critical Reading Power through Newspaper
      Reading—*Carl Sailer*   *258*
(34) Clustering Comprehension Skills to Solve Problems—
      Althea Beery   *264*

CHAPTER 8. ATTITUDES AND VALUES—AFFECTIVE DIMENSIONS

Introduction   *275*
(35) Reading Interest: A Function of the Law of Effect—
      William Eller   *276*
(36) Developing Interest and Taste in Literature in the Ele-
      mentary Grades—*Helen Huus*   *282*
(37) A Comprehensive Literature Program—*Charlotte S. Huck*   *289*
(38) Building Lifetime Reading Habits in an Individualized
      Reading Program—*Alvina Treut Burrows*   *299*
(39) Evaluating the Affective Dimension of Reading—*David
      W. Darling*   *303*

PART FOUR
SEQUENCE AND ORGANIZATION

CHAPTER 9. PRE-READING—EARLY READING

Introduction   *313*
(40) Philosophical Differences in Reading Concepts—*Dorothy
      B. Beckett*   *314*

(41) Discovering Reading Readiness—*John D. McNeil*   322
(42) Readiness Measures for Predicting Reading Achievement
      —*Samuel Weintraub*   329
(43) Studies in Reading Readiness—*Robert L. Hillerich*   334
(44) Perspectives: Teaching Young Children to Read—*Nila
      Banton Smith*   338
(45) Early Readers—Reflections After Six Years of Research—
      Dolores Durkin   347
(46) Let's Not Read So Soon! (Even Those Who Can)—
      Gerald G. Glass   353

CHAPTER 10. BEGINNING APPROACHES TO READING

Introduction   359
(47) How a Language-Experience Program Works—*Roach Van
      Allen*   361
(48) Philosophy of Individualized Reading—*L. C. Hunt, Jr.*   368
(49) Linguistic Approaches to First Grade Reading Programs—
      Charles C. Fries   372
(50) Phonics Emphasis Approaches—*Arthur W. Heilman*   383
(51) Programed Instruction and Automation in Beginning Read-
      ing—*Edward Fry*   400
(52) Why an Eclectic Approach in Reading Instruction?—
      Emerald Dechant   413

CHAPTER 11. PROGRESS TOWARD READING MATURITY

Introduction   421
(53) Effective Study—Its Nature and Nurture—*A. Sterl Artley*   422
(54) Patterns of Writing in Different Subject Areas—*Nila
      Banton Smith*   434
(55) Reading Instrument Usage—*Stanford E. Taylor*   446
(56) Devices to Improve Speed of Reading—*Miles A. Tinker*   453
(57) Flexibility in Reading—*Arthur S. McDonald*   459

PART FIVE
PROGRAMS IN TODAY'S SCHOOLS

CHAPTER 12. ADMINISTRATIVE ORGANIZATION FOR READING

Introduction   469
(58) The Nature of Individual Differences—*William R. Powell*   470

(59) Factors Affecting the Organization of Elementary School Programs—*Walter J. McHugh*   483

(60) A Conclusive Look at the Caring for Individual Differences in Reading—*Wallace Ramsey*   486

(61) Pupil-Team Learning: Objectives, Principles, Techniques— *Donald D. Durrell*   497

CHAPTER 13. READING FOR DISADVANTAGED AND URBAN PUPILS

Introduction   503

(62) Learning Problems in Cultural Deprivation—*Thomas J. Edwards*   505

(63) Some Conclusions About Teaching Reading to Disadvantaged Children—*S. Alan Cohen*   512

(64) An Experimental Reading Program for Disadvantaged Children Learning English as a Second Language—*Richard D. Arnold*   516

(65) Starting A Reading Program for Speakers of Sub-Group Dialects—*Roger W. Shuy*   522

(66) Progress in Developmental Reading for Today's Disadvantaged—*Helene M. Lloyd*   529

(67) The Preschool-Disadvantaged Child—*Queenie B. Mills*   536

CHAPTER 14. MEASUREMENT AND EVALUATION OF READING ACHIEVEMENT

Introduction   544

(68) Functional Use of Standardized Reading Tests—*William Q. Davis*   545

(69) Evaluating Diagnostic Reading Tests—*Priscilla Hayward*   552

(70) What Can Be Measured?—*Roger T. Lennon*   558

(71) New Developments in the Evaluation of Critical Reading —*Martha L. King*   572

Index   583

INTRODUCTION

For several years the International Reading Association has granted permission to a number of compilers and editors of books of articles on reading to use materials which first appeared in one of our numerous publications. At times over the years, the Board of Directors has considered publishing its own book of readings, but because of so many other important tasks, such a project was never brought to fruition. During my term of office as president, Mr. John Peters of Allyn and Bacon approached me and suggested that IRA compile a book of articles on elementary reading instruction, and that Allyn and Bacon would be willing to publish such a book. I brought the matter to the attention of the Board of Directors and they decided that we should enter into a contractual agreement with Allyn and Bacon. It was agreed that a committee of three, chosen from the membership of IRA, would be asked to compile the articles and edit the book. The Board would serve as an advisory group.

Dr. Althea Beery, who was then Director of Elementary Education in the Cincinnati Public Schools, was the logical choice for Senior Editor and chairman of the committee. Her broad background, her open mind, her ability to work with people, and her twinkling sense of humor would be compatible ingredients for the successful completion of such a project. Dr. Thomas Barrett, Associate Professor, Department of Curriculum and Instruction of the University of Wisconsin, and Dr. William Powell, Director of the Center for Reading Research and Instruction of the University of Illinois, were asked to complete the team because of their background in elementary education and their wide knowledge of research and trends in the field. Not only have these team members worked diligently over the past year, but, as I have observed, they have also stimulated one another and helped each other find the major contributions that would best reflect the framework they chose for the book. Their viewpoint, and one in which I heartily share, is reflected in a statement in the Preface where they indicate that they have brought together diverse ideas, so that the teacher, who is a professional person, may read critically and make his own decisions.

I am sure this book, with its important articles and the succinct introductory comments of the compilers, will meet the needs of those interested in reading instruction at the elementary level.

H. Alan Robinson, President, 1967–1968
International Reading Association

Part One
Foundations

Chapter 1.   The Major Aspects of Reading

Chapter 2.   Linguistic and Psychological Implications

Chapter 1

THE MAJOR ASPECTS OF READING

INTRODUCTION

One of the important problems confronting teachers of reading is the need for a rationale which undergirds the reading program. Such a rationale should come from what is known about the reading process and should answer the question: What is reading? Moreover, it should provide a point of departure for the development of the broad goals and the specific behavioral objectives which structure and give direction to the learning activities and evaluation techniques intrinsic to the reading program.

Although the articles in Chapter 1 will not resolve this problem entirely, they will provide a reasonable beginning for its resolution. In the first selection, for example, Strang deals with the reading process and its relationship to products of reading, prerequisites for reading, and teaching procedures. She provides insight and structure to the reading process, and in so doing, she provides a very useful paradigm which teachers of reading can use to analyze their instructional programs. The article by Barrett illustrates how an operational definition of reading can provide the basis for the goals of the reading program and how the goals interact and interrelate with the learning experiences and the evaluation techniques to be employed. Rentel, in the final selection, provides a very helpful discussion of the considerations one must be aware of when he develops specific objectives for reading instruction. His examples and illustrations are practical and should be useful to all teachers of reading.

In general, then, Chapter 1 deals with three fundamental questions. What is reading? How might the goals for the reading program relate to a rationale for or a definition of reading? How should specific behavioral objectives for reading be formulated?

(1) THE READING PROCESS
AND ITS RAMIFICATIONS*

Ruth Strang

Too often, I'm afraid, I talk like the woman whose husband wanted to get a divorce. The judge asked him, "What is the trouble?" "Oh, my wife just talks and talks and talks," he said. "What does she talk about?" asked the judge. "She doesn't say," the husband replied.

Sometimes, too, like the nurse in "Romeo and Juliet," I'm afflicted with total recall. Even after all these years, I have not learned what a French literary critic described as "the art of not saying everything." To include only the most relevant ideas is in line with the newer emphasis on composition which seems to be, not on sentence structure as presented by linguists, but on logic and rhetoric as set forth by Aristotle and Plato. It was the search for structure in the broad field of reading theory and practice that led me to attempt a synthesis of related aspects.

Let us start, as all effective reading instruction should, with the individual.

Marie is fifteen years old and in the ninth grade. She comes from a non-English speaking home. Her verbal IQ on the WISC is 81; her performance IQ, 99; and her total IQ, 88. Her reading achievement is far below her potential mental ability. On three silent reading tests her grade scores varied from 4.7 to 5.3. On the Gray Oral Reading Test, her grade equivalent was 4.0. This is the information about Marie that is available on the cumulative record. It tells us nothing about the processes by which she acquires—or fails to acquire—meaning from the printed page, nor about environmental conditions that may facilitate or inhibit her progress.

To understand how students read, we need a framework, a paradigm, a pattern that encompasses the major or contributory factors. If we focus on the reading process per se, we immediately see that it is a factor of the reader's goals, the degree to which he possesses or has acquired prerequisites for learning, and the effectiveness of the teaching procedures to which he is subjected. This broad, complex view of

*Reprinted from *Invitational Addresses*, 1965, pp. 49–73, by permission of the author and the International Reading Association.

reading may be discussed under four main headings: product, prerequisites, process, and procedures.

PRODUCT

Under product, we have included the main competencies, results, or goals that are to be achieved. These include (a) vocabulary—many words recognized instantly at sight; (b) word recognition skills gained through a systematic use of context clues, grapheme-phoneme correspondences, structural analysis, and the dictionary; and (c) comprehension—ability to derive meaning from words in sentences, paragraphs, chapters, and larger units. These abilities enable the individual to "read the lines."

However, the mature reader must do more than get the literal meaning of a passage. He must be able to interpret the author's thought, and to make critical judgments, evaluations, and inferences. This is "reading between the lines." "Reading beyond the lines" involves drawing conclusions, forming generalizations, and applying the ideas gained from reading. The end result of reading is the contribution that it makes to personal development and social welfare.

Of the four categories, the product has been studied most extensively, largely by means of tests. Of the 94 items in Traxler's comprehensive list of reading tests,[1] by far the largest number were silent reading tests of speed, vocabulary, sentence and paragraph comprehension. Next in order of frequency were tests of readiness, measures of study habits and skills, and diagnostic tests—ten of each type. There were seven oral reading tests. There was only one test of "reading capacity," library orientation, listening comprehension, dictionary skills, and logical reasoning. Although additional tests have appeared since Traxler's list was published, there is still a serious lack of instruments to measure the reader's ability to organize ideas while reading, to recognize the author's purpose, and to engage in critical, creative, and interpretive reading.

Several new tests may prove to be valuable supplements to tests of intelligence. In grades three, five, and seven, Braun[2] found a test of

---

[1]Ruth Strang, Constance M. McCullough and Arthur E. Traxler, *The Improvement of Reading.* New York: McGraw-Hill Book Company, 1961, pp. 352–359.

[2]Jean S. Braun, "Relation between Concept Formation Ability and Reading Achievement at Three Developmental Levels," *Child Development,* 34 (September, 1963), pp. 675–682.

concept formation to be more closely related to reading achievement than tests of mental maturity. The Cloze test proved superior to multiple choice tests as a measure of difficulties in comprehension.[3]

More emphasis is being placed upon informal or teacher-made tests, and upon the practice of making continuous appraisal and diagnosis while teaching.

From concern with reading status or product we often move directly to teaching procedures, with the result that we neglect a very important factor—the degree to which the student possesses or has acquired certain prerequisites for success in reading.

PREREQUISITES

Certain prerequisites underlie both product and process. Holmes[4] called these "sub-strata factors." He studied the relation of variables to high school students' reading speed and comprehension. Employing a technique of factor analysis, he grouped these separate factors into patterns or clusters. Most closely related to reading "power" were four factors: verbal analogies, vocabulary in isolation, vocabulary in context, and auding or listening comprehension—each of which contributed 16 per cent to the power of reading variance.

Other factors exerted lesser degrees of influence. But 25 per cent of the variance remained unaccounted for by all the factors put into the factor-analysis hopper. It is possible that such imponderables as the individual's value-system, his self-concept, his purpose or "set," and other motivations may be among the sub-strata factors that affect his reading process as well as what he reads and why he reads.

Reading difficulties have also been attributed to many other factors. Among these are physical defects, especially visual and auditory; retarded development in visual and auditory perception and discrimination; and neurological dysfunction or minimal brain damage. Lack of previously acquired knowledge and skills and the experience of repeated failure in reading also have a cumulative negative effect on the child's subsequent progress.

Several of these prerequisites deserve more detailed consideration:

[3]John Bormuth, "Cloze as a Measure of Readability," in *Reading as an Intellectual Activity* (J. Allen Figurel, Ed.). New York: Scholastic Magazines, 1963, pp. 131–134.

[4]Jack A. Holmes and Harry Singer, "Theoretical Models and Trends toward More Basic Research in Reading," *Review of Educational Research*, 34 (April, 1964), pp. 131–133.

prereading experiences, specific mental abilities, linguistic factors, listening comprehension, and concepts and values.

Readiness for Reading. Prereading experiences are a prelude to success in beginning reading. From the earliest years, the child's normal curiosity can be fostered, his sense of trust developed, his openness to experiences encouraged. He should come to school eager to learn to read. He should have the ability to understand and speak 2000-3000 words. He should have learned to distinguish small differences in word sounds. Without being specifically taught, he should have learned that meaning depends partly on the order, intonation, and stress with which words are spoken. It should not be necessary to "teach your baby to read." Children who have a rich background of prereading experience tend to catch up quickly with other children of the same ability who have had pre-school reading instruction.

However, many children come to school without having had the prereading experiences just described. These are children from educationally and culturally disadvantaged homes, and from homes where a language other than English is spoken. For them, beginning reading may prove difficult. They may fail in their first attempts to learn to read. This initial failure undermines their self-confidence. They become afraid to try. Their parents may respond by acting disappointed or punishing them. Their teachers may express disapproval. Their classmates may ridicule them. Any of these responses may intensify their concept of themselves as children who can't learn to read.

Pilot studies in New York City, at Peabody College, and in other centers have demonstrated the value of preschool or kindergarten prereading experiences. Programs under "Project: Head Start" are now underway in many communities.

Readiness is a prerequisite for any child who is about to take the next step in the sequential development of his reading ability.

Mental Abilities. Although individual intelligence tests are given less weight than formerly, they are still important diagnostic instruments. Analysis of subtest scores and patterns widens their usefulness and enhances their diagnostic value. The individual's total score or IQ often conceals wide differences in his mental abilities. A retarded reader may be weak on certain subtests, and strong on others. One of my doctoral students, Eldon Ekwald, is studying the relationship between the WISC subtests and certain reading abilities.

Retarded readers generally, though not always, score higher on the performance section than on the verbal section of the Wechsler

Intelligence Scale for Children (WISC) and the Wechsler Adult Intelligence Scale (WAIS). This discrepancy may be due to an inherent lack of verbal ability; to environmental, emotional, or other factors that are inhibiting the functioning of verbal ability; or to other circumstances that have prevented the individual from learning to read. To be significant, however, the difference between the verbal and the performance scores should be fairly large because the performance IQ has a general tendency to run higher than the verbal.

Of still more diagnostic value are the profiles of sub-test scores. These show graphically the patterns of strength and weakness in the individual's mental functioning. Each represents some mental process involved in reading that *may* be improved by practice and instruction.

Studies of the relationship between reading ability and scores on the sub-tests of the Wechsler have shown a characteristic pattern for retarded readers. They tend to score low on the sub-tests of Information and Arithmetic, and also relatively low on Digit Span and Coding. On Picture Arrangement, Block Design, Picture Completion, and Object Assembly, retarded readers often score relatively high. Conflicting results were reported on the Vocabulary sub-test.

Each sub-test might well be examined for its significance to the teaching of reading. A low score on the Information test might indicate lack of mental ability to gain information as normal children do. Or it might reflect lack of reading ability—the means by which older children in our culture gain much of their information. Both the Information and the Arithmetic sub-tests are closely related to school learning.

Since the Coding sub-test involves visual discrimination and memory abilities that are also required in decoding printed words, we should expect retarded readers to score low.

The Digit Span sub-test requires a mental ability somewhat similar to that involved in getting the meaning of a sequence of words arranged in a sentence. A low score on this sub-test may indicate that the individual has a short attention span, difficulty in concentration, or the habit of thinking slowly and reacting slowly to any stimulus that involves visual motor skills.

The two sub-tests on which retarded readers generally score relatively high—Block Design and Picture Completion—measure the subject's response to stimuli that are always at hand. These tasks are less abstract than those set by other sub-tests in the WISC. Poor readers, as a group, tend to approach a learning situation in a more concrete manner than do good readers; they are less able to handle abstractions.

Analysis of any test of mental maturity indicates strengths and weaknesses in areas that are often associated with reading disability. Strengths can be developed; weaknesses remedied. To improve visual-motor ability, the Frostig and the Kephart programs are useful. To increase visual and auditory discrimination, teachers give children practice in recognizing details in pictures, and in distinguishing similar forms, letters, and words. Older pupils may be helped to develop the mental abilities that are prerequisite to mature reading by using the Thurstone exercises published by Science Research Associates.

Since reading tasks that resemble other school instruction are often associated with negative attitudes toward the teacher, toward school, and toward reading, we try to make remedial work as different from regular school instruction as possible. We use concrete, multi-sensory approaches. For example, we use word, phrase, and sentence cards to build sentences and paragraphs. Since retarded readers are weak in information, we build up their reservoir of meanings through avenues that require no reading pictures, trips, discussions, and listening to stories and articles read aloud.

Thus examination of the mental processes of our readers enables us to find appropriate methods and materials to build the prerequisites for success in reading. Bearing in mind the characteristic patterns of retarded readers, we can study individual profiles to observe deviations that may have special significance.

Linguistic Factors. Linguists put primary emphasis on the spoken language. They call attention to the meanings conveyed in speech by pauses, by differences in pitch and stress, and by intonation and rhythm. Although listening and speaking come first in a child's language development, are prerequisite to reading, and even though there is scientific evidence that vocal cords move very slightly even in rapid reading, we would question the statement by some linguists that the reader must first reconstruct the spoken sound of a printed sentence before he can comprehend its meaning.[5] This would seem to be a slow. laborious process that would be incompatible with rapid reading. Is it not possible for the mature reader to make a direct association between the printed words and the author's meaning? It would seem that rapid readers achieve speed through clue reduction, and that their reading vocabulary exceeds their speaking vocabulary.

A related factor that linguists emphasize as a prerequisite to reading

---

[5]John B. Carroll, "The Analysis of Reading Instruction: Perspectives from Psychology and Linguistics," in *Theories of Learning and Instruction.* The Sixty-third Yearbook of the National Society for the Study of Education, Part I. Chicago: University of Chicago Press, 1964, p. 338.

for meaning is an understanding of sentence structure, i.e., syntactic construction—the meanings conveyed by various arrangements of words in English sentences. It is their contention that knowledge of these grammatical meanings combines with vocabulary knowledge to unlock the full linguistic meaning of a selection. Children should learn to think of sentences as constructions within constructions, rather than as strings of separate words. Comprehension in reading does depend upon one's capacity to use the English language, as well as upon one's familiarity with the vocabulary of the area of knowledge with which the passage is concerned.

Listening Comprehension. The third cluster of factors that Holmes and Singer found to be significantly related to reading speed and power may be designated as ability to comprehend the meaning of a passage when it is read aloud. Listening with understanding carries over into reading for meaning. Tests of listening comprehension are useful in appraising reading potential, and training in listening has been found to contribute to reading improvement.

Value Systems, Motivation, and Self-concept. These three are interrelated. The desire to read is a resultant of present need, the push of the past, and the pull of the future.

For the little child, desire for approval by teachers and parents is a strong motivation. Intrinsic interest in the content is a more permanent life-time motivation. A specific need to fill out an application blank for a part-time job, to get a driver's license, or to pass the Army classification tests, often spurs a previously indifferent teenager "to get down to work on this reading business." When asked why he wanted to read better, one slow learner gave these reasons: "So no one will laugh at me, so as not to be stupid, so no one will cheat me." In his study of the nature of mature reading, William S. Gray[6] came to the conclusion that the mature reader "has acquired many compelling motives for reading and focuses his attention on the meaning of what he reads."

The most persistent and pervasive influences are the individual's self-concept and self-ideal. The self-concept may be predictive of, a cause of, or a result of reading achievement. In a primary group, the children's self-concepts were, in general, more predictive of their reading achievement than were their scores on the Detroit Beginning First Grade Intelligence Test, which was given near the end of

---

[6]William S. Gray, "The Nature of Mature Reading," *The School Review*, LXII (October, 1954), p. 394.

Kindergarten.[7] On all age levels, evidence is accumulating about the relation between an individual's self-concept and his achievement in reading.

THE READING PROCESS

What do we really know about the chemistry, physiology, and psychology of the reading process? What kinds of thinking go on in a student's mind when he reads a short story, a popular article, a textbook in science or history? How does he distinguish the main ideas and the supporting details? What associations does he make between what he reads and what he already knows? What kind of questions does he ask? What reasoning takes place? Does he comprehend better when reading aloud or silently? By what process does a child learn to read, and by what process does he continue throughout life to get meaning from the printed page? These important questions have been too long neglected. Satisfactory answers to them would help us determine what teaching methods to use. "The teaching process must take its clue from the learning process." If we can determine the learning process that the child uses, then we can try to create conditions that capitalize on the process.

The reading process may be explored on several levels—chemical, neurological, psychological, and behavioral.

The Chemical Level. Attempts are being made to assess the influence of body chemistry on the functioning of the nervous system, with special reference to reading. It seems possible that the child's nutrition and the stresses and strains that affect the chemistry of his body may modify synaptic transmission, which may govern the speed with which he reads.[8] However, Staiger[9] obtained no evidence that the administration of a single drug, deanol, improves the performance of retarded readers.

Neurological Processes. Much more extensive work has been done on neurological impairment with reference to severe reading disability. Rabinovitz has recognized two levels of neurological disorganization—

[7]William W. Wattenberg and Clare Clifford, "Relationship of the Self-concept to Beginning Achievement in Reading," *Child Development*, 35 (June, 1964), pp. 461–467.

[8]Donald E. P. Smith and Patricia M. Carrigan, *The Nature of Reading Disability.* New York: Harcourt Brace, and Co., 1959.

[9]Ralph C. Staiger, "Medicine for Reading Improvement," *Journal of Developmental Reading*, 4 (Autumn, 1960), pp. 12–16.

the minimal type that is difficult to diagnose, and the more easily recognized brain injury. Rabinovitz, de Hirsch, and others emphasize the importance of detecting neurological impairment at an early age; this will help to prevent the secondary emotional disturbance that often results from expecting the child to accomplish learning tasks that are too difficult for him.

The Psychological Process. This includes all that goes on from intake—the stimulus of the printed word—to output—the individual's response in thought, spoken or written words, or action. Output may take many forms: a mental image evoked by the passage, an answer to a question, a written summary, an illustration or drawing of a character or scene, a motor response to a direction.

The first stage is what Samuel Kirk has called *visual reception*, a process necessary to produce a clear visual impression. When the sensory impressions, visual and auditory, pass to the cerebral cortex, they combine with traces already imprinted on the nervous system to produce meaning. The words have now been perceived.

Perception is a learned process; it is not simple. It is affected by the attention, the previous experiences, the needs, and the expectancy of the individual. Important individual differences in perceptual style have been summarized by Helen Robinson.[10] Three types of perceivers may be distinguished: (1) those who see the word as a whole—these are the more able learners and better readers; (2) those who perceive word parts and tend to be preoccupied with unimportant details—these tend to be poor readers; and (3) those who focus on the sequence of letters in the word as a whole. Tachistoscopic studies have shown that familiar syllables and words can be recognized almost as quickly as individual letters, and short passages almost as readily as single words. As children mature, they perceive longer and more complex spelling patterns as units.

Conceptualization is the process by which the individual puts a single perception in a more inclusive setting. He relates the observed phenomenon to a class of objects or events. A new word is an "empty category" which can be invested with more and more meaning as new experiences enter the mind. This is the beginning of abstract thinking, and the basis for generalization.

There is a reciprocal relation between perception and conceptualiza-

[10]Helen M. Robinson, "Perceptual and Conceptual Style Related to Reading," in *Improvement of Reading Through Classroom Practice* (J. Allen Figurel, Ed.). Newark, Delaware: The International Reading Association, 1964, pp. 26–28.

tion. Concepts screen or filter impressions as they come into the mind. Thus the individual avoids dealing with a bewildering diversity of separate impressions. Traits extracted from perceptions are synthesized into concepts; concepts aid in the interpretation and organization of perceptions.

There is a positive relation between conceptual ability and reading proficiency. Children who fail in reading in the upper primary grades are often deficient in the ability to form concepts.

Research has clarified the first stages of the reading process—sensory impression, perception, conceptualization. What happens next is still a psychological "no-man's land." It has been explored primarily by speculation and by experiments in animal psychology.

It has been hypothesized that at *the higher level of association* there are patterns, schema, or circuits—memory sub-systems that are interrelated. These become larger and better organized when they are activated simultaneously. Thus the "whole perceiver" has an advantage over the "part perceiver." The individual's reading ability increases as the inter-facilitation of the working system improves. The word-by-word reader makes each association in isolation, rather than activating numerous connections within and among his memory patterns. The way a thing is learned helps to determine how it is used or applied.

Behavioral Level. This refers to the way individuals actually read. Do the gifted use different processes than the less able? Can the less able learn the more efficient methods, or are the methods they have evolved the best for them? These are fascinating questions to which we have no answers. Fortunately there are many ways in which we can gain insight into students' reading processes. These will be briefly described.

1. Observe the individual's eye movements. Since Buswell's[11] pioneer work on eye movements, more than one hundred similar studies have been reported. These studies explain how the eyes function during reading. We have learned that the span of recognition increases during the school years, but that even adults do not usually recognize more than two words per fixation. Eye movements may provide objective evidence that a reader is having difficulty, but introspection is necessary to show what the difficulty is. The eye movement camera does not show how the mind works. Consequently the informal "peephole method" of observing the reader's eye movements through a tiny hole in the center of the page he is reading is more useful in studying the reading

[11]Guy T. Buswell, "The Process of Reading," *The Reading Teacher*, 13 (December, 1959), pp. 108–114.

process. When he oscillates on a certain word or makes a regressive movement, the observer can stop him and ask what was going on in his mind at that point.

2. Observe how students respond to reading situations during the school day. During silent reading periods, the teacher may note the way the student approaches the reading assignment, and may chart his periods of attention and distraction. From the student's own questions and from his answers to questions that call for facts, generalizations, or interpretations, the teacher may draw inferences about his reading process. To verify these, the teacher will make further inquiries: "How did you happen to know this unfamiliar word?" "Why did you choose this answer rather than another?"

You will be amazed to see in what devious ways children acquire their vocabulary.

3. Ask the student to read a short selection aloud. As well as obtaining the usual diagnostic information afforded by oral reading, the teacher may also make inferences based on the student's facial expression, bodily movements, side remarks, and answers to questions involving comprehension.

For example, Marie, the ninth-grader whom we briefly described earlier, showed embarrassment when asked to read the paragraphs on the Gray Oral Reading Test. She made many errors in pronunciation, a few repetitions and substitutions, and two omissions. The repetitions seemed to stem from her struggle with the pronunciation of the words. On the easier paragraphs, her substitutions made sense. On the comprehensive questions, her difficulties became serious at the fifth paragraph when there was a marked increase in the number of key words that she did not know. The examiner could have learned more about her reading process by asking her to "tell what happened" when she pronounced a difficult word correctly, or made a given kind of error. This could have been done very easily while she was being examined in the individual testing situation, or immediately after the test had been administered according to standardized instructions.

4. Analyze the student's responses on standardized silent reading tests. Most of the diagnostic value of tests is lost when we neglect to study individual responses. This kind of study gave E. L. Thorndike[12] his famous insight into the reading process.

On the multiple choice questions of the vocabulary section of the

[12]E. L. Thorndike, "Reading as Reasoning: A Study of Mistakes in Paragraph Reading," *Journal of Educational Psychology*, 8 (June, 1917), pp. 323–332.

Metropolitan Intermediate Reading Test, Marie made many errors. She associated "glorious" with "independent" rather than "splendid." Perhaps to her, being independent was a glorious feeling. She marked "future" as the correct meaning of "ancient" instead of "old." Here she may have been misled by a vague conception of both words as associated with time. In marking "cause" instead of "result" as the meaning of "effect" she apparently reversed the meanings of two words commonly used together.

These are only tentative inferences that could be made from the analysis of a student's response on a multiple choice vocabulary test. To understand her actual thought processes, it would be necessary to ask her to try to explain how she arrived at the answers that she marked.

On the word discrimination part of the same test, we obtained further understanding of Marie's reading process. In the sentence "Be sure to ———— your raincoat" she selected "were" instead of "wear." Similarly, in many of the other items, she inserted a word that begins with the same letter as the correct word. Moreover, she showed little awareness of structural or grammatical clues to meaning; she chose "terminate" instead of "terminal" in the sentence, "The truck driver delivered the trunk to the railroad ————." From this section of the test, it was possible to infer that Marie tended to use initial consonants as her sole method of word attack, to be unconcerned about whether the word she chose made sense in the sentence, and to neglect grammatical clues to meaning.

In the paragraph reading section of the test, Marie seemed sometimes to show a similar disregard for appropriateness in her answers. Some of her choices were reasonable. She said "Some of the boats were probably not very *well made*," instead of *big*, which was considered the best answer. In another paragraph she supplied an idea of her own—"be in a parade," instead of the correct response, "greet visitors." In still another item, she gave overpotency to the word "bicycle" and made up her own conclusion instead of giving one that could be properly derived from the paragraph as a whole.

From the analysis of Marie's responses on this standardized test, we could make several tentative inferences about her reading behavior. She seemed to be misled by irrelevant or partial word associations. Apparently her only method of word attack was recognition of the initial letter. In reading a paragraph, she grasped at any straw that might enable her to make a response. It seemed as though her main concern was to mark some answer, whether correct or not.

5. Analyze the student's answer to the unstructured or creative-type question on an informal reading test. The question, "What did the author say?" may lead a student to reveal a great deal about his reading process. In studying responses to this type of question we find many different reading styles or approaches:

> Some students select a few isolated, unimportant, or irrelevant details.
> Some select the main ideas.
> Some select the main ideas, and cite supporting details.
> Some compose a brief, terse summary.
> Some offer a vague, general summary.
> Some tend to be carried away by their emotional response to the passage.
> Some tend to elaborate on details that are purely personal in significance or interest.
> Some use a passage as a springboard for creative thinking.
> Some make a well-organized summary of the author's pattern of thought.
> Some compose a full and accurate summary, and supplement it with their own reflection, and critical evaluations.

You will find examples of all of these reading styles in any heterogeneous class.

Although the unstructured question does not systematically measure the reader's comprehension of simple and definite facts, it may have the more important value of yielding insights into the student's thought processes; it may give a glimpse, as Paul Diederich admitted, into how the reader's mind works.

6. After students have read and completed the comprehensive questions on an informal group reading test or inventory, ask them several questions about the reading method that they used. Although many students, especially the less able readers, find it difficult or impossible to identify and describe their reading methods, others make revealing comments—such as the following, made by a boy in the eleventh grade:

Question: What did you do to get the main idea?
  "I thought about the main idea as I went along."
Q.:   What did you do to get important details?
  "I tried to correlate them with something I already knew."
Q.:   What did you do when you met a word you did not know?
  "I got the idea from the context. If it's a particularly puzzling one, I try to think up a Latin derivative."
Q.:   Do you like to read books of this kind? (a social studies text)

"No, I like to read plays and biographies. I got a big blast out of Van Loon's books. But, in general, I'm bored stiff by this type of stuff."

7. Ask them point blank: "How do you read a given assignment?" Many years ago I asked all the graduate students at Teachers College who had made straight *A* records to describe their methods of getting the author's thought. It became evident that these successful students used a variety of methods, some of which represented wide departures from those commonly recommended. The following is one student's description:

> I find my method of gaining ideas from reading is comparable to building a skyscraper. I first read the material through completely and quickly. On the way, I get a general outline or skeleton of the material. After this reading, I go back and start over more slowly. This time I argue my way through the book and fill in the skeleton which I built the first time. This seems to be my method for reading material which is rather difficult.[13]

Each reader appeared to have certain idiosyncratic methods that were helpful to him.

A similar procedure was used by Michaels[14] to ascertain what methods high school students used in reading four subjects—English, chemistry, plane geometry, the United States history. They were asked to describe their usual method of reading different kinds of assignments in each subject. Two representative responses will give us some idea of their study processes:

> First, I look at the question I am to answer. Then I will look up the subject in the index of a book and turn to the page that has the information on the question. I then read the information available in that book. I usually follow the same procedure with three to five other books. When I have finished these books, I take the most important information from each and begin to compose my answers to the questions.
> I always read my text first. Next, I select several books on the subject, noting their differences in details and general feeling about the subject. I then write what I feel are the essential ideas that I would be likely to

[13]Ruth Strang, Constance McCullough, and Arthur Traxler, *The Improvement of Reading.* New York: McGraw-Hill Book Company, 1961, p. 20.

[14]Melvin L. Michaels, "A Study of Similarities and Differences in Student Perceived Reading Difficulties in Selected Secondary School Subjects." Unpublished doctoral project, Teachers College, Columbia University, New York, 1963.

forget, and the major differences in the references in which I found "my" point of view.

8. Use an unstructured interview to gain understanding of how students have read certain selections and answered questions on them. In a study of interpretation of poetry, Letton[15] established the value of retrospective verbalization in identifying the reading processes. She recorded the subjects' oral interpretive responses in a systematic way, and identified differences in the introspective and retrospective verbalizations of high-level readers and low-level readers.

Using a similar technique, Rogers[16] studied the responses of three classes of eleventh grade students—high, average, and low—to a selected short story. She began with a completely unstructured approach—"Try to tell me everything you thought and everything you felt as you read this study. Just go ahead and talk about the story." This approach elicited a wide range of responses,[17] such as the following:

Response on a symbolic level:

> I thought as the story went along the symbolism of the snake became more clear and kind of stood for—for evil, perhaps. . . . But it also symbolizes something deeper. . . . I think it stands for all bad. The snake is black, and black always stands for bad. . . . The mate symbolizes something which all of us would want to find. . . .

Response on a literal level:

> In a way, I thought it was bad, you know, for the dog to kill the snake, but in a way he was doing what the boy's father told him to do. . . .

After the students had responded to this invitation to talk freely, Rogers[18] asked a number of specific questions such as these:

> What are the main events in this story?
> How did you discover these main events?

[15]Mildred Letton, "Individual Differences in Interpretive Responses to Reading Poetry at the Ninth Grade Level." Unpublished doctoral dissertation, The University of Chicago, 1958.

[16]Charlotte Dee Rogers, "Individual Differences in Interpretive Responses to Reading the Short Story at the Eleventh Grade Level." Unpublished doctoral dissertation, University of Arizona, 1965, p. 40.

[17]*Ibid.*, p. 113.

[18]*Ibid.*, p. 40.

What is the main point in this story?
How did you arrive at this conclusion?
How do you know what kind of a person he is?

In addition, Rogers used a questionnaire to obtain information about the students' attitudes toward short stories, and their habits of short story reading.

A variation of this technique, combined with several others, was employed by Cafone[19] with an extremely uncommunicative group of ninth grade students who were five or more years retarded in reading, who had a history of school failure, and who scored below average on the verbal section of the WISC or the WAIS. Although silence or "I don't know" were their most common responses to the invitation to tell how they arrived at an understanding of the selections, some of them, including Marie, occasionally brightened these interviews with significant insights.

Marie's attention to context clues seemed to improve as her interest in the story increased. However, she tended to remember the main ideas that were personally significant to her, rather than to distinguish the main ideas logically from the many supporting details. This approach sometimes led her to make errors in interpretation. For example, she said that one main idea of the story was that the boy "should not drop out of school." This was not a main idea; in fact, the author implied that he might as well drop out of a school that had no meaning or utility for him. Her extremely personal approach also led her to insert ideas that were not in the story at all. For example, she said that the reason for the boy's losing his job was his inability to speak well. This was one of Marie's own problems, but it was not mentioned in the story.

The technique of retrospective-introspective verbalization may be modified in various ways. Starting with an unstructured approach, the interviewer may allow the subject free expression of his reflections, thoughts and feelings about the selection, and then ask questions designed to promote clarification and elaboration, somewhat like those used by Piaget in his study of children's language and thoughts. This procedure is also comparable to the "Inquiry" technique of the Rorschach test. The interviewer follows up the subject's comments with such questions as these:

[19]Harold C. Cafone, "Individual Differences in the Reading Processes of Ninth Grade Retarded Readers." Doctoral project in progress, University of Arizona, 1965.

How did you know that?

Why didn't you say _____?

How did you know it wasn't _____?

Did you know this before?

Were you especially interested in this (the right answer)? Why was it interesting to you?

The final step, as in the Rorschach, might be a "testing the limits" by asking the subject to respond to a series of "yes" or "no" questions such as: Did you think about the title before beginning to read? Did you skim the selection before reading it carefully?

To delve more deeply into the process that a student actually uses, the interviewer may ask him to introspect while he is reading. By use of this introspective method, in combination with other techniques, doctoral students at the University of Chicago have conducted several very significant researches. Swain[20] asked twenty-nine college students to think aloud as they read passages of literature, social science, and science, and then to answer questions on them. She recorded their verbalizations about how they analyzed the words and restructured the meaning. This approach encouraged the subjects to reveal their conscious thought processes.

Pickarz[21] used a similar procedure with able sixth grade students. She asked the subjects to verbalize freely their thoughts and feelings about the selection as they read it.

Using introspection as supplementary to a more objective approach to ascertaining students' specific purposes in reading certain kinds of material, Smith[22] learned much about their reading processes. For example, she found that some students persisted in reading for the main ideas even when the instructions were to read for details.

In 1956 at the University of California, Berkeley, James R. Squire studied "The Responses of Adolescents to Literature Involving Selected Experiences in Personal Development." His study is now published in

[20]Emeliza Swain, "Conscious Thought Processes Used in the Interpretation of Reading Materials." Unpublished doctoral dissertation, University of Chicago, 1953.

[21]Josephine Pickarz, "Getting Meaning from Reading," *Elementary School Journal*, 56 (March, 1956), pp. 303–309.

[22]Helen K. Smith, "The Responses of Good and Poor Readers When Asked to Read for Different Purposes." Unpublished doctoral dissertation, University of Chicago, 1964.

pamphlet form. In interviews lasting several hours, Squire[23] obtained responses of ninth and tenth grade students to each segment of four short stories. They were asked to respond freely and completely in describing the "feelings, ideas, opinions, or reactions" which occurred to them while reading or at the end of the story. The transcripts were analyzed according to seven categories: literacy, judgment, interpretational responses, narrational reactions, associational responses, self-involvement, prescriptive judgments and miscellaneous. Wilson[24] used a similar analysis in comparing the responses of college students to three novels before and after class discussion of the novels.

Introspective methods in a case-study setting were employed by Strang[25] in an exploration of reading patterns, and by Gray and Rogers[26] in a study of different kinds and degrees of maturity in reading.

Jenkinson[27] used a "cloze test," in which words were omitted within the reading passage at regular intervals. The reader was asked to supply the precise word that the author intended. After taking the test, each student was asked in an interview to explain the reasons for his insertions as he again completed the cloze passages. The students who were able to supply the largest number of correct words also tended to be the students who saw more relationships among the various ideas, had a better understanding of the language structure, and made better use of the grammatical and syntactical clues to meaning. They were, in general, less subjective than those who scored low.

Much can be learned about the reading process through students' retrospective and introspective verbalization. Various methods of studying the reading process have yielded a number of insights:

Able readers differ from those who are less able in many respects:

In their ability to analyze language and reconstruct the meaning of a passage.

[23]James R. Squire, *The Responses of Adolescents While Reading Four Short Stories.* Research Report No. 2. Champaign, Illinois: National Council of Teachers of English, 1964.

[24]James R. Wilson, "Responses of College Freshmen to Three Novels." Unpublished doctoral dissertation, University of California, Berkeley, 1962.

[25]Ruth Strang, *Exploration of Reading Patterns.* Chicago: University of Chicago Press, 1942.

[26]William S. Gray and Bernice Rogers, *Maturity in Reading.* Chicago: University of Chicago Press, 1956.

[27]Marion Dixon Jenkinson, "Selected Processes and Difficulties of Reading Comprehension." Unpublished doctoral dissertation, Department of Education, University of Chicago, 1957.

In their ways of integrating newly acquired ideas with previous experience.

In the intensity of their responses to what they read, and in their application of new insights to their own lives.

In their grasp of symbolic meanings: The more able readers respond about equally to literal meaning, implied meaning, and opportunities to offer critical evaluations; whereas the less able readers respond almost exclusively to literal meaning. The more able also tend to be more objective and impersonal in their interpretations. The less able are more likely to confuse their own ideas with those of the author.

In the positiveness of their attitudes toward literature.

In their background knowledge of poets and poetry.

In the degree of satisfaction they have derived from their previous experiences in reading literature.

It should be emphasized that individual differences as well as group differences are to be found among able readers and less able readers.

Since the reading process demands an ever active intelligence, it changes according to the nature and difficulty of the reading material. The reader "must select, repress, soften, emphasize, correlate, and organize, all under the influence of the right mental set or purpose or demand."[28]

Adult readers are highly influenced by their interests and attitudes, which affect their interpretation of the author's ideas.

Reading achievement—the product—depends upon the prerequisites that the individual possesses for a given reading task, the processes he uses, and the skill of the teacher.

PROCEDURES

What are the optimal procedures for teaching reading to children at a given chronological or mental age? To answer this we must have an understanding of the product—of what the learner can do when he has realized the objectives: we must know what prerequisites he brings to the learning situation; and we must know what processes he uses. I have often described the teaching process by using this formula:

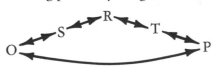

[28]Thorndike, *op. cit.*

The focus is on *O*—the individual student. His physical condition, his need and desire to read, his mental ability, his previously learned skills and previously acquired knowledge, his concept of himself—any or all of the underlying factors already mentioned may make him more or less responsive to the teacher's instruction.

Starting with an understanding of the student, the teacher is next concerned with the situation—*S*. This is the classroom situation over which the teacher has most control—attractive physical conditions, an atmosphere conducive to learning, and reading material of suitable format, difficulty, and appeal.

The student responses—*R*—are to the situation. Each experience leaves a trace—*T*—on his nervous system; this affects his general perception—*P*—of the next situation in which reading is involved.

This, I sometimes tell students, is the psychology of teaching reading in a nutshell, to which one sprightly student responded: "The psychology of teaching reading is too complex to put in a nutshell, even a coconut shell!"

CONCLUDING STATEMENT

I have outlined the main stages in the reading process, as I understand it, from intake—the stimuli of a printed page or passage—to output in the form of vocal or motor responses.

The first sequential stages have been quite clearly defined: auditory reception, visual reception, perception, and conceptualization. The higher association processes involved in the reading process are beginning to be explored through observation, analysis of errors, the reader's responses to unstructured questions, and introspective and retrospective reports.

I have become more aware of the necessity for a case study approach to an understanding of the reading process by my recent work with ninth grade severely retarded readers, who have experienced years of failure and frustration in learning to read. Marie, to whom I have previously referred, is one of this group. The variation in their responses in different reading situations is astonishing. One boy whose score initially on the Gray Oral Reading Test was on first grade level was, after twelve hours of individual instruction, able to pass the official driver's license examination with a score of 96. In the first individual session, the worker, Mrs. E. Louise Knopf, asked him whether he would prefer to learn word attack skills in connection with a story he wanted to read, or begin with systematic instruction in reading and go ahead as fast as and as far as he could. He chose the first of the alternatives. This approach was not successful. The book he had chosen was written on third to fourth grade level of difficulty, and it was not as interesting as he had anticipated. He stumbled over almost every word.

In the course of conversation with the worker, he mentioned his desire to get a driver's license. As a first step he collected and learned a large number of road signs. Then he tackled the driver's manual. The worker read him a section at a time: they discussed it; they formulated questions that might be asked on the examination; he faced and mastered difficult key words like *vehicle* that might be included in the test. Then he would give orally his answer to each question. When he was satisfied that the answer was complete and correct, he dictated it to the worker. She wrote it and typed it for him to read the next period. In this way he made his own driver's manual which he could read and reread fluently and with full comprehension.

Another boy initially scored below fifth grade level on standardized silent reading tests and still lower on the Gray Oral Reading Test. In a series of individual conferences he read and comprehended far more difficult material. He read aloud with few errors paragraphs from Mark Twain, Lincoln's Gettysburg address, a selection from a biology high school text, and articles in *Hot Rod* magazine. Under the stimulus of a friendly tutor, he began to read the newspaper—as much as he could understand of the sports page, the comics, and the front page news.

We can only speculate concerning this discrepancy between test results and performance under the most favorable conditions. Here are some possible explanations:

> Interest in the content of the more difficult material generated his maximum of effort.
>
> Content that had little or no meaning, use, or interest to him, was rejected and consequently evoked no effort.
>
> Content that was immature and read by younger children decreased his self-esteem and aroused his resistance to reading.
>
> Previous instruction in phonics, syllabication, and other word recognition skills may have lain dormant until he had a real need or sufficient motivation to apply them.
>
> Although his concept of himself had been lowered by being called "dumb" and "stupid" and by repeated experiences of failure, he still may

have retained a deep-seated desire to make himself as "good" and complete as possible. When the opportunity to develop his potentialities was offered and the boy experienced some success, he was stimulated and challenged to do his best.

The negative influence of his classmates was not operating in the individual learning situation.

The relationship with the worker—a relationship of friendly, sincere, positive regard and an expectation that he could and would improve his reading, supported him in his efforts to use the abilities he did possess in getting the meaning of selections of real interest to him.

Experiences like these have convinced me that what I have called product or goals, prerequisites, process, and teaching procedures are all interwoven. To understand an individual's reading development, we need to be aware of all of these interacting aspects.

(2) GOALS OF THE READING PROGRAM: THE BASIS FOR EVALUATION*

Thomas C. Barrett

Since the purpose of this Perspectives in Reading volume is to consider various dimensions and means of evaluating the reading behaviors of students, it seems appropriate to focus attention on the goals of the reading program which should provide the basis for the evaluative process. A prerequisite to this undertaking, however, is a common understanding of the definition of reading that will be used as a point of departure in the discussion of the goals of a reading program. Thus, this presentation will have two purposes. First, it will present contrasting definitions of reading and will delineate the definition which will constitute the foundation for the remainder of the chapter. Second, the discussion will deal with some selected goals of a reading program which appear to be important with respect to the definition.

*Abridged from *The Evaluation of Children's Reading Achievement*, Perspectives 8, 1967, pp. 13–26, by permission of the author and the International Reading Association.

WHAT IS READING?

The necessity for dealing with the question, "What is Reading?" is based on two hypotheses: (a) that the term *reading* means different things to different people; and (b) that the way in which a teacher consciously or unconsciously defines reading is reflected in the goals of the reading program he provides for his youngsters. Whether these hypotheses can or cannot be validated empirically is open to question, but it does seem logical that the data for such an undertaking are available. For example, at the beginning of the semester I have each of the students enrolled in a graduate course in developmental reading write a definition of reading. As might be expected, the results are quite divergent. Moreover, the fact that different definitions of reading do exist in the minds of teachers suggests that it might be possible to observe the impact of these stated definitions in the goals they emphasize in their reading programs.

Although the argument as to whether the hypotheses can be validated empirically is purely academic at the moment, it is not speculation to state that the professional literature is replete with definitions of reading, that the definitions do in fact differ, and that they do have differing implications for instruction. In an extreme and somewhat facetious sense, an anecdote offered by Huey (5) in his early book, *The Psychology and Pedagogy of Reading* may help to illustrate the point:

> To the early peoples, reading was one of the most mysterious of the arts, both in its performance and in its origin. We recall how, even in modern times, Livingstone excited the wonder and awe of an African tribe as he daily perused a book that had survived the vicissitudes of travel. So incomprehensible, to these savages, was his performance with the book, that they finally stole it and ate it, as the best way they knew of "reading" it.

Whether Huey's anecdote can be accepted as a legitimate definition of reading is doubtful. Nevertheless, it would certainly simplify the task of determining the goals for a reading program.

In a more serious light, the literature related to the psychology and the teaching of reading reveals three points of view when it comes to defining reading: (a) reading is decoding; (b) reading involves perception and cognition; and (c) reading involves a perceptual response, a cognitive response and an affective response.

Reading Is Decoding. Bloomfield (2) among others presented the idea that reading is basically relating sounds to symbols. He contended that the alphabetic nature of the English language more or less demands that reading be viewed in this light. Furthermore, he suggested that meaning is not uniquely inherent to reading, but that it is related to all uses of language. The implication here is that to perceive reading as anything other than breaking a written code is to confuse the issue.

In its purest form, then, a decoding definition of reading indicates that the student must develop habit patterns which permit him to automatically transform written signals into their oral counterparts. In other words, the primary task of a teacher of reading, when this is the accepted definition of reading, is to enable pupils to develop an understanding of the alphabetic nature of the language and to develop, either inductively or deductively, skill in producing sounds for symbols. Thus, the implications the decoding definition of reading holds for the reading program are quite definite with respect to the operation of the teacher and his students. First, it seems reasonable that there would be a great deal of emphasis on sound-symbol relationships in such a classroom. Second, there undoubtedly would be a considerable amount of oral reading for the purpose of determining the accuracy of decoding. Finally, the reading program would deal with cognition only in an incidental way. These operations, it appears, would be standardized from group to group and from grade level to grade level.

Reading Involves Perception and Cognition. In contrast to the decoding definition of reading are those definitions which view reading as a two dimensional act. Smith and Dechant (10) and DeBoer and Dallmann (3) as well as others have taken this position. The definitions which fall into this category suggest that reading involves not only visual perception of the written symbols, but also thoughtful responses on the part of the reader. They also imply that the intent of the reader and the background he has to work with in responding to what he reads will permit him to develop new understandings and modify old concepts.

The implications the two-dimensional definition holds for the reading program are far different from those projected by the decoding definition. Basically, it extends the concept of reading purveyed by the decoding definition by placing strong emphasis on meaning and levels of thought. Therefore, this definition suggests that the classroom teacher should be concerned with word perception skills and with the ability on the part of the reader to interact with the author in a variety of thoughtful ways. A reading program which is congruent with the two-dimensional definition would provide learning activities of this nature at all grade levels.

Reading Involves Perceptual, Cognitive and Affective Responses. The third type of definition that can be found in the literature is more complex than either of the other two types. It suggests that reading has three dimensions; namely, a perceptual dimension, a meaning dimension, and an emotional dimension. With these criteria in mind, reading can be defined in the following manner:

> Reading involves the visual perception of written symbols and the transformation of the symbols to their explicit or implicit oral counterparts. The oral responses then act as stimuli for a thoughtful reaction on the part of the reader. The type or level of thought induced by the stimuli is determined, in part, by the intent and the background of the reader and the nature of the materials. In addition, the effort expended in the perceptual act and the intellectual impact of the written materials on the reader is influenced by his interest in the specific selection and by his attitude toward reading in general.

The definition of reading noted above has rather definite implications for a reading program. Basically, it suggests that a reading program which is congruent with this definition should have three strands. One strand should be concerned with the perceptual skills of reading. A second strand of the program should deal with the cognitive dimensions of reading, while a third strand should be devoted to the affective dimensions of reading. Not only should there be three strands in terms of goals for the reading program, but there should also be evidence of learning activities in the program which are explicitly designed to aid youngsters in attaining these goals. Thus, an analysis of the biweekly or monthly program, in terms of time allotted to different endeavors, should reveal a relative balance with respect to the three strands of goals. An optimum balance would, of course, depend on the grade level and the types of pupils involved; nevertheless, the three strands should always be visible. Moreover, the ongoing evaluation of the reading program should focus attention on each of the three dimensions of the program. To clarify this position, the following sections present a more analytical discussion of the specific goals of the reading program using the three dimensional definition as a conceptual framework.

GOALS OF THE READING PROGRAM

Educational goals have often been viewed as uninspiring fare by people who should be deeply concerned with them. This feeling may come from several sources. First, there are some people who consider goals to be the artifacts of some theoretician's thoughts. This reaction may come about because the goals are imposed on teachers from outside sources, such as curriculum guides and teachers' manuals. The end result is that teachers do not become ego involved with implementing goals, because they have had nothing to do with creating them.

A second possibility for the general lack of enthusiasm for goals is that they are frequently stated in such a fashion that they do not give adequate guidance to the person who is to help children accomplish them. In some cases, the goals are so gross that they leave a great deal of latitude for interpretation or misinterpretation. In other instances, they focus attention on teacher behavior and not on pupil behavior; thus, they distract the teacher's attention from behavioral outcomes on the part of his students and draw it to his teaching techniques. There is no doubt that a relationship exists between teaching technique and pupil behavior, but goals should be stated in terms of pupil behaviors so that attention is focused on the pupils primarily and on the teacher secondarily.

A third reason why educational goals appear to carry negative connotations may be that the relationships among the philosophy guiding the educational program, the goals of the program, instructional decisions governing the learning activities, and the evaluation process have not been clearly perceived. As a case in point, consider these relationships with respect to the reading program again. In this instance, the definition of reading provides the basis for the scope of the goals. The goals, in turn, indicate the kinds of reading and reading related behaviors that children should demonstrate as a result of the reading program. In other words, the goals of the program should guide the teacher in the types of learning activities he selects and the evaluation procedures he follows.

Although the remainder of the article will not resolve the problems inherent in a discussion of educational goals, what follows is designed to accomplish two things: (a) the goals of the reading program will be put into perspective with regard to the three-dimensional definition of reading; and (b) the nature and instructional implications of selected goals of the reading program will receive consideration.

GOALS OF THE READING PROGRAM IN PERSPECTIVE

In an effort to put the goals of the reading program into a frame of reference, Figure 1 was created. Specifically, it was designed (a) to show the relationships of the goals to the operational definition, the implementation of the goals, and the evaluation process and (b) to provide some descriptive information about the categories of goals and their relationship to one another.

Figure 1 shows that, in the first instance, the flow of action, as indicated by the arrows, is from the definition of reading, to the goals, to the implementation of the goals, to the evaluation of the desired reading behaviors, and back to the goals. This suggests that within certain limits the program has some flexibility in as much as the results of the evaluation may give new directions to some goals and may suggest increased emphasis on others. Such changes in these elements will have a direct influence on the types of and time allotted to certain learning activities. This circular flow of action is constant and is what keeps the reading program up-to-date.

With regard to the second purpose of Figure 1, it should be noted that the three categories of goals are briefly described so that they reflect the essence of the instructional goals appropriate to each dimension of the program. For example, the perceptual dimension of the program is concerned with skills in word perception. Although perception is used rather broadly here, the intent of this dimension of the program is rather precise, since it focuses on the ability of children to demonstrate flexibility, accuracy, and variability of rate in word perception. The cognitive dimension of the program, on the other hand, indicates that children should demonstrate different levels of thought in their reading. Finally, the affective goals of the reading program deal with the child's feelings about reading, particularly the feelings that reading is worthwhile and self-fulfilling.

In addition, Figure 1 shows that the three types of goals are interrelated. The implication here is that the type or level of thought demonstrated by the reader is dependent on his perceptual skills and on his feelings about reading at the moment or in general. Moreover, how well a child understands what he is reading and the way he feels about

FIGURE I

INTERACTIONS AMONG A DEFINITION OF READING, CATEGORIES OF GOALS OF THE READING PROGRAM, IMPLEMENTATION OF THE GOALS, AND EVALUATION OF PUPILS' READING AND READING RELATED BEHAVIORS

DEFINITION OF READING

Reading involves the visual perception of written symbols and the transformation of the symbols to their explicit or implicit oral counterparts. The oral responses then act as stimuli for a thoughtful reaction on the part of the reader. The type or level of thought induced by the stimuli is determined, in part, by the intent and the background of the reader and the nature of the materials. In addition, the effort expended in the perceptual act and the intellectual impact of the written materials is partially controlled by his interest in the specific selection and by his attitude toward reading in general.

CATEGORIES OF GOALS OF THE READING PROGRAM

Perceptual Goals	Cognitive Goals	Affective Goals
are concerned with the flexibility, rate, and accuracy of word perception.	are concerned with the types and levels of thought generated during reading.	are concerned with the feelings children have toward reading.

IMPLEMENTATION OF GOALS

Making pupils aware of the goals to be achieved

Selecting learning activities designed to achieve specific goals

Organizing time, space, materials, children and teachers to carry out the learning activities

EVALUATION OF PUPILS' READING AND READING RELATED BEHAVIORS

Evaluation of the perceptual goals of the reading program	Evaluation of the cognitive goals of the reading program	Evaluation of the affective goals of the reading program

reading influences his efforts in the perceptual area. In other words, the three types of goals and their behavioral outcomes do interact and are interdependent upon one another. This does not preclude the possibility, however, that we can think about and organize the reading program in such a way that three types of goals will receive varying degrees of emphasis at different times.

In general, then, the purpose of Figure 1 is to support the position that the goals of the reading program should be three-dimensional in nature and that the goals are interdependent on one another and interrelated with a definition of reading, the implementation of the goals, and the evaluation process.

REFERENCES

1. Bloom, Benjamin S., *et al. Taxonomy of Educational Objectives-Handbook I: Cognitive Domain.* New York: David McKay Company, Inc., 1956.
2. Bloomfield, Leonard, and Clarence L. Barnhart. *Let's Read.* Detroit: Wayne University Press, 1961.
3. DeBoer, John J., and Martha Dallmann. *The Teaching of Reading.* New York: Holt, Rinehart and Winston, Inc., 1961.
4. Guszak, Frank James. *Relations Between Teacher Practice and Knowledge of Reading Theory in Selected Grade School Classes* (USOE Cooperative Research Project No. S-437). Madison, Wisconsin: University of Wisconsin, 1966.
5. Huey, Edmund Burke. *The Psychology and Pedagogy of Reading.* New York: The Macmillan Company, 1908.
6. Krathwohl, David R., *et al. Taxonomy of Educational Objectives-Handbook II: Affective Domain.* New York: David McKay Company, Inc., 1964.
7. Letton, Mildred C. "Evaluating the Effectiveness of Teaching Reading," *Evaluation of Reading*, Helen M. Robinson, Editor, Supplementary Educational Monographs, No. 88. Chicago: The University of Chicago Press, December, 1958, pp. 76–82.
8. Otto, Wayne, Theodore L. Harris, and Thomas C. Barrett. *Transfer Effects of Training Intermediate Grade Pupils to Adjust Reading Speed to Reading Purpose* (USOE Cooperative Research Project No. 3137). Madison, Wisconsin: University of Wisconsin, 1966.
9. Sanders, Norris M. *Classroom Questions.* New York: Harper and Row, 1966.
10. Smith, Henry P., and Emerald V. Dechant. *Psychology in Teaching Reading.* Englewood Cliffs, N.J.: Prentice-Hall, Inc., 1961.

(3) ENDS AND MEANS: DEVELOPING SPECIFIC OBJECTIVES FOR READING INSTRUCTION*

Victor M. Rentel

T. H. Huxley once remarked that the great end of life was not knowledge but action. This statement is only partly true, for action, to be purposeful, must be directed by knowledge. The two, knowledge and action, cannot be separated so easily, even if the match at times becomes awkward. This balance between knowledge and action is a major concern for educators who must constantly keep the balance mechanism adjusted to the social and philosophical changes that influence education in every period. If, in the coming years, educational technology holds our fancy, as it seems likely to—given our lust for specialization and our preoccupation with measurement—specific behavioral objectives in education will increasingly shape society's larger goals as they are interpreted by the schools.

Because the objectives of reading instruction will play so large a part in determining both the academic and human possibilities of the children we teach, formulating these objectives demands careful and sensitive thinking. Objectives commonly serve four functions: a) they define and give direction to learning; b) they provide a mechanism for selecting content and experiences for the curriculum; c) they focus on the kinds of learnings which will receive emphasis; and d) they detail specifications for evaluation (10).

There is almost universal agreement that society's needs and demands are the primary sources of educational goals; but at this point universal agreement ends. The development of objectives, based on deep convictions arising out of previous experience and an interpretation of society's ideals, methods of thinking, attitudes, and current needs, is a matter of choice on the part of a teaching staff (1). Final selection of objectives ultimately depends upon a faculty's convictions and its philosophy of education.

*Reprinted from *Forging Ahead in Reading*, 12, Part I, (1967 Convention Proceedings), pp. 187–91, by permission of the author and the International Reading Association.

LEARNING AND LEARNERS

What is known about learning and learners, as well as the nature of content and its contribution to the education of an individual, will determine in part the selection of objectives, but, even more, will order, relate, and give them dimension (1). Most educators consider what we know about learning to be crucial in the selection of objectives to such an extent that current methods of teaching reading retain vestiges of nearly every learning theory which historically has achieved some prominence. The psychology of learning, in one guise or another, forms the basis for most instruction in reading—regardless of the timeliness or established proof of the theory. Taba makes this observation:

> The study of the psychological principles underlying curriculum and teaching is somewhat akin to an archeological expedition: one can find the fossilized remains of almost any learning theory that ever existed, no matter how outdated or how discredited it may be (14).

The warning here is clear. Before objectives are selected for reading instruction, their theoretical antecedents should be examined carefully, for quite possibly, the theories underlying these objectives may be little more than historical curiosities.

Briefly, is there a precise, consistent, unified theory of learning upon which the formulation of objectives in reading can be based? While many advances leading to a greater understanding of the learning processes have been made over the past few years, the answer to this question still remains a rather unsatisfactory *no*. If this is the case, of what practical value are theories of learning to instruction in general and reading in particular? Cantor, writing on the contemporary status of research in learning, skeptically concludes:

> In this writer's opinion, an honest appraisal of basic psychological research on learning indicates that, at the present time, such research activity produces little of significance for educational practice. (2).

Mowrer, in this connection, advised students of learning theory that they would do better in practical fields to make use of "enlightened and informed common sense." On the other hand, Hilgard does not regard differences among theorists as particularly vexing. Instead, he suggests that on many important points crucial to educators, most theorists are in substantial agreement. Theorists may differ with regard to interpretation, but they agree in principle on most matters. Havighurst, too, believes that sufficient "ground work" has emerged from research of the past few decades to enable educators to relate "intellectual development" to practical instruction (5).

Because of the intramural conflict between learning theorists, a tendency arises among those who are responsible for developing programs of reading instruction to ignore research findings in the psychology of learning. This is an extreme view. No unified theory of learning is likely to emerge from basic research for years to come, but where current theory is incorporated into curriculum planning, where the best evidence available is considered, where objectives consonant with theory are subjected to a rigorous tryout before their acceptance, the selection of objectives using learning theory as one of the bases seems to me to be sound.

Attempts to develop suitable objectives for instruction must be based on selection criteria which include, in addition to what we know about learning, what we know about the learner. In particular, objectives must be based on what is both logical and appropriate to the growth potential of a given level of maturity: specific objectives are developmental statements of general objectives. Mirroring the physical, social, and emotional concomitants of these needs, they reflect basic needs at various developmental levels. Then, to be attainable, objectives must also be statements of *behavior* which students at a given level of development can achieve.

OBJECTIVES—GENERAL OR SPECIFIC?

Both curriculum experts and specialists in educational measurement generally recommend that specific instructional goals be defined in behavioral terms. But this advice conceals a major problem. It is all but impossible, nor is it advisable, to specify fully and exactly all of the behaviors that might apply to a skill or concept. Ebel makes this observation:

> Behavioral definitions tend to be books, not paragraphs, sections, or even chapters. . . . The virtue of concreteness involves the burden of complexity. Abstractions for all their faults do have the virtue of simplicity. The virtue of definiteness involves a danger of over-emphasis on conformity (3).

The level of generality appropriate for an objective is one of the most troublesome questions facing educators today. Fifteen years ago it was popular—and still is if my topic today is any reflection of current thinking—to draw a contrast between highly specific objectives and those whose reference is a more generalized mode of behavior. Tyler suggests that it may be more useful to think of defined levels of generalization, verified experimentally, and aimed "at as high a level of generalization as experiments show to be successful." The purpose would be to help students use generalized modes of behavior as those modes are reflected in the ability to cope with specifics. An objective might then be "stated in the curriculum plan with specifics used as *illustrations* [italics mine], rather than treating the specifics as ends in themselves" (15).

This matter suggests that the goals of reading should be concerned with processes as well as products, with perspective as well as pertinence, and with simplicity as well as specificity. Most important, in relation to Tyler's suggestions, reading instruction needs to focus on adaptability, not merely on an adaptation.

Where specific behaviors are used to illustrate objectives, their function is largely one of clarifying the verbal meaning of a larger outcome. There have been at least three productive attempts to define educational goals in behavioral terms, one at the elementary level (7), one at the secondary level (4), and one (most appropriate) at the college level (1). These classification systems may be of great value to those responsible for the development of reading instruction in helping them to define substantive content, to specify objectives, and to plan learning activities for specific units of work. Referring to Bloom's *Taxonomy*, to which he was a contributor, Krathwohl (8) sees the *Taxonomy* as a concise model for the selection, analysis, and refinement of objectives. Further, it provides a system by which objectives can be compared both with learning content and the means used to measure the mastery of that content.

Though a possible "hierarchy of learning experiences" from the lower to the upper levels of the *Taxonomy* is suggested, only general support has been demonstrated in research for this hypothesis, but in no instance has the hierarchical structure of the *Taxonomy* been supported by various factor matrices (12, 13). If this system or similar classification ones suggest a readiness relationship between lower and higher objectives in the hierarchy, then these systems can hardly be ignored in framing objectives for reading instruction.

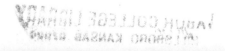

BEHAVIORAL ILLUSTRATIONS IN READING

There are listings in the literature of reading which catalog and classify the outcomes of reading instruction. In most of these lists, little or no attempt has been made to distinguish between general and specific goals, between content and behavior, or between lower and higher order objectives.

French provides many excellent examples of these distinctions and illustrates general objectives with specific behaviors. One such example states the general objective and illustrates behavior as follows:

> Commands and uses the basic skills of reading for information, ideas, opinions, stimulation, and leisure.
> Illustrative Behaviors
> a. Adjusts his reading rate and his method of reading (skimming, taking notes for detail or for enjoyment only) to the material at hand.
> b. Seeks consciously to attain his best reading rate and comprehension.
> c. Reads with increasing speed, comprehension, and appreciation.
> d. (Other illustrative behaviors are included) (4).

At the primary level, as one of the goals of modern reading instruction, David Russell states that teachers should provide "for the gradual increase in skills and acquisition of valuable habits in silent and oral reading" (11).

This objective may be illustrated behaviorally as follows:

> 1. Reading
>   a. He does assigned reading by himself.
>   b. Anticipates the story from its title, picks out chief sentences, and is able to tell what each says.
>   c. Reads to find answers—what, when, where, and why.
>   d. Distinguishes the chief elements in a story and can repeat them.
> 2. Word Recognition
>   a. Recognizes and produces the individual letter signs for consonants and consonant blends.
>   b. Can fuse two- or three-letter sounds into a single word and can recognize letters by their sound.
>   c. Uses context to pronounce and locate meanings for words.

After developing specific illustrations for set objectives, the next logical step would involve placing these objectives in some hierarchy consonant with what is known of development and maturation. If the objectives selected are consistent and noncontradictory, they can then be compared with and classified according to one of the previously mentioned systems.

A CONCEPT OF THE LEARNER

Systems, however, can only aid in the *formulation* of objectives. They cannot insure what will happen when objectives come face-to-face with a learner. Tyler, speculating on the changes that have occurred in his thinking over the past two decades, notes that beyond the planning of objectives students must have the chance to do what is implied in the objective, that what they do must be satisfying to them, and that what they have done must become an impelling force, stimulating them to try new ways to reach the same objectives (15). He urges that the learnings be sequential and that each learner set standards that compel him to go beyond his past performance. Finally, if learning is to continue beyond the teacher's "poor power to add or detract," the individual must have some means of judging his own output.

No recognition, no concept, no insight is more meaningful than the realization that in education we must deal with a live, squirming, purposeful human being in whom go our hopes for critical judgment, our needs for creative innovation, and our freedom to change as the world changes. And humans exert a powerful influence on one another, regardless of their ages. When we plan and develop programs of reading instruction, children and young people must be the constant focus of our attention.

If our attention is fixed on curriculum, on technology, and on reaching specific goals at every turn, students who vary from our conception of them but who, nevertheless, are expected to conform to a pattern of objectives will find themselves lodged on one of Procrustes' infamous beds. And if you recall, Procrustes had a marvelous way of fitting a traveler to his bed. If the traveler was unfortunate enough to have his legs extend beyond the footboard, Procrustes and his men would cut them off to make the sleeper fit the bed. If, on the other hand, he was too short, ropes were tied to his head and feet and Procrustes would conveniently stretch him until he reached the proper length. When we adjust students to programs rather than programs to students, when the curriculum in reading becomes a rigid lockstep sequence of goals, what happens to the child is analogous to what happened to Procrustes' travelers. We all need to remember that what happens to the child in schools is the final criteria for judging what we have practiced there. Children do not learn an objective but what they do in response to one.

REFERENCES

1. Bloom, B. (Ed.) *Taxonomy of Educational Objectives: The Classification of Educational Goals Handbook I: Cognitive Domain.* New York: David McKay Company, Inc., 1956, 26–28.

2. Cantor, G. M. "Basic Learning Research and Mental Retardation," in E. Trapp and P. Himelstein (Eds.), *Readings on the Exceptional Child.* New York: Appleton-Century-Crofts, Inc., 1962, 172.

3. Ebel, R. L. "The Relation of Testing Programs to Educational Goals," *The Impact and Improvement of School Testing Programs.* National Society for the Study of Education. Sixty-second Yearbook, Part II, University of Chicago Press, 1963, 34.

4. French *et al, Behavioral Goals of General Education in High School.* New York: Russell Sage Foundation, 1957, 96.

5. Havighurst, R. J., *et al.* "The Nature and Needs of the Disadvantaged," *The Educationally Retarded and Disadvantaged.* National Society for the Study of Education. Sixty-sixth Yearbook, Part I, University of Chicago Press, 1967, 33–35.

6. Hilgard, E. *Theories of Learning.* New York: Appleton-Century-Crofts, Inc., 1956, 486–487.

7. Kearney, N. C. *Elementary School Objectives.* New York: Russell Sage Foundation, 1957.

8. Krathwohl, D. H. "Stating Objectives Appropriately for Program, for Curriculum and for Instructional Materials Development," *Journal of Teacher Education,* 16 (No. 1) (1965), 83–92.

9. Mowrer, O. H. *Two-Factor Learning Theory: Reviewed, Revised, and Extended.* Urbana, Illinois, 1955 (Mimeographed).

10. Ragan, W. B. *Modern Elementary Curriculum.* New York: Holt, Rinehart, and Winston, 1963, 86–89.

11. Russell, D. *Children Learn to Read.* Boston: Ginn and Company, 1961, 144.

12. Smith, R. B. "An Analysis of Scability, of the 'Knowledge' and 'Comprehension' Levels of the *Taxonomy of Educational Objectives: Cognitive Domain,*" paper read at the National Council of Measurement in Education, 1965.

13. Stoker, W. H., and R. P. Kropp. "Measurement of Cognitive Processes," *Journal of Educational Measurement*, (No. 1) (1964), 39–42.
14. Taba, H. *Curriculum Development: Theory and Practice.* New York: Harcourt, Brace, and World, Inc., 1962, 77.
15. Tyler, R. W. "New Dimensions in Curriculum Development," *Phi Delta Kappan*, 61 (September 1966), 26–27.

Chapter 2

LINGUISTIC AND PSYCHOLOGICAL IMPLICATIONS

INTRODUCTION

To develop a defensible theory of reading, the field must be viewed in its larger setting as a facet of language. The way reading is taught must also be in harmony with what psychologists and students of child development have discovered about the conditions and strategies which best promote learning. This chapter, therefore, brings together articles which carry implications from linguistics and psychology for the teaching of reading.

Although not a new science, the application of linguistics to the field of reading is relatively recent. Many linguists have been primarily interested in describing how our language works, rather than in encouraging its application to the teaching of English and reading. Some who offer advice to teachers have a narrow view of what reading involves or lack sufficient knowledge of how children learn. Psycholinguistics is concerned not only with linguistics as a science but also with how individuals learn to use their language.

Typically, the treatment of linguistics has been ignored or slighted in courses in the teaching of reading. Many classroom teachers are meeting the term, linguistics, for the first time in university classes, reading conferences, and periodicals. Specialists in reading have sometimes ignored the relevance of the science of language or have criticized the efforts of linguists to point out findings that should affect the way reading is taught. It is fortunate that this situation is changing, since linguistic scientists have many insights to offer the field of reading.

Entire books have been written on the psychology of reading, and at least one course in psychology has generally been included in the pre-service preparation of teachers. Of the two articles on psychology included here, the one by Ziller views learning to read in its social setting and highlights the influence of the teacher, the reactions of classmates, and the interaction between the reader and the author. The second article describes the process of learning to read in the light of Gestalt psychology.

The papers presented in this chapter do not begin to exhaust the effect which these two disciplines can have on reading. Scattered throughout the volume are other selections which will give added insight. This chapter should serve to make teachers more cognizant of the relationships between reading and other allied fields and more alert to pertinent writings in professional magazines.

(4) READING OUR LANGUAGE PATTERNS: A LINGUISTIC VIEW—CONTRIBUTIONS TO A THEORY OF READING*

Carl A. Lefevre

Reading theory is of interest to all of us. My presentation here is adapted from discussions of reading theory in a book-length manuscript I have just completed writing in collaboration with Professor Donald Lloyd. The title of the book is *Linguistics and the Teaching of Reading*. Publication plans are still tentative, but we hope the book will be made available in 1962. Persons who have previously been interested in my work in linguistics and reading will find in the following remarks a summary of my present thinking. My earlier suggestions were first reported in talks at two national conventions, followed by publications in the *Journal of Developmental Reading* and the *I.R.A. Conference Proceedings*.[1]

Reading theory generally does not concern itself *rigorously* with language; instead, it concerns itself largely with psychological matters, with visual perception especially. The question is, visual perception of what, exactly, if not of the graphic counterparts *in printed form* of meaning-bearing language patterns? To comprehend printed matter, the reader must perceive entire language structures *as wholes*—as unitary meaning-bearing patterns. Short of this level of perception, he simply does not perceive those total language structures that alone are capable of carrying meaning; short of this level of perception, he may perceive individual words as though words were meaning-bearing units in themselves—

---

*Reprinted from *Challenge and Experiment in Reading*, 7 (1962 Convention Proceedings), pp. 66–70, by permission of the author and the International Reading Association.

[1] Carl A. Lefevre, "Reading Instruction Related to Primary Language Learnings: A Linguistic View." A paper read at the Golden Anniversary Convention of the National Council of Teachers of English, Chicago, Illinois, November 25, 1960. Published in *The Journal of Developmental Reading*, Spring 1961.

Carl A. Lefevre, "Language Patterns and Their Graphic Counterparts: A Linguistic View." A paper read at the 6th Annual Convention of the International Reading Association, St. Louis, Missouri, May 6, 1961. Published in *Changing Concepts of Reading Instruction*, International Reading Association Conference Proceedings, Vol. 6, 1961.

one of the most serious of all reading disabilities—or he may group words visually in structureless pattern fragments that do not and cannot bear meaning. What he does not do is read *total language patterns for total comprehension of meaning.* My basic assumption is that reading must be regarded as a language-related process; that reading must be rigorously studied in relation to language. Today, rigorous study of language means structural linguistics.

Current reading methods and materials reflect little or no acquaintance with the structural linguistic rationale. This basis of twentieth-century advancement in language scholarship was foreshadowed in Sapir's *Langauge* (1921) and then catalyzed in 1933 by Bloomfield's *Language.* This is thirty to forty years ago now. Since 1933, the scientific study of languages, including American English, has laid the foundation for a new approach to language learning, both native and foreign. In essence, structural linguistics is cultural-anthropological: language is studied objectively and systematically as a learned arbitrary code of vocal symbols through which men in a given culture communicate with each other, interact, and cooperate.

It makes little difference whether a language has an ancient and honorable tradition of literacy, or is simply the speech of a people who have never developed a writing system. Language is viewed as a vocal symbol-system from which a graphic system may or may not have been derived. Handwriting and print are seen as secondary, derivative codes of visual symbols that reflect the basic language learned before formal schooling begins. This is a position of far-reaching consequences for education, pointing toward new theories of language and teaching, new methods, and new materials.

But linguists cannot do this vital educational work; we must do it ourselves. Professionally qualified, experienced teachers must study linguistics and discover for themselves how to apply new knowledge to old problems. We must teach ourselves and we must teach the teachers—teachers in being and teachers on order—for a more effective attack on the development of literacy in our schools. This whole range of activity is the professional concern of teaching, not of linguistics. Few linguists are capable language arts teachers; and they have problems of their own, including narrowness and insularity. Let us solve our problems, let them solve theirs. In the meantime, their discipline has much to offer that we need: it is there for the taking. Let us make full use of it.

As for myself, I am primarily a humanist rather than a linguistic scientist, though I do not feel that science is alien to the humanities. On the contrary, science is one of the humanities—or should be. As a scholar-teacher of English, I have made it my professional business to apply relevant findings of structural linguistics in teaching language and literature to students of all ages. I have also tried to determine just what and how much linguistic knowledge of English is needed by persons who introduce the young to literacy. In language arts methods and other college English courses I have made it a point to integrate linguistic knowledge with the more traditional content. Structural linguistics can enrich as well as clarify many areas of the language arts.

A number of broad substantive and methodological assumptions underlie my approach to a theory of reading. Two basic substantive assumptions are as follows:

1. Language is human behavior.
2. Each language has its own independent and unique structure; it requires its own independent and unique description. This structure or system, taken as a whole, is the grammar of the language.

Four basic methodological assumptions are as follows:

1. Language may be studied objectively and systematically.
2. Objective study of a language yields an accurate, orderly, comprehensive description of the language system, or structure.
3. Structural linguistics is not just another nomenclature for "the parts of speech" of traditional grammar, or another way of parsing and diagramming sentences. It is an entirely new way of looking at language, of sorting out the data, of classifying findings.
4. Structural linguistics leads to new data, new knowledge, new insights, new understandings.

Such broad substantive and methodological assumptions have illuminated my classroom experience as a teacher of literature and the skills of literacy—*and as a teacher of teachers*. They have led me to close study of basic linguistic principles and data, and eventually to the view of reading summarized in this presentation.

Precise linguistic principles are embodied in the basic Smith-Trager system of language analysis at three levels: (1) phonemes, (2) morphemes, and (3) syntax.

1. *Phonemes.* Phonemes are the basic sound units of language; a phoneme is the smallest class of significant speech sounds. The "segmental" phonemes are the nine simple vowels and the twenty-four consonants of American English. Linguists also refer to four levels of stress, four levels of pitch, and four junctures of terminals, as phonemes. The total number of phonemes is thus forty-five.

2. *Morphemes.* Morphemes are the basic meaning-bearing units of language; a morpheme is an indivisible language element patterned out of phonemes. Morphemes include word bases ("roots"), prefixes, suffixes, and inflections. A "free" morpheme may pattern by itself in larger language structures; a "bound" morpheme must combine with another morpheme. Such single words as *cat*, *go*, and *green* are examples of free morphemes; *in*-and-*here* in *inhere* are examples of bound morphemes.

3. *Syntax.* Syntax includes the various patternings of morphemes into larger structural units: noun groups, verb groups, noun clusters, verb clusters, prepositional groups, phrases, clauses, sentences.

Moreover, sentence-level utterances in American English make use of four signaling systems, listed here in descending order of importance: (1) intonation, (2) syntactical function order in sentence patterns, (3) structure words, and (4) word-form changes.

1. *Intonation.* Intonation is the generic term for significant and distinctive patterns of pitch, stress, and juncture. Comprising intricate patterns of obligatory and optional features, intonation is perhaps the least understood signaling system of American English.

2. *Syntactical function order in sentence patterns.* There are possibly no more than four basic sentence patterns in American English. Variety is achieved through nearly endless possibilities of modification and substitution.

3. *Structure words.* About three hundred "empty" words, having no referents outside the language system itself; contrasted to "full" words having referents in the real world outside language. Structure words include many sets, such as noun markers, verb markers, phrase markers, clause markers, question markers, and sentence connectors.

4. *Word form changes* ("grammatical inflections"). Form changes include noun plurals, possessives, verb parts, adjective "comparison," and the like.

I make explicit use of the three levels of language analysis and of the four signaling systems in my explanation of the interactions of speech and reading.

Beyond reading readiness, six "methods" of basic reading instruction have been traditionally suggested. Usually a sort of warning is added to the effect that an "eclectic" method is best: "There is no one method of teaching reading." The terms *alphabet, phonic, word, phrase, sentence,* and *story* methods seem to refer to categories of language or disclosure; but so far the "eclectic" method has not proved eclectic enough to include an accurate description of our language structure. Actually, all six methods attempt to reach meaning virtually without analysis of meaning-bearing language structures. Discussions of reading methodology abound with such expressions as *fused thought content, eye span, meaning units, fusing single words into sequences of meaning,* and so on. The missing part in all these explanations is simply the meaning-bearing structural patterns of American English. It is almost as though meaning could be reached by visual perception of graphic symbols unrelated to the structure of the language they represent.

Current reading methodology, so far as it concerns itself with "language" at all, in fact focuses on letters and words as the most significant units. This holds true even of the several linguistic treatments of reading that limit themselves largely to basic sounds and spelling; these works substantially accept the traditional "phonics" approach, but do provide accurate linguistic data in place of inaccurate information on sound-spelling relationships in English. The main concern is still the single word.

On the other hand, in my approach to reading instruction, the word is treated as a minor language unit for many reasons, some linguistic, others pedagogical. In English the word is an unstable element, whether it is taken as semantic or structural; the most significant structures are intonation patterns, grammatical and syntactical word groups, phrases, clauses, and sentences.

Single words, analyzed and spoken in isolation, assume the intonation contours of whole utterances; they lose the characteristic pitch and stress they normally carry in the *larger constructions that comprise the flow of speech and bear meaning.* This automatic upgrading of words may lead many learners to "read" word by word, or by pattern fragments, without regard for whole structural patterns that carry meaning; this automatic upgrading may thus contribute to the frequency and extent of serious reading disability among pupils of all ages. So far, little has been done to develop reading of American English by its known structures instead of by its "vocabulary."

A structural linguistic approach to reading and to reading instruction appears very promising, however, and there is some experimental evidence to support it. Like any other explication, the present one has an immediate context that helps to locate and define it. Five important elements of this context may be stated as follows:

1. Not enough is known about why some students learn to read while others do not; or in particular, why many bright children do not learn to read well.

2. Reading ability does not correlate reliably with intelligence, nor with any other measurable human trait.

3. Profound confusion prevails in English and in language arts instruction over the relationship of reading and writing to speech; educated but linguistically unsophisticated persons regard the graphic system as the "norm" for both speech and writing.

4. Lacking a rigorous theoretical base, the so-called "eclectic" theory of reading instruction and of the "multiple causation" of reading failures begs many questions and tends to avoid the responsibility for solutions.

5. Consequently, efforts should be made to develop a reading theory comparable in rigor to theories in other disciplines; structural linguistics can make a major contribution to such a theory.

Within this broad context, the following fourteen substantive assumptions comprise the basis of this approach to reading according to my present understanding. These statements are offered as contributions to a theory of reading and reading instruction.

1. Reading is basically a language-related process.

2. a. Language is speech, an arbitrary code or system of vocal symbols. It is non-instinctive behavior; it must be learned.
   b. Graphic symbols of writing and print comprise a secondary, derivative system;
   c. Thus, a dual set of symbol systems interact, the manual-visual with the audio-lingual.

3. a. Infants and young children naturally learn playfully, they enjoy the game and they enjoy themselves as they play it.

   b. This natural spirit of play should be encouraged and developed fully at all levels of language instruction.

4. a. Simply by talking, normal children from five to seven years old demonstrate their mastery of the basic structures of American English.
   b. Children should learn to read and write the language they already speak and understand.

5. a. Learning a native language is quite different from learning a foreign language. Similarly, developing literacy in the mother tongue is different from learning to read and write a foreign tongue.
   b. Developing literacy in the native language should proceed on the analogy of learning native speech as infant and child.

6. a. Graphics—the representation of language in writing and print—is essentially a "shorthand," a mnemonic device which can effect recall of entire meaning-bearing language patterns, sentences predominantly.
   b. Efficient reading requires consciousness of the relative equivalence of the graphic counterparts to spoken language structures.

7. Accordingly, some reading problems can be solved by developing consciousness of pertinent language processes and their interrelationships with graphics; this statement applies especially to the relationship of written and printed symbols to their equivalent speech segments.

8. The sentence is not merely a sequence of words, but a unitary meaning-bearing pattern of grammatical and syntactical functions: the individual words are relatively minor elements in such unitary patterns.

9. a. Individual words have less significance to hearer or reader than is commonly attributed to them.
   b. The significant elements are grammatical and syntactical structures: noun and verb groups and clusters, phrases, clauses, sentences.

10. Analytical slicing of larger language segments and their graphic counterparts into smaller segments should be done only to the extent that the reading process itself requires it.

11. a. The language learner, like any other, learns what he practices.

If he practices analyzing, spelling, and "sounding" words and word-parts, that is what he will learn. He may learn something else accidentally, or incidentally; and he may not.

b. The child learning to read should practice reading meaning-bearing language patterns at the sentence level.

12. Mastering the graphic system by giving his main attention to larger patterns, a learner would develop his own inductive generalizations of sound-spelling relationships (and this largely through his writing); in reading he would need formal spelling instruction only to get him over difficulties.

13. The American English sentence should be read not as a sequence of words but as a unitary meaning-bearing series of structural functions clearly signaled and patterned by (a) intonation; (b) syntactical functions in basic sentence patterns; (c) structure words; and (d) word-form changes.

14. In developing literacy in the native language, mutual reinforcement of skills may be achieved by coordinating teaching of auding, speaking, reading, and writing in the same lessons, so far as practicable.

The view of reading developed in this book is not offered as a "panacea," but for study and reflection, and as a stimulus to research and experimentation. If it is deeply and widely considered, I believe it may contribute qualitatively to modification and basic improvement in reading theory and instruction. It is time for the field of reading to reflect the great contribution made by twentieth century language scholars to our understanding of all language processes—and of reflective and conceptual thought.[2]

---

[2] I refer to such well-known linguistic works as Sapir's *Language* (1921), Bloomfield's *Language* (1933), Fries' *American English Grammar* (1940), Bloch and Trager's *Outline of Linguistic Analysis* (1942), Pike's *Intonation of American English* (1945), Trager and Smith's *Outline of English Structure* (1951), Fries' *Structure of English* (1952), Gleason's *An Introduction to Descriptive Linguistics* (1955), Paul Roberts' *Patterns of English* (1956), Lloyd and Warfel's *American English in Its Cultural Setting* (1956), Noam Chomsky's *Syntactic Structures* (1957), W. Nelson Francis' *The Structure of American English* (1958), a volume of articles edited by Allen, *Readings in Applied Linguistics* (1958); and a number of newer books by Carroll, Gleason, Hockett, Roberts, Warfel, Whorf, and others. This is a selective list; a complete bibliography of books and articles published during the last thirty years would run to many pages.

(5) STRUCTURAL LINGUISTICS: PRACTICAL TEACHING SUGGESTIONS*

Sarah M. Irvin

A small boy once boasted, "I have the smartest dog in the world. All I have to say to him is, 'Are you coming or aren't you?' and he either comes or he doesn't."

If we used just one method of teaching beginning reading we would, in effect, be like this small boy. We would be saying to children, "This is how I teach reading. Are you going to learn, or aren't you?" And they either would or they wouldn't. But primary teachers use many different approaches to reading, all of which are successful with some children. Our concern is that all children find success in reading. Teachers are discovering techniques for using certain linguistic knowledge to help us toward this goal.

Linguistics is a scientific study of the nature and functioning of spoken language. To say that we use a linguistic approach to reading means that we take advantage of certain knowledge and insights accumulated by linguists. Since reading is a language-based process, it is a logical approach. Applying linguistic principles in teaching beginning reading helps children find true enjoyment in discovering the versatility of their own voices. It helps children have fun in looking at language in many different ways. It also provides means for skill development.

CAPITALIZE ON THE LANGUAGE HE BRINGS

In his study of children's language Dr. Walter Loban found that all children, regardless of cultural or socioeconomic background, had acquired the basic structures of language before entering first grade (7). The child may say "He don't want none" instead of "He doesn't want any," but he is in full control of his language system as he learned it in his home and neighborhood. His dialect may not be that of standard English, but if we hope to help him succeed, we must make him feel

*Reprinted from *A Decade of Innovations: Approaches to Beginning Reading* 12, Part 3 (1967 Convention Proceedings), pp. 192–201, by permission of the author and the International Reading Association.

accepted first; and to make him feel accepted, we must accept his dialect. He may say he had "corn pone" and "clabber cheese" for lunch, or that he stayed home from school because he "ketched cold" (8), but no matter what "different" words he uses, if we reject these differences, we are also rejecting him, his family, and his community. Donald J. Lloyd, in his search for what is applicable to instruction in literacy (6), says that change of dialect will only follow the child's decision "to make his way out of the world he was born to."

Before children learn to read we must help them understand the relationship between talk and print. First, however, teachers must realize that written language and spoken language are seldom the same. Almost any sentence can help us prove this point. Try reading the following one aloud:

My dad lost his job because he got picked up by the cops.

Now pretend you're telling someone what happened. The sentence probably sound something like this:

Mə Dad lost'iz job 'cuzee got pickup by thə cops.

Words become blended together and sound as one. Some sounds in words are omitted entirely. Teachers are apt to become upset and say we are encouraging careless speech habits. They may even insist that children pronounce every sound and syllable of a word in reading. Then we have an artificial situation such as the one described by Ethel Strainchamps in her autobiographical sketch, *Don't Never Say Cain't* (9). She grew up as a hillbilly in the Ozarks, but became an avid reader at an early age. In telling of her experiences with language at about the time she was in the third grade, she says, "I had by that time picked up the notion that there was not necessarily much connection between the way teachers expected you to pronounce words in oral reading and the way they were pronounced in real life. Teacher speech in general struck me as a special lingo, lying somewhere between book language and normal speech."

It seems that much confusion could be avoided if we follow the advice of Dr. Lloyd (6) when he says, "In any event, each person must at all times read his own speech off the page of his standard English print and put his own speech on the page when he writes."

It is important for the very young child to learn that print is talk written down, that the written symbols can be read, and when they are read they become talk again. He learns this by watching his teacher write his own spoken thoughts about the experience, a picture, or maybe just a feeling. If he has a great deal to say, his teacher may listen, and then ask him to tell her which part of his story he would like to have her write. Then she writes his exact words whether they come up to her standards or not. Her purpose is to show him that his own talk can be written down and read back.

A little six-year-old boy dictated this thought to his teacher (4):

HURTING

It doesn't hurt no place when I'm sad.
I just know I'm sad.

It must have taken courage for the teacher to leave it alone and let it be truly his. But would it, honestly, have improved the thought if she had changed one word of it?

USE HIS SENTENCE PATTERNS

Children who are of school age already use the common basic sentence patterns of American English in expressing themselves. We take advantage of this in teaching them to read. In an activity period the teacher may overhear some children talking about the new pet rabbit. One says, "Floppy is soft." Later, when children come together for a group discussion period the teacher says, "While you were working I heard Billy and Jack talking about our bunny. Billy said, 'Floppy is soft,' " and she writes the sentence on the chalkboard. Then she allows each child to say the sentence, substituting a different word for "soft." Each time she writes the new word like this:

Floppy is soft.
white
furry
little
wiggly
new
shiny
clean

The children have said, seen, and heard eight sentences, each in the same pattern, each with a different meaning. They could then substitute appropriate words for Floppy, arriving at sentences such as these:

> The kitten is soft.
> My dress is white.
> A puppy is furry.
> Johnny is little.
> A snake is wiggly.
> My coat is new.
> Our car is shiny.
> The floor is clean.

By means of similar exercises children soon learn to expect certain kinds of words in particular positions in sentences. They learn to read sentence patterns and note the differences in meaning when words are substituted.

Sentence stretching exercises can help children vary sentences, which will prepare them for reading longer sentences. Dr. Loban told how one teacher used a clothesline and pinned word cards to it to form a basic sentence pattern, like this:

Bob		ran

By asking children,

> Where did Bob run?
> When did Bob run?
> How far did Bob run?
> Why did Bob run?

the teacher was able to help them stretch their sentence to sound like this:

| Today | | Bob | | ran | | all the way | | home | | to see his puppy. |

Yet the basic pattern can still be seen and heard in the sentence.

DEVELOP HIS INTONATION PATTERNS

Some linguists have called intonation the melody of speech. Dr. Lloyd (5) offers the hypothesis that "the ability to relate the melody of speech to the written page is the key to good reading. Good readers do it. Poor readers don't do it."

This statement is supported by Dr. Loban's study. He found that groups who were high in language ability were also high in reading ability, and that these high groups were likewise superior in handling the intonation patterns of pitch, stress, and juncture (7).

Dr. Lloyd reminds us that children entering first grade know intonation as far as oral language is concerned. It is so much a part of them that they are not consciously aware of it. Their sense of the more obvious intonation contours of their native American English was established before speech fluency developed, and refinements have been taking place ever since (5). It is intonation which can give a different meaning to an utterance, distinguish sarcasm from praise, tell us to push some words together while cutting others apart, and mark the end of a sentence or phonological unit.

Linguists can be very technical in describing intonation patterns in varying degrees of pitch, stress, and pause. It isn't necessary for the reading teacher to make such fine distinctions. What is necessary is to help the child become consciously aware of the principal intonation patterns of his language and to be able to use them as he reads.

A rule which we all must understand is that normally there is only one major stress from the beginning of an utterance to a pause, or between pauses. When a word or syllable is stressed, pitch normally rises unless it is the final word before a pause, when pitch normally falls.

Nó |↘|
I'm nót going |↓|
I've seen that show befóre. |↓|

Shifts in stress can change meanings in sentences and in certain words. Note this example:

After the kitten drank the *contents* of the saucer, it was *content.*

Open juncture, which cuts off one word or syllable from the next, works with stress and pitch to give meaning to this sentence:

The Greens, who own the *greenhouse,* live in the *green house* on the corner.

Open junctures also make the difference between words like *ice cream* and *I scream; a name* and *an aim.*

A reference which can help teachers learn more about the intonation patterns which are helpful in teaching reading is chapter five in Dr. Carl Lefevre's book, *Linguistics and the Teaching of Reading* (3).

Let's turn our attention now to the six-year-old. How can we help him become aware of the intonation patterns of his own speech? I think we must first let him hear in our speech what we call "stress," and "pitch," and "pause," pointing them out one at a time. For example, we can ask him to listen to simple directions, tell us the word with hard stress, and then follow the direction.

Bring me a book.
Put the book on the table.
Bring me a red book.
Go open the door.
Please shut the door.

After children have heard a favorite story the teacher may choose particular phrases which have been repeated over and over, and ask children to use their hands to show the ups and downs of her voice. To illustrate, take the refrain from *The Gingerbread Man*:

Run, run, as fast as you can

You can't catch me

I'm the Gingerbread man.

To help children realize that changing the stress within a sentence can change its meaning, ask them to say the following sentence with stress on different words.

You said I could feed the rabbit.

Yoú |↗|	Who said so?
You sáid |↗|	Please keep your word!
You said Í | ↗|	Not someone else.
You said I coúld |↗|	Now you say I can't.
You said I could féed |↗|	Someone else can clean the cage.
You said I could feed the rábbit|↘|	Someone else can feed the bird.

I like to put each word of a sentence such as this one on a separate card and distribute the cards to children in random order. Children must arrange themselves so their words make a proper sentence. I designate a word to be stressed by holding my hand over the head of a child. Children discuss the different meanings they have voiced.

To show how pitch and stress indicate mood you might ask children to show how their mother calls them to dinner:

When she is just letting them know dinner is ready.
When she has already called twice.
When dinner is getting cold!

The tape recorder is invaluable in helping children hear their own intonation patterns. Record examples of their oral reading and help them compare these with recordings of their informal talk. This helps children hear the differences between their intonation patterns in reading and in talking.

Before we leave intonation, I would like to point out some pitfalls which must be avoided in teaching. We sometimes tell children that a question mark indicates a question and calls for the voice to end in rising pitch. Note the following examples:

What is the name of your school? |↓|	Barlow.
How much did your new hat cost? |↓|	Ten dollars.
Where did you put my pencil? | ↓|	On the table.
What are we having for dinner? |↓|	Steak and salad.
Do you like ice cream? |↗|	Yes.
Are you going home? |↗|	No.

We can help children by leading them to make the generalization that questions requiring a "yes" or "no" answer usually end in rising pitch. Others normally fade and fall at the end.

Words in a list for drill purposes are seldom pronounced correctly, as each word receives a heavy single word stress. This encourages children to be word callers without any understanding of structural patterns or meaning. I would avoid excessive isolated word drill.

Punctuation marks in print indicate a pause. All pauses are not signaled by punctuation, however, and children should be taught to recognize this. They must learn to associate automatically the punctuations of their own speech with the graphic representations of language.

TEACH HIM THE WORDS

It is important that children develop skills in word recognition. Charles Fries, in *Linguistics and Reading*, outlines some specific principles which he says take priority. He says that because written words consist of sequences of letters from the alphabet it is necessary for children to learn to recognize the letters by configuration and name (2). Some educators believe that we have sufficient evidence to support this.

Some of the most difficult words for children to learn are those the linguists call structure words. They are the words which make up nearly half of the Dolch list of 220 most commonly used words. They are such words as *that, this, who, how, in, on,* etc. These words should not be taught in isolation, but always as they function in the language. Some structure words consistently receive weak stress in sentences. *A* and *the* are structure words which tell us a noun will follow in the sentence. I doubt that a preschooler has ever heard them as separate words. If he is taught to read them in phrases, as "a boy," "a dog," "the cat," we can avoid the mispronunciations they are often given in reading.

Teachers are concerned that children learn phoneme (sound) -grapheme (symbol) relationships in order to be able to decode words. Linguists and educators have called attention to the irregularities of these relationships in some words. Examples are: *come, sure, shoe,* and *again*. Very many American English words do, however, fall into specific spelling patterns. Examples of the three most common patterns follow:

1. consonant—vowel—consonant

bat	bit	bet	but
can	pan	fan	ran

2. consonant—vowel—consonant—e

same	game	lame
hide	side	ride

3. consonant—vowel—vowel—consonant

heat	bait
feed	road

Fries identifies groups of words which fall into subpatterns of each of the three main patterns given (2). Regular spelling patterns are being used predominantly in several sets of linguistic readers currently on the market. Controlled vocabularies are used to present sentences and stories composed of words of the same spelling pattern. There is not agreement among linguists as to this approach. Some of them questioned Leonard Bloomfield's method as outlined in *Let's Read* (1), and these newer approaches appear to be very similar to it.

We do know, though, that children need to learn the common sounds represented in words by letters. We know that we cannot teach them in isolation without distorting the sounds. We know how difficult it is for children to blend together separate sounds to make words. Try saying the sound of the letter *b* alone, and it sounds like "bu." In blending the sound of *b* with *at* to make *bat* the child says "bu-at." He still doesn't know the word *bat*. By teaching spelling patterns we can avoid this. We can teach consonant sounds by helping children hear similarities of sounds in words, and by substituting letters to make new words. We can help children know which vowel sound to expect in a word pattern. These techniques can be used as the child's reading progresses and meaningful opportunities for teaching arise.

SOME CONCLUSIONS

We have examined some of the ways certain principles from the science of linguistics can be applied to the teaching of beginning reading. These principles involve the patterning of language. They include sentence patterns, intonation patterns, and word patterns. We have given examples of some specific teaching procedures which we feel can help children read with fluency and understanding.

Success can come to teachers using these techniques if they have developed insight into some of the basic structures of language. Certain erroneous concepts must be dispelled and a more realistic view of spoken American English accepted.

Some attempts have been made to write linguistic readers for children. Very little use of our knowledge of sentence patterns and intonation patterns is seen. It is in these areas especially that we feel the resources offered by linguistics are being neglected.

The science of linguistics is relatively new. Educators have only begun to ask, "What's in it for us?" We must accept the challenge of this new knowledge, and through experimentation, select that which can help us gain our objective—success and enjoyment in reading for all.

REFERENCES

1. Bloomfield, Leonard, and Clarence L. Barnhart. *Let's Read.* Wayne State University Press, 1961.
2. Fries, Charles C. *Linguistics and Reading.* New York: Holt, Rinehart and Winston, 1962, 190, 171–182.
3. Lefevre, Carl A. *Linguistics and the Teaching of Reading.* New York: McGraw-Hill, 1964. 79–115, 10.
4. Lewis, Richard. *Miracles, Poems by Children of the English-speaking World.* New York: Simon and Schuster, 1966, 167.
5. Lloyd, Donald J. *Reading American English Sound Patterns, A Monograph for Elementary Teachers,* No. 104. Evanston, Ill.: Row, Peterson, 1962.
6. Lloyd, Donald J. "Sub-Cultural Patterns Which Affect Language and Reading Development," *Language, Linguistics and School Program,* National Council of Teachers of English, 1963, 37–54.
7. Loban, Walter. *The Language of Elementary School Children.* National Council of Teachers of English, 1963, 84, 88.
8. Malstrom, Jean and Annabel Ashley. *Dialects U.S.A.,* National Council of Teachers of English, 1963, 18–23.
9. Strainchamps, Ethel. *Don't Never Say Cain't.* Garden City, N.Y.: Doubleday, 1965, 10.

(6) THE SOCIAL PSYCHOLOGY OF READING*

Robert C. Ziller

For too long, thinking and reading have been viewed as lonely academic pursuits. It is unfortunate in some respects that Rodin depicted his thinker as a solitary, closed figure. In this paper, *The Thinker* will be recast (in ink) as *The Thinkers*; more than one person and at least one book will complete the contemplative scene. Within this social cognitive environment reading will be discussed as social imitation, group problem solving, social interaction, and as search for self.

*Reprinted from *The Reading Teacher* 17 (May 1964), pp. 583–87; 573, by permission of the author and the International Reading Association.

READING AND SOCIAL IMITATION

People in general, but particularly children, are by definition members of a social group. Thus, to ignore the social variables involved in any observation of human behavior is to increase the amount of uncertainty in predicting human behavior. The process of learning to read is, from the outset, a social process. Usually the child has observed others in his social environment picking up, holding, and peering at a printed page. As is the child's wont, he will attempt to duplicate the adult behavior. Thus, the foundation of the reading process is imitation, a social learning process. In the pages which follow, a series of ideas collected and expanded by Bandura and Walters (3) will be further expanded to include reading behavior as a socialization process.

Imitation may be reduced to an interaction between self and other in which the imitator identifies with other (3). The identification process is assisted by behaving in a manner similar to the other. Learning may be merely incidental in the process. Yet, imitation is, in general, a most efficient method of learning.

For example, in contrast to methods of selective reinforcement, it is not necessary in the imitative process to await the occurrence of the desired behavior on the part of the student. Moreover, assuming an appropriate model, the imitative process avoids the risk of learning undesirable responses. Some forms of instruction, for example, in order to bring the desired behavior into the foreground, place undesirable behavior before the student as a contrast effect. In this process, however, there is a risk that the contrasting behavior will have greater salience than the expected behavior (3).

The efficiency of observational learning is such that it suggests itself as the optimum approach in rapidly raising the effectiveness of the learner to a level where independent instruction and refinement of the set may operate, thereby relieving the burden of the teacher as well as avoiding student ennui. Accounts provided by anthropologists are replete with examples of the importance of imitation in the socialization process. In fact, in many languages "the word for teach is the same as the word for show, and the synonymity is literal." In many cultures "children do not do what adults *tell* them to do, but rather what they *see* other adults do" (13).

Some of the disadvantages of imitation of a human model are that a single individual performer is often observed, a performer who may embody some behaviors less desirable than others. Moreover, the negative facets of the model may be overlooked because of the mesmerizing effects of emotional attachment. Finally, the human model may not be as available as symbolic models.

Some of these difficulties are less evident in symbolic models. Symbolic models may be presented through oral or written instruction, pictorially, or through combinations of these. Thus, reading in this sense may be viewed as a symbolic model 'for imitation. Reading, then, is a symbolic socialization process whereby the norms of society are conveyed to the neophytes. Indeed, reading itself may be viewed as normative behavior in Western society and a concrete aspect of the socialization procedures; that is, a child is not perceived or does not perceive himself as an accepted group member unless he has learned to read and unless he can discuss topics which he has read (11).

With regard to reading behavior, a study by Almy (1) may be reinterpreted in support of the imitation framework. She found a significant positive relationship between success in reading and such experiences as looking at books and magazines, having someone read aloud, and showing interest in words, letters, and numbers. The origin of such behavior is of greatest interest. It is proposed here that the parents of the more successful readers provided a better model for success in reading; that is, the parents of successful readers were more frequent users of books and were fond of words.

Ryans' exhaustive study (15) with regard to the characteristics of teachers (model here) may also be interpreted within the imitation framework. Some of the personal qualities which appeared to characterize a group of elementary women teachers highly selected with respect to overall classroom behavior included (a) expressed admiration of such qualities as friendliness, permissiveness, definiteness, and fairness in teachers; (b) typically appeared to be "accepting" and generous in appraisals of other persons; (c) saw good points of a person rather than bad. Moreover, personal warmth tended to differentiate the elementary school teacher from the secondary school teacher. Thus, again, these results may be interpreted as supporting Bandura's and Huston's thesis that exposure to a model possessing rewarding qualities facilitates imitation.

Similar evidence comes from an experiment with leaders of military teams (17). These leaders were charged with the optimal development of *all* members of the group, as is the classroom teacher with heterogeneous ability groups. In the military study the leaders of the higher rated teams showed more encouragement to the less effective members; the leaders tended to be more positively disposed toward group members as a whole and were therefore superior models for the imitation process.

In a study by Ehart (7) it was concluded that the tendency to acquiescence was characteristic of good student teachers. She suggested that acquiescence as a manifestation of a generalized tendency to accept, agree, and to approach the total environment in a positive way may elicit imitative responses which result in increased learning.

Other characteristics of the model which relate to imitative behavior on the part of the observer have been subjected to experimentation. For example, differences between the sex of the model and the sex of the child must be considered in assessing or predicting imitative behavior. Rosenblith (14) established, for example, that a male leader was more effective, in general, than a female leader with regard to imitative responses of children. Moreover, high prestige persons are more effective than low prestige persons in inducing imitative behavior (12). This suggests, of course, that if the teacher is accorded high status in the community, regardless of the bases for the status, the teacher may be expected to be more effective.

Finally, the characteristics of the observer also influence imitative outcomes. Thus, the socialization of the child may influence his susceptibility to reinforcement or modeling procedure. Rosenblith (14) noted that more imitation was found in children of nine and ten than in those fifteen and sixteen years old. Extrapolation of these results suggest that even more imitation may be expected by younger children. What supplants imitation as a learning process in older children has not been explored. It is suggested, however, that imitative behavior is inconsistent with the need for independence and the development of a stable and unique self identity.

Another characteristic of the students which has been investigated with regard to imitative behavior is dependency. In a laboratory study by Cairns (6) children with high and low dependency needs were observed in a classroom setting. It was expected that the group low in dependency inhibition would readily seek the experimenter's help in solving a non-solvable puzzle task, while the group high in dependency inhibition, in contrast, would resent any help seeking behavior. The independent group not only reluctantly imitated dependency bids, they also tended flatly to reject help when it was offered.

GROUP PROBLEM SOLVING AND READING

Reading may be described as an individual problem solving process wherein the reader responds to a felt difficulty, searches for information which bears upon the problem, proposes a solution, and evaluates the solution. Similarly, a reading group of children or adults may be described as participating in a group problem solving session. Furthermore, it is proposed that group problem solving processes may serve as a model for individual problem processes and as a superior technique for teaching individual problem solving (2). Again, we will invoke the imitation model with a special concern for role playing as imitation.

One of the difficulties encountered in analyzing the problem solving processes of individuals concerns the inability to observe individual non-verbalized thought. Three methods used to reveal these thought processes are thinking aloud (4), objective techniques of measurement (5), and structured questioning (9). A fourth technique, however, which may be particularly applicable to reading groups, involves observation of group problem solving processes.

One of the mental sets developed by most readers who have learned to read in a standard classroom is an unconditional positive acceptance of the written word. Stauffer describes this phenomenon as the habit of credulity (16). The textbook writer assumes the figure of the teacher in the eyes of the reader, which again tends to reinforce the perception of the inviolability of the typewritten word (it is possible that young students who typewrite may not hold as high a regard for the typewritten word, however). The teacher as the embodiment of the writer presents a powerful differential in comparison with that of the student which is sufficiently disparate as to discourage any kind of critical thinking. It is suggested here that guided group problem solving may facilitate group and individual critical thinking.

In a guided group problem solving reading session, the teacher is viewed as an exemplary model for imitation. Thus, in the group discussion the teacher may shatter teacher-author synonymity by critically evaluating the writing and the writer. Having presented the model for critical evaluation, conforming students may be expected, to imitate the teacher's critical behavior. The third stage of class involvement occurs when a large number of children identify with the exemplary model and peer model imitators and initiate criticism themselves.

In a similar manner other problem solving roles may be introjected by the class members. These roles may include information search, ideation, offering opinions, asking for opinions, and summarizing group progress. Through a process of multiple identification, each student may adopt various problem solving roles as they become embodied in various members of the group who characteristically assume these group functions. Eventually, each independent reader may evoke the appropriate problem solving role through recall of and identification with the role as it was enacted by a group member.

The imitation paradigm suggested throughout this paper assumes that appropriate peer models are available within the classroom group. Thus, the problem of homogeneity as opposed to heterogeneity of the classroom members becomes relevant. It is suggested here that a degree of heterogeneity of classroom members with regard to ability, attitudes and values may facilitate identification with an appropriate peer model and facilitate the positive imitation process which evolves from the teacher as a learning model. If, on the other hand, the classroom is composed of children who are homogeneous in abilities and attitudes, the imitation process may be retarded because of the absence of a peer model who is sufficiently different to encourage the observer to contrast the self with the other and yet sufficiently similar to encourage identification and positive imitation. Thus, in a homogeneous classroom, the teacher becomes a more critical exemplary model for imitation. However, identification with the exemplary model is not facilitated in homogeneous classrooms by the peer model intermediary.

READING AS SOCIAL INTERACTION

Throughout, reading has been described as social interaction between the author of the book and the student. Indeed, two way interaction from author to student and student to author was described as one of the advantages of a group reading approach. However, interaction between reader and author may be achieved without the group's physical presence. Thus, the reader may be encouraged to write running comments in the book's margin; or the child may play the role of the author by summarizing the content and expressing his personal reaction to the author's statements.

All communication is in some sense designed to be persuasive. Even the most bland textbook in reading is attempting or at least indirectly managing to convey normative social behavior. Through interaction with the writer, the persuasion process (reading) is intensified.

By playing the role of the author, the student is reinforced by approval for imitating the behavior of the model. In fact, as the role in time becomes a part of the self concept, imitation of his own former responses may become rewarding to the imitator. In effect, role playing is doubly reinforcing (3).

Through role playing procedures, then, the imitator actively participates in persuading himself of the author's point of view. Indeed, the effectiveness of role playing as a persuasive process has been noted repeatedly by social scientists (8). In the usual experiment, opinion change is tested under two experimental conditions using (1) "active participants" who are induced to play a role which requires them to deliver a persuasive communication to others, and (2) "passive controls" who merely read and listen to the same communication. The results have indicated that active participants were more influenced than the passive controls.

The parallel with a reading class is obvious. Active participation on the part of the readers encourages imitation of the role behavior suggested by the reading, but only when the participants are required to take a position supporting the writer's point of view.

READING AS SELF SEARCH

Finally, reading may be interpreted as a process of self search or self discovery or as a change agent, as has just been described. The student exposes the self to a new experience. Information is provided in the course of this experience as to the relative success or failure of the student in comparison with other students. Thus, new information about the self becomes available and must be integrated within the self concept. Moreover, success and failure are decided by the peer group and a new authority figure other than the parents. This process requires a reorientation of the power structure of society and the location of the self within it. Finally, through reading information is programmed at a far more rapid rate than has heretofore been possible in the child's work, and the information is collected from an enormous number of persons other than the parents. The student is confronted with strangers who have become his teachers and parent surrogates or reinforcing agents in general. It is now proposed that acceptance of these new sources of information and reinforcement probably depends on earlier social relationships and an acceptance of self reorientation.

This position is supported by the results of a study by Long, Ziller, and Henderson (10) concerning the self-social constructs of nonreaders or pupils having severe difficulties in reading in comparison with a sample of readers matched for intelligence. Using a nonverbal descriptive measure of the self-social concepts, it was found that children with reading problems tended to be less independent and tended to cling to the parent relationship. Thus, for example, the nonreaders tended to locate the self within a parent-teacher-friends equilateral triangle rather than outside the boundaries of the triangle; they avoided taking a journey alone and located themselves nearer their parents and teachers than did the children with no reading problems.

SUMMARY

Reading has been described as a social learning or imitative process, as social interaction with the writer, and as a self defining process. Finally, group problem-solving in a reading context was discussed in terms of imitation, identification, and role playing. These discussions are merely illustrative of the efficacy of the more global view of the reading process achieved through the consideration of social psychological factors.

REFERENCES

1. Almy, M. C. *Children's Experiences Prior to First Grade and Success in Beginning Reading*. Contributions to Education, No. 954. New York: Bureau of Publications, Teachers College, Columbia University, 1949.
2. Bales, R. F. *Interaction Process Analysis: A Method for the Study of Small Groups*. Cambridge, Mass.: Addison-Wesley, 1950.
3. Bandura, A., and Walters, R. H. *Social Learning and Personality Development*. New York: Holt, Rinehart and Winston, 1963.
4. Bloom, B., and Broder, H. *Thinking Processes*. Chicago: University of Chicago Press, 1949.
5. Bruner, J. S., Goodnow, J. J., and Austin, G. A. *A Study of Thinking*. New York: John Wiley, 1956.
6. Cairns, R. B. "The Influence of Dependency Inhibition on the Effectiveness of Social Reinforcers." *Journal of Personality*, 29 (1961), 466–488.
7. Ehart, M. E. *Cognitive Complexity-Simplicity in Teachers Perceptions of Pupils in Relation to Teaching Effectiveness*. Doctoral dissertation, University of Illinois, Urbana, Illinois, 1956.

8. Hovland, C. I., Janis, I. L., and Kelley, H. H. *Communication and Persuasion*. New Haven: Yale University Press, 1953.

9. Inholder, B., and Piaget, J. *The Growth of Logical Thinking*. New York: Basic Books, 1958.

10. Long, B., Ziller, R. C., and Henderson, E. "Studies of Individuation: Some Demographic and Psychological Correlations." Unpublished manuscript, 1964.

11. Martin, W. E., and Stendler, C. B. *Child Behavior and Development*, p. 383. New York: Harcourt Brace, 1959.

12. Prince, A. I. "Relative Prestige and the Verbal Conditioning of Children," *American Psychologist,* 17 (1962), 378. (Abstract)

13. Reichard, G. A. "Social Life," in F. Boas (Ed.), *General Anthropology*, pp. 409–486, esp. 471. Boston: Heath, 1938.

14. Rosenblith, J. F. "Learning by Imitation in Kindergarten Children," *Child Development*, 30 (1959), 69–80.

15. Ryans, D. G. *Characteristics of Teachers*. Washington: American Council on Education, 1960.

16. Stauffer, R. G. "Reading and the Habit of Credulity," in S. Hook *et al., The Science and Philosophy of Reading and Role of Tests in Reading*, pp. 2–14. Newark, Del.: Reading Study Center, University of Delaware, 1961.

17. Ziller, R. C. "Leader Assumed Dissimilarity as a Measure of Prejudicial Cognitive Style," *Journal of Applied Psychology*, 48 (1963), 243–248.

(7) PSYCHOLOGICAL CORRELATES OF THE READING PROCESS*

Katrina de Hirsch, L.C.S.T.

I shall try in this paper to discuss some of the structures and processes involved in the reading act in the light of Gestalt psychology. I shall then try to apply some of the general concepts to children who are learning to cope with printed words.

*Reprinted from *Challenge and Experiment in Reading*, 7 (1962 Convention Proceedings), pp. 218–26, by permission of the author and the International Reading Association.

DEFINITION

Reading is the successful response to the visual forms of language. The goal of reading is the understanding of graphically fixed language units.

VISUAL ASPECTS

Reading is obviously more than and different from seeing. More is involved than simple ocular functioning. The visibility of letters is not the same as their readability. Dyslexic children do *see* letters but they do not grasp their symbolic significance. Reading is not only a matter of perception, it is, in the last instance, an intellectual act.

There are, of course, some reading disabilities which are related to visual problems. Robinson and Cleland refer to farsightedness and lack of binocular vision, to difficulties with visual fusion and depth perception which contribute to reading problems.

The 1940 report of the Los Angeles County Medical Association takes a different stand. "Only if visual acuity is reduced to 50% or more will the child have trouble with interpretation of symbols he does not see well. Except in farsightedness of a marked degree, the child's power of focusing is sufficient to give adequate but not perfect vision. Crossed eye with normal vision in one eye has little effect on reading ability."

The discussion whether or not faulty eye movements are responsible for reading difficulties is still going on. Orton and Tinker deny the significance of faulty eye movements in the etiology of reading disorders. Research has shown that the difference in number of eye fixations in excellent and poor readers is surprisingly small. The Los Angeles report quoted above says: "So-called faulty eye movements as judged by regressions depend primarily on poor understanding of subject matter, not on uncoordinated eye muscles, not the eye but the brain learns to read."

Kainz also maintains that the number of eye movements is a function of ability to grasp meaning and not the other way around. In other words, visual processes in reading are largely of a central rather than of a peripheral nature.

CORTICAL FUNCTIONS

Earlier concepts of the central processes pertinent for reading have undergone considerable modification. Neurologists no longer believe that precisely pinpointed brain areas are responsible for specific performance. We do know that in lesions of the angular gyrus the interpretation of printed material is impaired or lost. We also know that the areas adjacent to the angular gyrus do subserve processes involved in reading. However, we no longer believe that we deal with separate and summative cortical excitations. Rather, we assume the existence of highly complex activities involving the whole brain. We know that in aphasic patients who suffer from severe receptive speech disturbances, reading is often impaired as well.

RELEASE OF MEANING

The fact that in cases of language pathology loss of speech is usually accompanied by difficulties with reading comprehension has important implications. For the beginning reader the visual and the auditory structure of the word are intimately bound up with each other and the graphic sign has to be translated silently or aloud into auditory verbal form. The printed word "mat"—a series of letters seen—a sequence in space is transformed overtly or in inner speech into a series of sounds heard—a sequence in time—which in turn release the concept of "mat." Schilder found an increase of electrical activity of the vocal muscles in slow readers.

While Kainz believes that the highly skilled reader proceeds directly from the printed symbol on the page to the underlying concept, that the written word itself is a carrier of meaning, many studies show that even the fluent reader evokes the auditory and motor images symbolized by letters, but that these images are so fleeting and of so short a duration that the individual is not necessarily aware of them. Even the practiced reader will resort to vocalization when he meets an unknown word or tries to understand a difficult passage. Inner speech phenomena are probably never entirely eliminated. How many vocal clues are needed may be a matter of reading proficiency.

PARTIAL PERFORMANCES
INVOLVED IN THE READING PROCESS

However, evoking the auditory image of the word during reading is only part of the total performance. Kainz, in analyzing the reading process, finds a number of partial performances: there is the perceptual grasping of letter and word configurations, there is their evocation in inner speech, there is the comprehension of syntactical relationships, the construction of anticipatory schemata as to what the sentence is going to say, there is finally the assimilation of content into an already existing framework. All of this constitutes an integrated performance, each part influencing the others. It is only in unsuccessful reading experiences—as when someone reads a text aloud but does not grasp its significance—that one can separate out partial performances.

GLOBAL VS. SYNTHETIC READING

One of the basic problems in reading research is the question whether the skilled reader adds letter to letter or rather sound groups to sound groups in order to comprehend the word, or whether the printed word is experienced globally. An answer to this question is obviously pertinent in terms of the battle now raging between the people who teach reading in a global fashion and those who believe that words should be broken up into their phonetic elements and then blended into larger units.

The philosophical foundation for the global approach is based on Gestalt psychology, and it is thus imperative to discuss briefly how this theory influenced the different systems of teaching reading.

SOME GESTALT CONCEPTS

Gestalt psychology, as originally conceived by Wertheimer, defines Gestalt as that function of the organism which responds to a given constellation of stimuli as to a whole. There is an innate tendency in human beings to experience whole configurations. We respond to a given series of separate musical tones as to a tune—a melody—even when it is transposed into a different key. The single element—the separate notes—are different, but the essence of the configuration stays constant, the "figure" as Wertheimer calls it, the tune, in this particular case—remains the same. We respond to an arrangement of pencil strokes as to a square even if the square is presented at a different angle. As defined by Gestalt psychology, visual forms obey certain laws:

1. Form is characterized by being separated and standing out from the ground.

2. The whole and its parts mutually determine each other's characteristics.
3. The various parts of a form have different values, some are indispensable if wholeness is to be retained, others are relatively unnecessary.

These are only a few of the Gestalt laws.

APPLICATION OF GESTALT CONCEPTS TO READING

The original Gestalt experiments were done with simple visual forms like circles and squares. Although letters are, of course, more complex— quite apart from the fact that they have symbolic significance—much of what is true for simple forms, is also true for letters and words. We do not see all the single elements in a word, we see its characteristic features. Words have a physiognomy, derived from the particular relationship between the whole and its parts. This physiognomy makes it possible to recognize these words, no matter whether they are printed large or small, black or red, whether the print is good or relatively poor. We know that if one tears a word apart and prints it in separate syllables it takes 66% longer to read, because, as a result of the syllable division, the Gestalt quality gets lost. In one of his experiments Korte presented words from a long distance so that they were at first quite indistinct and diffuse. The first impression of the word was a global one, including Gestalt qualities like length, density, and so forth. The second phase of recognition began with the moment when characteristic details were recognized as physiognomic and as definitely influencing the total Gestalt.

Because fluent readers are global readers, educators and psychologists have concluded that the best way of learning to read is by the global approach. However, it is only the proficient reader who sees words in a structured and organized way. The beginning reader does not—his ability to differentiate and to integrate is as yet undeveloped and as a result he often cannot cope with long and complex configurations in the form of words. Shorter configurations as represented by letter and letter groups are often easier to take in for the beginning reader. A letter, of course, is a Gestalt also, a partial Gestalt it is true, but possessing, nevertheless, the same qualities as do whole words. We see the single elements in a letter as little as we see the single elements in a word —we only see characteristic features which enable us to recognize the letter as such—whether printed in black or in red, written in one handwriting or in another. Like a word, the letter also has a Gestalt in the sense that it is separate, that it stands out.

What it amounts to is this: There is no essential difference between the recognition of letters and that of whole words. The process is the same: letters as well as words are grasped on the basis of their determining features. Proficient readers tend to take in more complex Gestalten, but even if they grasp them as wholes, they still must be able to analyze them quickly and reliably into their elements. Reading requires both integrative and analyzing competence.

Thus, the dichotomy between the reading of parts and the reading of wholes is largely an artificial one. In normal reading the grasping of complex configurations and the integration of partial ones goes forward simultaneously. It is the combination of both which makes for good reading. The approach depends largely on the age of the reader and on the reading goal. A research paper is read differently from a light novel. When one has to read a large number of newspapers one takes in only the essential words. However, the beginning reader is unable to "skim"— this is a technique he still has to learn. Integrative and differentiating functions develop only slowly. In the light of this statement what happens to the young child who is first confronted with the printed word?

READING READINESS

Reading readiness is a much discussed concept and has numerous facets. Language growth—and reading is one aspect of such growth—is closely related to the emotional climate of the home. The quality of the mother-child bond is a significant factor in early ego organization and basic to verbal communication.

Some children fail in reading because of severe psychopathology, much of their psychic energy is blocked off and not available for learning of any kind. Severe diffuse anxiety, extremes of aggression and submissiveness, psychological infantilism, may all result in a learning disability. Some children are so passive, so phantasy-ridden, that they have little to invest in academic work. However, these children will tend to do poorly in all subjects not in reading only, their difficulties are usually non-specific.

In some homes there is little verbal communication. The cultural level is low, there are few, if any books available, the children are never read to; theirs is an environment deprived of important verbal experiences.

For such children language is not a comfortable tool and reading is likely to present problems.

The correlation between intelligence quotient and reading readiness has been discussed extensively and it has been shown that intelligence is by no means always a reliable indicator of future reading performance. Lately the concept of mental age has been stressed rather than that of I.Q. Most investigators feel that the child must have attained a mental age of between six and six and one-half years in order to successfully deal with printed words.

However, by no means all children with a mental age of six and one-half years are able to cope with visual verbal forms. Our guidance clinics, our schools, and our private offices are filled with youngsters whose mental age is ten years or older and who fail in reading, writing, and spelling for a variety of reasons.

The author feels that "developmental age" is a better yardstick for reading prediction than either intelligence quotient or mental age. There are many lively, reasonably well-adjusted youngsters with excellent reasoning ability, whose developmental age in important areas is lower than that of their peers. These children suffer from what Bender calls a "developmental lag." Language growth and development do not exist apart from organismic growth. Learning to read depends more on maturation than on I.Q., although these two are, up to a point at least, related. Dyslexic children are often neuro-physiologically immature. In order to integrate successfully the visual and spatial patterns as they are represented to the child on the printed page, physiological functions underlying such complex activities as reading, writing, and spelling must have reached a degree of maturation.

MOTILITY

There is, to begin with, the youngster's motility patterning. A young child's movements involve the total organism, they are random and little organized. The ability to move isolated parts of the body develops later out of this generalized pattern. Young children are normally immensely active, their postural reflexes and their tonus reflect a primitive state of organization. They respond to external stimuli in an undifferentiated, global, and sometimes explosive way. Learning to pattern motor and behavioral responses, however, is required in first grade where the youngster is expected to sit still for a considerable length of time.

FINER MOTOR CONTROL

Orton was the first to point to dyspraxic features in dyslexic children. Rabinovitch refers to their non-specific awkwardness and clumsiness. Movements require patterning. A skilled motor act, as Gestalt theory points out, is not merely a summation of isolated events; a series of separate movements will not necessarily result in a fluid rhythmic performance. To hold a pencil and learn the rudiments of writing requires a degree of finer motor control which not all children have reached at the age of six and a half years. Youngsters with severe writing difficulties lack the control needed for the rhythmic flow of pressure and release required in the writing act. Indeed, we find many older dyslexic children whose written compositions look like those of youngsters who have just begun to write. Their letters are crudely executed and in some severe cases we find continuing difficulties not only with spacing, but with the formation of the letters themselves.

PERCEPTION

Not only the formation but the very recognition and identification of letters is difficult for some children. Perception starts out as an only crudely differentiated process and becomes more precise as time goes on.

Intact sensory equipment is not all the young child needs in learning to speak and read. It is not sufficient for the three-year-old to *hear* words, he has to differentiate between a bewildering variety of phonemes contained in words. In the same way, it is not enough for the six-year-old to *see* letters and words. His peripheral and central visual apparatus must be mature enough for him to discriminate between minute differences in the shapes of letters and words.

For some children nothing on the printed page stands out—in Gestalt terms the "figure" and the "ground" are fused, and as a result, the printed page looks like an undifferentiated and meaningless design.

Beginning readers and immature older children do not perceive words as structured wholes, but as a jumble of details lacking organization. As Langman puts it, "they do not perceive the complex and distinct internal designs of words, nor do they respond to their general shape and outline." Young children are often unable to grasp the physiognomic features of words, the specific relationship between the whole and its parts which, according to Gestalt theory, makes a word or a letter look familiar. They sometimes recognize a word in one situation, perhaps in heavy black print against the background of a white card. However, the perceived Gestalt is unstable and the child might fail to recognize the same word when it is embedded in a page. For successful reading the youngster's perceptions must be mature and stable enough to allow him to transpose the word or letter configuration into different situations, so that he can differentiate between a *t* and an *f* or a *d* and a *b*, whose only discriminating feature is orientation in space.

SPATIAL ORGANIZATION AND PRINTED LANGUAGE

Since reading is a pattern laid out in space, it is pertinent to discuss briefly spatial organization in young children. The point of origin for all spatial relationships is the child's body image. His own body is the frame of reference. Between the age of three and four the child's image of his body—its parts and their relationship to each other—still is fairly undifferentiated. Body image is determined by laws of growth and development. It unfolds in the course of a maturational process by integration of the child's sensory, motor, emotional, and social experience. Spatial organization in the pre-school youngster still is at a primitive level. Many five-year-olds are unable to see the difference between the picture of an object and its mirror image. Furthermore, the child acquires only slowly the verbal concepts expressing spatial experiences. He has to learn what "upside down" or "right side up" means. As a matter of fact, acquisition of these verbal labels helps to fix the relationships themselves.

Laterality implies an internal awareness of the two sides of the body, directionality is the ability to project this awareness into extrapersonal space.

Ambiguous laterality is an expression of difficulty with spatial orientation and is frequently found in combination with disturbances in understanding and formulating of spoken and printed language. Most young children are ambidextrous and only slowly develop a functional superiority of one hand over the other. Thus it is of interest that Subirana reports that E.E.G.s of strongly right-handed children are more mature than those of ambidextrous ones. This would tend to prove that laterality has its maturational aspects as well as the genetic ones emphasized by Orton. Zangwill resolves the apparent dichotomy between a genetic and a maturational point of view by postulating a constitutionally determined maturational weakness in children whose laterality continues to be ambiguous.

Most researchers do feel with Harris that failure to develop a superiority of one hand over the other usually results in difficulty with consistent left to right motor and perceptual orientation which is essential for reading, writing, and spelling. Most people will agree that there is a significant relationship between poor lateralization and reading and spelling disabilities.

VISUO-MOTOR ORGANIZATION

One of the ways we judge spatial organization is by means of the Bender Gestalt test, which is designed to evaluate visuo-motor organization. The evolution of visuo-motor Gestalten is primarily a developmental process, and the youngster who is expected to cope with reading and writing must have visuo-motor experiences similar to the adult's. The Bender Gestalt test correlates highly with existing reading readiness tests and it has been shown that the visuo-motor competence of poor readers is inferior to that of good ones. Difficulty with arrangement of the Gestalten on paper, tendency to rotation, and verticalization all bespeak the dyslexic child's troubles with spatial patterning.

TEMPORAL ORGANIZATION AND ORAL LANGUAGE

Language in its different forms is organized in a time-space pattern. Chesni and Simon say that dyslexia is a disturbance in spatio-temporal organization, which consists, according to Hardy, in failure to "perceive and reproduce the serial order of auditory and visual information." As discussed earlier, speech, which demands sequential organization of linguistic units in time, is intimately linked to reading.

Disorders of auditory memory span and difficulties with auditory discrimination interfere not only with speech, but also with reading and spelling. For spelling the simple recognition of visual configurations is not sufficient. Spelling requires reproduction of these configurations, and if their temporal representation is inadequate, spelling difficulties are bound to follow. Vernon says that bad spelling reflects a lack of phonetic appreciation. Reversals of sounds in speech show up in reading reversals. Trouble with the intonational and melodic aspects of oral language are usually reflected in arrhythmic and non-fluent reading. It is quite possible that the same basic disturbance in temporal patterning underlies the rhythmic disorders of both reading and speech.

There is an abundance of literature dealing with the relationship between poor articulation and dyslexia. It is less well known that inadequate inner language structure and grammatical deficits will tend to interfere with the formation of anticipatory schemata in reading.

Another aspect which has been largely overlooked, and which we have long felt is an important factor in dyslexia, is word-finding difficulties. The child who has trouble evoking familiar word concepts when presented with pictures, is bound to have difficulties with the printed symbols representing these concepts. Rabinovitch feels, as does the author, that anomia—word-finding difficulty—is a significant and often neglected cause of reading disabilities. Dyslexic children's vernacular may be adequate, but they are frequently unable to remember not only the letters of the alphabet, but also the names of weeks and months. Since naming is a conceptual function, difficulty with naming would reflect not only trouble with all types of sequences, but also problems of a categorical nature.

Another and very important speech disturbance is cluttering, which is characterized by extremely fast, arrhythmic, and disorganized verbal output and is frequently associated with severe spelling disabilities. The clutterer's reception and reproduction of auditory configurations is usually diffuse and poorly structured—he will tend to say "monstry" for "monastery," and this is the way he will spell the word. His poor auditory discrimination is directly reflected in his inferior spelling.

INDIVIDUAL ENDOWMENT IN THE DIFFERENT MODALITIES

We know that normal individuals' endowment differs in terms of the various sensory modalities. I now refer to the auditory, visual, and motor types described by Charcot and discussed by Freud in his paper on Aphasia in 1886.

Children vary enormously in ability to deal with the various sensory modalities. Some show excellent competence in the visual-spatial area, in striking contrast to their weakness in the auditory-motor realm. Others show a different pattern: excellent auditory ability while visual-spatial performance lags.

We are now testing approximately 100 children by means of a battery of 42 maturational tests for a reading prediction study on the kindergarten level,* and we are trying to get an impression of each child's maturational pattern in the various modalities and in the following areas: motility, gross and fine muscular coordination, laterality, visuo-motor organization, body image, figure-ground discrimination, auditory competence, receptive and expressive aspects of oral language, and matching ability. So far we have observed a number of phenomena:

1. There is a striking difference in children's performance from month to month, between the ages of five and six, before they have been exposed to formal learning. Apparently this age span is a crucial one in terms of maturation.

2. Some of the children's maturational patterns are bizarre in the sense that they are far advanced in one modality and quite slow in another one.

3. Some youngsters seem to mature slowly in *all* modalities in spite of good reasoning ability. One gets the impression that they have trouble with the structuring of Gestalten on different levels and in various areas. Their immature motor patterning, their trouble with organizing auditory and visual stimuli into sharply and clearly delineated configurations, their primitive perceptual and motor experiences, and their difficulty with reception and expression in oral speech seems to reflect some basic Gestalt weakness —perhaps as Bender and Subirana suggest—some inherent maturational deficit.

IMPLICATIONS FOR TEACHING

What then are the implications for the teaching of reading? Most children learn to read regardless of the method of teaching. They learn to integrate short configurations into larger ones and analyze wholes into their determining parts, simply by being exposed to them over a period of time and by being given some organizational principle to help them unscramble printed patterns. The majority of bright youngsters learns to integrate and differentiate toward the middle or end of first grade, and as time goes on they acquire a stable enough perceptual organization to enable them to maintain a "linguistic Gestalt."

*Grant from the Health Research Council of the City of New York, Contract No. U-1270.

However, there are many other children for whom specific teaching approaches will make a world of difference. And only if we study the various sensory modalities differentially will we find out what type of learning a child can use best. The work done by Hardy and Wepman in the auditory realm and the very important new investigations done by Birch in the visual and motor sphere have significant implications for learning of both normal and handicapped children.

Since, as the author tried to show, reading requires both the grasping of wholes and the analyzing of parts, there is no real dichotomy between the teaching of whole configurations and that of separate units which are blended into larger entities. What method is best depends entirely on the individual child, his specific competence and weakness, and his differential maturation in the various modalities.

The youngster who has "physiognomic" troubles, as it were, for whom words do not easily become familiar even after many exposures, the child whose visual-spatial competence is lagging, will do better with phonics, which involves temporal rather than spatial organizational principles. If the child's auditory ability is adequate, phonics will make it easier for him to link the visual with the auditory structure of the word. Moreover, since the learning of smaller units reduces the complexity and length of Gestalten, such a child will find it easier to cope. Phonics does not, of course, mean the simple adding of sound to sound—after laboriously blending short units, there comes a moment when the process changes qualitatively and the Gestalt "jells"; only from that moment on the child is actually reading.

On the other hand, there are children who cannot possibly be taught by phonics. Children, for instance, who have trouble with analysis and synthesis, whose intellectual potential is low, whose auditory competence is weak, whose frustration level is too low to build up words slowly and patiently from their determining parts, will undoubtedly do better with the whole word approach.

It is not easy for the overburdened classroom teacher to investigate each child's competence and weakness. On the other hand, an awareness that avenues of approach are not necessarily the same for all children, has significance for all teaching, not only for reading. Such awareness is especially important in dealing with those children whose maturational pattern is markedly uneven. Much time and effort could be saved by careful study of the differential maximal learning modality in children.

Kofka says any perceived Gestalt is a product of organization and maturation and is promoted by training. Such training contributes to the formation of essential sensory-motor patterning in the Central Nervous System. We know from animal experiments that the non-use of a function leads to atrophy. Thus, the emphasis on maturation should not be understood to mean that one should sit back and let development do the rest. The clinician's and educator's task is to study carefully the maturational level of the different modalities in each child who has difficulties. Thus, in the framework of a warm and supportive relationship the teacher can help the child perform at the highest level of his potential.

TO SUM UP

Reading is one segment of the interrelated skills which we call language. It requires a relatively high degree of integration and differentiation. If viewed as immaturity of Gestalt functioning, many of the correlates of reading difficulties like reversals, poor auditory discrimination, figure-ground difficulties, and poor oral speech become a comprehensible part of the total picture.

Differential study of the maturational level of the various sensory modalities will prove to be helpful not only for remedial work, but will also, in the last instance, provide another avenue for exploration of educational tools and methods.

Part Two
The Teacher's Task

❖❖❖❖❖❖❖❖❖❖❖❖❖❖❖❖❖❖❖❖❖❖❖

Chapter 3. Classroom Diagnosis and Correctional
            Strategies

Chapter 4. Classroom Management and Teaching
            Techniques

Chapter 5. Materials

Chapter 3

CLASSROOM DIAGNOSIS AND CORRECTIONAL STRATEGIES

INTRODUCTION

All instruction begins with a diagnosis. The diagnosis may be simple or complex, but any decision is made on an analysis of the data or the presenting situation. Decisions reached may be correct or incorrect; but in any instance, they normally will be no better than the information on which they are based.

Can teachers learn to constantly collect data, diagnose, and make effective decisions in daily teaching? The articles in this section are addressed to the premise that teachers can and should become proficient in solving the intricate problems which arise in everyday classroom situations in teaching reading. To achieve this goal, teachers must be committed to the concept of differentiated teaching and formulate plans to achieve it. Differentiated instruction based on diagnostic operations does not just happen. Such instruction must be made to happen by the teacher first adopting a diagnostic attitude.

Probing, constant probing, for further information about each student through informal and standardized measures as well as through critical observations is an essential criterion for diagnostic teaching. Learning to interpret each measure correctly and accurately must occur to avoid wrong instructional decisions. Knowing the purposes and limitations of each tool and their interrelationships, such as the relationship between standardized test scores and instructional reading levels, fosters accurate interpretation of classroom measures.

Making a timely diagnosis of a potential reading problem before the problem becomes serious can arrest or prevent many a disability case. Each lesson or practice session offers several opportunities for classroom diagnosis. But diagnosis and decision-making are hardly enough. Action must follow! Corrective strategies must be formulated, applied, adjusted, readjusted if necessary, according to the problem situation.

Differentiated instruction and diagnostic teaching depend upon five essential elements. These "5-D's" are: 1) discernment, 2) data-gathering, 3) diagnosis, 4) decision-making and 5) doing. A constant cycling and recycling of these processes leads to effective diagnostic teaching and improved reading instruction.

(8) THE CLASSROOM TEACHER
AS A DIAGNOSTICIAN*

Richard W. Burnett

The concept of the teacher of reading as a diagnostician in the classroom is not a new concept. However, it is a point of view which needs to be continually restated because of the many narrower definitions of the teacher's role vying constantly with it for attention in the market place. Unfortunately, the restating of a point of view which has been around for some time is closely akin to preaching from the pulpit. Certainly, the field of reading has had more than its share of sermon preachers and evangelists—too many people with all the answers. Some are just hucksters peddling a product; others are zealots devoted to an organizational pattern or a single approach to reading instruction.

We have had the strident voices of the *Why Johnny Can't Read* era with us now for some time. We have patiently endured such books as *Reading: Chaos and Cure, Tomorrow's Illiterates, What Ivan Knows That Johnny Doesn't,* and *Reading Without Dick and Jane.* We have watched fundamentalist evangelists band together into a corporation dedicated to keeping a "phonics vs. no phonics" argument alive even when the issue as they chose to define it has been demonstrated time and time again not to exist. Even now those with simplified solutions to all reading problems find support in the equivocations of the latest controversial book, *Learning to Read: The Great Debate.*

We have weathered a revision of *The Writing Road to Reading* which preaches that the only way to teach children to read is to teach them to write and spell first. In the early 60's we had the emotionally charged writing of the evangelists who preached "individualized reading," which many took to mean "burn the basal texts and have every child reading out of his own little book." In the mid 60's we had the British invasion of the much promoted and publicized ITA or Initial Teaching Alphabet. At about the same time, Words in Color with its multi-hued charts and glittering promises hit press and classroom. Throughout the

---

*Reprinted from *Methods of Evaluating Reading* 13, Part 4 (1968 Convention Proceedings), in press, by permission of the author and the International Reading Association.

60's we have shuddered as the "neurological reorganization" disciples have continued to call attention to their crawling exercises as reading-related therapy. At present, we are bombarded from all sides with this set of "linguistically sound" readers or that set of "scientifically programmed" kits or workbooks. The din of the drumbeats grows louder as corporations grow larger and as university professors fight for "visibility" above the clamor.

My message is based on the results of a research study, partly on observations made as an elementary teacher, and partly on experience in working with teachers and disabled readers in schools and clinics during the past twelve years. A major point of this "sermon" is to suggest that you reflect carefully on any sermons you read or hear preached in the reading field before rushing to embrace a new cult or sect.

PATTERNS OF TEACHING READING
IN THE CLASSROOM

My observation has been that elementary teachers in the approach they take to reading instruction arrange themselves on a continuum from A to Z.

At point A we have the teacher who has 37 pupils in his classroom. He has heard someplace that it is normal to expect a wide range of differences in reading performance within any class. But there are just so many hours in the day! How can he do individual work with 37 children? Besides, there is a set of readers for his grade and all of the pupils, according to the principal, should read the stories before they move on. So, the teacher has one big reading group. They all read out of the same book for thirty or forty minutes each day, preferably in the morning because that is the best time, according to the curriculum guide.

At point Z at the other end of the continuum, we have a very busy, anxious teacher who goes to all the conventions and workshops he can possibly attend. He reads all the research monographs and journals. He is extremely interested in causal factors in reading disability and the relationship between handedness, eyedness, and cerebral dominance factors and reading problems. He is also concerned about vision and hearing problems, gross and fine visual-motor perception deficiencies, endocrine and metabolic inbalance, mental age factors, growth patterns, reversal tendencies, personality variables including intro- and extrapunitiveness, hereditary factors, socio-economic status of the home, sibling rivalry, sex identification, and anything else that anybody has seen fit to relate to reading instruction in the past forty years. In his fifth grade class, he may be using Frostig materials, ITA, and Fernald's kinesthetic approach all at the same time. In short, he is so anxious and changes his methods and his own objectives so frequently to conform with theories that he does not begin to understand, that his approach is an even more ineffectual "do nothing" approach than the one at point A.

Back at point B, we have the teacher who recognizes that some differentiation in instruction should take place, so he has two reading groups—the slow and the fast, or more commonly, the "eagles" and the "hawks." Both are reading out of the basal reader but one group is going through a little slower.

At point Y, we have a teacher who believes in individualized reading instruction. He will not permit a basal reader or any kind of a workbook in his classroom. He has 37 pupils, so he secures three times thirty-seven library books every two weeks for the class. He believes in self-selection, so the pupils pick out their own books to read. Luckily, this teacher is a rather fast reader himself, so by next year he will have read nearly all of the books and will know a little better what the pupils are reading. It is a good thing for his sake, too, that the children are all using the same arithmetic book, social studies text, health book, and speller.

With a little more common picture at point C, the teacher has three reading groups—"eagles," "hawks," and "crows." The top group is reading in the fifth grade level basal readers. This middle group is reading in another fifth grade series but taking it a little slower. The third group is reading in some old third grade books the teacher just happened to find in the storeroom. He is not very satisfied. Neither are his students.

Right next to our previous teacher, at point D, we have an ambitious teacher with something almost revolutionary taking place in his room. Not only are there different numbers of reading groups with considerable changing back and forth, depending on the teaching purpose, but children are all reading individually or in groups out of different level books and materials at different times. Weaker readers are working in varying materials in accordance with their specific skill strengths and weaknesses. Most surprising of all, top achievers are reading out of library books as well as other materials at a level two or more years beyond the class's actual grade placement.

The illustrations could go on for, actually, there are hundreds of possible instructional approaches and classroom organizational patterns that could be described along such a continuum. Furthermore, at any point on this continuum, short of the extremes, effective classroom instruction can take place and is taking place. But it is not because of the materials being used or not used or the organizational pattern followed that instruction may be effective. It is because there is a teacher, who, within the framework of his classroom organization, is looking for individual problems that come up in the course of instruction. He varies his instructional approach enough from day-to-day to strengthen weaknesses that become apparent, and to expand and reinforce certain basic learnings that have been covered before but now need expansion and reinforcement. This effective kind of teaching approaches what has been called "diagnostic teaching."

As stated before, the idea of diagnostic teaching is not new. It is simply the idea that the classroom teacher must be able to assume the responsibility for planning and carrying out a program of instruction based on his analysis of the strengths and weaknesses of each pupil. But it is obvious from the popular controversies in reading instruction such as phonics vs. no phonics, basal reader programs vs. individualized reading, Joplin plans vs. homogeneous grouping within the classroom, filmstrips vs. primers, ITA vs. traditional orthography, or "meaning emphasis" vs. "decoding emphasis" that the principles underlying a diagnostic approach are often lost sight of in looking for "all or nothing" answers to how to teach reading.

TEACHING COMPARED TO OTHER PROFESSIONS

A brief comparison between teaching and other professions is appropriate here. There are certain problems that a doctor is expected to be able to cope with as a consequence of his training and experience. He has to diagnose an illness, prescribe a remedy, and evaluate the effectiveness of his decisions in bringing about a cure. The lawyer who has a case in court is faced with a problem situation also. He has to size up the situation and weigh alternative in each separate case before proceeding on a certain course of action. Teaching a class of children to read presents an analogous situation. Each class, as well as each individual in a class, poses a unique problem for the teacher. As a professional, he must first of all be equipped to size up the class as a group as well as each individual in the class in terms of strengths and weaknesses, and, secondly, know how to keep up a constant appraisal while carrying on a program of instruction designed to bring about improved performance in the reading skill areas being taught. The utilization of a problem solving approach should underlie the teacher's planning when he faces the class at the beginning of the year, when he plans each lesson throughout the year, and anytime that he looks at the performance of an individual pupil in his class.

We are not likely to be satisfied with a doctor that prescribes the same medicine for different illnesses. Nor are we inclined to consult a lawyer who handles a divorce case in the same way he handles a criminal case. Yet many teachers keep expecting to find the one "sure fire" way to teach reading to all children.

THE BASES OF DIAGNOSTIC TEACHING

A research venture I engaged in some years ago (reported in the January 1963 *Reading Teacher*) had the underlying objective of trying to define operationally what is meant by the diagnostic teaching of reading in the elementary classroom and to construct an instrument for measuring a teacher's proficiency at solving problems related to the teaching of reading. The work that took place was part of a much broader study of teacher problem solving proficiency. The particular instrument I worked on, in order to measure what we wanted it to measure, had to be valid for assessing the teacher's problem solving proficiency regardless of the administrative plan or grouping procedure overlaid on the actual reading instruction. These kinds of questions were considered pertinent:

Can the teacher pick out information from a pupil's record file that is critical information in making judgments regarding his reading ability?

Can the teacher formulate classroom diagnostic procedures that are applicable in giving him more information about a particular child's reading skills?

Can the teacher interpret the information after he accumulates the data?

Can he make meaningful recommendations as to how to remedy certain kinds of weaknesses or problems?

There remains, of course, a final question that unfortunately could not be answered by any paper-and-pencil tests we were able to devise. That is, can the teacher carry out effectively all of these steps in an actual teaching situation? It appeared logical then, as it does now, to assume that the teacher who knows best what to do will be more likely to do it than one who cannot identify the problems, interpret data, and formulate a course of action.

These problem solving instruments have been given over the years to several hundred teachers and elementary education students. A shocking finding is that the performance of experienced teachers in terms of mean scores on the problems is only slightly higher than that of students in undergraduate courses. However, the performance of people who are trained and experienced in remedial reading procedures appears to be significantly higher on the problems testing each level of operation, i.e., recognizing critical data, calling for additional information, interpreting data, and recommending a plan of instruction. A question emerging from this study is why do people after several years of classroom experience in teaching reading seem to be performing in their problem solving about the same way they might have performed as undergraduate students. To respond to that question requires speculation beyond the research data. Such speculation is reprehensible for a researcher but is pretty much a matter of policy for "preachers" in the reading area. I, also, shall speculate. It may be that as teachers we are accustomed to thinking in terms of preestablished patterns or methods of classroom organization for instruction to take care of individual differences which we know to exist. We may not be oriented to preparing ourselves to be flexible, to identify problems as they arise in our classes, and to change our courses of action, sometimes drastically, in accommodating our techniques to the problems rather than forcing the child with problems to accommodate himself to our procedures.

IMPLICATIONS FOR THE CLASSROOM TEACHER

The frequent reaction from classroom teachers is "Well, it's easy enough for a reading clinician to say be flexible, look for individual problems, teach to meet individual differences, when he is working with one or two children at a time while I have a room filled with 35 different problems." And, of course, this reaction is justified, up to a point. Those teachers are correct that in a clinic children are instructed one or two at a time. Ordinarily, though, the only cases worked with are those who are pretty much beyond the reach of group instruction in a classroom. Methods and materials are adapted to meet their needs and are used only as long as they work. Approaches to instruction are modified or replaced if they do not seem to be getting results. Constant evaluation, both formal and informal, takes place to determine if progress is being made and if the instructional techniques are working. In extreme cases, anything that conceivably might work is utilized. But, short of the fact that he may be working with only one or two children at a time, the clinician has nothing miraculous, no wonder-drugs, no teaching devices, no machines, that are not available to any classroom teacher. Many times, the wide gulf that exists between good remedial teaching and the teaching that takes place in the classroom is attributable to an attitude that our problems must conform to our limited supply of available solutions rather than our solutions conform to our problems.

What are some of the skills that we ought to legitimately expect any teacher of any grade to possess and make use of? There are several levels of proficiency in coping with a problem situation. One level would be to grossly identify the problem in this manner. "Johnny has a problem. He is in the fifth grade and he cannot read fifth grade material." That is as far as some go in their diagnosis. At the next higher level, the problem is broken down and interpreted. "Johnny has a problem. He is in the fifth grade and he cannot read fifth grade material. He is of normal intelligence. He has a well-developed sight vocabulary and makes good use of context clues. However, he cannot consistently apply phonic principles to sound out strange words beyond recognizing initial consonant sounds. His instructional level is about third grade, while he is completely frustrated with fourth grade material. Independently, he can handle controlled vocabulary reading material of a middle second grade level." Some teachers accumulate this much information about a child in a semester, but that is as far as they go in coping with the problem. At the highest level of problem solving proficiency, the teacher, besides identifying and interpreting the problem, can suggest specifically what can be done within the framework of available time, materials, and school policy to help Johnny overcome his weaknesses, and can carry out such a program.

Underlying the assumption that we can expect qualified teachers to perform at the highest level of proficiency are many teaching skills that we need assume. For example, a teacher has to know what the difference is between an independent and an instructional reading level. He has to recognize when a child has reached his frustration level. A teacher may not describe the child's reading behavior using these terms but, nonetheless, he needs to recognize the different levels of reading performance in each child. He has to be able to interpret standardized test results with all of their limitations. Ideally, the teacher should be able to listen to a sample of oral reading and determine whether a child is prone to be over-analytic in his approach to strange words or whether he is deficient in phonic analysis skills. He ought to be able to tell whether the pupil is a word guesser or whether he makes good use of context and structural clues to unlock new words. He has to be able to judge whether a child's performance is consistent with his ability. He has to recognize the difference between weaknesses in comprehension and weak word attack skills. He should be aware of the sequential development of skills that go into forming a confident and capable reader. He must be able to instruct in specific skills without throwing out the balance that must exist between unlocking words and understanding ideas. All of these and many more are necessary skills for effective reading instruction regardless of how the class is grouped, what textbooks or materials are used, or whether the teacher leans toward a strict program of phonics instruction for everyone or toward an individualized reading program.

CONCLUDING STATEMENT

To summarize, I want to emphasize that we, as teachers, should not limit ourselves to looking for "how-to-do-it" recipes or last word solutions. We should grow in professional competency, certainly, by looking at new materials and programs, and by reading new research and journal reports related to improved methods of reading instruction. But new approaches must be translated into our own teaching situations, weighed against our own understanding of the reading process, measured against our own personality and teaching style, and only then applied and formally evaluated.

In trying out new instructional approaches, we can take encouragement as well as find cause for caution in a couple of observations that are substantiated in nearly every study that is made of new approaches to teaching reading. One is that experimental groups usually show gains over control groups regardless of the new teaching method being used, often just because of the interest and enthusiasm generated by the teacher in trying to understand and make use of a new method. A second finding we can take heart in is that problem readers often respond favorably in terms of performance gains when any kind of attempt is made to individualize instruction.

Today, there is a sense of urgency in finding better ways to teach reading, just as there is a sense of urgency in finding an effective cure for cancer. In our inner cities we have the seemingly insurmountable problem of teaching hundreds of thousands of children who must not be turned out of our schools with substandard educations. Cultural pressures of a different sort in suburbia are resulting in thousands of children, especially boys, limping through their school experiences as underachievers seriously deficient in reading ability. In the face of this urgency, nothing is gained by recklessly abandoning our decision-making responsibility as to how reading shall be taught to the loudest and most recent of the hucksters or evangelists to arrive on the scene with their educational nostrums.

There are no programs, machines, kits or other novelties in the reading market place today that offer advantages that cannot be attained in several other different ways by informed teachers. The effectiveness of any one of the new tools rests on a teacher's proficiency at recognizing and solving problems that are different not only every school year but every school day. When the day comes that every teacher at all grade levels is concerning himself with diagnostic teaching, we can close our clinics and retire our remedial reading teachers, for we will have our diagnosticians in the classroom where they belong. Furthermore, our hucksters and preachers in reading will not continue to get rich on unwarranted claims and unfulfilled promises.

(9) CLASSROOM METHODS IN CORRECTING READING DEFICIENCIES IN ELEMENTARY SCHOOL*

Sister Mary Julitta, O.S.F.

Have educators today built up a wall of seclusion around the retarded readers? At times, it would seem that there is a tendency to place the problem of the retarded reader entirely in the hands of the specialist, leaving the teacher with either a feeling of impotency or a lack of responsibility for the retarded reader. This is unfortunate in many re-

*Reprinted from *Better Readers for Our Times* 1 (1956 Convention Proceedings), pp. 134–38, by permission of the author and the International Reading Association.

spects. From the statistical standpoint alone, the classroom teacher is needed to play a vital role in helping the 15 to 40 per cent of the class who may be retarded in reading. However, it is even more important that the classroom teacher be included in the program because, in the last analysis, she is the one who works directly with the child in all activities and knows the child's academic, social, and emotional maturation levels. Regardless of the efficiency of administrative plans, curriculum consultants, and reading specialists, the teacher is in the best position to reach directly all the children and to be sensitive to each child's needs. She is constantly watching his developmental characteristics to prevent retardation, diagnosing and correcting the reading ailments which are in the embryonic stage or emanate from external causes, and detecting serious remedial cases with deeply rooted causal factors for referral to the reading specialist.

This places the classroom teacher in a very important role in the lessening of reading retardation and correction of actual deficiencies. It implies that the classroom teacher will be prepared (1) to detect reading retardation, (2) to be diagnostic in her approach to reading disability, (3) to carry on a well-rounded, developmental reading program which meets individual needs, (4) to understand the child with reading problems, (5) to be acquainted with materials and techniques, and (6) to make provisions for the retarded reader in other content fields which require reading. As implied in the title of this paper we shall deal here only with the correction of reading deficiencies.

MEETING INDIVIDUAL NEEDS THROUGH A DIFFERENTIATED INSTRUCTIONAL PLAN

In situations where class size is reasonable and there are good or superior teachers, corrective work for the ordinary poor reader will not be thought of so much as remedial reading but as meeting the individual's need in a group situation. The work begins with the class and builds an atmosphere of oneness among the individuals through co-ordinated interests and with respect for the dignity of an individual and his contribution regardless of his reading level. In such a setting, the classroom teacher will be free to differentiate instructional procedures, assignments, and levels and types of work while each child feels accepted and is happy in the joy of success which he meets when work is planned in line with his functional reading power.

Although this friendly relationship is basic to success, it cannot succeed unless the teacher has some administrative ability to take care of various details within the total classroom picture. To meet individual differences, there will be need for groupings within the class.

Since the learning rates of individuals differ and there are varied needs within each similar instructional-level group, flexibility and variety in grouping will be necessary or the groups may become as lock-step as our present grade system. Probably the most basic type of grouping will be *that according to general instructional level.* At this time, the basic skills of reading can be taught in a well-directed developmental program allowing for development of the varied skills in reading. Many cases of simple retardation can be corrected if these developmental programs are initiated at the child's true instructional level. In fact, a very fundamental principle of good corrective reading is to begin at the child's instructional level of reading. There will be definite growth if intensive daily work is done in developing the lessons while gradually building the skills which will give the child power over the printed symbol, including both identification and interpretation. Care must be taken that the individual retains his identity within the group by constant study and re-appraisal of his reading so that emphasis in skills can be directed according to studied needs. There is no reason why each child would need to follow through with the same assignment. Instead, assignments should be made according to needs.

As the achievement-level group continues with a strong developmental program, there will always be individuals from any one of the groups who will require more work in certain areas. The need arises for another type of grouping, the *special skills group.* One small group of children may need help in word analysis; another group, help in assimilative reading; or another group, assistance in oral reading. These small groups are organized at any time without formality, and for any period of time simply to meet a need when and for the length of time the need exists.

At times, there will be *team groups* who work with especially prepared materials for needed practice on some problem, or even an individual child who is helped through pupil tutoring or by the teacher. The free-reading time, while stimulating pupils to wider reading, offers opportunity for the teacher to give time for assistance in skills to individuals at critical times.

Not all help in corrective work is given through group instruction. There should be opportunity for the entire class to meet together, not only to keep group solidarity and interests, but also to give the retarded reader status with the total group. Even the severely retarded readers should be a part of the class group. The important factor is that each child is able to contribute to the total group. From these class groupings will arise *interest groups* or committees which will work on different aspects of the general problem and report to the group. This is valuable as there will be a cross section of ability within these groups, which, though reading about the same topic, are working with materials of different readability levels appropriate to their stage of growth in reading.

This brings us to another point in the program of differentiated instruction—the amount and variety of materials required in a good reading program designed to aid all types of readers. There will be need for materials of a sequential nature to ensure a step-by-step development of the total reading skill. Small sets of different basal reader series will satisfy this need. However, it is highly advisable to reserve those sets which have higher interest levels and a more mature format for use with the retarded readers so that they will not be embarrassed using materials which are in the hands of children in the lower grades. These basal readers should serve, not as the developmental reading program, but as the springboard from fundamental skills to wider reading, utilizing the skills acquired in the basic work. At present, there is a growing collection of materials of low difficulty and high interest level to meet the needs of retarded readers. Lists containing titles and sources are available.[1] Present readability gauges for mechanical difficulty aid teachers in selecting books of various difficulty levels for any particular topic.

Aside from actual books, there are many types of materials to develop specific skills in a challenging manner.[2] These various skill builders and games enable the teacher to supply practice material for the skill groups and individuals.

Worksheets and workbooks for the development of skills are an additional aid to teachers. When used to meet a specific purpose for a certain group or individual, they offer valuable learning and practice situations. They may serve also for the development of skills with the entire class group, for example, in the improvement of rate and compre-

[1]Helen S. McEntee. "When Johnny Can Read—But!", *The Reading Teacher*, IX (February, 1956), 144–49.

George Spache. *Good Books for Poor Readers.* Gainesville, Florida: Reading Laboratory and Clinic, University of Florida.

[2]George Spache. *op. cit.*

hension. In that case, workbooks emphasizing a certain phase of reading at various difficulty levels such as the *Reading for Meaning* series[3] can be a learning situations for all the children, with each one, however, using the level suited to his particular reading power.

Then there are the broader educational aids such as filmstrips, movies, and pictures which furnish backgrounds for improvement of word meaning and interpretation, and also are the means of teaching different skills. Atlases, indexes, dictionaries, and encyclopedias are needed for background references and the teaching of locational skills in reading.

All in all, for a differentiated reading program to meet individual needs and help the retarded readers, an adequate supply of materials of many types and many levels of difficulty must be available. The school librarian can help tremendously not only in the distribution and checking of materials, but also in acquainting the classroom teacher with books, and guiding individual children in reading at their particular levels of growth.

We must conclude that a differentiated reading program is not merely a matter of group teaching. It is something much more personal and founded on the idea of the dignity of the individual and his particular growth pattern while at the same time he is an integral part of a total classroom situation. It requires a teacher who is acquainted with the psychology and method of teaching reading, who has administrative power, and who at the same time is highly sensitized to individual needs and growth patterns. In such a situation, the retarded reader is free to solve his problem. Here, too, there is time to devote to the child with the serious reading disability who is receiving help from the specialist. He, too, can be drawn into the group and have the opportunity to work with special skills groups as well as do his own practice work guided by the reading specialist without feeling different. For in this class, growth and development of the individual within his group is the standard.

CONCRETE SUGGESTIONS FOR GUIDING
THE RETARDED READER

It will be noted that in the class taught through a differentiated instructional program, the retarded reader is helped as an individual in the same basic manner as the reader who is working up to capacity. There are ways, however, in which the classroom teacher meets the retarded reader on the specific basis of his own problem. Usually, the retarded reader

[3]W. S. Guiler and J. H. Coleman. *Reading for Meaning*, Grades 4 to 12. Chicago: J. B. Lippincott Company, 1945, 1955.

has been frustrated; he has developed personality and emotional problems as a result of his reading deficiency or vice versa; and he has often developed poor work habits. Consequently, in helping the retarded reader, the classroom teacher will need to know how to assist him in solving his problems, relaxing his tensions, and building good habits. Specifically, the teacher:

1. Initiates a program which means success at the outset to build confidence
2. Begins with short assignments which the child learns to complete
3. Utilizes every means to restore status to the child in the eyes of his peers
4. Gives healthy encouragement and places real confidence in him
5. Discusses the particular problems directly with the reader in such a way that he realizes there are means of solving reading deficiencies and assists him in setting his goal
6. Places the responsibility for progress on the child's shoulder with the felt assurance that he will be backed by the teacher
7. Continuously shows progress in such concrete ways as through graphs and charts

Within the round of the day's work, there will be many situations in which the retarded reader must receive consideration outside the regular reading class. In the language arts areas, it is necessary to remember that there is a sequence in the facets of language, that adaptation in written expression must be made. The child cannot be expected to spell at his grade level when he is reading several grades below it, nor can he express himself adequately in written communication. Since he has not read so extensively, he may not have acquired a facile use of language unless his home background has provided this in the form of speaking vocabulary.

In the content areas, such as social studies and science, unit teaching lends itself well to the many reading levels. The concepts and the important facts in the lesson to be taught are the basis for planning. If these form the basis for the lesson, children can be directed to books of lower difficulty level for enrichment of concepts. Instead of studying the text, which is too difficult for the retarded reader, the ingenious teacher will find other means of conveying the ideas. Some suggestions are:

1. Sharing with each other the ideas gleaned from varied books read by members of the class at their particular difficulty level

2. Using movies, filmstrips, slides, and pictures related to the text content
3. Arranging for various contributions by class members, through maps, construction activities, dramatization, etc.
4. Class summarization of basic concepts and facts as a core of knowledge
5. Pictorial representation in the form of time lines, spatial representation of events, and charts of processes in development

In order to carry out effectively the work in content fields with many books and materials of various difficulty levels, the teacher will need to work in close co-ordination with the librarian. She will need to keep the librarian informed on the individual children's reading levels and difficulties, the topics to be studied, and the general plan for study.

Through these methods of adaptation and through direct teaching of related reading skills, the classroom teacher will be able to help children improve reading, not only during the teaching of the basic skills, but also during any class period throughout the day. This will necessitate alertness to situations in which basic reading skills are developed or applied. As general and technical vocabularies are introduced, special efforts can be made to introduce the word forms in relation to meaning and apply skills in word attack. Particular lessons will offer guidance in the use of textbooks. The text and smaller units within the textbook supply many occasions for the teaching of organizational skills. Even before the reader is able actually to follow through on the reading, he can be introduced to division of thought, the relationship of these ideas, and the method of development of ideas by means of class discussion. He then acquires the power to think in organized fashion and is ready to make a transfer of organization power to the reading situation when he has gained control over the mechanics of reading.

(10) EVALUATING PROGRESS IN READING THROUGH INFORMAL PROCEDURES*

Mary C. Austin and Mildred H. Huebner

Educators today recognize that growth in reading is a continuous process which should be measured periodically. They know that pupils and

*Reprinted from *The Reading Teacher* 15 (March, 1962), pp. 338–43, by permission of the authors and the International Reading Association.

teachers benefit from evaluations of reading progress which indicate what has been accomplished and what skills, methods, and materials should be presented next in the developmental sequence to assure further growth. They are aware also that their evaluations should combine the findings both of formal and of informal appraisal procedures.

In their efforts to provide better reading instruction for all children, teachers ask: What are the values of informal measures? Which types have been most useful? How can these procedures be used to greater advantage in the classroom?

VALUES OF INFORMAL MEASURES

Informal appraisals can assist teachers in a number of ways. The results of such procedures supply evidence regarding pupil reading levels, including pupil strengths and weaknesses. This information is useful in forming reading groups based upon instructional levels or special needs. It is helpful also in selecting appropriate materials for these purposes, as well as for independent reading activities.

When used in conjunction with other appraisal techniques, informal procedures assist teachers and pupils in assessing pupil growth over a period of time, thereby pointing to the possible need for reviewing and reteaching certain reading skills before the introduction of new ones. In other words, when informal appraisals are conducted skillfully, and when the results are interpreted accurately, they enable teachers to *program* reading instruction more effectively.

TYPES OF INFORMAL APPRAISALS

Whenever teachers note a pupil's reading ability or deficiency for planning purposes, they are using informal evaluation procedures. They observe pupil behavior for signs of inadequate sight recognition vocabulary, poor methods of word attack, vocalization during silent reading, unusual reading posture, comprehension problems. They discover the ease with which a pupil locates information in a card catalog and in reference books. They use teacher-made tests to determine a reader's depth of understanding and his ability to read critically.

Teachers also devise inventories, questionnaires, and checklists for additional data about pupil reading interests and abilities. Interest inventories, for example, may be developed by preparing statements to be completed by students, such as, "If I had three wishes . . . ," "During my free time I like to . . . ," and "My favorite book is . . . ." Study skills may be ascertained by informal small-group discussions of previously planned items, such as "I study best . . . ," "When I want to learn more about a topic, I . . . ."

A pupil's instructional level can be estimated quickly by means of a checklist which samples the vocabulary from several graded textbooks in reading, social studies, science, or other areas. The checklist may include from ten to fifteen words from the primary-grade texts and twenty words or more from the upper-grade texts. Words from several levels, both above and below the pupil's grade level, may be presented for flash recognition by means of a hand tachistoscope or by the teacher's manipulation of two small cards in such a manner that a single word is exposed rapidly. Usually the failure to recognize one or more words at a grade level will indicate the necessity for choosing easier materials for instructional purposes. Vocabulary checklists, then, can be helpful on several occasions: to test a pupil's mastery of words from previous reading levels, to form a tentative judgment of his independent and instructional levels, to provide reading materials with which he can succeed until further information is available about his ability, and to estimate the starting level for the administration of an informal reading inventory.

Because teachers frequently ask about informal reading inventories, two types are described somewhat in detail in the following sections of this paper.

GROUP INVENTORIES

As a first step toward the selection of appropriate materials for each pupil at the beginning of the year, teachers usually refer to the information about pupil achievement to be found on cumulative records and on reading progress sheets. In referring to these data, teachers recognize that changes probably have occurred in the pupil's reading status during the months following the last recorded items. They therefore plan to give a vocabulary checklist, similar to the one mentioned above. By using the results of the checklist, the scores from the most recently administered standardized tests, and the information of the student's completed reading list of the preceding year teachers can estimate the present reading levels of their pupils. Materials for developmental and independent reading, as well as for the content areas, can then be assembled.

During the first week or two of the school year, many teachers seek more reliable evidence of their pupils' reading levels by giving inventories based upon the reading materials tentatively selected. If, for example, a teacher has decided that a fifth-grade basic reader is appropriate for a number of her pupils, she can "try out" the new book by inviting four or five pupils to read orally at sight from a representative story. As each child presents a passage from the story, the teacher may note special characteristics of his ability to read with fluency, comprehension, and accuracy. Following his oral reading, each pupil can be asked a series of questions prepared by the teacher to determine the extent of his comprehension and his grasp of word meanings. The passage and questions below serve as an illustration:

Fifth Reader (3)

Oral: (140 words) p. 116

It was close to sunset in the woodlands of the Adirondack Mountains. Joseph Brant, the young leader of a group of Mohawk Indian boys, halted. The hunting trail that they had been following all day led into a small open space in the forest. Under a great tree, a spring of clear water trickled over mossy stones.

The leader raised his arm as a signal for his band to halt. "We will camp here for the night," he said. "It is a good place."

"Joseph Brant is very careful," said the boy next in line. "If I were leader of this hunting party, we would walk on until nightfall."

Joseph half turned. He began to answer sharply, but stopped. He knew that a leader must not let himself become angry. He was a sachem's son and must handle his men well.

1. Who was Joseph Brant?
2. What had the boys been doing all day?
3. What did the leader decide to do?
4. What did the next boy think about this decision?
5. Why didn't Joseph give the boy a sharp answer?
6. What do you think a sachem is?

Should the pupil make more than one word recognition error for every twenty words in the selection he has read, and should there be an obvious lack of story comprehension, the material probably is not suitable for him. In this way the results of the group reading inventory show the teacher immediately for which pupils the material is not appropriate for instructional purposes, either because of its difficulty for the less able reader or because of its lack of sufficient challenge for the more able one. On subsequent days she may regroup her pupils for an inventory based on more advanced reading for those whose achievement is at a higher level, and, similarly, she may present easier books to those who appear to need them. In a relatively short time the teacher is able to appraise the present reading levels of her pupils, to re-evaluate the suitability of the materials she has selected for their use, to form groups within her classroom, and to make plans for individualized work.

The above techniques are equally helpful in assessing reading levels in the content areas, particularly in social studies and science throughout the entire school program.

INDIVIDUAL INVENTORIES

While teachers would like to analyze the reading performance of each student by means of an individual inventory, class size may make such a procedure impractical. It will be especially helpful, however, for evaluating the ability of those pupils who do poorly on a group inventory and of those transfer pupils who enter during the year with incomplete records. In situations such as these, the individual inventory is an effective tool for the reading specialist and the classroom teacher to use in determining a pupil's specific strengths and weaknesses, as well as his readiness for reading at a higher level.

The informal inventory is typically a compilation of graded reading selections with questions prepared in advance to test the reader's comprehension. Graded textbooks in reading, or in the content areas, may provide the material for the inventory. At least two samples are chosen from each book. The length of each sample will vary from under one hundred words at the primary levels to more than one hundred at the intermediate and upper grade levels. One passage at each level is read orally without previous preparation by the pupil, and a second passage is read silently.

The starting level on the inventory may be estimated by the teacher through the use of a vocabulary checklist. As the pupil reads aloud, the teacher carefully notes the child's errors on a separate oral reading checklist or on a transparent paper placed over the page of her book. If the latter technique is used, the teacher will have prepared transparent sheets beforehand to correspond to the pages of the story, so they can be realigned easily for her appraisal at another time. Having a tape recording of the pupil's oral reading, if this can be arranged, is of great value for an accurate analysis of the pupil's reading performance.

The items listed below are illustrative of those which might be incorporated into an oral reading checklist. If the teacher places a mark after the errors as they occur, and writes an example, whenever possible, she will have a graphic picture of the pupil's performance.

1. Word recognition errors
    a. Mispronunciations
    b. Omissions
    c. Substitutions
    d. Words pronounced for the pupil (after a five-second hesitation)
2. Fluency
    a. Word-by-word reading
    b. Inadequate phrasing
    c. Punctuation ignored
    d. Repetitions
3. Observations
    a. Finger pointing
    b. Strained, high-pitched voice
    c. Marked insecurity
    d. Tension movements
    e. Poor posture
    f. Head movements
    g. Lack of interest
    h. Holding book too close

Detailed oral reading checklists both for sight reading and for prepared reading may be found in *Reading Evaluation* (1).

Following both oral and silent reading, the pupil's comprehension should be checked by asking previously determined questions orally and by having the child respond in a like manner. The number of questions usually will range from five to eight, the lower number accompanying the selections at the primary-grade levels. In formulating these questions, certain guides are helpful (4):

1. Questions should be based upon the reading material rather than on experiences the child may have had.
2. "Catch" questions should be avoided.

3. The language of the questions should be geared to the level of the material.

4. Unaided recall-type questions should be used.

5. Questions should be stated so that the exact wording of the story is not necessary.

Whenever possible, four types of questions should be included in the comprehension check: (1) Factual—those dealing with the child's ability to recall specifics in the story, (2) Inferential—those measuring the child's ability to draw inferences or make judgments based on events or implied occurrences in the story but which are not directly stated, (3) Vocabulary—those attempting to measure the pupil's knowledge of words used but not defined in the selection, and (4) Use of context clues—those attempting to measure the child's ability to use context clues to gain the meaning of presumably unknown words (4).

In evaluating the results of an informal reading inventory, teachers should clearly understand the differences between the pupil's *independent reading level* and his *instructional level*. In the first place, the child's independent reading level is somewhat lower than the one at which the teacher plans to carry on developmental reading instruction. Usually, the independent level is indicated by the pupil's ability to read orally without making more than one word-recognition error per one hundred words, to understand at least 90 per cent of what he reads, and to read without such symptoms as finger pointing, head movements, and poor phrasing. His *instructional level* is reached when he can read orally with no more than one word-recognition error per twenty words, with at least 75 per cent comprehension and recall of the material he has read, and when symptoms of difficulty are absent. Betts (2) discusses these levels in detail, and he provides instructions for constructing and administering individual and group reading inventories.

SOURCES OF INFORMAL INVENTORIES

Informal reading inventories may be developed by classroom teachers individually or by a school system for its own use, as has been done in Lakewood, Ohio, and in the Bucks County, Pennsylvania, Public Schools.

Several inventories have been published and may be examined for their content: (1) M. Austin, C. Bush, and M. Huebner, *Reading Evaluation* (New York: Ronald Press, 1961) pages 235–246. Includes an inventory based upon the Sheldon Basic Readers for grades 1–8, published by Allyn and Bacon, Inc., 1957. (2) E. Betts, *Handbook on Corrective Reading* (Chicago: Wheeler Publishing Company, 1956), pages 20–35. Includes an inventory based upon the graded American Adventure Series. (3) N. B. Smith, *Graded Selections for Informal Reading*: Diagnosis for Grades 1 through 3 (New York: New York University Press, 1959). An inventory for the primary grades. (4) R. Strang and D. K. Bracken, *Making Better Readers* (Boston: D. C. Heath, 1957). Includes examples of teacher-made tests in the content areas.

CONCLUDING STATEMENT

The wide range of reading achievement at every academic level is an accepted fact today. Awareness of this situation, and of the importance of adapting instruction to individual accomplishments, focuses attention upon two related instructional needs: (1) accurate appraisal of each pupil's level of reading achievement, and (2) the use of such information as a basis for the selection of suitable reading methods and materials.

Teachers who give more than "lip service" to providing for individual differences in the reading program recognize the valuable contributions of informal procedures in their evaluation of pupil progress. During the next decade they will use an even greater variety of approaches than in the past to assist them in meeting the needs of all pupils in their classes.

REFERENCES

1. Austin, M. C., Bush, C. L., and Huebner, M. H. *Reading Evaluation.* New York: Ronald Press, 1961. Pp. 10–11.
2. Betts, Emmett A. *Foundations of Reading Instruction.* New York: American Book, 1957. Pp. 438–485.
3. Sheldon Basic Reading Series, Boston: Allyn and Bacon, 1957.
4. Sipay, Edward R. "A Comparison of Standardized Reading Achievement Test Scores and Functional Reading Levels." Unpublished Doctor's dissertation. Storrs, Connecticut: University of Connecticut, 1961. Pp. 81, 83.

(11) HOW USEFUL ARE INFORMAL READING TESTS?*

Joseph P. Kender

Many reading authorities have acknowledged the usefulness of informal reading tests, or informal reading inventories (2) as they are often called, for evaluating the performance of pupils to insure their proper placement in reading materials for instructional purposes. Among the references to the efficacy of informal reading tests are those made by Austin and Huebner (1), Betts (2), Botel (3), Cooper (6), Durrell (8), McKee (13), Smith (14), and Sipay (15), to mention only a few. The brief discussion of the strengths and weaknesses of informal reading tests that follows, while admitting their usefulness, seeks to define the limitations within which these tests can be used.

It is argued that informal reading tests are valid because they are constructed from functional materials, that is, the textbooks or reading matter that the pupil is going to use. It is further argued that because of this factor they are more accurate than standardized tests, at least insofar as they are used to place pupils in reading materials for instruction.

There seems to be some evidence to support this position. In a study in which Betts (2) compared the grade equivalent scores of several standardized tests designed for use at the fifth grade level with the performance of pupils in functional reading materials, he found that the standardized tests were not adequate for determining the level of achievement of pupils at the lower or upper ends of the distribution. Chall (5) pointed out that standardized tests designed for a few grade levels often give a distorted impression of reading achievement especially for the poorest and the best readers. Killgallon's study (11) in which he administered an informal reading test to 41 pupils revealed that the standardized test did not discriminate well among the lower extremes of the distribution. One child, for example, scored 2.8 on the standardized test but was incapable of reading a pre-primer on the informal reading test. Sipay (14) compared the grade equivalent scores of three standardized reading tests with the grade placement scores yielded by an

*Reprinted from *Journal of Reading* 11 (February 1968), pp. 337–42, by permission of the author and the International Reading Association.

informal reading test. Although his general conclusion was that it was impossible to generalize as to the suitability of a particular standardized test to indicate the instructional level of a given pupil, he reported that the use of standardized reading test scores for selecting materials that are most suitable for instruction does not appear to be warranted.

These views illustrate the agreement among many reading authorities, regarding the usefulness of informal reading tests. But here the general agreement ends. The literature pertaining to the construction and scoring of informal reading tests is conflicting. For example, there are informal reading tests that consist of a series of grade passages, oral and silent; others that consist only of oral reading passages; still others composed of graded word lists; and some constructed from sentence samples. All of these instruments purport to do the same thing—determine the instructional level of pupils.

When one analyzes the criteria used to score informal reading tests, there is even more conflicting data. There is disagreement, for example, over whether or not to include certain types of errors such as repetitions when calculating percentages of accuracy in oral reading. There is disagreement over whether all oral reading errors should be counted or whether only significant errors, that is, those that alter the meaning of the sentence or passage, should be counted. There is disagreement over whether or not vocalizing during silent reading is a detriment to the reader and whether it should be considered in ascertaining instructional levels. Some feel that understanding of 90 per cent of the material is necessary at the instructional level; others feel that 75 per cent is adequate; while others contend that only 60 per cent is sufficient—and on it goes.

Perhaps some of the disagreement results from the dearth of research related to the subject. This writer found only three experimental studies devoted to the topic, and these have obvious shortcomings. A case in point is Killgallon's study (11) upon which at least a part of Betts' criteria for scoring informal reading tests is based. As one aspect of a larger investigation, Killgallon examined 41 fourth-grade pupils on an informal reading test in an effort to establish criteria for scoring any such instrument of similar construction. Peculiarly enough, he set up *a priori* criteria for the establishment of instructional levels, then tested his subjects, analyzed the performance of the subjects at the instructional level on the basis of his *a priori* criteria, and derived a new set of criteria. He found, for example, that the most suitable percentage of accuracy for acceptable pronunciation at the instructional level was 95 per cent. Despite the unorthodox manner by which this "criterion score" was derived, it is quoted widely in the literature (4, 7, 9, 12, 16).

Cooper (6) attempted to establish suitable criteria for scoring an informal reading test in a more scientific manner. He hypothesized that there is a direct relationship between the ratio of word perception errors and gains in reading. To test this hypothesis, he administered an informal reading test to approximately 1,000 pupils from the Boston area in grades one through six. He then placed them into five word perception groups ranging from those who made the fewest word perception errors to those who made the most. He compared the scores made by the pupils on two standardized reading tests that were administered at the beginning and end of the investigation and found that the group that made the fewest word perception errors made the greatest gains in reading achievement, and the reading group that made the most word perception errors made the least gains. He analyzed the performance of the pupils in each group and derived criteria for scoring an informal reading test.

Obviously Cooper's criteria were derived with greater scientific precision than were Killgallon's; however, their wide application is subject to some question. Because of the relatively small sample tested and the limited geographic and socioeconomic group represented in the study, application of these criteria to other pupils in other places must be made cautiously. Then, too, the materials that were used were taken from only a few basal reading texts. Whether Cooper would have arrived at the same criteria if he used different materials is questionable.

McCracken's research, which intended to establish a valid instrument for establishing instructional levels, seems to be one of the best reported to date. He based his validity on the vocabulary of three basal readers and tested the validity of his passages by using well-known readability formulas. He further corroborated his results by administering his test to 664 pupils in grades one through six and using the ratings of twenty-five nationally known reading authorities. One is aware of the care and scholarship that were involved in the study; but the shortcomings that were mentioned relative to Cooper's study are also applicable in this case. In addition, McCracken (12) stated that the standards used in his test were based upon the criteria recommended by Betts (2). In light of this fact, McCracken's findings must be regarded with some reservation if one considers the manner in which at least one of Betts' standards was derived by Killgallon as reported above.

Kender (10) attempted to determine how much agreement existed among the instructional levels of a group of eighth-grade pupils if he ascertained these instructional levels by using three different informal reading tests, two consisting of a series of graded passages and one consisting of a series of graded word lists, scored by three different criteria. The use of these dissimilar tests and criteria represented the lack of agreement that is evident when one reads the literature extant. It must be noted that all three of these tests are reported to be useful in determining the instructional levels of the pupils to whom they are administered. As one might expect, significant differences were found among the means of the instructional levels made by the same pupils on the three tests. In fact, the mean scores obscured the magnitude of the differences among individual instructional levels especially for the poor readers.

On the basis of the foregoing discussion, one can answer the question, "How useful are informal reading tests?" by stating that they are useful, but within certain limitations. They can be used for establishing the level at which a pupil can be instructed profitably and can yield other valuable diagnostic information. The conclusions that follow, though not a definitive prescription for all the problems mentioned in this paper, might serve as a guide within which informal reading tests might be used effectively.

1. Passages used in a test aimed at determining placement of pupils for instructional purposes should be taken from reading materials in which the pupil is going to be instructed. Obviously, placement of pupils in instructional materials is extremely important and must be as accurate as possible for all children. It is conceivable that the difference of even one-half of a level (the differences, say, between a 2^1 and a 2^2 basal text) could mean the difference between success or frustration in reading for some pupils. Therefore, using an informal reading test constructed from one set of materials to place pupils in other materials would result in inaccuracies that would be detrimental to the progress of these pupils. Undoubtedly, these inaccuracies would be greater if narrative materials were used to predict placement in content materials than if narrative materials taken from one basal series were used to predict placement in another basal series. If materials other than those to be used for instruction are employed, the results must be regarded as only highly tentative.

2. It is difficult to recommend any particular criteria for scoring an informal reading test because no one set of criteria has been

sufficiently validated. The few sets of criteria that have been derived experimentally are subject to some question. Use of these criteria would have to be based on a solid foundation in reading diagnosis—which leads to the next point.

3. Anyone who is expected to administer an informal reading test must be thoroughly knowledgeable about the reading process and thoroughly skilled in administering the instrument. The examiner must make his own judgments about what constitutes a sound reading performance on the part of any pupil. He must make decisions about a pupil's word analysis skills, his oral reading, his silent reading, his comprehension, and many other factors involved in the reading process. The usefulness, then, of an informal reading test is in direct proportion to the knowledge of the examiner who uses it; therefore, it is unlikely that just any classroom teacher can easily administer an informal reading test and judiciously interpret its results as is sometimes claimed.

REFERENCES

1. Austin, Mary C. and Huebner, Mildred H. "Evaluating Progress in Reading Through Informal Procedures," *The Reading Teacher*, 15 (March, 1962), 338–343.

2. Betts, Emmett A. *Foundations of Reading Instruction*. New York: American Book, 1957.

3. Botel, Morton. *Guide to the Botel Reading Inventory*. Chicago: Follett Publishing, 1961.

4. Caughran, Alex M. "Determining Progress in Basic Reading Skills," *Evaluation of Reading*. Supplementary Educational Monographs, No. 88. Chicago: University of Chicago Press, 1958, 98–101.

5. Chall, Jeanne S. "Interpretation of Results of Standardized Reading Tests," *Evaluation of Reading*. Supplementary Educational Monographs, No. 88. Chicago: University of Chicago Press, 1958, 133–138.

6. Cooper, J. Louis. "The Effect of Adjustment of Basal Reading Achievement," Unpublished Doctoral Dissertation, Boston University, 1952.

7. Daniel, John E. "The Effectiveness of Various Procedures in Reading Level Placement," *Elementary English*, 39 (October, 1962) 590–600.

8. Durrell, Donald D. *Improvement of Basic Reading Abilities*. New York: World Book, 1956.

9. Fletcher, Lillian B. "Using the Results of Standardized Reading Tests to Improve Instruction," *Evaluation of Reading*, Supplementary Educational

Monographs, No. 88. Chicago: University of Chicago Press, 1958, 144–148.

10. Kender, Joseph P. "Analysis of Factors Associated with Informal Reading Tests at the Eighth Grade Level," Unpublished Doctoral Dissertation, University of Pennsylvania, 1966.

11. Killgallon, Patsy A. "A Study of Relationships Among Certain Pupil Adjustments in Language Situations," Unpublished Doctoral Dissertation, Pennsylvania State College, 1942.

12. McCracken, Robert A. "The Development and Validation of the Standard Reading Inventory for the Individual Appraisal of Reading Performance in Grades One Through Six." In *Improvement of Reading Through Classroom Practice.* International Reading Association Conference Proceedings, 9. Delaware: International Reading Association, 1964, 310–313.

13. McKee, Paul. *The Teaching of Reading in the Elementary School.* Boston: Houghton Mifflin, 1948.

14. Sipay, Edward R. "A Comparison of Standardized Reading Scores and Functional Reading Levels," Unpublished Doctoral Dissertation, University of Connecticut, 1963.

15. Smith, Nila B. *Reading Instructions for Today's Children.* Englewood, New Jersey: Prentice Hall, 1963.

16. Wheeler, Lester and Smith, Edwin H. "A Modified Approach to the Informal Reading Inventory," *Elementary English,* 34 (April, 1957), 224–226.

(12) CLASSROOM HELP FOR CHILDREN WITH BEGINNING READING PROBLEMS*

A. Sterl Artley

For the sake of our discussion in this paper, we are placing children and youth with reading handicaps in categories depending on the nature and complexity of their problems.

In the first group are those whose reading problem is only one of a constellation of problems. Usually it is deep-seated, multi-causal, and multi-faceted. Related problems may be neurological, physical, sensory,

*Reprinted from *The Reading Teacher* 15 (May 1962), pp. 439–42, by permission of the author and the International Reading Association.

social or emotional. Where facilities are available it is not uncommon for several specialists to become involved in both the diagnosis and remediation of the problem. Fortunately, in terms of the total number of retarded readers, the number of children in this group is relatively small.

A somewhat larger group is made up of children whose reading problem, though of varying degrees of severity, is unencumbered with the related problems found in the first classification, or at least stands out as the primary problem. Frequently these are children whose individual instructional needs have been unmet over a prolonged period. Not only has reading growth been at a virtual standstill, but family pressures and the effects of frustration have added complications. These children may be referred to a reading center or to a specially trained reading teacher for diagnosis. Remediation may be carried out in special classes or in summer remedial programs where the services of a specially trained remedial teacher are required.

READING DIFFICULTIES BEGIN

A third group, a still larger one, is made up of children in the regular classroom who, in terms of specific skill areas, are failing to achieve as well as they should. These are children whose problem is just beginning and who will find themselves eventually in the second group which we have just described unless their needs are met through a planned program of instruction. These children and their problems are the responsibility of the regular classroom teacher. It is this group with whom we shall be concerned in this paper.

For the sake of clarification let us describe a few of the children comprising this group. Tom has completed his first grade readiness program but still shows limited ability to detect rhyming words and to indicate other words beginning with a given sound. Helen has been absent from school for a week with an illness and has missed the sequential instruction on several important reading skills. Mark fails to "catch on" to the application of an essential word attack skill. Jane has a persistent confusion between four groups of similar words. Pat runs roughshod over material he is reading orally, getting the meaning through context rather than through accurate recognition of words. Marie's oral reading is accurate, but her voice is high-pitched and she gives little thought to the interpretation of the story. Cathy is a fifth grade transfer pupil who is unable to use the dictionary to get the meaning or pronunciation of words.

One will observe that each child has a particular reading need—we can hardly call it a problem—which on the surface appears quite innocuous, or at the most only annoying. However, these innocuous difficulties have a way of combining and snow-balling until we have a major problem which may require specialized services for both diagnosis and remediation. From our clinical experience we have found that the majority of cases referred for diagnosis are not those caused by some obscure emotional problem, an uncorrected visual defect, or an involved neurological problem. Basically, they are an accumulation of unmet reading needs.

DETECTING BEGINNING PROBLEMS

To detect and diagnose these incipient problems is one of the primary responsibilities of the teacher. It is at this point that the prevention of major difficulties begins. She must be on constant watch for the child whose reading performance is alerting her to a possible problem.

One of the situations that lends itself to an assessment of needs is the directed reading lesson itself. In fact, every reading lesson should be a diagnostic lesson. It is here that the teacher may observe the application of skills that have been taught. Inability to recognize certain high-frequency words, to read for meaning, to use a familiar sight word to unlock an unknown one, to interpret implied ideas, or to apply a principle of syllabication are symptomatic of a lack of understanding or skill mastery. Both silent and oral reading situations will give the teacher clues to areas where instruction should be modified or adapted to particular children in the group.

Possibly one of the best diagnostic devices that the teacher has available is the practice or workbook. One of the functions of the workbook is to give the child opportunity to practice independently a particular learning or skill that has been taught in the directed reading lesson. Consequently, it will give the teacher an idea as to how effective that instruction has been and the kinds of additional help that a given child may need. If, on a fifteen-item page dealing with the short sounds of vowel letters, a child shows a preponderance of errors, the evidence is quite clear that additional teaching and practice are in order.

If the workbook is to be used to its maximum advantage, every page should be checked by the teacher or by a pupil-helper. If by the teacher, she may give needed reteaching help as the pages are being checked. If a pupil-helper checks the page from a key supplied by the teacher, only those items indicating incorrect responses need to be marked, so that in a free moment the teacher may note pupils who need more help.

The "unit" tests supplied by the publisher of the reading series are designed chiefly as diagnostic instruments. They give an objective measure of each child's readiness for the succeeding level and indicate areas where special guidance is needed. Administering and interpreting the test as recommended by its authors will give an indication regarding the effectiveness of the basic instruction and the adequacy of the day-by-day corrective help.

The personal reading record of each child may also be a means of indicating areas where special guidance is needed. Through individual and group discussions with the children the teacher will be able to get answers to questions such as these: What is the quality of the content being selected for personal reading? Has the child made the discovery that books and magazines are a source of information and pleasure? What is the quality of insight into the motives and behavior of story characters? What types of reactions does he freely make? What is the level of comprehension for main ideas and supporting details? Is the child being frustrated by persistent errors of word attack?

PROVIDING SPECIAL HELP

Assuming that the teacher is able to identify the specific problem, what action follows? With problems of the type we have been discussing the child seldom needs more than additional teaching or reteaching, directed specifically to the problem at hand. Tom, the boy who needed more work in ear training before introducing the sounds of initial consonants, can profit from activities similar to those that have been suggested in the guidebook of the readiness program. Jane, who was confusing groups of similar words, needs to be shown in one group at a time the features that differentiate one word from the other. This should be followed by practice sentences where the context calls for careful choices between the confused words.

Seldom will it be necessary to use reteaching techniques requiring special training. Excellent suggestions for reteaching and practice will be found in the teacher's manual. In addition, teaching activities and suggestions of materials that may be constructed for practice purposes may be found in such sources as Russell and Karp's *Reading Aids Through the*

Grades; Durrell's *Improving Reading Instruction*; and Harris' *How to Increase Reading Ability.*

Pages from workbooks of other series dealing with the skill on which one is working may be used to good advantage in particular instances. If the problem is one of word attack, selected pages from prepared workbooks such as Meighan, Pratt, and Halvorsen's *Phonics We Use* may be useful. Frequently the guidebook to the reading series will suggest activities to be used with children with special needs.

ORGANIZING SPECIAL HELP GROUPS

The question of organizing the class or group for additional help is one to be considered. Time is precious to any teacher and she seems never to have enough to do all the things that need to be done. Yet this is not the problem that it appears to be if one organizes special "help" groups made up of those children who require more help. In fact, the meeting of individual needs through "help" groups will provide the opportunity for the teacher to do some of her most effective and rewarding teaching. These groups are made up of the children who evidence the same need; they are designed to deal only with one specific problem, and as soon as that problem is resolved the need for the group no longer exists. Hence, it is temporary in nature.

To be more specific, let us assume that in the directed reading lesson we find two children who need reteaching and additional practice in attacking words where the vowel digraph principle applies. These two children might be called aside for help at a time during the day when the other children are engaged in independent work. Quite possibly one, or at the most several, short sessions are all that will be necessary to help these children over their hurdle.

In many cases the teacher may find that the problem is one that the children may work on together without her direct supervision. For example, several of the children may be having trouble recalling certain sight words. After each child identifies those particular ones that give him trouble, either he or the teacher should write or type the words on halves of 3-by-5 index cards. Meeting in pairs, each child "flashes" to the other his trouble words.

In cases where a problem is more persistent the teacher may need to keep a special group intact over a longer period of time. This may be the case where several children have been absent or where transfers show the need for the development of a particular ability.

SUMMARY

A high percentage of the reading problems that one finds in a typical classroom are a result of the failure of instruction to provide adequately for individual needs. Unless these problems are identified early and individual or small-group help provided, many of these children will experience serious retardation. The time to care most effectively for these cases is when the problem first appears, rather than later when special services may be required for diagnosis and remediation.

(13) CORRECTIVE READING IN
THE CLASSROOM*

Marianne Frostig

Three major approaches to the teaching of reading may be distinguished, principally on the basis of the materials commonly used. With the so-called basic approach the teacher uses the familiar basic readers, and the children are usually grouped according to reading achievement. During the reading lesson the children are told about the material they will read, and new words are introduced before they read. The individualized reading approach permits each child to make his own selection from a great variety of books, magazines, and pamphlets. The teacher gives assistance as needed. Each of these approaches has advantages and disadvantages for a total communication program. The language experience approach meets many of the disadvantages of the other two since in this approach the reading material is mainly composed by the children themselves. They tell their experiences in class and the teacher writes them down for later reading.

All of these approaches to the teaching of reading are valuable and each supplements the others. They are the three major lines of approach, and none can be neglected. Nevertheless, in teaching reading to children who have learning difficulties, whether the cause is emotional disturbance, brain damage or a developmental language disorder, it is neces-

*Reprinted from *The Reading Teacher* 18 (April 1965), pp. 573–80, by permission of the author and the International Reading Association.

sary to modify and augment these approaches. This paper is devoted to an account of a variety of ancillary methods which should be used to supplement these approaches when teaching children with learning difficulties. But I should like to state most emphatically that these additional techniques can be used very effectively in the regular classroom as well as with exceptional children. They can speed up the process of learning to read for all children and help eliminate nagging difficulties that might impede even a relatively proficient learner.

LABELING

During World War I, Kurt Goldstein developed methods to rehabilitate soldiers who had suffered brain damage because of gunshot or shrapnel wounds. He found that some of those who had lost their reading ability were unable to regain the skill when taught by the regular methods because the symbolic functions of their brains had been impaired. Reading involves a double symbolic process, for not only are the spoken words symbols, representing real things or events (the word *chair* stands for a real chair, *house* for a real house, *running* for a certain type of locomotion), but the printed words are symbols also, standing for the combination of sounds that make up the words.

To help soldiers whose ability to master symbols had been impaired by cerebral dysfunction, Goldstein introduced a method of matching words to pictures. Kindergarten teachers now often use a similar method by putting labels on objects or pictures in the room. When a child first sees the configuration of the word *chair*, it is meaningless to him, but when he sees it paired with either a real or pictured chair he can understand what it means. The child at this stage is only labeling, however; he cannot be said to be reading until he is able to recognize and understand the word alone, unsupported by the object or picture.

In teaching children with reading difficulties by this method, we usually start with just two words. The two words, cut out from an old workbook, and their matching pictures are put in an envelope fastened to the back of a page, ready to be matched with either the words or pictures pasted on the front of the page. When the child can match the words and pictures well, the identical two words are used again on the next page, but with a new word added, and this system is maintained. All three words are used on the third page, plus a fourth word. The matching can be repeated indefinitely, since the material to be matched is always available. The child should switch frequently between matching pictures with words. The words should be joined in as many ways as possible to form simple phrases or sentences. The words *run* and *Billy* can be written "Run, Billy," or "Billy, run," or "Billy, Billy, run!" for instance.

This method is, of course, limited by the fact that only words for concrete objects or depictable actions can be matched with pictures. Conjunctions and other parts of speech which exist for the purpose of organizing language cannot be illustrated. Such words as *the*, *to*, and *and* have to be added gradually to the illustrated words so as to make phrases and sentences. These words have to be learned by repetition, but only in the context of phrases or sentences in which their function is clear.

The labeling method has been found of particular value in teaching children suffering from specific dyslexia or more pervasive defects, such as mental retardation, who fail to learn by any other method. The process requires careful use and preparation by the teacher, but usually need not be maintained for an extended period. When the child has learned to match from nine to twelve words, he will very likely indicate that he has developed the ability to visualize words and will no longer need the help of pictures.

THE HIGHLY CONTROLLED VOCABULARY

All books designed for children just learning to read employ a vocabulary which is controlled to some degree, with new words being introduced slowly and with frequent repetition. But in teaching children who have learning difficulties, this process needs to be intensified. In preparing such children for reading a preprimer, for instance, it is advisable for the teacher to first compile original books for them, using the same vocabulary that is used in the pre-primer. The teacher thus has control over the pace at which vocabulary is accumulated and can eventually provide each child with encouraging success when he tackles the printed book.

The teacher should write in the right upper corner of each page of each child's book the words that the child has learned in the order of their original presentation. In the middle of the page the same words are presented in story form. As soon as the child knows a few words, this presentation is made in as lengthy units as possible—phrases, sentences, and finally paragraphs—rather than in the individual words or two-word phrases which necessarily characterize learning by the matching method.

Emphasizing larger word units avoids chopped and relatively meaningless learning, which lessens interest and fails to instill a feeling for the structure of language.

One or two new words should be introduced daily, and repeated daily for a sufficient period of time to insure overlearning. The list of words in the upper corner constitutes a record of the sequence. If a word is missed, the teacher can go back to the page on which this word was first introduced and review the succeeding pages. When necessary, a page is prepared without new vocabulary for the purpose of review. It is helpful to give the children familiarity with reading different kinds of print by composing the reading matter in the book from words cut from old textbooks, newspapers, and magazines, as well as from words written by hand in both articulated and cursive writing. Illustrations can be gathered similarly from a variety of sources or can be made by the children themselves.

Proper names which occur at this stage in most preprimers are best omitted, because they are not common vocabulary and because it is best to teach the children to think in a less specific way at first than by reading stories about a single family. The appropriate proper names can be introduced when the rest of the vocabulary has been learned and the child is about to read the book itself. When the child has learned to read one book in this way, he should learn to read others in a different series at a similar level before progressing to the vocabulary and stories of the next level.

Other commercially available books may be used in addition to primers and preprimers in such a way as to insure sufficient repetition of each word. For instance, the series called Easy Readers, published by Wonder books, New York, has a highly controlled vocabulary and a great deal of repetition, but as with all commercial books, some words are repeated as many as thirty times and other words only a few times. Before giving these books to the children, therefore, all words which are likely to cause difficulty should be written on flash cards and learned beforehand. Words which are missed by the child in reading the book should also be written on flash cards or listed on a chart and taken home by the child for review.

The Easy Readers may also be used to develop other reading skills. A list of printed questions concerning the text can be prepared glued to cardboard, and inserted in a pocket on the last page of the book. These questions help the child in developing certain areas of reading comprehension or reading skills, such as finding a certain bit of information on a particular page, finding the main idea of the story, finding a word which rhymes with a given word, and so on.

Teaching reading by the use of a highly controlled vocabulary can be adapted to work with both the usual basic readers and individualized reading programs. Insuring adequate mastery of the vocabulary beforehand greatly enhances the probability that the child will enjoy what he reads and will acquire increased motivation.

THE CHILD'S OWN BOOK

A third auxiliary method consists of constructing a book based on each child's own experiences and using it according to the principles of the language experience approach, in which reading, writing, and oral language are integrated. The fact that the child's own experiences constitute the subject matter does much to assure his interest and cooperation.

The child is presented with a booklet made from newsprint stapled between sheets of construction paper, and he is told that the teacher is going to help him to make his own book. The teacher will necessarily have to steer the child closely to make sure that the vocabulary is appropriate to the child's level and is augmented sufficiently slowly. On the first page is pasted a photograph of the child, or a picture of any boy or girl, and the name of the child is written beneath it. Then one or two more words may be added so that a simple sentence can be written: for example, "I am Billy," or "See Billy." In writing the next page, the child can be asked what he saw recently that interested him, and the sentence constructed accordingly. It might read, "Billy, Billy, see the car," or "I see a dog." The incident to which this new word, *car* or *dog* refers is discussed, and the simple sentence may have all the qualities of a real adventure for the child.

I recall how successful this method was with Jim, a little boy from Alaska who had been sent to us because he had not been able to learn to read. He was at first very homesick for Alaska. His teacher talked with him about what he liked best there, and he told how he went out in a boat to fish with his father. For the first page of Jim's book, the teacher put a picture of a father standing by a boat, and the words were, "Jim, see the boat." Jim and his teacher talked about the construction of the boat, how it would be launched, and so on. For the second page, the teacher wrote under a picture of a father beckoning his son: "Jim, ride in the boat. See the boat, Jim. Jim, ride in the boat. See, Jim, see! See the boat." Jim told how the first time he went out in the boat he was so excited that he could not sit still and his father told him not to jump in the boat. So his third page read: "Jim, ride in the boat. See Jim ride. See Jim jump, Jim, Jim, jump not in the boat. Jump not in the boat, Jim." In the upper right corner of the first page the words used were written: *see, Jim, the, boat.* On the second page, the words used were written in the same order in the right hand corner: *see, Jim, the, boat, ride, in.* The words on the third page were: *see, Jim, the, boat, ride, in, jump, not.*

In this way the story was developed, and the entire preprimer vocabulary introduced with sufficient repetition. For the adult the story may seem somewhat inane, but for the child it represented a series of most pleasurable experiences.

Besides learning to read the words, the child should be taught to write them as soon as possible, and he should be encouraged to read his book to the other children and discuss with them the contents of his book and theirs.

The Child's Own Book method need not be restricted to young children. It was found to be equally effective for teaching a group of non-reading adolescent girls between thirteen and seventeen years of age in a camp for juvenile delinquents near Los Angeles. These youngsters had not even mastered the preprimer vocabulary, and an attempt to teach them from a printed book would have evoked only a scornful refusal to work. The idea of making books of their own, however, caught their interest. Surprisingly, they did not choose as their subjects the lives of film stars or stories of crime or romance, as might be expected, but cooking, travel, and flowers.* When they had learned a basic vocabulary in the manner described above, they were told that they were now equipped to read a preprimer. They were at first reluctant to try, until it was suggested that they should imagine they were mothers wanting to read a story to their children, or older sisters reading to the younger members of the family. This imaginative touch stimulated them to read aloud in turn from a preprimer, and they were delighted with their accomplishment.

PHONICS

The purpose of teaching phonics is to help the child to recognize the association between the phoneme and the grapheme—between the audi-

---

*A catalog is often a most helpful source for illustrations. In this instance a Sears-Roebuck catalog and a National Park brochure were used.

tory stimulus, the sound, and the printed word or symbol. It is often possible to teach reading without the aid of phonics by using the whole-word method, but in our experience, the latter method is difficult, if not impossible, for children with certain disabilities in visual perception, nor does it give a child a tool with which to attack new words. It seems, therefore, that the whole-word method should be augmented by instruction based on phonics.

Teaching a child to associate the sounds of the language with written symbols is especially difficult in English, because of the great disparity between many of the spelling and phonetic rules. Even the greatest admirers and promoters of the phonic methods, such as the author of *Why Johnny Can't Read*, cannot claim that more than 80 per cent of the words in the English language are phonetically written, and many maintain that the proportion is less. It is even difficult to teach rules of exception, since there are exceptions to the exceptions. For instance, when the letter *i* appears in short syllables, it is pronounced as in the word *bit*, *except* when it appears before the letters *nd*, when it is pronounced with a long sound (as in *kind*), *except* in the word *wind*, referring to air in motion.

For this reason, we place greater emphasis upon a functional approach to phonics than upon a systematic teaching of phonetic rules, but it must be acknowledged that opinion on this question is divided. Sabaroff (5), for instance, found that an experimental group of low achievers made progress with systematic instruction in the rules of phonics.

COLOR CUES

Our usual method is to associate phonemes with graphemes from the beginning, writing each distinct sound in a word in different color. The first words to be introduced are, of course, phonetically "pure," and it is best to introduce words containing short vowels first, then words with long vowels, and finally more complex sounds, such as diphthongs and digraphs. Where letter groups are pronounced uniformly, as, for example, the combination *ur* in the words *hurt, curtain, turn*, the letters in the group are written in the same color, to help the child learn the pronunciation of that particular combination. Sometimes it is necessary to teach a child to read only the initial letter in a word, at first, then the last letter, and finally the middle letter or letters. In these cases, the appropriate letter only is colored. Colors can also be used to teach syllabification, each syllable of a word being written in one color. Silent letters, such as the *e* in *those*, can be indicated by an appropriately insubstantial stippled effect so that the letter does not stand out from the background. We have not generally found it necessary to use the same color for one sound consistently, except in a few instances in which a child shows a particular difficulty which he can be helped to overcome by receiving a consistent cue, but we have found it useful to use consistently one color for *all* of the long vowels, and one other color for all of the short vowels.*

KINESTHETIC METHODS

The sense modality basic to the reading process is of course vision. Accurate space and form perception are essential. But when a child has disturbances in visual perception, the visual modality can be supported by the auditory even at the beginning of reading (as with the phonic instruction described above) and also by the kinesthetic modality. As kinesthetic activities are largely a matter of tracing, they not only provide training in reading but serve also to further writing and spelling skills.

Kinesthetic methods have other advantages as well. They form a bridge between the experience of an act extended in time, which occurs when we hear, and the experience of an act extended in space, which occurs when we see. Whenever we say a word or read it aloud, we experience an act which is extended in time. The *v* at the beginning of the word *visual*, for instance, is heard before the *l* at the end of the word. But when we read silently, we usually take the word in at a glance, and all of the letters seem to be perceived at the same time. The word is no longer perceived as extended in time, but as extended in space. It may be that it is just this translation from a spatial dimension to a temporal one, and vice versa, which makes it difficult for a child to associate words which he hears with the printed word. The kinesthetic method helps overcome the problem by forming a bridge between the auditory stimulus and the visual one. When we write or trace a word, it takes time to write it; we perceive that a time span elapses while we are writing. We also experience a spatial dimension as we see the word "grow" from left to right on the page. When a word is presented kinesthetically, therefore, it has both a temporal and a spatial dimension,

*We have not discussed the use of the Augmented Roman Alphabet in teaching reading because we have had no experience with it. It would seem to be a very worthwhile method, however.

which makes it easier for the child to connect the two experiences of seeing and hearing.

There are many modifications of the kinesthetic method. Pulliam (3) has suggested that children write in grooves, experiencing in this way the movement of the word and learning its kinesthetic pattern. For children with severe motor defects, it is helpful to write in clay or on some similarly resistant surface. Many clinics advocate the Fernald method (2) of first tracing words with the fingers and then writing them.

BLIND WRITING

The blind writing kinesthetic method deserves a detailed account because of its effectiveness with children whoses visual perception is inadequate, as is often the case with children who have minimal brain damage.

Recent research (1, 4) has shown that even in small children the visual experience is stronger than the haptic one. ("Haptic" means the dual experience of touch and kinesthesia, which are combined, for instance, in taking an object in one's hand and feeling it totally while moving a finger over it to experience its shape.) When the children were first shown something which they experienced visually, and then felt the same object without looking at it, their final description of the object was in visual terms rather than in terms of touch. Because of this natural predominance of the visual modality, a child with a severely distorted visual perceptual sense is very seriously handicapped. It is necessary in these cases to train the child's less effective, but at least unimpaired, kinesthetic abilities so that he can perceive accurately by movement, as blind children can do. The kinesthetic modality can then be used to guide the visual one.

To teach the child to write and read by the blind writing method, the teacher first writes the letter or word on the chalkboard at a height which can easily be reached by the child. Then the teacher guides the child's hand while he traces the word with closed eyes. The elimination of visual stimuli enables him to concentrate entirely upon the kinesthetic experience. While the teacher guides the child's hand, she pronounces the word slowly, trying to use as much time for saying the word as the child takes in tracing it. With repetition, the teacher will feel the child's hand begin to follow the lines of the word independently. She can then remove her hand while he continues to trace, without opening his eyes and without her assistance. The next step is to have him make the connection between the kinesthetic and the visual modality by looking at the word as he traces it, and then as he writes it. The child is finally asked to find the word on a page in his book, to read the sentences in which it appears, and then to write it again. The use of cursive writing is a great advantage because of the uninterrupted flow of the kinesthetic pattern the child perceives, even though he has to make the association between the written and printed forms of the word.

Causes of Reading Difficulties. Difficulties in reading occur not only because of a specific difficulty with the reading process itself. They may be due to disabilities in comprehension or to a lag in any other area of development, such as in perception, motor skills (especially eye movements), language, and social and emotional development. The possible difficulties in any one of these areas are legion. But the corrective methods described above can be used with all children in the regular classroom during corrective reading.

REFERENCES

1. Birch, Herbert G., and Lefford, A. "Intersensory Development in Children," *Society for Research in Child Development Monographs*, Vol. 28 (1963).

2. Fernald, Grace M. *Remedial Techniques in Basic School Subjects*. New York: McGraw-Hill, 1943. Pp. 349.

3. Pulliam, Roy A. "Invented Word Cards as a Sensori-Motor Aid in Vocabulary Development," *Peabody Journal of Education*, 23 (July 1945), 38–42.

4. Rock, I., and Victor, J. "Vision and Touch: An Experimentally Created Conflict Between the Two Senses," *Science*, 43 (Feb. 1964), 3606.

5. Sabaroff, Rose. "A Comparative Investigation of Two Methods of Teaching Phonics in a Modern Reading Program: A Pilot Study," *Journal of Experimental Education*, 31 (Mar. 1963), 249–256.

Chapter 4

CLASSROOM MANAGEMENT
AND TEACHING TECHNIQUES

INTRODUCTION

Management of the classroom environment plays an important part in producing an effective learning situation. However, the learning process can be and often is affected by the number of pupils in the class, the number of reading groups necessary, the amount of materials available for instruction, and many other factors. Managing these factors and discovering the most appropriate way to structure them into a meaningful program is the perennial task of the teacher. The vitality and excitement of the classroom depends upon how well these management problems are handled.

Since in most classrooms basal readers are the main source of material used in the formal teaching of reading, the problem of avoiding the "basal reader rut" needs much attention. Learning to use readers and other teaching tools effectively with varying degrees of individualization, and in a weekly structure that offers variety and flexibility in operation, is one management problem with which a teacher must contend. Another related task is to use instructional time efficiently while giving proper emphasis to needed skills. Upper grade teachers in particular should give serious thought to whether they are providing ample time for direct instruction in reading skills. Several authors assert that included in the reading program should be time, books, and guidance for voluntary recreational reading. All teachers must constantly be striving for productive communication with their parent population. The final article describes trends in reporting reading progress to parents.

The articles in this chapter focus on those operations which influence the classroom atmosphere and structure. These operations contribute immensely to classroom management and permit effective teaching techniques to be demonstrated.

(14) WHAT CAN I DO WITH THE OTHER GROUPS WHILE I AM TEACHING ONE GROUP?*

Millard H. Black

"What can I do with the other groups?" This plaintive question always comes up when we talk about grouping. A teacher may be sold on the idea of having several small reading groups in her class. She may be able to divide her children into three or four reading groups. She knows she can give more effective help to a small reading group of, say, six or eight children. But what about the other 25 or 30 children in the room? What will they be doing while she is helping one group with reading?

This is an old question and one for which there is no pat answer, no simple formula. The way you solve the problem in your class will depend on many factors: the needs of your children, the extent of their maturity, the nature of their interests and drives, the materials and facilities which are available in your school and community, the leadership among your pupils, and their ability to help themselves and to work with each other.

To work effectively with one reading group, the teacher wants a minimum of interruptions from the other children. Unfortunately some teachers have made this the only criterion in planning for the "other groups." There have been times when those not actually reading with the teacher have been encouraged to do almost any kind of busy work that would guarantee an uninterrupted half hour for the reading group. But this is not enough.

All classroom activities should contribute to desired learnings whether or not they are under the immediate supervision of the teacher. Therefore the thoughtful teacher plans a variety of activities for a variety of educational goals.

Below I am listing six important reading goals with examples of the kinds of activities that can be carried on independently by those children or groups not actually working with the teacher.

DEVELOPING READINESS

To many people the term *readiness* suggests only the activities of first and second graders who are in the initial developmental stages. However,

*Reprinted from *The Reading Teacher* 5 (September 1951), pp. 10–11, by permission of the author and the International Reading Association.

the necessity of *readiness* for reading any story or beginning any unit extends into all grades.

Children with independent reading ability can develop such readiness by individual or unsupervised group research on the topic or unit being introduced. Such research will be much more interesting if children have a variety of interesting materials assembled by the teacher and by their own leaders and research groups.

The preparation of bulletin boards, posters, dioramas, maps, charts and the reading of related stories are all valuable activities designed to procure readiness.

IMPROVING WORD RECOGNITION SKILLS

A well-planned workbook specifically designed to accompany a modern basic textbook will often provide for the development of phonetic and syllabic analysis skills. However, several children will need supplementary practice before independence in these techniques is acquired.

Frequently specific exercises must be designed for the specific needs of certain children. For other children, certain exercises from the workbook should be selected for him to complete. No pupil will need every page of every workbook.

This means that the teacher must be constantly alert to the needs and capabilities of each child, giving him the practice materials best suited to his needs and shifting him to the group in which he will receive most help.

EXTENDING COMPREHENSION

Follow-up activities can contribute effectively to this objective. Questions, jointly posed by the class after the reading of a story, may be written on the blackboard or prepared in chart form to be answered by the group in independent reading or laboratory-type research.

Another procedure is to provide children with duplicated questions permitting a choice of answers, sentences which provide for a controlled choice of words to complete their meaning, and the matching of questions with pictures. These activities may be used to extend comprehension, either supplementing or complementing a specific story.

INCREASING SPEED AND PLEASURE IN READING

Free-time reading is ideal for this reading goal. But it means that children must have access to a variety of interesting books written for different reading levels. It also means the teacher must constantly guide and direct so that some children are not struggling to read books too difficult for them while others lose interest in books too easy.

In providing such materials it is well to consult such references as the following: *Guide to Children's Literature* published by The American Library Association and *Bibliography of Children's Books* published by the Association for Childhood Education International.

DEVELOPING CREATIVITY

Many activities encourage a child to express his own thoughts and feelings about the things he has read and done. Such activities may lead to genuinely creative expression that will give deep satisfaction to the individual and to others in the group.

Clay, finger paints, water colors, and oils should be available for children to use. Such materials as Lincoln Logs, Tinker toys, and blocks will suggest making models and dioramas related to the reading experiences.

Free dramatization and pantomime may be significant activities growing out of stories read by the group and units on which children are working.

Given a little encouragement, many children will enjoy writing a story or poem as an outgrowth of other activities.

DEVELOPING ORGANIZATION AND RESEARCH SKILLS

Even third graders can learn how to make one and two-point outlines. As language arts skills increase the complexity of the outline may also be increased. The ability to summarize in both oral and written form provides valuable exercise in the organization of data.

Functional use of a table of contents and index will grow out of the search for stories and pictures that are related to the topic being studied.

IN CONCLUSION

All of these activities can be carried on by individuals and by independent groups of children while the teacher is working with a reading group.

But such activities don't just happen. They grow out of long and careful planning by the teacher who is constantly alert to the needs of individual pupils and who sees new ways to spur children on to seek new materials and new skills.

(15) ACTUAL AND RECOMMENDED ALLOTMENTS OF TIME FOR READING*

Gerald W. Brekke

The problem in this study was to identify and compare current practices in time allotments for basal and other reading with the optimum amounts of time recommended by reading authorities.**

Specifically, the major questions to be answered by this study were: (1) How much time is allotted weekly in each grade for basal reading instruction? (2) How much time is used weekly in each grade for reading outside of those periods which have been designated for formal reading instruction? (3) How much time do reading authorities feel is most desirable for basal reading instruction, and for other reading? (4) How do the recommended practices compare with the practices followed by the schools? (5) Do states or regions differ markedly in their time allotment practices? (6) Is there an improvement in reading achievement when time allotments are increased?

Secondary questions asked were: (1) How do the over-all time allotments for this study compare with averages found in earlier studies? (2) Do time allotments progressively increase or decrease between grade levels? (3) What percentage of the total reading experiences is allotted to basal reading, and what percentage is employed for other reading? (4) What is the predominant method of giving reading instruction in the elementary schools?

Answers to these questions should be of assistance to school administrators when they are considering allotment of school time.

Basal reading was defined as that which occurs in a formal reading instruction period, usually making use of a basal reader series. Reading

*Reprinted from *The Reading Teacher* 16 (January 1963), pp. 234–37, by permission of the author and the International Reading Association.

**This report is an abstract of a dissertation prepared under the direction of Dr. Archie I. Gray at the University of North Dakota.

done outside of specifically designated reading classes—either in free reading periods, or in other subject areas—was termed "other reading."

METHOD

Normative-survey methodology was employed. The questionnaire to identify time allotment practices was validated among the schools in three states. The sample was then selected from eight geographic areas throughout the nation. Proportional sampling was used to select individual schools within each state. Respondents for the criterion measure were selected from officers and members of the International Reading Association. Twenty-five reading authorities were asked to validate the questionnaire identifying the recommendations of the reading authorities as to time allotments. An additional seventy-five respondents were then obtained.

Data were obtained from 1,224 schools for basal reading, identifying weekly time allotment practices in more than 8,000 separate grades. Responses were received from 1,087 schools for other reading, identifying weekly amounts of time employed in more than 7,000 grades. Sixty-five reading authorities forwarded recommendations for weekly basal reading time allotments, and 60 furnished responses for the optimum amounts of time which should be used for other reading. Data were processed in the University of North Dakota Computer Data Processing Laboratory. Analyses of variance were employed to determine differences in weekly time allotments among states. The t test was used to determine the significance of differences between these groups. Comparisons of averages and percentages were used to determine differences between other groups.

MAJOR FINDINGS

1. The table shows for each grade the actual time allotments reported by the schools for basal reading and for other reading, along with the time allotments recommended by our authorities for these two types of reading.

It will be noted that, for the most part, the schools reported spending more time on basal reading instruction than was recommended by the authorities. On the other hand, the schools reported spending in every grade less time on other reading than the authorities recommended. The

School Reported Time Allotments vs. Recommended Time Allotments for Basal Reading Instruction and "Other Reading"

Grade	Basal Reading Av. Minutes Per Week			Other Reading Av. Minutes Per Week		
	Reported	Recommended	Diff.	Reported	Recommended	Diff.
1	462	414	+48*	221	287	− 63**
2	431	409	+23	253	301	− 48*
3	364	324	+40*	295	319	− 51*
4	281	310	−29	344	400	− 56*
5	256	292	−36	365	437	− 72**
6	242	273	−31	379	456	− 77**
7	209	202	+ 7	376	490	−114**
8	208	205	+ 3	376	502	−126**

*Difference significant at the 5 per cent level.
**Difference significant at the 1 per cent level.

table shows that five of the differences between actual and recommended practices are significant at the 5 per cent level and five differences significant at the 1 per cent level.

2. Differences in the amounts of time allotted for basal reading weekly at each grade level in the schools were greater among various states than they were among the schools within each state. Statistically significant differences were found at the 1 per cent level among states in each of the first three grades, and at the 5 per cent level in the sixth and seventh grades. Differences among states at the fourth, fifth, and eighth grade levels were not found to be statistically significant.

Statistically significant differences were found at the 1 per cent level between each of the eight geographic strata in the sample, and one or more other regions, both for basal reading and for other reading.

3. Scattergrams constructed to show the relationships between median achievement scores in reading as measured by standardized reading tests did not, on inspection, show any correlation for this sample between increased time allotments for basal reading instruction, and improved reading achievement. On inspection, slight, but not significant correlation was noted for this sample at the third grade level between improved achievement and increased amounts of time for other reading.

SECONDARY FINDINGS

1. An over-all increase of sixty-eight minutes weekly was found between the average weekly identified time allotments for basal reading in this sample and the average of eight earlier studies.

2. Time allotments for basal reading are greatest in the first grade; least in the eighth. Time employed for other reading is least in the first; greatest in the sixth. Differences between the amounts of time allotted for basal reading at each successive grade level were found to be statistically significant at the 1 per cent level between all grades except the seventh and eighth. Differences between the amounts of time employed for other reading at each successive grade level were statistically significant at the 1 per cent level between the first four grades, and at the 5 per cent level between the fifth and sixth grade. Differences between other grades were not statistically significant.

3. Slightly more than 50 per cent of the total weekly time employed in reading experiences is allotted to basal reading, and slightly less than half is used for other reading.

4. The basal reading approach to the teaching of reading was used to some extent by 99.5 per cent of the schools in this sample.

RECOMMENDATIONS

The recommendations following from the data of this study are:

To conform with the recommendations of reading authorities, schools should (1) place less emphasis upon weekly time allotments for basal reading in the first three grades and more upon other reading, (2) provide more time for both basal and other reading in the intermediate grades, (3) employ more time in other reading in the seventh and eighth grades.

It is recommended that school administrators and curriculum directors seek to provide at least an equal distribution between the amounts of time allotted in basal reading and that employed for other reading.

The recommendations of this study pertaining to further research are: (1) that additional studies be made to verify the apparent lack of correlation for this sample between amounts of time for basal reading and measured reading achievement, (2) that additional studies be made to ascertain the extent of correlation between increased amounts of time for other reading and measured reading achievement, and (3) that additional studies be conducted to investigate the effects of increased time allotments in reading upon related subjects in other content areas.

(16) LET'S GET VARIETY IN THE READING PROGRAM*

Virginia M. Reid

To secure the greatest interest of children, there should be variety in the reading program. This means far more than a range of things for children to read. It also means variety in the way the teacher sets up her objectives and plans her procedures.

This point of view is reflected in the statement of one Oakland Curriculum Committee: "We believe reading must be a happy, broadening, and enriching experience. The reading program in the fifth and sixth grades should: arouse and extend interests, raise the child's reading tastes, develop the child's ability to use printed material intelligently and effectively."

VARIETY IN THE WEEKLY PROGRAM

The same program each week can become monotonous unless provision is made for variety in the materials as well as the activities connected with them. Many teachers plan each week to include:

Some library experiences such as looking at books, hearing the teacher read, later reading stories for themselves.

Some oral reading

Some work-type reading

Some enrichment experiences, doing something interesting with what they have read such as making a mural, dramatizing a story, writing their own stories

Some experiences in word recognition related to the reading material

Much silent reading for discussion and enjoyment

Many opportunities as a part of every lesson to discuss what they have

*Reprinted from *The Reading Teacher* 7 (February 1954), pp. 169–73, by permission of the author and the International Reading Association.

read, to make judgments as to its validity, to relate it to their own experience.

Opportunities to relate reading to the other language arts and to other areas of the curriculum, to integrate reading with all other experiences.

MONDAY	Class goes to library for reference work, training in library skills, exchanging individual books, browsing, and sharing.		
	Group I	*Group II*	*Group III*
TUESDAY	Silent recreational*	Silent study basic reader	Teacher-guided T
	Teacher-guided silent and oral reading T	Silent recreational or reference*	Silent study basic reader or workbook
WEDNESDAY	Silent study basic reader	Silent study basic reader	Teacher-guided T
	Silent Recreational*	Teacher-guided T	Silent study basic reader
THURSDAY	Silent basic or reference reading*	Silent recreational Teacher-guided	Silent recreational*
	Silent recreational	Teacher-guided T	Teacher-guided Reference or recreational T
FRIDAY	Whole-class activities which might include the following: Choral reading Book reports Appreciation activities Dramatization Audience reading Storytelling		

T shows where the teacher will be at each period.

*Possible times for individual, team, or small group working for a specific purpose.

To provide for such a variety of activities the plan illustrated was worked out as a suggestion for fifth and sixth grades:

VARIETY IN GROUPING

While this weekly program provides for three ability groups only, the teacher may be able to provide other types of grouping. For flexibility, intermediate grade teachers frequently use one or more of these additional types of groupings.

Interest Grouping. Children who are interested in rocks, for example, will meet as a group to pool the information they have gained from reading the science primer, first-grade science book, or third-grade science material about rocks.

Special Needs Grouping. Certain children from the three main groups mentioned in the chart above may need help in some type of word analysis. These children will be called together for specific instruction as a small sub-group.

Team Grouping. Two children work together on a specific need common to both.

Tutorial Grouping. One child, more advanced, helps his "reading pal" during the reading period. It is often wise to allow the one needing help to choose the one to assist him. It is also necessary for the teacher to guide the "tutor" in knowing what kind of help to give.

Research Grouping. Two or more children work together to give a group report on information they have found on their own.

Whole Class Grouping. Choral reading, reporting, listening, sharing, dramatization are times when the whole class will work together.

VARIETY OF READING MATERIALS

In the rush of trying to teach children how to read, it is often easy to forget the equally important tasks of teaching them what to read and when to read. The child must have the *how* or the skills, but he must also learn to select reading material that is worthwhile and significant for his purpose.

Since many children are unable to read for themselves books which are on their level of understanding or speaking, they must depend upon adults for stories or poems to challenge the mind and stir the imagination. Much can be accomplished by the teacher who reads aloud to her class each day.

While there is a great temptation to read aloud an entire book chapter by chapter, there is great advantage in varying the read-aloud materials to stimulate a much more extensive reading program. Often a child's interest is aroused by hearing one story from a collection of stories or one chapter from a complete book. With this interest in the book he may then go on to read the whole thing on his own.

In selecting books for children, it is often well to begin with the known and proceed to the unknown. Children of all ages like to hear realistic stories about their own age group.

First graders thoroughly appreciate the lost tooth theme of McCloskey's *One Morning in Maine.* Third and fourth graders find their lives mirrored quite faithfully in the Beverly Cleary's *Henry Huggins, Ellen Tibbits, Henry and Beezus.* Other reigning favorites are Haywood's "Little Eddie" series; the most recent two are *Eddie and Gardenia* and *The Mixed-Up Twins.*

Though most fifth and sixth graders can read these books to themselves, a teacher's enthusiastic introduction will help launch them on the independent reading. One chapter is usually enough to establish a waiting list.

McCloskey's *Homer Price* and *Centerburg Tales,* Estes' *Ginger Pye,* as well as her three earlier books about the Moffat family, and Enright's *The Saturdays* and two other Melendy family books are all good for the teacher to start with older children.

From these humorous beginnings the teacher can begin to extend into other realistic stories, sometimes based on biography, such as Judson's *Thomas Jefferson*; or on history, Garthwaite's *Shaken Days*; or science, Zim's *Alligators and Crocodiles.* Holing's *Minn of the Mississippi* combines science with history, while Levinger's *Galileo* is a thrilling duet of science and biography.

The teacher who is unsure of his class' response to poetry reading had better begin also with the humorous and the realistic rather than the whimsical or lyrical ones. Aileen Fisher's *Up the Windy Hill* should prove popular from kindergarten up. The older children enjoy poems intended for younger listeners. They enjoy feeling superior because they "know better" now. For more of these poems based on every-day happenings, teachers will welcome also *All Together,* the new volume by Dorothy Aldis. It includes selections from four previous volumes together with poems previously unpublished in book form.

Primary teachers will continue to make good use of that most satisfying collection, *Very Young Verses,* by Geismer and Suter. Upper grade teachers whose children have had an unfortunate introduction to poetry will welcome the robust verses, "In Samarcand," "The Little Cossack," "Robinson Crusoe's Story," and others in that delightful collection, *A Pocketful of Rhymes,* edited by Katherine Love.

It is said that whimsical stories have a limited appeal. They have a much wider appeal if the teacher likes them and reads portions of such books as *My Father's Dragon, Mary Poppins in the Park,* or *Charlotte's Web.*

By introducing such materials as these, it is often possible to encourage children to branch out on their own and do more independent reading than before.

VARIETY IN OTHER MATERIALS

The printed book is not the only source of effective reading for children in the elementary school. The dictated story or experience chart has long been effective in the primary grades. Children dictate, then read, and are proud to have an audience.

Intermediate and upper grade teachers may also capitalize on children's interests in their own writing and that of other children. For example, Jake, a fourth-grader, was a non-reader until he started to dictate, then copy in painful manuscript, short paragraphs on his experiences with goldfish, spiders, starfish, and other creatures. Here is one of Jake's stories:

Turtles live near the water.

They lay eggs.

They do not like to be bothered.

My turtle lives in a jar with a water dog.

After many such stories, Jake was introduced to phonics by finding "twins" (begin-alikes), such as *spins-spiders,* from his own stories.

Class books made up of stories contributed by individual children are tremendously popular. One sixth-grade class made a wonderful collection entitled "Heartbreaks and Sidebreaks"—their way of saying "Pathos and Humor." "Pet Peeves" was another interesting collection which proved good reading as well as an emotional outlet.

Children who have had the opportunity to read stories written in dramatic form, such as McCaslin's *Legends in Action* or any of those by Kissen, will enjoy writing and reading their own dramatic scripts. Some of these dramatizations of their favorite stories may be duplicated by the central office and distributed for the enjoyment of other classes as well.

The value of choral reading has been cited frequently for its effect on personality development, on speech improvement, and for the impetus it gives to poetry appreciation. It is true that poetry reading takes special skill, but choral reading may be introduced easily if the poem is written on the board or on a chart. The teacher's hand helps with the phrasing.

Later the teacher may mimeograph selections to be read by a group or by the class. The less able readers acquire surprising ability to recognize new words on the second or third reading. There is a certain thrill in being one of a large group all doing the same thing. This feeling of success is a powerful factor in making reading enjoyable.

IN CONCLUSION

There is really no end to the variety that the alert teacher can introduce in the reading program. To be sure, it takes more careful planning to provide such variety in materials and procedures. Probably even more difficult is maintaining the flexibility needed to meet each new interest and attitude developing within the group. But the dividends in increased pupil interest will be a very rewarding return on the investment of time and effort.

(17) REPORT CARDS AND PARENTS*

Mary C. Austin

"School report cards can be, and too often are, ambiguous and untrustworthy to a degree wholly unsuspected by parents," wrote Orville Palmer in a recent issue of *Parents' Magazine* (5). Interviews with parents frequently confirm this statement.

Similarly, there are those who share the point of view expressed by the mother of two young school children. "I don't pay attention to report cards because they are neither fair nor systematic. There are no norms to let parents know what the bases for grading are. We don't know whether the child is graded against his own class or with all children in that grade in the school. Besides not all teachers grade the same."

A mother of a second grader reported another type of difficulty. "I think my son reads well, but he got a *D* in reading. At home he reads the newspaper and library books. He relates stories to the family. I feel that he understands what he is reading, and we praise him for his good work. Now the *D* confuses us. When I asked the teacher about the

*Reprinted from *The Reading Teacher* 18 (May 1965), pp. 660–63, by permission of the author and the International Reading Association.

grade, she answered that his reading workbook was sloppy—yet she admitted that his answers to the comprehension questions were correct. She is grading him upon poor work habits rather than upon his ability to read with understanding."

Comments such as these show the great need for a better understanding of present practices and variations in the reporting of progress to parents.

TRADITIONAL REPORTING PRACTICES

The earliest report cards were developed as the school's major means of informing the pupil and his parents of the learner's progress. They were concise documents which used letters or numbers to rate the child's achievement in four or five subject areas. Having been devised prior to the 1900's, they naturally represented the educational philosophy of that period with its emphasis upon subject matter. The learner himself was overlooked, except as his behavior and personality were reflected in the ambiguous category of "deportment."

Viewing these early cards from our relatively sophisticated position today, we realize that the traditional reports contained several deficiencies. One characteristic weakness was an outgrowth of the fact that they included no description of the basis for evaluating the student's work. Confusions which arose often centered around the following questions: Did the grade relate to the student's potential or to the norm for the class? Did it indicate the pupil's present standing or his progress since a previous report? Did a high mark in a low ability group mean the same grade in a high ability group? Because grades were not objectively determined and defined, they were subject to many misinterpretations. As a consequence, parents often became antagonistic toward the school and the child since they had no real basis for understanding the grading system.

Frequently, early reporting practices resulted in poor attitudes on the part of parents and children. With the focus upon marks, too many people disregarded the values of learning and education; pupils prodded by adults (including teachers) worked to obtain good grades or to "get by." In the hands of well-meaning parents, reports could become lethal weapons to be used for bribery, cajolery, and to promote competition among children. Unfortunately, too, parents often withdrew love and reassurance from children whose grades were low. Cheating and cramming were inevitable byproducts of these situations.

TRENDS IN REPORTING PUPIL PROGRESS

Important trends in reporting pupil progress have emerged during the past twenty-five years. Through experimentation and revision of their procedures, school systems have attempted to overcome many of the objections to former types of reports.

The term "progress report" rather than "report card" is preferred today. The reports may vary at succeeding levels, with some schools using a different form for each grade. Other schools employ a separate form for every two levels or one for the primary grades and a second for the intermediate.

Owing to the variety of educational philosophies and social climates, the content of no one report form has been equally effective in all schools. Whatever the form employed, however, it is of utmost importance that the chosen method be understood by everyone concerned—teachers, parents, and pupils.

Among the items appearing on recent reports, the following appear to be making a contribution to improved understanding (2):

1. School philosophy and curriculum objectives are stated on the cards or included in an explanatory brochure.

2. Emphasis is placed upon the learner, with the inclusion of essential aspects of pupil growth—physical, social, emotional, and academic.

3. Descriptions and interpretations of grading accompany new cards, either as part of the card itself or in a separate bulletin.

4. Reasons for achievement and/or difficulty frequently are explained.

5. Subject headings are followed by items descriptive of several related skills.

6. Space is provided for comments by teachers and parents.

Designing a report card that everyone in the community will approve is no small task. Surveys of the desires of parents have led to the conclusion that parents want three basic types of information: (1) how well their child is doing in relation to his own abilities, (2) how well he compares with others in his grade, and (3) how well he is progressing toward the accomplishment of major academic and personal goals (3).

Aside from the problem of form, and in accordance with the wishes of parents, educators must decide whether a pupil should be graded in terms of his own capacity or in relation to some predetermined standard. Many schools have handled this question by using a double marking system. In this way, the child who may already be doing his very best can be recognized readily, as well as the one who may be doing average work when a higher quality could well be anticipated. In the example below, the letters correspond to traditional grades which indicate how well the pupil is achieving in comparison with an objective standard. The numbers tell whether the child is accomplishing as much as can be expected of him on the basis of his own potential (6).

	John		Janet	
Arithmetic	A	2	D	1
Reading	B	4	C	2
History	B	3	C	2
Science	A	2	D	1

At first glance, perhaps, John appears to be making good progress in each subject, while Janet is receiving low grades in all. Interpreting the letter grades only, John's parents might encourage him to continue his good work; Janet's parents undoubtedly would admonish her to "work harder" so she could have all *A*'s and *B*'s also. Careful inspection of both columns of this double marking system, however, should lead John's family to learn why he is not doing better in reading and history. Possibly he needs to turn off the TV and spend more time on these assignments. Without the numbers to qualify Janet's letter grades, her family would fail to realize that she is doing her best work in the subjects most difficult for her. Obviously, praise and encouragement should be forthcoming for Janet's efforts.

How one community resolved the report card dilemma is illustrated by Glencoe, Illinois. Since 1955 parents have been invited to select—and if necessary design—the report card they personally preferred. In the fall they are asked to come to school for a conference with the teacher. They are shown various types of report cards as the advantages and disadvantages of each are explained. Parents may then design another card if none of those available seems satisfactory. Although few parents choose to make their own, the opportunity to do so opens the channels of communication between parents and teachers and leads to a deeper mutual appreciation of the problems involved (4).

REPORTING READING PROGRESS

The second Harvard-Carnegie study of reading included a survey of current practices in reporting to parents the progress of elementary school pupils (11). According to the findings, a child's accomplishment in reading was shared in one of three ways: (1) progress reports (report cards), (2) parent-teacher conferences, and (3) a combination of progress reports and parent-teacher conferences. Occasionally, these practices were supplemented by telephone calls, informal notes, and home visits.

As mentioned earlier, school systems increasingly use subheadings under the major heading of "reading" on their progress reports. While wording varies, most of the subheadings can be classified under one of the following categories: (1) auditory discrimination (hears differences in sounds), (2) visual discrimination (sees differences in pictures, forms, letters, and words), (3) left to right progression (know how to read from left to right), (4) basic sight vocabulary (has learned a basic recognition vocabulary), (5) interest (shows interest in learning to read, enjoys reading on his own), (6) speed (reads with adequate speed, adjusts speed to type of material), (7) independent reading (reads silently with guidance for information and recreation), (8) library (uses library, reads a number of library books), (9) word analysis (works out new words), (10) oral reading, reads orally with expression), (11) comprehension (reads with understanding), and (12) phonics (uses phonics and other word attack skills (1). Obviously, these statements can be modified and improved by educators who are making revisions of their present forms.

INFORMAL PUPIL REPORTS

Undoubtedly, the most effective type of report to parents is the informal one given each day by the youngsters themselves. A common question in many households is "What did you do in school today?" Too frequently the reply is "Nothing." But this need not be the case if teachers will take time to discuss and evaluate each day's activities with their pupils. Children can then give positive answers, accompanied by appropriate details. When they share enthusiastically with their families what they are doing and learning, parents know that their children are finding that learning can be a very satisfying experience.

REFERENCES

1. Austin, Mary C., and Morrison, Coleman. *The First R:* The Harvard Report on Reading in Elementary Schools. New York: Macmillan, 1963.

2. Burton, William H. *The Guidance of Learning Activities.* New York: Appleton-Century-Crofts, 1962.

3. Johnson, Martha C. "Let's Get Rid of Report Card Jitters," *Parents' Magazine,* 37 (1962), 40–41, 119–123.

4. Misner, Paul J. "The Restoration of Report Cards," *PTA Magazine,* 58 (1964), 10–12.

5. Palmer, Orville. "What Report Cards Don't Tell," *Parents' Magazine,* 39 (1964), 50–51, 92–95.

6. Shuster, Albert H., and Ploghoft, Milton E. *The Emerging Elementary Curriculum.* Columbus, Ohio: Charles E. Merrill, 1963.

Chapter 5

MATERIALS

INTRODUCTION

Materials, both hardware and software, are vehicles used in the teaching of reading. Today's rapid publication process permits the school market to be flooded with all types of materials. Today's increased technology permits and encourages new devices, machines, and equipment to be designed for teaching reading skills. And today's financially supported state and federal programs permit schools to have available funds to purchase books and other materials for teaching reading on a scale not always possible in the past.

Increased potential for securing materials brings with it a corresponding need for more discrimination in selection. Rapidly produced materials may be lower in quality. Machines, while fascinating, may not facilitate long-term instruction nor be justified in terms of cost. The choice of material demands careful evaluation upon the part of school personnel.

The six articles in this chapter pertain to some of the issues in material production and selection. Prestwood discusses ten criteria to consider when selecting and evaluating reading materials. Among his criteria are the contribution, both immediate and long-range, which the use of the material will make to' the goals of the reading program; the scope and worth of the reading materials; and their appeal to the learner. Weintraub reviews the research relative to the controversial problem of vocabulary control in reading materials. He cites findings that would support control in initial instruction in basal readers but would question any severe limitation as children gain independence and meet an increasing number of words in other reading situations.

Durkin examines the reasons for the current proliferation of phonic materials and points out the necessity for the profession to evaluate the place of phonics in the reading program and the contribution, if any, the product under consideration will make to the total program.

How reliable are the grade levels indicated by publishers for children's books? Mills and Richardson attempt to answer this question by comparing the published grade levels with those obtained by the use of formulas dealing with vocabulary and sentence complexity. In a scholarly article Bormuth cites new facets of readability based on recent tools developed by psychologists and linguists. The chapter closes with an article by Gilbert which stresses the fact that fine books are the most important materials for teaching reading and suggests sources which will assist the busy teacher in finding them.

(18) CRITERIA FOR SELECTION OF READING MATERIALS*

Elwood L. Prestwood

Regardless of the amount of money spent by a district for reading materials, it is important that it be spent well. By adhering to a good set of criteria, a school should be able to secure an effective return for every dollar it expends for reading materials. An excellent set of criteria for selecting and evaluating reading materials, developed by Robinson and Rauch, can be found in their book *Guiding the Reading Program*. The discussion that follows quotes the criteria and is based upon them.

1. "Materials should be selected and evaluated for suitability in achieving the objectives of a reading program."

The objectives of a reading program should be determined cooperatively by the entire staff or by an adequate representation of it. They should provide for the reading needs of gifted students, normal students, slow-learning students, and disabled readers. To be appraised suitable the materials must help teachers achieve the objectives designed to meet the needs of all the students who can profit from reading instruction.

2. "Materials should be selected and evaluated in relation to a plan for continuous development. Materials directed toward reading instruction should provide for development of a systematic sequence of skills."

Growth in reading is developmental; that is, it follows a pattern whereby a specific phase appears at or about a certain period in the life of the individual, successful achievement of which leads to success with later phases. The learning of each new skill and ability builds upon previous learning. Consequently, materials should be selected that provide for well-organized, sequential development of the skills and abilities needed by the proficient reader. All materials must be examined critically to determine whether they do facilitate developmental growth in reading.

Criterion two applies to materials for corrective and remedial reading just as it does to those for reading in the regular classroom approach. All

---

*Reprinted from *Combining Research Results and Good Practice*, 11, Part 2 (1966 Convention Proceedings), pp. 147–51, by permission of the author and the International Reading Association.

materials selected for instruction, whether they are intended for use with a disabled reader or a gifted reader or any other kind of reader, should fit the plan the school follows for continuous development.

3. "Materials used for skill development in supplementing a basic program must be specifically related to the particular skill in which a given student or group of students is deficient."

Staff members must examine supplemental materials with a sharp critical eye, and not rely upon statements indicating their intent. Too frequently materials designed to improve comprehension use exercises that really call for the use of but one comprehension skill, for example, questions requiring the recall of details. Such materials may be of little value for pupils whose need lies in learning how to draw conclusions or how to secure implied meanings. Once the skill deficiency of a student is determined, the supplementary materials selected must have the elimination of that deficiency as their chief target.

4. "Materials should be at the appropriate level of difficulty (in terms of both skill and personal maturity) for the students concerned."

Not only must the materials be specifically related to the particular skill or ability in which a student is deficient, but also they must be at the appropriate level of difficulty if he is to learn. If they are too easy, he will be bored and will not profit from them; if they are too difficult, he will be frustrated and dislike the task set for him. A careful check of a student's personal maturity must be made if materials are to be appropriate in the concept load, a factor which all too frequently is disregarded when materials are selected. Unnecessary reading disabilities are sometimes created because little or no attention is paid to the appropriate level of difficulty of the concepts included in the reading materials given to a pupil in the instruction program.

Appropriate difficulty does not mean that materials should not be challenging. They should be stimulating. But a student, although challenged, should be able to experience success as he learns. Using criterion four effectively requires the use of keen insights by the person assigning the materials to pupils.

5. "Although all materials will not be of equal interest to all students, materials should be chosen and evaluated in accordance with realistic needs and interests of the student or group of students concerned."

If the reading program is to result in a student's reading at the independent level without the pressure of assignments, some attention must be paid to the interest that the materials arouse in the students. Of course, expert teachers can and do help pupils develop interests which can and often do create within them desires to read certain books. Interest created by the reading materials themselves generates effort.

The ultimate in reading materials will be achieved when they contain inherent motivation that entices the students to read. Although teachers will have to select materials that are related to the realistic reading needs of their students, they may not disregard the interest-appeal the materials have.

6. "Materials should be selected and evaluated in relation to broadening the students' intellectual and emotional experiences."

Obviously this criterion indicates that a teacher cannot rely on a single textbook to meet the needs of all students. Individual differences demand that a wealth of reading materials be available for expanding and creating both intellectual and emotional experiences.

To make criterion six effectively operable, according to Herrick, a school must "(a) provide for interest areas of reading, (b) provide content necessary to meet varied educational needs, (c) 'trigger' reading in different kinds of materials for the full range of purposes for which a child might read, and (d) adapt the level and rate of reading development to the wide range of differences that exist among children."

One of the best means of providing the kinds of material referred to by Herrick is the school library. Schools have much to do in this area. Today there is a great lack of libraries. In 1963 it was reported that over ten million American students were going to schools "bare of any libraries at all." Many of the libraries in existence were "appallingly inadequate." Provision of materials for broadening student intellectual and emotional experiences and for meeting individual differences can be made most adequately and usually most economically through well-stocked libraries.

7. "Practice materials should be appropriate to the purpose for which they are used and should maintain a balance between success and challenge."

Since a reading program should be designed to help all students who can profit from reading instruction, it must serve many purposes. Practice materials, when used, must be chosen to meet specific purposes if they are to assist students in the mastery of reading techniques. Materials that stress word-recognition skills, for example, should not be expected to develop the ability a student needs in tying interpretation to critical reaction.

Once materials have helped a student to begin his mastery of a skill or ability, subsequent materials used by him should increase in difficulty at a pace that will not defeat him in his task. As Bond and Wagner put it, "from time to time the child must have material with which he has to 'tussle'; but there should always be a reasonable chance that he will win the 'tussle.'" One may never forget that it is essential to maintain a balance between success and challenge for the student as he strives for higher levels of efficiency. Practice materials chosen for specific purposes and selected with this balance in mind are most valuable assets in the reading program.

8. "Materials should be varied enough in content, type, length, interest, and point of view so that students may have many different kinds of reading experiences, including abundant opportunities for voluntary reading."

Reading, a most complex process, requires a wide variety of materials if all the purposes of an effective program are to be realized. Obviously materials that vary in length are important. Usually short selections are most appropriate for the beginning of instruction intended to develop a new skill. Later, selections of considerable length can be used to cement the mastery of the skill.

Fiction and factual materials of all kinds must be among the reading materials if a school is to provide a wealth of reading experiences. They should include a variety of approaches and interpretations to enable students to secure a realistic understanding of the world. Materials presenting different views on a simple topic are essential in the development of critical reading.

Materials that give a realistic, truthful view of the world are particularly needed. They can be useful in helping today's mobile children and youth adapt to new environments. Thirty-eight million Americans, one of every five, changed residence between March, 1964 and March, 1965. Half of these moved from one state to another. Three out of five live in urban areas, most of which have multi-cultural populations.

9. "The authors of materials for both instructional and recreational uses should be experts in their field; authors of instructional materials, in particular, should also be aware of the developmental needs and interests of students."

When one stops to list just a few of the items an author of reading materials must keep in mind when he develops them, he must conclude that experts are indispensable in preparing what teachers require if they are to do an efficient job in teaching reading. Here are just a few matters that an author may have to consider as he writes: appropriateness of vocabulary for his reading audience; such reading skills as following directions, reading for details, determining the proper sequence of events in terms of time, and reading to make inferences; concepts appropriate for different ages of pupils; interests of boys and girls at different stages of development; and knowledge that provides accurate information for the content included in the materials.

10. "Students should have the opportunity to select and evaluate materials. These judgments by students are of value to the teacher in his own selection and evaluation of reading materials."

According to Herrick, one aspect of the sequence in the teaching of reading, "is found in the child and his reading experiences. . . . Here the learner assumes increasing responsibility for the continuity of his learning and for the relating of reading materials to his own development and purposes. There is an increasing body of knowledge about the ability of the child in self-selection [even] at the early periods of his education . . . any adequate program of reading instruction should help the child increase his ability to select and use his reading materials so as to achieve his reading purposes."

The pupil learns to read by reading. Freedom of choice may motivate a student to read far more than if he is compelled to rely completely upon teacher judgment. Given the opportunity, he will evaluate materials in such a way that a teacher will be able to use effectively the peer evaluations with other students.

Criterion ten is vitally important in a program designed to help students become independent readers. And this objective should be the key-stone of all reading programs!

Putting to effective use the ten criteria as briefly presented here requires skill, knowledge, time, and a wealth of materials from which to choose. If the school dollar spent for reading materials is to bring the returns in learning that it should, then school district staffs must be willing to apply such a set of criteria.

(19) VOCABULARY CONTROL*

Samuel Weintraub

The Problem. The issue of vocabulary control has produced almost as much heated controversy as has the phonics quarrel. Vocabulary control,

*Reprinted from the *Reading Teacher* 20 (May 1967), pp. 769–75, by permission of the author and the International Reading Association.

as considered in this column, refers only to the limiting of the number of new words introduced and to the planned repetition of those words. There are, of course, aspects of vocabulary control other than those considered in this column. The topic of word selection and the control of grapheme-phoneme correspondence are not discussed.*

Historically considered, the planned repetition of words in a form similar to that practiced today was first introduced in the McGuffey Readers (10). McGuffey also provided for a more gradual increase in the number of new words introduced per page. The most significant reduction in the size of primer vocabularies, however, appeared between the late 1920's and early 1930's. During this same period, authors of reading materials also provided for a higher percentage of repetitions of words. Such control appeared not only in first grade materials but oftentimes in readers written for grades two through six.

At least one critic of vocabulary control pointed to the size of reading vocabulary Russian children encounter in their readers during the elementary school years and found that American children, by contrast, met an extremely limited number of words (12). Other critics have felt that controlling the number of new words introduced and repeating them frequently causes the reading material to be dull and boring for elementary school children. Still other critics point to the fact that children enter first grade with large speaking and listening vocabularies and leave the elementary school with even larger ones (9). Because of the extensive vocabularies already developed by the age of five or six, this last group feel children can and should meet with unlimited numbers of words in reading materials.

Proponents of vocabulary control, on the other hand, feel that such control provides for fluency and ease of reading. Controlling vocabulary, they claim, programs for the child a gradual and systematic introduction into reading and helps him learn to read by phrase and by thought units rather than word by word. Furthermore, the point is often made that one needs to look at the number of failures in our reading programs prior to the introduction of vocabulary control to see how such control has been helpful (2, 5).

Faced with conflicting arguments and with what has often appeared to be an increasing pressure from parents and the lay public to do away with readers and other materials advocating vocabulary control,

---

*The author wishes to express his gratitude to Mrs. Debra Weiss and to Miss Ellen Thomas for reacting critically to this article and for their assistance in compiling references.

teachers and reading specialists often find themselves without a scholarly answer as to whether vocabulary control should or should not be practiced. Indeed, such control is probably unquestioned by most teachers. But this question remains: Is there any sound basis in the research literature for vocabulary control?

The Research. The important basic research on vocabulary control has been reported by Gates in a series of investigations covering a wide span of years.

In one of his earlier studies Gates noted that children vary markedly according to intelligence levels in terms of the number of repetitions needed in acquiring a reading vocabulary (3). He estimated the *average* minimum number of repetitions per word that need to be provided for first grade children at various intelligence levels, as shown in the table.

IQ	Number of Repetitions
120–129	20
110–119	30
90–109	35
80–89	40
70–79	45
60–69	55

Several cautions about interpreting the table were recommended by Gates. He felt that the reader should not infer that *every* word should be given the number of repetitions indicated. He suggested that some words will need more, and some, fewer repetitions. Obviously, too, interest and motivation are factors to be taken into consideration in estimating the number of times a particular child must be exposed to a particular word before it becomes part of his sight recognition vocabulary. The length of the word and the function it serves are other factors which play a part in determining the amount of exposure needed for various words.

In addition, Gates commented that readers typical of the late 1920's, introducing new words at rates between 1 in 10 to 1 in 17, could not be read by even the more gifted classes of students without considerable additional practice in various supplementary materials (3).

Somewhat later, Gates and Russell studied three groups of children who had been introduced to varying numbers of different words in first grade (6). The groups were approximately equal with respect to read-iness test scores, mental age, and sex distribution. On standardized tests using words not taught to anyone, the children who had encountered the smallest number of different words scored higher in both word recogni-tion and paragraph comprehension than the children encountering the largest number of different words in grade one reading instruction.

Moreover, when these pupils were divided into ability levels on the basis of readiness scores, the following findings were noted: (1) Children in the highest readiness score group given the medium amount of vocabulary diversity obtained the highest scores on the four reading tests administered. (2) Of the children scoring in the middle readiness ranges, the group receiving the restricted vocabulary scored highest on all four reading measures. (3) Among children in the low readiness group, the restricted vocabulary classes received the highest scores.

Clark and Monahan reported on two master's studies which yielded results contradictory to those of Gates and Russell (1). In one of the studies, stories, in which the words from four series of readers were used, were written at each of three levels—preprimer, primer, and first reader. At the preprimer level only a small number of children were able to read orally the words in the story that had not been included in their particu-lar basal reader. At the primer level and beyond, a number of children were able to read words not previously taught in the reader in which they had been working. Clark and Monahan concluded that vocabulary control did not seem necessary beyond the preprimer level. They failed to note, however, that they were dealing with a comparatively gifted group. When this factor is taken into account, their findings tend to agree with those of Gates and Russell.

More recently, Gates reported investigations beyond the first grade. In one study he found that third grade children of average ability or better had little difficulty in recognizing and grasping the meaning of words in the fourth grade book. Brighter pupils in the latter part of grade two experienced little difficulty with new words taken from third and fourth grade readers (4). A supplementary study of end-of-the-year second grade children of approximately average intelligence measured word meaning ability on samples of words taken from books covering grades one through four. Almost half of the children knew most of the words. Because there were pupils who scored low on the test, Gates comments that it behooves us "not to be too hasty in discarding every form of 'vocabulary control' in the basal readers of the lower grades" (5).

Summary and Conclusions. Children do learn to read words other than those in the basal reader. As Mason demonstrated, some first graders learn words from television (8), and Story pointed up other sources from which her first graders learned many words (11).

It would appear, then, that there is ample evidence for a controlled vocabulary for most children through second grade. For children of less than average ability, the control should probably continue even longer. Assuming that children have read extensively outside their formal reading program and have mastered most of the basic word analysis skills, there would seem to be little value in the planned introduction and repetition of a limited number of words beyond grade three or four.

REFERENCES

1. Clark, Faye M., and Monahan, Mary M. "A Controlled Vocabulary?" *Journal of Education*, 137 (May 1955), 15.
2. Dolch, Edward W. *Teaching Primary Reading*. Third Edition. Champaign, Ill.: Garrard Press, 1960.
3. Gates, Arthur I. *Interest and Ability in Reading*. New York: Macmillan, 1930.
4. Gates, Arthur I. "Vocabulary Control in Basal Reading Material," *Reading Teacher*, 15 (Nov. 1961), 81–85.
5. Gates, Arthur I. "The Word Recognition Ability and the Reading Vocabulary of Second- and Third-Grade Children," *Reading Teacher*, 15 (May 1962), 443–448.
6. Gates, Arthur I., and Russell, David H. "Types of Materials, Vocabulary Burden, Word Analysis, and Other Factors in Beginning Reading: II," *Elementary School Journal*, 39 (Oct. 1938), 119–128.
7. Hildreth, Gertrude. "Reading Programs in the Early Primary Grades." In Nelson B. Henry (Ed.), *Reading in the Elementary School*, pp. 54–92. Forty-eighth Yearbook of the National Society for the Study of Education. Chicago, Ill.: University of Chicago Press, 1949.
8. Mason, George E. "Children Learn Words from Commercial TV," *Elementary School Journal*, 65 (Mar. 1965), 318–320.
9. Seegers, J. C., and Seashore, R. H. "How Large Are Children's Vocabularies?" *Elementary English*, 26 (Apr. 1949), 181–194.
10. Smith, Nila Banton. *American Reading Instruction*. Newark, Del.: International Reading Association, 1965.
11. Story, Suetta B. "Does Johnny Know More Words Than Ivan?" *Reading Teacher*, 20 (Nov. 1966), 131–133.
12. Trace, Arthur S., Jr. *What Ivan Knows That Johnny Doesn't*. New York: Random House, 1961.

(20) PHONICS MATERIALS: A BIG SELLER*

Dolores Durkin

Even a quick stroll up and down the aisles of a convention exhibit hall provides ample evidence that educational materials are "big business." In fact, corporations like IBM, RCA, and CBS can now be viewed as the latest alphabet to dot the educational marketplace (4).

Predictably, the involvement of large corporations has led to some changes. Clearly apparent are more sophisticated advertising, more colorful materials, more urbane sales personnel—in fact, more of everything; for quantity is the very essence of big and successful business. In spite of the new and more glamorous façade, however, one thing remains unchanged: the unique importance of reading to the entire educational enterprise continues, making materials connected with the teaching of reading skills one of the most lucrative pieces to be found in the whole of the market place display. It is probably equally accurate to add that, of all the various skills comprising reading, phonics is the juiciest from an economic point of view. Why?

A variety of factors account for the special market value of phonics. For one thing, phonics instruction often is equated with reading instruction. While such an equation confuses a part with the whole, the association has still resulted in assigning to phonics a rather special place of honor. For the market place the confusion has resulted in "a big seller."

But there is another characteristic of phonics that makes it especially enticing to the publisher: its content can be packaged. It can fill up workbooks. It provides material for charts, cards, pictures, and filmstrips. It can be pressed into phonograph records. It can be put into the form of a "game." It can be used to take advantage of the current interest in programmed instruction. And, even more recently, it provides ideal material for the teaching kit. Could we expect such potential to be overlooked by the publisher? Hardly. But as a result the question of discriminate buying takes on paramount importance.

*Reprinted from *The Reading Teacher* 20 (April 1967), pp. 610–14, by permission of the author and the International Reading Association.

THE DISCRIMINATE BUYER

Discriminate buying, whether of a workbench or a workbook, always requires a knowledge of the product—what it can and cannot do, for instance. And this will not change. But what *is* changing, even as the nature of the market place changes, is an ever increasing need for the buyer to possess what might simply be called the will to resist temptation.

To be sure, temptation has always been the goal of the merchant and, correspondingly, the downfall of the buyer. But today the temptation held out to the man with money in his pockets must be, and often is, uniquely enticing and even manipulative. Reflecting the technological and affluent society which surrounds it and which also has created it, the modern market place no longer is characterized by the classical supply-demand relationship. The "good old days" in which what was produced was what was needed are now part of past history. Replacing them is an economic era in which the traditional sequence has been reversed. Today the first step is production, and the second step is the deliberate creation of a need for what has been produced. Indeed, the wares of Madison Avenue have never been so important—nor so effective.

Although in the past the schools have sometimes been accused of remaining apart from the realities of life, nobody now could deny that they are very much immersed in the reality of this new market place. There is not only a larger number of children to educate and teachers to help; there is also that "man with money in his pockets." Thanks to the generosity of federal funds, the educator has become a wealthy man, and so a most welcome customer in the aisles of the market. Perhaps it goes without saying that, among the counters devoted to reading, phonics materials are richly and enticingly displayed.

MOTIVES FOR BUYING PHONICS MATERIALS

While the allurement of the modern market place is undeniably great, it would be erroneous to think it is the sole reason why phonics materials are a big seller. Certainly other factors are at work too. One, for example, is related to the kind of public criticism that has been leveled at the schools for about the last ten years. Starting with the publication of

Why Johnny Can't Read in 1955, the focus of a surprisingly large amount of criticism has been the charge that the schools are not teaching phonics (2). This has been the case whether the complaint was about reading, as in the Flesch book, or something as broad as the possible inferiority of American schools as compared with those of Soviet Russia (5).

Within the past decade, too, phonics instruction has worked its way into public debates about manners and morals, and frequently into politically conservative publications. As recently as November 1966, for instance, Russell Kirk was writing in *National Review* statements like, "Among the educationists phonics is a dirty word," and, as he gave his description of elementary schools, ". . . actual teaching by phonics is taboo." (3).

That statements like these could never be documented has less effect on practice than ought to be the case. In fact, public accusation about too little phonics is one of the factors that has resulted in too much phonics, in certain schools. In their eagerness to have very visible phonics programs, for instance, some administrators have gone all-out in stressing phonics and in purchasing phonics materials. While these efforts to "prove a point" are psychologically understandable, they are not always professionally defensible. Just as some schools would profit from a little more and a little better phonics instruction, others could probably be improved simply by having less.

Related to the public indictment of too little phonics instruction is still another factor which sometimes enters into a school's decision to introduce more and more phonics and, as is generally the case, to buy more and more phonics materials. This source of influence is parents.

Typically, what a parent knows about reading comes from the newspaper or, perhaps, one of the monthly magazines written for women. When this popular press reporting deals with reading, it most often focuses on its beginnings and, in conjunction with this, the advantages of phonics instruction compared to what is called the "look-say" approach.

It is doubtful that the frequent selection of beginning reading as the topic of popular press articles is accidental: never is a parent so concerned about reading as when his child is just starting to learn. How well the child progresses at the beginning is viewed not only as an indicator of future progress in reading, but even as a forecast of how well the child will do in all areas of the curriculum. Such uncommon importance makes the parent eager to learn about beginning reading. And it also makes him somewhat gullible as popular press articles offer sure cures and even "guaranteed" results, if the cures are followed. Most of these prescriptions, of course, call for immediate and frequent instruction in phonics.

To think that parents' beliefs about the best way to teach beginning reading have no effect on a school's reading program would be naïve. As a minimum they encourage the administration to take another look at the way reading is taught in the early grades. At the other extreme, however, parents' beliefs about the special advantages of much phonics instruction have been known to result in obviously increased amounts in the schools, sometimes as early as the kindergarten year.

While nobody would deny the right of a parent to be concerned about his child's education, and even to have definite ideas about the way it ought to be effected, the priority of professionalism needs to be recognized when decisions about education are to be made. In the case of phonics instruction, decisions about its timing and, for instance, about whether it ought to be taught inductively or deductively are professional matters. When these decisions are affected by such factors as the desire to "pacify" parents, the results are not always what is best for the children learning to read.

There is still another reason motivating the purchase of volumes of phonics materials. It is neither a "right" reason nor a "wrong" one; but when it exists it ought to be recognized. This is the fact that some teachers are not prepared to teach phonics and, as a result, feel an unusual need for materials.

Citing the possibility of this source of motivation is not to be critical of teachers. Rather, it is to be aware that many were elementary school children when phonics was given scant attention. As a result, unless these teachers are lucky enough to have had a reading methodology course which actually taught them the content of phonics, they enter their own classrooms with feelings of inadequacy and insecurity. These feelings are natural, but they lead to overreliance on materials. And while this might be advantageous for the merchant, it is hardly good for the classroom. What the dependency creates is a situation in which the teacher is merely an assistant to materials—a role hardly worthy of a professional person, and hardly productive of the best kind of instruction.

SOME FACTORS IN CONSIDERING MATERIALS

If a school should decide to buy materials to help its faculty learn more about phonics—and this surely is laudable—the reason for the purchase ought to be taken into account as particular materials are selected. This is important because what might be suitable for educating teachers is not necessarily best for teaching children. With them, different criteria have to be kept in mind. With both, however, the requirements of prudent choices begin even before the customer gets to the market place.

Certainly the first step—whether the intent is to help children or teachers or both—is clarification of the role phonics is to play in a total reading program. In the opinion of this writer, phonics instruction is very important. It is one way to help a child develop independence as a reader and as a learner. But to recognize its importance is not to lay aside the fact that phonics is just one kind of reading instruction and, therefore, only one part of the total reading program. Without this perspective, phonics all too easily becomes isolated as an end in itself, actually losing its very reason for being: a means toward identifying unfamiliar words.

Once clarity about the contribution of phonics is achieved, decisions have to be made about whether its content will be taught inductively or deductively, and also when the teaching will begin. It is not the intention of this article to take a stand on these questions; that has been done with considerable detail elsewhere (1). Rather, the purpose is to recognize the existence of the questions, and to point out the need for a faculty to arrive at some answers, hopefully for "right" reasons. Once this is accomplished, a school is ready to consider whether there are materials in the market place that might be helpful.

When materials are being considered for children, the first kind to look for are those that might actually instruct. Assuming, for instance, that a school has some children who are able to learn at least part of the content of phonics from a book rather than a teacher, it then makes sense to try to find materials which allow for independent learning, and also for a pace of learning that can be matched to the abilities of individual children.

More frequently, though, schools will be looking for materials which review instruction given by a teacher, or which provide practice in the use of what has been taught. When materials are being considered to serve these functions, the most important requirement—and the only one that will be discussed here—is that they facilitate a teacher's efforts to individualize instruction.

For example, materials providing practice in the use of short vowel sounds ought to have enough coverage for the child who will need a great deal of practice. But, in addition, the various kinds of practice ought to be assembled in a way that allows a teacher to make selections on the basis of what is needed by individual children, and at a time when the need is identified. As practice material is now generally put together by publishers—in the typical workbook, for instance—individualized instruction is not only *not* facilitated; it is often made more difficult. In fact, materials like the typical workbook are the most prolific reminder that what is needed by a teacher is not always what is produced by the publisher.

A SUMMARY

This brief article has tried to enumerate a few of the reasons why phonics materials are an especially big seller in the educational market place. Its content has been developed on the assumption that an awareness of some of the factors that affect buying will make the buyer more perceptive and discriminating.

In no sense does the selected focus infer that educators must rely only on published materials to do their job. Certainly some of the best materials used by children are what they themselves make, or what a teacher makes out of her knowledge of what needs to be taught and practiced. However, it is unrealistic to think that all the materials required by classroom instruction can be "home made." This being the case, there is the need to look to the publisher for help. But, as this article has tried to show, there also is an ever increasing need to be wary of his products, knowing that the motivation of the educator and that of the publisher will not always be the same.

REFERENCES

1. Durkin, Dolores. *Phonics and the Teaching of Reading.* New York: Bureau of Publications, Teachers College, Columbia University, 1965.
2. Flesch, Rudolph. *Why Johnny Can't Read.* New York: Harper, 1955.
3. Kirk, Russell. "Why Don't They Teach Phonics?" *National Review*, 18 (Nov. 15, 1966), 1169.
4. Silberman, Charles E. "Technology Is Knocking at the Schoolhouse Door," *Fortune*, 74 (Aug. 1966), 120 ff.
5. Trace, Arthur S. *What Ivan Knows That Johnny Doesn't.* New York: Random House, 1961.

(21) WHAT DO PUBLISHERS MEAN BY "GRADE LEVEL"?*

Robert E. Mills and Jean R. Richardson

Teachers and remedial clinicians frequently express despair about securing from publishers materials that are accurately graded for level of difficulty. Nevertheless, most parents, and too often teachers, assume that what the publisher states is a "third grade" book is written at third grade level. Recent studies of readability variances between the publisher's grade listing of a book and the grade level as determined by a readability formula suggest the need of a common formula in the grading of books by a single publishing company and among various companies. It is true that factors such as concept load and individual differences within any school grade level add to the difficulty of evaluating texts. Too often, however, it would seem that publishers and educators excuse themselves from concern over level of difficulty because they are unable to control *all* variables. It is our contention that every effort should be made to control at least the more mechanical, objective, variables to get the selection of reading books and materials out of the realm of pure guesswork.

Two hundred basic readers and other texts recommended for use in grades one through three were graded by remedial clinicians using the Spache formula. This formula takes into account both vocabulary and sentence complexity and, with a little practice, can produce very consistent reliable gradings. These texts came from seventeen publishers and included most of the primary texts used in the United States today. While many of them agreed closely with the publishers' stated grade level, there were some wide disparities. There was, for example, a "primer" that turned out to be written at second grade-third month level. This seemed such a wide disparity that it was independently regraded by two other clinicians, with comparable results. There was also the series of three first grade readers which scored at second grade-forth month, second grade-sixth month, and second grade-ninth month.

*Reprinted from *The Reading Teacher* 16 (March 1963), pp. 359–62, by permission of the authors and the International Reading Association.

Attention was then turned toward books on higher levels. The books selected were from a group of children's books, grades four through eight, published by well known companies. These books were then graded by the Dale-Chall formula for books above fourth grade level, which like the Spache takes into account both vocabulary and sentence complexity. The results were comparable to those found in the study of elementary texts.

The findings indicated a need for examining the methods by which the publishers determine the grade level of their books. Twelve companies were then chosen from well established publishers of children's books, grades one through eight. These publishers were sent a letter and a questionnaire designed to secure only data pertinent to this study. The list of publishers included: Bobbs-Merrill, Grosset and Dunlap, E. M. Hale, Houghton-Mifflin, J. B. Lippincott, Charles B. Merrill, Macmillan, Row-Peterson, Scott-Foresman, Webster, and World Book Company.

The main part of the letter consisted of the following paragraph:

> We are requesting information regarding your formula for grading children's books, grades one through eight. A research study is being conducted on the need for a more consistent formula in grading books within a single publishing company, and between various companies. When your company lists a book as "for grades 1-3," it is difficult to understand such labeling because of the extreme difference in sentence complexity, vocabulary load, and interest level for a first grader as contrasted with a third grader.

The questionnaire posed six questions in three groups. (1 and 2) Do you use specific formulae for grading books? If Yes, what method is used and by whom is it done? (3 and 4) Is this formula used for all books, grades one through eight? What other procedures are used, i.e., experts in field grading books? (5 and 6) Do you employ specifically trained people to grade books? How is the level of interest established?

From the publishers to whom we addressed our requests, seven replies were received. From these seven only four completed the questionnaire. Second and third letters were sent to the five publishers who did not respond the first time, but to no avail.

We might speculate as to why five of the publishers gave no response whatsoever. Do they feel there is no need for a readability formula? Were they purposely avoiding the subject for some reason? Or is there an indifference on the part of publishers toward the readability of their books? Or did they "not have the time" to be bothered with research projects such as ours?

The replies we received were astonishing and somewhat discouraging. Two large publishing firms were unabashedly annoyed at our inference that a readability formula should be used. One publisher stated ". . . it is impossible to grade children's books exactly, for reading standards vary widely in different parts of the country and even in different parts of the same state, but those of us working in this field have found it necessary to use very elastic gradings—Pre-School to 3rd Grade, 4th to 6th, 7th to 9th, 10th to 12th. . . . We strive to make the reader stretch his mind, imagination and interest."

A child reading on a primer level cannot be expected to read and comprehend a book written on a third-grade level because of the tremendous development vocabulary between these grades. To give a child who is reading on a first grade level a third grade book is unwarranted, unfair, unrealistic, and damaging. A young reader's mind can be "stretched" only so far before he loses interest. Besides frustrating the child, these "elastic gradings" rob the teachers of a criterion for judging a child's reading. How many parents would accept a report card which read, "Your child is reading somewhere between a primer and third-grade level"?

Another publisher wrote: "The most important thing in determining actual readability is probably none of the mechanical factors which include the word list, sentence length, complexity of sentences, etc., but rather the motivational factors. These are quite hard to assess, but include such things as writing in conversational style, personalizing the material, giving dramatic openings and dramatic handling of material, and a considerable additional range of factors that make material interesting and easy to read and of particular appeal to particular grade levels."

It does not seem possible that motivational factors could determine to this extent the readability of a book. An adult who is a sailing enthusiast cannot read a book on sailing written in Arabic if he does not know Arabic; nor can a child who is reading on a first grade level read a third grade book with much profit. To present such books to the adult or child highly motivated in a particular field would only prove that much more frustrating. The problem is obviously a matter of vocabulary development.

About one-half the publishers reported that no standardized formulae were used; they relied on the judgment of their authors or educational consultants to determine the grade level of their texts. Authors and educational consultants are, however, too often out of touch with the school system and have too little opportunity to observe the child as he reads. They do not realize the obvious need for a consistent systematic progression of graded texts.

Furthermore, there is the problem of variations in texts at the same grade level. The assumption that books labeled by their publishers as third grade are actually written at third grade reading level has already been shown to be fallacious. This variance works a tremendous hardship not only on the student, but also on the teacher, for the teacher is thus required to work with virtually no universal criteria. Consistency in graded texts cannot be accomplished without the use of standardized, comparable formulae.

Books of all varieties from the publishers queried in this survey were graded by at least two evaluators. The results were then compared with the grade level listed on the individual publisher's catalogue. It is true that approximately 50 per cent of the two hundred books graded were appropriately labeled. A selection of twenty of the books which showed disparity is presented in the table to indicate some of the differences which exist. These books varied from the publisher's listing from one to four school years. One in every five books (20 per cent) was below the grade level listing; and four out of every five books (80 per cent) were above the grade level listing. Therefore, we would conclude that the tendency is to upgrade books, and that there are enough discrepancies in these gradings to warrant some positive action being taken to remedy this very real problem..

In these days when we are asking young readers to read more texts than ever before, it is our contention that providing them with a systematic progression of graded texts is an important step in developing confidence and minimizing frustration. Our findings certainly indicate the need for publishers to use some more consistent means of grading their texts. We believe that the use of comparable readability formulae is the best solution. It would be well if teachers, librarians, and others charged with the responsibility of selecting books for young readers started questioning publishers more closely as to what means they employ for grading their books and perhaps make purchases accordingly.

It would appear from the lethargy shown in the responses of publishers to this type of study that if anything constructive is to be done, it will have to be initiated by educators and parents.

GRADE LEVELS OF PUBLISHERS AND RESEARCHERS COMPARED

Book	Publisher's Grade	Researchers' Grade	Difference
Buckie's Friends	Pre	2.5	2½+
Making Friends	1	3.2	2+
Skipping Along	2	3.4	1½+
The New Round About	1	2.2	1+
The New Wishing Well	Pre	2.3	1+
The New Anything Can Happen	1	2.4	1½+
Runaway Home	6	5.2	1−
Parades	7	5.9	1−
New Days and Deeds	5.1	6.1	1+
Jack and Janet	1	2.0	1+
Bright Peaks	6	7.1	1+
Young Audubon	4.0	5.4	1½+
Molly Pitcher	4.0	2.5	1½−
Dan Webster	4.0	2.6	1½−
Boy Sailor	4.0	5.9	1½+
Little Fat Gretchen	1	3.3	2+
Stagecoach Sam	2	5.3	3+
Cowboy Tommy	3	5.6	2½+
Cowboy Tommy Roundup	3	5.9	3+
The Little Cowboy	1	5.3	4+

(22) NEW DATA ON READABILITY*

John R. Bormuth

Reading and language specialists are avid students of readability research, for this research attempts to discover what makes language easy or difficult to understand. Readability researchers study the correlations between various features of language and the difficulty children have in

*Reprinted from *Forging Ahead in Reading*, 12, Part I (1967 Convention Proceedings), pp. 488–92, by permission of the author and the International Reading Association.

understanding language. This provides the specialists with the information they need to tailor instructional materials to fit the reading abilities of their students. It also provides them with readability formulas by which they can determine if commercially prepared materials are suitable for their students. Finally, by studying how the many features of language influence comprehension, readability research provides insights into the nature of the comprehension process itself.

The last few years have seen rapid and somewhat startling developments in readability research. For example, the readability formulas available only three years ago could, at best, predict only 25 to 50 percent of the variation we observe in the difficulties of instructional materials. Today, we have not one but two prototype formulas, which are able to predict 85 to 95 percent of the variation. This represents a very high level of precision and an improvement of from 35 to 75 percent over the validities of older readability formulas. The purpose of this paper is to describe some of the results of this research and the efforts currently being made to forge our newly gained knowledge into practical educational tools.

Among the most important events leading up to the present developments was the publication of two books summarizing the readability research done up to that time. One was by Chall (1958) and the other by Klare (1963). From these books it became clear that the future readability research had to concentrate on three problems. First, a more reliable method would have to be developed for measuring the difficulty children have in understanding materials. Second, researchers would have to learn to measure and describe the linguistic features of materials that are really important in affecting comprehension. Third, investigators would have to analyze their data in far more detail than they had up to that time. What follows is an account of what resulted when efforts were made to attack each of these problems.

MEASUREMENT OF COMPREHENSION DIFFICULTY

Problem. Until recently, investigators used multiple choice tests to determine the comprehension difficulties of materials. They made a test over each passage they were studying, tested the students after they had read each passage, and then found the mean percentage of questions answered correctly. The test means represented the difficulties of the passages. This method presented two problems. First, because the test was itself a reading task, the investigator was never quite certain whether he was measuring the difficulty of the passage or just the difficulty of the test questions. Second, these tests could tell him nothing about how difficult each word, phrase, or sentence in the passage was.

Construction of Cloze Tests. Shortly before Chall and Klare published their books, Taylor (1953) reported his first work with the cloze procedure. The cloze readability procedure can be used to make tests from any verbal instructional material. To do so, the investigator selects the passage he wishes to study, deletes every fifth word, and replaces the deleted words with underlined blank spaces of a standard length. The test is given to children who have not previously read the passage, and they are instructed to write in each blank the word they think was deleted. Their responses are scored correct when they exactly match the words deleted, except that misspellings are disregarded.

Advantages. Cloze readability procedure does not confuse the measurement of passage difficulty by injecting an extraneous reading task into the process. It also has the added advantage that investigators could measure the difficulty of every word, phrase, or sentence in a passage.

Research. The cloze readability procedure immediately drew the attention of readability researchers who set about studying cloze tests to see if they were valid and reliable measures of the comprehension difficulties of passages. This research has become far too extensive to review here. Bormuth (1967) and Rankin (1964) have each published detailed analyses of this research. In general, the research showed that cloze readability tests are highly valid and highly reliable measures of the comprehension abilities of students and of the comprehension difficulties of materials.

DESCRIPTION AND MEASUREMENT OF LANGUAGE

Early researchers felt a need to make their formulas so simple they could be used even by clerks having little technical knowledge of language. For example, to determine the complexity of a word, the clerk either counted its syllables or looked it up to see if it was on a list of words thought to be easy. To determine the grammatical complexity of a sentence, the clerk had only to count the number of words, and sometimes prepositions, in the sentence. While it was, at that time, important for formulas to be simple, the old formulas vastly oversimplified the rich array of language features that influenced its comprehension difficulty.

The oversimplification also contributed to the fact that the old formulas were inaccurate.

VOCABULARY COMPLEXITY

Present investigators are probing more deeply into the question of what makes a word difficult to understand. It is not enough to say that the words on some list have been shown to be easier to understand, for this leaves us still asking which of a word's many meanings do children understand and why those words are easier for students. Nor is it practical to test all words directly on children, especially when we consider that most words have several meanings. What follows is a discussion of some of the features currently being investigated.

Word Length. Children have always thought of long words as hard and short words as easy, and researchers have recently rediscovered this fact and begun investigating word length as a variable. Coleman (1961) found that a word's difficulty has a correlation of -.90 with both the number of letters and the number of syllables in the words. Bormuth (1966) found correlations of -.76 and -.68, respectively, for the same measures.

Morphological Complexity. A word is often a complex structure which may be analyzable into a stem and a series of inflectional, derivational, and lexical affixes. It seems that this is an important source of difficulty in understanding words. Coleman (1961) found that word difficulty had a correlation of -.88 with the number of affixes and stems into which a word could be analyzed and a correlation of the same size with the number of inflectional morphemes.

Abstractness. Although there are almost as many meanings of the word abstractness as there are people who use it, nearly everyone agrees that, whatever it is, it has an influence on the difficulty of a word. Coleman (1966) devised a definition which permitted him to count reliably the number of nouns that referred to internal mental states and found that this number had a correlation of -.78 with passage difficulty.

Frequency. It has long been known that the frequency with which a word is used has some influence on the difficulty people have in understanding it. But frequency was thought to be a weak variable since Lorge (1949) had found only a correlation of .51 between it and difficulty. More recently, Bormuth (1966) has shown that frequency and difficulty have a curvilinear relationship and that, when this fact is taken into account, they have a correlation of .66. Klare (1967) has now taken a position that the frequency of a word may directly reflect most of the other characteristics of the word.

GRAMMATICAL COMPLEXITY

The degree of intricacy of the grammatical relationships between the parts of a sentence has always been considered an important source of the difficulty in understanding the sentence. Until recently, the chief means of assessing grammatical complexity consisted of counting the number of words in sentences.

Two major objections can be raised in considering sentence length as the sole factor affecting grammatical complexity. First, it forces us to accept the dubious proposition that all sentences containing the same number of words possess the same degree of complexity. Thus, we are asked to believe that the sentence, *The man saw the boy who found the penny which was lost*, has the same degree of complexity as, *The penny which the boy whom the man saw found was lost*. Second, the number of words in a sentence does not measure a natural unit of language. We cannot simply add or chop off a few words to make the sentence more or less complex.

The grammatical complexity of a sentence actually results from the grammatical structure of the sentence. Consequently, modern researchers are investigating measures of grammatical complexity based on the grammatical structures of sentences. This approach is given firm support by the experiments performed by Martin and Roberts (1966) and Johnson (1966a, 1966b) which demonstrate that people utilize the phrase structure of sentences as they process the sentences.

Syntactic Depth. Yngve (1960) developed a measure of syntactic complexity which obtains the number of grammatical facts a reader must temporarily hold in his memory as he reads a sentence. Presumably, the more grammatical facts the reader must remember as he reads a sentence, the more likely he is to forget one of those facts and the more likely he is to fail to comprehend some aspect of the sentence. Bormuth (1964) and Martin (1966) have each shown that people's responses to sentences are closely related to the depth measures of the sentences. Bormuth (1966) found a correlation of -.55 between depth and passage difficulty. Further, he found (1963) that the effects produced by depth were independent of those produced by sentence length.

Modifier Distance. A variation on the depth measure was developed by Bormuth (1967) and is being investigated by him and by Coleman and Aquino (1967). This variable measures the number of words occurring between a word or phrase it modifies on the theory that the longer a grammatical fact is held in memory, the more likely it is that it will be forgotten. Preliminary results indicate that there is a correlation of -.80 to -.90 between this feature and passage difficulty.

Transformational Complexity. A sentence such as *The little boy ran* may be represented as resulting from a transformation which embedded the kernel sentence *The boy was little*, into the kernel sentence, *The boy ran.* Chomsky (1965) has argued that to interpret a sentence people must transform a sentence back into its kernel sentences.

An interesting aspect of the transformation analysis is the fact that it can be used to measure what early researchers referred to subjectively as being the idea density of materials. Coleman (1966) found that the number of nominalized verb and nominalized adjective transformations had correlations of -.76 and -.57, respectively, with passage difficulty. Many parts of speech represent transformations, also. Bormuth (1966) found that counts of the various parts of speech had correlations as high as .81 with passage difficulty. His present studies are analyzing the effects associated with each of the transformations found in English.

CONTEXTUAL VARIABLES

Modern researchers are looking beyond the word and the sentence to find the features of language that operate over longer segments of text to influence comprehension. Rosenberg (1966) found indications that passages containing words which people tend to associate with each other are easier to recall. Coleman and Aquino (1967) are finding that anaphoric analyses yield variables that predict passage difficulty. Anaphora are repeated references to a concept in a passage. The use of anaphora indicates the extent to which a passage deals in depth with a single topic. Since the work in this area is only beginning, it is still too early to predict its outcomes. But it seems certain that gains in this area will have great value in increasing our ability to predict and control passage difficulty.

READABILITY FORMULAS

Early investigators had to defer the investigation of many important problems until research in other disciplines had made tools available for studying those problems. As may be seen from the preceding discussion, linguistic research provided readability researchers with new and power-ful tools for analyzing language. Similarly, research tools became avail-able for studying the problems involved in designing readability formu-las. As a result, we have now learned enough to design much sounder readability formulas.

Readability and Reading Ability

A problem long plaguing researchers was the question of whether the features that influenced readability for poor readers also influenced the readability of materials for more able readers. If the same features of language influence readability for both and by the same amount, then a single and fairly simple formula can be used to predict readability for all students, regardless of their level of accomplishment in reading. But if different features influence difficulty for students of differing levels of reading achievement or if the same features influence difficulty by differ-ent amounts, then we must develop more complex and materially differ-ent kinds of formulas. Bormuth (1966) studied this problem and found that, regardless of the person's reading ability, the same features of language that caused difficulty for him caused the same amount of difficulty for others.

Shapes of the Relationships

A second question was whether a given amount of increase in a feature of the language increased difficulty regardless of how much was already present. For example, is the difference in difficulty between two and three syllable words as great as the difference in difficulty between 7 and 8 syllable words? If not, the simple correlation techniques used by early researchers yield misleading results. Bormuth (1966) found the differ-ences were not always the same. Figuratively speaking, adding another syllable to a one syllable word increases its difficulty far more than adding another syllable to a seven syllable word. The same is true of many other features. Hence, future readability formulas must include appropriate transformations of measurements taken of these features.

Form of the Formulas

The traditional readability formulas are presented in the form of what is called a multiple variable, linear equation. These equations have a charac-teristic that makes them unsuitable for use as readability prediction formulas. To use them, the researcher must assume that any correlation observed between two variables, say sentence length and word length, must always exist. This simply is not true of the language features used in most formulas. The result is that the old formulas yield misleading results whenever the correlation is anything other than the correlation the formulas assume. Most future readability formulas will probably be designed to provide a profile of the level of difficulty represented by each of the language features in a passage.

SUMMARY

Readability researchers have made rapid strides in the past few years, increasing the accuracy of readability formulas by as much as 75 percent. The reason lies largely in the fact that researchers in several disciplines have developed research tools which have aided greatly the study of readability. Psychologists have developed the cloze procedure into an accurate and reliable method of measuring language difficulty. Linguists have developed descriptions of various features of language, and these descriptive devices have been further adapted into powerful new techniques for measuring the features of language that influence its comprehension difficulty. Finally, advances in our understanding of the mathematics used in our analyses have led to improved designs for readability formulas. The result of these advances is that, within a year or two, educators will have placed in their hands powerful new tools for determining if instructional materials are suitable for use with their students.

REFERENCES

1. Bormuth, J. R. *Implications of Cloze Procedure for the Evaluation of Instructional Programs.* Los Angeles, University of California Center for the Study of Evaluation of Instructional Programs, Occasional Report No. 3, 1967.

2. Bormuth, J. R. "Development of Readability Analyses." Project in Progress at the University of Minnesota, Sponsored by the U.S. Office of Education, 1967.

3. Bormuth, J. R. "Readability: A New Approach," *Reading Research Quarterly, 1* (1966), 79–132.

4. Chall, Jeanne S. *Readability: An Appraisal of Research and Application,* Ohio State University Educational Research Monograph No. 30, 1958.

5. Chomsky, N. *Aspects of the Theory of Syntax*. Cambridge, Mass.: M.I.T. Press, 1965.

6. Coleman, E. B. "Developing a Technology of Written Instruction: Some Determiners of Complexity of Prose," *Symposium on Verbal Learning Research and the Technology of Written Instruction*, unpublished manuscript, 1966.

7. Coleman, E. B., and M. R. Aquino. Communications Project. Project in Progress at the Southwest Regional Laboratory in Los Angeles, 1967.

8. Johnson, N. F. "The Influence of Associations between Elements of Structured Verbal Responses," *Journal of Verbal Learning and Verbal Behavior, 5* (1966), 361–368.

9. Johnson, N. F. "On the Relationship between Sentence Structure and the Latency in Generating the Sentence," *Journal of Verbal Learning and Verbal Behavior, 5* (1966), 369–374.

10. Klare, G. R. *The Measurement of Readability*. Ames, Iowa: Iowa State University Press, 1963.

11. Klare, G. R. "The Role of Word Frequency in Readability." 1967 (in press).

12. Lorge, I. "Readability Formulas—An Evaluation," *Elementary English, 36* (1949), 85–95.

13. Martin, E. and K. H. Roberts. "Grammatical Factors in Sentence Retention," *Journal of Verbal Learning and Verbal Behavior, 5* (1966), 211–218.

14. Rankin, E. F. "Cloze Procedure—A Survey of Research," *Yearbook of the Southwest Reading Conference, 14* (1965), 133–148.

15. Rosenberg, S. "Recall of Sentences as a Function of Syntactic and Associative Habit," *Journal of Verbal Learning and Verbal Behavior, 5* (1966), 392–396.

16. Taylor, W. L. "Cloze Procedure: A New Tool for Measuring Readability," *Journalism Quarterly, 30* (1953), 415–433.

17. Yngve, V. "A Model and an Hypothesis for Language Structure," *Proceedings of the American Philosophical Society, 104* (1960), 444–466.

(23) SOURCES OF CHILDREN'S BOOKS
OR FITTING THE BOOK TO THE CHILD*
Christine B. Gilbert

"The right book for the right child at the right time" has long been a familiar adage to teachers and librarians. What are the right books—those books worthy of a child's reading—the books which will, as Dr.

*Reprinted from *The Reading Teacher* 20 (April 1967), pp. 663–69, by permission of the author and the International Reading Association.

Taylor said in his article, "Call to Excellence," in the January issue, "extend a child's horizon and increase his being."

The ability to read the printed page is not enough. It is what the child reads that is of greatest importance. There are over two thousand children's books a year being published today. Many of these books are useful supplements to the curriculum but are not books which will extend the horizon or cherish the soul of anyone, be he child or adult. How then from out of this wealth of children's books does the teacher know which ones to select?

The selection of a fine book for a child cannot be computerized and selections made automatically. The selection of good books for a child requires a knowledge of a child's interests, his reading ability and maturity level, and a knowledge of the best books and materials to meet these interests. There is no substitute for personal knowledge of the books. The teacher who has read and enjoyed some of the finest books in children's literature can speak from enthusiasm and personal experience when introducing books to children. Children show a ready response to literature when a teacher cares enough about them to read "their books." Young people need to be introduced to books. They need to know a little of what a book is about, and a brief introduction, or preview, or sales talk concerning a book helps them gain this knowledge. In an age when a child can get satisfaction from a variety of media such as television, radio, and movies, the satisfaction a book can bring needs to be explored with them. This is done not by talking about the satisfactions but by discussing particular episodes, and this takes a personal knowledge of the books. Reading then becomes an art, not just reading for information but reading to satisfy the soul. All of the excitement, beauty, and wonder of the printed page unfold as children become more discriminating in their selection of books.

Where does the teacher go for suggestions for the best books? There are ample sources, and with federal money available to schools to build up libraries it is highly important that the money be spent for the finest books. Out of the wealth of book selection aids available, I would like to suggest the following basic lists. This is by no means a comprehensive list but one I think will prove useful to teachers.

The *Children's Catalog*, published by the H. W. Wilson Company, is the one book selection tool developed by a group of librarians and is a composite of their choices of the best books. It appears in a new edition every five years and is kept up-to-date by yearly supplements. There are approximately four thousand five hundred titles included in the 1961 edition and its supplements. Books are listed two ways: first, by the

Dewey decimal classification (subject arrangement), and second, by author, title, and subject. Full information is given for each title: publisher, date, price, grade levels, and a brief annotation. This is a highly selective list and is the basis for a great deal of the material found in school and public libraries. This list more than any other might be considered "the standard tool." A system of stars highlights the most important books.

Good Reading For Youth, a 1966 booklist published by the New Hampshire State Library, is a fine example of a selected bibliography for children in kindergarten through eighth grade. Limited to five hundred titles, the list was prepared under the direction of the Children's Services Division of the American Library Association in cooperation with the National Education Chairman of the United States Junior Chamber of Commerce. A single copy of this beautifully designed and printed booklist is free to libraries.

Books for Children 1960–1965. The books listed in this bibliography are those which were selected and reviewed by the *Book List and Subscription Books Bulletin*, the book selection publication of the American Library Association. Since the *Book List and Subscription Books Bulletin* selects only the better books for review, this five year compilation of their reviews of children's books automatically gives you the cream of the crop for these years. Books are arranged according to the Dewey decimal classification with full bibliographical entry. Books are graded and annotated. Three thousand sixty-eight titles were selected out of the approximately twelve thousand juveniles published during the first half of this decade.

The National Congress of Parents and Teachers and the Children's Services Division of the American Library Association cooperated in compiling a fine bibliography of children's books entitled *Let's Read Together* (published by the ALA, 1964). Books for home purchase and for a family to share together are stressed.

The American Library Association has published *Notable Children's Books 1940–1959*, which includes the most distinguished books of that twenty-year period. A list of notable books is published each year by the Children's Services Division of the American Library Association and periodically these lists are reevaluated. The list for 1940–1959 is the most recent re-evaluation; it appeared in 1966. There is a very helpful introduction by Elizabeth Nesbitt, which is a summary of the principles on which the selection of books has been made.

We Read is an interesting booklist prepared for the Office of Economic Opportunity by the Children's Services Division of the American Library Association and published in 1966. It includes a selected list of children's books and recordings. Books are arranged according to the following categories: Books for Pre-School Children; Stories to Tell; Recordings for Children; Books for Boys and Girls in the City; Books for Boys and Girls in Rural America; Books for Boys and Girls, 12 to 16 Years of Age, Who Need Special Encouragement to Read; Books for Spanish-speaking Children; and Other Useful Sources. One copy of this list is free to schools and libraries from the Office of Economic Opportunity.

Certain bibliographies emphasize a purpose or special point of view. Such a list is *Reading Ladders for Human Relations,* compiled by Muriel Crosby and the Committee for Human Relations of the National Council of Teachers of English, published by the Council in 1963. This is an unusual and most helpful bibliography since it lists books under special categories, such as, How It Feels To Grow Up; The Individual and the Group; The Search for Values; Feeling at Home; Living with Change; and Living as a Free People. Books are separated into those for Primary Readers, Intermediate Readers, Junior Readers, Senior Readers, and Mature Readers. Complete bibliographical information is given, and there is also an excellent annotation pointing out the particular value of the book in terms of the category in which it is placed. I can't praise this bibliography highly enough, for it opens vistas in the way books may be used with children, which will lead to many hours of enjoyment and understanding.

For a very brief booklist of about two hundred sixty titles of children's books that are classics or becoming classics I would recommend *Children's Books Too Good to Miss* by May Hill Arbuthnot (Press of Western Reserve University, 1966).

Each year the American Library Association awards two medals to outstanding children's books, the first, the Newbery Medal and the second, the Caldecott Medal. The Newbery Medal had its beginning in 1921 when Mr. Melcher of the Bowker Company first offered it as an incentive toward the development of better quality in children's books. Named after John Newbery, the famous eighteenth-century publisher and seller of children's books, it is given annually to the author of the most distinguished contribution to American literature for children published during the preceding year. In 1938 the first Caldecott Medal was also donated by Mr. Melcher. It was awarded to the artist of the most distinguished American picture book for children published in the United States during the preceding year. The name of Randolph Caldecott, the famous English illustrator of books for children, was chosen for the medal because his work best represented "joyousness of picture books as well as their beauty." The lists of Newbery and Caldecott awards in the form of a bookmark are available each year from the Children's Book Council in New York.

An excellent list of children's books appears in *Compton's Encyclopedia* under the heading of "Reading for Pleasure," prepared by Frances Clarke Sayers and titled "Bounty of Books." This article is available as a separate reprint, free of charge, from the F. E. Compton Company.

For outstanding books of the year I would suggest the annual listing of *Children's Books* published by the Library of Congress and compiled by Virginia Haviland, Head of the Children's Books Section of the Library of Congress, and Lois Watt, Chief of the Educational Materials Center of the Office of Education. This list of outstanding books of a given year for preschool through junior high school includes both fiction and nonfiction. The list is available from the Superintendent of Documents, Washington, D.C., for fifteen cents.

To keep up with the new books as they appear on the market, teachers will find the following four book reviewing publications of greatest help.

Horn Book Magazine, which is the only magazine devoted exclusively to children's books, is published bimonthly and includes a large section devoted to extensive reviews of children's books. Emphasis is on the literary quality of the books.

Booklist and Subscription Books Bulletin, published by the American Library Association, is published semi-monthly except for August, when there is a single issue. It reviews adult, children's, and young people's books. It is the library profession's own reviewing medium and is a recognized authority in the field.

The School Library Journal published by the Bowker Company appears monthly and reviews a large number of books for children and young adults. Reviews are written by practicing librarians throughout the country who are in the school or the public library field. This publication reviews a larger number of books than any other.

The *Bulletin of the Center for Children's Books* published by the University of Chicago Press has excellent book reviews. Books are reviewed in terms of the needs of schools.

Part Three
Components of Reading

Chapter 6.   Word Skills—Perceptual Dimensions

Chapter 7.   Comprehension—Cognitive Dimensions

Chapter 8.   Attitudes and Values—Affective
Dimensions

Chapter 6

WORD SKILLS—
PERCEPTUAL DIMENSIONS

INTRODUCTION

The ability to recognize known words in print rapidly is vital to becoming an able reader. Acquisition of rapid word perception skills enables the pupil to read more fluently and to derive more meaning from the printed form. However, to become an able reader involves the use of various methods in identifying words. A singular approach to word identification is hardly sufficient. Integrating simultaneously the several approaches that will function automatically is essential for a reader to secure independence in reading.

One of the first instructional tasks facing a teacher of reading is to assist pupils in acquiring and maintaining essential vocabulary skills. These are frequently listed as building a sight vocabulary; expanding vocabulary and word meaning; using context, picture, language, and configuration clues; employing phonetic and structural analysis; and learning the proper use of the dictionary. Each of these skills has numerous components which if merely listed would involve an extensive statement.

The selected articles in this chapter focus upon some of the major skill areas within the word perception dimension. The problem of developing a sufficient and meaningful sight vocabulary is presented by Chambers, together with techniques for its development. McCullough discusses the extension of word meaning and concept development. She provides background information and research data as well as offering suggestions for instruction. The value of context clues in word recognition, ways of classifying them, and specific teaching techniques are included in the first entry by Emans.

The irregularities of the English language add to the task of teaching reading whether the "decoding" concept is employed or useful phonic generalizations are sought. The second selection by Emans examines the values and priorities of phonic generalizations. Winkley asks a similar question about what is worth teaching in regard to accent generalizations. Again the issue of values and priorities based on possible frequency of use of a rule provides the basis for the author's recommendations in teaching accent. An inquiring student would be well advised to read further in this area by using the reference lists provided by the authors of the selections in this chapter and by noting relevant articles in Chapter 2 and Chapter 10.

(24) EXTENDING THE SIGHT VOCABULARY*

J. Richard Chambers

Sight vocabulary belongs under the broad category of word recognition regardless of the grade level span one considers. Disregarding grade level further, word recognition (and therefore, sight vocabulary) also implies word meaning since the necessity of understanding the meaning behind words read is without question. As everyone knows, there is no meaning on the printed page since only the symbols of meaning are there, stimulating the reader to make his own meanings. Therefore, word recognition becomes the ability of the reader to recognize the word as a form he readily knows (a "sight" word), to correctly pronounce the word, and to know the particular meaning of that word in its present context.

IMPORTANCE OF A SIGHT VOCABULARY

Lacking an adequate sight vocabulary, the child is without word recognition skills and necessarily then, without word meanings. When meaning is not present neither are comprehension and/or recall. The effect of the absence of an adequate sight vocabulary is also reflected in incorrect, inadequate phrasing or word-by-word reading resulting, then, in poor oral reading. Though one might approach the development of word recognition skills through word analysis, without immediate recognition of words, speed of reading is too slow and results in an interruption of flow of thoughts and, consequently, a reduction in memory of the content read.

Traxler's study[1] of the relationship between vocabulary and general achievement points out that a child's word meaning score on the Stanford Achievement Test is a reasonably good predictor of his total score on the complete test. It has also been suggested that, "Some psychologists

---

*Reprinted from *Reading and Inquiry* 10 (1965 Convention Proceedings), pp. 29–30, by permission of the author and the International Reading Association.
[1]Arthur Traxler, "The Relationship Between Vocabulary and General Achievement in the Elementary School," *Elementary School Journal*, XLV (February 1945) pp. 331–33.

think that we never have any ideas until we have words to express them. Words seem to be necessary tools with which to think."[2]

It appears that to read with comprehension, the ultimate goal of all reading instruction, one must be able to recognize words immediately and to transfer these symbols into their proper meaning as determined by the particular setting in which the words occur. Children should be given the responsibility of *demanding* meaning from material read even though historically it is known that children are often not good judges of words needing clarification. The scale becomes one of reading with comprehension on one extreme to verbalism on the other.

At the intermediate grade level, the problems associated with vocabulary are multiplied a hundred-fold as compared with those in the primary grades. The number of words met by the child in the middle grades is almost without limit, yet his power to learn words is obviously limited to a small fraction of this total. The sheer number of new words is further complicated by the specialized nature of the vocabulary associated with the content subjects of social studies and science and, indeed, with any of the many subjects taught within this three-grade span.

LIMITATIONS OF SIGHT VOCABULARY

Stockpiling words in his sight vocabulary permits the child to develop his reading power and increases his reading horizons. Yet, as he reads more widely, he must inevitably meet new words which are not a part of his ready supply of words. Here his "go-power" is limited and the usefulness of his sight vocabulary diminishes. Unless he has been taught some independent method of analyzing words his only alternatives are to ask his teacher what the words say (assuming she is available), to guess at the words, or to forget about them and to try to go on without figuring out what the new words might be.

Simply relying on his ability to remember the configuration of a word limits his knowledge to words already presented. If he has learned to examine the context surrounding the word he has increased his "octane" but still has restricted his potential power. These perception and association abilities must be implemented by the addition of analytical abilities. Structural and phonetic analyses become particularly valuable and necessary at the intermediate grade level when the range and frequency of

[2]Mabel Vinson Cage, *Reading in High Gear.* New York: Harper and Brothers, 1938, p. 30.

new words met in the many different types of reading materials increases.

TECHNIQUES OF TEACHING

As one considers ways in which upper elementary level children may be helped to extend their sight vocabulary it becomes necessary to consider the element of quantity or the practical question of the number of words children may be expected to successfully learn per day. The number of words met by children at this level is apparently high. Yet *all* of these words will not be learned by all of the children. This suggests that establishment of the learning rate of students at this level is just as necessary as it is at the reading readiness and primary levels. Teaching in relation to the established learning rate is an acknowledged method of providing for individual differences since it recognizes the existence of varying progress rates and is a sound criterion to consider when attempting to set up reading groups.

Children in the upper elementary grades must be encouraged and, if necessary, re-taught to make use of context clues as an aid in word recognition. Evidence indicates that students at this level do not appear to use these clues as frequently as they should even though they have probably been given this instruction in the primary grades.

Evidence suggests that tachistoscopic drill not only produces gains in quick word perception ability but also results in increases in rapid word recognition with meaning, speed of oral reading, reduction in the number of errors in oral reading, and overall reading achievement.

When teaching vocabulary it is important to add the dimension of depth to the existing one of breadth. Depth in this context means two things: a level of learning going beyond simple recognition, and a knowledge of the multiple meanings which most words have.

Word analysis ability, a necessary extension of skill in word recognition for the development of independence in extending sight vocabulary, offers many opportunities for middle-grade teachers. Exercises combining structural analysis (especially prefixes, suffixes, root words) and word meaning are probably the most valuable kind of word analysis practice for developing the reading vocabulary of intermediate-grade children. The relationship of these sub-skills to reading vocabulary is higher than the relationship existing among any of the other commonly taught word analysis skills and vocabulary.

Since studies show a positive relationship between phonic ability and reading achievement it is necessary to suggest, too, that phonetic analysis be added to the elements that need emphasis when developing independent vocabulary power. The inductive approach to word analysis as reflected in the Word Analysis Practice Cards by Durrell and others[3] will help children develop a "phonic sense" without the necessity of relying on a multiple rules-exception program.

SUMMARY

Procedures in word recognition must continually emphasize meaning and extend over into the area of word analysis with attention to the use of context clues and structural and phonetic analysis. The vocabulary demands placed upon children at these grade levels, because of the specialized nature of the content in the various subject areas and because of the lack of a rigidly controlled vocabulary, make it imperative that they become self-sufficient in their vocabulary needs.

(25) IMPLICATIONS OF RESEARCH ON CHILDREN'S CONCEPTS*

Constance M. McCullough

One has only to look at the more than 2500 references in Dale and Reichert's revised *Bibliography of Vocabulary Studies* (7) to be properly awed by the interest which investigators have shown in the vocabulary and concepts of children. Inflated egos may require an additional look at Russell's 900 references in *Children's Thinking* (22) to realize that a quick answer to the problem of children's ideas—the ways they are formed, and children's experiences with the symbols which represent them—is farther from our grasp than the moon today. The purpose of this article is to give the reader something of the knowledge that is

[3]Donald D. Durrell, Helen A. Murphy, Doris Spencer, and Jane Catterson, *Word Analysis Practice Cards.* New York: Harcourt, Brace and World, 1960.
*Reprinted from *The Reading Teacher* 13 (December 1959), pp. 100–107, by permission of the author and the International Reading Association.

available to teachers about the most basic ingredients in the reading program: the ideas which the child brings to the page and the ideas which he attaches to the words in their relationships.

WHAT A CONCEPT IS

Mr. Webster attempts to settle what we are talking about by describing a concept as "a mental image of a thing formed by generalization from particulars . . . an idea of what a thing in general should be" (36). Russell (22) helps by speaking of concepts as dealing with objects (chair, fish), qualities (honest, clean), and relationships (under, when, because). Jarolimek and Foster (16), refer to concepts as definite (one-half teaspoon of salt) and indefinite (a generous helping of salt). (Generous for what, generous in whose opinion?)

Facets of a concept can be numerous. Take the word *paws*. As a spoken word, of course, it must first be untangled from *pause*. Position makes a difference (front or back), kind (raccoon or dog), shape (long, broad), size (big, little), composition (three-toed, bare, furry), feeling (cold, rough), sound (thumping, stealthy), time (old, young), number (many, few). You can probably think of others.

The facets of a concept can sometimes be illuminated by pairs of words and their relationships to each other: ceramic—dish (general—specific), father—child (numerous facets), fish—fowl (flip versus flap), in—on (position), peace—war (complex opposites), glory—prize (state and symbol).

Russell (22, p. 162) reminds us that a concept may be known thoroughly (toothbrush?), partially (parents?), inaccurately (mother-in-law?), or not at all (income tax regulations?). He attempts to explore children's grasp of concepts by resorting to questions requiring classification, function, definition, appearance or description, characteristics, association with other words, and varied meanings of the same word (23).

How do concepts affect reading? Chall, in *Readibility* (5), points out that the more different words there are on a page, the more ideas, the more involved the sentence structure, the more abstract the words, the more remote the words from fundamental life experience—the greater the difficulty of the material for the reader. Authors can throw road-blocks before the concept builder. Since all types of reading matter do not require the same quantity or quality of comprehension, the varied reading activities in and out of school demand a readiness of the child for many degrees of challenge.

HOW CONCEPTS ARE FORMED

Some insight into the teaching of concepts may be gained by consideration of the manner in which concepts are formed. Russell points out that concepts are often developed slowly "out of percepts, memories, and images, and their development is aided greatly by language or other symbols." Some concepts help explain other concepts: "Concepts of time help explain concepts of social custom . . . aesthetic and humorous concepts grow in relation to social concepts" (22, p. 162). (Slipping on a banana peel is funny because it violates the social idea of the dignity of man). He further remarks that concepts "seem to move along a continuum from simple to complex, from concrete to abstract, from undifferentiated to differentiated, from discrete to organized, from egocentric to more social" (22, p. 249). The parenthetical remarks throughout this article are concrete examples offered to ease the shock of the abstractions which are being discussed. (I am reminded of the child skating along on one roller skate, his other foot occasionally on the "concrete" to push the "abstract" along.)

In developing his concepts "the child employs naming, counting, measuring, discriminating, abstracting, and generalizing." He must recognize the common elements in objects or situations, setting aside unrelated items in the process. (If he has known only short-haired dogs, he must mentally give a shaggy dog a haircut before he can see the generalization "dog"; but, at the same time, he must be ready to add shagginess to his original concept of what a dog can be.) The child gains concepts by an active process, during "sensory impression, muscular activity, motor manipulation, questioning, reading, and problem solving." The process "involves inductive thinking and, at least sometimes, deductive and creative thinking" (22, p. 249).

In books, concepts can be built by pictures which accompany the text, and by the way the words are used in the verbal context. Capitalization and punctuation may hint at the relationship of a strange word to those surrounding it. ("The Keeper of the Privy Seal" is clearly—to experienced readers—a compact title because of the capitalization.)

FACTORS INFLUENCING CONCEPT DEVELOPMENT

What factors influence the development of a concept? Clearly, a concept is based upon experiences, and the more direct these are, the better (28). There may be experiences with objects, processes, and lower-level concepts upon which the needed concept is built, or experiences with the world itself in hearing, speaking, reading, and writing situations. Of course, the mere use of a word by a child is no assurance of his grasp of its meaning. This goes for college students as well as others (18). That the teacher must have a part in book experiences is shown by the fact that many of the common words of multiple meanings used in primary readers are not accurately comprehended by primary grade children (12). If this is true of a controlled vocabulary, how much more true it must be of children's literature in general.

Children of higher socio-economic status tend to score higher on vocabulary tests than children of lower-socio-economic status (32). The opportunities which accompany the status partially account for this difference.

Age, probably a reflection of experience, also has been found to be a factor in concept development. Durkin (10), in investigating children's ideas of justice, found that older children (junior-senior high school) tended to be aware of many more factors to be considered in meting out justice. (He swatted me I'll swat him back . . . but he didn't mean it. Somebody pushed him. His arm just flew back. He thought I was that other guy.) Kruglov (17) found that, in Grades 3 through 8, younger children chose concrete definitions for words they were given, while older children chose more often the abstract definitions or synonyms of the words.

Intelligence, which makes it possible for a child to benefit from experience, to observe, to remember, to generalize, to deduce, to discriminate, and to hold images in mind, is also a factor in concept development (22, p. 25). While Durkin found no relationship between children's concepts of justice and their levels of intelligence, it is sensible to suppose that this lack reflects variations in education and opportunity rather than the unimportance of native ability to one's grasp of the environment. Similarly, McCullough (19), finding children of varied intelligence rather uniformly poor in getting meaning from context clues, supposed this finding to reflect the uniform lack of attention to this skill. So direct teaching as well as intelligence can be a factor.

Sex, with its cultural overtones, shows some influence in concept building. In Russell's study of the dimensions of children's vocabulary (23), boys showed some superiority to girls in their knowledge of vocabulary in science, sports, hobbies, and recreation. (He didn't examine the groups on the properties of Vel, Genie, and Mr. Clean.) Templin (32), studying children aged three through eight, found that the older boys had achieved greater average word knowledge than the older girls, while the latter had better average articulation. (The girls can say it better but the boys know what it means!)

Well-meaning attempts to generalize about factors influencing concept building are defied by the presence of individual differences. Differences are extensive in the same age group and become greater with the age of the children concerned (22). Fennema (11) reported different degrees of imagery among children, which would affect not only the development of concepts, but the ability to hold in mind the symbols representing them. Davis (8) stated that speech maturity had a direct bearing on meaning-getting in early reading activities; and the variations among children in speech at early ages is well known. Russell cites the importance of emotional factors, tensions, needs, and the presence of problems to be solved.

Written material itself contributes to the ease or difficulty with which a child develops understandings. Concepts explained by an author through difficult vocabulary and involved sentence structure may never filter through to the reader (30). Too much to learn on a page, and too frequent use of indefinite terms may result in inaccurate or incomplete concepts, or in none at all (27). On the positive side, Traxler reminds us that wide reading offers the opportunity for a reader to infer meanings from context (34); and Werner (37), that a word may lose its lexical meaning and gain new facets through context. On the negative side, Sachs (24) and others report that meanings are not always gained from context, whether the fault be with the difficulty of the passage, the absence of context clues, the lack of reading ability, or the lack of experience or effort on the part of the reader.

WHAT TEACHERS CAN DO

Materials. The literature on the development of concepts suggests a number of guide lines for teachers. Some of these relate to material.

Clyse (6), studying occupational ideas in eight third-grade readers, found over a thousand incidents which could be used to teach attitudes, skills, and appreciations essential for vocational success. Through discussion and other experiences teachers can capitalize on what is offered and round out partially-developed concepts.

In choosing materials for children we should realize that the presence of modifiers means enriched meanings, perhaps more complicated ideas, and, in either case, something to be asked about and noticed by the children. Books containing technical words, common words used in a technical sense, uncommon words used in the general vocabulary of the author, and different words used interchangeably for the same meaning, mean a job of concept-building and some direct teaching.

If a choice is possible between interestingly written material and material of the same content written in a less interesting way, the former selection means better understanding on the part of the child (2).

Understandings. Understandings can be built in a classroom which provides materials to be seen, handled, operated, discussed. An actual object, short of an elephant, is preferable to a movie (39), but films are indeed helpful in clarifying book meanings (21, 38). Our ears are tired of the cliché, "providing rich experiences for the child," and probably should be. We need to put a point on this weapon, giving experiences with pointed questions for the development of specific meanings for the child's current reading. First hand experiences should be used as much as possible (22).

If we are dealing with children of lower socio-economic level, we should expect to have to engage in more concept building (22). This, of course, does not mean that we should assume that children of higher socio-economic status have fully-developed concepts. We should, rather, ask them for meanings to see whether the grasp exists.

It is important that we ourselves speak clearly in naming the concept, and that we require clear speech by the children (8). *Goad* and *goat* are not the same, though they both provide propulsion from the rear.

Motivation. Since basic needs and favorable feelings grease the wheels of learning, we should as much as possible use the "hot moment," the time of keen interest, for providing the learning. (However, we should not be above starting a few fires ourselves.) The study of concepts which children's current text and recreational reading utilize, with the children fully aware that these are the needed concepts, means more efficient learning.

Group Learning. In working with groups we must expect a wide range of concept-grasp. We should use the children who do know, to explain, dramatize, demonstrate, experiment, and illustrate for those who do not know. ("Who can tell us about ————? Willy, didn't I see you watching that bulldozer yesterday?")

Sometimes in dealing with the meaning of a word, we can write down on the chalkboard the different definitions the children in the group offer (21), then help them seek verification (studying the actual object, rerunning the film, going to the dictionary, etc.), and choose or compose a proper definition.

Since brighter pupils seem to grasp prefix, root, and suffix meanings more readily than average or dull children (20), we might use the brighter pupils to lead in the group study of these aspects of word structure and meaning.

Group approaches to concept building are particularly valuable. Even we, "the omniscient," cannot with our one-life experience compensate for the facets other minds might bring to group discussion.

Exploration of a Concept. Children need guidance in studying meanings. In dealing with multiple meanings of words (9), such as *up*, we can say, 'Who can show us what up means in this sentence? (He went up the street.) In this one?" (He reached up to the high shelf). The presence of a word of many meanings is an opportunity for introducing the other common meanings of it. Younger children may have to demonstrate meanings rather than express them in words, but gradually they should be given the defining words to use, and be encouraged to use them.

In probing for the meaning of an abstraction like *justice* (10), we should probably ask questions which make children aware of the factors which affect it. "Why did he do it? What had just happened to him? What would this make him think?" Discussions of many situations involving justice gradually build the complex meaning.

To help children generalize (22), we must give them a number of examples to study for their common characteristics. ("What is true about all of these Fidos, Neros, Rovers, etc.?"—in getting at "dogness.") In the process of deduction we can help by saying, "If this is what a dog is, do you think this (showing another example) is a dog? Why or why not?" Measuring how many pints of water can be poured into a quart jar gives concrete evidence of the relationship between pints and quarts. Counting the number of eggs (Watch out there!) in a dozen builds the idea of dozen. Naming the parts of an object observed requires more thorough observation than a child might ordinarily give.

We must remember that we build more easily from the concrete to the abstract. In so doing we must be sure that we start with what is concrete to the child, not just to us. *Prize* may be to us a concrete aspect of *achievement*; but to the child prize *may* be the as-yet unrealized abstraction referring to the doughnut he won yesterday and the marble he won the day before.

Acquisition of Concepts. The concepts we get from reading may not automatically become the property of the children who read this same material (16). Jarolimek and Foster report that comparison, problem-solving, contrast, and interpretation of sentence meanings are useful techniques in word study. Sutton's study (31) suggests that we base word exercises on words the children encounter in their texts, have the children find the meanings in the dictionary, and build sentences using the words with these various meanings. Werner (37) proposes that we let children know that the meaning of a word changes with use through the years, introducing them to such books as Epstein's *First Book of Words* (Watts, 1954), Lambert's *Our Language* (Lothrop, 1955), and Laird's *Tree of Language* (World, 1957). Bloomer's study (3) leads to the conclusion that we should pay attention to modifiers: "What does the word *hungry* do to your idea of the lion?" Children can engage in creative activity with modifiers—changing the wording to other possibilities (the well-fed lion) and discussing what happens to the meaning.

We can hope that wide reading will build concepts, but cannot expect that all will be achieved by this means (34). Setting a standard of understanding clearly what is read, we can encourage children to bring puzzling words and expressions in context to the class for discussion. Many studies, including those by Vineyard and Massey (35), Gray and Holmes (13), show the effectiveness of direct systematic study of word meanings. Taking cue from several studies, we can require the classification of words (4), an expression of the function of an object, a definition or description of it, the enumeration of its characteristics, a discussion of its relationship to other concepts (23). Other suggestions are that children study words in context (28), the meanings of roots (1), prefixes (29), suffixes (33), stems, and the parts of a compound (15).

Application. Children should be urged to use a concept as a word and as knowledge which can be applied. We often permit children to use words loosely, vaguely, and even inaccurately (14), when we might be offering more exact words for the situations (a funny day, a funny accident, a funny look, a funny feeling, act funny). Since mastery and retention of new learnings are based upon frequent and proper use, we may deliberately set up situations calling for thinking about the new concept, using it in speech, listening to it, reading it, and writing it.

These are only samplings of the ideas research offers the teacher in this very important work. They may provoke us into further reading of such studies as well as inspire us to creative application of the practices they support.

REFERENCES

1. Barry, Robert F., and Smith, Paul E. "An Experiment in Ninth-Grade Reading Improvement," *Journal of Educational Psychology*, XLV (Nov., 1954), 407–414.
2. Bernstein, Margery R. "Relationship Between Interest and Reading Comprehension," *Journal of Educational Research*, XLIX (Dec., 1955), 283–288.
3. Bloomer, Richard H. "Level of Abstraction as a Function of Modifier Load," *Journal of Educational Research*, LII (Mar., 1959), 269–272.
4. Bradley, Martha, Cahill, Loretta A., Tate, Harry L. "Acquisition of a Reading Vocabulary," *Elementary English Review*, XVIII (Jan., 1941), 19–21, 32.
5. Chall, Jeanne S. *Readability: An Appraisal of Research and Application.* Bureau of Educational Research Monograph No. 34. Columbus, Ohio: Ohio State University, 1958. Pp. 202.
6. Clyse, Juanita. "What Do Basic Readers Teach About Jobs?" *Elementary School Journal*, LIX (May, 1959), 456–460.
7. Dale, Edgar, and Reichert, Donald. *Bibliography of Vocabulary Studies*, Revised Ed. Columbus, Ohio: Ohio State University, Bureau of Educational Research, 1957. Pp. 174.
8. Davis, Irene Poole. "The Speech Aspects of Reading Readiness," *National Elementary School Principal*, 17th Yearbook, 1938. Pages 282–289.
9. Dolch, Edward, and Leeds, Donald. "Vocabulary Tests and Depth of Meaning," *Journal of Educational Research*, XLVII (Nov., 1953), 181–189.
10. Durkin, Dolores. "Children's Concept of Justice: A Further Comparison With the Piaget Data," *Journal of Educational Research*, (March, 1959), 252–257.
11. Fennema, Elizabeth H. "Mental Imagery and the Reading Process," *Elementary School Journal*, LIX (Feb., 1959), 286–289.
12. Gammon, Agnes L. "Comprehension of Words With Multiple Meanings," *California Journal of Educational Research*, III (Nov., 1952), 228–232.
13. Gray, William S., and Holmes, Eleanor. *The Development of Meaning Vocabularies in Reading: An Experimental Study.* Publication No. 6

of the laboratory schools of the University of Chicago. Chicago: Department of Education, University of Chicago, 1938. Pp. 140.

14. Gunderson, Agnes G. "What Seven-Year-Olds Like in Books," *Journal of Educational Research*, L (March, 1957), 509–520.

15. Hunt, Jacob Tate. "The Relation Among Vocabulary, Structural Analysis and Reading," *Journal of Educational Psychology*, XLIV (April, 1953), 193–202.

16. Jarolimek, John, and Foster, Clifford D. "Quantitative Concepts in Fifth-Grade Social-Studies Textbooks," *Elementary School Journal*, LIX (May, 1959), 437–442.

17. Kruglov, Lorraine P. "Qualitative Differences in the Vocabulary Choices of Children as Revealed in a Multiple-Choice Test," *Journal of Educational Psychology*, XLIV (April, 1953), 229–242.

18. Lange, Philip C. "Study of Concepts Developed by Students in an Undergraduate Course in the Psychology and Practice of Teaching," *Journal of Educational Research*, (May, 1943), 641–661.

19. McCullough, C. M. "Learning to Use Context Clues," *Elementary English Review* XX (April, 1943), 140–143.

20. Otterman, Lois M. "The Value of Teaching Prefixes and Root-Words," *Journal of Educational Research*, XLVIII (April, 1955) 611–616.

21. Reid, Florence. "Films Provide a Rich Source of Vocabulary Study," *Journal of Educational Research*, LI (April, 1958), 617–23.

22. Russell, David H. *Children's Thinking*. Boston: Ginn and Co., 1956. Pp. 449.

23. Russell, David H. *The Dimensions of Children's Meaning Vocabularies in Grades Four through Twelve*. Publications in Education, Vol. 11, No. 5. Berkeley: University of California Press, 1954. Pages 315–414.

24. Sachs, H. J. "The Reading Method of Acquiring Vocabulary," *Journal of Educational Research*, XXXVI (Feb., 1943), 457–464.

25. Serra, M. C. "A Study of Fourth Grade Children's Comprehension of Certain Verbal Abstractions," *Journal of Experimental Education*, XXII (Dec., 1953), 103–118.

26. Serra, M. C. "Amplifying and Simplifying Instructional Materials: Effects on Comprehension," *Elementary School Journal*, LV (Oct., 1954), 77–81.

27. Serra, M. C. "The Concept Burden of Instructional Materials," *Elementary School Journal*, LIII (May, 1953), 508–512.

28. Serra, M. C. "How to Develop Concepts and Their Verbal Representations," *Elementary School Journal* LIII (Jan., 1953), 275–285.

29. Stauffer, Russell G. "A Study of Prefixes in the Thorndike List to Establish a List of Prefixes That Should Be Taught in the Elementary School," *Journal of Educational Research*, XXXV (Feb., 1942), 453–458.

30. Stolurow, Lawrence, and Newman, J. Robert. "A Factorial Analysis of Objective Features of Printed Language Presumably Related to Reading Difficulty," *Journal of Educational Research*, LII (March, 1959), 243–251.

31. Sutton, Rachel S. "The Effect of Vocabulary Building on Reading Skills," *Elementary School Journal, LIV* (Oct., 1953), 94–97.

32. Templin, Mildred. *Certain Language Skills in Children.* Minneapolis: University of Minnesota Press, 1957. Pp. 183.

33. Thorndike, Edward L. *The Teaching of English Suffixes.* Teachers College Contributions to Education, No. 847. New York: Teachers College, Columbia University, 1941.

34. Traxler, Arthur E. "What Does Research Suggest About Ways to Improve Reading Instruction?" In Arno Jewett, Ed. *Improving Reading in The Junior High School,* pages 5-15. Bulletin No. 10, U.S. Department of Health, Education, and Welfare. Washington: U.S. Government Printing Office, 1957. Pp. 165.

35. Vineyard, Edwin E., and Massey, Harold W. "The Interrelationship of Certain Linguistic Skills and Their Relationship With Scholastic Achievement When Intelligence Is Ruled Constant," *Journal of Educational Psychology,* XLVIII (May, 1957), 279–286.

36. *Webster's New Collegiate Dictionary.* Springfield, Mass.: G. and C. Merriam Co., 1953.

37. Werner, Heinz. "Change of Meaning: A Study of Semantic Processes Through the Experimental Method," *Journal of General Psychology,* L (April, 1954), 181–208.

38. Witty, Paul A., and Fitzwater, James P. "An Experiment With Films, Film-Readers, and the Magnetic Sound Track Projector," *Elementary English,* XXX (April, 1953), 232–241.

39. Yock, Douglas H., and Erlandson, Forrest L. "The Effectiveness of Visual Aids in Dental Teaching," *Journal of Educational Research,* LII (Sept., 1958), 11–15.

(26) CONTEXT CLUES*

Robert Emans

Mary had a little lamb,
Its fleece was white as _____.

Few four-year-old children would be unable to complete the sentence with the word *snow.* Likewise, "Becky and her mother wanted to go

*Reprinted from *Reading in the Total Curriculum* 13, Part 1 (1968 Convention Proceedings), in press, by permission of the author and the International Reading Association.

shopping. They climbed into the _____ to go to the store." Few children, even before entering school, would have difficulty with supplying any one of several words which would make sense; car, automobile, bus, streetcar. Children use context in their oral language, easily and naturally. Children, and adults too, use context clues to aid them in their reading.

It is easy to find testimonials to the importance of context clues in reading. Open almost any textbook on the subject and there are such statements as:

It would be difficult to overestimate the value of the context in children's word perception in reading.   (7, p. 16)

Contextual clues provide one of the most important aids to word identification and interpretation.   (6, p. 84)

Context clues are perhaps the most important single aid to word perception.   (11, p. 25)

Or to put it negatively,

The person who has not developed skill in the use of verbal context has not become a mature reader.   (22, p. 23)

It is important to know, however, that many children who are thought to be in difficulty in reading because of limited skill in analytical techniques or because they have insufficient knowledge of phonetic, structural, or visual elements are usually in difficulty because they are not using context clues well.   (4, p. 321)

Obviously, statements praising the worth of context clues are easily found. Much has been written about how the use of context helps the reader to develop the meaning of words. However, such is not the concern of this paper, as important as it may be. It is rather my purpose to attack the more elusive problem and explore what aid the use of context clues give the reader in respect to word recognition.

There are at least four uses of context clues in word recognition. These probably can be summarized as the following:

1. Context clues can help children to identify words they have identified before, but have forgotten. Most teachers can cite examples of a child having difficulty with a partially known word but who recognizes the word in a new setting when told that he has seen the word before and

that it makes sense. For example, if a child reads, "Bill was a cow" for "Bill saw a cow," asking him if what he reads makes sense will often enable him to correct himself.

2. Context clues may be combined with other word analysis clues, e.g., phonic and structural analysis, to check on the accuracy of words tentatively identified by the use of other clues. As Bond and Wagner state, context clues serve as "Checks on the accuracy of all the other techniques that are used" (5, p. 172).

3. Context clues help in the rapid recognition of words for all readers by helping us to anticipate what a word might be. The ability to draw an accurate inference to what a word is can serve as a time saver. It is a faster technique than other word recognition aids such as phonics. It enables the reader to use only those phonic and other analytical techniques which are necessary to distinguish one word from another. For example, instead of having to sound out a word, the efficient reader uses only enough phonic clues to recognize the word quickly when combined with the meaning clues.

4. Context clues are required for the correct identification of some words. As Gray states, "The pronunciation of many words (permit, for example) depends upon their meaning in a given context" (11, p. 148). Other words which require the use of context clues are: *lead* in a pencil, or *lead* the way; to *wind* a ball of string, or the *wind* blew; to *tear* a piece of paper or a *tear* flowed down her cheek; a piggy *bank*, or a *bank* to fish from.

HOW DO CONTEXT CLUES WORK IN WORD RECOGNITION?

So far we have discussed the importance of context clues and some of the uses of context clues in word recognition. However, we probably should ask ourselves, "How do context clues work?" By answering this question, we can gain a better idea as to how to teach the use of context clues.

To understand how context clues work it must be recalled that the child brings to reading a background of experience and oral language. Likewise, the child must bring to the reading situation a habit of demanding meaning from his reading. A child must combine his experience, his oral language, and the meaning he gets from his reading if he is to use successfully context clues in recognizing words. When he meets a word which he cannot recognize, he uses his experiences, oral language, and the meaning of the words, phrases, sentences, and paragraphs surrounding the word, to anticipate what it might be. As Bond and Wagner state, "Instead of having to recognize the word from the total of words in the English language, the use of context clues limits the choice of words to the few that would fit the meaning of the passage being read" (5, p. 172). By also using the other word recognition skills the child has at his disposal, he tentatively identifies the word and checks to see if the word makes sense. For example, if a child reads the sentence, "Jenny picked up her ——————— to draw," he can from his experience, the meaning of the sentence, and his oral vocabulary, limit the words to such possibilities as pen, crayon, pencil, or chalk, and would not have to select the word from the 800,000 or so possible words in the English language. By combining this information with various phonic clues the child could more quickly recognize the exact word than by using only phonics.

In respect to this last point, that context clues may be used in conjunction with other word recognition techniques, Bond and Tinker state that "Meaning clues alone are not enough for good reading at any level. They must be accompanied by the use of a flexible set of word recognition skills. It is the interaction of all the word-study skills that forms the foundation on which a competent reader builds his reading structure" (4, p. 322). DeBoer and Dallmann state, "Context clues are most effective when they are employed along with other methods of word attack" (8, p. 111). In actual reading the use of context clues is probably so closely tied in with other word recognition techniques that they can not be separated. Context clues alone are seldom adequate because they provide only one aid to word recognition. They may suggest one of several possible words, but seldom point to the specific word. For example, in the sentence, "The mouse nibbled a piece of ——————." Any number of possible words could fit the meaning. However, by combining the sense of the sentence with the phonic clue that the word begins with a *ch* sound, a reader would have to strain not to supply the word *cheese*. Children should probably be discouraged from using context clues alone. By combining them with other word recognition techniques a child would be discouraged from wild guessing. Therefore, in relation to the discussion that follows, it should be remembered that whenever context clues are taught they should probably be combined with other word recognition aids.

Some people might regard using context clues as untutored as guessing; and in a sense it is. However, it is probably more accurately described as inferential reasoning which must be developed and guided, and used in many areas of life. As Nila B. Smith states, "Surely this process of examining meanings, reasoning, and deducing an unrecognized word is not just a matter of chance guessing" (20, p. 186). Kolson and Kolinger state, "Guessing is the mainstay of the contextual clue skill and should be encouraged, but wild guessing is a symptom of a disability in contextual clue use" (14, p. 65). The sophisticated use of context clues, therefore, should probably be developed along with reasoning and the use of other word recognition skills.

THE CLASSIFICATION OF CONTEXT CLUES

Various attempts have been made to classify the wide variety of context clues. Although these classification schemes may be closely related to those for developing word meanings they also have relevance for the use of context clues in word recognition. Artley identified ten types of contextual aids the reader might find in printed matter: typographical (e.g. quotation marks, parenthesis), structural (e.g., appositives, nonrestrictive clauses), substitute words (synonyms, antonyms), word elements (roots, suffixes, prefixes), figures of speech (similes, metaphors), pictorial representation (e.g., pictures, diagrams, charts), inference, direct explanation, background of experience of the reader, and subjective clues (e.g., tone, mood, intent) (2). Likewise, McCullough identified two general classes of clues, idea and presentation. Idea clues included pictorial illustration, verbal, experience, comparison and contrast, synonym, summary, mood, definition, and familiar expression. The presentation clues included the position of words, the sequence of a sentence or paragraph, and the general organization of a selection (15). From a study of 500,000 running words Deighton identified four *key words* classes as being definition, examples, modifiers, and restatement, and *inferential clues* for which the reader has no direct clue except for his ability to draw inferences (9). In his dissertation, for which he won the IRA research award, Ames found fourteen clues from his case studies of mature readers using a variety of contextual situations (1). These clues are:

1. Clues derived from language experience or familiar expressions
2. Clues utilizing modifying phrases or clauses
3. Clues utilizing definition or description

4. Clues provided through words connected or in series
5. Comparison or contrast clues
6. Synonym clues
7. Clues provided by the tone, setting, and mood of a selection
8. Referral clues
9. Association clues
10. Clues derived from the main idea and supporting details pattern of paragraph organization
11. Clues provided through the question-and-answer pattern of paragraph organization
12. Preposition clues
13. Clues utilizing non-restrictive clauses or appositive phrases
14. Clues derived from cause and effect pattern of paragraph and sentence organization

However, Russell states concerning the Artley and McCullough classifications, "these are often too technical for systematic use in the elementary school . . ." (19, p. 300–301). Likewise, Ames states in respect to his own study, that "It must be stressed that much more research is necessary and one would be ill-advised to try to develop elaborate instructional procedures based on the present classification scheme." (2, p. 81). An appropriate task regarding the implementing of context clues in word recognition would appear to be the development of a simplified scheme for classifying the numerous kinds of context clues identified. The next few paragraphs will suggest such a possible scheme.

Most context clues for use in word recognition seem to fall into one of three main categories, meaning bearing clues, language bearing clues, and organization clues. The meaning bearing clues use the sense of the sentence or sentences surrounding the unrecognized word. The category includes such clues for recognizing unknown words as familiar expressions and idioms, definitions, descriptions, examples, synonyms, antonyms included in the text, as well as comparisons and contrasts, and the tone, mood, and setting of what is being read.

The language bearing clues use knowledge of syntax, the structure of sentences, as aids in word recognition. As Hildreth states, "The use of context clues has its roots in linguistics," (13, p. 156). There are a number of examples of language bearing clues. One such aid is the noting of phrases which may serve as a clue in recognition of modified unknown words. Another such aid is the recognition of unknown words through referral signal words such as *these* and *same* which refer to what has been stated previously. The associating of known words of one part of speech with closely related unknown words of another part of speech (such as nouns and verbs or adjectives and nouns) may serve as another clue. For example, birds fly and fish swim; grass is green and old ladies usually have gray hair. Finally the recognition of the relationship of non-restrictive clauses, appositive phrases, or prepositional phrases to other parts of a sentence may serve as another language clue.

Another group of clues involve how sentences or paragraphs are organized. Within this group are such aids as the realization that an unknown word is part of a series of words, and an appreciation of the relatedness of main idea to details, of questions to answers, and of cause to effect within sentences or paragraphs.

Therefore, it would appear that many context clues seem to fall within one of these three classifications, meaning bearing, language bearing, and organization. The scheme is not all inclusive. For example, the scheme does not include contextual aids from pictures or the typography. However, it seems to simplify the complex classification schemes previously suggested. The belief is that children will learn to use context clues better if they only have to learn three classes of clues than if they are burdened with many types. Although a child would need to be given experience in using the many various types of clues, he would not need to learn the many technical names which are confusing even to the adult.

Possibly to date sufficient emphasis has not been placed on the role that context clues plays in word recognition because the classification schemes have appeared to be too complex. The above simplified, yet comprehensive, scheme for the classification of context clues is proposed in hopes that it will foster further investigation in this area. Because of the simplification, teachers may feel encouraged to teach the use of context clues as knowledge of the structure and implications for teaching context clues is more attainable.

TEACHING CONTEXT CLUES

Although the teaching of context clues seems complex, there is evidence that teachers should attempt to do so. McCullough (15) concluded that adults fail to use context clues because they were never taught how to use them. In a study by McKee, children were found to use context clues effectively in only about one-third of the opportunities presented; (17, p. 73) while Porter (21, p. 316) found that third grade children could give an appropriate meaning of a word left out of context in about 80 per cent of the cases. Since children may not develop the skill of using context clues without specific training, they should be given help in its development. As Hester states, "Systematic guidance is necessary to help him learn this important technique for recognizing words." (12, p. 138)

The goal of instruction for the use of context clues in word recognition is probably to develop such skill that context clues are used easily and automatically. If a child makes as many errors in contextual reading as he does in reading a list of words he is probably failing to make extensive use of context clues. The problem becomes one of developing instructional procedures.

There is little evidence that children will use context clues more effectively if they have knowledge of sentence patterns. As McKee states, such knowledge "contributes little if anything to the pupils' comprehension of the sentences." (18, p. 185) However, children will probably benefit from knowing that, 1) a word makes sense within a sentence, 2) readers can use sentence meaning to help recognize an unrecognized word, and 3) more than one word may fit the meaning of a sentence and therefore, structure, and phonic clues are often necessary.

In preparing to teach the use of context clues materials should be carefully scrutinized to determine if the content gives adequate clues to words which children have not yet learned to recognize in their reading but possess in their speaking-listening vocabularies. Only a few such words should be presented at any one time, as too many unknown words make using the context difficult and might encourage wild guessing. The exact ratio of unknown words to known words probably depends on the children's intelligence, maturity, and background, although Bond and Tinker suggest that about one word in every forty running words should be unknown. (4, p. 321.) Nevertheless, the materials used should be easy enough for children to recognize the unknown word without too much difficulty.

The materials should reflect the language patterns of the child whenever possible, be at a concept level appropriate to the children and have the unknown words evenly distributed throughout the text. There should be an obvious connection between the unknown word and the context which suggests it. The portion of the context which serves as the clue should be reasonably close to the unknown word. Some clues should be included before the unknown words and some after. A variety of unknown words from the three categories of context clues, meaning bearing, language bearing, and organizational clues should be included.

After the materials have been selected, provisions need to be made, as in any reading activity, to assure that children have the background to read the materials through prior direct and vicarious experiences including discussions, explanations, demonstrations, and field trips. The children need then to be given direct guidance in reading using context clues. Such guidance may include talking about the idea that knowing the meaning of a sentence or paragraph will help in recognizing unknown words, encouraging children to read the entire sentence before deciding on an unknown word, showing how context clues can be combined with other word recognition techniques such as phonics, reading the exercises orally to the children and having the children supply the unknown word, covering a few lines in a story and having the children anticipate what will come, asking which part of a sentence or paragraph gives a clue to an unknown word, and showing that some words must be recognized in context such as *wound* the clock and *wound* a deer. In addition specific exercises may be presented.

Pictures may be used in the lower grades to develop an orientation toward the use of context clues. As Hildreth states, "The use of picture clues is similar to the use of context clues for deriving the meaning of new or forgotten words." (13, p. 156) In the lower grades much of the content is carried by pictures in the readers. However, Weintraub found that children do not make as much of illustrations as they might. (23) Therefore, children may be taught to look at pictures to get clues for unknown words since pictures are a part of the total context and since they may be helpful in demonstrating to children the concept of using context clues. Picture-word cards, picture dictionaries and introducing new words in advance of reading with the aid of pictures can be helpful in getting children to use pictures as aids in word recognition. Other ideas are as follows:

1. Have children find in a picture each of a number of items named.
2. Have the children match a series of pictures and words or sentences by drawing a line from each picture to the corresponding word or sentence.
3. Have children complete a sentence by drawing a picture, e.g., "The _____ helped the children across the street."
4. Leave the adjectives out of a story. Have the children make a picture of what they think the scene would look like.
5. Give sentences with incomplete pictures. Have the children complete the pictures to correspond to the meaning of the sentences.

As soon as children have developed enough sight words to read sentences pictures become less, and sentences become more, important for developing the use of context clues. Sentences, paragraphs, riddles and stories with parts of words omitted may be given to children. Emans (10) found the following hierarchy of exercises, easiest to most difficult, to be significant at the .001 level of confidence for children from grades three to ten:

1. No clue given other than context
2. Beginning letter given
3. Length of word given
4. Beginning and ending letters given
5. Four word choice given
6. Consonants given

Teachers can probably think of variations to the exercises. For example, in the multiple-choice type of exercise words with the same sounds or words with similar configurations may be used.

In summary, this paper has tried to show the importance of helping children to develop skills in the use of context clues in word recognition and has made some suggestions as to how to teach them. We opened this paper with Mary's little lamb. It is only fitting that we should close with him too.

> Mary had a little lamb,
> His life was filled with woed
> He sat upon a block of ice,
> Like his, my tale is told.

REFERENCES

1. Ames, W. S. *A Study of the Process by Which Readers Determine Word Meaning Through the Use of Verbal Context.* Unpublished doctoral dissertation, University of Missouri, 1965.

2. Ames, W. S. "The Development of a Classification Scheme of Contextual Aids," *Reading Research Quarterly*, 1966, 2, 57–82.

3. Artley, A. S. "Teaching Word-Meaning Through Context," *Elementary English Review*, 1943, 20, 68–74.

4. Bond, G. L. and Tinker, M. A. *Reading Difficulties: Their Diagnosis and Correction.* New York: Appleton-Century-Crofts, Inc., 1967.

5. Bond, G. L. and Wagner, Eva B. *Teaching the Child to Read*, third edition. New York: The Macmillan Co., 1960.

6. Carter, H. L. J. and McGinnies, Dorothy J. *Teaching Individuals to Read*. Boston: D. C. Heath and Company, 1962.

7. Cordts, Anna D. *Phonics for the Reading Teacher*. New York: Holt, Rinehart and Winston, Inc., 1965.

8. De Boer, John J. and Dallmann, Martha. *The Teaching of Reading*. New York: Holt, Rinehart, and Winston, Inc., 1964.

9. Deighton, L. *Vocabulary Development in the Classroom*. New York: Teacher's College Bureau of Publications, 1959.

10. Emans, R. and Fisher, Gladys Mary. "Teaching the Use of Context Clues," *Elementary English*, 1967, 243–46.

11. Gray, W. S. *On Their Own in Reading*. Glenview, Illinois: Scott, Foresman and Company, 1960.

12. Hester, Kathleen B. *Teaching Every Child to Read*. New York: Harper and Row, 1964.

13. Hildreth, Gertrude. *Teaching Reading: A Guide to Basic Principles and Modern Practices*. New York: Holt, Rinehart and Winston, 1958.

14. Kolson, C. J. and Koluger, G. *Clinical Aspects of Remedial Reading*. Springfield, Illinois: Charles C. Thomas, 1963.

15. McCullough, Constance M. "Learning to Use Context Clues," *Elementary English Review*, 1943, 20, 140–143.

16. McCullough, Constance M. "The Recognition of Context Clues in Reading," *Elementary English Review*, 1945, 22, 1 5.

17. McKee, P. *The Teaching of Reading*. Boston: Houghton Mifflin Co., 1948.

18. McKee, P. *Reading: A Program of Instruction for the Elementary School*. Boston: Houghton Mifflin Co., 1966.

19. Russell, D. H. *Children Learn to Read*, 2nd edition. Boston: Ginn and Company, 1961.

20. Smith, Nila B. *Reading Instruction for Today's Children*. Englewood Cliffs, New Jersey: Prentice-Hall, Inc., 1963.

21. Spache, G. D. *Reading in the Elementary School*. Boston: Allyn and Bacon, Inc., 1964.

22. Tinker, M. A. *Bases for Effective Reading*. Minneapolis: University of Minnesota Press, 1965.

23. Weintraub, S. *The Effect of Pictures on the Comprehension of a Second-grade Basal Reader*. Unpublished doctoral dissertation, University of Illinois, 1960.

(27) WHEN TWO VOWELS GO WALKING
AND OTHER SUCH THINGS*

Robert Emans

From time to time, research reports will stimulate the thinking and actions of other investigators. Such was the research reported in an article, "The Utility of Phonic Generalizations in the Primary Grades," in *The Reading Teacher* by Theodore Clymer (1963). Clymer selected forty-five generalizations and developed a word test from four widely used sets of readers in the primary grades. Then he set two criteria, admittedly arbitrary, as to what was meant by a "reasonable" degree of application. The first criterion was that there must be at least twenty words to which the generalization might apply. The second criterion was a percent of utility of at least seventy-five.

Only eighteen of the forty-five generalizations met the criteria of usefulness in Clymer's study. A number of generalizations which had long been considered to have merit were among those which did not meet the criteria. For example, the "When two vowels go walking, the first does the talking" or "When there are two vowels side by side, the long sound of the first one is heard and the second is usually silent," generalization was one of these. Clymer concluded that "some time-honored customs in the teaching of reading may be in need of revision." The need for revision has been interpreted by some people to mean that many commonly taught phonic generalizations should be discarded.

In a study supported by the Cooperative Research Program of the Office of Education (Emans, 1965) and reported in *The Reading Teacher* (Emans, 1967), this investigator replicated Clymer's study, but used a random sampling of words beyond the primary level. The writer reasoned that, although some phonic generalizations may not be useful with words in the primary grades, these same generalizations might have utility for the words which the child is required to recognize later.

The results of the two studies showed that thirteen generalizations demonstrated their usefulness at both primary and upper grade levels; at least four generalizations which met the criteria of usefulness on the

*Reprinted from *The Reading Teacher* 21 (December 1967), pp. 262–69, by permission of the author and the International Reading Association.

primary level failed to do so for words beyond the primary level; and three generalizations, which were found not to be useful at the primary level, were useful for words beyond the primary level. Hence, when the results of the two studies were combined, only twenty-one of the forty-five generalizations identified by Clymer were found to be useful.

As this investigator's study progressed, he became increasingly aware that if certain changes were made in Clymer's generalizations, their utility could be raised. In some cases a simple rewording of the generalization could increase the utility from a few percentage points to nearly a hundred. Also, since generalizations need not be applied in isolation, but can be applied in conjunction with each other, their usefulness could be increased greatly by combining them.

Therefore, this paper reports some possible modifications in Clymer's generalizations which may increase their utility. Its purpose is not to encourage keeping practices which are basically weak, but to avoid discarding practices which may require only modification and not abandonment. In some cases, the writer suggests the rewording of generalizations which already have a fairly high percent of utility. Sometimes, such rewording increases the utility even more.

RELATED LITERATURE

Various attempts have been made to find consistencies in the English language to serve as aids in word recognition. Ironically, probably more inconsistencies than consistencies have been discovered.

One of the first studies (Vogel, Jaycex, Washburne, 1923) was conducted by a group of teachers in the Winnetka Public Schools, Winnetka, Illinois. The study, which was later expanded (Washburne and Vogel, 1928), listed common phonograms to be taught in the primary grades. In a similar study, Atkins (1926) examined the relation between the phonetic and unphonetic occurrences of high frequency symbols. He found sounds which were most apt to accompany the various symbols and concluded that the then often-taught phonetic elements were frequently not the most common elements.

More recent studies of English have shown it to be complex and seemingly inconsistent. An examination of even a few common words such as bread, once, laugh, straight, and knife reveals silent letters, inconsistent spellings and exceptions to established rules.

Hildreth (1958, p. 153) states that there are no unvarying sounds and that vowel sounds depend on associations with the other letters within words. She states that only 200 of the 350 commonest words can be written as they sound (1958, p. 152). Armstrong (1949) found that the twenty-six letters in the alphabet give rise to at least 117 sounds. Anderson (1964) states that there are three hundred different combinations which express the seventeen vowel sounds; for example, *ow* has one sound in owl, cow and clown, but another sound in grow, flow, and snow. Horn (1954, pp. 129–132) points out that the short *i*, as in *hit*, is spelled twenty-two different ways. And of course, the classic example of *ough* has different sounds in ought, rough, though, and through. Furthermore, nearly all letters of the alphabet are silent at some time. Hildreth (1958, p. 153) notes that about two-thirds of the words in an unabridged dictionary contain silent letters, e.g. here, were, through, once, one, enough, doubt, and sleigh. Sartorious (1931) found more exceptions than examples of the silent *e* rule. Clymer (1961) reported that in 35 percent of the cases involving the most common 220 words, the first of two vowels was not long when the second was a silent *e*. Dolch (1951, p. 35) found that there are about as many exceptions to the two vowel rule as there are instances when it applies. However, the rule does often apply, he found, for specific vowel situations such as *ai*, *ee*, *ea*, *oa*, and *ay*.

Although many studies have shown inconsistencies in the English language, others have demonstrated consistent patterns. For example, Hanna and Moore (1953) found English to be 86.9 percent phonetic, as they defined it. They found that single consonants are represented by regular spellings about 90 percent of the time.

A number of other specific studies have been conducted. Dolch (1938) lists 200 common syllables after determining that 81 percent of words studied were of more than one syllable. Osburn (1954) found the most common syllables in children's written vocabulary to be *ing*, *ed*, *er*, *by*, *es*, *tion*, and *y*. A study by Hildreth (1958, p. 154) showed that 25 percent of the words in English are composed of base forms with varied prefixes or endings. Thorndike (1941, p. 115) lists the common suffixes as *ion*, *tion*, *ation*, *er*, *y*, *al*, *ent*, *ful*, *ity*, *ty*, *ure*, and *ous*. Stauffer (1942) found that fourteen prefixes make up 82 percent of the total number of prefixes. These are *ab*, *ad*, *be*, *com*, *de*, *dis*, *en*, *ex*, *in*, *pre*, *pro*, *re*, *sub*, and *un*.

In respect to phonograms, Dolch (1938) showed that the twenty-four most commonly taught phonograms make up only 28 percent of the syllables in words children are likely to find in their textbooks. He recommended that teachers should, therefore, teach syllabication. Gunderson (1939) listed the phonograms found in the ten reading manuals for teaching in grades 1 and 2. Spache's (1939) study revealed that the three and four letter phonograms such as *ake* and *ight* are more phonetically constant than the two letter combinations such as *in, on, at, an*.

Oaks (1952) computed the frequency of vowel sound combinations in basal readers. She concluded that one-third of vowel situations appear as early as the primer. Anderson (1964, p. 130) states that the *schwa* vowel sound is found in half of the multisyllabic words. In respect to consonants, Black (1952) reports that they are evenly distributed between initial and final positions in syllables with very few consonants appearing in the middle of a syllable.

In a fairly recent article, Fry (1964) summarizes the findings of studies by Black (1952) and others in respect to phonic rules. He also presents a study of his own on 300 words usually taught in the primary grades and suggests twenty-one rules which he found to be worth teaching.

POSSIBLE MODIFICATIONS

In the discussion that follows, Clymer's original rule will be stated and the possible modifications will be given. Practical use of the modifications would probably indicate still other ways of restating them to correspond better with the understandings of children.

1. *When there are two vowels side by side, the long sound of the first one is heard and the second is usually silent.*

A total of 480 words were identified in the author's study as being words to which this generalization could apply. Only eighty-seven words conformed; there were 393 exceptions. Therefore, for the words beyond the primary level, it exhibited a utility of only 18 percent. Clymer found a utility of 45 percent for words in the primary grades. When the specific vowel combinations of *ai, ea, oa, ui,* and *ee* were omitted, 318 words remained to which one might hope to apply the generalization. Of these 318 words, only eight, or 3 percent, followed the rule. Therefore, the usefulness of this generalization must be questioned.

Nevertheless, a number of specific vowel combinations had a high percent of utility. The vowel combination *ai* had a percent utility of 83; *oa* had a percent utility of 86; *ee* had a percent utility of 100. In addition, a detailed study of the exceptions to the two vowel generalization indicated other possible generalizations which might be useful. Out of a total of 131 words, the vowel combination *io* had a short *u* sound as in *nation* 113 times, or a utility of 86 percent. The vowel combination *ui* was found to have a short i sound 79 percent of the time. In addition, the *oo* combination had the sound as in *food* in 74 percent of the words and the sound as in *good* in the remaining 26 percent of the time. Hence, the following generalizations replace, to some extent, the "When two vowels go walking the first does the talking" generalization.

a. When the first vowel in a word is *a* and the second is *i*, the *a* is usually long and the *i* silent.

b. When the first vowel is *o* and the second is *a*, the *o* is usually long and the *a* is silent.

c. Words having double *e* usually have the long e sound.

d. The letters *io* usually represent a short *u* sound as in nation.

e. The letters *oo* usually have the long double *o* sound as in *food* or the short double *o* sound as in *good*. They are more likely to have the double *o* sound as in *food*.

f. The vowel combination *ui* has a short *i* sound.

2. When a vowel is in the middle of a one-syllable word, the vowel is short.

This clue had a 73 percent utility for words beyond the primary level, as determined by this study, and a 62 percent utility for words within the primary level, as found by Clymer. However, of the thirty-eight exceptions for words beyond the primary level, thirteen had an *r* following the vowel. An important generalization found in both Clymer's and this study was that the vowel sound may be modified if it precedes an *r*. Therefore, if the clue is changed to state, "When a vowel is in the middle of a one-syllable word, the vowel is short except that it may be modified in words in which the vowel is followed by an *r*," it has a utility of 80 percent, increasing its usefulness considerably.

3. When words end with silent "e," the preceding "a" or "i" is long.

As stated, this generalization was found to have a utility of only 48 percent in this study. If words ending in *le* were excluded, the utility could be raised to 67 percent; to 71 percent if words ending with *le* and words with *ive* were excluded. These exceptions warrant further investigation in that Clymer found that his generalization had a 60 percent utility for words on the primary level. If the proposed exceptions were applied, Clymer's generalization might become useful in the primary grades, measured aginst the criteria used.

4. *The two letters "ow" make the long "o" sound.*

The generalization as stated had a 50 percent utility. However, if it were changed to, "The two letters *ow* make the long *o* sound or the *ou* sound as in *out*," it would have 100 percent utility in the sample of this study.

5. *When "y" is the final letter in a word, it usually has a vowel sound.*

This generalization had an 84 percent utility using words in the primary grades and a 98 percent utility using words above the primary grades. In all exceptions in this study, the *y* was silent, following the generalization that in *ay* the *y* is silent and gives "a" its long sound which Clymer found to be a useful generalization. Therefore, the two generalizations together would have 100 percent utility for words above the primary level. Similar findings might have been noted had Clymer applied the two generalizations together in his study—perhaps increasing the rules' usefulness on the primary level.

6. *When "y" is used as a vowel, it sometimes has the sound of long "i."*

Stated this way, this generalization has a utility of only 4 percent. However, if it were changed to read, "When *y* is used as a vowel, it sometimes has the sound of long *e*," it would have a utility of 92 percent.

7. *The letter "a" has the same sound (ô) when followed by "l," "w," and "u."*

As stated, the percent of utility is 24. Only four of the *al* words follow this clue, all but twelve of them having either long or short *a* sounds. Therefore, the *l* does not seem to modify the long or short *a*. However, of the thirty-two *au* and *aw* words, all but five, or 84 percent, follow it. If the generalizations were changed to state, "The letter *a* has the same sound (ô) when followed by *w* and *u*," its usefulness would be greatly increased.

8. *When "c" is followed by "e" or "i," the sound of "s" is likely to be heard.*

Eighty-eight words of the sample were possible applications. The clue had a 90 percent utility, meeting the established criteria. In the nine exceptions, the sound of *sh* was heard rather than *s*. Therefore, if the generalization were to be restated as "When *c* is followed by *e* or *i*, the sound *s* or *sh* is likely to be heard" the utility in this study would be 100 percent.

9. *When two of the same consonants are side by side only one is heard.*

This generalization was applied to 300 words with a 91 percent utility and, therefore, deemed to be useful. Of the twenty-six exceptions, all but three were a result of a prefix or suffix being added, for example, illegal. Ten of the twenty exceptions had an *ly* added to a root word ending in *l.* and both *l*'s were sounded, as in dreadfully.

10. *In most two-syllable words, the first syllable is accented.*

This clue met the criteria for usefulness in both this study and the previous study by Clymer. Approximately a third of the exceptions can be accounted for through application of the generalization that "If *a*, *in*, *re*, *ex*, *de*, or *be* is the first syllable in a word, it is usually unaccented" which was found in both studies to be useful. Additional prefixes such as *con-* and *pre-* could explain still other exceptions.

11. *One vowel letter in an accented syllable has its short sound.*

This clue applied to 1,490 words analyzed for this study and had a utility of 64 percent. If it is reworded to read, "One vowel letter in an accented syllable has its short sound if it comes before the end of the syllable and its long sound if it comes at the end of the syllable," the utility would be raised to 78 percent. Addition of the phrase, "Except when it is followed by an *r*" raised the percent of utility to ninety-two.

12. *When "y" or "ey" is seen in the last syllable that is not accented, the long sound of "e" is heard.*

As the generalization is stated, only three (1 percent) of the 269 applicable words conformed to its claim. However, if it is read "short *i*" instead of "long *e*" 261 words (87 percent) would have conformed.

13. *When "-tion" is the final syllable in a word, it is unaccented.*

This clue supports the original thinking which prompted this study— that the usefulness of phonic generalizations may differ for words above and below the primary level. Clymer found only five words from his list to which this rule might apply, while eighty-five words from this study's shorter word list conformed. In both studies the utility was 100 percent. Apparently, it is useful for words beyond the primary level, but it may be of questionable value, as defined in this study, for words within the primary level.

A *-tion* at the end of a four syllable word seems to indicate a secondary accent on the first syllable with a primary accent on the syllable preceeding the -tion. This held true in forty of forty-two words, indicating a 95 percent utility. The primary accent failed to fall on the second to last syllable only three times out of all the *-tion* words on the list. The primary accent was on the second to last syllable in all the three-syllable words, all but two of the four-syllable words, and all but one of the five-syllable words. Similar results were found with words ending with *-sion*. Therefore, the generalization "When *-tion* or *-sion* is the final syllable in a word, the primary accent is likely to fall on the second to last syllable," would indicate the location of the primary accent in many words to which it would apply.

14. *In many two- and three-syllable words, the final "e" lengthens the vowel in the last syllable.*

Of the total number of words in the sample, this clue would be applied to 227 with a 42 percent utility; ninety-five words conformed and there were 132 exceptions. Of the exceptions, fifty ended with *le* and eleven ended with *ive*. In that no *le* or *ive* words followed it, their omission would increase the utility to 64 percent. Other consistent exceptions might be found to make the generalization more usable.

15. *If the first vowel sound in a word is followed by two consonants, the first syllable usually ends with the first of two consonants.*

Clymer found that this generalization had only 72 percent utility with the words he studied. In this study, it could be applied to 811 words, meeting the criteria of usefulness with 80 percent utility. However, of the 163 exceptions, twenty-four words included vowels modified with an *r*, thirty-six words had a double consonant with one of them silent, twenty-one words had a *ck* with the *k* sound, twenty were found to have common prefixes, and twenty-two words had one of the sounds *th*, *ch*, or *sh*. All five of these generalizations were found by Clymer to be useful. If these generalizations were applied in conjunction with this generalization, it would have a utility of 96 percent.

16. *If the first vowel sound in a word is followed by a single consonant, that consonant usually begins the second syllable.*

This generalization could be applied to 659 words of the list with a 47 per cent utility. Clymer noted like results. Of the 346 words which were exceptions, ninety-three were root words plus a prefix, and 240 had beginning syllables which ended with a consonant with a short vowel sound. Consequently, if it read, "Except in some words with a prefix and a root word, if the first vowel sound in a word is followed by a single consonant, that consonant begins the second syllable and the vowel sound in the first syllable will be long, *or* if the consonant ends the first syllable the vowel sound will be short," the percent of utility would be 84. Of the 240 beginning syllables ending with a consonant and containing a short vowel sound, 227 or 95 percent are accented. Of the 237 beginning syllables ending with a long vowel, 138 or 58 percent are unaccented.

17. *If the last syllable of a word ends in "le," the consonant preceding the "le" usually begins the last syllable.*

This clue met the criteria of usefulness in both studies. In this present study a total of sixty-eight words could be applied to it with a utility of 78 percent. Of the fifteen exceptions, ten had double consonants, as in squabble, before the *le.*

18. *When a word has only one vowel letter, the vowel sound is likely to be short.*

This generalization could be applied to 136 words in the sample with a 70 percent utility, as compared with 57 percent in the previous study. However, of the forty-one exceptions, fourteen words had vowels which were modified by an *r*. Omitting these exceptions would raise the percent of utility to seventy-eight.

This article has suggested modifications and substitutes for some of the commonly taught phonic generalizations. There are probably other modifications which would also be helpful. The belief underlying this effort has been that greater improvement will come about in helping children learn to read if we first attempt to eliminate the weaknesses in existing practices before deciding that they should be discarded.

References

Anderson, P. S. *Language Skills in Elementary Education.* New York: Macmillan, 1964.

Armstrong, S. *How Words Get into the Dictionary.* New York: Funk and Wagnalls, 1949.

Atkins, Ruth E. "An Analysis of the Phonetic Elements in a Basal Reading Vocabulary," *Elementary School Journal*, 1926, *26*, 596–606.

Black, E. B. "A Study of the Consonant Situations in a Primary Reading Vocabulary," *Education*, 1952, *72*, 618–623.

Clymer, T. "The Utility of Phonic Generalizations in the Primary Grades," *Changing Concepts of Reading Instruction.* New York: Scholastic Magazines, 1961. P. 156–159.

Clymer, T. "The Utility of Phonic Generalizations in the Primary Grades," *The Reading Teacher*, 1963, *16*, 252–258.

Dolch, E. W. "Phonics and Polysyllables," *Elementary English Review*, 1938, *15*, 120–124.

Dolch, E. W. *The Teaching of Sounding.* Champaign, Illinois: Garrard Press, 1951.

Emans, R. *The Usefulness of Word Pronounciation Rules: Cooperative Re-*

search Project, No. S-340. Unpublished research report, Cooperative Research Program of the Office of Education, United States Department of Health, Education, and Welfare, 1965.

Emans, R. "The Usefulness of Phonic Generalizations Above the Primary Level," *The Reading Teacher*, 1967, *20*, 419–425.

Fry, E. "A Frequency Approach to Phonics," *Elementary English*, 1964, *41*, 759–765.

Gunderson, Agnes G. "Simplified Phonics," *Elementary School Journal*, 1939, *39*, 593–606.

Hanna, R. R., and Moore, T., Jr. "Spelling—from Spoken Word to Written Symbol," *Elementary School Journal*, 1953, *53*, 329–337.

Hildreth, Gertrude. *Teaching Reading.* New York: Holt, Rinehart & Winston, 1958.

Horn, E. "Phonics and Spelling," *Journal of Education*, 1954, *136*, 233–235.

Oaks, Ruth E. "A Study of the Vowel Situations in Primary Vocabulary," *Education*, 1952, *72*, 604–617.

Osburn, W. J. "Teaching Spelling by Teaching Syllables and Root Words. *Elementary School Journal*, 1954, *55*, 32–41.

Sartorious, I. C. *Generalization in Spelling.* New York: Teachers' College, 1931.

Spache, G. D. "A Phonics Manual for Primary and Remedial Teachers," *Elementary English Review*, 1939, *16*, 191–198.

Stauffer, R. G. "A Study of Prefixes in the Thorndike List to Establish a List of Prefixes That Should Be Taught in the Elementary School," *Journal of Educational Research*, 1942, *35*, 453–458.

Thorndike, E. L. *The Teaching of English Suffixes.* New York: Teachers College, 1941.

Vogel, Mabel, Jaycex, Emma, and Washburne, C. W. "A Basic List of Phonics for Grades I and II," *Elementary School Journal*, 1923, *23*, 436–443.

Washburne, C., and Vogel, Mabel. "A Revised List of Phonics for Grade II," *Elementary School Journal*, 1928, *28*, 771–777.

(28) WHICH ACCENT GENERALIZATIONS ARE WORTH TEACHING?*

Carol K. Winkley

As a technique of word identification, several reading specialists and authors of basal reader manuals have advocated teaching children to

*Reprinted from *The Reading Teacher* 20 (December 1966), pp. 219–24; 253, by permission of the author and the International Reading Association.

apply certain accent generalizations to locate the accented syllable in unfamiliar multi-syllabic words. Recommendations have been made although there has been no evidence providing justification for teaching the application of accent generalizations as a word-attack method. Two studies conducted by Clymer (1) and Groff (5) raised questions regarding the advisability of teaching principles of accentuation at either the primary or the intermediate grade levels. There has been no agreement among reading experts as to whether accent generalizations should be taught.

A recent study (7) has provided the first experimental evidence of the value of teaching accent generalizations as a word recognition technique. Two groups of pupils of average ability and above at the intermediate grade levels were compared. Pupils in one group received instruction in applying accent generalizations to unfamiliar words (the "accent-generalization group"). Children in another group in a neighboring community learned only the dictionary skill of pronouncing words in which the accented syllables were marked (the "market-accent group"). Compared with pupils who had not been taught the accent principles, pupils in the "accent-generalization group" were found to have greater "power" in (a) ability to attack unknown words, (b) vocabulary development, and (c) comprehension. It was concluded, therefore, that the reading proficiency of intermediate grade pupils with average ability was improved by a word recognition program that included the teaching of accent generalizations.

THE PROBLEM

From the findings presented, indicating that accent generalizations were helpful in the identification of unknown words, it was inferred that such generalizations should be taught to pupils of average ability and above at the intermediate grade levels. The question then arose as to *which* generalizations should be taught.

Of the reading specialists, Gray has presented the most comprehensive plan for teaching "clues to accent." These are fully explained in his 1960 edition of *On Their Own in Reading* (4) and were incorporated in his basic reader series for Scott, Foresman. Although linguists have discussed a few of the "stress patterns" of isolated words, their chief interest has been in the stress patterns of connected speech and the effects of shifts of accent on intended meaning. Because isolated words have been the main concern of reading specialists, these were investigated in this study. Eighteen accent generalizations proposed by Gray were tested. The generalizations appear in the accompanying table.

The relative merits of each generalization were assessed in two ways. First, a word count was used to determine the percentage of multisyllabic words complying with each generalization and the percentage of words which were exceptions to each principle. Second, an attempt was made to determine the relative usefulness of each generalization to children faced with the actual task of identifying unfamiliar words of more than one syllable.

The applicability of accent generalizations to multisyllabic words, through the use of word counts, has been reported elsewhere (7).

Columns one and two of the table show which accent generalizations had the highest percentage of words complying with the clue and those having the highest percentage of exceptions.

The findings of this aspect of the study seem to lend support for the teaching of the accent generalization clues numbered 3, 4, 8, 13, 15, 16, and 18. Since Clues 1 and 10 had a relatively high percentage of exceptions, they were not considered to be of value.

As the second step in determining the advisability of teaching the principles of accentuation, the relative merits of the generalizations were assessed through the administration of a written Accent Test, constructed by the experimenter. This test required the pupils to perform three tasks in relation to each unknown word: (1) to underline the accented syllable, (2) to select the right vowel sound for the accented syllable, and (3) to choose the correct meaning for the word.

The unknown words for the test were secured from two word lists—Dale and Eichholz, *Children's Knowledge of Words* (2), and Diederich and Palmer, "Difficulty in Grades 11 and 13 of 4,800 Words from 6,000 Through 20,000 in Frequency" (3). A total of 10,896 multisyllabic words which could be considered unknown to an average fourth grader were classified according to the accent generalization that was applicable.

The Accent Test was constructed using a random selection of words from the lists obtained for each generalization. The number of test words exemplifying each accent generalization reflected the percentage of words of that type in the total sample at each particular grade level. The "foils" originally used by Dale and Eichholz in their testing were obtained and used as the multiple-choice items of the test. The administration of the test in pilot studies provided an additional check on the familiarity of the words and made it possible to improve the content of the test and refine the procedures of administration.

Face validity, supplemented by evidence obtained in individual interviews with selected subjects, and reliability coefficients of .92 and .95 (using the Spearman-Brown "split-half" technique) established the Accent Test as a dependable instrument of measurement.

The subjects of the study were 409 pupils at the fourth, sixth, and eighth grade levels. Approximately half of these pupils (207), using the Scott, Foresman basal readers, had been taught accent generalizations as a part of their word recognition program at the intermediate grade levels (the "accent-generalization group"). The remaining 202 students, using the Lyons and Carnahan basal readers, had received instruction in pronouncing words which had their accented syllables marked (the "marked-accent group"). Each subject had an IQ of 100 or more, had attended his present school system since the beginning of fourth grade, and had been taught by teachers in the intermediate grades who had had at least two years of experience in that school system. The reading consultant and the principals in each system encouraged the use of the basal reader manuals and believed that concepts concerning accent were taught as suggested.

Following the administration of the tests, all data were coded and punched on IBM cards. An item analysis of test responses related to each generalization was made. Proportions were then computed comparing the total responses that were correct with the total possible responses for all of the test items exemplifying each generalization. A statistical analysis of the differences between the resulting proportions revealed any differences that were significant. The relative merits of each accent clue were thus assessed.

Statistically significant superiority in proportions was shown for the "accent-generalization group" over the "marked-accent group" in many generalizations at the end of fourth and sixth grades. In the fourth grade at the beginning of the year and in the eighth grade at the end of the year differences were not consistently in favor of either the "accent-generalization group" or the "marked-accent group," and the differences did not reach the 5 per cent level of significance in any instance.

Since the differences found at the end of the fourth and sixth grades were frequently statistically significant and, for each generalization, proportions were higher in the "accent-generalization group" than in the "marked-accent group," the data for the two grade levels were combined

ACCENT GENERALIZATIONS AND THEIR USEFULNESS

Clues to Accent Generalizations	Highest Percentage of Words Complying With Clues	Highest Percentage of Exceptions to Clues	Clues Most Useful to Accent-Generalization Group	Clues Considered Worth Teaching
1. Compound Word Clue—In compound words, a common pattern of accent is a primary accent on or within the first word and a secondary accent on or within the second word. (foot″ hold′)	x	x		
2. Noun-Verb Clue—In two-syllable words which may be used either as a noun or a verb, the accent is usually on the first syllable when the word is used as a noun and on the second syllable when the word is used as a verb. (con′ test *vs.* con test′)				
3. "Ion" Clue—In words ending with—ion, the primary accent falls on the next to the last syllable. (tu i′ tion)	x			x
4. Varied Suffix Clue—The primary accent usually occurs on the syllable before the suffixes —ity, —ic, —ical, —ian, —ial, or —ious and on the second syllable before the suffix —ate. (vi tal′ i ty, ty ran′ ni cal)	x			x
5. Dropped Final "e" Clue—A single consonant letter following a single vowel letter before an ending or suffix (beginning with a vowel) may be a clue that a final "e" was dropped and the last syllable of the root word is accented. (pro cur′ ing)				
6. Unaccented Syllable Before Ending Clue—A single consonant letter following a single vowel letter before an ending or suffix (beginning with a vowel) may be a clue to an unaccented final syllable in the root word. (cov′ et ed)				
7. Two Consonants Before Ending Clue—Two like consonants before an ending or suffix are a clue to an accented final syllable in the root word. (con trol′ ler)			x	x
8. Twin-Consonant Clue—Two like consonant letters following the first vowel letter are a clue to an accented first syllable. (ag′ gra vate)	x			x

ACCENT GENERALIZATIONS AND THEIR USEFULNESS   (Cont.)

Clues to Accent Generalizations	Highest Percentage of Words Complying With Clues	Highest Percentage of Exceptions to Clues	Clues Most Useful to Accent-Generalization Group	Clues Considered Worth Teaching
9. "ck" Clue—The letters "ck" following a single vowel letter are a clue to an accented first syllable. (flick' er)			x	x
10. Final "e" Clue—Two vowel letters, one of which is final "e" in the last syllable of a word, may be a clue to an accented final syllable. (con trive')	x	x	x	
11. Two Vowels Together Clue—Two vowel letters together in the last syllable of a word may be a clue to an accented final syllable. (im peach')			x	x
12. Final "y" Clue—In a two-syllable word that ends in a consonant followed by "y," the first syllable is usually accented. (pal' sy)			x	x
13. Common Beginning Clue—If de—, re—, be—, ex—, in—, or a—, is the first syllable in a word, it is usually unaccented. (re sort', a dieu')	x		x	x
14. "ture" "le" Clue—If the final syllable in a word is —ture, or —le preceded by a consonant, that final syllable is usually unaccented. (nur' ture, am' ble)			x	x
15. Root-Word Clue—In inflected or derived forms of words, the primary accent usually falls on or within the root word. (list' less, un mixed')	x		x	x
16. Long Word Clue—In words of three or more syllables, one of the first two syllables is usually accented. (cat' a pult)	x			x
17. Two-Accent Clue—In longer words where there is a secondary as well as a primary accent, often the secondary accent falls on the first or second syllable, which is then followed by one unstressed syllable before the primary accent. (su' per sede')				
18. Two-Syllable Word Clue—In a word of two syllables the first syllable is usually accented unless it is a prefix. (mer' chant)	x			x

and new proportions computed for the "accent-generalization group." The purpose of combining the data was to secure a single proportion for each generalization which would make it possible to compare one generalization with another. Thus, the accent clues which were most helpful to the pupils to whom they had been taught could be determined.

Eight of the generalizations had proportions significantly higher than the remaining generalizations. These generalizations are indicated in the third column of the table. The principles that appeared to have the highest utility, listed in the order of their apparent usefulness, were: (9) "ck" Clue, (11) Two Vowels Together Clue, (10) Final "e" Clue, (12) Final "y" Clue, (13) Common Beginning Clue, (14) "ture," "le" Clue, (7) Two Consonants Before Ending Clue, and (15) Root-Word Clue. (Clue 18 was not tested since the children in the "accent-generalization group" had not been taught to apply it.)

DISCUSSION

Comparing the whole list of generalizations with those identified as "useful" through word counts, one finds Clues 13 and 15 identified as useful by both techniques. Although the generalization clues numbered 3, 4, 8, and 16 were not as helpful to the subjects of the "accent-generalization group" as were the eight clues enumerated above, their applicability to a relatively high percentage of multisyllabic words warrants consideration in the final selection of accent generalizations worth teaching.

Because about one-third of the words to which Clues 1 and 10 were applicable were found to be exceptions, the advisability of teaching these clues was questioned. Omitting these clues, the possible "utility" of twelve of the generalizations was demonstrated.

CONCLUSIONS AND RECOMMENDATIONS

Twelve generalizations (Clues 3, 4, 7, 8, 9, 11, 12, 13, 14, 15, 16, and 18) appeared to be worth teaching to children. With these findings in mind, the recommended list of accent generalizations to be taught was shortened and simplified by combining and rewording the twelve generalizations.

The following seven generalizations are proposed as those worth teaching to children because of their applicability to multisyllabic words or because of their demonstrated usefulness to children in the identification of unknown multisyllabic words. Examples of words to which the clues are applicable are provided.

1. When there is no other clue in a two syllable word, the accent is usually on the first syllable. (Eliminates need for teaching Clues 8, 9, 12, 14, and 18) Ex.: basic, program.

2. In inflected or derived forms of words, the primary accent usually falls on or within the root word. (Clue 15) Ex.: boxes, untie.

3. If *de-, re-, be-, ex-, in-*, or *a-* is the first syllable in a word, it is usually unaccented. (Clue 13) Ex.: delay, explore.

4. Two vowel letters together in the last syllable of a word may be a clue to an accented final syllable. (Clue 11) Ex.: complain, conceal.

5. When there are two like consonant letters within a word the syllable before the double consonants is usually accented. (Clues 7 and 8) Ex.: beginner, letter.

6. The primary accent usually occurs on the syllable before the suffixes *-ion, -ity, -ic, -ical, -ian, -ial*, or *-ious*, and on the second syllable before the suffix *-ate*. Clues 3 and 4) Ex.: affectation, differentiate.

7. In words of three or more syllables, one of the first two syllables is usually accented. (Clue 16) Ex.: accident, determine.

Further research should be conducted to assess the usefulness of the generalizations, as restated above, in unlocking unknown words; to determine the advisability of teaching accent generalizations to pupils of below average ability; and to recheck the merits of teaching the generalizations eliminated in this study. In the meantime, the list of seven clues presented above can serve as a useful guide to the accent generalizations worth teaching.

REFERENCES

1. Clymer, Theodore. "The Utility of Phonic Generalizations in the Primary Grades," *The Reading Teacher*, 16 (Jan. 1963), 252–258.
2. Dale, Edgar, and Eichholz, Gerhard. *Children's Knowledge of Words.* Columbus, Ohio: Bureau of Educational Research and Service, 1960.
3. Diederich, Paul B., and Palmer, Osmond E. "Difficulty in Grades 11 and 13 of 4,800 Words from 6,000 Through 20,000 in Frequency." Princeton, N.J.: Educational Testing Service, 1956.
4. Gray, William S. *On Their Own in Reading*, pp. 121–225. Chicago: Scott, Foresman, 1960.

5. Groff, Patrick. "To Teach or Not to Teach Accents?" *Elementary School Journal*, 62 (Jan. 1962), 218–221.

6. Winkley, Carol K. "The Applicability of Accent Generalizations," *Academic Therapy Quarterly*, 2 (Fall 1966), 2–10.

7. Winkley, Carol K. "Utilization of Accent Generalizations in Identifying Unknown Multisyllabic Words." Unpublished doctoral dissertation, University of Chicago, 1965.

Chapter 7

COMPREHENSION–
COGNITIVE DIMENSIONS

INTRODUCTION

One of the ultimate goals of reading is to respond in an intellectual fashion to what is read. In other words, the reader must comprehend what the author is saying, must extend and refine his concepts and understandings, and must apply what he learns through reading in his daily living. The purpose of the present chapter is to provide insights into the theoretical and applied aspects of this important facet of reading, the cognitive dimension.

To begin, the articles by Guilford and Lorge provide two theoretical structures of thinking that will aid the teacher in conceptualizing the many dimensions of intelligence and the aspects of comprehension to be considered in the teaching of reading. Guszak and Melnick go on to highlight the significance of appropriate teacher questioning as a means of helping elementary children think in different ways about their reading. They point out that thoughtful, open-ended questions will result in more spirited classroom discussion and more critical reading by pupils.

Sailer in a provocative article, illustrates how advertisements and cartoons furnish interesting materials for developing critical reading power. Finally, Beery identifies some comprehension skills needed in reading to solve problems and some practical ways in which teaching can develop the spirit of inquiry.

In general, then, Chapter 7 should help the reader to deal with two questions about reading comprehension: What kinds of comprehension abilities should the reading program emphasize? How can such comprehension abilities be taught?

(29) FRONTIERS IN THINKING THAT TEACHERS SHOULD KNOW ABOUT*

J. P. Guilford

There is little doubt that the teacher of reading has a wealth of opportunities to teach the child to think. The teacher who has only the very general and rather vague objective of "teaching the child to think," however, is not likely to do justice to the task. In the past, the prevailing conception has probably been that thinking is a single kind of activity and that the ability to think is intelligence. Some relatively recent developments in research on the analysis of intelligence indicate that there are a great many different thinking abilities. If we look upon each of these thinking abilities as a distinct kind of thinking skill, and if we know what kind of skill it is, we have a much more definite objective at which to aim in teaching how to think.

COMPONENTS OF INTELLECT

During the past twenty years numerous investigations by the methods of factor analysis have brought to light some sixty different abilities having to do with intellectual activities. The large number is rather overwhelming to those who have been accustomed to the simple idea of one ability—intelligence—or at the most, the few primary mental abilities of Thurstone. Fortunately, it has been possible to find a definite system in which to organize the intellectual abilities, with some interesting new principles (1, 2). The system is known as the "structure of intellect," which is represented in the figure on the next page.

There are five classes of abilities depending upon the basic kind of operation or activity involved. A group of cognitive abilities have to do with discovery or recognition of information. They are ways of understanding or comprehension. A parallel group has to do with retention of information. Two parallel groups are concerned with productive thinking. Given certain information, we not only understand it but we can generate from it some new information. An important new distinction is

*Reprinted from *The Reading Teacher* 13 (February 1960), pp. 176–82, by permission of the author and the International Reading Association.

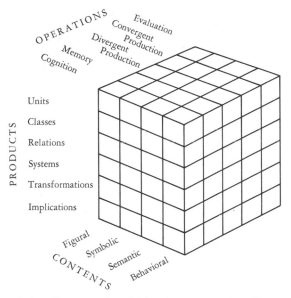

A three-dimensional model for the structure of intellect

that between divergent production and convergent production. In divergent production the goal is to produce a variety of ideas, all of which are logically possible in view of the given information. In convergent production the conclusion is completely determined by the given information, or at least there is a recognized best or conventional conclusion. A fifth group has to do with evaluation, which, in more familiar ways of speaking, means critical thinking. We continually evaluate what we know, what we recall, and what we produce by way of conclusions.

A completely different classification of all the abilities cuts across the first. It is in terms of the kind of material in which the information comes. Some information is concrete, being in the form of things that we can see or hear. We may call this kind of material "figural." Other information is in abstract form, either in the form of symbols such as letters, words, and numbers, or in the form of the things for which they stand—meanings or ideas. The two categories are called "symbolic" and "semantic," respectively. A fourth content category, "behavioral," has been added on the basis of theory only, to take care of the obvious information that we have concerning the behavior of ourselves and of others: our thoughts, desires, and feelings, and intentions, and those of other individuals.

Still a third cross classification is concerned with products of information. These are forms in which the individual casts his information—units, classes, relations, systems, transformations, and implications. The technical meanings of these terms are so close to their common meanings that they will not be defined here. Their applications in connection with reading will be pointed out later.

One more word should be said on the "structure of intellect" as a system before taking the next important step in this discussion. When the three cross classifications are combined in the three-dimensional model, the intersection of a certain kind of operation, a certain kind of content, and a certain kind of product, is represented by a single cell. Each cell is expected to represent its own kind of ability, whose properties can be stated in terms of the three category concepts to which the ability belongs.

For example, there is an ability to cognize semantic units, which has been generally known as "verbal comprehension," and which is tested by means of a vocabulary test. It is the dominating ability represented in tests of verbal intelligence. Another ability can be described as the divergent production of semantic transformations. A simpler, prior term for the ability has been originality (in dealing with ideas). There are other such abilities for dealing with kinds of content other than semantic. Semantic originality can be tested by asking examinees to give a list of titles for a short story and by counting only the number of clever titles in scoring their work. To gain numbers of clever titles the examinee must have some drastic changes (transformations) of his conception of the story and in the meanings of words that he uses in titles.

There are 120 cells in the structure of intellect as now conceived, and at present we know only half as many intellectual abilities. It is expected that future research will bring to light others. The greatest doubt pertains to the behavioral category, for which no abilities have as yet been segregated. But it seems reasonable that "social intelligence," which the behavioral category no doubt represents, will break down into a number of different abilities and that this breakdown will be along the same lines that apply in the other content areas. At any rate, in later discussion this will be assumed.

COGNITIVE ABILITIES IN READING

Reading, when fully developed, is one of our most complex intellectual activities, involving many of the intellectual abilities, which we may also regard as intellectual functions. It does not begin that way in the young child. The preschool child has had considerable experience with visual forms, including letters, which he learns to discriminate. At this stage he is applying, and also perhaps developing, his ability to recognize visual figures, an ability that fits into the cell in the upper left corner of the structure of intellect. His readiness to start learning to read depends upon this basic ability.

In learning to recognize combinations of letters in syllables and words, the child depends upon and perhaps develops his ability to cognize symbolic units, the ability in the next cell to the right. Unusual reading difficulty may stem from a special weakness in this ability. The average IQ test should not be expected to predict progress in this particular respect, since this symbolic ability is not represented in the usual IQ test. Obtaining meaning from the printed symbolic unit involves abilities in the semantic column, first the meaning of single words, which is a matter of word recognition or recognition vocabulary. This is the aspect of reading development that is best predicted by an IQ test. But there is more to reading than recognition of word meaning. If we follow down the column of the semantic abilities in the cognitive category alone, we find a number of ways in which meaning can be enriched. There are relations to be understood, also class ideas. Sentences and paragraphs offer systems of ideas to be comprehended. Poetic and other literary writings, particularly, offer transformations of meanings and vague hints of implications that must be completed by the reader if he is to understand and enjoy his reading to the fullest.

READING AND PRODUCTIVE THINKING

Reading for understanding and enjoyment is a worthy objective and one that satisfies perhaps the great majority of those who read. There are multitudes of others, however, for whom reading is a means to other intellectual goals. The student who learns the material of his subject-matter courses largely from reading, and the scientist who enlightens himself about the discoveries of his fellow scientists, must go beyond comprehension. Even the reader who indulges for his own enjoyment, if he is at all philosophically inclined or if he enjoys making his own reactions to the thoughts of others, must do more than understand. All such individuals need to acquire skills in taking off from what they read into flights of thought of their own making.

Good teachers, of reading or of anything else intellectual, have always taken advantage of opportunities for the student to exercise his thinking equipment. Good teachers have felt their responsibility to contribute to the intellectual development of their pupils, whatever the subject matter. When we look upon the pupil's intellect as being an organized collection of distinguishable skills, each with certain properties, we are in a good position to decide what kinds of exercises are needed to develop those skills. These statements imply considerable faith in the possibility of developing intellectual abilities, including thinking abilities, through exercise. Until we learn something to the contrary, it is best for us as educators to proceed on that assumption.

From the learning theories that have been propounded by psychologists over the years, we have derived little in the way of substantial suggestions on the training of intellects. The prevailing model of behavior has been that of stimulus-response associations. The learner has been conceived as something on the order of a vending machine. You put in a certain coin and a certain thing comes out. Such a model has worked very well in instruction such as teaching the numerical operations. But even there, some added comprehension of the principles involved would be very desirable. Comprehension of principles is a matter of cognition and takes us at once beyond the stimulus-response model.

The major types of thinking, as indicated by the structure of intellect, are divergent production, convergent production, and evaluation. We shall now consider the possible relations of the thinking abilities to reading. In part, whether the reading material stimulates productive thinking on the part of the reader will depend upon the nature of the material. The teacher can therefore encourage pupils to think in response to their reading by selecting the more provocative materials. Does the material stir the imagination of the reader, and does it leave something for the reader to do? Does it open up alternative inviting avenues that would suggest divergent thinking? Does it, in other instances, carry the reader along step by step in logical sequences that point toward an inevitable conclusion? Such material should provide exercise in convergent thinking. Does still other material challenge belief and call for checking and testing of facts and arguments? Such material should automatically call for critical thinking or evaluation.

Even when the reading material does not itself obviously induce these types of thinking exercises, the alert teacher who is not a stranger to ingenuity will invent ways of turning that material to good use as the basis for thinking exercises. Skillful questioning should do the trick, as all good teachers know. Can the awareness of the abilities in the structure of intellect suggest types of questions that might be asked? Perhaps a survey of the possibilities represented in the semantic column, in connection with the two production categories and the evaluation category can suggest kinds of questions that may have been slighted. Let us consider a few examples.

SOME GENERALIZED THINKING TASKS

The examples to be given come directly from certain psychological tests that are known to indicate each ability, or from ideas of new tests that should be expected to indicate the ability if it is still unknown. In the latter case, we can readily suggest such tests by analogy to other tests for parallel abilities. In applying each task that is mentioned, the teacher will need to think of similar tasks and questions that can be utilized incident to the teaching of reading as a procedure for exercising each ability.

The divergent production of semantic units describes an ability more commonly known as "ideational fluency." This is the ability to produce a quantity of ideas in limited time in response to a specification of some kind. For example, we ask the examinee to name all the objects that he can think of that are white, hard, and edible, or we ask him to list all the uses he can think of for a common brick. In either case, the number of suitable responses given in a limited time is the score.

The ability to produce a variety of class ideas is indicated by a test called Unusual Uses. An item reads: "A newspaper is commonly used for reading. What other uses can you suggest for it?" The answers might be: "To swat flies," "To line shelves," "To wrap garbage," "To stuff packages," or "To make up a kidnap note." Notice that each response is in a quite different category.

The ability to produce a variety of responses involving relationships can be assessed by a test called Associational Fluency. The examinee is told to list as many words as he can which mean about the same as the word "high." In another test the examinee is given two words and is asked to state a number of different ways in which they are related, for example, the words "man" and "daughter."

The hypothetical factor of divergent production of systems has no known tests as yet, but it is expected that a test in which we give the examinee several facts and ask him to state a number of different problems that could be involved would apply. Another possible semantic system may be a story plot, in which case we might ask, given the same list of characters, what different story plots could reasonably apply.

As stated earlier, the divergent production of transformations means originality. This can be tested in a number of ways, one way having been mentioned earlier. In another test we ask the examinee to write "punch" lines for cartoons. In another we ask for clever interpretations of riddles. In still another we ask for simple symbols to represent meaningful words, such as "ring" and "bell," in the sentence "Ring the bell."

The divergent production of implications involves elaboration upon given information in different directions. One test presents the bare outlines of a plan (as for a school function) to which the examinee is to add as many details as he can. In another test we give a simple line or two, which the examinee is told to make into a familiar object. He is scored in both instances in terms of the number of additions he offers.

The convergent production area of abilities offers less exciting activities, but the development of carefully reasoned conclusions has always been recognized as an important objective in education. In each task that indicates abilities of this kind, we call for one right answer, or a best or most conventionally accepted answer. In the case of the production of semantic units we have an ability known as "abstraction naming." The examinee is presented with objects of a class, to name the class, or with two objects in relation, to name the relation.

A test of the ability to produce unique classes presents a list of perhaps a dozen words that the examinee must put into three classes, using all the words and putting no word in more than one class. This is in contrast to a test for divergent classification, in which the examinee must reclassify words in as many ways as he can, using each word as many times as he wishes.

Items of the following types indicate the ability to produce unique responses involving relationships: "What word means the exact opposite of *cold*?" "What is the wife of a king?" "Fish is to water as bird to what?" In each case only one best answer is accepted.

The production of a unique system can be tested by calling for arrangement of given events in their most reasonable or optimal order. The events may be presented pictorially, as by using the scrambled pictures of a cartoon strip, or verbally, as in stating several steps involved in changing a tire, planting a new lawn, or building a dog house. Temporal order is one kind of system.

Transformations in the semantic area involve shifts of meanings or uses of objects. "Which of the following objects could be most reasonably used in making a needle: onion, book, fish, wheel, pansy?" The bone of a fish, when given an eye, would serve the purpose. "What more complex object could be made by combining a coil spring and a basket-ball?" This could most clearly be a punching bag. An object or part of an object must be redefined in order to use it in some new way.

Unique implications are fully determined conclusions. The item might be: "Frank is older than Jim and younger than Sam. Who is older, Jim or Sam?" Many readers who enjoy detective stories probably like to indulge in this kind of reasoning, and they probably want their stories to be logic-tight so that unique conclusions are possible.

In the evaluative or critical-thinking area we are less certain of the basic abilities, but most of them that are known are in the semantic column. In the case of figural or symbolic units we have two abilities that apparently have to do with deciding whether two given units are identical or not identical. One might give two proverbs, or a proverb and a non-proverb expression, the examinee to say whether they express the same idea. We are not sure, as yet, what kind of evaluation or standard may pertain to the judgment of classes.

The evaluation of semantic conclusions where relationships are concerned rather clearly involves the standard of logical consistency. Given a syllogism, with two statements of relationships and several alternative conclusions, one of which is determined by the premises, the examinee is to say which conclusion is sound.

In the evaluation of a system two criteria or standards are found to apply. One is whether the system is complete, and the other is whether the parts are internally consistent. In one test we show a simple picture, the examinee to say "What is wrong with this picture?" In one picture the doorstep is missing from the house, and the smoke from the chimney and the clothes on the line are flying in opposite directions.

The ability to evaluate transformations has often been called simply "judgment," or sometimes "commonsense judgment." Tests that seem most suitable for it involve decisions as to which improvisations are best. Workability seems to be the standard or criterion.

Evaluation of implications or evaluation involving implications represents a very interesting kind of ability. When first found, it was called "sensitivity to problems." One test asks the examinee to give two things that are wrong with such common devices as telephones, toasters, or refrigerators. Another asks what is wrong with social institutions such as tipping and divorce. Being sensitive to defects and deficiencies is the apparent quality involved. The sensitive person has evaluated unfavorably, and the person who sees no defects has evaluated positively the implication that things are all right as they are. The former feels problems still exist, while the latter feels they are solved.

In the short space of this article it has been impossible to bridge the gap between the kinds of exercises presented by tests of the semantic factors and teaching operations in the subject of reading. It is hoped, however, that a systematic exposition of the varieties of general thinking skills will be sufficient to extend the boundaries of conceptions of thinking activities and also to delineate each kind of thinking skill clearly enough to enable the average teacher to observe it and to help the student cultivate its development.

REFERENCES

1. Guilford, J. P. *Personality*. New York: McGraw-Hill, 1959.
2. Guilford, J. P. "Three Faces of Intellect." *American Psychologist*, 14 (1959), 469–79.

(30) THE TEACHER'S TASK IN THE DEVELOPMENT OF THINKING*

Irving Lorge

In arriving at a definition or conceptualization of thinking I tried to list as many verbs about thinking and thought as I could. This list was supplemented by an active search for other verbs which should be added to fill out my working definition of thinking. The list contained forty-nine verbs. The next step was to try to bring together verbs that seemed to have common elements, and, then, to organize the sets in a sequence. My grouping may not be yours—but it may suggest a process by which you can synthesize your own categories and your own sequences. The content analysis comprised twenty sub-clusters as follows:

List A

attend   orient
observe   regard

*Reprinted from *The Reading Teacher* 13 (February 1960), pp. 170–75, by permission of the author and the International Reading Association.

relate   recall   associate
abstract   conceive   conceptualize
generalize
comprehend   understand
review   reorganize
know   believe
evaluate   appreciate

List B

concentrate
seek   search
ascertain   analyze
deliberate   contemplate   ponder   meditate
speculate   consider   guess   imagine
judge   reason   surmise   infer   hypothesize   deduce
restructure   plan
solve   discover
verify   decide   conclude   confirm
act   resolve

The two lists give some impression of the complexity of the thinking process. The act of thinking, indeed, is more complicated than the verbs in the sub-clusters. Nevertheless, the classification suggests a comprehensive structure for the behaviors subsumed under the verb *think*.

For me, two large blocks of ideas emerged to define thinking: first, in List A, the sequence represents the behaviors exhibited in learning for mastery; and second, List B shows the sequence of behaviors involved in solving problems, coming to decisions, in inventing, and in creating.

Learning and thinking are interrelated. The verbs in List A seem to parallel in sequence those in List B, although the emphases and goals differ. In learning for mastery, the steps begin with attending, and continue with observing and regarding, utilizing past knowledge and experience in recall, and relating the common elements through to the active processes of concept-formation and generalizing, to the important phases of comprehending and understanding. In the learning sequence, viewing the materials and skills in new ways will deepen knowledge and belief in terms of evaluation and appreciation—the genuine learning of the philosophers.

List B usually implies an obstacle that has to be overcome. The list suggests Dewey's famous five steps: experiencing a felt difficulty, locating and defining the difficulty, evolving suggestions for the solution, reasoning about possible outcomes for the solution, and, on verifying the solution in thought, concluding and taking action.

The range of terms related to the act of thinking gives ample evidence of the great variety of behaviors involved in thinking. In addition, contemplation of the terms serves to emphasize the importance for us in understanding what a child, or a teacher, means by thinking. The child who is attending to what his neighbor is doing, or who is trying to recall the number of products that can be made from coal, or who is contemplating in retrospect the swimming test he passed last summer can say that he is thinking—and he is! Many teachers, of course, have an expectation that thinking usually means the solving of a problem in arithmetic, or the suggesting of the reasons why cotton is produced in California or beef cattle are raised in Florida, or the consecutive steps in writing a composition or creating a poem.

Thinking involves all these—and much more. Teachers must appreciate that the behaviors involved in the acquisition of an idea, the recognition of similarity or difference, or the deepening of a meaning are as much thinking as are the behaviors in solving a puzzle, planning for a picnic, or discovering a new process in chemistry. The implied gradient, of course, suggests that all of us think at different levels at different times. Some of us become aware of a new fact and try to fit it into our store of knowledge; and the same person may also be working out a procedure for simplifying the recording of grades, the giving of assignments, or the staging of a play.

Thinking, however, must be learned—and in the learning, the consequences of successful thinking must be satisfying. Thinking always involves some activity on the part of the thinker, whether it be recalling, or getting at the principles, or whether it be reorganizing material or developing a new methodology. Thinking can be taught by stimulating the learner to overcome obstacles within his intellectual range at his developmental stage and his intellectual level.

In teaching the child to think, the problem or task should be difficult enough to stimulate the learner—but not so difficult as to frustrate the child. Fortunately, the teacher can help the child by providing cues, hints, suggestions, and clues for the solution of the problem. In textbooks in arithmetic and algebra, authors usually provide hints or suggestions. Sometimes they provide the answer so that the learner may verify his thinking and obtain the satisfaction of solving the problem. Thinking and reasoning can occur in any subject or skill, in school and outside. Thinking requires the rearrangement of ideas, principles, and skills in finding the path from what is known to what is to be discovered. Teachers not only must encourage thinking, but, more important, they must teach thinking as an active process not only in every school period but also on the playing field and in the home.

Basically, the teacher has the responsibility of giving each learner the attitude that he can grow by giving thought to his life—by thinking and reasoning about his experiences, applying his knowledge to new situations. Every subject and every class can provide the stimulation for thinking and the satisfaction of solution.

The teacher can guide the learner's thinking about any problem by suggesting, through questions and by hints, the need to clarify the problem, to seek parallels, to open new vistas. Since much of the child's learning comes either through reading or listening, the teacher can help the child appreciate the important steps in thinking as they apply to his reading of a specific passage. Below is a passage from one of my unpublished reading tests. The teacher may suggest some questions which not only would motivate the reading but which might also suggest possible answers that would involve critical thinking. For example, the teacher may ask, "What is the passage all about?" "What was the influence of standing armies on the manufacture of clothing?" "What would be possible actions of a union if somebody invented a way of making something quicker or better?" Here is the passage:

"The first ready-made clothing establishments were set up for the manufacture of uniforms, the need for which arose with the coming of standing armies. After the Thirty Years War, Austria, for instance, maintained a standing army of 33,000 men. The uniforms were tailored partly in regimental workshops, partly in state or private factories, partly even in prisons and penitentiaries. The large number of measurements made by the military tailors enabled them to establish standard dimensions, which were utilized to produce for stock.

"The first large firm producing ready-mades for civilian needs was founded by Pierre Parissot in Paris in 1824. Thus was situated near the Pont Neuf, one of the busiest bridges across the Seine, and also near the flower market, hence the name: 'La Belle Jardiniere.'

"Parissot, who sold cloth and haberdashery, aimed at the manufacture of plain men's clothes designed to be cheaper than made-to-measure goods and little more expensive than second-hand apparel. As the handicraft tailors refused to work for him, Parissot was forced to have his first trousers and jackets sewn in prison workshops. By the end of 1824 he already had a complete line of ordinary working clothes for men. They sold so fast that he was hardly able to satisfy demand, and it was at this point that the master tailors decided to work under him. Parissot's small shop soon proved too small for the business. In 1830 he bought up the neighboring houses and in 1854 added a further block of twenty-five existing buildings. All his productions were hand-sewn and about half of the output was destined for the provinces and for export. Parissot was the first manufacturer to charge a fixed and clearly marked price for his goods. Also, he demanded cash payment, whereas previously prices were arrived at by bargaining with customers, who also were allowed credit. About 1850 the working capital of the firm was three million francs, a very considerable sum for those days. By that time Parissot also had branches in the provinces."

After the reading, the teacher could ask questions like the following: (1) What would be a good title for this passage? (2) Around 1820 how did a workingman get, or where did he buy, his work clothes? (3) Why was it that dealing in secondhand clothing was an important business in the 1700's and 1800's? (4) What is the value in "standardizing measurements"? Can you give examples that would apply today? (5) What invention was needed to speed and reduce the cost of making clothes? (6) Why was this passage written? (7) How can you find out whether the author was accurate and fair?

The questions are directed to provide a scheme by which the reader and learner can think with text materials. Indeed, the formulation of the questions parallels the analysis of any communication: Who says what to whom via what channels for what purpose and with what effect?

Basically, the questions are graded. The first few are designed to ascertain whether the child understands the material generally, e.g., author's main point or conclusion, general idea, details that support or lead to the conclusion. The second sort of questions are directed to relating the child's previous learnings and experiences to the problem, e.g., Are there situations now existing like this? Can any of the processes and conclusions be applied today in other areas? Can you predict what happened after this event? Are there any of the consequences still to be found?

A third set of questions could be directed to implications from the passage, e.g., Does this passage give any understanding of the prejudices of people? Why would people differ about the relative advantages of these ideas or this invention or this process? What values do you see in getting at the history of an idea?

A fourth set of questions might be directed toward formulating of hypotheses, e.g., Why did this event take place? How can you account for it?

The teacher's task in the development of thinking is important and significant. The steps must, by suggesting, hinting, or questioning, lead the learner through the phases of understanding the problem, suggesting hypotheses or reasons for the existence of the problem, and formulating hypotheses for the solution of the problem. Here the teacher can help the learner by asking him to formulate questions. Good questioning is good hypothesis formulation. The learners can be helped by being asked to formulate questions seeking additional information or inquiring about motives or prejudices or special pleading.

The art of questioning can be directed toward seeing similarities or differences (concept formation), or seeing common elements among concepts (generalization), or recognizing the limitations or advantages (evaluation). Questions can be formulated toward seeing sequences (structure and restructure), toward evidence and proof (verification). Indeed, each line of verbs in Lists A and B should suggest the direction of the thinking-learning process.

The development of thinking in pupils is a responsibility of all the teachers who meet the pupils. The emphasis should be upon developing in the child the ability for critical thinking. Even in the lowest grades children can be given the challenge of finding out how to attack a new word, how to infer the meaning of a word as used in context, how to recognize common elements among words, both in configuration and in meaning. The child should be made aware that critical thinking is an active process in which he can participate by collecting data, or suggesting examples of a principle, or demonstrating equivalences or similarities. He should be encouraged to see that one of the first steps in critical thinking is to organize information and experiences about problems by recognizing similarities or differences.

One of the most provocative experiences children can have is the challenge of suggesting hypotheses for a set of outcomes or facts. These could range from accounting for the pattern of rainfall in eastern Puerto Rico, the probable reasons for the Union Army's failure at the Battle of Bull Run, to the efficiency of a bicycle over a tricycle. The children should be encouaged to challenge some generalizations in terms of: What are the facts? Are they grouped properly? Did the author make an error in generalization or in inference? The matter of proof depends to a large degree on the respect for evidence. Can the children be led to recognize that not all the evidence has been adduced for a particular generalization or that the generalization does not consider all the available evidence? Undoubtedly, many opportunities will be found for understanding and criticizing advertisements and their claims, or for the understanding of propaganda, both positive and persuasive.

Since thinking is to be encouraged with reference to all experiences of the child, all teachers must cooperate in making the child aware of the importance of critical thinking, not only with reference to school learning but also with reference to experiences outside the school. This means that the child should be taught to test his own attitudes and interests. He ought to try to find out why he has certain attitudes toward people from other countries or toward a particular professional baseball team or toward one political party. For maximum transfer to be effected, all teachers must encourage and reward critical thinking. This, of course, implies that the teacher is competent to think critically in her subject area so that she is able to give illustrations of the way generalizations are developed, how evidence is organized, how hypotheses are formulated, how the requirements for proof are utilized.

In a significant sense, it will not be easy for teachers to reward critical thinking if they themselves are less than fully competent in the process.

One of the most exciting ways for the teacher to become aware of the aspects of critical thinking relevant for her in her particular area of competency is in the making of reading tests. As the teacher tries to formulate the kinds of questions suggested in the treatment of the passage used earlier, she will become aware of the fact that she is making hypotheses, suggesting organization of data, seeing relations that exist between the passage and past experience and knowledge. If the teacher were to try to make multiple choice questions, she would see that some of the most likely errors in thinking could be anticipated. For example, the following three items are items made to evaluate the child's understanding of the passage:

1. The best title for this passage is (a) Sweat Shop Labor, (b) *Ready to Wear Clothing*, (c) Military Uniforms, (d) Unfair Competition, (e) Dangers of Prison Labor.

2. The experience of the military tailors in manufacturing uniforms for the Austrian Army gave the tailors the experience for (a) producing large stocks, (b) establishing fixed prices for clothes, (c) opening branch stores, (d) *standardizing measurements*, (e) training master tailors.

3. The development of mass production of clothing on a large scale awaited the (a) development of retail stores, (b) elimination of prison labor, (c) improvement of clothing design, (d) growth of labor unions, (e) *invention of the sewing machine*.

Again, it is always stimulating to try to determine if given facts can be organized in terms of common principles or in sequences. The illustration given at the beginning of this article on the organization of verbs about thinking represents one attempt to show the generalization emerging from an active search for organization. Some forms of content organization can be widely applied. In the United States Air Force, for instance, the use of a general scheme applied to any problem became the basis for improvement in quality of the solution produced for problems by officers.

Thinking is an active process. It seeks and searches. It organizes and generalizes. It collects and solves. Thinking does not always produce a set answer. It is not memory, although it uses what is remembered; it is not generalization, but the process of arriving at generalization. Thinking is basically an attitude of suspended judgment about the problems all of us face.

(31) TEACHER QUESTIONING AND READING*

Frank J. Guszak

In 1917, Thorndike outlined a classic definition of reading in three words when he said, "Reading is thinking." Fifty years later, the conversation on the reading scene is still concerned with reading as thinking with regard to how varied reading-thinking skills can be developed within the classroom. Despite the numerous treatments of such reading-thinking skills as "critical reading skills" in the professional press, contentions abound that classroom teachers are doing little to develop a variety of reading-thinking skills. Rather, according to Austin and Morrison (1964) and Henry (1963), teachers appear to equate reading-thinking skills with the most narrow of literal comprehension skills.

Because standardized reading tests tend to measure literal comprehension skills, it is difficult to make wide assessments of pupils' abilities in various reading-thinking areas. In the absence of such test results, it seems advisable to examine the interaction between teachers and students in the reading circle as they engage in the development of reading-thinking skills. Thus, the current study was initiated in an effort to make

*Reprinted from *The Reading Teacher* 21 (December 1967), pp. 227–34, by permission of the author and the International Reading Association.

determinations about the state of reading thinking skills development as it occurred in the context of the reading group in the elementary grades. Observation and study were guided by the following questions:

1. What kinds of thinking questions do teachers ask about reading assignments in selected second, fourth, and sixth grade classrooms? In what frequencies do the various question types occur?
2. How frequently are teacher questions about reading assignments met with congruent or correct student responses?
3. Do teachers employ certain questioning strategies as they question students about reading assignments? If so, what are the characteristics of these strategies?

SUBJECTS AND PROCEDURES

From a population of 106 second, fourth, and sixth grade teachers in a public school system in Texas, a sample of four teachers (and their respective students) at each of these grade levels was randomly selected for the study. The mean class size of the three grades was as follows: second grade, 29.7; fourth grade, 24.7; and sixth grade, 28.5. Three-reading-group structures were operant in all of the second and fourth grade classrooms while such a functional structure was found in only one of the sixth grade classrooms. Each reading group in the twelve classrooms was observed and recorded over a three day period (an average of approximately five hours per classroom). The taped recordings were subsequently transcribed to written protocols and analyzed in accordance with the research questions.

RESULTS

Results of the study are discussed in accordance with the three basic question areas. Because each set of results is based upon a conceptual framework, the initial part of each discussion will deal with these frameworks which were subsequently utilized in the measurement process.

Question 1. The initial study task was one of making a determination of what kinds of questions teachers ask about reading assignments. An extensive survey was made of the following: reading-thinking skills as identified in basal series, reading-thinking skills as identified by reading authors, and representative thinking models. From these sources, the most pertinent conceptualizations of reading-thinking skills were synthesized into the model that subsequently was called the Reading Comprehension Question-Response Inventory. After repeated testing, the instrument was found to possess face validity and reliability when applied to teacher questions and student responses in a pilot study.

READING COMPREHENSION QUESTION-RESPONSE INVENTORY

Recognition. These questions call upon the students to utilize their literal comprehension skills in the task of locating information from reading context. Frequently, such questions are employed in the guided reading portion of a story, i.e. Find what Little Red Ridinghood says to the wolf.

Recall. Recall questions, like recognition questions, concern literal comprehension. The recall question calls upon the student to demonstrate his comprehension by recalling factual material previously read. Generally, such activity is primarily concerned with the retrieval of small pieces of factual material, but the size of the pieces may vary greatly. An example of a recall question would be the following where the answer to the question is clearly printed in the text, i.e. What was Little Red Ridinghood carrying in the basket?

Translation. Translation questions require the student to render an objective, part-for-part rendering of a communication. As such, the behavior is characterized by literal understanding in that the translator does not have to discover intricate relationships, implications, or subtle meanings. Translation questions frequently call upon students to change words, ideas, and pictures into different symbolic form as is illustrated in the following from Bloom (1956).

> Translation from one level of abstraction to another; abstract to concrete, lengthy to brief communication, i.e. Briefly re-tell the story of Little Red Ridinghood.
> Translation from one symbolic form to another, i.e. Draw a picture of the first meeting between Little Red Ridinghood and the wolf.
> Translation from one verbal form to another; non-literal statements to ordinary English (metaphor, symbolism).

Conjecture. These questions call for a "cognitive leap" on the part of the student as to what will happen or what might happen. As such, the conjecture is an anticipatory thought and not a rationale, i.e. What do you think that Little Red Ridinghood will do in the future when she meets a wolf in the forest?

Explanation. Explanation questions, like conjecture questions, are inferential in nature. However, the inference involved in the explanation situations calls upon the student to supply a rationale. The rationale must be inferred by the student from the context developed or go beyond it if the situation is data-poor in terms of providing a rationale. Instances of explanatory behaviors are found in the following: explanations of value positions, i.e. Explain why you like Little Red Ridinghood best; conclusions, i.e. Explain why the wolf wanted to eat Little Red Ridinghood; main ideas, What is the main idea of this story?

Evaluation. Evaluation questions deal with matters of value rather than matters of fact or inference and are thus characterized by their judgmental quality (worth, acceptability, probability, etc.). The following components of this category are adapted from a classification scheme by Aschner and Gallagher (1965).

> Questions calling for a rating (good, bad, true, etc.) on some item (idea, person, etc.) in terms of some scale of values provided by the teacher, i.e. Do you think that this was a good or bad story?
> Questions calling for a value judgment on a dimension set up by the teacher. Generally, these are "yes" or "no" responses following questions such as "Would you have liked Tom for a brother?"
> Questions that develop from conjectural questions when the question is qualified by probability statements such as "most likely." 'Do you think that it is most likely or least likely?"
> Questions that present the pupil with a choice of two or more alternatives and require a choice, i.e. "Who did the better job in your opinion, Mary or Susan?"

With the determination of the categories of the Reading Comprehension Question-Response Inventory the first question concerning the kinds of questions asked by teachers was answered. Comparative frequency of the six question types is reported in Table 1.

Total questions recorded numbered 1857—878 in grade two; 725, grade four, 254, grade six. The teachers spent the greatest portion of their questions on the literal comprehension realms of "recall" and "recognition." Seemingly, the observations tend to support the contention that elementary reading teachers dwell on literal comprehension. It should be added that "dwell" is imprecise as is any determination about what percentage of questions should be asked in each category.

Although 15.3 per cent of the teachers' questions were spent on

TABLE 1. PERCENTAGES OF EACH QUESTION TYPE IN
GRADES TWO, FOUR, AND SIX

Grade	Recog.	Recall	Transl.	Conjec.	Explan.	Evalua.
	%	%	%	%	%	%
Two	12.3	66.5	.2	5.7	3.8	11.5
Four	16.3	48.4	.6	6.9	7.4	20.4
Six	10.2	47.6	2.4	7.9	8.1	13.8
Total	13.5	56.9	.6	6.5	7.2	15.3

evaluation questions, there seems to be some legitimate doubt about the thinking depth they required. A close inspection of the questions in this category revealed that nearly all called for a simple "yes" or "no" response. Thus, the measure of higher level thinking seemed to be the incidence of questions in the inferential categories of "conjecture" and "explanation." These combined categories accounted for 13.7 per cent of the teachers' questions.

The old adage that "children learn to read in the primary grades and read to learn in the intermediate grades" seems to be borne out if one interprets an increase in inferential questioning as an increase in "reading to learn." There was a pattern of decrease in literal questioning as children reach the higher grade levels. The supplementary observations of the researchers indicated that second grade teachers spent many questions upon the minute, developing details of most story sequences. This close comprehension check is further evidenced by the greater frequency of questioning in the lower grades.

Question 2. A study exclusively devoted to teacher question types would indicate little about the effect of such questions upon students. Therefore, an effort was made to check the student responses against the teacher questions that initiated such responses. If responses satisfied the substantive intents of the teacher-initiated questions, these question-response sequences were said to be congruent or correct. If the responses failed in some way (incomplete, inaccurate) to meet the intent of the teachers' questions, they were termed incongruent. Thus, congruence was a measure of the reciprocity between questions and responses. It should be pointed out that whereas response patterns were very narrow in terms of literal comprehension questions they were very loose in terms of inferential questions that allowed for numerous responses. Patterns of question-response congruence in the three grades are illustrated in Table 2.

Possibly one of the most interesting observations relating to the con-

TABLE 2. PERCENTAGES OF QUESTION-RESPONSE
CONGRUENCE IN GRADES TWO, FOUR, AND SIX

Grade	Recog.	Recall	Transl.	Conjec.	Explan.
	%	%	%	%	%
Two	94.6	92.5	100.0	95.1	80.0
Four	91.9	88.1	50.0	91.5	86.0
Six	100.0	84.4	80.0	100.0	88.1
Total	93.9	90.3	75.0	94.2	85.5

gruence patterns is that the highest incidence of congruence was found in
the second grade. A close inspection of the category frequencies reveals
that the total congruence percentages are the result of the congruence
percentages in the recall category. Second grade teachers obviously had
higher percentages in the recall category. Second grade teachers obviously had higher percentages of congruence at the recall level than did
fourth and sixth grade counterparts. As indicated previously, the second
grade teachers tended to question more precisely than did the upper
grade teachers in that they questioned frequently about the factual
material on a given page. While the upper grade teachers seemed to
question specific factual bits also, it appeared that they lacked the control
over the story details because of the difficulty of the memory task created
by the greater quantity of words. Consequently, this factual questioning
mode resulted in several situations wherein the upper grade teachers
accepted as congruent certain responses which were indeed incongruent.
The second grade teachers had no such problem because of the readily
apparent answers in the simple reading materials.

Question 3. Many hours of observation revealed that teachers employ
two basic kinds of strategies as they question children about reading
assignments. First, they control the nature of the exchange relative to
each question. Second, they may pattern such individual question-
response exchanges into larger wholes.

In order to describe the strategy elements involved in the single
question the concept of the Question-Response Unit (QRU) was developed. The QRU represented the boundaries wherein the anatomy of
an exchange could be illustrated. As such, it contained the following
elements: the teacher's initiating question; any subsequent remarks on
the part of the teacher that might serve to extend, clarify, or cue
subsequent student response; the referent in the reading materials for the
question; the way in which the student subsequently dealt with the

question; and finally the phase wherein attention was shifted away from the initiating question.

Conceivably, every initiating question can be met by a congruent response on the first response attempt. However, such is not always the case. In some instances, the teacher may move the focus before a student can respond. In other instances, response time may be allowed, but none may be forthcoming. In this case, the teacher may drop the unit or invoke a sustaining statement that will either clarify the question or offer some cues as to the correct response. These examples represent a very small number of alternatives that may happen in the context of a QRU.

Many QRU patterns were identified. Because so many were seen in only one or two instances, the decision was made to focus upon those which occurred in at least three instances. Table 3 presents a frequency report of such patterns. The following symbols are used to identify the patterns:

Q—teacher's initiating question
R—student response
/—a clarifying, extending, or cueing remark by teacher
+—congruent response
——an incongruent response
(—)—response allowed but only silence heard
(0)—teacher did not allow time for student response
|—separate responses

TABLE 3.   FREQUENCIES OF QUESTION-RESPONSE UNIT PATTERNS

Patterns	Recog.	Recall	Transl.	Conjec.	Explan.	Evalua.	Total
SR+	74	681	4	56	50	189	1054
S(O)/R+	5	34	0	1	4	2	46
SR—	4	41	0	0	1	0	46
SR—/R+	6	15	0	4	1	1	27
SR+/R+	0	5	0	3	3	4	15
SR+|R+	1	1	0	2	0	6	10
S(—)	0	6	1	0	1	1	9
S(—)/R+	0	5	0	0	0	0	5
S(O)/(O)/R+	1	2	0	0	1	0	4
SR+|R—	0	4	0	0	0	0	4
S(O)/R—/R+	1	2	0	0	0	0	3
S(O)/(—)	1	1	0	0	1	0	3
Total	93	797	5	66	62	203	1226

A question followed by a single congruent response (SR+) was the dominant pattern of interaction. Furthermore, observation indicates that the pattern tends to be closely associated with "recall" questions. Because "recall" questions were most abundant in the second grade classes, the SR+ pattern was likewise most prominent in the second grade.

A second focus relative to teacher questioning strategies was the concept of the Question-Response Episode. The Question-Response Episode represented a combination of two or more Question-Response Units which tended to be related in the following ways:

Setting Purpose Follow-up. These episodes occur when a teacher follows-up a "setting purpose" question (S(O)) with a parallel question calling for a response. The teacher asks the first question as a guide for the students and then repeats the question in a manner that calls for response.

Verification. Verification episodes involve questions wherein congruence can be verified by referring to the text. As such, it is the reverse of the previous episode type. In verification episodes, the teacher follows up a student response with a question that calls for the verification or finding of the referent for the response to the previous question.

Justification. These episodes appear when a teacher calls upon a student to justify his own or somebody else's previous response by the use of explanation. This explanation most frequently follows a judgmental or conjectural response to a previous question.

Judgmental. These episodes occur in situations wherein a teacher asks for an evaluation of the student response to the preceding question. Thus, judgmental episodes constitute a reversal of the order employed in the justification episodes.

Of the 142 Question-Response Episodes tallied (Table 4), sixty-seven were "setting purpose follow-up" episodes. "Judgmental" episodes represented the least observed type.

TABLE 4. FREQUENCIES OF QUESTION-RESPONSE EPISODES IN GRADES TWO, FOUR, AND SIX

Grade	SP Follow-up	Verification	Justification	Judgmental	Total
Two	26	11	11	3	51
Four	35	14	23	2	74
Six	6	8	2	1	17
Totals	67	33	36	6	142

CONCLUSIONS AND IMPLICATIONS

Although the following conclusions and the implications based upon them are aimed specifically at the sample teachers, it is the feeling of the researcher that these items may be keenly appropriate to a much wider group of teachers.

1. Conceivably, the expenditure of nearly seventy of a hundred questions in the literal comprehension areas may be justified. Unjustifiable, however, is the involvement of these so-called literal comprehension questions with retrieval of the trivial factual makeup of stories. In real life reading situations, readers seldom approach reading with the purpose of trying to commit all the minute facts to memory. Rather, the reader is more interested in getting broad understandings of the material, finding out specific things commensurate with his interests or other needs, etc. It would appear, then, that much of the recall questioning actually leads the students away from basic literal understandings of story plots, events, and sequences. It seems quite possible that students in these recall situations may miss the literal understanding of the broad text in their effort to satisfy the trivial fact questions of the teachers. Seemingly, if teachers want to get at utilitarian aspects of literal understanding, they would offer many situations (rather than the few evidenced) for translational activities wherein they could really determine the extent to which children were understanding the literal elements. Of course, before teachers can employ more comprehensive questioning patterns, they must be aware of such. Thus, reading series should clearly spell out their comprehension structures in such a way that classroom teachers can have some clear insights into their task in comprehension development.

2. Students invariably are sensitive to "what teachers want" and generally do a good job of supplying it. This appears very evident with regard to questions about reading when one notes that over 90 per cent of all literal comprehension questions are met with congruent responses on the first student try. Presumably, the programmed learning buff would comment that this is the way it should be. However, inspection of the makeup of the questions proves the folly of such a notion. About the only thing that appears to be programmed into the students is the nearly flawless ability to anticipate the trivial nature of teachers' literal questions. As evidenced by the high congruence of immediate responses, the students have learned quite well to parrot back an endless recollec-

tion of trivia. It would be interesting to measure the same students' understandings of the story line via a translational question.

3. If educators want to condition students for irresponsible citizenship, it seems quite appropriate to ask children for unsupported value statements, a practice which is very frequent in the reading circle according to this study. It seems imperative that teachers pattern the all-important "why" questions after students take positions. Until such is the common practice it seems that teachers will condition students to take value positions without the vital weighing of evidence that seems to separate the thinking individual from the mob member. Perhaps the use of a tape recorder would indicate to teachers their patterning practices with regard to such potentially dangerous questioning practices.

REFERENCES

Aschner, Mary June, Gallagher, J. J., Perry, Joyce M, Afsar, Sibel S., Jenne, W., and Farr, Helen. *A System for Classifying Thought Processes in the Context of Classroom Verbal Interaction.* Champaign, Illinois: Institute for Research on Exceptional Children, 1965.

Austin, Mary C., and Morrison, C. *The First R: The Harvard Report on Reading in Elementary Schools.* New York: Macmillan, 1964.

Bloom, B. S. (Ed.) *Taxonomy of Educational Objectives: Handbook I: Cognitive Domain.* New York: McKay, 1956.

Henry, J. "Reading for What?" *Teachers College Record,* 1963, 65.

Thorndike, E. L. "Reading as Reasoning: A Study of Mistakes in Paragraph Reading," *Journal of Educational Research,* 1917, 8, 323–332.

(32) THE FORMULATION OF QUESTIONS AS AN INSTRUCTIONAL-DIAGNOSTIC TOOL*

Amelia Melnik

A basic concept of reading, which should underlie instruction at all levels, is that reading is a thought-getting process and as a thought-getting process, reading involves comprehension. To comprehend, the reader must judiciously select, organize, and relate the author's pattern of

*Reprinted from *Reading and Inquiry,* 10 (1965 Convention Proceedings) pp. 36–9, by permission of the author and the International Reading Association.

thought. To be selective, the reader must raise significant and appropriate questions relevant to the material as a basis for establishing a purpose for reading. His questions determine what he reads, how he reads, and what he gets out of his reading. In short, questions underlie and guide the readers' quest for understanding as he engages in a dialogue with the author. In this sense, then, reading is inquiry.

What, then, is the role of questions? And how are they formulated to serve their multiple purposes?

THE ROLE OF QUESTIONS

Questions function in both reading and teaching situations. In reading, questions establish a basis for identifying and clarifying a reader's purpose which influences his method of reading, the degree of comprehension, rate of reading, and the skills employed in reading. More than anything else, a reader's purpose influences what he reads and how he reads.

In instructional situations, the role of question is by far the most influential single teaching act. According to Taba, "A focus set by the teacher's questions circumscribes the mental operations which students can perform, determines what points they can explore, and what modes of thought they can learn."[1] Moreover, students' concept of reading is largely influenced by the types of questions asked by teachers. For these reasons questions play a crucial role in affecting the level of the teaching and reading process. Yet there is little evidence to suggest that teachers are well prepared in the formulation and analysis of fruitful questions as a diagnostic and instructional tool.

For example, in examining 17 newly published or recently revised professional reading textbooks, only four of them identified the topic of questions in either the table of contents or the index. Even here, however, the treatment of questions was rather brief and superficial, with a four- or five-paragraph descriptive and prescriptive discussion rather than analytically with appropriate application. Perhaps in our textbooks too much attention is paid to the content of reading instruction to the neglect of how teachers teach reading.

If teachers are not competently trained in the formulation and use of questions, it is not surprising to find that investigators of teachers' use of

---

[1]Hilda Taba et al., *Thinking in Elementary School Children.* Cooperative Research Project No. 1574. San Francisco State College, 1964, p. 53.

questions report that they were found to ask regularly 150 questions per class hour.[2] Findings of this kind clearly suggest that the quality of teaching in these situations is at the level of memory of facts and details. Such an emphasis encourages students to read with a mind set to memorize as many isolated details as possible. Unfortunately, even our most able readers reflect a detail-oriented concept of reading which largely results from the types of questions they have encountered in the classroom. In a study of 1500 Harvard and Radcliffe freshmen, Perry[3] made the following observations:

1. The typical approach of 90 percent of these students was to start at the beginning of the chapter and read straight ahead. No attempt was made to survey the chapter, note marginal headings, or first read the recapitulation paragraph in which the whole structure and summary of the chapter was given. Thus, none of the clues and signals provided as a basis for raising questions were used to identify specific purposes for reading.
2. Their performance on a multiple-choice test on details as far as they were able to read in this manner was impressive. But only one in 100—15 in all—were able to write a short statement on what the chapter was about. Perry describes the reading performance of 99 per cent of these students "as a demonstration of obedient purposelessness in reading."

Obviously, setting a purpose is a potent influence on reading comprehension. But a purpose for reading can only be defined and established if the reader knows what kinds of questions to ask the author. According to both the Harvard study and the analysis of teachers' questions, it seems evident that students and teachers need to improve the quality of their questions. Perhaps in our teaching we need to shift our emphasis from giving the right answers to raising relevant and significant questions.

THE PURPOSES AND FORMULATION OF QUESTIONS

As a tool in the teaching of reading, questions have two main functions, diagnostic and instructional:

(1) *As a diagnostic tool*, they are unstructured, allowing the student to

[2]William H. Burton, *The Guidance of Learning Activities*, 3rd edition. New York: Appleton-Century-Crofts, Inc., 1962, p. 436.

[3]William G. Perry, Jr., "Student's Use and Misuse of Reading Skills: A Report to the Faculty." *Harvard Educational Review*, Vol. 29, No. 3, Summer 1959, pp. 193–200.

respond in his own fashion, thus giving the teacher opportunity to observe the variety of individual responses in a natural reading situation.

(2) *As an instructional tool,* questions are more precisely formulated and logically organized to uncover the author's pattern of thought, develop discussion, and clarify meaning.

Questions also serve to evaluate learning, but in these situations, questions are primarily concerned with the content rather than the process of reading, and for that reason will not be considered at this time.

It is the teacher's responsibility to understand these two separate functions of questions so that she may use them independently and concurrently in appropriate situations to stimulate thinking and help the student increase his awareness of the reading process. To do this, it is essential that the teacher first decide for which of these functions she will be using her questions. Her purpose will determine what types of questions to ask and how to formulate them. In each situation, students should also be made aware of the purpose of the questions. Otherwise, they perceive questioning as testing and the classroom atmosphere is charged with tension as the teacher conducts a threatening inquisition instead of a natural discussion.

DIAGNOSTIC QUESTIONS

As a diagnostic tool, questions are formulated to elicit the maximum response from an individual. In analyzing his response, the teacher gains insight into his process of reading, which provides a basis for planning appropriate individual instruction. In obtaining evidence of the student's ability to select, organize, and relate ideas gained from reading, Strang[4] has long advocated the use of the free response. In her study of reading interests and patterns, she used as a stimulus the question, "What did the author say?" This question is purposely somewhat vague in order to leave the subject free to express his habitual response to printed material. From analyzing the responses to this question, she concluded that all aspects of reading are involved in answering it, thus giving the most revealing single picture of the individual's reading ability.

More recently, this unstructured question has been used to diagnose reading proficiency by Gray and Rogers[5] in their study of mature readers.

[4]Ruth Strang, *Explorations in Reading Patterns.* Chicago: University of Chicago Press, 1942.

[5]William S. Gray and Bernice Rogers, *Maturity in Reading.* Chicago: University of Chicago Press, 1956.

Adapting Strang's stimulus question, "What did the author say?", and a scale for rating the responses, their diagnostic procedure also emphasized more encouragement of the free response and less dependency on formally structured questions.

While the formulation of the unstructured question poses no difficulty, the analysis of the response does require the teacher to be skillful in identifying which reading skills appropriate to the material should be noted in the response. Among the insights revealing reading proficiency, the teacher may note the following:

1. The student's approach to a reading passage
2. His tendency to relate ideas rather than merely seize on isolated details
3. His ability to uncover the author's pattern of thought
4. His ability to organize and show the relation among details
5. His tendency to let his emotions or prejudices and personal experiences influence his comprehension
6. His tendency to relate what he reads to other knowledge he has gained
7. His ability to communicate in writing what he has gained from reading

Diagnostic questions, then, reveal rather than conceal individual differences.

INSTRUCTIONAL QUESTIONS

As instructional tools, questions serve the purpose of guiding the reader to select, organize, and relate the author's pattern of thought during or following the reading experience. In these situations, questions are primarily concerned with identifying the types of thought relationship developed to unify the content. In other words, the central purpose of questions at this time is to focus on the process rather than the content of reading.

How is this accomplished? First of all, the teacher must be able to analyze the author's structure of thought to identify the type of relationships around which he has organized his ideas. For example, ideas that are related through comparison will be identified through key word combinations such as: *some-others*; *either-or*; *as-so*; *one-both*; *all-none*;

few-many. In this instance a question may ask for a comparison in which details are related according to likenesses and differences. If a contrast is stressed, then the question asks for a response in which just the differences are related. Frequently, details are related in a time sequence, as indicated by key words such as *long ago, later, now.* In this case, the question is formulated so that the response relates details to indicate development and/or change. In other thought patterns, sequence according to process rather than time is significant. Here the student reports details logically organized in a specific series of steps. Other types of relationship are cause-effect; problem-solution; main idea-detail. In each case the type of relationship suggests the formulation of a single question which requires the student to select and relate relevant details in his response rather than a series of specific questions which elicits a simple yes-no answer or an isolated factual detail.

Profitable instructional questions then guide and clarify various types of relationship which result in comprehension. Discussion begins with a global question which focuses on the essence of the selection and serves as a point of departure for evolving further related questions which serve to clarify, modify, or illustrate meaning. Challenging questions stimulate students to report relationships among ideas and lead to fruitful discussion. Here more time is spent in listening and supporting answers to questions than in asking them.

If the effective reader is a questioning reader, more and more opportunity should be given to students to formulate and analyze questions themselves. Perhaps in this changing world of expanding knowledge, it is more important to learn how to formulate significant questions than it is to know all the answers.

What effect does training in the formulation and use of questions have on teaching performance? Here are some insights student teachers at the University of Arizona have reported:

1. One of the most important things this experience has taught me is not to expect a particular answer. I feel very strongly that the diagnostic question should allow a *free* response. When I first started, I would keep on asking different people if they know *the* answer when I didn't receive the answer I had decided was logical. I often found myself, having run through the whole group, giving the answers myself with loaded questions. Now I accept all ideas and then have students refer to the text in search of evidence for the best answer. The students read with much

more comprehension and enter into discussion more enthusiastically now, for there is a real controversy to solve. They understand that any of the reasons could be possible but the question is which ones can be justified.

2. In becoming aware of the importance of questions during my semester of student teaching, I have noted several changes in approach. Before presenting the story I try to begin with at least one free response question and other supplementary questions. I've noticed that the pupils have more to say lately, and with more expression. I have also found that one effective question seems to lead to another as if it were a natural sequence so there's more continuity in our discussion. I feel I have also applied this knowledge in answering pupils' questions. When they ask questions about their work, I try to answer them with instructional questions in return, instead of answering their questions without stimulating thought.

3. From actual instruction, I found that the children were "detail" oriented. I mean that most of the questions were asked primarily to find out if the children knew the specific facts in a particular selection. I found in my own instruction that not enough questions were thought-provoking and that they did not promote inductive reasoning or divergent thinking. The questions did not cover many of the comprehension skills, especially inference, conclusion, and generalization. After observing and asking general questions over a period of time, I did initiate some action in formulating questions in the instructional situation. I have seen results in increased interest and enthusiasm. In teaching the proper motivation and keeping the pupils' interest is essential. The most useful technique I have found to develop motivation is thought-provoking questions.

4. I have used the information from this class almost every day in my student teaching. I used to be the type who would try to diagnose and prescribe on the basis of impressions, suspicions, feelings. I wasn't always wrong or right; that is beside the point. However, I was inaccurate, non-specific, and possibly unjust in some of my decisions. I now feel more professional. I now have a specific process to follow no matter what the reading material may be. For that matter, the process applies to many instructional areas other than reading. Making my decisions about diagnosis and prescriptions on the basis I now use, gives me a sense of

security. I feel I could explain and justify what I am doing to a parent or a principal now, much better than I could before.

I now try to give my students a guide to their reading by having them ask questions before they read. After they have read, we spend more time listening to the answers to questions than we do asking them. I attempt to ask them questions which will guide their future reading, and I think I notice an improvement in attitude and in reading. This approach takes reading beyond interest and makes it challenging no matter what the material is.

(33) DEVELOPING CRITICAL READING POWER THROUGH NEWSPAPER READING*

Carl Sailer

My favorite way to start developing critical reading power through newspapers is with a careful consideration of the claims made in advertising. Let us look at a few examples to see several things which can be done to stimulate thinking about what has been read in an ad.

INTRODUCING OUR JENNY LIND
COLLECTION EARLY AMERICAN
ELEGANCE IN LAMPS
$24.88 to $35.88
Regularly $32.50 to $44.95

"How do you read this ad?" can be the opening question. Differing interpretations will get the discussion going. Does this advertisement mean that the lamps were formerly priced at the higher figures and are now reduced? That may be the impression some uncritical readers get, and that may be the one the writer wishes to create. But the ad does not say that the lamps have been marked down, and we readers would be well advised to consider the "regularly" as mere "sales talk"—if not purposefully misleading.

*Reprinted from *Forging Ahead in Reading* 12, Part I (1967 Convention Proceedings), pp. 118–22, by permission of the author and the International Reading Association.

In the same category is "usually." Other phrases to be wary of include: "manufacturer's list price," for it is a misleading price to be marked down from; "special bargain," for it has little value; "special purchase" *may* indicate a real sale with savings but, "specially priced" has little validity. From this study of the meaning of words in varying situations it is an easy step to the fascinating fabrication of the realm of semantics, a step which can be an enjoyable and revealing excursion.

Now what about this ad?

STIR, PUREE, GRATE, CHOP,
MIX, BLEND, LIQUEFY
This 5-cup Oster blender has 8 recipe-tested speeds
You get 4 bowls at no extra charge
SALE $39.88 reduced from $49.88

Questions: Believable? Reasonable reduction? Verifiable?

Thinking: The original or standard price can be easily checked at another store. The reduction is probably less than the usual markup, the difference between the store's purchase price and selling price. It is, therefore, believable.

There are complications, however, when we read about a toaster reduced from $13.99 to $10.99 when no brand name is given and when we cannot check the stated original price. Moving from the relatively simple to the more complex, read this ad on a much higher priced article.

MINK JACKETS
SALE-PRICED TOMORROW
$400 $500 $600

With every fur you receive a guarantee regardless of price. We'll replace and repair skins that wear out through natural causes for two whole years from date of purchase. We'll refund your money in full for any reason at all up to six weeks from date of purchase.

Intelligent buying requires the aid of critical reading and critical thinking. After cost and need have been considered, comparative shopping must be done. The critical reading problem involves untangling terminology such as natural cerulean, bleached white mink, natural blue mink, silverblue, natural pastel, autumn haze, ranch, dyed, let-out, etc.

The critical reading problem continues with this question: What does the guarantee mean in terms of protection? What does it mean to the purchaser and does it mean the same thing to the advertiser? Interpret "natural causes." Does this phrase mean ordinary, daily, double or normal wear? What does "wear out" mean? Does it mean completely worn out or worn through or easily visible or somewhat ragged or shabby or what? Can it be both replace *and* repair or must it be replace *or* repair? Who decides? Here there is room for close reading and closer reasoning.

By design I would not talk about the refund aspect of the guarantee, I would wait for a student to mention that this ought to be discussed. But if I did not get the question from the group, I would raise it myself.

THE 3-C AND THE 3-D WAYS

A critical reading of the ads is not quite so simple as it seems at first sight. To protect our own best interests, we must be able to distinguish the good ad from the poor, the better ad from the bad, and the best from the misleading. This skill demands both penetration and reservation, much intellectual penetration and more mental reservation. My further recommendation is that every reader use the 3-C and the 3-D ways of critical reading or critical decoding. The 3 C's are careful, circumspect and critical. Careful means cautious, thorough; circumspect means considering all sides; critical means involving skillful judgment as to truth and merit. All these are dictionary definitions. The 3 D's are decode, dissect, and discount; decode the advertising jargon; dissect minutely the terminology; and discount the claims.

Armed with a sword having the blade of keen penetration and the handle of substantial reservation, protected by the breastplate of 3-C and the buckler of 3-D, with all these on your side, you are ready to engage in an interesting and challenging "battle of wits" with the ad writers. Be advised that they are sharp and that you, too, will need to be. Be sharp—stainless steel sharp—and cut your cost of living. With a little practice in this critical reading skill you can "eat higher on the hog" and "live beyond your means" without landing in jail.

If better living were indeed to be the outcome, then I agree with *The Wall Street Journal*, "The best thing that ever happened to an advertising program: a creative (critical) reader."

CARTOONS: THE MORE MANAGEABLE MATERIAL

Assuming you have reluctant readers and you are looking for easier and more manageable material, try starting with cartoons. Regular cartoons, better known as "the funnies," could be a point of departure from which to go to editorial cartoons. Ask the students to point out the absurdities and the incongruities which they see in such three-to-four panel cartoons as *Nancy, Ferdinand, Donald Duck, The Girls, Big George,* and *Grin and Bear It.*

Several examples will suffice, Nancy and two of her friends are at ski school, and the instructor appears on the scene with his arm in a sling, bandages around his head and left leg, and using a crutch as a ski pole. He says, "Now for the first lesson." If the students make application—even current and localized—of the main thrust of the cartoon, be prepared to concede the truth in whatever degree it exists. Some of us do teach writing but do not write well. Some of us do teach reading without doing too much of it. And let's not talk about speaking or listening. Are we teachers good listeners in our classes?

Ferdinand is paddling up the river in a birch-bark canoe, and he is passed by an Indian going down stream in an rowboat propelled by an outboard motor. (Title the cartoon "Curriculum"?) Donald Duck, stranded on a tropical island, sees a huge wooden packing crate float up to his little island refuge. His unpacking reveals a compact auto from which he uses the tires for his raft. The last panel shows Donald paddling away—to home presumably. (Whither, Education?) Two women, passing a taxi stand, say, "Since our husbands want us to economize this year, why don't we just walk the five blocks to the hat shop?" (Fill in your own title.) In a school room a mother, accompanied by her son, is saying, "I don't see why Junior is a problem, Miss Finch! Good grades are due to heredity and bad ones to poor teaching."

EDITORIAL CARTOONS AS TRANSITIONALS

These cartoons would of course be fun, but they would also be mild, intellectual gymnastics for flexing somewhat flabby mental muscles. They could be introductory to editorial cartoons, which demand a mature type of interpretation. Let me try to describe one of these in a few sentences. One is a picture of a hallway showing several doors with names on them and 1968. One door has Nixon's name on it and outside is a pair of spiked running shoes. The next door down the hall has what appears to be Romney's name and a pair of shoes—not spiked. Further down the hall is an indistinct name and a pair of loafers. Here there are a few subtleties to challenge the mind.

A second editorial cartoon is a drawing of an auto speeding down the highway with two passengers, Mr. Taxpayer and Mr. Economy. They have just passed over a road-wide wire which leads up to a timing device and a motorcycle policeman named Income Tax Hike who is standing behind a billboard labeled Prices. "I think you slowed down just in time," says Mr. Taxpayer. Some knowledge of rising prices and inflationary pressures is needed here to stimulate thinking.

"Then high school, college, marriage, Vietnam . . ." says the father to the mother about the baby in the crib. With this situation most high school students can identify and react.

Editorial cartoons, not side-by-side with an editorial, are intermediate ("funnies" first) to editorials and commentaries by columnists. Start with an editorial which has a cartoon to accompany it, probably on the same page. Discuss the cartoon first and then the editorial.

Seated at a desk is a man labeled Congress holding a report entitled "President's Plan to Finance Educational and Non-Commercial TV." Another man standing beside the desk is urging "Why not? After all, we're dealing with a disaster area!" The editorial is called "For Better TV" and offers comments on a number of points: shortcomings of commercial TV, excise tax on new TV sets, diverting income from satellite relay of commercial TV, how to spend the limited funds of $9 million, and freedom from government interference. Even if there is agreement that there should be more educational and non-commercial TV, there is obviously plenty about which the students can read critically and react. Read and react. Read and think. These are the key processes.

THE CRITICAL READING CONCEPT

And isn't this what we want when we try to develop critical reading power? Don't we want the students to weigh and consider, to reflect upon, to line up the pros and cons, to assess the value of the arguments and reasons, to assay the fine metal in the ore, to determine the strong and weak points of the exposition, and to run up a box score of the runs, hits, and errors? This, then, brings me to my major premise: Reading is thinking, and critical reading is critical thinking. A companion basic idea, if not a corrollary, is that teaching must result in student thinking; i.e., teaching is student thinking.

Now it will be easy to "get students going" on another companion cartoon and editorial, for it is about Adam Clayton Powell. Here the teacher's problem will be to keep the discussion on the track and to slow it down so that it can be looked at thoughtfully and thoroughly, completely and deeply. Here the teacher's problem will be to keep down the heat and friction and to turn on the light, enlightenment, and tolerance. A difficult and monumental task! One possible way is to use a wide range of different newspapers so that several editorials, a number of columnists, and many points of view are represented and available. This task will constitute a real test of critical reading, critical thinking by the students, and a stern test of masterful teaching. It is here that the teacher must be a superb example of a rational appraisal of all the facts and all the arguments given on both sides of the question.

But do not try one as difficult as the Powell discussion is bound to be until you have done a number of others on less emotionally charged areas, ideas, or persons. Both the teacher and the students need practice before they plunge. Here you will have to feel your way and be sensitive to the stage of development of the ability of your group to discuss subjects more rationally than passionately. Perhaps California's Clark Kerr represents a good intermediate step between educational TV and Powell.

The Powell controversy had its center in the East, whereas the Dr. Clark Kerr case had its origin in the University of California. Both cases, however, became national and international. Both are fine but difficult material for students practicing the art of critical reading and thinking. The student has to function in reading on at least three different (but not necessarily distinct) levels: He must first comprehend, then interpret, and finally evaluate. Any reader must first understand what has been said; secondly, he must be able to interpret its significance; and then he must evaluate its importance. Without this depth of three-fold reading, a student cannot be said to be reading critically. And he must have the patience to learn how. This will entail a great deal of practice from day-to-day, over an extended period of time, and on many kinds of materials.

OTHER ELIGIBLE MATERIAL

What are some of these materials over and beyond the ads, the cartoons, the editorials, columns, controversial issues, and persons? Several present themselves immediately: political news; the sports pages, particularly sports editorials and columns; certain kinds of news articles and stories where there is an admixture of straight, strict reporting coupled with unwarranted editorializing; feature and human interest stories; and certain special, syndicated features and columns.

Most certainly the student must be exposed to the two (or more) sides of the political news, to a Republican and a Democratic newspaper, to a conservative and a liberal point of view, to the sports pages, editorials, and columns of more than one newspaper. The student must be taught how to detect the intrusion of opinion into news items where it does not belong. He must have repeated practice in discovering it for and by himself. To better understand illicit editorializing the student might try his hand at writing an opinion-filled news story. Human interest and feature news stories can be evaluated against a background of "hard news." The syndicated columns and special features offer golden opportunities for critical reading.

USE PLENTY OF EXAMPLES AND DISCUSSION

While learning the art of reading critically and creatively is going on—with its daily ups and downs, its monthly progress and regressions—the teacher must practice patience. He must have understanding and insight, give opportunities for reactions and encouragement to thinking, and be exemplary. In fact, and in the final analysis, the teacher may have only two major functions to perform in terms of developing critical reading power: exemplification and discussion. Set the example many, many times and give all the students time to talk and plenty of time to discuss. With these two "fists" a strong teacher can knock out "Knuckle-Head," the non-critical reader.

(34) CLUSTERING COMPREHENSION SKILLS TO SOLVE PROBLEMS*

Althea Beery

Implicit in the wording of this topic are several assumptions: 1) that elementary children can solve problems and that it is desirable for them

*Reprinted from *Forging Ahead in Reading* 12, Part I (1967 Convention Proceedings), pp. 109–115, by permission of the author and the International Reading Association.

to have training in doing so; 2) that reading will help in children's inquiry; 3) that comprehension skills in reading are necessary in this quest; 4) that these skills are not separate and disparate but tend to cluster around related skills. Let's examine these assumptions for a moment.

First Assumption: Elementary children can solve and should have training in solving problems. Those of us who have worked with children need no further evidence that children *can* attack problems and that, within the limits of their experience and a challenging situation, they enjoy the opportunity with considerable success. Research backs this up (17, 22). In fact, the characteristics and attitudes favorable toward inquiry can be developed in quite young children. Banta (2) has built and is norming a test (CATB) for children from three-to-six years of age that measures the following characteristics which he considers significant for problem solving and believes to be amenable to training: curiosity, exploratory behavior, persistence, resistance to distraction, control of impulse, reflectivity, analytic perceptual processes, and innovative behavior.

Second Assumption: Reading helps in children's inquiry. Provided that children have the requisite literacy skills, reading is an important tool which children use in problem solving, whenever their search extends beyond their previous experiences or one immediately at hand, including observation or inquiry of adults or other children (21, 26). How limited, indeed, their search for answers to their problems would be without access to the printed page.

Third Assumption: Comprehension skills are necessary for solving problems. Children use a great variety of comprehension skills when they read to find answers to questions, including reading for general ideas, for significant details, for the author's plan of development, to summarize, to judge or evaluate, to identify possible solutions and test them out, to use reference skills, to get the literal meaning of a sentence or paragraph, etc.

Fifty years ago Thorndike (28), from a study of errors which elementary school children made in reading single paragraphs, concluded that reading a single paragraph with understanding involves many elements of thought, including the weighing of words in terms of the context, the organization of each element in its proper relation to others, the selection of certain connotations of words, and the rejection of others. He said that in effective reading the mind selects, softens, emphasizes, correlates, and organizes—all under the influence of the right mental set or perspective. He compared the processes required in comprehending a paragraph to those of solving a problem in mathematics.

Fourth Assumption: Comprehension skills are not used separately but tend to cluster. Fortunately for children and teachers alike, these skills can be grouped around basic steps involved in problem solving. They do not need to be taught in isolation. In fact, for the most part, they should be developed together. A flexible reader shifts from one skill to another as he gains insight into the nature of the problem, the difficulty of the reading matter, and its development by the author and as he develops or rejects "hunches" he has concerning the best solution. Not only does the understanding of what is read involve many of the higher mental processes it also involves them in close conjunction with one another. As the situation demands, we analyze, organize, criticize, reject, reason, and judge with one process merging imperceptively into another and employing the appropriate reading or study skills.

WHAT PROBLEM SOLVING INVOLVES

Where does problem solving fit into all this? Reading to solve problems is never a simple form of comprehension. It involves many of the skills needed for critical reading. Indeed, problem solving *is* a form of critical reading although it may impose more restrictions than some other types of careful reading. Dale (5) gave *problem centered* as a characteristic of critical reading.

The essential steps in problem solving have been listed in different ways by authorities in reading and psychology. In this article, they have been classified under those centering around the problem itself, locational skills, comprehension of the printed page, organizational skills, evaluation of materials in relation to the problem, and finally, application of findings so that attitudes, values, and behavior are changed.

THE PROBLEM SITUATION

Reading for problem solving emphasizes the *purpose*, in this case the problem to be answered. Whether the problem originates with the introductory material in the text, with the teacher as an assignment, by the class setting the problem, or even with an individual pupil himself is not crucial, so long as the child accepts the problem as his own. The clarification of the problem may include exploratory reading and class discussion or some other method of sharpening so that the direction of the search is clearly defined.

If the solution of a problem is to call forth effective reading, the problem or purpose must have relevance to the pupil and his interests. Roma Gans (9) in a landmark study discovered that high achievement on a standard test is no guarantee that the pupil has the ability to reject material which does not contribute information on a selected topic. It should be equally clear that the problem should not be so simple as to require no thought or investigation nor yet so complex that it cannot be truly understood; nor should the reading materials and thought processes involved be too complex for him to handle. If reading is to be a part of problem solving, there must be appropriate material available.

Location of Suitable Reading Materials

In the early elementary grades, guidance may well be given in a group situation with children reading a given selection in search of pertinent facts. Or, following the reading of the selection, the group may discuss whether the facts in the article supported or contradicted information gleaned from a previous selection.

For a successful quest, a child must have at his command a variety of reference skills such as using a card index in the library, a dictionary, an encyclopedia, chapter headings, side headings, and the index of a book. None of these abilities is spontaneously acquired. On the other hand, neither does each of them have to be taught meticulously and sequentially to every child in every class. Needed, of course, is a teacher who is adept at diagnosing the level which different pupils have attained in these skills and at knowing when to give guidance in a particular skill to an individual, a small group, or even the entire class.

Comprehension of Material Read

In the first place, comprehension in any real sense involves the ability to recognize words and attach meanings to them in relation to other words and their function in an English sentence. The richer the word meanings, the more likely that full comprehension will be achieved.

Except for a small minority who would *limit* the term "reading" to simple decoding of letters to sounds, there is general agreement that reading involves getting information from the printed page. Many persons call this "literal comprehension." Edgar Dale (4) calls it "reading the lines." A few writers would also include under literal comprehension some elements of the higher thought processes, such as seeing the relationship between ideas and sensing the purpose which the writer had in mind. Constance McCullough (15), in an article in a recent issue of *Elementary English,* points out how necessary to even literal comprehension is the knowledge of our language and how it works, i.e., *linguistics.* She illustrates with the following sentence: "In . . . its . . . hose-like . . . gray . . . trunk . . . the . . . little . . . figure . . . on . . . the . . . match-box . . . carried . . . a . . . Republican . . . banner." In her own inimitable way she gives the steps which the listener or reader might take in understanding this sentence—cumulative, tentative, revised steps with later words in the sentence modifying or expanding earlier meanings. The example illustrates that the reader leans heavily, although often unconsciously, on his knowledge of our language and how it patterns itself.

ORGANIZATION OF MATERIALS

Too many children read along absorbing the ideas as they appear without building mentally an outline of the selection. Studies show that children tend to read all material at the same rate, regardless of their purpose or of the nature of the material itself (6, 12). Certainly, as elementary teachers, we are responsible for helping children decide whether a particular selection should be scanned rapidly merely to locate material which is important in the solution of a given problem or should be read more carefully for pertinent matter. At the same time children must carry in their minds some feeling of where this point fits into the general problem. At first this activity can probably best be done as we guide a group of children in reading a common selection. Later they should be responsible for the same activity when reading or studying independently. Certainly by the end of the elementary school at least the better pupils should be able to organize the information which they have obtained from several sources without duplicating ideas.

EVALUATION OF MATERIALS READ

In a third-grade-class discussion about wild animals, one child said in response to another's statements, "But that isn't a *fact.* I read something different in another book." This remark led naturally to a discussion of which author was better qualified to make such a statement and to a comparison of the copyright dates of the two books. Further investigation involved the use of additional books and encyclopedia and included an interview with the director of the local zoo. Of course, pupils do not always need to go this far in deciding between fact and opinion.

In evaluating, the reader must constantly check the statements of the author against what he has learned from experience or other reading. As he reads critically, he weighs what the author said and challenges his ideas. He notes whether the author is making sweeping generalities which he does not back up with sufficient facts or whether he uses propaganda devices. The reader follows the author's line of reasoning and accepts or rejects his conclusions. He asks whether the material is written from a biased point of view. Studies have shown that young people color what they read by their own attitudes and biases (3, 11, 16, 18). Even so do we as adults. The least we can do is to be on guard against letting prejudice color our own reading and to be committed to giving pupils opportunities to weigh what they read or hear reported on the scales of objectivity in an honest search for truth.

APPLICATION

When children are reading to solve a problem they test what they have read by checking whether they have solved the problem they set for themselves. Young children are tempted to accept the first solution that they find. Older boys and girls are increasingly able to hold hypotheses tentatively and to test them more logically. Even when they have reached an apparently satisfactory solution, they learn to limit it by a statement such as, "This seems to be the answer . . . ," *or* "As far as we can find out, the solution seems to be. . . ." Gray (10), Gans (8), and others stress the fact that reading should make a difference in attitudes, values, and behavior. When children read wisely and thoughtfully and reach a conclusion, they must learn to incorporate it into their attitudes and values, contingent upon subsequent experience and evidence from further reading. Too few of us act on the basis of what we have learned from our reading. We should teach children to stand up and be counted when a controversial problem they have studied is under discussion. Further, reading should influence what children *do*. For example, it is of little use for a child to learn how bacteria are spread if he continues to be negligent in personal cleanliness, the handling of food, and the like.

PROBLEM SOLVING RELATED TO SUBJECT FIELDS

Whatever the content field in which reading is done to solve problems, it will require certain comprehension skills. Examples are recognizing and understanding the general and technical vocabulary; getting the sense of the material; evaluating it in the light of the purpose or problem, such as judging the relevance and worth of the ideas; and seeing the relationships among ideas.

Granted that there are comprehension skills common to all content areas, there is still variation from field to field in the skills to be emphasized. The nature of the reading material and its function tend to differ from subject to subject, as Nila B. Smith and others have pointed out (23, 24).

Science and Arithmetic

Science and arithmetic texts are typically compact in form with a rather heavy burden of technical terms and with precise, sequential steps to be followed. Usually a varying but slow rate is required (7).

Social Studies

Social studies materials can often be read at a faster pace, but not always. Frequently, the pupil must interrupt his reading to study a picture, a graph, a chart, or a map. Cause and effect, especially in historical writing, must be traced. Here, too, authenticity is important (14, 20).

Children's Literature

We are accustomed to think of critical, evaluative reading in relation to arithmetic, science, and social studies—the so-called content fields. Recently, increased emphasis has been placed on analysis and a more probing interpretation of literature by children. Some of us have feared that this emphasis might result in lessening children's love for good stories and books, if such analysis is within their powers. Evidence is accumulating, however, that with careful selection of materials and wise guidance elementary children can learn to use the problem solving approach in evaluating materials: comparing characters in two books with similar themes, tracing the development of plot and character, and reacting to the quality of a selection. Children seem to enjoy savoring the appropriate word and the vivid description and examining the point of view of the author. All this without lessening their competence in reading and at the same time increasing the range and amount of voluntary reading! An interesting study has been in progress at Ohio State University under a grant from the U.S. Office of Education (13, 29, 31). In fact, this study group has developed and normed a test on the critical reading of literature. The study was a comprehensive one which included control groups and guided classroom observation. To members, evaluation of literature to be valid must be done in accordance with criteria, hopefully criteria which the children have helped to set up.

Children compared Madeline, quite a character but always the same, with Crow Boy who changes believably into a more mature yet still shy boy. They learned how to identify realistic *vs.* imaginative roles. They found that trying their hands at writing their own modern folk tales or fables enhanced their ability to discriminate. Such problems as why the author chose to write a story from a given point of view proved interesting and profitable.

Van Gilder (30) found that the differences in the skills required in various fields lie not so much in the materials themselves as in the type of thinking required. He rejects the notion that the reading act can be packaged, parceled, or isolated into separate compartments. The teacher not specifically charged with the development of reading power may take comfort from Artley's (1) statement that the teacher need only ask himself, "What competencies must my students have to carry out the learning tasks in this course as I teach it?"—and then, presumably, help students build the competencies when lacking. We would hope that the tasks set would frequently be problem solving in nature.

INQUIRY AS AN INDIVIDUAL MATTER

Suchman (27) defines inquiry as learning that is initiated and controlled by the learner himself as a means of expanding his own understanding. He believes that the more active, autonomous, and responsible the learner becomes for decisions regarding the collection and interpretation of the information, the more meaningful the learning and the better motivated the pupil. Stauffer (25) also distinguishes between group and individual inquiry.

CONCLUSION

In summary, can children in the elementary grades be taught to use reading and other modes of inquiry to solve problems? The answer to this question is affirmative (19)—granted that young children, as indeed any of us, cannot think beyond the acquired experiential background and that they do not always have the verbal skills with which to express their ideas; their thinking nevertheless, does not vary in kind from that of adults.

Problem solving skills are not limited to reading. If we wish children to use these skills when they do read, we must capitalize on every opportunity for them to develop a spirit of inquiry through manipulation, observation, conversation, and discussion. Situations throughout the school day and in out-of-school life give countless opportunities for children to practice the skills involved in critical thinking. As adults, we must permit differing opinions and cherish a questioning attitude.

A recent convention of this Association was centered around the theme "Reading and Inquiry." *The Annual Proceedings*, issues of *The Reading Teacher*, and other IRA publications, contain numerous articles related to critical, discriminative reading, many with practical suggestions for classroom procedures. Let us apply what we have read and what our experience has taught us as we guide children's reading in the classroom. If we do, in addition to *who, what,* and *when* questions, we will add ones which ask *why* or *how*. We will release imaginations as we give such leads as *I wonder why . . . ? What if . . . had not finished his job?* Above all, we will strive to create an atmosphere in which "reading between the lines" and "reading beyond the lines" (4) are taken for granted, a climate in which children's ideas are encouraged and examined. In these ways we make reading and all learning an adventure which leads to lifetime commitment to inquiry.

REFERENCES

1. Artley, A. Sterl. "Influence of Specific Factors on Growth of Interpretation," *Reading: Seventy-five Years of Progress*. Proceedings of the Annual Conference on Reading. H. Alan Robinson, (Ed.) Supplementary Educational Monographs. Chicago: University of Chicago Press, 1966.
2. Banta, Thomas J. "Tests for the Evaluation of Early Childhood Education: The Cincinnati Autonomy Test Battery (CATB)," *Educational Therapy*, Vol. 2, Special Child, Chapter 2 (in press).

3. Crossen, Helen J. "Effects of the Attitudes of the Reader upon Critical Reading Ability," *Journal of Educational Research*, 42 (December 1948), 289–298.

4. Dale, Edgar. "The Art of Reading," *News Letter*, 32 (December 1966). Columbus: Ohio State University, School of Education.

5. ———. "The Critical Reader," *News Letter*, 30 (January 1965). Columbus: Ohio State University, Bureau of Educational Research and Service.

6. Ellinger, Bernice, and Charlotte Huck. "Does Johnny Evaluate?" *Grade Teacher*, 82 (March 1965), 101–105.

7. Fay, Leo. "Reading Study Skills: Math or Science," *Reading and Inquiry*, International Reading Association Conference Proceedings, 10 (1965), 92–94.

8. Gans, Roma. *Common Sense in Teaching Reading*, Indianapolis: Bobbs, Merrill, 1963.

9. ———. *A Study of Critical Reading Comprehension*, Contributions to Education, 811. New York: Bureau of Publications, Teachers College, Columbia University, 1940.

10. Gray, William S. "Theme of the Conference," *Promoting Growth Toward Maturity in Interpreting What Is Read*, Supplementary Education Monograph 74. Chicago: University of Chicago Press, 1951, 2–5.

11. Groff, Patrick J. "Children's Attitudes Toward Reading and Their Critical Reading Abilities in Four Content-Type Materials," *Journal of Educational Research*, 55 (April 1962), 313–318.

12. Herculane, Sr. M. "A Survey of the Flexibility of Reading Rates and Techniques According to Purpose," *Journal of Developmental Reading*, 4 (Spring 1961), 207–210.

13. Huck, Charlotte S., and Martha L. King. "Observation of the Critical Reading of Children," *AERA Paper Abstracts*, American Educational Research Association, 1967, 45.

14. Huus, Helen. *Skill Development in Social Studies*, 33rd Yearbook of the National Council of Social Studies, National Education Association, 1963, 94–113.

15. McCullough, Constance. "Linguistics, Psychology, and the Teaching of Reading," *Elementary English*, 44 (April 1967), 353–362.

16. McKillop, Anne S. *The Relationship Between the Reading Attitude and Certain Types of Reading Response*, Contributions to Education. New York: Bureau of Publications, Teachers College, Columbia University, 1952.

17. Payne, Rebecca. "Primary Children Can Solve Problems," *Childhood Education*, 41 (May 1965), 479.

18. Piekarz, Josephine. "Getting Meaning from Reading," *Elementary School Journal*, 56 (March 1956), 303–309.

19. Raths, Louis E., *et al. Teaching for Thinking: Theory and Application.* Columbus, Ohio: Charles E. Merrill, 1967.
20. Robinson, H. Alan. "Reading Skills Employed in Solving Social Studies Problems," *The Reading Teacher*, 18 (January 1965), 263–269.
21. Russell, David H. "Research on the Processes of Thinking with Some Applications to Reading," *Elementary English*, 42 (April 1965), 370–378, 432.
22. ———. *Children's Thinking.* Boston: Ginn and Company, 1956.
23. Smith, Nila B. "Patterns of Writing in Subject Fields I," *Journal of Reading*, 8 (October 1964), 31–37.
24. ———. "Patterns of Writing in Different Subject Fields II," *Journal of Reading*, 8 (November 1964), 97–102.
25. Stauffer, Russell G. "Reading as a Cognitive Process," *Elementary English*, 44 (April 1967), 342–348.
26. ———. "Reading as Experience in Inquiry," *Educational Leadership*, 24 (February 1967), 407–412.
27. Suchman, J. Richard. "Learning through Inquiry," *Childhood Education*, 41 (February 1965), 289–291.
28. Thorndike, Ed. L. "Reading as Reasoning: A Study of the Mistakes in Paragraph Reading," *Journal of Educational Psychology*, 8 (June 1917), 323-332.
29. Usery, Mary Lou. "Critical Thinking through Children's Literature," *Elementary English*, 43 (February 1966), 115–118, 120.
30. Van Gilder, Lester L. "Meeting Reading Demands of the Content Subjects," in *Vistas in Reading*, J. Allen Figurel, (Ed.) International Reading Association Conference Proceedings, 11 (1966), 39–42.
31. Wolfe, Willavene. "Teaching Critical Reading to Elementary School Children," *Paper Abstracts.* Washington, D.C.: American Educational Research Association, 1967, 44.

Chapter 8

ATTITUDES AND VALUES— AFFECTIVE DIMENSIONS

INTRODUCTION

If all the reading programs in the United States were to be analyzed today, what would be the relative emphases given to the development of various reading and reading related student behaviors by such programs? Although one can only hypothesize about the results of the proposed study, it seems reasonable to conjecture that the vast majority of reading programs in operation today place far greater emphasis on the development of word analysis and comprehension skills and abilities than they do on the affective behaviors related to reading.

There appear to be at least three reasons why such a finding seems plausible. First, approximately 60 per cent of our elementary schools do not have libraries. This means that a variety of reading materials are not readily available to teachers and students for classroom use. The net result of a school without a library may very well be a sterile reading program built around one, two, or, at the best, three sets of instructional reading materials. Second, word analysis and comprehension skills and abilities in reading are fundamental to academic success in our schools as they are presently constituted. In other words, students do not have to enjoy or appreciate reading, although it obviously would help, to be successful academically. Third, word recognition and comprehension skills and abilities are relatively easy to evaluate while affective reading behaviors are not. Consider, for example, the standardized reading achievement tests used by school systems to evaluate the success of students, teachers and reading programs. How many such tests give even a passing nod to the assessment of affective behaviors related to reading? The answer is none.

With these assumptions in mind, the present chapter was designed to highlight the importance of helping students to value reading. It suggests ways to develop (a)interest and taste in and appreciation for literature, (b) interest in reading as a leisure-time activity, (c)appreciation for the contributions reading can make to self-realization and self-fulfillment, and (d)the ways in which affective behaviors related to reading might be evaluated. The point of Chapter 8 is, then, to encourage teachers to evaluate for themselves the significance of placing adequate emphasis on developing students who appreciate reading for what it is.

(35) READING INTEREST:
A FUNCTION OF THE LAW OF EFFECT*

William Eller

One reason, among several, for the widespread conviction that teacher training courses are easy and lacking in worthwhile content is the disarming notion that much of the psychology of teaching is just "common sense." When a student in an educational psychology course, for example, hears the instructor's explanations of the law of effect—the principle of rewards and punishments—he may think that he has nearly always understood this principle and may feel so confident of his understanding that he allows his attention to drift. Later, an examination may reveal that the student apparently did not understand the law of effect thoroughly, either before or after the classroom explanation.

While many of the principles of learning and teaching seem fairly obvious when presented by a good methodologist, they are not sufficiently obvious that most people could formulate them, even in everyday language, without some instruction. And these common-sense learning principles which are allegedly so apparent are often poorly applied by practicing teachers.

If a student in a college classroom overestimates his awareness of the principles of learning, it may not be very important at that moment. On the other hand, it appears that many American children and adults have *learned* their lack of interest in reading, at least partly because of faulty application of the common-sense laws of learning in schools.

It is, of course, possible that lack of interest in reading is not a problem of sufficient magnitude to provoke an examination of its causes. There are abundant statistics which show that increasing numbers of books and magazines are published and sold in this country, that more than 90 per cent of adults read a daily newspaper, and that library services are being extended in various ways. Whenever educators wish to silence a Rudolf Flesch, they point to the mounting sales of children's books and to the superior performances on reading achievement tests by pupils of the present generation. All these items indicate that Americans have both the ability and the materials to read if they wish. However,

*Reprinted from *The Reading Teacher* 13 (December 1959), pp. 115–20, by permission of the author and the International Reading Association.

they must have the inclination to read, and the research into the reading actually performed by Americans suggests that this inclination is often lacking.

Presumably, young adults provide the best indices of school success in developing a life-long reading interest, because young adults are no longer directly guided by the school in their reading habits, yet the attitudes toward reading which they developed in school should still influence them. Berelson (1) reported a survey which revealed that during a given month a group of high school students averaged about three times as much use of the library as a matched group just out of the secondary school (and not in college). Fifty-six per cent of the adults in this same survey sample indicated that they had been more active library users when they were in school. Berelson further reported that among a group of young women who had recently graduated from high school and who also indicated that they were not current library users, 90 per cent had possessed library cards when they were in school but had allowed their cards to lapse.

Of course, library usage is not a perfect indicator of reading interest, because reading materials can be acquired from many other sources, and because some would-be users do not have access to a library. Further examination of the research removes the relief which may be offered by either of these explanations, however, as Campbell and Metzner (2) discovered that more than half the adults in the nation live within one mile of a public library, yet less than a fifth of them had visited a library during the year preceding the survey. While reading materials can be acquired from other sources, the evidence indicates that much of the adult population is not inclined to read books or the higher level magazines. Link and Hopf (4) found that the nonreading half of our population reads only 6 per cent of all books consumed. As for the reading of the serious magazines, last year *Harper's* reported the results of a survey of its readers which demonstrated that they are a highly select group (3).

Scarcely anyone who had examined research of the type cited would argue with the observation that a large proportion of Americans do not read very much printed material of quality. Because reading interest is not a convenient experimental variable such as chronological age, it is rather difficult to determine the extent to which interest or the lack of it influences the differing reading patterns of active readers and non-readers. However, when adults in the Campbell-Metzner sample were asked why their use of the library had declined since their younger years, 65 per cent responded to: "Read less; less interested in reading." It seems safe to conclude that a majority of students do not possess a lasting reading interest when they leave the schools. Many have unwittingly been taught to avoid reading because they have encountered a succession of teachers who adhered to certain out-dated practices and ignored the implications of the common-sense laws of learning.

Consider the law of effect. It might be paraphrased to state that when students are rewarded through their reading, they will tend to read more in the future; contrariwise, if they are unrewarded or punished by reading, they will be less likely to turn to reading in the future. Presumably, any time a student receives satisfaction from reading, his attitude toward reading matter in general, and toward the teacher who led him to the particular satisfying reading matter becomes more favorable by some amount, however small. The primary reward in reading comes from the information or entertainment (or both) which satisfies the reader's motives for reading. A secondary type of reward which may be associated with reading comes from teacher, pupil, or parent approval or praise springing from outward evidence of the reading.

If a student is to achieve a life-long interest in reading as a result of the rewards received in school, the preponderance of these rewards should be of the direct sort, since the less direct rewards are not so likely to be earned, once the reader has left the schools. Thus, the twelfth-grade reading program should strive to provide students with direct satisfactions from reading, and should not depend upon social rewards, such as giving certificates for the reading of a specified number of books.

If teachers can strengthen reading interests by leading pupils into articles and stories which are intrinsically rewarding, they can also minimize or destroy interest in reading by teaching procedures which either reduce the magnitude of the reward or actually constitute a type of punishment. Assume that a pupil has read a book which was highly satisfying to him: his interest in reading this particular type of material is at a peak. But his teacher requires students to prepare extensive formal book reports of each book they read. After a young reader has completed two or three such reports the prospect of future book reports is so distasteful that he is reluctant to read any books that are not required. The formal book review in this case has become a punishment strong enough to offset the anticipated rewards of further reading.

Through the use of less formal, more imaginative methods for book reporting, the teacher could have extended the rewards—and interests—instead of stifling them. For example, if two pupils had read the same story or book, they might be invited to prepare a simple dramatization of a particularly exciting or amusing portion of the story for their class-mates—perhaps a mock radiocast or crude puppet show. With this more creative means of reporting on books the readers receive first the intrinsic reward yielded by the story and then the secondary rewards of classmate approval and even self-expression.

Another sort of punishment which can be inflicted upon young read-ers is the routinized study of the lives of authors. The pleasures of many a story have been wiped out by a teacher's insistence that students examine the life of the author according to a standard procedure which does not vary from one author to the next. Students' retention of information about an author's early life and his other not-very-important works is rather poor, although their failure to remember is not as disturb-ing as the damage to their general reading interest.

Instead of hampering reading interests through uniform study of the biographies of almost all authors whose works are to be read, teachers can reinforce reading interest by more extensive, but flexible, consider-ation of just a few authors whose lives were either particularly interest-ing or conspicuously reflected in their literary efforts. In its seventh-grade basal reader Ginn exploits this strategy with interesting treatments of episodes in the lives of Mark Twain and Armstrong Sperry.

Still another punishment which can offset the rewards of an interesting bit of prose or poetry is over-analysis of the meaning of small segments of the writing. Sometimes teachers, anxious to be certain that the stu-dents understand a literary selection, spend considerable time on the microscopic probing of a single phrase or word. "Why did the author use this particular word?" or "What did the writer mean by this phrase?" Quite often the teacher can only speculate wildly as to the reasons for an author's choice of words; indeed, sometimes the author himself could not answer the question directed to the student readers. Admittedly, there are occasions which call for analysis of prose or poetry selections in order to clarify subtle meanings, but even the better-than-average student some-times appreciates a story best as a whole and may find it less appealing and meaningful under analysis.

Most of the punishments mentioned in preceding paragraphs are somewhat specific to instruction in reading and literature. The depend-ence on a single textbook for reading material in all content fields represents another application of the principle of rewards and punish-ments as it relates to interest in reading. When a teacher relies upon a basic textbook to provide all or almost all the reading content for a given course, no allowance is being made for the varying reading abilities represented in the class (unless the school classrooms are organized homogeneously by reading ability). If the textbook is two or three levels too difficult for the poorer readers, it is quite apparent that the assignment constitutes a punishment for them, as far as reading interest is concerned. The declining reading interest of the poor reader is a near-perfect illustration of the law of effect.

The single textbook assignment if not embellished with supplementary reading materials can also affect adversely the interest of the excellent reader. If a teacher of eighth-grade science assigns a text chapter on electricity and magnetism, the top-flight readers in the class will, of course, read it in just a few minutes. A thoroughly unenlightened teacher might then "punish" these good readers for their efficiency by suggesting that they read the assignment again, although certainly few teachers would make this error. More commonly, the good readers just remain unchallenged as they proceed to some sort of busywork. For some of them, there was not even any appreciable reward in the content of the assigned chapter, because they were good students and already knew more about electricity than the chapter divulged. If these outstanding eighth-grade readers are to receive rewards from their science reading, they must be provided with content that answers the questions that matter to them, questions that go beyond the conceptual level of the eighth-grade textbook.

Reliance on a single textbook deprives young readers of rewards since the single text provides no opportunity for critical reading. If the textbook constitutes an undisputed source, students have no chance to observe that authors differ in their emphases, differ on minor points of detail, and occasionally differ on major philosophical views. The element of controversy which weaves in and out of the lessons on critical reading is quite invigorating to many juvenile readers. Sometimes a critical reading exercise takes on the flavor of a game, and thus interest is rewarded in much the same way that it is in games and contests.

Compared to the single textbook assignment, then, the differentiated reading assignment in content subjects would appear to help the young reader learn increased interest in reading in these ways:

1. The differentiated reading assignment provides more opportunities for the student to be rewarded by the intrinsic values of the reading material.

2. Unusually good or poor readers are rewarded instead of punished, since they read materials which have value for them.

3. The poor reader gleans more from his reading, is able to make a

greater contribution to class discussions, and is thus rewarded both by his own sense of achievement and by his classmates' approval.

4. Elements of controversy in critical reading lessons excite students and provide rewards in a number of ways, including some that are not clearly defined.

The logic which requires differentiation of content field reading assignments also underlies the need for materials of various levels for recreational reading. If anything, a range of difficulties is even more important among the recreational materials, because there is less teacher help available and the pupils are motivated to read mostly by their own interests, not by teacher-made study guides.

Four or five years ago the principal of a small high school in Oklahoma realized that the great bulk of his students were below-grade-level readers. As part of his plan to upgrade reading ability throughout the high school he placed in the library a number of easy books, including the American Adventure Series. In this school of ninety students, the (then) fourteen titles of his series were checked out thirty-nine times in a single week, and by the end of the semester they were worn to the point that they had to be replaced. Some teachers, knowing that the books in the American Adventure Series are designated for grade levels from second through sixth, might be horrified to find them in a high school library. It may very well be that the reading ability of some of the pupils in this Oklahoma backwoods community could properly be described as horrifying, but the principal acted wisely when he provided easy, interesting material for the library. With easier materials many students enjoyed for the first time the rewards of reading for pleasure, and while they continued to read easy material for a time, the general level of reading ability and taste steadily improved in that high school.

Certainly one of the best ways in which a teacher can reward and strengthen a pupil's interest in reading is through personal effort to locate materials which will be likely to appeal to the pupil, and to place them in his hands with the suggestion that he will find the contents to his liking. The difficult element in this procedure is the requirement that the teacher know considerable about the interests, habits, and hobbies of each pupil. Once this information is acquired, the teacher can be on the lookout for books and articles of interest to specific readers. The search does not necessarily require a great deal of time; in fact, it may work better if the teacher tries only to keep each pupil's interests semiconsciously in mind, so that when suitable materials are encountered they will be recognized.

When a teacher takes the trouble to present to a pupil material that obviously reflects some concern for his interests, the situation can be very rewarding. In addition to the yield from the reading itself, his ego benefits from the personal attention. There is probably no better way to reward and increase interest in reading.

There are assorted additional reasons for the lack of reading interest among so many American children and adults. Some of these reasons hinge upon rudimentary principles of learning, others upon principles which are not clearly understood at present. The obstructions to reading interest which have been considered in this discussion exemplify the fundamental law of rewards and punishments, a principle which teachers and prospective teachers consider to be rather obvious. These few reminders of the negative results achieved when the law of effect is ignored in the development of reading interest may alert some teachers to employ methods which maximize the rewards and minimize the punishments accompanying reading.

REFERENCES

1. Berelson, Bernard. *The Library's Public.* New York: Columbia University Press, 1949.
2. Campbell, Angus, and Metzner, Charles A. *Public Use of the Library.* Ann Arbor: Edwards Bros., Inc., 1950.
3. Fischer, John. "The Editor's Easy Chair," *Harper's*, 217 (Sept., 1958), 14–20.
4. Link, Henry C., and Hopf, Harry Arthur. *People and Books.* New York: Book Manufacturers Institute, 1946.

(36) DEVELOPING INTEREST AND TASTE IN LITERATURE IN THE ELEMENTARY GRADES*

Helen Huus

WHY CHILDREN READ

Why will children read? For the same reason they will do anything: because they really want to. But what makes them *want* to read becomes

*Reprinted from *Reading as an Intellectual Activity* 8 (1963 Convention Proceedings), pp. 46–50, by permission of the author and the International Reading Association.

a complex question to answer, for the basic motivation of individuals varies greatly. There are at least five good reasons that lead children to read books.

Our Culture Expects It

First of all, in America our prevailing culture, both in and out of school, demands that children learn to read—and then read. In fact, that is why most of them look forward to school, particularly first grade, because now they will at last learn to read.

Children who have pleasant experiences with reading at home will want to read. As they see other people reading, it becomes only natural that they also do. A four-year-old, whose lawyer father was always quoting from his legal journals, surprised his family at a dinner party one evening by asking the guests if they had seen the new article about trucks in the latest *Saturday Evening Post.* When they admitted they had not, he said that after dinner he would be glad to show it to them. So when the time came, he produced the magazine, turned to a big double-page spread containing an ad with two huge trailer-trucks, and proudly showed the guests the "new article" on trucks. Reading? Yes, to him, at this level. "Reading" picture books is only the beginning, however, but with the fancy fare available today, who wouldn't want to read?

Older children, too, read because it is expected of them, just as mother reads the books required for her Book Club and father keeps up with the AMA *Journal,* the company's house organ, or the "Union News."

So, the first essential in getting children to read, if they do not, is to submerge them in a reading environment where they cannot escape reading. Surround them with good books—and I mean literally—on top of, inside of, underneath. Read yourself, read to them, get parents themselves to read and to children. Then, just try teaching one whole day—perhaps you can last only one period—without reading. You'll see—so will the children!

To Satisfy Curiosity

Another reason why children will read is to satisfy their curiosity. Children by nature are curious. If you are skeptical, follow a three-year-old around for a day and tabulate how many times he asks "What's that?" or "Why?" Unfortunately we adults get too busy to appreciate these active little minds and brush off the questions with a hurried half-answer. This leads children to conclude that asking is a bother, and they better find out for themselves. So by the fourth grade, or so, they have learned so well *not* to ask, that to get them started again often poses a problem for teachers. Books will help satisfy their curiosity, though sometimes perhaps to excess, as in the case of the now-classic story of the boy who returned the library book with the comment that this book told him "more about penguins than he cared to know!"

What can children learn from books? Just about anything from archaeology to zebras, about the world they live in, today and long ago, about how things work, about interesting experiments.

To Help Solve Problems

That books can help solve problems is a third reason why children will read, for they, too, find in books ideas that help them in learning how to act and in learning how to work with other people. A book that comes to mind first is *The Hundred Dresses* by Eleanor Estes, with pathetic little lonesome Wanda Petronski, who wore the same faded blue dress to school each day but bragged that there were a hundred in the closet at home. Not until she had moved away and the drawings of her hundred dresses won the art contest did the class feel sorry for the way they had treated her.

Older boys and girls alike thrill to the way in which Johnny Tremain finally faces up to his problem of having a maimed hand and becomes a young man with a purpose and a goal. That the story is laid during the American Revolution and has historical events and characters is also interesting and helps children feel that this all could have happened; but the real import of the book is Johnny's growing up.

Helping children adjust to new circumstances—new mothers, adoption, new homes, chronic illness in the family, and other problems of living—can often be done better through a book that preserves the child's privacy, yet gives him courage and suggests a course of action for him. And it is often through story friends that children gain an image of what they would like to be themselves.

For Escape

Children will also read to escape. Quite soon some learn that reading is considered by their parents as a legitimate use of leisure time not to be interrupted for errands and chores, as television is. So they escape work.

Others escape into books when it is too rainy to play outdoors, or when they want to prolong the actual turning out of the light at night. Adults escape to evade making decisions, to "kill" time, or to take one's mind away from vexing problems. And often what serves as escape literature for one is serious reading for another.

Children may use fairy stories and fanciful tales as a means of escaping into a world where the villain is always punished and everyone "lives happily ever after." One of the amusing modern fairy tales is *Many Moons* by that master of the whimsical, James Thurber. The Princess Leonore wants the moon, and the King wants to get it for her so she will be well again. But when the Royal Mathematician is asked to get it all he does is list the things he already has done since 1907. But this does not help, and the King summons the Court Jester, who neatly solves the problems by asking the Princess what she thinks. Children are delighted when this underdog of the court turns out to be so clever.

Adventure and mystery stories are often escape literature for children, as are the series books and comic books. But if they read quality books as well, I would not worry. The teacher's job is to see that there are books enough.

For Fun

The most important reason why children *will* read I have left until last. Of course they read for fun! And there are books that provide all sorts of fun, from the hilarity of Dr. Seuss to the gentle glow engendered by Little Bear, Winnie-the-Pooh, Mole in *Wind in the Willows*, or Little George in *Rabbit Hill*.

The lure of books is often their illustrations, and a book like Helen Borten's *Do You See What I See?* helps children understand what lines, shapes, and colors can be and do.

The appeal of sound and rhythm is found both in prose and poetry. Ann Nolan Clark's *In My Mother's House* conveys—through the steadiness of the beat, the repetition, and the simplicity—the stability of the Indian and the security the little girl feels as she describes her Mother's house. The cadence of the prose in James Daugherty's biographies, particularly, I think, in *Abraham Lincoln*, is most fully savored when read aloud.

Enjoyment is composed of many things—appreciation of beauty, the feel of words rolling around one's tongue, the sounds that tumble over one another, the protectiveness of large and able creatures for the small and weak, the buoyant good humor of healthy, happy children, with the added spice of nonsense.

So I maintain that children *will* read, because we expect them to, in order for them to satisfy their own curiosity, to help solve their problems, as an escape, and just for fun. But we must give them good books they can read and a chance to read them!

HOW TO DEVELOP TASTE

According to Webster "taste" is defined this way:

> The power of discerning and appreciating fitness, beauty, order, congruity, proportion, symmetry, or whatever constitutes excellence, esp. in the fine arts and belles lettres; critical judgment, discernment, or appreciation.[1]

Elsewhere I have recently reported the research studies that relate to the development of taste, and so I shall not repeat them here.[2] But what I shall do is to suggest ways (based upon the research findings) by which you can help children progress to higher levels as they continue reading.

To begin with, children have what might be called an "indigenous taste." When given a chance to choose, they usually prefer that which is good. A fourth-grade teacher found this out when she collected four versions of Pinocchio and put them on the reading table: the comic book, the Walt Disney version, one of the "rewrites," and a standard translation containing the original illustrations by Attilio Mussino. Later, when she asked which one she should read to them, the children immediately wanted the "regular" edition—the version that has made it the classic it has become. They recognized the quality of the detailed descriptions and the development of plot that made the story good.

Although children do have inherent good taste, there is still room for improvement. They must learn to recognize *why* one book is superior to another: what is appropriate and congruent, what has order and beauty, proportion and symmetry as they look at and compare books. But before they can do this, they need first to understand what they read, and here is where the basic reading skills loom so important. Their lack can hamper

---

[1] *Webster's New International Dictionary of the English Language.* Second Edition. Unabridged. Springfield, Mass.: G. & C. Merriam Co. Publishers, 1957, p. 2585.

[2] Helen Huus, "Developing Taste in Literature in the Elementary Grades," *Elementary English*, XXXIX (December, 1962), pp. 781–789; XXXX (January, 1963), pp. 56–67.

a child from reading a book he really *needs*. But once he reads it, he then must become involved in the book—really live it with the characters the way many third-graders do as they silently weep when Charlotte, the spider heroine of *Charlotte's Web*, gasps her last breath, or the way older children rocket off into space with Robert Heinlein. Once the reader becomes involved, he is aware of the quality of writing—vivid images, believable characters, a fast-moving plot or at least one that has things happen, a satisfactory ending, and throughout, a basic ethic that recognizes enduring values and moral right. These are little Puritans, these children!

SURROUND THEM WITH BOOKS

The easiest way to improve taste is just to put enough good books where children find them. And if you are clever and know your children well, you will "plant" those books on their pet interests right where they can find them—the Bronson book on *Turtles* for the budding zoologist; a biography of Byrd or *Mr. Popper's Penguins* for that Antarctic fan; *Children of Odin* for that one who loves adventure stories, and so on. By making such quality books available and by judicious recommendations, you can do much to keep them reading.

BE ENTHUSIASTIC YOURSELF

When teachers get excited over books, it rubs off on the children—even on college students. I regularly find that my students in children's literature read those books I promote, and one term there was a student who waxed eloquent on "ants." Never before nor since have so many students read the "ant books" as they did that term! Nor is it any wonder that a child who knows you have read a book will want to discuss it with you when he finishes it. And so you get an oral book report without even an assignment.

Then there was the sixth-grade boy who could hardly wait to tell me, for I was a rather regular visitor to the class, all about *Atoms and Molecules*, which he said was the best book he had read recently. Fortunately, I also had read it recently, and we could share our ideas; but as I left the room, the teacher shrugged her shoulders and said, "I don't even know what he's talking about." My first thought does not bear repeating in this company, but it seems a pity if teachers cannot (or worse yet, do not want to) understand what even a good elementary pupil can.

READ TO CHILDREN

Even the most naive student teacher learns quickly that the best way to get the group quiet is to start "Once upon a time. . . ." And this fondness for listening to good stories does not stop with the elementary grades. Adults listen to Lynn Fontanne reading "The White Cliffs of Dover," or to Robert Frost or Carl Sandburg or Dylan Thomas or any number of other poets reading their own poems. So read to children regularly, every day, and more than once a day if you can squeeze it in. What you start reading in class they will get from the public library and be finished long before you are, but will savor each chapter none the less the second time they hear it.

Poetry, of course, is meant to be read aloud, and besides, it has the advantage of being varied enough in length to be easily fit into the many little "in-between" periods of the day.

PRESENT LITERATURE LESSONS

Plan your lessons so that children learn what makes books good. Spend time on descriptive phrases, idiomatic language, or figures of speech.

Or plan a series of lessons that will relate the books or poems to music and art. In one sixth grade, the teacher used the record "The Glow Worm" with the poems "Fireflies" by Fawcett and "The Firefly" by Elizabeth Madox Roberts.[3] In another class, the teacher played "The Anvil Chorus" from Verdi's *Il Trovatore* and used Rosa Bonheur's picture, "The Blacksmith," with Longfellow's poem "The Village Blacksmith."[4] (You can almost date this report from these titles!) Annis Duff reports similar experiences in her book *Bequest of Wings*, which is a description of their family's reading together.[5]

BUILD LADDERS OF TASTE

Finally, but not really the last for there are many other good ideas, gradually introduce the child to better and better books. Get the girls to go from *Nancy Drew* to *Misty of Chincoteague*, to *Caddie Woodlawn*, to

[3]Fern H. Bowes, Florence Painter, and Vesta Lynn, "Use of Recorded Music to Introduce Literature to Children," *Elementary English Review*, XIX (May, 1942), pp. 178–180.

[4]Merrill Bishop, "Appreciation Classes in Sixth and Seventh Grades," *Elementary English Review*, IX (June, 1932), pp. 151–152.

[5]Annis Duff, *Bequest of Wings*. New York: Viking, 1944.

The Three Musketeers, as Dora V. Smith suggests.[6] Or counteract the comics by substituting the bold and exciting Norse myths—like the edition by Sally Benson—and they are well on their way.

Why do children read? Because it serves their needs at the time until the habit becomes so fixed that they feel cheated if they cannot continue. And how do teachers help? By saturating the environment with books, by showing enthusiasm for books themselves, by reading aloud to children, by presenting lessons that focus on the qualities that make books literary or that relate them to the other arts, and by gradually leading children to books of progressively higher quality. Thus is taste developed, and thus do children come into their inheritance.

(37) A COMPREHENSIVE LITERATURE PROGRAM*

Charlotte S. Huck

Great stress is given to the teaching of reading in elementary schools, and all of us agree to its vital significance. Less attention is given, however, to providing children with the opportunity to read widely once they have developed fluency, and almost no attention is given to the quality of what children read. Individualized reading promises the time and opportunity for extensive reading but it in no way guarantees the quality of children's reading. Too frequently, teachers and students are impressed with the quantity of books which have been read rather than the quality of the experience in reading the book. It is not the number of books which we have read which is important, but the number of books which we have read that have made a difference in our lives.

Those of us who know and love children's literature realize that there are many such significant books in the juvenile field. Frequently, however, the great books may be hidden from view by the forest of mediocre ones which appear on the market each year. Teachers complain that they do not have time to read and evaluate the some 1500 new titles which represent the yearly output of juvenile literature. Parents, if they buy books at all, buy what is readily available in supermarkets, drug stores,

---

[6]Dora V. Smith, cited in Ruth Strang, Constance M. McCullough and Arthur E. Traxler, *Problems in the Improvement of Reading*. New York: McGraw-Hill Book Company, Inc., 1955, pp. 150–152.

*Reprinted from *Children, Books and Reading*, Perspectives 3, 1964, pp. 111–20, by permission of the author and the International Reading Association.

and airports. These books are not our best children's literature—far from it. All that is golden may not glitter. I am convinced we are raising a generation of children that are over-Seussed with Seuss, but how do parents choose? Even the suggestions of the sales persons are no longer available since most of the book sections of department stores utilize self-service. Children's librarians continue to be the greatest source of information and help, but there are far too few of these.

Children themselves have established few guidelines for selecting their books. Frequently they make their choices by the picture on the cover, the title, the amount of conversation or the size of the print. Even the best readers are not discriminating readers. A fifth grader may thoroughly enjoy Virginia Sorensen's beautifully written story, *Miracles on Maple Hill*, and the next day be equally engrossed in a Nancy Drew mystery.

There is nothing wrong with reading a mediocre book, except as it robs you of the time which you might have spent in reading a better book. Time in a child's life is a precious commodity, particularly since the period of childhood is so limited. Time controls the amount of reading a child does each day, and the length of the period in which he is interested in reading children's books. Both of these aspects of children's time for reading are decreasing. First, children's days are so filled with dancing lessons, French lessons, homework and TV that there is less time for children to read. Secondly, children are growing up faster than they used to and they are beginning to read adult books at an earlier age. As C. S. Lewis so aptly said in *The Last Battle*, we spend all our time rushing to reach the age of eighteen, and the rest of our lives trying to stay that age. The favorite books of one sixth grade, for example, were *Gone With the Wind* and *The Diary of Anne Frank*; most of these students had ceased reading children's books. We seldom catch up with the books which we missed as children, for no adult voluntarily reads Gag's *Millions of Cats* or Gates' *Blue Willow*. If children miss reading or hearing a book at the appropriate age for them, it is generally missed forever. Today, with the number of titles available, it is quite possible for a child to have read widely and never have read a really good book. The quality of children's reading experiences should not be left to chance alone. They should have an opportunity to choose from a wide variety of excellent books; hopefully, they should receive some guidance in making their selections and interpreting their reading.

Literature is one of the few areas of knowledge which receives very little attention in the elementary school. Many teachers consider the teaching of reading and the development of literary appreciation as synonymous. They are not. Some teachers believe that if you provide ample time for free reading, children will automatically develop literary taste. They do not. Naïvely I once assumed that if children were exposed to many books, they would learn to compare and contrast them, to become critical readers. Now I am sure this does not happen. We have no wide-spread literature program in our elementary schools when we compare it with our carefully planned developmental programs in reading, spelling, arithmetic and the social studies. Only a seriously planned literature program from kindergarten through grade twelve can begin to develop the kind of discriminating readers which are needed for our modern world.

MAJOR PURPOSES OF A COMPREHENSIVE LITERATURE PROGRAM

Developing a Love for Reading. The development of a love for reading should be a prime purpose of a literature program. Teachers have been more concerned with teaching children *to read* than with the development of children who do read. And yet Russell (5) suggests that if a child has not developed the *habit* of reading by the time he is twelve years old, the chances are pretty good that he will not do so. While there are some studies (4) which indicate that both American children and adults are reading more than they have ever read before, other studies would indicate that our reading habits are woefully inadequate. For example, in one study (6), nearly one-half of the adults in the United States had not read one book during the year. Another one contrasted American reading habits with that of adults in other countries and found that only 17 percent of the Americans had been reading from a book the previous day whereas 55 percent of the English sample had been engaged in this activity (2). This fact leads to a major concern—what are the reading habits of teachers.

A teacher can do much to stimulate an enthusiasm for reading; she can also do a great deal to militate against it. The enthusiasm of the teacher who loves books is always contagious. She will share favorite books with boys and girls and provide time for them to share their favorites with her and with each other. She will not penalize a child for reading a book by requiring him to write a book report on every book he completes. Nor will she demand tangible proof of his reading the book by requiring a project for each one. Why must we always *do* something with every book we've read? There is a place for an occasional mobile or diorama depicting the scenes from a favorite book, but some classrooms become veritable mobile jungles and defeat the very purpose of creating interest in books. Dora V. Smith (7) points out that "The reading interests with which pupils come to school are our opportunity but the reading interests with which they leave school are our responsibility."

Knowledge of Our Literary Heritage. A second major purpose of the literature purpose is acquaintanceship with our literary heritage. Such knowledge begins with literature for children. Common literary allusions have their origin in children's stories and if we have not read those books, the meanings are not clear. Think of such common expressions as:

Mad as a hatter	Cheshire grin
Sour grapes	Your man Friday
Whitewash your fence	Lilliputian
Goose that laid the golden egg	Insatiable curiosity
"Don't count your chickens before they're hatched"	

Acquaintanceship with mythology, folklore and legends is also necessary to the future understanding of many literary allusions. The roots of all literature are derived from the primitive beginnings of the folk tale, fable, myth and legend. It is these stories which show children that the concerns of man today are exactly the same as they were before recorded time. Man is still searching for a satisfactory explanation of his beginnings and his end. Trial and triumph, fear and hope—these are the elements of myth and of life itself.

Children develop common reference points as they share modern day literature also. One sixth grade boy made a telling point in a heated debate on book censorship by suggesting that censorship was the beginning step of giving in to *IT*. All the children who had read *A Wrinkle in Time* recognized his reference and his point. A shared experience with a book had given these children a common set of values and criteria by which to judge a particular act.

Certain modern stories build a foundation and a readiness for some of the books which belong to our classical heritage. Today's children should meet Henry Huggins, Homer Price and Henry Reed, before they are introduced to Tom Sawyer and Huckleberry Finn. A knowledge and appreciation for the evocative beauty of Grahame's *Wind in the Willows* is developed best by building an appreciation for animal fantasy with such books as Lawson's *Rabbit Hill* and Stolz's *Belling the Tiger*.

Children who have read George's *My Side of the Mountain* and O'Dell's *The Island of the Blue Dolphin* may be more ready for *Robinson Crusoe.* We must have readiness for what we read as well as readiness for reading itself.

Developing Appreciation for Good Books.—The development of literary appreciation should be a major goal of the elementary school. Bruner (3), in his much discussed book, *The Process of Education*, emphasizes the importance of identifying the basic principles and concepts of each discipline and building upon these in a spiral type curriculum. Children can be taught to appreciate and recognize the elements which constitute fine writing if they have been exposed to good literature from childhood and if these elements of excellence have been discussed. Mere exposure is not enough to develop an understanding of the structure of writing.

Even young children can be helped to appreciate the delineation of the character of *Madeline* or recognize the conflict faced by Mako in Matsuno's *A Pair of Red Clogs* as she deliberately tries to spoil her cracked clogs and deceive her mother. Children in the second and third grades might compare the convincing character development of Yashima's *Crow Boy* with that of the stick-like Bobbsey Twins. Older children can be helped to appreciate the effect of different circumstances and relationships on characters as they contrast the two books by Mary Stolz which present the same story but from different points of view, namely, Stolz's *A Dog on Barkham Street* and *Bully on Barkham Street.* The grim story of the seven Sager children's struggle to reach Oregon in Van der Leoff's *Oregon At Last!* presents authentic background and carefully drawn characters. The enormous responsibility of caring for his six brothers and sisters almost overpowers John's physical and mental strength, and the reader lives every step of that arduous trek with the orphaned children.

Children can be helped to recognize the story that is organic, that is held together with a basic underlying truth. Mere episode or exciting adventure may be characteristic of series books but not of good writing. A comparison of the adventures of any of the Hardy Boys with Sperry's *Call It Courage* would be an enlightening undertaking. Fifth and sixth graders could readily identify the underlying theme of overcoming fear in *Call It Courage*; they might have more difficulty in identifying the inner truth of the Hardy Boys!

For children to develop appreciation for an author's style is more difficult but it can be done. After reading De Jong's *Hurry Home, Candy* and *Along Came a Dog* to one fourth grade, the children identified the author's compassion and deep understanding of animals and people. His ability to create the pathos of the story is established in his opening paragraph of *Hurry Home, Candy*. (Listen to the cadence of that paragraph and compare it with the first five verses of the Book of John: "In the beginning was the Word.")

> The dog had no name. For a dog to have a name someone must have him and someone must love him, and a dog must have someone. The dog had no one, and no one had the dog. The dog had only the silent empty countryside of the few houses. The dog had only the crumbs and cleaned bones he could pick up at the few houses. The dog had only himself, so the dog had nothing, and he was afraid. (14b)

This same group of children understood De Jong's use of the symbolism of the broom to represent everything that was terrifying to the dog. The captain, too, had had "brooms in his life" and this the children knew represented his fears, not actual brooms. The ironic symbolism of the gulls winging free over the ship which brings the chained slave, Amos Fortune (Yates), into the port of Boston has been recognized and discussed by middle graders. Children enjoying knowing and being able to identify some of the techniques of fine writing. They come to understand that by means of symbol and imagery, an author can say more than actual words state.

A beginning understanding and feeling for simile and metaphor could be undertaken with younger children. Tresselt's *White Snow, Bright Snow* contains excellent samples of each in the following passage:

> Automobiles looked like big fat raisins buried in snowdrifts. Houses crouched together, their windows peeking out from under great white eyebrows. Even the church steeple wore a pointed cap on its top.

The new quiet story by Charlotte Zolotow *The White Marble* includes this interesting simile:

> On a summer evening when "the heat sat like a feathered bird over the city" John and Pamela met in the park. (40)

Obviously, primary teachers are not going to have lessons on metaphors and similes, I hope! However, they can savor these passages and help children to visualize them or draw them. As children respond to such metaphor as that in Sandburg's Poem "The Fog," they are beginning to develop a foundation for literary appreciation. Bruner (3) states ". . .

that the foundations of any subject may be taught to anybody at any age in some form."

Developing Socially Through Reading. Personal social growth through reading has always been a major purpose of childen's literature. In a planned literature program, teachers will attempt to unite the right book with the right child at the propitious moment. Introducing a child to a book in which a character faces and solves a problem similar to his own may help him to understand his own problem better and to face it with courage and determination. Reading may help children to explore living, "to try on" various roles vicariously and to accept or reject them as they search for their own identity. Some of our overprotected white children may experience the hurts of prejudice for the first time as they read and identify with the main character in Dorothy Sterling's *Mary Jane* which tells of desegregation in our public schools in the South. Louisa Shotwell's new book, *Roosevelt Grady*, is a poignant story of poverty and prejudice, told with a quiet dignity which will be shattering to the sensitive. Some of the feelings of grief and death may be first faced through literature. How many modern day children have wept at the death of Charlotte, the large grey spider in White's *Charlotte's Web?* Nowhere in children's literature is there a more compassionate statement of the way to help a loved one overcome the pangs of death than the advice given to Juya by his father on what to do for his friend who has just seen Buck's *The Big Wave* engulf his home and family. These books are as real as life itself. They do not preach; they do not patronize. Rather they portray the harsher realities of life in a way which makes their readers more able to face and understand them.

INFUSING CHILDREN'S LITERATURE INTO THE CURRICULUM

The use of children's literature should permeate every curricular area and all teachers should be committed to this objective. Social studies is greatly enriched through reading books which authentically picture the social problems of our world. Children may develop increased appreciation for the educational dilemma of rising nations as they read such books as Arora's *What Then, Roman?* and Sommerfelt's *The Road to Agra.* They can hardly imagine a situation in which only one boy in a whole village knows how to read, or where a thirteen-year-old boy determines to walk 300 miles in order to take his seven-year-old sister to a hospital. Geography books may tell of the immensity of the problems of these nations, but these literary books focus upon the lives of one or two individuals and throw the light of understanding upon the many. History, too, may gain a new perspective through the re-creation of a period and events in historical fiction or biography. Children may be helped to understand that history is always someone's interpretation, as they read Tunis's *Silence Over Dunkerque*. For in this story the author had the courage to admit that our men were sometimes less than brave in their desperate struggle to survive. Children who read books which present different points of view will have a better understanding of their historical heritage than the child who is limited to a single textbook approach. For historical fiction clothes the bare bones of historical fact and makes it come alive. Periods remote in time and place such as England in the days of the Romans and Saxons come alive through the superb writing of Rosemary Sutcliff. Harry Behn's hauntingly beautiful story, *The Faraway Lurs*, makes the people of the Bronze Age believable and authentic.

The words of archeology, anthropology, medicine, chemistry, physics and others have all been presented in children's trade books which enrich the study of elementary school science. The most recent information in these fields can be found in such books, for single titles can be revised much more readily than can a text series or a set of encyclopedias. The amazing flood of informational books is a recent phenomenon in the field of children's literature. Outstanding examples of some of the best of these books include De Borhegyi's *Shops, Shoals and Amphoras*, the young people's edition of Carson's *The Sea Around Us* and Anne Terry White's *Lost Worlds*.

The hearing of much good literature affects the quality of children's writing and vocabulary growth. Creative writing may frequently grow out of children's personal reading. Children may wish to write further adventures of a particular storybook character; or they may create their own story based upon a certain theme in literature, such as Kipling's *Just So Stories*. We have seen the responses which children have made to Mary O'Neill's lovely color poems presented in *Hailstones and Halibut Bones*. Recent research in the development of creativity has demonstrated that we should look at all the possibilities and dimensions of a particular object or event. The poems of Myra Cohn Livingston in *See What I Found* explore many dimensions of such familiar objects as a feather, a rubber band, a key and many more. Young children may be inspired to look at their world in a new way after they have heard these poems.

The Need for a Comprehensive Literature Program. At the beginning of each quarter I ask the elementary education majors in my class of children's literature to list the books which they remember reading as children. Most of them look at me in dismay and then slowly push away the cobwebbed memories of required reading in both college and high school to reveal a pitifully inadequate knowledge of the literature for children. Their lists usually contain Mother Goose rhymes, stories by Dr. Seuss, frequently characters from well-known basic readers, The Bobbsey Twins, Nancy Drew mysteries, Clara Barton stories, sometimes *Little Women*, and *The Little House* books by Laura Ingalls Wilder. Occasionally, one or two students will have very extensive lists that include such well-known classics as *Peter Rabbit, Winnie the Pooh, Peter Pan*, all of the Alcott stories, and modern classics such as McCloskey's *Homer Price*, Brink's *Caddie Woodlawn*, White's *Charlotte's Web,* Lawson's *Rabbit Hill* and many others. Almost invariably, the students who have a rich background in children's literature attribute their knowledge to their family's interest in reading and love for books. Schools appear to have played a relatively insignificant role in leading children into the world of books.

The Requirements of a Planned Program. Obviously, such a comprehensive literature program would make many demands upon teachers, their time and the school program. Only as teachers are committed to the value of literature in children's lives will they give serious consideration to such purposes. They will have to know and love books more than the majority of our teachers do now. Hopefully, the quality of both pre-service and in-service courses in children's literature will be improved. Graduate courses in literature for children need to be offered to the teachers who have not had a course in this area for some twenty years. Teachers should be encouraged to do voluntary reading of children's books and then share their favorites with their colleagues. Surely every teacher could read a minimum of one new children's book a month. Shared with two other teachers at the same grade level, this would add some 27 to 30 new books a year to each one's basic knowledge of the field.

We shall have to have many more books, and many better books than are currently available in the majority of our schools. I predict that the growth of school libraries in the next ten years will be tremendous. Every school needs a central school library, and every classroom needs a small changing group of books immediately available. I am appalled at the money we have spent on school cafeterias, lighted football fields, and inter-communication systems when two-thirds of our elementary schools do not have libraries. The 1960 *Standards for School Library Programs* (1) are not unrealistic and hopefully may lead the way to school libraries for all.

Such a comprehensive literature program as has been suggested here will take time—time for children to read and share books and for the teacher to share books with them. Some schools are already providing the time for such activities, but there must also be purposive planning of these activities. Is there a group of books which we feel elementary students should not miss? Could the teachers in one building or system develop such a working list, from which they could select books to read aloud in the story hour, or books to discuss with their children? Could teachers agree on some basic elements of fine writing, some criteria by which books may be evaluated? Instead of the usual free reading period, teachers could talk with children about their reading, help them evaluate the unique aspects about their books, and make suggestions for future choices. What books will be useful in other curricular areas and how can they be used to their best advantage? These and other questions will need to be resolved as teachers cooperate in bringing children and books together through a comprehensive literature program.

Each and every one of you here love children's literature or you would not be here—but there are too few of us. How can we extend our influence so that the children in schools today will not become the teachers of tomorrow with little or no background in children's literature?

I am reminded of that challenging statement in *What Then, Ramon* when Ramon, the little Indian boy who is the only child in his village that knows how to read talks with his friend, the American lady, and tells her that when he grows up, he just wants to read and read and read. And his friend waits a moment and then says, "And what then, Ramon?" To each of you who have attended this meeting, I can only say. "*And what, now?*"

REFERENCES

1. American Association of School Libraries. *Standards for School Library Programs.* American Library Association, 1960.
2. Asheim, Lester. "A Survey of Recent Research," *Reading for Life.* (Edited by Jacob M. Price). University of Michigan Press, 1959, pp. 3–4.
3. Bruner, Jerome. *The Process of Education.* Harvard University Press, 1960, p. 12.

4. National Society for the Study of Education. *Adult Reading*, Fifty-fifth Yearbook, Part II. University of Chicago Press, 1956.
5. Russell, David. *Children Learn to Read*. Ginn, 1961, p. 28.
6. Russell, David. "We All Need to Read," *Saturday Review*, XXXIX (February 18, 1956), p. 36.
7. Smith, Dora V. "Current Issues Relating to Development of Reading Interests and Tastes," *Recent Trends in Reading* (Edited by W. S. Gray). University of Chicago Press, 1939.

(38) BUILDING LIFETIME READING HABITS IN AN INDIVIDUALIZED READING PROGRAM*

Alvina Treut Burrows

Lifetime attitudes and values are the human responses I should like to try to build rather than habits. It might be wiser to expect habits to change with the years. Lifetimes are longer now than they used to be, and who can say how we'll need to change them by the year 2000? Perhaps instead of going to a library, in the electronic era now aborning, we shall press a button in our home and flash book pages upon a screen standing on our desk within comfortable eye range. But regardless of the format of book, screen, or page; regardless of whether books remain on paper or become a combination of film and electric impulses, and regardless of the size and shape of libraries of the future, I trust that our children now in school will retain their eagerness to enlarge the world of mind and heart through the writing of other minds and hearts.

READING PROGRAMS IN THE CONTEXT OF LONGEVITY

Before proposing some of the ways in which an individually oriented program can contribute to such values, let us look at three directives toward the sequences and the climate in which reading values grow. I

*Reprinted from *Reading and Inquiry* 10 (1965 Convention Proceedings), pp. 151–54, by permission of the author and the International Reading Association.

submit three directives: 1. Start young. 2. Expose the reader to families and friends who love reading. 3. Look long years ahead.

By starting young, I do not mean to begin formal reading instruction at two or four or even necessarily at six. It has never been less important to rush an early attack upon reading than it is today. There are more non-reading sources of learning for young and old in the year 1965 than ever before in human history. Nor does anything in our technology suggest that these sources are about to wither on the vine—the electronic vine, that is—if we can judge by the increase of inventions in the last decade. Pictures in books and magazines and on billboards; pictures on television and movie screens, both indoors and out; pictures on newspapers, on dress fabrics, and on the walls of buildings! The world of graphic symbols has burgeoned beyond the most extravagant predictions of a century ago. In addition to pictures, still and moving, children have more toys to learn from than ever before. Some of them are bad, but some of them are so good that they almost force children into discovery and learning. In addition to the many visual stimuli, are all the media of sound transmission. Indeed, children are often so surfeited by these sources of learning that they tune us out with devastating skill.

Some of the best examples of starting young occur in nursery schools where children live a vigorous program of first hand experience and uses of language for the joys of self-expression as well as for the satisfactions of utilitarian communication. Here are the raw materials and the processes out of which pupils build the knowledge they need to bring order into their booming, blooming world. Here they forge the concepts that are the life-links of reading. When three- and four-year-olds play out the daily work rhythms of Farmer Small, along with planting gardens (or at least window boxes); when they visit a farm, see and hear a tractor, see and smell the cows and watch the milking done either by hand or by machine, they are blending reality into words spoken and heard, words seen in books, and ideas shown in pictures.

The second directive proposed before, to expose readers to others who read, takes us into the sociology of persuasion by example. I need not remind you that high achievers in reading quite generally come from reading homes. Since we seem to learn our values from those who value us, it is axiomatic that children whose parents love them and who also love books, are likely themselves to become readers. Statistics bear out the logic of this observation.

When a community supports its libraries and uses them widely, a reading climate becomes pervasive. It is natural to see people carrying books, going in and out of libraries and book stores, and to hear parents, friends and neighbors talking about books. These are part of the accustomed and visible signs of literacy. Where these activities do not go on, both schools and children are at a disadvantage. Exploration is sorely needed today of ways and means of making reading important in adult affairs. Today's emphasis upon literacy all around the world may well open up opportunities for research in this essential matter. Many a town could today be lead to see the economic importance of libraries and reading that would have scoffed at the idea some years ago. From economic values to humane ones is a road often traveled.

My third directive, to look ahead, means to look to the years that are no longer assigned to old age but to "dynamic maturity." The term has already been popularized as a movement, an organization, and as a magazine title. The name holds importance for anyone alert to the role of reading for new life designs. How much of social interaction do octogenarians want tied into their reading? What changes should the older reader expect in himself *as a reader?* Whatever the changes may be, flexibility as to purpose and content seems certainly to be related to age as well as to youth. With the ever extending life span, it behooves us to learn as much as we can about beginning and sustaining the individual as a reading person from his first efforts with print throughout life.

HOW INDIVIDUALIZED PROGRAMS
FACILITATE LIFETIME READING

Where does an individualized program of instruction fit into this lifelong sequence? What are its unique potentials in contributing to the lifetime of a person who increases the maturity of his reading as he increases in age?

By making learners' choices and decisions central in the instructional program we are increasing the potential for lifelong reading, for reading is inescapably concerned with making choices. One must choose what one reads, what to pursue during the process, and afterwards, what use to make of it. Whether one needs mere literal information, whether one wants to weigh accuracy or values inherent in what one has studied; or whether one feels compelled to make a creative response of some kind, the choices are the readers'. Or they should be! Often decisions are so rapid as to seem intuitive. At times, selection of response is more deliberate. In any case, reading to be profitable must engage the individual in making decisions.

I propose that an individualized program has a better chance to further the making of decisions than does any other organization. I do not stake an exclusive or a monolithic claim here, but I do propose that any organization that does not consciously provide for a broad range of decision-making by the learners, thwarts the actual process of getting meaning from the printed page. Choices involve selection of content, rate of work, purposes in reading, and overt or covert responses. In a well individualized plan, the reader most often works in a solitary fashion. Sometimes he elects to read with a group. Occasionally he is assigned to work with others on a specific common need, but he helps to decide when and if the goal has been reached. And even in a directed study group, the individual can and should find his own purposes, bring them to consciousness, judge his own success, and the value or appropriateness of his processes. But the novice spends most of the available time in reading by himself, and for himself, even if the goals are as social as finding a good story for the class to dramatize. If reading is to be a lifelong affair, such personal identification with the process—through making and testing choices time and time again—is of the essence.

Specifically, the satisfaction of making choices contributes dynamically to the reader's self-image rather than threatening that image. Selection, we are told, is never accidental. Given some range of content to choose from, what a child chooses is *on purpose*. Compensating for deficit, extending oneself or consolidating gains, exploring human relations, seeking new knowledge, escaping pressures, enjoying adventure or excitement; in any case the values are personal. Reading that helps an individual build himself in positive ways rather than lessening himself in his own eyes has a good chance of survival in his life design.

One of the specifics through which this process operates is through identification with characters met in print. The girl who reads and becomes one with the heroine of *The Island of the Blue Dolphin*, or with Wanda of *The One Hundred Dresses* takes something of their strength into her own fibre. The boy who helps Little Toot withstand the buffeting of wind and tide to get the liner off the rocks is never quite so fearful again. He has stood a test; he has proved himself adequate. Children reach out for such opportunities at home and at school and inevitably in books. We need to know infinitely more about this complicated process of identification as a literary comprehension skill. Without it there is little appreciation, if any. How it works precisely, eludes us. But the opportunities for identification rest in no small measure upon choice of what is read as well as how to respond. Contribution to one's image of one's self, to the pursuit of lifetime reading are inextricably intermeshed.

In answering the two questions as to how an individualized program of instruction fits into lifetime sequences of reading, and of what its unique contributions are, the values of personal choice, of exposure to almost infinite variety of content and style loom large. But above all, in my judgment at this moment, is the importance of identification. Little understood as it is psychologically, the poets have committed themselves to it long ago. One of the recent assertions of this route to understanding is to be found in Paul Engle's sonnet about his daughter. "She became these books," the poet-father says of his child.[1] We, too, have been made by the books we have read. As teachers, may we continue to make and to re-make ourselves and to help youth to find joy in their own building.

(39) EVALUATING THE AFFECTIVE DIMENSION OF READING*

David W. Darling

THE AFFECTIVE DOMAIN

Thanks to extensive research, quite a lot about teaching the cognitive reading skills is known. Due to the lack of extensive research, very little about teaching for affective behavior in reading is available. It appears that we have fallen into the trap of which John Mann recently warned; we are putting all our energy into that about which we know the most at the expense of that about which we care the most (3).

Four things must be done to correct this deficiency: (a) teachers' editions and manuals of reading textbooks must put greater emphasis on

[1]Paul Engle, *American Child.* New York: The Dial Press, 1956.

*Abridged from *The Evaluation of Children's Reading Achievement*, Perspectives 8, 1967, pp. 127–41, by permission of the author and the International Reading Association.

affective questions and testing; (b) extensive research must be carried out to bring about a balance in what we know about both the affective and cognitive aspects of reading; (c) pupils' affective growth in reading must be tested and reported; and (d) teacher education programs should be expanded so that those entering teaching will have competence in teaching the basic skills and in guiding the learner's affective development.

The acceptance of a general taxonomy of affective behavior or one specifically for reading would be a distinct asset in accomplishing these four tasks. To analyze its applicability, it would be interesting to use the Krathwohl Taxonomy as a basis for affective evaluation in reading (2).

An attempt has been made to use the term *affective* in the same sense it is used in Krathwohl's handbook. Affective behavior emphasizes a feeling tone, an emotion, or a degree of acceptance or rejection. Learning activities which are aimed at developing interests, attitudes, values, and appreciation are all in the affective realm.

It may be recalled that there are five levels in the hierarchial continuum of the affective taxonomy: (a) *Receiving*, (b) *Responding*, (c) *Valuing*, (d) *Organizing*, and (e) *Characterization.* The continuum extends from a simple *awareness* on one extreme to *complete internalization* on the other.

One way to view the taxonomy is in terms of personal involvement. If a learner is sporadic in his attentiveness during reading, if he is *receiving* sometimes—but not all the time—then his degree of personal involvement is very low. On the other hand, if he is an avid reader and seeks to immerse himself in reading, then he is committed to reading and is personally involved to a high degree. The taxonomy represents a continuum of varying degrees of personal involvement.

Another way to look at the taxonomy is in terms of internalization. This is the organizing thread Krathwohl and others have accepted (2). Internalization describes the process by which the act of reading may progressively become an integral part of the individual.

Reading can be valued for itself or it can be used to study and evaluate the other parts of one's total value system. Thus, one can learn to value reading itself and one can be committed to utilizing reading to build a consistent value system. Both are legitimate objectives of education and both should be evaluated.

In the Receiving category, three levels of behavior have been identified: (a) *awareness*, (b) *willingness to receive,* and (c) *controlled attention.* These are close to being cognitive behaviors. It is not generally necessary to test or ask questions to ascertain learner behavior at this level. The day dreamer, the sporadic listener, the one who is occasionally with you and occasionally not—each is on this level. These persons show a lack of interest *as well as* skills. The teacher can usually spot these by consciously reflecting on each child and his overt behavior during reading instruction.

Three levels of behavior have been identified in the Responding category: (a) *acquiescence in responding,* (b) *willingness to respond,* and (c) *satisfaction in response.*

These behaviors are most evident when the learner has an opportunity to respond during reading instruction. A teacher can check this fact occasionally by keeping a small chart to tally pupils' responses. Each time Sally must be requested to answer, a tally goes in the *acquiescence in responding* box. When she volunteers a response but indicates no strong feeling about having responded, a tally goes in the *willingness to respond* category. If Sally volunteers a reply and indicates she feels good or happy about having answered, the mark goes in the *satisfaction in response* box. A total of tallies in each box will render a rough indication of the child's responding level. This informal evaluation is simple and will help focus the teacher's attention on affective behavior. Evaluating responding behavior should be of major importance to teachers, and informal assessment should be made periodically.

The three levels of Valuing behavior, (a) *acceptance of a value,* (b) *preference for a value,* and (c) *commitment to a value,* are rather high levels of affective behavior. These usually develop over a longer period of time.

Elementary teachers often use charts to record books pupils have read and to give an added incentive for pupils to read trade books. These teachers are attempting to get the students *to accept the value* of reading. Billy reads more trade books so he can be ahead of Mary on the chart. In the process, he finds that there is satisfaction to be gained from reading. Later, hopefully, when the stimulus chart is removed, the pupil will continue to prefer reading to some other activities. At this point, it can be said that if the learner likes to read, he is *accepting the value* of reading.

To determine whether a student has acquired a *preference for reading,* he needs to be given the opportunity to make a choice. Many teachers have a reading table, an activity table, and the like in their rooms. If Susan has the choice of reading a book, working a puzzle, or writing a story, and if she chooses reading, it could be said that Susan is operating at the second level of valuing. She has developed a *preference of reading*, at least over the stipulated alternatives. Keeping a record of free time choices made by students could give another indication of the students' affective development in reading.

This category also lends itself to paper and pencil testing. Reading preference inventories could be used, or it would not be difficult to find personal preference inventories that could be adapted for assessment in this area.

Developing a *commitment for reading* is a high and noble aspiration. This is the highest level of Valuing behavior. It is usually not difficult to determine when a pupil is committed. When he has a free moment, he is reading. Reading is *very* high on his list of preferred activities. He has a tendency to channel his reading in a special area and shifts to a new area only after he has probed deeply into his current interest. A teacher can evaluate a commitment by observation, much the same as she can evaluate Receiving behavior by observation. The teacher should look for (a) constant reading, (b) depth reading in special areas, and (c) a dependence on reading as a means of recreation as well as a means of becoming informed.

A person that has become committed to reading may use reading as a means of exploring and further refining his whole value system. That is, a reader committed to reading may use reading *for* developing, ordering and structuring a comprehensive, consistent value system that becomes his person.

Raths' (4) clarifying response strategies assess behavior and require the learner to operate at the three highest levels of the affective taxonomy—Valuing, which we have just been discussing; Organizing; and Characterization. This contention is consistent with the idea that the Taxonomy is a continuum of progressive internalization. External measures and standards may be used to evaluate the first three levels: Receiving, Responding, and Valuing. Internal measures and standards may be used to evaluate at the three highest levels: Valuing, Organizing, and Characterization. Notice that Valuing is the transitional link on the internalization continuum where both external and internal evaluation may take place.

The major referent used here for evaluating at these three higher levels is essentially Raths' clarifying response strategy. The substance being evaluated shifts generally from reading as a behavior to the material one has read. The technique uses the content of what one has read to help him recognize commitments, help him conceptualize what he values, and aid him in organizing his value system.

Returning to the second Valuing level, *preference for a value*, teachers' questions such as "What is good about this book (or story)?" or "What books did you reject before you settled on your present selection?" are asking the learner to clarify his preference for a value. The first question asks the learner to reflect on what is "good" about his choice, while the latter asks him to relate his choice to discarded choices.*

A teacher is asking the reader to test his *commitment to a value* when he asks such questions as "Are you willing to recommend that author to the class?" or "Would you be willing to write a paper supporting the author's point of view?" These questions tend to test the student's commitment by asking him to reflect on the extent to which he is willing to make his own views and values public information and to take action on them.

Moving to the fourth level of the Taxonomy, there are two levels of the Organizing category: (a) *conceptualization of a value* and (b) *organization of a value system*.

Questions like "Is this what I understand you to say about that book . . . (interpret the reader's previous statement)?" and "Where do you suppose you first got interested in that kind of story?" aid the student in *conceptualizing a value*. In this first instance the student is given a chance to see what he has said and thus conceptualize more objectively the meaning of his utterance. In the second question, the student is asked to search his present conceptual structure to see if his statement fits into a pattern that is developing in his reading habits.

The teacher is helping the learner *organize his values* by asking, "What's really good about this book (or story) which makes it stand out from the other possibilities?" or "Is what you say consistent with what you said earlier?" The first clarifying response in essence asks the student to fit his choice in with his organized set of beliefs. The second is testing consistency in the student's organized set of values.

Again, these questions do not necessarily relate directly to reading, but they may grow out of a student's reading. The student needs an opportu-

---

*Many of the clarifying questions quoted in this section were adapted from Louis E. Raths, *et al.*, *Values in Teaching*. The attempt to classify Raths' questions into categories of Krathwohl's Taxonomy is the responsibility of the author. Neither Raths nor Krathwohl has indicated that such a possibility exists, or that the author's attempt is valid.

nity to respond personally to what he reads. The teacher ought to ask questions which will help the reader understand and evaluate his ideas, emotions, and values.

The top level on the internalization continuum, Characterization by a Value or Value Complex, is so intricate as to be almost mysterious. The Characterization category can best be described by quoting from the Taxonomy:

> At this level of internalization the values already have a place in the individual's value hierarchy, are organized into some kind of internally consistent system, have controlled the behavior of the individual for a sufficient time that he has adapted to behaving this way; and an evocation of the behavior no longer arouses emotion or affect except when the individual is threatened or challenged (2).

The two levels of Characterization are (a) *generalized set*, and (b) *characterization*. The *generalized* set gives an internal consistency to the system of attitudes and values at any particular moment. Such questions as "Have you felt this way about reading for some time?" and "Will you read this author again?" help the student to evaluate his set. The prior response asks him to reflect on the durability of his feelings, while the latter helps him to see the pattern that has developed in his behavior.

Characterization, the highest level of internalization continuum, is the totality of what a person is and what he is becoming. The master configuration of his generalized set of values and how the individual relates these to the larger world represent his character. As stated in the taxonomy,

> The great humanitarian figures of history—Socrates, Christ, Lincoln, Ghandi, Einstein—have achieved the characterization we refer to at this level. Each is universally held in high esteem precisely because his philosophy of life characterizes and pervades all of his behavior (2).

It is doubtful whether any questions or any way of evaluating behavior can be offered at this level. However, one can guide a student in developing other affective behaviors. At this level it is felt that the individual is independent; the valuing process is completely internalized; and the individual's own internal mechanism for processing, ordering, and selecting what he values takes over. The *characterization set* can be affected by influencing the learner at other affective levels, but whether or not he is led to restructure his character is an internal matter. Questions recommended by Raths are likely to help a learner come closer to realizing his transactive character and may lead one to develop a consistent value pattern. The clarifying response strategy appears to offer greater potential than any other technique at the moment.

Teachers may use observations, charts, tables, questions, and tests to measure and evaluate a learner's affective behavior at the first three levels of the Affective Taxonomy: Receiving, Responding, and Valuing. Teachers may ask questions and construct tests to help learners clarify and evaluate their own values about reading and what they have read at the three higher levels of the Taxonomy: Valuing, Organizing, and Characterization.

Some external rewards are likely to be necessary in guiding affective growth at the levels of Receiving, Responding, and Valuing. A learner must become dependent on internal rewards as the clarifying response strategy is used to encourage development of affective behavior at the levels of Valuing, Organizing, and Characterization.

CONCLUSION

Teachers are generally doing a good job of teaching the cognitive reading skills. If teachers are given leadership and encouragement in developing the learners' affective behavior, they will do a good job there, too.

Researchers need to provide teachers and textbook writers with information about affective behavior and how it is learned.

Professors and supervisors need to provide rational and practical strategies for teaching and evaluating the student's affective behavior in reading.

If the teacher-student interactions and the teacher-made tests analyzed here are representative of reading evaluation in general (and there is no strong reason to suspect otherwise), it appears that little or nothing is being done which assesses or evaluates the feelings, emotions, or values the learner has about reading or derives from reading. This lack represents a severe imbalance in reading instruction. The lack of evaluation of affective behavior is likely the cause of the erosion of interest on the part of teachers in affective learning.

There is evidence on college campuses across the country of the behavior that manifests itself when learning is depersonalized. The new frontier in education and in reading instruction is in the affective realm. Inventing new alphabets and applying linguistic techniques to reading instruction may improve the learning of cognitive reading skills, but the impact on affective behavior is far from clear. (Some linguistic readers I have seen don't do much to get me personally involved in reading.) The major concerns facing our country today are affective in nature. They are problems that relate to man's emotive forces, his attitudes, feelings, and values. The importance of being able to read is undeniable. It is any less important to value reading and to use reading to develop one's character?

REFERENCES

1. Guszak, Frank J. "A Study of Teacher Solicitation and Student Response Interaction About Reading Content in Selected Second, Fourth, and Sixth Grades," unpublished doctoral dissertation, University of Wisconsin, 1965.
2. Krathwohl, David R., Benjamin S. Bloom, and Bertram B. Masia. *Taxonomy of Educational Objectives: Handbook II: Affective Domain.* New York: David McKay Co., Inc., 1964.
3. Mann, John S. "Functions of Curriculum Research," *Educational Leadership, 24* (October, 1966), p. 85.
4. Raths, Louis E., Merrill Harmin, and Sidney Simon. *Values and Teaching.* Columbus, Ohio: Charles E. Merrill Books, Inc., 1966.
5. Robinson, Helen M., and others. *More Roads To Follow.* Chicago: Scott, Foresman, and Company, 1964.
6. Russell, David H., and others. *Finding New Friends.* Boston: Ginn and Company, 1964.

Part Four
Sequence and Organization

Chapter 9.   Pre-Reading—Early Reading

Chapter 10.   Beginning Approaches to Reading

Chapter 11.   Progress Toward Reading Maturity

Chapter 9

PRE-READING—
EARLY READING

INTRODUCTION

Among the most controversial topics for discussion by people interested in reading are the nature of pre-reading programs and the decision as to whether reading should be taught prior to first grade. Although Chapter 9 will not resolve the controversy, it is composed of selections which present diverse points of view.

Beckett, McNeil, and Smith point out the present confusion concerning what is meant by reading readiness and the act of reading. Weintraub and Hillerich cite the conflicting evidence concerning the factors that are predictive of initial success in reading. McNeil argues the case for empirical validation of the relationship of a readiness skill to specific achievement in reading.

Impetus has been given to early introduction of reading instruction (a) by dissatisfaction with traditional programs in kindergarten still being carried out in some places which ignore the expanded world of today's five-year-olds and (b) by recent studies by psychologists and others of ways in which even infants respond to more visually stimulating environments. Durkin, Glass, and, especially, Smith place the introduction of reading in a larger setting of the overall needs of particular children and the kinds of kindergarten programs that will nurture those needs.

Hopefully, the chapter will stimulate the reader to pursue the answers to such questions as: What is reading readiness? What kinds of pre-reading programs are appropriate for different kinds of children? When and where should various types of pre-reading programs be introduced? How can readiness for reading be determined? When should initial instruction in reading be introduced? Who should receive early reading instruction?

(40) PHILOSOPHICAL DIFFERENCES IN READING CONCEPTS*

Dorothy B. Beckett

One of the trends resulting from the myriad of pressures on education is the earlier introduction of learning tasks, with earlier formal reading occupying a significant place among these trends. This activity has moved into many kindergartens and even nursery schools. In connection with this practice one finds the term "readiness" in wide but variable use. How, and with what meaning, do teachers use the term? Do their interpretations affect their classroom procedures? These important questions bear directly on one of the major issues in elementary education today: shall formal reading be a part of the kindergarten program?

HISTORICAL BACKGROUND

To speak ex cathedra on the current concept of readiness without considering its historical origins and development foreshortens perspective and limits insight. In the eighteenth century Pestalozzi in his principle of Anschauung repudiated Locke's *tabula rasa* theory on the basis that "the child is a real, living, spontaneous force which acts organically on its own development." The contemporary flavor is evident in this statement:

> Because stimulating experiences cause development, there must be graded progress in the way these experiences are presented to the child if the development effect is to be achieved; they must keep pace with his developing powers and never precede them. . . . Only after he has acquired a readiness consisting of perceptual and speaking knowledge is it reasonable to teach him to read and write (18).

Herbart and Froebel both expanded the idea of self-activity as inner-directed, based on the child's experiences and interests. Even though an elaborate symbolism formalized the free activity in his kindergarten,

---

*Reprinted from *The Reading Teacher* 18 (October 1964), pp. 27–32, by permission of the author and the International Reading Association.

from Froebel came the first indication that knowledge and the mind do not exist in isolation from the rest of the child personality. In G. Stanley Hall's study (the first of its kind in the United States) he commented: ". . . we seem to have an illustration of the law that we really see not what is near or impresses the retina, but what interests are awakened and words found for" (4).

Dewey wrote at length on interest which he viewed as a unified activity with a moving, developing nature. To him interest was not a method nor an end, but the result of the child's natural, developmental activity.

Thorndike's first Law of Learning contributed significantly toward making educators "readiness-conscious," but the lag between research and its application delayed for more than a decade the appearance of articles on readiness using the term per se. The earliest ones in the twenties were concerned with testing for reading readiness.

In 1946 Anderson cited the extremes of the two theories which had persisted in the past—one that education's sole purpose was to prepare the child for adult living, paying no particular attention to his present needs; the other, developing education around the child's immediate needs and interests. He strongly advocated not projecting adult values, attitudes, and goals into child behavior (1).

READINESS DICHOTOMY DEFINED

The preceding illustrations show from a historical standpoint how deeply rooted are the differences in interpretation of readiness. The differences center essentially around the issue of whether readiness is an intrinsic state of the organism, or whether it is an extrinsic acculturation of the organism. Both of these quite diverse ideas are widely present today. Furthermore, each can be rationalized on the basis of research in educational psychology. For the sake of clarity, the term "developmentalists" is used here to refer to those who believe that readiness waits upon maturation. Those who believe proper activities can cultivate readiness are referred to as "social learning theorists." Gesell and Sullivan represent these two points of view respectively. Limitations of space forbid more than passing mention of their theses. In his principle of ontogenesis Gesell proposes that behavior develops as a part of the total growth process, with age as the most significant developmental determiner (3). Sullivan's theory is not so much concerned with physical growth as the principal developmental determiner as it is with the adjustment of the child to the social pressures around him and the resultant interaction. In this theory, pressures from any authority figure have an impact on learning (17).

SAMPLING OF CURRENT LITERATURE

Opinions among reading authorities today are not characterized by an either-or philosophy. They arrange themselves along a continuum, from developmentalism to social learning theory. There is, however, one point throughout upon which all are agreed: it is unwise to begin teaching reading to children who are not ready (however they choose to describe this condition). The issue is: readiness *cannot* be built vs. readiness *can* be built.

Hildreth discusses the deviation of readiness programs from the original goals set for them.

Within recent years teachers overburdened with large classes have tended to interpret "the readiness period" as a daily practice period with expendable booklets for marking, cutting, and pasting, preparatory activities with the ABC's, auditory exercises for ear training, drills for visual word discrimination and for left-to-right directional orientation, and other exercises to precede and prepare for the use of the first preprimers.

This, she says, is a narrow interpretation of readiness, which presents no conclusive evidence of value as preparation for reading (6).

Olsen, noted for his work in child development, says he cannot find good evidence that parents and teachers can speed a child through the stages of readiness unless deprivation has existed (11).

Hymes, the most extreme protagonist of developmentalism, claims that the term "building readiness" is simply "pedagese" since the two words are mutually exclusive and contradict each other.

All the evidence says: Readiness comes as a healthy child grows and matures. Time is the answer—not special drills or special practice (7).

His view is documented by the research of those who first drew attention to readiness—Carmichael, Dennis, Hilgard, McGraw, Shirley, Strayer, *et al.*

Russell, Fuller, and others make qualifying exceptions, saying that the time to start formal reading should be decided on an individual basis, with weight given to aims of parents and schools (14). This turns from pure developmental theory toward the social learning theory. Sheldon has contributed significantly to exploring the literature advocating the formalizing of the kindergarten curriculum, although he does not endorse such change:

> The work of Piaget and others related to the education of five-years-olds seems to indicate that, at this stage in his life, each child needs individual attention. This cannot be accomplished in a rigid atmosphere wherein children are grouped together for formal instruction. . . . From the research which is pertinent, . . . there seems to be little or no justification for introducing reading into the curriculum at the kindergarten or five-year-old stage (15).

He acknowledges, however, the strong pressure of public opinion which often overrides the weight of research and attributes this pressure to the "national syndrome of anxiety over Russian technological advances."

Heilman believes, as do many others, that the readiness period is a highly structured, deliberately teacher-planned program, not a waiting period. He sees it, not as removing individual differences, but as a way to remove blocks to learning, fill gaps, and synthesize new experiences with past ones (5).

McKee and Harrison have recently prepared a prereading program for kindergarten, intended to "put the pupils months ahead on the road to independence in reading." It is their intent that at the end of kindergarten the children should be able to look at a printed word, listen to the spoken context, think the beginning sound, and decide what the word is (10).

Progressing along the continuum, the next degree of emphasis is: *not* permitting a child to begin to read early is actually harmful. McCracken, author of the New Castle Plan, believes that readiness is meaningless and queries, "Are we on the wrong track when we place so much emphasis on readiness for reading . . .? I certainly think so" (9). He theorizes that the time pupils lose in prereading activities is never regained. Walcutt indicts even further, saying that the only way to find out whether a child is ready to read is to try teaching him some words. If he learns them, he is ready. Reading readiness, he claims, was a "fad" invented to excuse poor reading instruction:

One day, when education comes to its senses regarding reading instruction, some determined researchers will devise an entirely new approach to the teaching of the subject. When educators finally take that . . . step we can forget about the many things that reading experts now think are wrong with the American child because then he will learn to read excellently and rapidly (19).

PRESSURE SOURCES

Current articles are creating pressures on the public school. The articles which describe experiments in teaching young children to read are read by parents who, in turn, become dissatisfied with existing kindergarten programs and urge reforms. A case in point is the recent publicity given to the Initial Teaching Alphabet, which originated in England. The revival of interest in the Montessori schools is another. Rambusch, active in this movement, defends the encouragement of formal learning activities:

> . . . learning to read at three can be for some children as exciting as stringing beads or jumping. Many a child eager to begin reading at three or four is being re-routed into bead-stringing and block play by teachers completely convinced that a child is not ready to learn, when frequently it is the teacher who is not ready to teach him (13).

Moore's project with "talking typewriters" is an extreme example of starting children to read early. In reporting, Pines comments: "If future experiments prove as successful as these to date . . . what passes for early-childhood education in most nursery schools may come to seem a terrible waste."

The sense of pressure to which Sheldon referred is well illustrated by Moore's words:

> We have no time. We can't stand pat. We have more new problems today than we can even name . . . and we must turn out larger and larger numbers of youngsters who can make fresh inductions about our world. . . . A new kind of person is needed to handle the present rate of change. This is our chief trouble today: Technological change but intransigent behavior. It's too late for us—our generation can't make it. At best we are just the transition group (12).

The foregoing examples drawn from current literature available to teachers for their use and guidance represent the spectrum of opinion and show the diversity in kindergarten philosophy. The implications for the curriculum are not readily observable, but as Sheldon has said:

> Certainly we are ready for a thorough study of the kindergarten as it now exists. Such a study might lead to a redesign of the kindergarten in terms of modern objectives and the five-year-olds of today. . . . When teacher after teacher in the kindergarten departs from standard practices and begins to teach reading to five-year-olds, it is time that we re-examine both the philosophy of the kindergarten and the objectives as set forth by leaders in the area of early childhood education (16).

TEACHER CONCEPTS OF READINESS

Having looked at the literature and noted the ambiguity surrounding the term "readiness," the inquiry naturally leads next to teachers to see if any discrepancy is evident between their teaching methods and philosophy, possibly as a result of the literature. The results of a questionnaire sent to teachers from selected public school kindergartens in Ohio show some striking inconsistencies. Some teachers who emphatically claim not to favor the formal teaching of reading said they had used such an approach for more or less than two years. Others who deny having used a formal approach elaborate on their practices—use of readiness workbooks, etc. There are several references from teachers who write about "building readiness" but who are opposed to teaching reading:

> I feel that kindergarten should be a time for building readiness.
> No. I feel it [the formal teaching of reading] should be correlated with kindergarten activities which naturally build readiness (2).

The following statement certainly illustrates a type of confusion:

> Some of these children who were kept out of school because of their birthdays' occurring the first of the year are actually over age when they enter kindergarten as far as reading readiness is concerned.

A few teachers' answers are consistent with developmental philosophy and show no confusion in the meaning of readiness. This fact tends to show by contrast the difference a clear-cut philosophy makes in methods used:

Lots of science and experiments, lots of manipulation of tools and materials, lots of social graces, lots of exploring the community, lots of problem solving (how and why), these are the teaching for kindergarten. Education is a long, developmental process. Let's not try to teach everything in kindergarten (2).

IMPLICATIONS

Evidence from the past and present which might illuminate the present state of affairs in this controversy has been sampled here. There has been no presumption that "this one is right and that one is wrong." There has been an attempt to demonstrate that teachers themselves are not sure of what they understand readiness to be, and that this unsureness affects actual teaching practices. At present, when reading activities are introduced into the kindergarten, they are called part of a "readiness program." This is not merely a case of "What's in a name?" Rather, it involves a real diversity in practice. Assuming reading readiness to be construed as a state of the organism, such acts as formal reading are generally inappropriate as a kindergarten task. On the other hand, if readiness is interpreted as a state of preparedness resulting from teaching, then reading may be indicated for the kindergarten child. It would seem that the definition accorded "readiness" becomes important in deciding whether or not reading is desirable for a particular group of children. Perhaps it might clarify things if the term "readiness" were reserved to describe the intrinsic state of the organism, and "prereading activities" were used to refer to efforts directed toward extrinsic modification.

One fact emerges clearly at the present: unless something happens to divert the course of events as now progressing, the kindergarten will, without reference to specifically defined limits, begin the teaching of reading. If this occurs there is always the possibility that all children, ready or not, will be subjected to reading instruction. Implications for administrators include the provision for individual differences, either by grouping within the grade or by using a nongraded plan. Further implications point to the necessity of protecting teachers from undue pressures to alter what they know to be sound teaching practices. A good public relations program will accomplish this.

If the present trend continues, publishers of reading materials for beginners should give considerable attention to revisions in their readiness programs in terms of five- rather than six-year-olds. Using materials for first grade will not do.

Although there are only 241 teachers involved in this particular sampling, the children affected by their practices number more than 16,000. If the activities are, as some believe, detrimental to the welfare of the child, then widespread reforms are in order. If changes are coming about because they seem to benefit the child who, for his part, seems ready for them and welcomes the chance to read sooner, then some revision is needed in the thinking of those who oppose the early introduction of reading.

REFERENCES

1. Anderson, John. *Forty-sixth Yearbook, Part II.* Chicago: The National Society for the Study of Education, 1947.
2. Beckett, Dorothy B. "The Concept of Readiness as Related to Present Practices in Early Childhood Education." Unpublished doctoral dissertation, Western Reserve University, 1963.
3. Carmichael, Leonard (Ed.). *Manual of Child Psychology.* 2nd ed., revised. New York: John Wiley, 1954.
4. Hall, G. Stanley. *The Contents of Children's Minds on Entering School.* New York: E. L. Kellogg, 1893.
5. Heilman, Arthur. *Principles and Practices of Teaching Reading.* Columbus: Charles E. Merrill Books, 1961.
6. Hildreth, Gertrude. *Teaching Reading.* New York: Holt, Rinehart and Winston, 1958.
7. Hymes, James L., Jr. *Before the Child Reads.* New York: Row, Peterson, 1958.
8. Kilpatrick, William H. *Twenty-fourth Yearbook, Part II.* Bloomington: Public School Publishing Co., 1925.
9. McCracken, Glenn. "Have We Overemphasized the Readiness Factor?" *Elementary English,* May 1952, pp. 273–275.
10. McKee, Paul, and Harrison, Lucile. *Getting Ready to Read.* Boston: Houghton Mifflin, 1962.
11. Olson, Willard. *Child Development.* Boston: D. C. Heath, 1959.
12. Pines, Maya. "How Three-Year-Olds Teach Themselves to Read—And Love It," *Harper's Magazine,* May 1963, pp. 58–64.
13. Rambusch, Nancy. *An American Approach to Montessori.* Baltimore: Helicon Press, 1962.
14. Russell, David H. *Children Learn to Read.* Boston: Ginn & Co., 1949.
15. Sheldon, William D. "Research Related to Teaching Kindergarten Children to Read," *Reading in the Kindergarten??* p. 17. Washington: ACEI, 1962.

16. Sheldon, William D. "President's Report," *Reading Teacher*, January 1962, p. 287.
17. Sullivan, Harry Stack. *The Interpersonal Theory of Psychiatry*. New York: W. W. Norton, 1953.
18. Walch, Sister Mary Romana. *Pestalozzi and the Pestalozzian Theory of Education*, Washington, D.C.: Catholic University of America Press, 1952.
19. Walcutt, Charles. *Tomorrow's Illiterates: The State of Reading Instruction Today*. Boston: Little, Brown, 1961.

(41) DISCOVERING READING READINESS*

John D. McNeil

In this paper two things are intended: (1) to contrast viewpoints regarding reading readiness and to show how these positions influence strategies for dealing with problems in beginning reading, and (2) to describe in detail three guidelines for conducting empirical inquiry in the area of reading readiness.

TWO OUTLOOKS REGARDING READINESS

The "naturalist" tends to emphasize physical and intellectual changes in learners that occur independently of deliberate instruction. By attending to such factors as skeletal growth, height, and weight on the one hand and reading achievement test scores on the other, he attempts to find the optimum time for introducing formal instruction in reading. At the extreme, he characterizes readiness as something to wait for.

In contrast, the programmer or empiricist tends to stress nurture, whereby the instructor undertakes to shape the learner's behavior. The empiricist's approach is threefold: (1) to make an operational definition of what the beginning reader must be able to do when confronted with printed symbols or other situations, (2) to specify the constituent sequentially dependent parts or *learning sets* that are subsumed in the complex behavior of beginning reading, and (3) to deliberately elicit from the learner responses to particular situations so that each component in the overall task is mastered. In short, the programmer characterizes readiness as prerequisite skills for which the teacher, not nature, must assume responsibility for producing in learners.

*Reprinted from *Research Designs in Reading*, Highlights, 1966, pp. 39–44, by permission of the author and the International Reading Association.

Reported correlation between success in beginning reading and selected physiological, emotional, or intellectual factors is likely to be interpreted differently in accordance with one's philosophical outlook. When confronted with a learner's scores on dimensions which indicate an unfavorable prediction regarding success in reading, an investigator who is closer to the naturalistic outlook is likely to say that it is uneconomical at this time to pursue instruction in reading with this child. Instead the learner would be invited to continue with activity in which he is successful, even though his activity is not releated directly to reading. The empiricist would react by saying: "What can I do to circumvent or close the gap on this individual's emotional, physiological, or intellectual deficiencies? If I do this, can I demonstrate that elimination of the deficiencies will bring success in reading?" The underlying assumption of this paper is that improved practice in the teaching of beginning reading is more likely to occur as a result of the latter outlook.

DESCRIPTIVE STUDIES AND EXPERIMENTAL STUDIES MAY BE COMPLEMENTARY

There are those who are content to describe children's behavior and not change it. Careful descriptions of children's behavior in a range of settings and in time (e.g., longitudinal studies associated with a developmental point of view as opposed to the manipulative studies of the experimenter or empiricist) should provide data useful to those who seek to control individual learners. For example, data regarding prevailing interests, concepts, and motor movements of young children serve as useful information in drawing inferences or hypotheses regarding ways to present instruction to these learners. Likewise, by changing the conditions of instruction or the presentation, we find that capacities of children formerly thought to be bounded by nature were, in fact, only limited by our ignorance of instructional technology.

CORRELATIONAL DATA INDICATE WHAT MIGHT BE DISCOVERED; EXPERIMENTS AFFIRM THE DISCOVERY

We will have better instruction in reading when factors identified as associated with success in the initial reading experience are demonstrated to be causative, not merely correlational. Causal relations exist when the desired effect occurs in response to the prescribed treatment. Only when we can produce the desired results in reading can we say we understand the process. Correlational studies advance our understanding of this process provided they are coupled with empirical tryout in which the associative factor is developed in the child and predicted consequences are checked out. For example, it has been found that upon entrance to the first grade those children who are able to name the letters of the alphabet generally achieve greater progress in beginning reading than do those children without this initial ability. The fact that knowledge of letter names and success in a particular program are associated does not allow one to say that such knowledge is a contributing cause to successful reading. It may be that those children who enter school with a knowledge of letters come from homes where reading is more valued; where parents are more ambitious for their children, etc. The importance of being able to name letters can be validated by experimentation: (1) by randomly selecting children from the population of those who cannot name letters; (2) by instructing these selected children so that they can name the letters while giving their peers equivalent instruction in all but the naming of letters, and (3) by assessing the relative degree of success both groups have when confronted with specified tasks of beginning reading. Correlational studies help one identify variables or reading skills which may prove to be important. Evidence that a true variable has been discovered is provided by the experimental study.

GUIDELINES TO EMPIRICAL VALIDATION OF A READINESS SKILL

CLEAR DEFINITION OF BOTH THE READINESS SKILL AND READING TASK WILL REVEAL THE LIKELIHOOD OF A RELATIONSHIP

One should not talk of a reading readiness skill independent from the reading task to be demanded. Both the readiness skill and the reading task must be specified. A given child may learn to orally pronounce printed words to imitate the behavior of another without being able to recognize the correlation between letters and sounds. It is not likely, however, that this child would have been able to independently pronounce these words without the prerequisite skill of associating phonemes to the constituent letters or printed syllables of the words. The first task requires memorization; the latter, decoding. A prerequisite to decoding is not necessarily a prerequisite for memorization.

There should be a logical connection between the criterion that indicates the possession of a prerequisite skill (treatment variable) and the test which measures success in reading task (dependent variable). Were this condition met, there might be fewer charges that teachers of beginning reading are engaging in a fraud when they relegate a child to an activity termed "reading readiness" such as coloring geometric shapes, when there is no common element between the activity and the reading task. What are the arguments for assuming that certain skills are prerequisites? On what basis does one hypothesize that training on Task A (readiness) will enhance preformance on Task B (reading)? One can answer by showing how activity in Task A equips the learner for reading by (1) familiarizing him with details or instructions common to both procedures; (2) by giving him a principle, special vocabulary, or way to attack classroom problems including reading; (3) by predisposing him to reading by rewarding him with initial success in the preliminary work and reinforcing his curiosity and sense of challenge for school learning; and (4) by allowing for spaced practice and review so that what is learned in A will be more fully retained in B.

Much of today's literature refers to the importance of "auditory perception and discrimination" as a prerequisite skill to reading. There is no way to test the hypothesis that auditory perception is a prerequisite skill to reading until two steps are taken. First, there must be an operational definition or criterion for reading. One such definition might be, "Given a number of trigrams never seen before, the learner will be able to correctly pronounce them" (reading as texting). Another definition might be, "Given a number of printed words unfamiliar in the written form, the learner will be able to point to the visual referent for these words" (reading as meaning). Second, there must be an operational definition of auditory perception and discrimination. Following are four such definitions currently in practice:

1. Given 40 matched pairs of words such as *tub-tug, zest-zest* and asked if two words are exactly the same, the five-year-old child should be able to make no more than six errors; the six-year-old, no more than five.

2. Given a number of sentences, each of which contains a number of words that begin with either the sounds for *b, f, t,* and *c* (Betty saw a baby bird that was not very big), the child will be able to

clap his hands each time he hears a word that begins with the same sound as the first word in the sentence.

3. Given a series of word pairs, children will be able to tell which one rhymes—*cake-rake, cake-dog*.

4. Given a number of environmental sounds played on a tape recorder (e.g., sound of bird whistling, sound of dog barking) and, for each of the sounds, directions to point to one of the four pictures that represent the sound just heard, the child will be able to do so.

Examination of the above list should throw light on the reason there is a lack of agreement on the importance of auditory perception as a readiness skill for reading. Different treatments are subsumed under the same rubric-auditory discrimination and perception. Further, these treatments may be conflicting with one another. The child who is taught on one set of exercises to respond to the stimulus *log-dog* by saying "yes" (they do rhyme), must on another occasion respond to the same stimulus by saying "no" (they do not sound exactly the same).

There are many readiness variables which one could validate. Activities representing these variables include traditional practices such as pointing to one or more objects from left to right, comparing pictures as like or different, recognizing names as written, reciting jingles, retelling a story, drawing pictures of objects illustrating sounds, or inferring behavior in pictures. Also, we have only started to show the value of newer readiness activities that call for the use of such language concepts as negation, verbal mediation, self-correction, and the vocabulary of instruction. However, in selecting a variable for experimentation the researcher will be more likely to get positive results if he will examine the post-test to be used in measuring successful reading and select the variable that most clearly approximates an aspect of the complex kind of competence demanded on the post-test.

EVIDENCE THAT THE READINESS SKILL HAS BEEN MASTERED DURING TRAINING IS NECESSARY TO DEMONSTRATE ITS POWER

The experimental strategy for discovering readiness skills requires that the researcher be successful in teaching the skill to those who do not possess it. Measures must be taken to indicate whether the instruction in the prerequisite skill was effective after training. Occasionally, a researcher will fail to find differences in performance on a reading program between those who had training in readiness activity and those who did not. If, in this case, the researcher is unable to show that the learners indeed acquired the readiness skill as a result of training, then he has made no contribution. Only when he can provide evidence that learners have acquired competency in the readiness variable can he demonstrate its effect on subsequent tasks. A post-test following training on the readiness variable is necessary as well as a post-test following instruction in reading.

REPRODUCIBLE "BASELINE" PROGRAMS IN READING ARE TOOLS FOR DETERMINING THE VALUE OF READINESS SKILLS

Reproducible sequences of instruction, oral and visual stimuli, and confirming comments are available in many forms. Programmed work-books, scripts for teachers to follow, taped lessons with accompanying filmstrips, and self-instructional programs via teaching machines are cases in point. In some instances it can be shown that learners are unable to perform certain tasks of reading before being introduced to these kinds of materials, but that upon completion of the sequence, the learners respond to the reading task at a specified level of proficiency. Evidence of the learner's performance upon completion of the program is "baseline" data from which one can introduce variations such as preliminary train-ing in learning set and note the effects.

Essentially all that is required is that prior to introducing a learner to the reproducible program, the experimenter succeed in training the learner on the variable he believes will improve performance on the reading program itself. The research design can be made more precise by preparing an alternate training program for other learners (controls). In which case it can be said that changed performance on the reading task is due to the readiness skill and not to other factors such as familiarity with instruction or exposure to a sustained task.

Designs using a baseline program may include the following:

(1) $A + B > B$ (where B is the baseline program and A is the prerequisite skill)

(2) $A + B > B + B$ (where additional training in the baseline program is not held to be as valuable as training in the prerequisite skills)

(3) $A + B > C + B$ (where A and C are both prerequisite skills).

It is most desirable to develop a reproducible program that will produce the readiness skill in the intended population of learners. The program will be of use in studies of replication, in comparative studies involving other prerequisites, and in answering questions regarding the optimum order in which to introduce the prerequisites in relation to the hierarchical task of reading.

CONCLUDING COMMENTS

A noteworthy trend in research in reading readiness is empiricism using reproducible instructional programs. Any material which produces demonstrable reading achievement among learners can provide a baseline for showing how much might be gained by mastery of the presumed readiness skill. Additional instructional material which will develop the prerequisite skill is administered prior to the reading program. Evidence that learners achieve more and in less time from the reading program after mastering this skill confirms the discovery of a valid prerequisite.

A concomitant of empirical research using reproducible materials is that when a crucial variable has been discovered there is little time-lag in utilizing the finding in the development of instructional materials; the material itself is a valuable instructional product from the research.

As with all research, the technique is only as good as the logic of the researcher. Clear definition of the prerequisite skill and the teaching task should increase the probability of the researcher obtaining significant results. Operational definitions may reduce attempts to relate variables which have neither obvious nor theoretical connections. Empiricism and its desire for precision brings some loss of generalization. For example, operational definitions of auditory discrimination will not permit the researcher to generalize his findings to all situations and cases that bear the rubric.

The point of view underlying the empirical research procedure is that the development of readiness in reading is a responsibility of the instructor, not the learner. The search for better ways to develop readiness can be enhanced by naturalistic descriptive studies of the child and by correlational studies which point to promising variables. The results of empirical tryout with experimental controls is, however, the ultimate test that a readiness skill has been discovered.

REFERENCES

1. Bereiter, Carl. "A Beginning Language Program for Disadvantaged Children," paper presented at the American Educational Research Association, Chicago, February, 1966.

2. Elkonin, D. B. "The Psychology of Mastering the Elements of Reading," in Brian and Joan Simon, (Eds.), *Educational Psychology in the USSR.* Stanford, California: Stanford University Press, 1963.

3. Evans, J. L. "A Behavioral Approach to the Teaching of Phonetic Reading," paper presented at the International Reading Association Convention, Miami, Florida, May, 1963.

4. Feigenbaum, E. A. and Simon, H. A. "Performance of a Reading Task by an Elementary Perceiving and Memorizing Program," *Behavioral Science,* 8(1), January, 1963, 72–76.

5. Galperin, P. Y. "An Experimental Study in the Formation of Mental Actions," in Brian Simon (Ed.), *Psychology in the Soviet Union.* Stanford, California: Stanford University Press, 1957.

6. Gorelick, Molly. "The Effectiveness of Visual Form Training in a Prereading Program," *The Journal of Educational Research,* Vol. 58, No. 7, March, 1965.

7. McNeil, J. D. "Programmed Instruction as a Research Tool in Reading: An Annotated Case," *The Journal of Programed Instruction,* Vol. 1, No. 1, (October, 1962), 37–42.

8. McNeil, J. D. and Keisler, E. R. *Value of the Oral Response in Beginning Reading: An Experimental Study Using Programed Instruction.* Grant No. 1413. Washington, D.C.: U.S. Office of Education, Department of Health, Education, and Welfare Report, 1962.

9. Muehl, S. "The Effects of Letter-Name Knowledge on Learning to Read a Word List in Kindergarten Children," *Journal of Educational Psychology,* 53(4), (August, 1962), 181–186.

10. Silberman, H. F. *Exploratory Research on a Beginning Reading Program.* SDC TM-895/100/00. U.S. Office of Education, Department of Health, Education, and Welfare Report, June, 1964.

(42) READINESS MEASURES
FOR PREDICTING READING ACHIEVEMENT*

Samuel Weintraub

The prediction of behavior has long been one of the goals of scientific investigation in psychology and education. A major concern of teachers and reading specialists has been the prediction of success in beginning reading. Measures that would give unerring prediction of achievement in

*Reprinted from *The Reading Teacher* 20 (March 1967), pp. 551–58, by permission of the author and the International Reading Association.

reading would enable teachers to identify the children who were certain to succeed and those who were destined to fail without having more help. With the former group, the teacher could proceed with formal reading instruction while the latter group continued in a readiness program until success in reading was assured.

The most commonly used predictive measures of success in learning to read have been readiness and intelligence tests. Unfortunately these tests have been far from perfect predictive instruments. Readiness tests tend to correlate somewhere between .4 and .6 with later measures of reading achievement, while intelligence tests, for the most part, show an even lower relationship at the early reading levels. The readiness tests do an adequate job of identifying the extremes on the normal curve, those who will probably succeed and those who will probably fail. However, the large group of children in the middle may go in either direction when placed in a reading program. In addition, there is some question about the validity of current instruments for use with children who come from deprived backgrounds. The question of the validity of these instruments may well be raised when they are used with any group other than with children from middle-class backgrounds. The need therefore is two-fold: (1) to find instruments for use with children from different cultures, and (2) to find instruments that are better predictors of achievement than those now in existence.

Because considerable writing already has appeared concerning the usual measures of readiness and of intelligence and visual discrimination as predictors, little time will be spent in discussing these measures. The major emphasis will be on newer or different attempts to measure readiness factors and on bringing attention to studies that have not been published.*

One important finding about readiness tests deserves mention. Several recent studies (8, 11) have reported that one of the subtests on readiness tests seems to be the best single measure of prediction. The number subtest has been found to correlate better with criterion measures of reading than any of the other subtests. Reed (13) found the "Quantitative" score on the SRA Primary Mental Abilities Test as good a predictor of grade 1 reading achievement as the total score. He postulates, among other things, that recognizing quantitative relationships may involve some of the same reasoning ability called for in certain beginning reading skills. Perhaps the quantitative measures on readiness tests also

---

*The author is again indebted to Mrs. Debrah Weiss for her aid in locating and compiling references.

call for certain abstractions and reasoning abilities related to those necessary in the early stages of learning to read.

Various measures of visual discrimination have for some time been identified as at least as good predictors of reading achievement as readiness tests. A comprehensive review of the research in this area has been presented by Barrett (1).

Another perceptual skill consistently reported as closely related to beginning reading ability is auditory discrimination. However, Dykstra (4) reported comparatively low correlations between the tests of auditory discrimination he used and achievement on a first grade reading test. Indeed, he found a group intelligence test to be the best predictor of both word recognition and paragraph reading. When all his readiness measures were combined, they accounted for only 32 per cent of the variability in paragraph reading scores. Thus, he noted that a great deal (68 per cent) of success in reading is dependent on factors other than the auditory discrimination abilities measured by the tests he used. He felt there was relatively little need to test for auditory discrimination abilities if intelligence test data were available.

Buktenica (2) investigated the relationship between auditory and visual perception and concluded that the two were not substantially related. When auditory and visual perceptual variables were combined, they accounted for 37 per cent of the variance in reading. The two nonverbal perceptual variables accounted for more of the variance than did the combined auditory variables. On all tests, middle-class children performed better than did children from lower socioeconomic areas.

Reports on other visual-motor measures have included studies on the Bender Gestalt as a screening device for use with kindergarten and beginning grade 1 pupils. Koppitz *et al.* (9) reported that the Bender appeared to be less influenced by social and cultural factors than the readiness measures they used and felt that it more nearly revealed potential ability in visual-motor perception They found a correlation of .68 between scores on the Bender and reading test scores at the end of grade 1. Keogh (6, 7), on the other hand, evaluated the Bender given in kindergarten as a predictor of grade 3 achievement test scores and found negligible correlations between the two sets of scores when the effect of intelligence was held constant. It is possible that the differences in results between these two studies are due in part to the differences in the grade levels at which prediction was measured. By the end of grade 3 other factors appear to be better discriminators of good and poor readers than visual-motor skills.

While Robinson (14) reported that the Goodenough Draw-a-Man Test gave reliable results when used with disadvantaged children, Shipp and Loudon (16) found it correlated only .51 with one measure of reading achievement. It, therefore, does not appear more promising than other measures.

Martin (10) and Winter (18) recorded the oral language of beginning first grade children during an informal sharing period and tabulated the total number of words used, the number of different words spoken, and the average sentence length. At the end of first grade correlations with reading achievement were reported as negligible. Low relationships were also found at the end of grade 2.

Sampson (15), in a study done in England, reported a correlation of .69 between children's speech patterns as related by teachers at the age of two and one-half and performance on a test of reading comprehension at age eight. Vocabulary and language measures obtained at five years of age also showed relatively high (.67 and .58, respectively) correlations with later reading achievement. However, Sampson stated that the speech factor was not operating in isolation. Socioeconomic factors, emotional maladjustment, and intelligence were all involved in the language factors measured. It would appear, therefore, that the measures of speech, language, and vocabulary used by Sampson might have limited value for use with children from other than middle-class cultures.

In approaching the measurement of readiness from another viewpoint, Davey (3) observed the attention which kindergarten children gave to such daily activities as viewing movies, solving puzzles, listening, and playing. The coefficient of correlation reported between various attention ratings and later reading achievement scores was .69. She felt the results were significant enough to warrant further investigation with larger samples as well as with children from socioeconomic environments other than the upper-middle-class group she studied.

SUMMARY

Even a cursory glance at the literature indicates that current predictive measures of success in beginning reading are not so good as one would desire. The research suggests strongly the need to investigate other types of measures than those now in existence. Obvious, too, is the fact that the classroom teacher must interpret results of various readiness instruments with considerable caution. They are not infallible even with children from middle-class backgrounds. They are decidedly fallible with children who come from lower socioeconomic backgrounds.

Based on the findings of his study, Johansson (5) pointed out that ". . . there is no firm ground for the conviction that one factor is more important for school readiness than another. . . ." Various factors interact in the development of readiness for reading. It is unlikely that any one measure will be an accurate predictor.

A survey of the literature on prediction, then, leads us to conclude that there is an urgent need for the development of better measures or batteries of measures than we now have. This development calls for creativity on the part of researchers and reading teachers in general. New directions need to be investigated. The areas of attention and of oral language have by no means been thoroughly investigated. Children themselves have much to tell us about readiness for reading. And children from various subcultures have many different things to tell us about how they reach readiness for reading. Perhaps our best clues for future measures will come from careful observational, longitudinal case studies.

REFERENCES

1. Barrett, Thomas C. "The Relationship between Measures of Pre-reading Visual Discrimination and First Grade Reading Achievement: A Review of the Literature," *Reading Research Quarterly*, 1 (Fall 1965), 51–76.
2. Buktenica, Norman A. "Relative Contributions of Auditory and Visual Perception to First-Grade Language Learning." Unpublished doctoral dissertation, University of Chicago, 1966.
3. Davey, Elizabeth P. "Attention and Reading Readiness." Unpublished master's paper, University of Chicago, 1961.
4. Dykstra, Robert. "Auditory Discrimination Abilities and Beginning Reading Achievement," *Reading Research Quarterly*, 1 (Spring 1966), 5–34.
5. Johansson, Bror A. *Criteria of School Readiness.* Stockholm, Sweden: Almquist and Wiksell, 1965. Pp. 333.
6. Keogh, Barbara K. "The Bender Gestalt as a Predictive and Diagnostic Test of Reading Performance," *Journal of Consulting Psychology*, 29 (Feb. 1965), 83–84.
7. Keogh, Barbara K. "Form Copying Tests for Prediction of First Grade Reading." In Malcolm P. Douglass (Ed.), *Reading is the Process of Making Discriminative Responses*, pp. 141–144. Twenty-Seventh Yearbook of the Claremont Reading Conference, 1963.
8. Kingston, Albert H., Jr. "The Relationship of First-Grade Readiness to Third- and Fourth-Grade Achievement," *Journal of Educational Research*, 56 (Oct. 1962), 61–67.

9. Koppitz, Elizabeth M., Mardis, Verdena, and Stephens, Thomas. "A Note on Screening School Beginners with the Bender Gestalt Test," *Journal of Educational Psychology,* 52 (Apr. 1961), 80–81.

10. Martin, Clyde. "Developmental Interrelationships among Language Variables in Children of the First Grade," *Elementary English,* 32 (Mar. 1955), 167–171.

11. McCall, Rozanne A., and McCall, Robert B. "A Comparison of First Grade Reading Tests," *Illinois School Research,* 2 (Oct. 1965), 32–37.

12. Morrison, Ida E. "The Relation of Reading Readiness to Certain Langauge Factors." In J. Allen Figurel (Ed.), *Challenge and Experiment in Reading,* pp. 119–121. Conference Proceedings of the International Reading Association, VII, 1962.

13. Reed, James C. "An Analysis of the Interrelationship of Certain Components of the Primary Mental Abilities and Reading Achievement." Unpublished doctoral dissertation, University of Chicago, 1958.

14. Robinson, H. Alan. "Reliability of Measures Related to Reading Success of Average, Disadvantaged, and Advantaged Kindergarten Children," *Reading Teacher,* 20 (Dec. 1966), 203–208.

15. Sampson, Olive C. "Reading Skill at Eight Years in Relation to Speech and Other Factors," *British Journal of Educational Psychology,* 32 (Feb. 1962), 12–17.

16. Shipp, Donald E., and Loudon, Mary Lou. "The Draw-a-Man Test and Achievement in the First Grade," *Journal of Educational Research,* 57 (July-Aug. 1964), 518–521.

17. Townsend, Edward Arthur. "A Study of Copying Ability in Children," *Genetic Psychology Monographs,* 43 (Feb. 1951), 3–51.

18. Winter, Clotilda. "Interrelationships among Language Variables in Children of the First and Second Grade," *Elementary English,* 34 (Feb. 1957), 108–113.

(43) STUDIES IN READING READINESS*

Robert L. Hillerich

Reading readiness has been defined directly and by implication in many ways. Generally speaking, it represents progress in two areas of living: one area is time—time for growth and development; the second area is experience or training. Whether a given school emphasizes the time or

*Reprinted from *Reading and Inquiry* 10 (1965 Convention Proceedings), pp. 47–49, by permission of the author and the International Reading Association.

the experience factor, reading readiness may be judged successful or not in terms of the eventual success or lack of success of pupils in reading.

Current research in reading readiness and early reading instruction has made us question many traditional practices relating to the readiness of children. First, the mental age criterion (11) has been refuted on several counts: Schram (16) pointed out the influence of television on the vocabulary of pre-school children; Anderson (1) found that mental age was not a significant factor in learning certain pre-reading skills; a number of studies show low correlations between mental age and beginning reading. Second, Karlin (8) and Bremer (3) have indicated that general reading readiness tests have little predictive value. Finally, Eames (5) reported that visual maturity of five-year-olds was adequate for reading.

RESEARCH EMPHASIS TODAY

Crucial questions in research today seem to revolve around two related points: what kind of pre-reading instruction is most effective, and when should formal instruction begin? The research evidence may seem contradictory in respect to this double question, but I believe a pattern is apparent.

A number of studies have investigated the relationship between knowledge of letters and reading achievement. Nicholson (13) found that most children can discriminate letter forms prior to instruction. Olson (14) and McHugh (10) found that knowledge of letter names prior to instruction correlated more highly with reading achievement than did a reading readiness test.

In contrast, Linehan (9) reported that teaching letter names did not lead to significantly higher reading achievement. Muehl (12) found that knowledge of letter names actually interfered with learning to associate nonsense words with pictures.

Considering the findings of these studies, one might conclude that, while knowledge of letter names may be a good predictor of future success in reading, it is not necessarily a causal factor.

FORMAL INSTRUCTION IN KINDERGARTEN

Studies of formal programs in kindergarten and of the use of workbooks for reading readiness instruction appear to be even more contradictory.

I'd like briefly to review five studies and then attempt to describe a pattern.

Blakely and Shadle (2) compared the use of *We Read Pictures* with an informal program. While there were no significant differences in the case of girls, boys gained more in the informal program.

Ploghoft (15) reported no significant differences in a similar comparison, although the unspecified workbook was used for only nine weeks. Both of these studies involved only one section of children in each treatment group.

Brzeinski (4) reported a large-scale study of the effectiveness of a formal skills program in kindergarten. Using *Getting Ready to Read*, he found that the formal program in kindergarten followed by an adjusted first grade program resulted in significantly higher scores on the Gates Reading Tests at the end of first grade.

In another study with the same program, Hillerich (7) reported on several aspects of formal reading readiness in kindergarten. He found that 83 per cent of the children developed adequate skill in kindergarten, that retention was good over the summer, that workbooks were significantly more effective than the same program was without workbooks, and that the program in kindergarten led to significantly higher scores on the Primary Reading Profiles at the end of first grade.

In contrast to these findings, Fry (6) found that children who received no reading readiness instruction scored significantly higher on a word recognition test than did those who received readiness instruction. His "readiness" group used *Before We Read, We read Pictures*, and *We Read More Pictures* in first grade, while the "non-readiness" group began the readers immediately.

SOME CONCLUSIONS

First of all, what kinds of readiness experiences are necessary for success in reading? Of the studies we've examined, the programs that contribute to success are two kinds: an experience approach when the latter involves interpreting pictures and/or gross kinds of discrimination; a program teaching the use of context and consonant-letter-sound associations seems better than an experience approach, and the use of a workbook with this kind of program was the most effective. The studies consistently separate in terms of this difference in readiness content. This division suggests to me that the traditional experience approach and the general kind of readiness workbook are teaching relatively the same thing. Neither develops specific skills, but the experience approach has the advantage of spontaneity and enthusiasm.

A second point from these studies relates to tests used. If reading readiness is viewed as a collection of skills or abilities, general readiness tests will not measure these skills. While a number of the studies reported did use readiness tests, the low correlation between these tests and reading achievement makes their use questionable. Furthermore, the true test of any reading readiness program lies in its contribution to success in reading. One might even speculate here that general readiness tests and general readiness programs are a circular process wherein each has helped to perpetuate the other.

Third, in any study, we leave an element uncontrolled when the groups compared use different programs. For example, Fry was comparing groups on the effectiveness of reading readiness as opposed to no reading readiness. Yet, another variable was the use of two different reading programs with the groups.

Finally, and by far the most important similarity in these studies, the age at which children *begin* instruction in reading seems to be a significant factor. In Fry's study, for example, the readiness work itself—or the differences in the reading programs—is probably not nearly so significant as the factor of time. At the mid-December testing all but three of twelve readiness groups were already in primers.

Some guidelines for future research are apparent from these studies. Selection of tests ought to be made in terms of what is being measured; one cannot truly evaluate the success of a readiness program with a general readiness test, nor does a word recognition test adequately measure reading achievement. Care must also be taken to control such obvious variables as the type of reading program which follows a comparison of readiness treatments. The reported differences in the success of various approaches to readiness points up the importance of specifying the programs being compared in any study; failure to state the program used makes a research study worthless to the reader.

More longitudinal studies such as those in Denver and in Glenview are needed to investigate other programs.. Are these two programs successful merely because of a running start—as many synthetic phonic programs seem to be—or will youngsters continue to progress more rapidly in reading as they advance in the grades? Success is not a short-term affair, but perhaps neither is failure. Would some of the other studies which showed no significant differences at the end of kindergarten have produced different results on a long-term basis?

Although the issues are not resolved, we have made great strides in recent years. Reading readiness is becoming less nebulous as we identify certain pre-reading skills which lead to success in reading. The old taboos are being broken down as we learn more about early reading. Yes, we live in an exciting age; youngsters today and tomorrow will reap the benefits.

References

1. Anderson, D. M., A Study to Determine if Children Need a Mental Age of Six Years and Six Months to Learn to Identify Strange Printed Word Forms When They Are Taught to Use Oral Context and the Initial Sound of the Word. Unpublished Ed. D. Dissertation, Greeley: Colorado State College, 1960.
2. Blakely, P. W., and Shadle, E. M., "A Study of Two Readiness-for-Reading Programs in Kindergarten," *Elementary English*, XXXVIII (November, 1961), pp. 502–505.
3. Bremer, N., "Do Readiness Tests Predict Success in Reading?" *Elementary School Journal*, LIX (January, 1959), pp. 222–224.
4. Brzeinski, J. E., "Beginning Reading in Denver," *Reading Teacher*, XVIII (October, 1964), pp. 16–21.
5. Eames, T., "Physical Factors in Reading," *Reading Teacher*, XV (May, 1962), p. 432.
6. Fry, E., "Are Reading Readiness Materials Necessary in the First Grade?" Paper presented at American Educational Research Association meeting, Chicago, February, 1965.
7. Hillerich, R. L., "Pre-Reading Skills in Kindergarten: A Second Report," *Elementary School Journal*, LXV (March, 1965), pp. 312–317.
8. Karlin, R., "The Prediction of Reading Success and Reading-Readiness Tests," *Elementary English*, XXXIV (May, 1957), pp. 320–322.
9. Linehan, E. B., Early Instruction in Letter Names and Sounds as Related to Success in Beginning Reading. Unpublished Ed. D. Dissertation, Boston: Boston University, 1957.
10. McHugh, W. J. "Indices of Success in First Grade Reading," Paper presented at American Educational Research Association meeting, Chicago, February, 1962.
11. Morphett, M. V., and Washburne, C., "When Should Children Begin to Read?" *Elementary School Journal*, XXXI (March, 1931), pp. 496–503.
12. Muehl, S., "The Effects of Letter-Name Knowledge on Learning to Read

a Word List in Kindergarten Children," *Journal of Educational Psychology*, LIII (August, 1962), pp. 181–186.

13. Nicholson, A., Background Abilities Related to Reading Success in First Grade. Unpublished Ed. D. Dissertation, Boston: Boston University, 1957.

14. Olson, A. V., Jr., Growth in Word Perception as it Relates to Success in Beginning Reading. Unpublished Ed. D. Dissertation, Boston: Boston University, 1957.

15. Ploghoft, M. H., "Do Reading Readiness Workbooks Promote Readiness?" *Elementary English*, XXXVI (October, 1959), pp. 424–426.

16. Schramm, W., Lyle, J., and Parker, E., "Television in the Lives of Our Children," Palo Alto: Stanford University Press, 1961.

(44) PERSPECTIVES: TEACHING YOUNG CHILDREN TO READ*

Nila Banton Smith

There are strong surges of thinking in regard to all aspects of education at the present time. We seem to be experiencing a veritable crescendo of new ideas about improving instruction in science, social studies, mathematics and reading. Fresh schools of thought are emerging, novel materials are being developed, opinions pro and con are being advanced with vigor, and educational controversy is running rampant.

Among present controversial issues perhaps no one of them is more widespread among parents and educators than that of teaching young children to read There are some who are forcefully arguing for the early teaching of reading; others are opposing this practice with vehemence.

What troubles me is that the arguments seem to be *all* black or *all* white. There are many variables in this complex situation and numerous shadings of gray between the two extremes of thought. Yet most people talk, speak and write in terms of one or the other of two broad alternatives: Shall we teach young children to read or shall we not teach young children to read? We need to be more specific. I am convinced that this controversy would be mellowed, reduced, in many cases resolved, if we would break down into specifics the broad implications of this topic as a whole. What do we mean by the generic term *children*?

*Reprinted from *Vistas in Reading*, 11, Part I (1966 Convention Proceedings), pp. 581–86, by permission of the author and the International Reading Association.

What do we mean by the broadly applied adjective *young*? What do we mean by the prepositional phrase *to read*; and lastly, and perhaps most important, what do we mean by the word *teaching*? It is hoped that pointing out some of the shades of meaning in each of these terms will serve to clarify the concept of the overly-generalized subject, "teaching young children to read."

WHAT DO WE MEAN BY *CHILDREN?*

When we talk about teaching reading to young *children*, are we talking about the great mass of offspring representing the plural of *child*? Or are we talking about some particular group or some individuals having certain characteristics of their own but still classifiable under the generic term of *children*?

Are we talking about children like John, the son of a professor who is a colleague of mine? Upon going to the home of this colleague I was introduced to Nancy who is in the second grade and to John who had just turned four. Mrs. Miller said, "Nancy is reading at fourth grade level, and she spends hours reading to John. He begs her to read to him." "Can you read, John?" I asked. The answer was forthright, "Not yet but I will be soon." And I am pretty sure that he will be reading soon. The children evidently have high intelligence, they live in a cultured home, they have had rich experiences, they have an ample library of children's books. The father, mother and sister are all avid readers. John lives in a stimulating reading environment.

John and Nancy represent the kind of children whom most investigators are talking about in their studies of early readers. Plessas and Oaks (1) summed up the characteristics of children in these studies and stated:

> . . . these early readers can be characterized largely as having superior intelligence, having fathers who have mainly clerical and professional positions, living in homes with many encouraging and stimulating activities relating to reading . . .

Bob and Janice are children in another home that I had occasion to visit recently. Janice is eight and Bob is three. Their mother finished high school; their father quit at tenth grade. Both parents work at non-professional and non-clerical jobs. Janice went to school on the day of my visit. Bob spent the day with a woman who does babysitting in her own home.

"Do you ever read to Bob?" I asked Janice. "Oh, no" replied Janice. "We don't have any books, and besides I hate reading." Finally I edged this question across to Mrs. Steele. "Do you read to your children when they are little?" "Goodness, no. I'm too tired and when I have a little time at home I have too many other things to do to bother reading to them. I hardly find time to take a few looks at television, myself." Imprudently, I pursued the matter further, "Do you think Bob might be more interested in reading in school if he had some children's books, and if you or Janice might squeeze out a little time to read to him?" The answer was disappointing. "When he goes to school the teacher will take care of his reading. That's her job."

May we ask, do Janice and Bob represent the kind of children we are talking about when we glibly discuss the topic of teaching young children to read?

Here is another example. It is a description which a first grade teacher gave me concerning her class:

At least two-thirds of the children would be termed disadvantaged. There are perhaps a half-dozen in the class who are blessed with both a mother and a father in the home and who are reasonably well clothed, fed, and loved. Of my twenty-nine children, fifteen are Puerto Rican, five are Negro from poverty homes, and the remaining nine are low-middle-class white. They have a median I.Q. of 86. I suspect they would rate low on a maturity test. At the end of the school year last spring, my children in a similar class indicated a beginning kindergarten level of maturity on the Peabody Vocabulary Test. One child in the class is emotionally disturbed, three youngsters have severe speech problems, and all are meager in their language expression. They are creative, however, in such areas as music, art and dramatic play. We have the best finger-painters in Jackson County. On the other side of the ledger I must say that when it comes to reading they just don't catch on; and I am often confused by such expressions as "My Mudder, he . . . ;" "My toof jess fall down . . . ;" "I gots de stomick ache in my froat . . . ;" "Land where da Peelgrims fried . . . ;" and so on.

Now, when we are talking about teaching reading to young children, are we including in this broad concept the kind of children that this first grade teacher has in her class?

For years research has revealed again and again vast individual differences in children physically, intellectually, emotionally, linguistically, in rates of growth, and in degrees of motivation to learn. Research also has shown that reading success is related to these factors. Children are different from one another and reading ability differs as children differ.

A striking example of individual differences is apparent in a longitudinal study which has been under way for several years. Durkin (2), the investigator, has followed groups of children who read before coming to kindergarten as they proceeded through the grades, and she has found that they have been consistently higher in reading achievement than the children in her control groups who did not read before first grade. The non-early reading groups were matched with the early reading groups in intelligence, in chronological age, and in the school which they attended. An important question yet to be answered is why didn't the children in this comparably bright control group learn to read early? Some differences between these children and the early readers did come out in interviews with parents. The early readers walked and talked at earlier ages; they tended to come from smaller families; they spent fewer hours before television sets; they were more often content with quiet activities (drawing, coloring, looking at books) while the non-early readers had been more involved in active play, being fascinated with toys rather than coloring books, blackboards, pencil and paper.

The differences mentioned above were obtained through interviews and are significant. When additional research of this nature proceeds with its objective being to probe deeply into individual differences with a variety of appropriate tests, undoubtedly many differences will be found in regard to the fundamental growth areas mentioned earlier.

The need for adjustments to different kinds of children was evidently strongly sensed by Mason and Prater (3) in their review of 43 studies having to do with children and early reading.

In their summary the authors ask the question of "whether or not we should teach reading to preschool and kindergarten children." Then they draw some preliminary conclusions from the comparative studies included in the summary. Some of their conclusions are:

> When exposed to the same program younger children make less progress than older ones with similar levels of intelligence.
> That the best age for beginning reading is dependent upon several other variables such as the instructional materials, class size, the pacing of the program, and teachers' expectancies.
> That the control of attention is apt to be difficult for young children, and that attempts to force learning may lead to emotional reaction.
> Unless we improve in gearing our instruction to the student's ability to learn and to the amount of his previous learning, the answer to the question posed at the beginning of this paragraph will be *no*.

In regard to the last conclusion, particularly in so far as the kindergarten is concerned, I am not satisfied to leave this matter in the subjunctive mood. In my opinion we should be taking immediate and constructive steps "in gearing our instruction to the student's ability to learn and to the amount of his previous learning" and to many other individual differences. In doing this the answer may well become "yes" for certain children, provided that the "instruction" is carefully defined. Later on in this paper an attempt will be made to sketch broad outlines of possibilities of instruction for different types of children.

WHAT DO WE MEAN BY YOUNG?

Webster defines *child* as "a young person at any age between infancy and maturity, but most commonly one between infancy and youth." According to this definition "young" covers a pretty wide spread of ages. Authorities in childhood education and child psychologists are generally agreed that the period of early childhood extends from birth through the eighth year of life.

When we speak of young children do we mean the two-year-olds whom one writer suggests as subjects for word-card flashing? Do we mean the three- and four-year-olds of nursery school age? Do we mean the five-year-old in kindergarten? Do we mean the six-year-old in first grade or the eight-year-old in third? Technically "young" used in modifying the word "children" covers a lot of territory, and age makes a tremendous difference in teaching reading. When we are talking about teaching reading to "young" children we had better specify whether we are referring to two-year-olds, five-year-olds, six-year-olds or eight-year-olds.

And even if we do specify chronological age, we must go further and indicate the kind of children at this chronological age whom we have in mind; and, if possible, give some information in regard to their stage of development in many growth areas other than chronological age.

WHAT DO WE MEAN BY "TO READ"?

Many people seem to labor under the impression that "to read" means to recognize a few words on the television screen, on flash cards, or in a book. This is an exceedingly limited and distorted viewpoint.

What does "to read" really mean? What are the chief constituents of the reading process?

First, and of basic importance, is the development of interest in reading. Thousands and thousands of individuals today possess the skill of reading but never read a book or anything else, not even a newspaper. Studies repeatedly show meager reading habits in many students in school and college, in adults in life, and even in the aged whom we might expect to welcome leisure time in which to read. Without a thirst for reading, the skills perform only a minor part of the function which they should serve.

Little John, the professor's son who was surrounded with books and who begged his sister to read to him, was probably establishing an interest that will remain with him throughout life. Bob, who had no children's books in his home, whose mother was too busy to read to him, and whose sister hated reading, may wind up completely lacking in reading interest as are many adults at the present time.

May I ask is the development of thirst for reading uppermost in the minds of many parents who are now teaching their preschool children reading skills? Judging from the large numbers of students and adults who can read but do not, is it possible that we, as teachers, haven't been doing as good a job in kindergarten and primary grades as we might have done in establishing this primary constituent in the learning-to-read process? It would be of great significance if all of us would work toward greater improvement in this area.

Another fundamental needed in acquiring the process of reading is word recognition, the ability to decode words. This skill, however, is only a medium to use in realizing the other components of the reading process. Nevertheless, it appears that this one skill is considered by many people to be the end point in teaching young children to read. It is regrettable, indeed, that so many advocates of early reading mean word recognition only when they speak of reading. Overemphasis on this extreme concept of the reading process limits the reading growth possibilities of the child in other ways.

A third constituent of the reading process is that of understanding meanings given through word symbols on printed pages. This is the real purpose for which reading is carried on. Yet, one rarely hears any mention of comprehension by those advocating the teaching of reading to young children. We might inquire seriously, "Why is it that this very significant element in efficient reading is so often disregarded in accounts of teaching reading to young children?" This isn't quite understandable.

We have some evidence that early readers cannot grasp meanings commensurate with their ability to pronounce words. For example:

McCracken (4) recently reported a study in which eight children who read before first grade were observed and tested over a two-year period. Their average I.Q. was 132. They quickly mastered word-pronouncing and oral reading skills and made test scores above average. However, the investigator reported, "The ability to comprehend materials which they could read fluently orally was a problem for three of the children in March of first grade and for seven of these children at the end of second grade."

If gripping national and international problems are to be faced and solved, the adults of tomorrow must be keen interpreters and critical evaluators. May we ask, then, is it fair to the young children of today to implant in them the impression that all there is to reading is word-calling as is often done? Pronouncing words is not enough. Meanings are worthy of consideration, also.

This brings us to a discussion of concepts. Comprehension is based on concepts. Through the use of concepts the child in early stages brings meanings to symbols rather than getting meanings from symbols. Concepts of young children need development, enrichment and clarification.

A study that was carried out several years ago was very significant. It was conducted by Cantor (5) and it had to do with concept development in the kindergarten. The investigator analyzed the preprimers and primer which kindergarten children would use in the first grade, for concepts. Then she planned a series of excursions designed to acquaint kindergarten children with these concepts. Next, she organized matched groups of kindergarten children. Some groups were taken on the excursions; others were not. The groups having the excursions made higher scores on their readiness tests, and later in first grade on their reading tests than did the others. This is convincing evidence that concept development contributes to beginning reading.

One more constituent of the reading process will be mentioned—that of implications for developing rate in reading. In this age of speed, rapid reading is a desirable skill to develop and while young children definitely should not be subjected to speed pressure, the foundations should be laid from the beginning Does pronouncing individual words or an overemphasis upon scrutinizing words for phonetic elements serve to develop fluency? Research says that it doesn't. Experiences in reading words in phrases and in sentences is necessary in laying the foundation for fluency.

In summarizing different viewpoints in regard to the meaning of the reading process, two questions will be asked:

1. When we speak of "to read" in discussing the topic of "teaching young children to read" do we mean that reading is simply a matter of saying words in response to a visual presentation of printed symbols?

2. When we speak of "to read" do we mean the broad process of developing deep and abiding interest, skill in identifying words, ability to grasp meanings, and habits of reading phrases and sentences?

My readers may decide for themselves to which of these meanings they subscribe, and which one they support in practice.

WHAT DO WE MEAN BY THE WORD "TEACHING"?

"Teaching" is perhaps the most significant word in the whole controversial topic of "teaching young children to read," and the one concerning which there are the largest number of shadings in meaning.

When we think of *teaching* young children to read, do we mean:

1. Flashing word cards before the child, saying each one, and asking him to repeat it?

2. Drilling the child on the sounds of phonetic elements, presenting them on cards or paper, having him repeat them, and then telling him how to apply them when sounding words?

3. Having children work through a phonics workbook or kit designed for kindergarten?

4. Having children use a readiness workbook that accompanies a basal reading program?

5. Organizing a kindergarten class into three groups and following a teachers' manual in teaching the children to read from the successive preprimers and primers of a basal reading series?

6. Building a permissive reading environment, whetting interest by much reading to children from books, providing abundant contacts with reading symbols in functional and meaningful situations, recognizing and encouraging those who already read or begin to read, being willing to wait for readying maturation to come in those who don't?

All six of the above practices are in use in different parts of this country at present. So "Teaching" means different things to different people. When one person is talking about teaching to young children he may have in mind any one of the six practices I have mentioned. The person to whom he is talking may have an entirely different one in mind. How futile it is to talk in general terms about the "teaching" of reading to young children.

The great majority of specialists in early childhood, kindergarten teachers, and reading authorities are deeply concerned about *pressures* to teach formal reading to young children *indiscriminatively*. These people recognize the present trend to raise skills to higher levels of achievement in all fields. They are earnestly seeking ways to meet this demand of society at the kindergarten level without sacrificing their philosophy arising from great funds of knowledge in regard to the characteristics and needs of young children and in regard to the complexity of the reading process. Perhaps clearer understandings of the shades of meaning in the concepts of "Teaching Young Children to Read" will help in reconciling these viewpoints and in working out prudent applications of the concept as a whole. If this paper has contributed anything at all to this end, its purpose will have been accomplished.

REFERENCES

1. Plessas, Gus P. and Oaks, Clifton R., "Pre-reading Experiences of Selected Early Readers," *The Reading Teacher*, 17 (January, 1964), 241–45.
2. Durkin, Dolores, "Children Who Read before Grade 1: A Second Study," *The Elementary School Journal*, 64 (December, 1963), 143–148.
3. Mason, George E. and Prater, Norma Joan, "Early Reading and Reading Instruction," *Elementary English*, XLIII (May, 1966), 483–489.
4. McCracken, Robert A., "A Two-Year Study of the Reading Achievement of Children Who Were Reading When They Entered First Grade," *The Journal of Educational Research*, 59 (January, 1966), 207–10.
5. Cantor, Alma, *An Historical, Philosophical, and Scientific Study of Kindergarten Excursions as a Basis for Social Adaptation and Reading Readiness.* Master's Thesis, p. 191, Cincinnati, Ohio: University of Cincinnati, 1935.

(45) EARLY READERS—REFLECTIONS AFTER SIX YEARS OF RESEARCH*

Dolores Durkin

For the past six years I have been working on two longitudinal studies of children who learned to read at home, prior to their entering first grade. The first of the studies began in September 1958. The subjects were

*Reprinted from *The Reading Teacher* 18 (October 1964), pp. 3–7, by permission of the author and the International Reading Association.

children who just started first grade in the Oakland, California, public schools. The second study was begun in September of 1961, with first grade children enrolled in New York City public schools as subjects.

In June of 1964 both studies were concluded. The California children were then completing sixth grade; the New York children were spending their last month in the third grade.

Over the years central questions in the research have focused on the frequency of preschool readers in the population, on the factors that encourage early reading, and on the future advantages—or problems— of an earlier start.

Data in the studies have been collected from a variety of sources. Many findings have come from tests designed to assess intelligence, creative thinking ability, memory, perceptual skills, personality characteristics, and, of course, reading achievement. Other data have come from home interviews and teacher rating scales.

Since the research was first begun, periodic reports have been published. Some of the reports concentrated on research findings (1, 2, 3, 4, 7, 10, 11). Other reports were more concerned with the possible implications of these findings for the kindergarten curriculum (5, 6, 8, 9).

Now I would like to comment on some of the accidental and incidental things I have learned and noticed as I worked on the studies. There is no pretense about the profundity of these comments. For many of you, in fact, the comments and observations might only recall what you learned and noticed a long time ago.

ATTITUDES TOWARD EARLIER READING INSTRUCTION

In 1957, when plans for my research were still somewhat vague and indefinite, the general response to the topic selected for study was an unenthusiastic response to say the least. It was as if to think about the possibility of earlier reading instruction was to encourage a return to the era of child labor abuses. Consequently it has been very interesting to observe over a period of only seven years, the great change in attitude and acceptance. Today, the climate that surrounds educational thinking and decision-making is so full and heavy with demands that cry, "Let's have more and let's have it sooner" that a matter like teaching reading in the kindergarten is now a very popular topic. One might even call it a dangerously popular topic because its popularity often discourages the careful and objective probing that is necessary for intelligent decisions about kindergarten. Too often, today, intelligent decisions are replaced by the rush to be modern or, on the other hand, by the rush to defend what is traditional.

When the topic is reading and the kindergarten, the "rush to be modern" sweeps along with a point of view that assumes all five-year-olds are ready to learn to read. For the few children who might not be ready, or interested, the remedy usually offered is the use of reading readiness workbooks.

In this particular rush, the picture of reading instruction itself looks very much like a typical first grade picture. The job is simply to transfer to kindergarten what is now in grade one.

The rush in the opposite direction—that is, the rush to defend what has been traditional for kindergarten—often moves along a road marked by nostalgic thinking and sentimentality. On this road the youngness of young children is highlighted, as is their need for social and emotional development. Overlooked, very often, is the obvious presence of preschool children who are very much aware of the written language in their world, and who are curious about it. Overlooked, too, are the preschool children who want to write, who ask how to spell, and who could learn to read with ease and enjoyment.

However, for the traditionalists the entrance of reading into the kindergarten marks the inevitable entrance of a formal program. And, though the term "formal" is almost never defined with preciseness, it is commonly used to denote instruction that is book-centered, group-centered, and rigid—and, therefore, most inappropriate for five-year-old children.

To think about the practices promoted either by those who want to be modern or by those who are traditional is to face the temptation of supporting the opposite position. Kindergartens that are cluttered with workbooks and that are noisy with phonics certainly tempt one to urge, "No reading in the kindergarten, please!" On the other hand, kindergarten programs that are totally empty of opportunities to learn to read but which, very often, are full of activities that some children abandoned even before they came to kindergarten—these programs, too, tempt one to move quickly away and to the opposite extreme

But these extremes are the easy reactions. They should remind us, nonetheless, that extreme and opposing positions in education do not naturally counteract one another in such a way that they are then replaced by a more sensible and balanced position. Instead, it would seem, the position that makes sense is one that emerges only after the important questions are asked, and when these questions then get attention that is as full of objectivity and scholarship as it is empty of bias and sentimentality.

IMPORTANT QUESTIONS

What are some of the important questions that need to be considered in any discussion about reading and the kindergarten? I personally feel the initial questioning should concentrate on the total kindergarten curriculum before the focus ever shifts to one possible piece. Otherwise the emphasis will be on curriculum patchwork rather than on fundamental questions about the purpose and appropriateness of the whole.

If one accepts, as a fact, that the kindergarten program today is almost exactly like the earliest of the American kindergarten programs—even though the pre-kindergarten life of children has changed—then it is both fair and fundamental to ask whether this is as it ought to be.

IMPLICATIONS FOR KINDERGARTEN PROGRAMS

In the parent interviews I have done for my research (in the second study the interviews were with parents of both early and nonearly readers) it became commonplace to hear about five-year-olds who had expressed disappointment with what they found in kindergarten. For the children who had already attended nursery school, kindergarten was often either a repetition of the previous year or, in a few instances, a year of reduced challenge and interest. For the children who had not attended nursery school, the kindergarten program which offered them games and coloring and singing and storytelling was interesting for a while, but not for a year.

Very often, when the content of kindergarten programs was compared with the preschool activities of the children, there was either very little difference or, if there was much difference, the preschool activities generally looked better in variety and challenge. When differences favored the kindergarten, it was because the abilities the children brought to school were recognized, and the kindergarten program then moved on to extend them.

The few kindergarten programs that offered challenge certainly showed no scorn for the importance of social and emotional development. Instead, it seemed, they reflected the assumption that maturity is not accomplished in a vacuum. In the case of these better programs, the vacuum was filled with a curriculum that neither bored nor frustrated the children.

If kindergartens, as a whole, are to avoid both boredom and frustration, and if they are to build on the abilities the children bring to school, then at least some kindergarten programs should offer opportunities to learn to read, either because the children arrive with the beginnings of reading ability or because, over time, they show an interest in learning. For other five-year-olds other kinds of learning opportunities should be provided because these children show special interest and ability in art, for example, or because they are fascinated with simple arithmetic.

Within this framework, then, reading in the kindergarten becomes one possibility. Within this framework, too, kindergarten instruction in reading becomes one of the possible ways in which differences among five-year-olds are both recognized and utilized.

KINDERGARTEN INSTRUCTION IN READING

Were I to try to put into kindergarten programs the kinds of things that encouraged the early reading ability of children in my research, I would begin with a kindergarten teacher who not only answers questions about written language but who also plans ways to increase the questioning. In the research, the preschool questions of children were frequent, and the questions were about street signs and car names as often as they were about words appearing in books. When books did help, it was generally while a parent read to a child and, on occasion, pointed out words that were of special interest or importance.

Actually, more than half of the preschool readers in the research were interested in writing before they ever showed any interest in reading. For these children writing seemed to be the extension of a still earlier interest in scribbling. Over time, the scribbling changed to drawing of people and things; later, to the drawing of letters of the alphabet. Here, small blackboards were often used for "practice."

Still other early readers, according to their parents, showed interest in playing with oral language and with sounds. For some of the children this interest resulted in the ability to respond to requests like, "Tell me a word that begins with the way 'bird' begins." For a very few children the interest in sounds and in letters eventually led to some independence in spelling.

Were I to try to move from research findings to kindergarten programs, I would also be quick to remind teachers that the preschool children who were interested in reading, or in writing, were not necessarily interested every day. On some days, according to their parents, the children would be occupied for an hour or even longer with the kinds of questioning and with the kinds of pencil and paper activities that can lead to skill in both reading and writing. On other days the interests of the children were very different, and might go in the direction of playing house or of building with blocks. But even here, playing house occasionally included attempts to make out a grocery list, while block building sometimes included the making of signs to identify what had been built. In both instances, interests of the children were made productive by parents who gave help when help was requested.

If kindergarten education is also to give help—whether with reading or with something else—then there is work to be done. Immediately needed, for example, is more research that will tell us in detail about the preschool years of children who are living and learning in the 1960's. Hopefully, this research will have an excellence that leads to an increase in the number of facts about young children and, in turn, to a reduction in the number of myths.

With these facts, it seems safe to predict, our conception of the role of kindergarten education will be broadened to include much more variety in the curriculum and, consequently, much more need for small-group and individual activities. And this immediately suggests what all kindergarten teachers know: If a truly worthwhile job is to be done, kindergarten classes must be reduced in size and, in some instances, extended beyond a two- or three-hour period.

If a "worthwhile job" is made possible, one can also predict an attitude toward kindergarten which views it as an integral and very important part of the total elementary school program. For too long, now, kindergarten has been either isolated or put on the sidelines. It has been—as I heard a parent say just the other day—"a good time for catching measles and mumps because not much of importance goes on there." This is unfair to kindergarten children, and to kindergarten teachers.

References

1. Durkin, Dolores. "A Study of Children Who Learned to Read Prior to First Grade," *California Journal of Educational Research*, 10 (May 1959), 109–13.

2. Durkin, Dolores. "The Precocious Reader," *California Journal for Instructional Improvement*, 2 (Dec. 1959), 24–28.
3. Durkin, Dolores. "Children Who Read Before Grade One," *Reading Teacher*, 14 (Jan. 1961), 163–66.
4. Durkin, Dolores. "Children Who Learned to Read at Home," *Elementary School Journal*, 62 (Oct. 1961), 14–18.
5. Durkin, Dolores. "Some Unanswered Questions About Five-Year-Olds and Reading," *Changing Concepts of Reading Instruction*, pp. 167–170. IRA Conference Proceedings, 1961.
6. Durkin, Dolores. "Kindergarten and Reading," *Elementary English*, 39 (Mar. 1962), 274–76.
7. Durkin, Dolores. "An Earlier Start in Reading?" *Elementary School Journal*, 63 (Dec. 1962), 146–51.
8. Durkin, Dolores. "Reading Instruction and the Five-Year-Old Child," *Challenge and Experiment in Reading*, pp. 23–27. IRA Conference Proceedings, 1962.
9. Durkin, Dolores. "Should the Very Young Be Taught to Read?" *NEA Journal*, 52 (Nov. 1963), 20–24.
10. Durkin, Dolores. "Children Who Read Before Grade I: A Second Study," *Elementary School Journal*, 64 (Dec. 1963), 143–48.
11. Durkin, Dolores. "A Fifth Year Report on the Achievement of Early Readers," *Elementary School Journal*, in press.

(46) LET'S NOT READ SO SOON!
(EVEN THOSE WHO CAN)*

Gerald G. Glass

The teaching of beginning reading is on a track system! One track. As the "new insight" choo-choo goes speeding along it is getting to be the only track "do-it-sooner, do-it-sooner, do-it-sooner" system, leaving all others either by the wayside or far behind damned as "lock-stop" or "underestimators-of-young-minds." The hottest fireman of them all, Jerome Bruner, began shoveling on the coal with "our schools may be wasting precious years by postponing the teaching of many important subjects" (1). And how about this for power to run a run-away train by: "delay in teaching reading to *some* children wastes not only precious time

*Reprinted from *Vistas in Reading*, 11, Part I (1966 Convention Proceedings), pp. 458–61, by permission of the author and the International Reading Association.

but also the precious spark of enthusiasm that teachers are always trying to light" (2). An examination of the literature and the trend in the changes instituted in beginning reading programs in the past five years leave no doubt that today it is considered "good" to look for ways to bring youngsters to reading sooner rather than later.

ARE WE READING TOO SOON?

This paper is not going to enter the current dialogue in opposing this trend by asking the usual questions *Why?*, *To What advantage?*, *For whom?* What about those who are "normal" and can't learn earlier? Can we keep from them the message that they are already failures at five and six? (Would you believe four, in the "new" nursery school?) Moffit asks these and many other pertinent questions elsewhere (3).

We have other concerns. We seriously question whether teaching children to read and to use reading before *second* or *third grade* is advantageous to the developmental nature of reading. The utilization of reading as a form of communication before it should be used may potentially have a long lasting negative effect upon the child's growth in reading. These concerns result from an examination of the apparent reasons that young ones have for reading and also a serious unbiased look at what six or seven year olds can derive from reading.

WHY READ?

Why does a youngster in primary school read? To enjoy story line? Maybe, but he can usually *hear* stories that offer much more in the way of descriptive vocabulary and complexity of plot. An adult, teacher or parent, is not controlled by the problem of word analysis and also can give immediate help with what might be difficult concepts. (And, at this age, the contact with an adult in a non-evaluative atmosphere is always fun and sort of confidence producing.) Maybe the early grader reads because the books are pretty. Of course, but it is not the words in print that are pretty—it is the whole book itself—and the person reading out loud can show the pictures and discuss them when appropriate. Maybe a youngster wants to know about the world around him. He wants to use reading to extend himself and learn. But why a book? He can learn more about *anything* by hearing someone with more knowledge than himself (a teacher) tell about it. He can see a film that he can easily understand which tells him so very much more and usually in a more inviting way. He can "do" by planting or building or comparing actual phenomena, rather than guess what the world is about through someone else's words. Reading would give relatively little. In short, reading, for a youngster in primary school, is the *least* effective medium of all the communication media that can be used for learning about things or for enjoying stories pleasing to the thoughts and imagination.

Of all the communicative skills the primary child develops, reading is the least mature. It is merely in its beginning stage. A young reader cannot deal with material beyond the level at which he can analyze the sound of words. He can think and be made to think at a much higher level if reading is not the stimulus. The main thing a primary youngster seems to be missing when he reads instead of hearing and seeing is practice in sounding out words, even if the words in their book setting almost always have to be at levels lower than words he can hear without help.

How can you learn more about a frog? By reading about him in a second or third level book or by seeing a film strip or a film? Better still, have a frog before you and compare him to the anatomical chart you have right next to the frog. Or why not compare the chart to the actual discoveries you make when you dissect a frog? Yes, learning can be really interesting!

READING MORE AND ENJOYING IT LESS?

Learning that the learning process can be both satisfying and educative is crucial in the education of a youngster. If a youngster depends primarily upon "reading" to learn in his early years he will not only be cheated of using his highest level cognitive skills (at that stage in his development) but he might initially (and forever) associate reading with the *act* of reading and not expect that it can give him learnings and joys beyond the other ways of communicating (which reading cannot do in the early grades). There is so very much a child can learn through actual experience, through listening, and speaking, and seeing—and so relatively little the child can learn through *reading material* that can be introduced even in the most advanced early grades. Almost every primary school youngster can listen and speak at least two years beyond the level at which he can read. Reading here can be a drag on learning.

There is ample evidence that in the upper grades—where reading should be the medium through which the student develops his cognitive potential—many youngsters already have associated the act of reading with something they are expected to do instead of what they feel would be more interesting and informative. These readers may not, because of the materials they have read in the primary grades, expect to deal with writing that includes the thoughts, evaluations, descriptions, and ideas which cannot and should not be introduced to youngsters not mature enough to deal with them. For how long are we going to continue to develop readers who "skip the parts where people do not talk." At about age nine or ten development allows for maturing cognitions that can best and often only be obtained from reading—not through a picture, actual experience, or visual examination. To a great extent the nine or ten year-old has played out what he can get from "non-reading" and needs to deal with thoughts and ideas not available to him without reading. Great men of ideas have long passed away and the middle grader is now ready to give them a hearing—through reading. Persons he could never hope to meet are "listened" to—through reading. The immediate environment is becoming less adequate for the student's conceptual, experiential and vocabulary growth. He is now ready to learn and experience—through reading. It is ironic that *before* fourth or fifth grade, when reading should be least important in the education of the child, the most intensive reading instruction is given. But in the upper grades, when reading becomes crucial in the education of the child, reading instruction is offered to a significantly lesser extent.

FIRST THINGS FIRST!

In today's primary grade classroom the craze to teach reading sooner is inundating the rest of the curriculum. It is more reading, often at the expense of other communication skills! Youngsters are working in a medium that is relatively new to them. Ideas cannot be explored nor can new ideas be acquired through reading, because word-analysis ability needs about three or four years to catch up with what a youngster can understand. As stated, most first graders are reading at least two years below their comprehension level.

Therefore, if reading is not important to the immediate education of the early grader and if other media can more effectively educate the child, why do we not stop and ask: Why are we pushing reading so heavily in the early grades? Why not push (not just include) learning through listening *before* reading. Actually, to a youngster listening is the same as reading, only easier and more productive. Words mean the same whether they are spoken or written. Youngsters have been listening all their lives—it would be (and is) sheer ignorance not to utilize listening to its fullest when it can do the job. Almost anything that can be read by a youngster through second grade could be handled at a much more advanced and interesting level through listening. If we were to wait until a youngster's word analysis ability caught up to his conceptual ability before we "pushed" reading, the youngster would, from the start, feel the power, strength, and uniqueness of reading. His only control would be his own interests and strivings.

Also, think of the dimensions in learning we could reach if we developed materials to listen to with the same dedication that we develop material to read. It is conceivable that the level of ideas handled at first grade through listening would be more like those introduced at our present third grade. The primary aim, then, of early reading instruction would be the teaching of the "decoding" so that the youngster can, as soon as possible, drop the need for an auditory cue and become effective in handling language through visual (written) cues. If, during that time, he has developed vocabulary, concepts and interpretive skills through listening, seeing and doing, he will be catapulted to much higher levels when reading becomes appropriate. But to keep the youngster tied to reading before word-analysis ability matures is to hamper his educative process.

The writer has elsewhere described an approach to the teaching of reading that holds the "use" of reading in abeyance until the teaching of word analysis is completed (4). This is not only possible but, as has been discussed here, also desirable.

SUMMARY

This writer feels that the early teaching and emphasis upon reading has within it inherent factors which may account for the relatively poor record we have as "readers." (How often do adults turn to reading for what it alone can give?) Because of the developmental nature of reading versus the other communication media, "reading" ability is years behind in the primary grade youngster. Thus what the youngster can "read" is usually not nearly as rewarding to him as what he can hear, see, examine, or do.

The only task unique to early reading is that of learning the word-analysis skills. If, in the early grades, concepts were to be developed solely through listening, speaking, feeling, seeing (instead of through reading), the potential for growth would indeed be great. Later when the child has become proficient in word analysis, he can be presented with material to read at levels truly commensurate with his stage of development and truly able to fire his imagination and thought processes. Then perhaps we can hope for a nation of "readers."

REFERENCES

1. Bruner, J. *The Process of Education.* Cambridge: Harvard University Press, 1961.
2. Pincus, M., Morgenstern, F. "Should Children be Taught to Read Earlier?", *The Reading Teacher*, 18 (Oct. 1964).
3. Moffitt, M. "Is It True That Children Can Be and Should Be Taught to Read at a Younger Age Than Before?" Elementary Division, N.Y.C. Bd. of Ed., Apr. 1962.
4. Glass, G. "Teaching Word Analysis Thru Perceptual Conditioning." Proceedings of the International Reading Association, "Reading for Inquiry," 1965.

Chapter 10

BEGINNING APPROACHES
TO READING

INTRODUCTION

The articles in this chapter describe current approaches to teaching beginners to read. Several descriptions include evaluation of the particular approach. The final decision on the way children are taught to read must be made locally. In making a choice, full consideration should be given to the following questions:

How comprehensive a view of reading does this approach assume?

Will the method and materials promote growth toward maturity in reading?

How appropriate is the approach to these particular pupils?

Does the staff understand and accept the plan?

Are teachers prepared to interpret the selected approach to parents and the public?

Will the materials and procedures contribute to the child's feeling of progress and success in learning to read?

Before a particular approach is adopted, educators should take a hard look at the evidence of its effectiveness in similar situations. Pilot studies should precede general use and teachers should be involved in the decision. In-service education will need to accompany any drastic change in emphasis. It is obvious that changes in initial reading instruction will call for appropriate adjustments in the program in grades beyond the first.

Primary teachers will wish to become acquainted with the twenty-seven studies of first grade reading sponsored by the U.S. Office of Education and carried out during the 1964–65 year, as well as the follow-up studies in second and third grade. It seems that there is probably no single best approach for teaching reading to all children, although early decoding emphasis appears significant. Certain combinations of approaches tend to prove more effective than the use of a single method in isolation. In the article which closes the chapter, Dechant argues for an approach that is many-faceted. The teacher who accepts the point of view that the best teaching is diagnostic will be sensitive to the learning styles and particular needs of individuals and will adapt her procedures accordingly.

The present ferment among parents and teachers concerning the best initial approach to reading has led to a rather general reappraisal of present programs in teaching beginners. If this reappraisal is thoughtfully done, with changes in procedure constantly checked for effectiveness, the result will revitalize the process for both teachers and children.

(47) HOW A LANGUAGE-EXPERIENCE PROGRAM WORKS*

Roach Van Allen

A language-experience approach to instruction in beginning reading makes no distinction between the development of reading skills and the development of listening, speaking, spelling, and writing skills. All are considered essential in the instructional program and are viewed by teachers as providing reciprocal reinforcement. All facets of language are used as experiences related to the reconstruction of printed materials. All experiences of a child which he can express, especially in oral language, are included as the raw material out of which reading refinement grows. During the instructional program he conceptualizes:

What I can think about, I can talk about.
What I can say, I can write (or someone can write for me).
What I can write, I can read.
I can read what others write for me to read.

A language-experience approach recognizes in daily practice that the oral-language background of each child is a basic ingredient in word recognition. As implemented in most programs

- the thinking of each child is valued, regardless of how limited, which leads to
- encouraging each child to express his thinking in many forms, but especially in oral language, which can be
- represented in written form by a teacher or by the child which can be
- reconstructed (read) by the author and others, which leads to
- reading the written language of others from a variety of sources, which should
- influence the thinking and oral language of the reader so that his spelling, writing, and reading improve.

*Reprinted from *A Decade of Innovations: Approaches to Beginning Reading* 12, Part 3 (1967 Convention Proceedings), pp. 1-8, by permission of the author and the International Reading Association.

EACH CHILD BECOMES INCREASINGLY SENSITIVE TO HIS ENVIRONMENT

The basis of children's oral and written expression is their sensitivity to their environment, especially their language environment, both within the classroom and in the world at large, The continuing responsibility of the teacher is to help children at all levels of ability become increasingly aware of the world in which they live—to "talk" about it in many media and to relate their observations and impressions to their own experiences. They should learn through repeated experiences that our heritage of literature, art, music, and science are the products of men and women who viewed the world with sensitive eyes and ears. For this reason there is a continuing program in a language-experience approach that urges every teacher to

- read something of children's literature each day
- provide a place for children to express their ideas with art media throughout the school day
- discuss topics of interest with children,
- provide a time and place for children to record in writing and in illustrations what they see, hear, taste, smell, feel, imagine, discover
- tell stories from real experiences
- write books which record the real and imaginary experiences of the children in the class

CHILDREN SUCCEED THROUGH A VARIETY OF EXPERIENCES

Children's communication skills, including word-recognition skills, are promoted through numerous activities, experiences, and devices. A major goal is that of increasing the chances of success for more children, and to do this it is expected that every teacher will know multiple ways of working with individuals. Positive attitudes which result from repeated success are viewed as being as significant as any method or material which might be employed.

The classroom is operated as a language laboratory that extends throughout the day. Language skills are extended and ideas are refined as children listen to stories and recordings, view films and filmstrips, make individual and class books, dictate stories to each other, study words, develop flexibility in using the letters of the alphabet to serve their spelling needs, and begin to record their ideas in writing independently. They view filmstrips and provide the commentary before listening to the accompanying recording. They view motion picture films with the sound track turned off and discuss their own meanings and interpretations prior to hearing the commentary. They build confidence in their own ability to use language at the same time that they are making progress in recognizing the language of other people—people who are not present but whose ideas have been recorded with writing.

Children have frequent opportunities to read their own writing to the entire class, to small groups within the class, and to other groups in the school. The child who is reading his own writing (the meaning of which he already knows) can devote his energies in oral reading to clarity of expression, effectiveness of presentation, interpretation of punctuation, and other necessary details that make listening to oral reading a pleasure.

Motivation for improving language form and usage comes as children's writing is read by others. Pride in "published" work stimulates the young authors to seek language forms that will be understood by others. They are also influenced by what they read and what they hear read to them from hundreds of authors.

As children study the English language—its alphabet, its spelling, its sentence patterns, and the flexibility of meaning in English words—they come to realize that other people use words very much like their own to express ideas. The study of words of high frequency in English to the point of mastering them at sight, correctly spelled, becomes a meaningful experience.

As children express their own ideas, they are interested in finding out, through reading, what other people think and say about topics of interest to them. Wide reading, in turn, stimulates individual authorship, which is handled in the classroom through a variety of publishing procedures.

Understanding the nature and flexibility of the English language to a degree that one can look at printed symbols and reproduce the language of another person is considered to be a lifelong process. Understanding does not always result from "exercises" in reworking other people's language; it is more likely to develop as a child works with and reworks his own language. As he writes to say something important or interesting, he is dealing with the language letter-by-letter, word-by-word, and sentence-by-sentence. It is when he has been helped to improve his own language that he makes significant gains in understanding the strengths and weaknesses of that language. Repeated success in this process of writing and refining language gives the child confidence to view reading materials as another person's language. He can approach the act of reading with an attitude of "being able to reproduce the talk of someone who is not present."

TEACHERS SELECT ACTIVITIES THAT
EXTEND LEARNING

Through numerous studies, including the San Diego County Reading Study Project (1958–1967), researchers have identified twenty language experiences which contribute to the balanced development of language skills, including reading skills. These twenty language experiences are grouped in three categories as an aid in helping teachers select activities and materials. In well-planned programs some activities are selected from each category each day. During the progress of several weeks, the teacher is careful to choose activities which are related to all twenty experiences.

The three major categories with their emphases are listed below.

Group One. *Extending experiences to include words*—through oral and written sharing of personal experiences, discussing selected topics, listening to and telling stories, writing independently, and making and reading individual books.

Group Two. *Studying the English language*—through developing an understanding of speaking, writing, and reading relationships, expanding vocabularies, improving personal expression, studying words, and gaining some awareness of the nature of the use of high frequency words and sentence patterns.

Group Three. *Relating ideas of authors to personal experiences*— through reading whole stories and books, learning to use a variety of printed resources, summarizing, outlining, reading for specific purposes, and determining the validity and reliability of statements found in print.

Resource books for teachers, which insure that all three categories are dealt with frequently and that all twenty language experiences are extended through the elementary grades, are now available.*

---

*Roach V. Allen and Claryce Allen. *Language Experiences in Reading*, Teacher's Resource Book, Level I, Level II, and Level III. Chicago: Encyclopaedia Britannica Educational Corp.

FLEXIBLE ORGANIZATION IS VITAL

Learning situations must be designed so that each child can view himself as worthy and able to succeed in reading tasks of increasing difficulty. How a child feels about himself and his relations to others—his family, his teacher, and other members of the class—will determine to a great extent what he is able to say, write, and read.

School practices that make reading achievement the measure of success in the early grades, such as grouping techniques that *highlight* lack of this success, may destroy the child's self-image rather than improve his reading skills. Ability grouping for daily reading instruction can negate any positive attitudes that may be developed in other language experiences. Since every child individualizes his reading whether the teacher wants him to or not, the sensible attitude toward building good learning situations is one that emphasizes each child's success and provides for flexible groupings.

A language-experience approach allows great flexibility in organization and scheduling. The activities are selected to help the teacher use three basic patterns of classroom organization, singly or in combination, depending upon the nature of the work of the day.

The teacher works with the entire class. This arrangement works well for the following:

- reading aloud to children
- permitting children to read their stories or compositions aloud
- encouraging children to compose stories orally
- directing class discussions on topics of interest
- extending experiences through films, filmstrips, and field trips
- introducing and playing games
- singing and rhythms
- conducting seminars on the development of various skills

The teacher works with small groups—

- completing activities initiated in the large group
- taking dictation from one while others observe
- letting children read their own books as well as those of others
- giving special instruction in skills to some children identified as needing them
- playing games to practice skills

- practicing effective oral reading
- choosing appropriate books

The teacher serves as a resource person for individual and independent activities—

- suggesting ideas for individual books
- helping with spelling
- furnishing words for independent readers
- helping children choose and organize an independent activity
- conferring about reading and writing progress

LANGUAGE-EXPERIENCE APPROACHES HAVE ADVANTAGES

Whether a language-experience approach is used as the major reading program or whether it is used in conjunction with other programs, it has inherent in it certain advantages.

A language-experience approach does not require standard English as a basis for success in the beginning stages. Children who use language greatly divergent from standard English are not placed at a severe disadvantage. Children with great fluency in language do not experience, when they enter school, a period of language regression while they take time to develop a small sight vocabulary and learn a few word-recognition skills.

The approach does not require, nor does it recommend, ability grouping in the class. Teachers can proceed without administering readiness tests or using valuable time to place children in ability groups. This type of grouping serves a questionable purpose in overall language development.

Materials already available can be used effectively. There is no need for large expenditures for special materials for children with reading problems. Basal readers, supplementary readers, recordings, films, filmstrips, trade books, picture sets, children's newspapers, reference materials, and word-study programs can be used to advantage within the basic framework.

Children can begin to read using a sight vocabulary which has been developing in the home and community environment. Brand names, labels, signs, and other words are seen often on television. To this vocabulary can be added words of high frequency which most children do not acquire independently.

The method allows for the effective use of aides to the teacher. Semiprofessionals, older children in the school, interested parents, and other volunteers are examples of teacher aides.

Team teaching arrangements can be used to great advantage. A division of activities into large and small groups can continue through most of the day, thus making maximum use of all team members and their ideas.

The language-experience approach is ungraded in the sense that much of the direct language teaching is done with material produced by the children. Each child produces at a level which he can understand and thus learns to recognize words at his own level. Frustration is avoided. Also, children are helped to choose their own stories and books for independent reading from the beginning. They spend little, if any, time keeping the place while another child reads something which might be too easy or too challenging.

Children learn to spell the words of highest frequency at the same time that they learn to recognize them as sight words.

Phonics is an integral part of the daily program. Children learn about the relationships between sounds they make when they talk and the symbols used to represent the sounds in writing. They view phonics as a natural, normal language experience. The flexibility of sound-symbol relationships in English becomes a challenge in self-expression. Teachers who wish to reinforce and extend phonics learning with a more structured program can do so and still use a language-experience approach.

Children develop a level of independence in making choices in the daily program. This is seldom observed among those who study with highly structured reading programs.

The program requires that all children participate in a variety of expressive activities. What appears to be additional time scheduled for language study includes art, music, dramatization, and rhythmic activities. These are media for the expression of ideas which might later be written and used for reading development.

Children choose writing as an independent recreational activity as often as they choose reading. Self-expression is as important to them as contact with the ideas and language of other people.

Children who live in a classroom with these major emphases in language development do have an advantage! They develop desire and resources for self expression; they learn how to study the English language as a lifelong pursuit; they are influenced in their own thinking and their own language by the ideas and language of many authors whom they view as friends.

(48) PHILOSOPHY OF INDIVIDUALIZED READING*

L. C. Hunt, Jr.

The paramount issue is whether our current emphasis on intensive reading instruction can be brought into balance to some extent through a program of extensive reading. A basic characteristic of the basal text program is that each lesson is developed in a highly structured, comprehensive fashion—an approach best described as intensive reading instruction. Every selection is read and reread in great detail—word by word, line by line, page by page, story by story, and book by book—in a seemingly endless study. There is a great need to balance this intensity of study with a program which builds reading instruction in a broader, more natural fashion.

Certainly a child's mind needs to brush up against a multitude of ideas; he needs periods of continuous uninterrupted silent reading in order to pursue ideas in larger gulps, in more continuous development. Providing children with opportunities to read widely in the extensive world of literature available for them can best be accomplished through the program most frequently termed Individualized Reading.

What precisely is the individualized reading program and how does it differ from the typical basal textbook program?

Individualized reading is a program organized to give particular attention to the needs and interests of each individual student. Certain aspects of the program may vary considerably among teachers, however. Some basic principles of individualized reading are common to nearly all class room situations where it is used. Typical common elements are:

1. Literature books for children predominate (rather than textbooks series) as basic instructional materials.

*Reprinted from *Reading and Inquiry* 10 (1965 Convention Proceedings), pp. 146–48, by permission of the author and the International Reading Association.

2. Each child makes personal choices with regard to his reading material

3. Each child reads at his own rate and sets his own pace of accomplishment

4. Each child confers with his teacher about what he has read and his progress in reading

5. Each child carries his reading into some form of summarizing activity

6. Some kind of record is kept by teacher or child or both

7. Children work in groups for an immediate purpose and leave the group when that purpose is accomplished

8. Word recognition and related skills are taught and vocabulary is accumulated in a natural way at the point of the child's need

PHILOSOPHY

This program is markedly different from the textbook program wherein children are assigned to groups according to reading levels. Once grouped, directed reading instruction is presented to all children simultaneously according to a highly defined procedure within the manual. Each child, bound by the pace of this group, must accomplish material according to the teacher's directions. In individualized reading opposite conditions prevail; children spend blocks of time reading extensively. The individualized reading program is based on a premise that a child's pattern of learning cannot be predetermined in either rate or manner and can best be guided within a highly flexible framework allowing for considerable pupil choice and teacher judgment.

With all the materials of wonder, beauty, and breadth of knowledge available to children in the great variety of literature written for them, it is vital that they be given the opportunity, under guidance, to bring their world and the world of books together. They should have time to explore the books that abound and to select those that touch their "growing edges" in terms of what they want to investigate and learn and enjoy.

By contrast most of our reading textbooks are anthologies of short stories or are collections of excerpts from well known original stories and books, a common and defensible practice. But it does seem advisable to give children opportunities to come to grips with total presentations as they appear in original works rather than always to select a part or the best part of the total selection.

ORGANIZATION

If each child is permitted to choose his own reading material according to his own interests, development, and proficiency reading, he must assume certain responsibilities as a member of the class. Each freedom is balanced by a corresponding responsibility to himself—and to others. He cannot behave so as to interfere with the responsible behavior of his classmates.

Each child must sense how he fits into this kind of program. In addition to sustained silent reading, he may be recording his reading, discussing his reading with teacher or classmates, writing creatively about his reading, choosing his next book, and so on.

PROCEDURES

1. *Book Selection*: Varying degrees of guidance are needed in helping children select books. Some children need almost no assistance, others initially need a great deal of teacher direction in choosing books which are appropriate in level of difficulty, value of content, and even in interest-appeal.

2. *Reading*: Children usually read independently in the materials they have chosen. The teacher directs or controls the reading of those not sufficiently independent to pace themselves. Usually the child sets his own purposes and reads silently at his own rate. It is necessary, however, for each child to show through a variety of activities that his reading is being done in a responsible manner.

3. *Recognition vocabulary*: The accumulation of a recognition vocabulary in the textbook program is built on the concept of a controlled vocabulary. Vocabulary control consists of presenting a limited number of carefully selected words which the child is to learn at the time they are introduced. Success or failure is dependent upon whether these preselected words are learned at the time they are presented. In the individual reading, a child meets words naturally within the context of the story he has chosen to read. He learns them usually because he needs them to get the important ideas in his reading.

A teacher who departs from the method of presenting preselected words must be able to discern whether or not a child is
accumulating a recognition vocabulary at a reasonable rate and
utilizing word study skills effectively. If a child is accumulating a
vocabulary at a rapid rate, he can be encouraged to learn many
words through wide reading. If a child is stagnated, then careful
and organized teaching must take place.

4. *Conference*: The teacher-child conference is central to the individualized program. In the conference the teacher uses all of her
talents and knowledge to intensify children's involvement with
words and ideas. During this time teacher and child may discuss
appealing aspects of the books, ideas presented by the author, and
implication of these ideas as guides for living. The teacher determines whether the child knows what is happening and is able to
select the important ideas in the book. The child is often requested to read aloud a particular passage of interest or importance. Frequently preparation is made for sharing the book with
the class. The teacher may make a note about the need for
particular kinds of help or may provide some on-the-spot instruction. The success of the conference depends on the art of questioning developed by the teacher.

5. *Related activities and sharing*: Hearing about books read by
others can foster in children a desire to do something on their
own with the new ideas, new learnings, and knowledge contained
in books being read. Stimulation to reading widely is gained as
children learn from others about new books through creative
work, panel discussion, dramatizations, etc.

6. *Record-keeping*: Teachers who use individualized reading instruction have found it necessary to devise ways of keeping records of
the children's development in reading. Such records serve as a
guide for planning and as a basis for reporting to parents on
pupil progress.

7. *Skills groupings*: When several children are identified by the
teacher as needing help in the same area, they are grouped
together temporarily for this specific instruction.

8. *Interest groupings*: Children often like to work together. Frequently, several children decide to read the same book independently and then meet to discuss the important ideas, what the
book has meant to them.

9. *Evaluation*: In every instance where individuals are asked to take

responsibility for their actions, their own evaluation of accomplishment is of utmost importance. Where children are expected to be developing independence, the need for continuous evaluation cannot be overstressed. The teacher must develop with her children criteria for determining whether or not they are improving in their abilities to select books, read independently, use time wisely, and to respond to meanings and implications from what has been read.

The individualized reading program then differs sharply from the basal textook program; differs in philosophy, in classroom organization, in utilization of printed materials, and, above, all, differs in procedures employed by the teacher. Basically, the difference lies between reading instruction conceived as an intensive activity as contrasted to instruction based on broader extensive reading by children.

REFERENCES

Hunt, L. C. "Can Teachers Learn About Individualized Reading Instruction Through Educational Television?" *Changing Concepts of Reading Instruction*, J. Allen Figurel, Editor, International Reading Association Conference Proceedings. Vol. 6, 1961, pp. 145–147.

Lazar, M.; Draper, M.; Schwietert, L. *A Practical Guide to Individualized Reading.* Bureau of Educational Research, Publication No. 40, October 1960. New York: Board of Education of the City of New York, 110 Livingston St., Brooklyn, N.Y.

Veatch, Jeannette. *How To Teach Reading With Children's Books.* 1964. Bureau of Publications, Teachers College, Columbia University, New York, New York.

(49) LINGUISTIC APPROACHES TO FIRST GRADE READING PROGRAMS*

Charles C. Fries

On the whole linguists have produced very few materials for actual series of reading texts from which to teach beginning reading.

*Reprinted from *First Grade Reading Programs*, Perspectives 5, 1965, pp. 45–55 by permission of the International Reading Association.

LINGUISTIC APPROACHES

Robert A. Hall, Jr. *Sound and Spelling in English*, Chilton Co., Philadelphia and New York, 1961.

Frances Adkins Hall [Series of developmental readers], *Linguistica*, Ithaca, N.Y. 1956.

Henry Lee Smith, Jr. and Clara G. Stratemeyer. *The Linguistic-Science Readers, A Basic Reading Program*, 1955. Now expanded by Jack E. Richardson and Bernard J. Weiss and published as *The Linguistic Readers* by Harper and Row, Publishers, Evanston, Ill., 1965.

Leonard Bloomfield and Clarence L. Barnhart. *Let's Read, A Linguistic Approach*, Wayne State University Press, 1961.

Ralph F. Robinett, Pauline Rojas, and Staff. *Miami Linguistic Readers*. Ford Foundation Project, Dade County Public Schools Board of Public Instruction, Miami, Florida, 1964. (The Miami Linguistic Reader Series is designed to help teach beginning reading to pupils whose preschool language was other than English.)

Charles C. Fries, Agnes C. Fries, Rosemary G. Wilson, and Mildred K. Rudolph. *A basic reading series developed upon linguistic principles.* Eight Readers, Eight Practice Books, A Manual and Guide entitled To Teach Reading: The Transfer Stage, and a book for teaching the letters of the English alphabet.

SPECIAL MEANINGS OF THE WORDS WE USE

1. The term *linguistic* in our discussion here must be clearly separated from its popular use in English as meaning "anything and/or everything that has to do with language."

2. The term *linguist* here must also be clearly separated from its popular use in English as meaning anyone who can speak one or more foreign languages.

3. *Linguistics*, as used here, means the *body of knowledge and understanding concerning the nature and functioning of human language* achieved by the scientific study of the structure, the operation, and the history of a wide range of very diverse human languages. (This body of knowledge and understanding has been called "linguistic science," "Sprachwissenschaft," for more than a hundred years.)

4. A *linguist* as used here is one who is a specialist in this body of knowledge and understanding—one who, by *profession*, teaches it and/or, by research, contributes to its advancement. (A *linguist* is one who

knows about the structure, forms, and operation of a great many languages, although he may not have developed the special habits necessary to use any of those languages in conversation.)

A *linguist*, then, is one whose special field of scholarship is linguistic science. *Linguistic science* is here understood to be a body of knowledge and understanding concerning the nature and functioning of human language, built up out of information about the structure, the operation, and the history of a wide range of very diverse human languages by means of those techniques and procedures that have proved most successful in establishing verifiable generalizations concerning relationships among linguistic phenomena.

In this much loaded and difficult definition there are five essential features that cannot be separated, for each succeeding feature is a qualifier of what has preceded. Perhaps the following arrangement of the parts of this definition may serve to give these important features their relative prominence.

Linguistic science is

(a) *a body of knowledge and understanding,*
(b) (knowledge and understanding) concerning the *nature and functioning of human language,*
(c) (this knowledge and understanding) built up out of *information* about the *structure*, the *operation*, and the *history* of a *wide range of very diverse human languages,*
(d) (this knowledge and understanding built up) *by* means of those *techniques and procedures* that have proved *most successful* in *establishing verifiable generalizations,*
(e) (verifiable generalizations) concerning *relationships among linguistic phenomena.*

5. By *linguistic approach* to a first grade reading program we mean here a body of materials designed to teach beginning reading which

(a) is definitely selected and arranged according to the principles and assumptions of language learning derived from the body of knowledge and understanding indicated above as the substance of linguistics (linguistic science);
(b) is taught by methods, procedures and practices which are in harmony with this knowledge and understanding, and, in which conflicting methods and conflicting habit-forming pupil exercises are rejected.

6. The linguist's *professional field of competence* is the body of knowledge and understanding concerning the nature and functioning of human language. To apply that knowledge and understanding to the problems of effective "doing" in any sector of human activity, the linguist needs another competence in the "engineering" aspects of that application.

In similar fashion, the professional field of competence for specialists in psychology or in reading is not "linguistic science." To deal with problems that concern the nature and functioning of human language such specialists also need a second competence in the field of linguistics.

THE LINGUISTIC NATURE OF THE READING PROCESS

The usual child of five has learned to talk. We are not concerned here with those who do not talk well enough to get along in their community. They constitute a different kind of problem.

The actual control of his native language by the five-year-old child is much more complete than persons other than linguists have assumed. From the point of view of a reading program we are concerned primarily with what the child *understands* as it is said *to* him, not what he himself says. His receptive language control is much greater than his productive language control. The basic question concerning his language becomes the following. "Just how much meaning and what meanings does the child receive or recognize when his parents, his teachers, his companions talk to him? If you read to him or tell him a simple narrative about going to a familiar store to get a ball, just what will he understand?" A five-year-old child will get some meanings from that "talk." The basic question for his reading becomes the following. "Just what must that five-year-old child learn to do now in order to get, by means of his own reading, the *same meanings* that he can get when he hears it? When he can get from his own reading the same meanings he can get from your telling him, he can *read* up to his language ability of that time. From our linguistic point of view a person can read in so far as he can get from special sequences of graphic symbols on a printed page the same fullness of meaning that he gets when these meanings are told to him in talk.

The process of learning to do reading, is the process of learning to transfer the already achieved ability to get meanings from talk in a time sequence to a new ability to get the same meanings from seeing representations of this same talk in a direction sequence on a surface. His reading progress and achievement is most realistically measured with his respective language achievement as the base.

Learning to read is not learning to *know* something, it is learning to *do* something. No amount of knowledge about a language, however great, will, of itself, enable one to speak that language.

The materials and methods here set forth assume as their primary objectives *not knowledge about reading but ability to do reading.* They aim at a step-by-step building of specific habits and abilities that lead directly to independent reading on the part of the pupils—*independent reading with a feeling of security in what they are doing.*

Learning to read must begin with and build upon the language control already achieved by the pupils. The reading must at every step be tied to the language of the child. Word recognition means a recognizing of the "word" as it appears spelled in letters as the same "word" that the child knows in his "talk." It is a recognition of an old friend now appearing in a mask—one whose "tone of voice" is recognized well.

The beginning steps in reading must all have this same fundamental character—the "words" as they appear in the spelling, and the "sentences" in which the "words" are joined together must all be recognized by the pupils as familiar, although somewhat masked, parts of the language they use every day. The first stage of learning to read consists of a building up by the pupils of the habits of identifying the "words," in their spelling-pattern dress, as the same words as those they know very well when they hear them in talk.

It is assumed that much of the school time outside the "reading period" itself will be given to the stimulating of "talk" by the children, for the sake of having them grow both in the vividness with which they can react to their experiences, and also in the fullness with which they can communicate those reactions. But the materials, *of the reading period itself,* in the "transfer" stage of the child's growth can be most effective by being adequately controlled. Within this control there is plenty of room for well-formed sentences in *coherent sequences.* A very few words, which the child knows orally, are presented as fitting into one of the types or matrixes of a pattern, and then immediately practiced by being read in sentences that belong to a sequence. There is no learning of lists of words at any time. The precise, rigorous controls of selection and sequence are embedded in the reading materials and not easily apparent in a hurried or superficial examination.

The most important first step in *preparing to learn to read* is the building up of high speed recognition responses to the letters used for the printing of English. It is true that adults who have learned to read well are usually not conscious of the separate letters of the words as they read. This fact, however, does not furnish any basis for concluding that the pupil at the beginning stage can learn to read by ignoring the special sequences of the letters that identify the separate words. He must master the whole set of letters by learning to recognize the special shape that identifies each letter and separates it from all other letters.

The instant recognition of individual letters as they stand alone is, however, not enough. Letters must be recognized as they appear in sequences. The order of the letters in the directional sequence of left to right acts as a fundamental marker for the discrimination of lexical units. This significant means of the identification and the discrimination of words in print are not only the different letter units that compose the sequence unit but also the order within that unit always seen from the single point of view established by English writing.

THE LINGUISTIC SIGNIFICANCE OF PRESENT-DAY ENGLISH SPELLING

English spelling changed drastically during the period between the death of Chaucer in 1400 and the birth of Shakespeare in 1564. This changed character of English spelling is revealed in the vigorous arguments in the middle of the 16th century concerning the deviation from "reason-ableness," and in the measures devised for bringing it back to its "due order and reason," "howe to write or paint the image of mannes voice most like to the life or nature." "The vices and faultes of our writing" were listed and condemned—"the use of the same letter for many sounds," "the use of many letters for the same sound," the "abuse" of "some letters to put a difference betwixt . . . wordes of one sound," "the superfluity of letters in writing," and to "shew the derivation and spring of some wordes borrowed or taken forth of strange tongues."

The new feature of this change was the fact that the *old spellings remained as patterns* and now represented the new pronunciations. This continuation of the use of the old spellings to represent the vowel phonemes, as now changed by the shift, put Modern English spelling out of line with the use made of the "Roman" alphabet by other languages. It even put it out of line with the English use of that alphabet during the Old English and the Middle English periods. By the end of the 16th century English spelling had accepted and extended for part of the vocabulary the "etymological" principle and, with it, the use of letters "silent to the ear" but "eloquent to the eye."

A new principle of representation became dominant. The spelling-patterns that developed historically pulled exceptions into conformity. The actual basis of the representation of the vowel phonemes changed from *items* of graphemes to *patterns* of graphemes.

The spelling-pattern approach used here, to a superficial examination, may seem to show features quite similar to those of a variety of the other approaches and "methods" that have been used in teaching beginning reading. However, this spelling-pattern approach is, in fundamental principle, quite different from any of them.

This spelling-pattern approach does explore and use the relation between the language as heard and spoken and the language as read and written. It is not, however, any of the *phonic* methods commonly discussed, nor is it any of the so-called *phonetic* approaches. It does not seek and emphasize correspondences of individual letter-individual sound. It does give attention to whole words rather than to isolated sounds but it is not any of the well-known "word" methods. At the beginning it uses a considerable proportion of the so-called "three letter words with short vowels" but it it is not the "word family" approach.

One major special characteristic of this spelling-pattern approach is the fact that the attention is not centered upon the learning of individual words; nor is success measured by the number of the words the child has learned to recognize. For such a learning of individual words it is essential that these particular words themselves be repeated over and over, and it is only the word itself that is learned. On the contrary, in the spelling-pattern approach it is the pattern itself that is repeated frequently, using a variety of different words and matrixes. The response to the spelling-pattern through different words is made so frequently that that response becomes a fixed habit. With such habits of responses to the patterns and the matrixes, the pupil can be led to make instant extensions of recognition or other individual words in the same pattern and to read words of his receptive vocabulary that he has never seen written before.

The separate spelling-patterns are enforced by constant repetition in minimum contrast with other spelling-patterns. The objective is the building up of habits of rapid recognition responses, not only to contrastive items in a pattern, but to contrastive items in a system of contrastive patterns.

The spelling-pattern approach takes maximum advantage of all the *regularities* that the orthography of English has developed throughout the history of English writing. The patterns of Modern English spelling are primarily those that arose during the Early Modern English Period, i.e. from the beginning of printing in England to the latter part of the seventeenth century. In the spelling-pattern approach the criteria for identifying the separate words are not vague and general shapes but precise and sharp—the criteria of the language itself. The major and the minor sets of spelling-patterns include all but a very few English words.

By the end of the first 325 pages of our reading materials the pupils have become familiar with sets of words that exemplify most of the matrixes or types of spelling-patterns that make up what has been called here "the first major set of spelling-patterns." By this time the pupils will have, therefore, not only learned to recognize rapidly the particular 523 words that they have used in their readers but also will have developed the habits of recognizing rapidly any and all words of their receptive vocabulary that in the context of their reading, fit the various spelling-patterns of the first major set. Pupils are therefore able to read many words that they have never seen written before. Developing this ability from the beginning is one of the chief objectives of the spelling-pattern approach.

READING FOR MEANINGS

From the very beginning, reading is developed as a means of acquiring meanings—not only the meanings of the separate words, but also the grammatical meanings that attach to structures in sentences, and the cumulative meanings of sequences of sentences in connected discourse.

The approach here assumes that language is man's chief device for storing and sharing meanings. With the invention of writing, the storehouse of man's knowledge has attained enormous capacity. Reading is the only key to that immense storehouse. The "words" as written have meaning for us only as these written "words" are connected with the "words" of our spoken language. But the isolated word alone can be used in so many situations that only as these "words" appear in the grammatical patterns that make sentences, do they actually convey precise meanings.

It is not, however, isolated sentences that convey the most important meanings we share, but rather sentences in sequence with the cumulative meanings of connected discourse. This series, therefore, begins the reading not with lists of words to be pronounced, but with three "words" to be recognized and at once used in three or four sentences with consecutive meaning.

The three basic words all fit a single type of spelling-pattern.

cat	Nat is a cat.
Nat	Is Nat fat?
fat	Nat is fat.
	Nat is a fat cat.

The "reading" thus begins with such a sequence as the following, using in addition to the three patterned words the familiar word *is* and the phrase *a cat.*

The significant elements of the meanings here are "words" in sentences which are joined in a sequence. All these elements of meanings are in the language forms that the pupil already knows. The reading process which the pupil is learning is the recognizing of the written forms in their directional sequence as standing for the "words," "sentences," and "sequences of sentences," the meanings of which he already knows and uses.

All the words that are introduced are thus not only immediately put into sentences, each one of which has a meaning, but the three sentences in sequence have cumulative meaning which is summarized in a fourth one. For the series, the very first book given the pupil (equal to the usual first and second preprimer), therefore, contains only some forty words; but these forty words are used in more than two hundred and sixty sentences through which the use of reading for meanings is developed from the very opening lesson.

These more than two hundred and sixty sentences appear, *not* as separate unconnected sentences, but in some fifty sequences or units of three or more sentences each.

Real reading is "productive reading." It is not only an active responding to all the signals of meaning represented in the writing, but also the carrying forward and building up of such a complete understanding of the sentences in sequence as will make it possible to fill in the patterns of tone, the special stresses, and the pauses of grouping that the live language of speech uses. Real reading is never a *passive* process of receiving meaning and saying words.

In order to make sure that pupils move easily into this sort of "productive reading," without having to correct interfering habits, attention to "expression" begins immediately. "Reading with expression" means nothing more than using in oral reading the intonation sequences (the sequences of musical pitch or tone) that characterize the ordinary talk of English speakers.

Normal English speech is not in a monotone. These variations of tone in the sequence of speech, however, are not haphazard and lawless. "Reading with expression" is more than avoiding a monotone. The sequence of tone in normal English speech follows certain major patterns within which there is considerable individual variation. It is essential that these major patterns of tone sequence be followed in oral reading by the teacher and by the pupil from the very beginning.

Using the major patterns of English intonation is *not* for the pupil (or for the teacher) learning to do anything new. As a matter of fact, fitting into the tone patterns of the intonation sequences of English is perhaps the very first thing the child learns of the language. Most normal children of six speak their language using all the intonation patterns of their linguistic community.

We do not aim to teach the pupils the facts concerning intonation patterns nor to make them conscious (or self-conscious) of their use of these patterns. Children will, however, use the patterns of intonation naturally *if they realize the meaning of what they are saying.* The *oral reading* must become the *telling* of the meaning which they have received from the written words. Their intonation will demonstrate whether they have really got the meaning or are simply pronouncing words which as a group do not for them stimulate any recognition responses.

Pictures have been excluded as a matter of principle from the readers of this series in order to force the pupils to *read* for the meanings rather than have them obtain the situational meaning from the pictures and then guess at the identity of the words that usually accompany the pictures.

The Readers of this "linguistic" series center attention upon the clues furnished by the words alone, that is, by the spelling-patterns that represent the linguistic units which the language itself uses to separate and identify the words. Pupils do not need the crutches that the ordinary use of pictures thrusts upon them. In fact, such pictures furnish a distracting element in the process of learning to read. They attract the attention of the pupil away from the spelling-patterns that must be learned and take away from him the necessity of getting the situation meanings from the sequences of the sentences to be read.

In these materials the ordinary process of starting with pictures is completely reversed. From reading the words as they appear in the sentence sequences the pupil must grasp the situation presented in the story. And then, in order to strengthen his imaginative realization of that situation, he is asked to draw pictures himself that will illustrate parts of the story. Many, even those of the slower learners, do very well with these exercises.

REFERENCES

1. Hanna, Paul, and Moore, James T. "Spelling—From Spoken Word to Written Symbol," *Elementary School Journal* LIII (Feb. 1953), 329–37. Also in *Education Digest,* May 1953, 16–19.

2. Hall, Robert A. *Sound and Spelling in English,* Chilton Company, Book Division, Philadelphia, Pa., 1961.

3. Hall, Robert A. "Graphemics and Linguistics," Symposium on Language and Culture, Proceedings of the 1962 Annual Spring Meeting of the American Ethnological Society (1963), 53–59.

4. Voegelin, C. F., and Voegelin, F. M. "Typological Classification of Systems with Included, Excluded, and Self-Sufficient Alphabets," in *Anthropological Linguistics,* III, Jan. 1961, 55–96.

5. Hanna, Paul, and Hanna, Jean Schuman. *Phoneme-Grapheme Correspondences,* (a detailed analysis of 17,000 different American English words). A Cooperative Research Project of the U.S. Office of Education, 1962.

6. Higginbottom, Eleanor. University College, London Univ., "A Study of the Representation of English Vowel Phonemes in the Orthography," *Language and Speech,* III, Pt. 2, April-June 1962.

7. Garvin, Paul, and Trager, Edith Crowell. Machine Translation of Speech into Orthographic English, Nov. 1, 1963, "The Conversion of Phonetic into Orthographic English, a Machine Translation Approach to the Problem." Final Version issued Nov. 1963, TRW Computer Division, Thompson Ramo Woolridge Inc., Canoga Park, Calif.

8. Hodges, Richard E., and Rudorf, E. Hugh. *Phoneme-Grapheme Relationships,* National Council of Teachers of English, Nov. 1964.

9. Weir, Ruth Hirsch. *Formulation of Grapheme-Phoneme Correspondence Rules to Aid in the Teaching of Reading,* (Cooperative Research Project No. S-039), Stanford University, 1964.

10. Dolby, James L., and Resnikoff, Howard L. "On the Structure of Written English Words," *Language,* 40 (1964), 167–196.

11. Various reports of studies of phoneme-grapheme correspondences from "A Basic Research Program on Reading, Cornell University, 1963." E. J. Gibson, C. F. Hockett, H. Levin, R. L. Venezky, and others.

(50) PHONICS EMPHASIS APPROACHES*

Arthur W. Heilman

Two objectives of this discussion are to identify salient features of a limited number of phonic approaches to beginning reading and to stress the educational issues which are related to the debate on phonics emphasis which has characterized the past decade.

BACKGROUND

The problem of what is the proper role of phonics in reading instruction is not new. Undoubtedly the pressures on schools and teachers today, which are traceable to this issue, are unprecedented. In general, the most vociferous critics of present day reading instruction start from a number of erroneous premises which suit their purposes. These premises include:

1. There is a sight word method of teaching reading which makes no provision for teaching phonic skills.
2. All words met at various instructional levels are taught exclusively as "sight words."
3. There is an educational conspiracy in American education which is opposed to the teaching of phonics.
4. Phonics instruction is "good" and childen cannot get too much of a good thing.
5. If we go back to the phonics emphasis of the 1890's, present reading problems in our schools would disappear.

To illustrate the present state of affairs we will turn to the Council on Basic Education, a non-profit organization dedicated to the improvement of American education. In so far as the Council on Basic Education has been concerned with reading instruction, that concern has focused entirely on the issue of phonics. In the January 1964 *Bulletin* (p. 1) of the Council we read:

*Reprinted from *First Grade Reading Programs*, Perspectives 5, 1965, pp. 57–71, by permission of the author and the International Reading Association.

Perhaps the most encouraging development of the year (1963), was the increasing understanding on the part of the public of what the phonics *versus* sight reading controversy is all about. The issue has often been confused in the public mind, especially when the advocates of the sight, or look-and-say method, insist that they also are believers in phonics instruction.

In the CBE *Bulletin*, February 1962 (p. 2), one finds:

> From our observation of good teachers in the fields of reading and language we discern a few guiding principles and methods of operations.
> 1. The good teacher of beginning reading, where she is not bound by an imposed methodology, operates on the theory that *beginning* reading is not a 'thought getting' process but is based on translating letters into sounds.

No evidence was cited as to source of this data.

In discussing an article by Paul Woodring, (*Saturday Review*, January 20, 1962) which made a plea for less heat and less name calling in the discussion of reading methodology, the editor of the council's *Bulletin* stated, "It seems to us that anyone who suggests, even by indirection, that the present reading controversy does not involve fundamental issues but is merely a reflection of temperamental differences between reading theorists, misreads the true nature of the controversy. There is a real war on in reading, and for the future well-being of American education it is *important that the right side win.*" [Emphasis added.] CBE *Bulletin*, March 1962, pp.8-9.

The individual who wants to make beginning reading a meaningful and enjoyable experience may have cause to feel threatened by the almost unlimited number of phonic systems which deal only with this limited facet of reading. This factor, coupled with the emergence of the philosophy that a "fast start" in beginning reading based on early stress of phonics is an unmitigated virtue, poses an educational issue of major importance.

The writer has long been of the opinion that phonics is second in importance to no other reading skill, and that "the reader must have the ability to pronounce or to approximate the pronunciation of words he does not know as sight words. This is ample reason for teaching phonics and sufficient justification for teaching it well" (9). Nevertheless, holding such a view does not preclude resistance to critics and materials which would push us into:

1. Teaching more phonics than is necessary for the child to learn to read.
2. Neglecting procedures for differentiation of phonics instruction.
3. Overemphasizing phonics in *beginning* reading.
4. Teaching phonics "steps" in illogical sequence.
5. Developing an over-reliance on phonics, (or context, or any other word analysis skill), as all such extremes are uneconomical and indefensible.
6. Behaving as if we believed that a child's memorizing phonic rules assures the ability to apply these rules in reading situations.

With these cautions in mind we move to a brief analysis of a limited number of phonic-emphasis approaches to first grade reading.

THE CARDEN METHOD

The Carden Method is a set of materials and a methodology developed and published by Mae Carden (4). Although the method stresses composition and spelling, its chief aim is the teaching of phonics. Book I deals primarily with the two-vowel rule. Book II teaches the sound of single vowels, and Book III introduces combinations which include *r* and *w*. The author suggests that *after* pupils have completed the Carden readers they move on to basal readers. Thus, the initial stage of reading is saturated with letter sound analysis. This approach:

I. STRESSES RULES

Initial teaching is limited to "regular spellings," or words which follow the given rule. The child is taught to "cross off" silent vowels and the famous two-vowel rule is modified to read: "When there are 2 vowels in a word the second vowel is crossed off and the first vowel keeps its name sound."

The following steps are utilized in teaching two-vowel patterns:

A. The term *vowel* is not used until after children have studied all vowels.
B. *a, e, i, o, u* = "The little letters that change their sounds."
C. Find the two letters that change their sounds.

1. Think! Which one comes first in the word and which one comes second in the word?
2. Cross off the one that comes second.
3. Sound out the word letter by letter (*coat* = cuh′ o tuh).

Later a goodly number of amendments or new rules are advanced or taught. Examples:

A. "There are *ea* words where the *a* drops out." (head, bread)

B. "There are words in which the *o* drops out in the *ou* combination and has the sound of *u*." (double, trouble, country)

II. Stresses Synthetic Sounding

Each consonant (or digraph) is given the weight of a syllable, (b—*buh*; j—*juh*; g—*guh*; th—*thuh*; ch—*chuh*; etc.). The word *the* is pronounced *thuh* and once the sound of a few letters have been introduced the child is ready to read a sentence:

suh′ e	thuh	buh′ o tuh
see	*the*	*boat*

(*preprimary manual*, p. 42)

Since an ordinary three- or four-letter word is sounded as though it consists of three syllables, the teacher is instructed to place the accent on the initial letter. (*boat* = buh′ o tuh; *coat* = kuh′ o tuh)

III. Stresses Writing and Spelling from the Beginning of Instruction

The letter *c* plays an important role in the teaching of letter forms. The child is taught that:

A. "Seven letters begin with *c*." These are: *c, a, d, g, q, o, e,* (The point is that there is a *c* imbedded somewhere in each of these letters.)

B. "Two letters make a *c* backwards." There are: *b, p.*

C. "The letter *s* is a *c* up in the air and a *c* backwards."

The following is from "A Note on Learning to Spell." The teacher constructs a word letter by letter applying the two-vowel rule. Example:

> The word *dime* is given.
> The teacher says, "Write *duh*."
> She adds, "What did you write?"
> The pupils answer, *"D."*
> The teacher says, "Write *i* next to the *d*."
> Then she says, *"m*, write *m, m—m."*
> The pupils write *m*.
> The teacher asks, "How do you make the *i* stay *i*?"
> The pupils answer, "Add an *e*." (*The Carden Method, A Brief on How To Get Started*.)

In the opinion of the writer, this approach is extremely mechanistic and ritualistic. However, it should not be concluded that children exposed to this type of instruction in grade one will not "learn" what is commonly measured at the end of grade one as "reading achievement." This is a tribute to children, but perhaps an unfortunate education phenomena since the fact that "learning takes place" is often cited as a justification for the use of such procedures.

WORDS IN COLOR

Words In Color (7) is a system developed by Caleb Gattegno who also developed *Numbers in Color* based on the Cuisenaire Rods for teaching arithmetic. These materials are discussed as a "phonics emphasis approach" because instruction begins and continues with the systematic teaching of letter sounds. The child is exposed to a dual visual stimuli: (1) the letter configuration, (2) in color. He hears hundreds of repetitions of each letter sound while his attention is focused on the *letter configuration* in color.

In this approach 39 colors are used, each of which represents a speech sound in English—regardless of what letters represent that sound. Initial teaching is done entirely at the blackboard using different colored chalks. and through the use of some 29 large wall charts done in color. On these charts the various letters and letter combinations in a given word are shown in different colors. Thus, the word *and* utilizes three colors: *sand*, four colors; and *impossible* calls for the use of seven colors. (The writer being color-blind could not verify this latter fact for himself, but accepted the word of a trusted colleague.)

The following are some pertinent facts about *Words In Color*:

1. Sounding, or the association of colored-letter *forms* with speech sounds, is taught in a most systematic, repetitive fashion. The term *drill* used in this setting would not be an overstatement. In the teaching of letter sounds the individual consonants are not taught in isolation but are blended with vowel sounds.

2. At this moment there is, to the best of the writer's knowledge, not a single piece of research which even hints that the addition of color to *letter forms* adds one iota to the learning of letter sounds or phonic principles.

3. The child actually never reads anything in color (except letters and words on the wall charts or in blackboard drill). All reading materials used are printed black on white!

4. Thirty-nine colors is a goodly number of colors. It is a tenable hypothesis that children might develop problems in discrimination of just noticeable differences in color in the absence of letter configurations. Examples of one series of colors include: cadmium green, yellow green No. 15, yellow green No. 47, dark green, olive green, light green, deep green, emerald green No. 45, emerald green No. 26, leaf green, gray green, yellow ochre, brown ochre.

5. Materials include: for teachers, *Background and Principles*, *Teacher's Guide*, 21 Wall Charts, 8 Phonic Code Charts; and children's materials (printed black on white), Books 1, 2, 3, *First Book of Stories*, set of worksheets.

PROGRAMMED READING (2)

While there are a number of materials which might merit the designation *programmed reading* our discussion is limited to one set of materials which meets the criterion of being a phonics emphasis approach to beginning reading (*Programmed Reading*, Webster Division, McGraw-Hill Book Co.). These materials are primarily a program for grades one and two, and for remedial instruction. The program begins with the teaching of word symbols which have "a constant sound value." Thus, we meet again the "word family" of previous eras or "regular spellings" of one linguistic approach.

However, before beginning to work with the programmed materials the child must have mastered a sizeable portion of word analysis or the phonic skills program which includes the following:

1. The names of the letters of the alphabet (capital and small).
2. How to print all the capital and small letters.
3. That letters stand for sounds and what sounds to associate with the letters *a, f, m, n, p, t, th*, and *i* which are used as the points of departure for the programmed readers.
4. That letters are read from left to right and that groups of letters form words.
5. The words *yes* and *no* by sight; how to discriminate the words *ant, man*, and *mat* from each other, and how to read the sentences, I *am an ant, I am a man, I am a mat, I am a pin, I am a pan, I am thin, I am tan, I am fat.*

These skills are taught in a stage called programmed pre-reading which, by the nature of what is taught, emphasizes the association of letter symbol with corresponding letter sound.

The programmed materials are workbook type exercises calling for the child to circle the correct word or write a letter or letters. For instance, a picture of an ant is followed by the sentence: *I am an ant.* A later frame will be *I am an -nt.* It should be noted that these materials rely heavily on visual discrimination and that there is considerable emphasis on "word parts" or individual letters.

Without doubt programmed materials hold some promise for teaching certain facets of beginning reading. A promotional brochure heralds these particular materials as "the most significant breakthrough in the teaching of reading in 50 years!" This might be an overstatement. One of the virtues of programmed learning is the fact that the child can instantly check his response to see if he is correct. As the child writes a vowel, a consonant blend, or a word in a blank space he can look to the left on the same frame and see if he wrote correctly. He can also look before he writes if he learns this approach.

One strength of programmed reading is that it could be called an individualized approach. However, in this case every child uses the same material or book, but each goes through it at his own rate. Programmed materials deal with mechanical aspects of the reading process. These are important, but they are not all there is to reading. There has been little, if any, programming of critical reading or thought processes.

THE PHONOVISUAL METHOD (14)

The Phonovisual Method is a supplementary phonic instruction program designed for use with existing basal and other approaches. The authors offer their materials as a "middle course" stating, "The Phonovisual Method is not intended to be used instead of sight reading, but as a parallel teaching" (14, p. 6). As is the case with many other phonics instructional materials there are no major differences in the "content" of the phonics program of phonovisual and basal materials. The major differences are:

1. The degree to which phonic teaching dominates beginning reading instruction.
2. The emphasis on *drill* in associating letter sounds and graphic letter symbols.

It should be noted that the teacher is cautioned to always use the material as a game, not as drill. Yet, it is obvious that the amount of emphasis on teaching letter sounds makes this a difficult goal to achieve. "For best results the teaching [of letters sounds] should begin the very first week of school, if possible the very first day. At the demonstration school one half-hour daily is given to each of these two subjects, (a) sight reading and (b) phonetic instruction . . ." (14, p. 11).

Materials. The Phonovisual materials are described as a phonics program for kindergarten, primary, and remedial instruction, and include the following:

1. Two 26" x 40" wall charts—one for teaching consonant sounds, the other for vowel sounds.
2. Phonovisual method book (a teacher's guide).
3. Pupils' books: Readiness book, transition book (preprimer), separate consonant and vowel workbooks.
4. Miscellaneous items: Phonograph recording, "Sounds on the Phonovisual Charts," skill building flash cards, consonant and vowel filmstrips, magnetic boards, phonic rummy games, and the like.

Of all the numerous phonic approaches, phonovisual probably most closely parallels the philosophy of a majority of basal materials. Consonant sounds are taught first, auditory-visual training is coordinated, learning words as sight-recognition units is encouraged. One of the major potential drawbacks in the use of phonovisual is that the actual instruction can easily go beyond simply systematic teaching and become a ritual.

The matter of differentiation of amounts of phonic instruction for different pupils is not stressed. Despite the warnings of the authors, and particularly in light of the procedures outlined, the teaching of sounding can easily become an end in itself rather than the means to achieving a balanced program whose goal is fluent, critical reading. On the other hand, the materials provide a concrete step-by-step program which introduces practically all of the phonics teaching in grade one. Some teachers may profit from this systematic approach while at the same time modifying techniques so as to minimize rote teaching.

PHONETIC KEYS TO READING

Phonetic Keys to Reading (8) is a quite accurate description of the materials which bear this title. The "keys" are the multitude of "rules" that have accumulated over a number of decades as a result of attempting to deal with the vagaries of letter sounds in written English. *Phonetic Keys* provides for teaching children all of the known rules including some which have very limited application. The data reported by Clymer (5), Oaks (13), and Burrows/Lourie (3), relative to the per cent of time various phonic rules actually apply, should be kept in mind as prospective users attempt to evaluate the materials under discussion.

Phonetic Keys is not a method of teaching reading but a set of supplementary phonics materials. The first two months of beginning instruction are devoted to teaching approximately forty separate phonic skills including both long and short vowel sounds, all consonant sounds, and a number of blends and consonant digraphs. For the first several weeks children are taught to sound letters (vowels) which are invariably located in the middle of words. Following this unique experience they are taught initial consonant sounds.

A reasonable rationale for attacking the middle of words has never been advanced. Promotional materials point out, "Since each word contains one or more than one vowel, no words can be sounded independently by the pupil until he has a knowledge of the more common vowel sounds." It might be pointed out that all words except *I*, *a* and *eye* contain consonants which must be noted if the word is to be solved.

As a result of the emphasis on sounding in beginning reading the child is in essence taught, and many learn, to acquire a set to sound out words. The same word is sounded out time after time, long after it should have been mastered as a sight word. The teacher's manual in discussing the use of experience charts cautions teachers against teaching words as sight words, "At first these charts are to be read by sight, but as soon as the children have learned enough sounds and phonetic principles to analyze words with the help of the teacher, teaching experience charts and reading charts by sight should be entirely eliminated" (*Teacher's Manual for First Grade*, 1964, p. 18).

Materials. First grade materials consist of three paperback workbook-type books, *Tag*, *Dot and Jim*, *All Around with Dot and Jim*, and a teacher's manual. The materials were developed by Cornelia Sloop, an elementary teacher in Texas.

The major educational issues with which users and prospective users of these materials should be concerned include:

1. Should beginning reading instruction concentrate on sounding letters to the degree these materials advocate?
2. Should initial sounding begin in the middle of words?
3. Should children learn dozens of complicated phonic rules in the process of beginning reading?
4. Can sounding be "overemphasized" to the detriment of future reading facility?
5. Can beginning instruction result in pupils' developing a "set" to sound out each word met?
6. All facile readers recognize words as units and sound out only those few words they do not recognize as sight words. Should children be taught to sound out all words to the neglect of developing a sight vocabulary?

LINGUISTIC APPROACH
(Emphasizing Speech Sounds in Words)

This discussion does not attempt to deal with all linguistic theory and suggested practices which relate to beginning reading instruction. Reference is made only to one approach, that of limiting initial teaching to words which enjoy "regular spellings" in English. While the term *phonics* might be offensive to the linguist-authors, the materials merit discussion here since their chief aim is the early association of speech sounds with written letter combinations.

The first such serious proposal by a linguist was presented publicly in 1942. The April and May issues of *The Elementary English Review* contained articles by Leonard Bloomfield in which he outlined what in essence was later published in 1961 under the title, *Let's Read—A Linguistic Approach* (1). Reduced to its essentials this approach simply advocates teaching beginning reading through the process of teaching words which follow "regular spellings" in English.

This approach relies on a very rigid vocabulary control. Each lesson introduces and stresses what in the past was called "word families," such as *cat, rat, fat, mat, bat, sat*. The child first learns words in isolation, then phrases and sentences: *a bat, a cat, a rat, a mat, a fat cat, a fat rat, a fat cat ran at a fat cat* (*Let's Read*, Bloomfield and Barnhart, p. 61).

In 1963, Charles Fries' book *Linguistics and Reading* was published. There are minor differences between Bloomfield's and Fries' approaches. The former advocated that children learn letter names and learn to distinguish both capital and lower case letters, while Fries advocated teaching only capital letters in beginning reading. However, in regard to methodology Fries and Bloomfield advocate almost identical content. The same words, phrases, and sentences are found in both sources, for examples in Fries, *"a cat, a rat, a fat rat, pat a fat rat, cats bat at rats,* (6, p. 203).

Both Bloomfield and Fries (in the materials referred to above) oppose the practice of making beginning reading instruction a meaning-making process for the reader. In the words of Charles Barnhart, coauthor of *Let's Read*, we find: "Bloomfield's system of teaching reading is a linguistic system. Essentially, a linguistic system of teaching reading separates the problem of the study of word-form from the study of word-meaning" (p. 9).

In Fries we find: "Seeking an extraneous interest in a story as a story during the earliest steps of reading is more likely to hinder than to help the efforts put forth by the pupil himself" (6, p. 199)*.

---

*Certain other linguists do not reject meaning in reading. Lefevre stresses "that language is meaningful behavior and that reading is the reproduction of sound patterns which carry meanings." In addition there has been a considerable body of writing which stresses the various *signal systems*. Under this heading the linguist discusses *intonation patterns, pitch, stress, juncture, transitions, pauses*, and the like. Teachers of reading have used different terminology without neglecting these important facets. (Reading terms might be, "reading with expression," "read it like you would say it." Juncture—pause—stops would be taught as functions of punctuation and phrasing.

When a person in reading raises questions as to the actual contributions made by linguists he is put in the position of a mere educational practitioner questioning the role of the scientist. When a linguist has reservations about the contributions of linguists to reading we might listen. Raven I. McDavid of the University of Chicago stated:

> I am diffident about how much the linguist can contribute to the complex operation of teaching reading, which may utilize everything from information theory to the doctrine of original sin. Like many of my colleagues, I am disturbed that linguistics is currently fashionable, often considered a panacea for all the woes of education and society. For with the supply of professional linguists low and the demand for their services high, we find a proliferation of store-front linguists clamoring to perform these services . . . And when the linguist attempts to produce readers, he can expect them to be criticized on both linguistic and other grounds (10).

THE AUGMENTED ROMAN ALPHABET

The objective of the Augmented Roman Alphabet is to present an initial teaching medium which approximates a one-to-one relation between letter-symbol seen and speech-sound heard when a word is pronounced. To accomplish this, 19 new letter characters were added to the present English alphabet after dropping the letters *q* and *x*. (For ITA materials see Mazurkiewicz and Tanyzer, 12.)

Some of the methodological features of this system are:

1. Phonics or letter sounds associated with graphic symbols are taught systematically and thoroughly.
2. Child learns symbol sound, not letter name.
3. Children write this new symbol system from the very beginning of instruction.
4. Separate capital letters are not used. Capitals are indicated by making the letter larger.
5. Children are expected to make a transition from this initial teaching alphabet to traditional orthography and spelling within a year; four to five months for the rapid learners; seven to eight months for the average pupils. In data reported from England, the transition was reportedly made without difficulty. However, pupils transferred from Augmented Roman to the same materials printed in regular or traditional orthography.

Some Issues:

1. *Teaching children to write the Augmented Alphabet.*

A very important question is, "If the child is to transfer from the initial teaching medium to traditional in from 4 to 8 months, why should he learn and reinforce the Augmented Alphabet in his own writing?" The ITA is much more difficult to write as one meets symbols such as:

ꞔh, æ, rg, œ, Ɬh, ie, ꭍ, ꬲ, ꞷ.

2. *The compatibility of ITA and Traditional Orthography.*

In the promotional materials for ITA it is claimed that there is a high degree of compatibility between spellings in ITA and traditional spellings. A fact that is often overlooked is that in addition to the changed alphabet in ITA a great number of words are changed to phonetic spellings, some of which do not involve any of the new letters. The re-spellings result in visual configurations which are radically different from those the child will meet once he transfers to traditional English. This is, in essence, not a system for "cracking the code" but rather the teaching of a substitute code. Do no children experience difficulty in transferring from phonetic spellings to the traditional irrational spellings? The following examples come from one small first-grade book of less than primer difficulty.

was – wox	watched – wotꞔht	walked – waukt
excited – eksieted	enough – enuf	also – aulsœ
wife – wief	sixth – siksꞭh	right – riet
called – caulld	find – fiend	thought – ꝑhaut
large – larj	crossed – crosst	next – nekst
pleased – plꬲꬲꭍd	climb – cliem	boxes – boksex
busy – bixy	night – niet	George – jorj
quieter – kwieter	castles – caslx	six – siks

(a seesied holidæ for jæn and tœby, ann Ɬhwaite, ꞔunstabl and ꞔumpany limited, lundon.)

In the promotional material the question is asked, "Is the traditional alphabet and spelling of English an important cause of failure in beginning reading?" It might be stated that failures do not stem primarily from the traditional alphabet, but from spellings of words. As noted above, ITA does not rely solely on a new alphabet but actually utilizes a considerable number of re-spellings of English words.

ITA actually attempts to follow the traditional "rules" found in most phonic approaches, particularly with regard to the "two vowel" and "one vowel in medial position" rules. When words do not follow the rules they are spelled phonetically:

one—wun	half—hav	come—cum
some—sum	have—hav	money—muny
said—sed	head—hed	once—wunz
more—mor	were—wer	

3. *Emphasis on teaching Phonics.*

A point that is seldom stressed on the popular writings about ITA is the fact that in this approach sounding or phonic analysis is taught both early and systematically. A large number of letters (consonants) are the same in structure and sound in both the augmented and traditional alphabets (b, d, f, h, j, k, m, n, p, r, t, y). The digraphs *ch, th, sh, wh* have the same sound and are very similar in visual pattern, although joining the two symbols in writing is more difficult.

The early stress on sounding or phonic analysis thus becomes a contaminating factor in research which purports to demonstrate that use of the Augmented Alphabet is the primary independent variable in comparative studies. The efficacy of the Augmented Alphabet could be tested only if the traditional alphabet approach with which it is compared included the same amount of early phonics emphasis.

4. *Results of instruction using ITA.*

There have been many reports in the popular press which contain suggestions, intimations and projections which often result in a reader's inferring that initial instruction using ITA, followed by transfer to traditional print sometime in grade one, will lead to significantly higher reading achievement at the end of grade one. The data covering the Bethlehem, Pennsylvania study, 1963–64, reported by Mazurkiewicz does not bear out this assumption, although that writer's tentative conclusions continue to be optimistic.

There was no significant difference in reading achievement between groups taught by ITA and traditional basal instruction:

Table I (11)

Total Raw Scores	ITA		Traditional		T. Test
	Mean	*S.D.*	*Mean*	*S.D.*	
California Reading Test (Lower Primary)	59.60	17.42	61.15	16.15	0.433
California Reading Test (Upper Primary)	41.11	19.28	41.29	16.90	0.064

Summary. The above phonic emphasis approaches cannot justifiably be labeled "methods of teaching reading." Each deals primarily with one important reading skill, namely, phonic analysis. To qualify as a method a set of materials would have to embrace a broad teaching program which attempts to deal with all of the essential skills which need to be taught in the entire program. A second criterion of a method would be that learning to read would of necessity be treated as a developmental process, extending over a relatively long period of time.

Each of the above approaches, as is the case with other phonic materials not discussed, deals only with beginning reading and attempts to saturate this instructional period with analysis of letter sounds. This extensive and intensive drill on sounding letters often has a salutary effect on reading achievement scores during the early stages of formal instruction. Standardized reading tests for grade one deal primarily with word recognition, and thus tend to measure what phonics-emphasis approaches teach.

Reading vocabularies of pupils at this stage of development do not approximate their capacity for dealing with oral language. The point of view of this paper is that this fact of human development does not serve as a justification for the position that beginning reading need not be a meaning-making process. Language is a system of agreements as to the meaning ascribed to particular speech sounds *as found in words and words-in-combination.* Meaning is the only thing that *can* transfer from oral language usage to facile reading of the graphic representation of oral language.

This question, as to whether beginning reading should be a meaning-making process is one of the major educational issues in the present controversy over the proper role of phonics instruction. Starting from the premise that *students must acquire the ability to sound out words not recognized as sight words,* other questions teachers of reading should answer as they think of methodology and materials are:

1. When initial reading instruction centers on letter-sound analysis is it not likely that a number of pupils will develop a "set" to sound out all words met?

2. Will some pupils continue to sound out the same words long after they should have been mastered as sight words?

3. Is it not true that smooth, facile reading is characterized by a minimum of recourse to "sounding out words"?

4. Do some phonic-instructional materials overemphasize what teaching letter sounds can actually accomplish in reading English?

5. Does the large number of irregular spellings in English militate against teaching over-reliance on sounding?

6. Do phonic instruction materials tend to under-emphasize the value of combining phonic analysis and context clues in solving unknown words?

7. If a set of materials and instructional procedures results in higher first-grade reading achievement, is this *prima facie* evidence that this approach is a better learning experience than any approach which achieves lesser results over this relatively short segment of the total educational continuum?

8. Specifically, is the "fast start" which may accrue from hours of drill on analyzing letter sounds inevitably the best *introduction* to the long-term developmental process called *learning to read*?

The point of view emphasized in this presentation is that the educational issues in phonics instruction center around (1) initial learning *set* which materials develop; (2) that letter-sound analysis is limited by the nature of written English; (3) over-reliance on phonics can be taught; (4) that not to use all word-analysis clues (context, structure, pictures) is uneconomical; (5) the sequence in which steps are taught should be based on a psychologically sound rationale.

If one concludes that numerous phonic approaches err in saturating initial reading instruction with letter-sound analysis, and over-emphasize what this can accomplish in learning to read English, the original premise still remains intact. Namely, that children must learn sounding techniques and that these should be taught effectively.

Simply because approaches A, B, C, etc. over-emphasize analysis in beginning reading does not establish that materials which present much less phonic analysis have hit upon the "right combination." To not systematically teach vowel sounds in grade one is a methodological decision which handicaps a majority of pupils in first grade.

All reading-instructional-materials are offsprings of the free enterprise system. Promotional materials which describe and sell reading materials are often much more imaginative than the materials themselves. "Let the buyer beware" applies as well to the adoption of teaching materials as it does to the purchase of a used car. Education will have nothing to fear from this philosophy and practice when teachers and administrators develop the professional competency to ask the right questions and evaluate materials in light of their questions.

REFERENCES

1. Bloomfield, Leonard, and Barnhart, Clarence L. *Let's Read—A Linguistic Approach*, Detroit: Wayne State University Press, 1961.
2. Buchanan, Cynthia Dee, *et al. Programmed Reading*. St. Louis: Webster Division, McGraw-Hill Book Co., 1963.
3. Burrows, Alvina T., and Lourie, Zyra. "Two Vowels Go Walking," *The Reading Teacher*, XVII, (November 1963).
4. Carden, Mae. *The Carden Method*. Glen Rock, New Jersey.
5. Clymer, Theodore. "The Utility of Phonic Generalizations in the Primary Grades," *The Reading Teacher*, XVI, (January 1963).
6. Fries, Charles C. *Linguistics and Reading*. New York: Holt, Rinehart and Winston, Inc., 1963.
7. Gattegno, Caleb. *Words in Color*. Chicago: Learning Materials, Inc., 1962.
8. Harris, Theodore, Creekmore, Mildred, and Greenman, Margaret. *Phonetic Keys to Reading*. Oklahoma City: The Economy Company, 1964.
9. Heilman, Arthur W. *Phonics in Proper Perspective*. Columbus, Ohio: Charles E. Merrill Books, Inc., 1964.
10. McDavid, Raven I., Jr. "Linguistics and Reading," *Reading and the Language Arts*, Supplementary Educational Monograph No. 93, University of Chicago Press, 1963.
11. Mazurkiewicz, Albert J. "Lehigh-Bethlehem ITA Study Interim Report Six," *Journal of the Reading Specialist*, Vol. 4 (September 1964).
12. Mazurkiewicz, Albert J., and Tanyzer, Harold. *ITA Program*. New York: ITA Publications, Inc., 1963.
13. Oakes, Ruth E. "A Study of the Vowel Situations in a Primary Vocabulary," *Education*, LXXII (May 1952).
14. Schoolfield, Lucille D., and Timberlake, Josephine B. *Phonovisual Method*. Washington, D.C.: Phonovisual Products, Inc.

(51) PROGRAMED INSTRUCTION AND AUTOMATION IN BEGINNING READING*

Edward Fry

Trying to find research in programed instruction for beginning reading materials is most frustrating. The main problem is that there is very little reported research. Hence, my plan is to tell you what I have been able to dig up and then make a few general comments about programing and automation in reading.

Programed instruction, since its very inception, has been long on learning theory rationalizations and heartwarming discussions but relatively short on hard-core data. A scholarly example of this is the current 1967 NSSE Yearbook, which is entitled *Programed Instruction* (13).

BUCHANAN PROGRAMED READING

The biggest and best controlled study that has been done is one by Robert Ruddell at the University of California at Berkeley (24). It was one of the first grade studies sponsored by the U.S. Office of Education. In this study Ruddell used the Buchanan Programed Reading series in six classrooms and the Sheldon basic readers in six other classrooms. Two other groups of classrooms were getting special supplementary linguistic materials, but we will not concern ourselves with those.

The Stanford Achievement Test was given to all children. Ruddell reports raw scores for four of the five subtests related to reading. They were Paragraph Meaning, Word Reading, Word Study Skills, and Spelling. Of the four, probably Paragraph Meaning is the most important since it represents a nearly true-to-life reading situation, in which a student reads a paragraph silently and answers some questions about it. On this test the 132 children who had had the Buchanan Programed Reading scored 1.6, and the 132 children who had had the Sheldon basic readers scored 1.7. The difference between the two is not significant and, as you can see, they are both about normal for children near the end of

---

*Reprinted from *A Decade of Innovations: Approaches to Beginning Reading*, 12, Part 3, (1967 Convention Proceedings), pp. 212–26, by permission of the author and the International Reading Association.

the first year. Incidentally, these scores are just about the same as those obtained in other first grade projects in other parts of the country using other basal readers—i.t.a., DMS, and various phonic and linguistic methods.

In the Word Reading section of the Stanford, the programed reading children scored 1.8 and the basal reading children scored 1.7. Ruddell found this difference significant. I must hasten to add that Ruddell reported only raw scores, and I simply took his raw scores and followed the directions given in the teacher's manual to convert to grade-level scores. This is an excellent illustration of what Clark Trow was talking about when he pointed out the difference between educational significance and statistical significance (31). Here we see a difference of one-tenth of a year, which hardly any classroom teacher or experienced educator would consider significant in terms of the reading ability of two groups; yet by tests of "statistical significance" it is significant at the .05 level. It should be remembered that the statistical significance between means only tells us that two means that far apart could not have occurred by chance except five times in a hundred. It tells us nothing about the size of the difference between the two means. Classroom teachers, of course, are concerned with the size of the difference between the means. They want to know—does one method teach reading better than another method?

Another section of the Stanford is the Word Study Skills, which is a mild mixture of some phonics word attack skills. Pupils using both the programed reading and the basal readers scored 1.7. In spelling there was the same lack of difference; both groups scored 1.7.

A subsample of the same population consisting of about 44 students was given some individual oral reading tests. The raw Gilmore Oral Reading accuracy scores were 16.6 for programed readers and 17.7 for the Sheldon readers. On the Gilmore Oral rate score the programed reading students scored 46.8 and the Sheldon readers scored 51.8. Even though the differences seemed to favor the basal readers, there is a lack of statistical significance in the difference. There is also probably a lack of educational significance in the difference.

The subsample was also given a list of high frequency words prepared by Arthur Gates, and the programed reading children scored 11.8, while the basal-taught children scored 10.8—again, a nonsignificant difference. A statistically significant difference was found for a list of phonetically regular words which were read orally, with the programed children scoring 9.1 and the basal reading children scoring 5.4.

TABLE 1

PROGRAMED READING COMPARED WITH BASAL READERS
AT THE END OF FIRST GRADE

(Data taken from Ruddell 1965)

Group Reading Test Means	Buchanan Programed Reading	Sheldon Basic Readers
Stanford Achievement Test		
Primary I (N=about 132 per cell)		
Grade Scores		
Paragraph Meaning	1.6	1.7
Word Reading	1.8	1.7*
Word Study Skills	1.7	1.7
Spelling	1.7	1.7
Individual Reading Test Means		
Raw Scores (N=about 44 per cell)		
Gilmore Oral Accuracy	16.6	17.7
Gilmore Oral Rate	46.8	51.8
Gates Word—Oral (Words not selected		
for phonic regularity)	11.8	10.8
Phonetically Regular Words		
Oral Reading Test	9.1	5.4*

*Ruddell found raw scores with statistically significant differences between means at the .05 level.

In summary, there does not seem to be much difference in the reading achievement of the students taught by programed reading and students taught by the Sheldon basic readers. The Buchanan Programed Reading series does emphasize the phonetic regularity of words and uses a kind of a phonics or, if you prefer, linguistics approach, and this does seem to give the students some advantage in terms of reading phonetically regular words only, but this advantage does not show up on more important segments of reading tests such as comprehension of paragraphs read silently or in the accuracy and speed of oral reading.

Harry Silberman published a rather extensive review of the research and related theoretical articles entitled "Reading and Related Verbal Learning" in *Teaching Machines and Programed Learning II*, published by the NEA in 1965 (25). As part of this article he describes only one program evaluation of beginning reading that has any type of test results. This again is a description of the Buchanan beginning reading materials, which were used at Crittenden School in Mountainview, California. A remedial class of fifteen, first through fourth grade children, used the program for twenty-five minutes a day, five days a week for three weeks. They showed a mean gain on the Gates Reading Test of four months. Since this report has no other citation, presumably it was submitted to Silberman directly by the publisher or the author of the materials. This type of report is probably loaded with most of the errors that are to be found in any kind of educational research. First of all, it is unsigned and it was presumably done by the materials seller. Second, it reports on only fifteen students, which is too few to give much reliability. Third, there was no control group. Next, it lasted for only three weeks, which is certainly not enough time to use a standardized reading test and measure any gain at all (the standard error of measurement on most achievement tests for groups this size would be over three months). I do not deny that the Buchanan materials can teach reading. What I am saying is that little studies like this don't prove much. However, when you can get no other data, I guess you have to use what is available.

TALKING TYPEWRITER

An interesting demonstration project has been carried out by O. K. Moore (25) with his "talking typewriter." This device is a special typewriter attached to something like a small computer. When the student presses a key, the machine says the name of the letter. It can also be programed so that if the student types a word, the machine says the word. Moore likes the term "responsive environment" because the student is allowed to come in and simply hit keys at random, listening to the letters. The environment (the talking typewriter) responds to the child's inquisitive little fingers and this, according to Moore, is the best learning situation. The ideal free choice mode, however, is shortly terminated for as soon as the machine tells him or shows him on a visual display a certain letter to hit and he learns to hit the correct key, all others will be silent and inoperative. In this manner the child is then taught to copy words and eventually sentences.

I have visited Moore's laboratory in Connecticut and have seen that children working with typewriters can, indeed, learn to read. However, the little boy they gave me to test, who was about four and reading on the third grade level, had an IQ of about 150. I would hesitate to generalize on a sample of one, but I must, in all honesty, say that I have never seen any studies reported by Moore which included intelligence tests. The next time I saw the talking typewriter was in a Harlem kindergarten, and after several weeks of instruction the children had mastered only three letters of the alphabet in a phonetic type of reading lesson. The type of children in the Harlem experiences carried on by Lessar Gotkin are certainly a far cry from the type of children that Moore likes to show off on television and in his films.

Gotkin did publish a smidgen of data to the effect that eight children who were exposed to nine lessons ranging in length from about 40 to 125 responses showed gains from 2.75 to 45.50 percent on a letter naming pre-test of the nine letters taught. Hence, there is some evidence that disadvantaged kindergarteners can learn slightly less than half of nine letters taught in nine lessons (10).

OTHER PROGRAMED STUDIES

Along this same vein, in the demonstration type of approach to teaching beginning reading, James Evans has reported that he taught one three-and-a-half-year-old how to read 218 short phonetic words using a Multi-Max teaching machine (5). Evans aided in the development of the program called *"Reading, a Programed Primer,"* published by Grolier (21).

Not all investigators of beginning reading using programed instruction believe in phonics. McNeil and Keislar used essentially a whole-word approach on a teaching machine, in which 40 everyday words were taught to 182 nonreading kindergarteners (18). The study was really an attempt to see if oral responses aided the learning of the words, and their investigation concluded that they did. The authors also suggested that oral responding aided the motivation of children of IQ's below 100.

A teaching machine was also used by Falconer, who conducted a study using eight deaf children who were about six and seven years of age. Using the machine for about five minutes daily for about two weeks they learned fifteen nouns (6).

Robinson, Weintraub, and Smith in their monumental collection of research findings in reading published annually in the *Reading Research Quarterly* report only two studies using programed instruction in the past two years (22, 23). In the first study, Blackman and Capobianco taught reading to nineteen mentally retarded youngsters using a teaching machine (2). They did not learn to read any better than seventeen equated students in the control group, who used traditional special class procedures. The second study was the Ruddell study.

PROGRAMED TEACHERS

The studies we have reported thus far use material that is programed; that is, the student interacts with the material either in book form or on a machine with the teacher acting only as an overseer or, at best, a supplement to the instruction. However, Ellson, Barbar, Engle, and Kampwerth attempted to program the whole tutoring situation including the untrained teacher (4). In a little series of experiments and demonstrations some 400 children were taught to read. These children included groups of slow learners and retarded children, as well as normal kindergarten and first grade readers. They report only one "failure." Gains tend to be reported in cumulative curves after the fashion of Skinner and his pecking pigeons. The authors felt that their programed tutoring was most successful when it was used as a supplement to regular classroom teaching.

Perhaps at least a brief description of one of Ellson's experiments will give an idea of a type of programed tutoring. The tutor sits behind a wooden screen and holds up a word in a window. If the child calls off the word correctly, a light is flashed, meaning "correct," and the tutor shows the next word. If, however, the child does not know the word, the tutor places a picture alongside the word. If the student can now name the word with the help of the picture, the tutor removes the picture and sees whether the student can say the word without having the picture present. If the student cannot say the word, the tutor helps him to say the word correctly, then a new word is shown.

A similar kind of procedure of a human operated teaching machine has also been used by Statts (26). Only, instead of rewarding the student with a flashing light, Statts is somewhat more lavish with his reinforcement budget and hands out tokens which are exchangeable for toys.

COMPUTER ASSISTED INSTRUCTION

From a programmed tutor to completely automating the processes is but a short technological step. Today the letters CAI standing for Computer Assisted Instruction are becoming almost as well known as various other trigrams such as IRA, ITA, and SOB. The idea of putting tutoring, or at least the function of a teaching machine, into a computer has been with us since at least 1959, when Rath, Anderson and Brainerd used a

typewriter input-output station in the manner of a more or less traditional teaching machine (20). Hence, we can say that at its simplest,
computer assisted instruction for an individual needs simply a typewriter
connected to a computer. Of course, the type of decision-making process
inside the computer can become extremely complex. The simplest type of
procedure would be to ask the student to respond to a question or picture
by typing in a word and having the computer tell him whether or not he
had responded correctly. A slightly more complex bit of programing
would not only tell him when he was correct but, when he was wrong,
what the correct answer was. The next degree of complexity would be to
try to understand his wrong response, and if egregious enough to refer
the student back for review or remedial work.

Recently, a much more complex decision-making process, on the part
of the computer, has been theorized and at least partially programed by
such workers as Stolurow, Lewis and Pask, Glaser, Atkinson and Hansen, and Simon and Kotovsky (11). Atkinson and Hansen are interested
in developing quantitative learning models that can be used to develop
optimal instructional sequences and thus maximize learning.

Duncan Hansen in his article, "Computer Assistance with the Educational Process" in the December 1966 *Review of Educational Research*
lists about a dozen universities that have active and ongoing CAI projects (11). There are at least three CAI projects that have beginning reading as one of their major emphases; these are the projects at Stanford with
Suppes and Atkinson, the project at the University of Pittsburgh directed
by Robert Glaser, and the project at Harvard directed by Larry
Stolurow.

Most of the CAI projects related to reading have a good deal more
input and output equipment than just a typewriter; for example, the
Stanford project has for each of sixteen student's booths a picture projector,
a cathode ray tube which functions much like a television tube, a light
pen, a typewriter keyboard, a set of earphones, and a microphone. It is interesting to note that even the "boob tube" has been educated so that now
it can accept feedback from the student. For example, the computer can
display three words on the tube and ask the student to underline the
word which would correctly answer a question given aurally. The student
takes his light pen and underlines the word; then the computer tells him
whether or not his response was correct.

I have not seen any results that say whether or not a computer can
teach reading better than a teacher in a tutoring situation or in a whole
class situation. I have, however, seen plenty of reports about the expense

of running a computer for instruction. Machine rental for just the equipment is very expensive and only feasible for research purposes. There is always the possibility, of course, that computers will become much cheaper, and with time sharing which allows a number of students to work off one computer, plus the economical connections that can be made between a classroom and a central computer using just telephone lines, it is not inconceivable that classrooms or at least remedial reading rooms will have some CAI in the not too distant future.

In the development of curriculum material, Glaser and his colleagues at Pittsburgh are working on a system known as IPI, which stands for Individually Prescribed Instruction. They have broken reading down into a number of skill-oriented tasks by an educational type of job analysis, and have used a large number of materials, such as a number of parts of the Sullivan Programed Reading. At present, IPI is more of a "systems approach" which uses flow charts and a number of individully assigned tasks to progress children through the reading curriculum. Once worked out, it is possible that a good bit of both the decision making for the "next step" as well as the actual curriculum materials, such as the reading paragraphs and phonics sounds and symbols, can be placed in the computer memory system.

Atkinson and Hansen have also published an article in the recent *Reading Research Quarterly* describing their CAI project in initial reading and giving samples of computer and student behavior (1).

PROGRAMED MATERIALS

The publishing industry seems to have taken some formal notice of programed instructional materials in reading. The 1967 edition of *Textbooks in Print* (29) has a section under Reading entitled Programed Learning. It lists nine different sets of materials. However, the bulk of the programed reading materials mentioned seems to be either the programed reading materials prepared by Sullivan Associates or the Lessons for Self-Instruction in the Basic Skills published by the California Test Bureau. (See list at end of References.)

The listing of the reading programed instruction materials in *Textbooks in Print* is probably not completely thorough or up-to-date, but it is a kind of objective measure of progress in the field. Earlier compilations of programs in all fields have been done by the Center for Programed Instruction that is now merged with Teachers College at Columbia University and by Carl Hendershot (12).

Not all programed instruction is at one extreme or the other; that is, it doesn't have to have a computer and it doesn't have to be just a book. Some interesting materials are being developed that use sight and sound or just sound. For example, Imperial Productions has developed a set of forty tapes which teach reading skills ranging from reading readiness up to third grade skills (19). Each tape has an accompanying four-page worksheet. The reading readiness tapes tell stories and ask students to do tasks similar to those found in traditional reading readiness workbooks. The difference is that no teacher is needed; the tape guides as many children through as are plugged into the listening post. For older students, for example, the stories are read by the student and then comprehension questions are asked orally, with the student writing the answers on his worksheet. After time has been allowed for the student to write his answer, the tape tells him the correctness of his response. Needless to say, with only forty short tapes to cover four years of reading instruction, this is intended as a supplementary program; but it does give some interesting thoughts to any teacher with a tape recorder who wishes to either purchase a prepared program or develop her own in conjunction with a set of printed materials.

A slightly more elaborate system is the Aud-X device developed by EDL, which displays words as well as reads them to the child. An interesting modification of the cloze technique that the Aud-X system uses is to tell the students a story orally, then the voice leaves out a word and the word is presented visually by the machine. Thus, the student is given semantic clues to help him read the symbol. The Aud-X has also a set of workbooks which can be used in conjunction with the machine so that the student is interacting by following directions given by the machine, such as circling a *yes* or *no* or writing a word in a space. After allowing for the student to respond in his workbook, the machine can then tell the student the word and show him the correct word on its screen.

ATTITUDES TOWARDS PROGRAMED INSTRUCTION

Teachers seem to be leery of machines and automation; perhaps of new devices in toto. Table 2 shows the results of a study done by Tobias on teacher's attitudes toward programed instructional terms. He found that such terms as "teaching machine" and "automated instruction" were the most disliked by teachers (30). Slightly less threatening were such terms as "programed text" and "programed instruction." But the teachers really felt more at home with terms like "flash card" and "workbook." Though this study was not done on reading teachers per se, presumably it applies to them equally.

TABLE 2

ATTITUDE OF FIFTY TEACHERS TOWARD PROGRAMED INSTRUCTION

(TOBIAS 1963)

Terms	*Mean Rating*
Teaching Machine	26.09
Automated Instruction	23.80
Mechanized Tutor	22.16
Technological Terms	24.13
Programed Text	30.31
Tutor Text	28.65
Programed Instruction	31.73
Programing Terms	29.94
Flash Card	31.77
Exercise Book	33.33
Workbook	33.78
Traditional Terms	32.97

(Maximum score 42)

There have been numerous studies done on students' attitudes toward programed instruction, though none specifically in the field of reading. A typical study would be the one by McGuigan and Peters which surveyed some four hundred elementary and secondary students and found that 55 percent of their responses were favorable toward programed instruction, 26 percent were neutral, and 19 percent were negative (15).

While the attitudes of teachers and pupils are important, there are forces outside the school which may be of great importance in the next few years. I would like to quote directly from a report entitled "Automation and Technology in Education" prepared after hearings by the Joint Economic Committee of the Congress of the United States (27):

Educational technology is now a major field of corporate research and investment. It is not only the business equipment manufacturers who are involved, but a great variety of corporations, many of them among the giants, ranging from steel and chemicals to publishing firms, who are directing their efforts more to the burgeoning education market. One witness stated:

"The American economy was built around the railroads in the last half of the 19th century, around the automobile in the first two-thirds of this century, and it will be built around education in the balance of this century."

This statement may seem a little strong, but one doesn't need to walk much further than the convention floor or to read much more technical material than the financial pages of the newspaper to know that there is at least some truth in it, and reading teachers had best be aware of this trend.

CONCLUSIONS

There seems to be plenty of evidence that programed materials and their technological neighbors of computer assisted instruction and talking typewriters can teach beginning reading. There is no proof, however, that programed instruction can do any more for beginning reading than regular classroom teaching or human tutoring. In fact, in the only well-controlled study we were able to find (Ruddell), programed learning and basal texts came out in a dead heat. Thus, the classroom teacher should feel free to use as much programed instruction or automated procedures as her temperament and budget will allow.

REFERENCES

1. Atkinson, Richard C., and Duncan N. Hansen. "Computer-Assisted Instruction in Initial Reading: The Stanford Project," *Reading Research Quarterly*, Vol. 2 (Fall 1966).
2. Blackman, L. S., and R. J. Capobianco. "An Evaluation of Programed Instruction with the Mentally Retarded Utilizing Teaching Machines," *American Journal of Mental Deficiency*, Vol. 70 (1965).
3. Bundy, Robert F. "Computer-Assisted Instruction: Now and for the Future," *Audiovisual Instruction*, Vol. 12, No. 4 (April 1967).
4. Ellson, D. G., Larry Barber, T. L. Engle, and Leonard Kampwerth. "Programed Tutoring: A Teaching Aid and a Research Tool," *Reading Research Quarterly*, Vol. 1 (Fall 1965).
5. Evans, James L. "Teaching Reading by Machine: A Case History in Early Reading Behavior," *AV Communication Review*, Vol. 13 (Fall 1965).

6. Falconer, George A. "A Mechanical Device for Teaching Sight Vocabulary to Young Deaf Children," *American Annals of the Deaf*, Vol. 106 (March 1961).

7. Fry, Edward B. *Teaching Machines and Programed Instruction: An Introduction.* New York: McGraw-Hill, 1963.

8. Fry, Edward B. "The Use of Programed Learning in the Teaching of Reading," in J. Allen Figurel (Ed.), *Reading as an Intellectual Activity.* International Reading Association Conference Proceedings, Vol. 8, 1963.

9. Gentile, Ronald J. "The First Generation of Computer-Assisted Instructional Systems: An Evaluative Review," *AV Communication Review*, Washington, D.C.: Department of Audiovisual Instruction of the National Education Association, Vol. 15, No. 1 (Spring 1967).

10. Gotkin, Lessar G., Joe McSweeney, and Alice Richardson. "Acquisition of Pre-Reading Skills in Five Year Old Children From Disadvantaged Backgrounds Using the E.R.E. Automated Teaching System," *National Society for Programed Instruction Journal*, Vol. 4, No. 3 (March 1967).

11. Hansen, Duncan N. "Computer Assistance with the Educational Process," *Review of Educational Research, 36*, No. 5 (December 1966).

12. Hendershot, Carl. *Programed Learning: A Bibliography of Programed and Presentation Devices*, 3rd Ed. University Center, Michigan: Published by the author, 1964.

13. Lang, Phil C. *Programed Instruction.* Sixty-Sixth Yearbook of the National Society for the Study of Education, Part II. Chicago: University of Chicago Press, 1967.

14. Loretan, Joseph O. "Programed Instruction in Reading," *High Points, 45* (December 1963).

15. McGuigan, F. V., and Robert J. Peters, Jr. "Assessing the Effectiveness of Programed Texts—Methodology and Some Findings," *Journal of Programed Instruction*, Vol. 3, Nos. 1 and 2 (1965).

16. McNeil, John D. "Programed Instruction as a Research Tool in Reading: An Annotated Case," *The Journal of Programed Instruction*, Vol. 1, No. 1 (1962).

17. McNeil, John D., and Evan R. Keislar. "Individual Differences and Effectiveness of Auto-Instruction at the Primary Grade Level," *California Journal of Educational Research*, Vol. 12 (December 1961).

18. McNeil, John D., and Evan R. Keislar. "Value of the Oral Response in Beginning Reading: An Experimental Study Using Programed Instruction," *British Journal of Educational Psychology*, Vol. 33 (June 1963).

19. *Primary Reading Program.* Kankakee, Ill.: Imperial Productions, Inc.

20. Rath, Gustave J., Nancy S. Anderson, and R. C. Brainerd. "The I.B.M. Research Center Teaching Machine Project," in Eugene Galanter (Ed.), *Automated Teaching: The State of the Art.* New York: Wiley & Sons, 1959.

21. *Reading: A Programed Primer.* TMI-Grolier Self-Tutoring Program. Distributed by Teaching Materials Corporation, a division of Grolier, Inc., New York, circa 1964.

22. Robinson, Helen M., Samuel Weintraub, and Helen K. Smith. "Summary of Investigations Related to Reading, July 1, 1964 to June 30, 1965," *Reading Research Quarterly*, Vol. 1, No. 2 (Winter 1965).

23. Robinson, Helen M., Samuel Weintraub, and Helen K. Smith. "Summary of Investigations Related to Reading, July 1, 1965 to June 30, 1966," *Reading Research Quarterly*, Vol. 2, No. 2 (Winter 1966).

24. Ruddell, Robert B. *The Effect of Four Programs of Reading Instruction with Varying Emphasis on the Regularity of Grapheme-Phoneme Correspondences and the Relation of the Language Structure to the Meaning on Adjustment on First Grade Reading.* Report of Research Project #2699. Berkeley: University of California, 1965.

25. Silberman, Harry F. "Reading and Related Verbal Learning," *Teaching Machines and Programed Learning*, Vol. 2, Washington, D.C.: National Education Association, 1965.

26. Staats, A. W., and C. K. Staats. *Complex Human Behavior*, 2nd ed. New York: Holt, Rinehart, and Winston, 1966.

27. Sub-Committee on the Economic Progress of the Joint Economic Committee, Congress of the United States, Wright Patman, Chairman. (A Report) *Automation and Technology in Education*, Washington, D.C.: Government Printing Office, August 1966.

28. Suppes, Patrick. "Modern Learning Theory and the Elementary School Curriculum," *American Education Research Journal*, Vol. 1, No. 2 (March 1964).

29. *Textbooks in Print—1967.* Including Related Teaching Materials. New York: R. R. Bowker and Co., 1967.

30. Tobias, Sigmund. "Teachers' Attitudes Toward Programed Instructional Terms," *Journal of Programed Instruction*, Vol. 2, No. 3 (1963).

31. Trow, William Clark. "Letters to the Editor," *Educational Psychologist*, Vol. 4, No. 2 (March 1967).

READING PROGRAMED INSTRUCTIONAL MATERIALS LISTED IN TEXTBOOKS IN PRINT

Allen, R. V. and Claryce. *Language Experiences in Reading* (Grades 1–2). Encyclopaedia Britannica Press.

Bostwick, Gracecarol, and Miles Midloch. *Lessons in Self-Instruction in the Basic Skills* (Various titles Grades 3 to High School). California Test Bureau.

Carroll, Lucy. *Programed Phonics* (2 books). Educational Publications.

Loesel, W. G. *Help Yourself to Read, Write and Spell* (2 books). Educational

Development Corporation. Ginn.

Glassman J. *Programed Reading*. Globe.

Loretan, Joseph O., and New York City Schools staff. *Building Reading Power* (kit). Merrill.

Sullivan Associates. *Programed Reading* (Grades 1–3). Webster-McGraw-Hill.

(52) WHY AN ECLECTIC APPROACH IN READING INSTRUCTION?*

Emerald Dechant

Eclecticism is generally defined as "the selection and orderly combination of compatible features from diverse sources," the combination of valid elements from various theories into an harmonious whole. It is definitely not syncretism nor an unsystematic and uncritical combination of data. Unfortunately, even the most charitable evaluation of the actual situation in the teaching of reading forces us to conclude that few teachers have arrived at such a synthesis. Few teachers can honestly say that the approach which they are using is a systematic and orderly synthesis of data from various theories. And yet, eclecticism of some kind seems necessary.

We thus propose an eclecticism for the teacher that encourages him to select from the great variety of approaches that one approach, or combination of approaches, which best meets the needs of the pupil. We propose that the selection of method should be based on the individual differences of the learners. Perhaps, instead of the word *eclecticism*, we should borrow the phrase of Elizabeth Vasquez, a principal at Homestead School in Garden City, New York. She speaks of an "All-Method Method" of teaching reading.

THE RATIONALE FOR ECLECTICISM

We believe eclecticism makes sense because:

1. Children do in fact learn to read through a variety of approaches.

*Reprinted from *Vistas in Reading* 11, Part I (1966 Convention Proceedings), pp. 28–32, by permission of the author and the International Reading Association.

2. Children are different.
3. Teachers are different.
Let's look at each of these.

As one scans the literature, listens to experts in the field, or observes practices in the classroom, he is dazzled by the bewildering array of methods of teaching reading. Each method is proposed as an answer to a reading problem; perhaps not *the* answer, but nevertheless an answer. There is not one advocate of a method who submits that his or her method does not work or who is unable to adduce evidence as to its effectiveness. And the fact is that children have become readers, indeed good readers, through analytic, synthetic, or combination approaches.

Thus, unless one is willing to call every researcher or practitioner who claims to have success with a given method a cheat, one has to accept that success may come by many paths. Since many different roads can and do eventually lead to reading proficiency, we are unwilling to accept that only one method, one approach, or one technique is successful with all children. We cannot agree with Terman and Walcutt that with their method all children learn to read. We cannot agree with Delacato that only his method is without its poor readers. We cannot agree with Sullivan that his programed learning approach will eliminate all reading failures. We simply do not have sufficient evidence in support of one approach that warrants universal allegiance to it as the supposedly best or only way of teaching reading. On the other hand, we must admit that Terman and Walcutt's, Delacato's, and Sullivan's methods have worked with some children.

A second argument for eclecticism is the fact that children are different and learn differently. It seems unwise therefore to standardize or communize reading method. If children were all alike, we might look for the method. Indeed, we would have found it long ago. But, the simple fact is that children are different from one another intellectually, physically, emotionally, socially, and perceptually, and they seem to be differentiated on the basis of the method that is beneficial to them.

We have gone through a period in which there has been frequent debate over phonics. Today, this debate has generally subsided, and the reason for this is that we have come to accept the fact that children react differently perceptually. Each child reacts to a "perceptual whole," but for some the perceptual whole is a word; for others, a part of the word. The whole child reacts, but he is not necessarily best stimulated holistically. What constitutes a whole is different from individual to individual and is determined by the meaningfulness of that unit and the ability, experiences, purposes, maturation, and perceptual skill of the learner.

The really successful teacher is one who has developed an extraordinary sensitivity to the differences among children in the classroom and makes adjustments for them.

Teacher differences are a third reason for eclecticism. The teacher's preferred mode of reaction may be as significant as the method of teaching that he is using. Two equally competent teachers may not be able to use the same method with equal effectiveness. It may be as significant in the education of future teachers (and in your own personal success in teaching) that you and prospective teachers develop competency in method in line with your own natural style of responding and communicating. Some one of you, because of your personal make-up may do a beautiful job with individualized reading; others, because of their personal characteristics, may almost be doomed to failure.

The teacher does make a difference. On the days when we don't feel well students often seem to be doing the poorest, are ill-mannered, and the least cooperative. They seem the smartest on the days when we feel best. Of course, on those days we feel that the world is lucky to have us in it and that our method is the best there is.

CONSEQUENCES OF ECLECTICISM

What does the acceptance of eclecticism imply? It implies, among other things:

1. That the teacher understands the differences in children;
2. That the teacher become familiar with a host of reading methods.

KNOWING THE PUPIL

The effectiveness of the teacher with a given method depends to a great degree on his understanding of the pupil. This differential in knowledge of the learner quite frequently accounts for the fact that one teacher is successful with a given method and another teacher fails with it. A method of teaching is adequate only if the teacher knows enough about the child so that he can adapt the method to the needs of a specific child. In addition to an understanding of the pupil's maturational, experiential, intellectual, neural, physical, social, emotional, motivational, language, and sensory characteristics, knowing the pupil means knowing his pre-ferred mode of learning. Identification of the child's mode of learning may well be the end goal of all classroom diagnosis.

THE PUPIL'S MODE OF LEARNING

As early as 1860, Fechner noted differences in imagery. In the 1880's Calton found that scientific men have feeble powers of visual representa-tion. In 1886 Binet described an auditory type and a motor, or kinesthetic type. He noted that the latter remember a "drawing better when they have followed the outlines with their finger." William James noted of himself that he was a poor visualizer and that he seldom could call to mind even a single letter of the alphabet in purely retinal terms. He noted that he must trace the letter by running his mental eye over its contour.

Children likewise differ in auditory, visual, and motor imagery. Some children simply cannot rely on a visual image; others rarely depend on auditory imagery. When the latter read a word, they may see the word; the former hear the word; and those with motor imagery feel the word. They recognize the word as one they traced previously.

Furthermore, the maturational pattern for each of those sensory modalities may fluctuate from one to another. A pupil may develop slowly in one, more rapidly in another. Others mature slowly in all despite good intellectual ability.

Research tends to indicate that a person's preferred mode may be determined culturally, experimentally, or constitutionally. Frank Ries-man, in the *Culturally Deprived Child*, suggests that the culturally-deprived child is physically oriented and learns better through aural learning. Walters and Kosowski[1] have found that difficulties in symbolic learning may be a function of reduced inability to attend to visual stimuli resulting from monotonous stimuli. There is evidence also that continued use of one modality for learning may make the use of other modalities of limited value.

Preschool children can learn to recognize geometric shapes much more readily if they feel the cutout forms. Young children learn to deal with the environment by "saying what they think," and we have found that progress in spelling is aided by saying the word to oneself. Slow learners

[1]Richard L. Walters and Irene Kosowski, "Symbolic Learning and Reading Retarda-tion," *Journal of Consulting Psychology*, 27 (February 1963), 75–82.

tend to learn best through kinesthetic approaches; brilliant youngsters, through visual approaches. Listening is generally preferred over reading as a medium for learning up to about the fifth grade.

Wepman[2] notes that auditory training to correct articulatory inaccuracies is not too useful until auditory discriminatory abilities have matured. This occurs sometime after the age of eight. He thus recommends that we emphasize in early learning experiences the modality that is preferred while training the underdeveloped or impaired pathway separately.

He adds that intermodal transfer is necessary in learning:

> Thus, a child who sees the printed word "dog" must evoke not only previous visual stimuli of printed forms but life forms as well; he must shift from the visual input to previously received and stored auditory patterns making up the word "dog" and perhaps to the tactile sensations of petting a dog, of his small and even his frisky movements, before the printed word has full meaning for him. Without this shift to other modal learning, little integrative meaning may be attached to the printed word. Intermodal transfer, then, seems to be vital to the learning act. Katz and Deutsch,[3] in an extensive study of good and poor readers on a variety of perceptual tasks, concluded in part that "poor reading is associated with difficulties in shifting from one sensory mode to another" (p. 30).

Since everyone is truly a unique learner, it seems reasonable to introduce materials through the pupil's stronger sense modality. It would seem reasonable to utilize instructional materials which are congruent with each learner's particular strengths in perception, imagery, and recall.

The pupil's preferred sensory mode of learning may be identified by using the Mill's *Learning Methods Test.* The Learning Rate Test of the *Durrell Analysis of Reading Difficulty* might be used to identify the child who will profit from a visual emphasis. Other recent tests with possibilities in this area are the *Frostig Developmental Test of Visual Perception* the *Illinois Test of Psycholinguistic Abilities*, the *Chicago Test of Visual Discrimination*, the *Roswell-Chall Auditory Blending Test,* and the *Wepman Auditory Discrimination Test.*

We all realize that, other things in the educational situation being

---

[2]Joseph M. Wepman, "The Perceptual Basis for Learning," *Meeting Individual Differences in Reading.* Ed. by H. Alan Robinson, Chicago: University of Chicago Press, 1964, 25–33.

[3]Phyllis Katz and Martin Deutsch, Visual and Auditory Efficiency and Its Relationship to Reading in Children. Cooperative Research Project No. 1099 Washington, D.C.: Office of Education, 1963, 45.

equal, the child must have reached a more advanced developmental stage to succeed in reading in a class of 36 pupils than in a class of 12 or 13 pupils. He will need greater maturity. The same might be said of reading method. A child might not be ready for reading—he might not be mature enough—because we are asking him to use a sensory modality which is less developed than another. Some children are more ready to learn through a phonic approach; and still others through a visual approach; and still others through a kinesthetic approach. The fact that children have different sensory strengths suggests that one-method teaching is questionable. We need to identify the child's differential ability to learn by ear, eye, or touch before choosing a given reading method to use with him.

KNOWLEDGE OF A VARIETY OF METHODS

A second major consequence of accepting a position of eclecticism is a need to become familiar with a great variety of methods of teaching reading.

The teacher needs to ask himself: What method works best with Jane, who has completed the readiness program, but still cannot identify rhyming words? What method works best with Dick, who has an abnormal amount of difficulty with similar-appearing words such as *them* and *then*? What method works best with the pupil who does word-by-word reading, who constantly back-tracks, or who blocks when he meets certain words? What method works best with the pupil who constantly reverses words, who cannot blend sounds or letters, or who cannot name letters?

These are not serious problems, but these innocuous difficulties tend to snowball. Most remedial cases are probably instances of an accumulation of unmet reading needs. The teacher of reading needs to be able to provide proper remediation all along the way. This means he needs to know what is best for a given child. It is not enough to know *a* method of teaching. It is necessary to know *the* method that is best for a *given* child. This means he must become familiar with a host of methods.

Teachers with the most novel approaches to teaching reading claim to be unusually successful with their method. It may be, and indeed often is, that these teachers work harder or are more enthusiastic than the average teacher. But, it may also be true that a novel approach may be especially effective with some child because it meets his need in a special way. There are methods, or specific teaching approaches, that make a world of difference for the *individual* child. One child benefits from one type of instruction, another may not.

There probably is some good in every approach. I don't know of any method that may not be useful with *some* child. The Initial Teaching Alphabet (i|t|a) approach, originated by Pitman, has already demonstrated its usefulness by simplifying the alphabet. It is interesting to note that systems similar to the i|t|a began as early as 1551, and by 1845 there were 26 phonetic alphabets, including those of Benjamin Franklin and Brigham Young. Davis' system, as propounded in *k-a-t speltz cat*, the Diacritical Marking System of Fry, and Gattegno's Color approach may each help some child to learn and remember better.

A child who has difficulty associating meaning with what is read may be especially helped by a linguistic approach such as Lefevre's.[4] It may help the reader to translate the printed text into the writer's intonation pattern. Another child may be aided by linguistic approaches such as those proposed by Bloomfield, Soffietti, Daniels and Diack, or Fries, which stress the phonetic consistencies of the language.

The teaching machine approach, originally proposed by Pressey, and programed learning approaches in general, may help a child who has special need for a detailed, sequential presentation of learning tasks and a need for confirmation of his progress.

Another child, who has a special need to be interested in what he is reading, may learn best through the language-experience approach, originally suggested some sixty years ago by Flora F. Fooke at the Chicago Institute.

Some children may not learn readily because certain internal events have gone awry. We cannot emphasize enough that learning, and indeed reading, occurs in the brain. Children think and learn differently because of differences in neural development.

Reading difficulties are thus said to be caused by damage to, or dysfunction of, certain localized areas of the brain such as the angular gyrus (Hinshelwood, 1917), the frontal gyrus (Wernike, 1947), or the parietal and parietal-occipital areas (Rabinovitch, 1959). Penfield and Roberts (1959) suggest that the difficulty is in the connection between the cortical speech mechanism and the brain stem system. Some suggested that reading deficiency results from underdevelopment of directional function (Hermann, 1959) from psychological disturbances, especially of an unconscious or subconscious nature (Jarvis, 1958, Namnum and Prelinger, 1961, Walters, Van Loan and Crofts, 1961), from dis-

---

[4]Carl A. Lefevre, "A Comprehensive Linguistic Approach to Reading." *Elementary English*, 42 (October 1965), 651–659.

turbed brain wave activity (Kennard, Rabinovitch, and Wexler, 1952), from prenatal and paranatal factors (Kawi and Psasmanich, 1959), from ocular inefficiency (Leton, 1962), from delayed development of the parietal lobes (Drew, 1956), from a slowness of neuromuscular maturation (Eustis, 1947), or from minimal brain injury (Strauss and Lehtinen, 1947). The Smith's Synaptic Transmission Model suggests a chemical basis for reading deficiency, and Delacato, following the early lead of Orton, emphasizes dominance factors.

Each of these people suggests that neurological factors are key factors in language and reading development. Delacato notes that the basic difference between man and the animal world is that man has achieved cortical dominance rather than cellular quantity. He probably summarizes the thinking of this group of specialists when he notes that peripheral activity . . . such as vision, dexterity, skills, *phonetics, various reading techniques*, are meaningless in remediation if the neurological organization is defective.

SUMMARY

When the teacher accepts the student, when he respects the individuality of the pupil, shows understanding and empathy, has deep faith in the improvableness of the pupil, and identifies the pupil's area of confidence, we find that his pupils are generally successful. We also know what a great effect a teacher can have if he is an interested and an interesting teacher. Because learning occurs in a relationship, the teacher's personality and his ability to enlist the child's active cooperation are often more important than the specific method used.

We propose that another key attitude of the successful teacher is a willingness to change his method to fit the learner's preferred mode of learning. Success in teaching is built on a willingness to be eclectic. We don't give much credence to a physician who seeks to alleviate all ailments with aspirin. Is the aspirin man less scientific than the one-method teacher?

Eclecticism is not easy, but I don't think that we can return to the "good old days," when we were content to dish out the same thing to all children. The greatest challenge in education today is the individualization of instruction. There is nothing quite so unequal as dishing out the same education to unequals. We need to personalize education. We need to be eclectic in the true sense of the word.

Chapter 11

PROGRESS TOWARD
READING MATURITY

INTRODUCTION

Progress toward reading maturity may mean different things to different people. In the context of the present chapter, however, it has to do with four important questions which confront teachers of reading whose pupils are on the road to maturity in reading: (1) What is effective study and how can it be developed? (2) What reading skills and abilities must be employed to deal effectively with the patterns of writing used by authors in the subject areas? (3) What mechanical aids are available to teachers of reading, how effective are they, and how can they best be used? (4) What is flexibility of reading and how can it be taught?

The first of these questions is dealt with in a thorough and practical manner by Artley. Smith focuses on the second question with her lucid discussion of the patterns of writing used by authors in the subject areas. The third question is attended to in the selections by Taylor and Tinker, who provide somewhat divergent points of view with regard to the efficacy of mechanical aids. Finally, McDonald provides a number of thought-provoking ideas which will help the reader to answer the fourth question posed. Upon completion of Chapter 11, then, the reader should have a reasonable picture of the instructional dimensions that must be considered and implemented in the classroom to promote power in reading.

(53) EFFECTIVE STUDY—ITS NATURE AND NURTURE*

A. Sterl Artley

In the days of computerized education, programed learning, and audio-visual aids of various sorts and types one begins to wonder if in the year 1967 a paper on study has any place on the program of IRA. Yet, on second thought, the process of assembling ideas and using them in forming generalizations and resolving issues is one that will be forever with us regardless of how the ideas are clothed and regardless of whether we are referring to a third grader or a graduate student. The Education Research Information Center (ERIC) may reduce some of the tasks involved in study, particularly in locating and summarizing information; but the major task of synthesizing and using it cannot be reduced to a mechanical process.

Much has been written already about the process of study; but in spite of the attention it has received as a specialized reading activity, major changes in school programs designed to improve study procedures have not taken place in widespread fashion. A few sporadic and transient programs are the best we can find. Karlin (8) in a paper presented at the Miami meeting of IRA quoted Ruth Strang as saying, "The most discouraging circumstance is that so little has been done to implement sound ideas that were advocated and tried years ago." In the same paper Karlin also refers to a survey made by McGinnis in 1961 in which she reported 61 percent of a total 1,029 college freshmen said that their high school teachers had not showed them how to improve reading skills. In addition, less than 10 percent of the high school surveyed claimed to have had any training in teaching reading and study procedures.

It is not to be presumed that another paper on study will effect major changes in practice. However, there are several aspects of study that have not been sufficiently emphasized. These I would like to explore with you.

*Reprinted from *Forging Ahead in Reading* 12, Part I (1967 Convention Proceedings), pp. 10–19, by permission of the author and the International Reading Association.

THE NATURE OF STUDY

First, I should like to discuss the use of the term study. Literature uses several terms somewhat synonymous in reference to this subject—*study, study skills, reading-study abilities,* and *reading abilities in the content areas.* All these terms relate to what one uses in terms of skills, abilities, and understandings in the process of study. But study itself, what is it? What does one do or should one do when he studies, whether at the fifth grade level or the eleventh? Strangely enough it is at this precise point that some of our study-skills problems lie, for we are not in agreement as to what the process is, in the first place. Even dictionaries are of limited help, for they define the process in different ways. One states that it is ". . . a process of acquiring . . . knowledge of a subject." Another defines it as ". . . the application of the mind to the acquisition of knowledge, as by reading, investigation, or reflection." The *Dictionary of Education* defines it as "the application of the mind to a problem or subject." Note that the first two definitions stress the idea of study as the process of "getting" knowledge, while the last one connotes the idea of problem solving.

In reading a number of articles and reports dealing with the subject, I have been particularly sensitive to the definition of study that the writer either states or implies. In the majority of cases it seems to be assumed that study is the act in which one engages to accumulate facts, information, or ideas. The end result is a score on a test of factual information or the number of questions that can be answered correctly after one has read a geography or science text. A study-skills course may be devoted to teaching the pupil or student how to locate information or to use a table of contents or to secure data from charts, graphs, diagrams, and the like, after which a study-skills test is administered and progress is noted in the learner's ability to engage in each of these tasks more efficiently, the implication being that he now has at hand a set of skills that will enable him to acquire facts more expeditiously.

On the other hand, we find statements to the effect that study should be considered as something more than information gathering, or as the dictionary says, "knowledge acquisition." Fay (4) wrote, "Students must be shown that there is more to study than merely reading the pages of an assignment." He contends that study in social studies is an active thinking process of following an author's line of reasoning in relation to a well-defined and clearly understood purpose. In other words, the process of study is engaged in when there exists some purpose or need to be satisfied.

In like manner, Robinson (11) in an article in *The Reading Teacher* said, ". . . a meaningful reading program in social studies or the other content areas will focus on problem-solution as the end, and skill development as the means, not vice versa." He, too, sees study in broader terms than the acquisition of information.

In a paper that I fear has been lost in the welter of literature on reading and study is the one presented by Preston (10) as the keynote speech at the Miami meeting of IRA. In "Reading for What?" Dr. Preston discussed what he called the "low ebb of reading as an intellectual activity." As an intellectual activity, he said, reading was at a low ebb for several reasons, one being that reading people are preoccupied with technical problems, the mechanics of the act, information getting, rather than the end result. He wrote, "We should not take our chief satisfaction in bringing about mere literacy, desirable though literacy is. It is only half the job. We need to conceive of our role in broader terms and not rest content until the learner is eagerly *applying reading to some worthwhile* goal. [italics mine] The real miracle of reading lies less in the process than in what can be accomplished through it." Translating this concept of reading into the language of study, we have the generalization that study is being carried on at its highest level when the reader is doing something with the writer's ideas.

In fact it is almost in these terms that Nila Banton Smith (15) defined study. In differentiating between reading and study she described a housewife perusing a household periodical for entertainment. Later the housewife returned to the magazine and studied an article having a recipe which she wanted to use in preparing the evening meal. In the latter situation she has put information to work and has utilized skills where the intent was "to do something" with the content read.

What we have then are two points of view with regard to the means and the end of the study act. One, that information, knowledge, facts, and ideas are the end; the other, that these are the means to the end of use, application, problem solving, question answering, or issue resolving. One has engaged in the act of study when he has derived information or ideas and has put them to use for some purpose that has relevance and significance to the learner.

Perhaps if we were to look at the study act apart from reading, it might be helpful; for we engage in study many times where no reading as such is involved. Many of us engaged in study when we faced the question as to whether we would attend the Seattle meeting of IRA. For some there were deterrents: it is a long way to Seattle from New York, Florida, and even Missouri, and cost was a major factor. Some were engaged in major projects where time away from the job had to be considered. But at the same time there were reasons why we should come: there were excellent meetings to attend; there was a paper to present; there were friends that we see only once a year; and the State of Washington is pleasant in May. And so we assembled facts from various sources: we used our past experiences; we talked with friends; we checked to see if there was money in the travel fund; we looked over the program; we may even have read the promotional literature about Seattle, and eventually we came to a decision. Can anyone say that this activity was not the process of study in every sense of the word?

On analysis, what was involved in this act? What were the steps? First, there was a problem, a question, or an issue. Second, there was the securing and marshalling of facts and information needed to solve the problem. Third, there was the evaluating and weighing of the bits of information, since each bit was not necessarily of equal value or merit. Finally, there was a resolution of the problem. All of this together composes the act of study.

Take note, if you will, of the second step in the study act. We called it the securing and marshalling of facts and information. There is no doubt that this was a very important part of the study process; but there would have been very little, if any, reason for it *had there not been a problem to resolve*. Study took place when there was a purpose or motive, and the collection of information was a means to the end of problems solving. Isn't meaning hereby given to Robinson's generalization that study should focus on problem solving as the end and skill development as the means? And in the same way isn't a partial answer provided, at least, to Preston's question, "reading for what?"

I don't wish to labor the place of idea intake in study or in the receptive area, as Herber (7) calls it, yet I do feel that it is in this step that the study act on all levels of instruction—from the elementary grades through college—so frequently begins and ends. It is reflected in the sixth grade teacher's assignment, "For tomorrow study to the middle of page 126," meaning that tomorrow be prepared to hand the material back in a discussion. It is reflected in the high school teacher's admonition, "Be sure to 'cover' the material carefully, for tomorrow we are going to have a test," which frequently ends up being a series of true-false items measuring little other than factual recall. It is reflected in research in which the researcher matches a control and experimental group to which he gives a series of lessons on the use of the card catalog, use of the dictionary, and map reading. After post-testing the two groups, he enters the data on Hollerith cards, puts them through a computer, and comes out with the fact that the 3.78 points of difference between the two groups is statistically significant at the one percent level. Truly, studying for what?

Facts, knowledge, ideas, all are useful, in fact essential, in the study act because they constitute the raw material in the process of problem solving. But accumulated for their own sake to be regurgitated later, they are no better than miser's coins which he counts each Saturday night and returns to his sack since they serve neither himself nor society to any useful purpose.

In fact, they represent a kind of pseudo erudition dramatized in radio days by the Quiz Kids and today in television on the College Bowl program, where for preparation the group dredges up every particle of isolated and undigested information that the questioner might possibly ask. Understanding the process of study would in a dramatic way modify the assignments that we make, the study act in which the students engage, and our teaching methods in general.

THE READING-STUDY PURPOSE

The term *purpose* in relation to reading and study also is used in different ways by different writers. Some speak of study as being a purposeful activity when the reader approaches his material with a definite question in mind; such as, "To what extent did Germany's decision to attack the Soviet Union and Japan's decision to attack the United States make possible the defeat of the Axis in World War II?" Others use the term in reference to the reading set or study objective that the reader keeps in mind as he studies, as, for example, to note details, to verify a statement, and to answer a specific question. Still others refer to purpose as adjustments that the reader makes in reading, such as to skim or to recognize devices and words that indicate certain types of idea relationships. Certainly before one can help students establish a purpose for study one needs to know what a purpose is to begin with.

Perhaps the following may help in clarification. The student begins with a study *objective* or study task, which may be a question for which he wants an answer or a problem situation in need of resolution. It is the reader's basic motivation for reading. Examples of these kinds of reading tasks might be: Why does a satellite orbit the earth? What steps are involved in baking a cake? or, What factors made possible the defeat of the Axis in World War II? The reading or study objective, on the one hand, may be met with a minimum amount of reading; or it may require the use of several sources and a prolonged period of study. It may be one that is established by the teacher as part of an assignment. It may be one set by the student himself as something he needs to find out or understand. At any rate it is an essential prerequisite for study. Being without it is like beginning a vacation trip with no idea of where one is going or what one wishes to see.

The study task or objective determines, in turn, the study *purpose*. The purpose may be to determine the main idea, to note details or facts, to trace out the writer's organization, to distinguish between fact and opinion, or to sense idea relationships. The purpose supplies the mental set for the act of study. If the study objective or task calls for tracing out the writer's organization, the student puts his mind to the job of searching for the main ideas being developed and the various levels of subordination used by the writer in developing his ideas. But, of course, a reading purpose cannot be determined until the student clearly has in mind his study objective.

Knowing the study objective and the study purpose, the student now needs to make certain adjustments as he proceeds. An obvious adjustment would be in the area of rate, for some purposes may call for rapid reading while others may call for a slow, study-type reading. The student may need to reread to determine the level of subordination of a given point, or he may need to skim to determine whether a particular bit of information is supplied by the article. The adjustments, then, are those required in order to satisfy the study purpose which in turn is conditioned by the study objective.

The most recent and possibly the most complete piece of research dealing with reading purposes is that of Helen K. Smith (14). She was concerned with student ability to identify appropriate reading purposes from the nature of the content, to comprehend material, and to make necessary reading adjustments in the light of the reading purpose. Using ninth graders from a suburban Chicago high school, Smith divided them into experimental and control groups, fourteen classes composed of 204 students being experimental and fifteen classes of 307 students being control. From these two sets of classes she matched two groups—an experimental group of 62 students and a control group of like number. All comparisons were between both experimental and control classes and groups. All students were pre- and post-tested with the Cooperative English Test: Reading Comprehension, and a "Test of Purpose" developed by the researcher. This test was made up of two parts: Part I, to assess the ability of students to identify appropriate reading purposes for which a given selection should be read; and Part II, to determine the ability to comprehend passages when given a pre-stated purpose, as well as to determine the procedures and adjustments used in reading those passages. Over a period of a year the experimental students were given instruction in purposeful reading through work in their regular English classes.

Comparisons made at the end of the experimental period indicated that those between the experimental and control classes were much more significant than those between the smaller groups of experimental and control subjects. As a result of the instruction given in the experimental classes, the students were better able to identify appropriate purposes for reading, to read significantly better for the purposes studied, and to comprehend on a higher level than could the students in the control classes.

As an overall conclusion from this comprehensive study, Smith concluded that well-planned assignments should be made in which students are given reading purposes or are given direct instruction and guidance in setting their own purposes. Moreover, she recommended that instruction in purposeful reading should be given below and above the ninth grade, the grade in which this study was carried out.

Other studies than Smith's confirm the value of study objectives and purposes. Schlesser and Young (13) working with college students found that higher levels of achievement accrued from helping students develop motives for study than from instruction in specific study techniques. They said, "steady, vigorous, highly motivated effort is the outstanding trait of the student whose achievement is high relative to his abilities."

Spache (18) made several pertinent observations concerning study objectives. He pointed out that accurate comprehension assumes clear-cut purposes (reading objectives), established either by the teacher or by the student himself. "Without directions," he wrote, "he is likely to retain neither main ideas, nor details, nor relationships since he knows not what he is seeking." And then he continued discussing the importance of clarifying study objectives for each assignment. He suggested that the instructor ask himself, "What are the reasons for having the pupils read this assignment?" And then he added a statement with which I thoroughly concur, "If the instructor has not a particular purpose in mind, it is doubtful whether the assignment is justifiable."

To my way of thinking, the point Spache made regarding the importance of reading objectives underlies one of the most troublesome problems facing a student in the act of study. When questioned about their study problems, students frequently list as one of the first their inability to concentrate. What they don't know and what we many times don't realize is that unless they are asleep, they are always concentrating on something; but what they are concentrating on may have little relation to the learning task. Rather than thinking about the precipitating causes of the Civil War, the major problem is "How will I ask Susie to go to the spring formal, and what will I do if she says, 'No'?"

It is a well known principle that one focuses his attention (concentrates) on those things that are of most significance to him. Consequently, if one is to concentrate one must make the learning task preeminent. Granted this is difficult to do when the learning task is in competition with the spring prom, but the principle still remains. If learning tasks are to be competitive with other questions and problems confronting the learner to which his attention might be drawn, two things must be kept in mind. First, the learning task or study objective should be one that focuses on problem solving, issue resolving, or generalization forming rather than memorization of details. Tyler (19) showed, for example, that facts and rote learnings were eroded away by the passage of time while generalizations and principles were retained to a much greater degree. Second, and most important, the learning task must have relevance to the learner. It must be one to which he sees some point, some purpose in doing. Otherwise it becomes another assignment to do, to get out of the way, and to forget. As Spache says, if there is no good purpose for doing it, it is doubtful whether the assignment is justifiable.

When discussing reading-study objectives, the question frequently arises as to whether, to be most effective, the study objectives should have their origin with the teacher or the student. A study reported by Henderson (5) throws some light on this question. Taking 24 good readers and 24 poor readers on the fifth grade level he subjected them to four different types of purpose-setting behavior. In one of these situations the subjects read the first half of a story and then conjectured and declared a reading purpose. In another the reading objectives were supplied by the teacher. A check of comprehension indicated that the differences between the two treatments were insignificant whether the pupils set their own purposes or were given purposes by the teacher.

Similar findings to those above were reported by Smith (14) in the study to which we have already referred. From her findings, you will recall, she concluded that well-planned assignments should be made in which students either were given reading purposes or were given direct instruction and guidance in setting their own purposes.

It would appear logical to assume that the younger children would profit from study objectives supplied largely by the teacher. Eventually the objectives will be cooperatively derived by teacher and pupils; and still later, as pupils become more mature, they will assume increasing responsibility for formulating their own study objectives.

SKILLS INVOLVED IN STUDY

In the area of study skills, there is likewise confusion growing out of the inconsistent use of terminology and the overlapping of skills from one learning area to another. Nila Banton Smith (16) helps to clarify the issues here by categorizing skills needed to study effectively as common reading skills, common study skills, and specialized skills and competencies needed for study in the various curricular areas. The common reading competencies utilized in study are those used in any type of reading in any type of content, nontextual as well as textual, and for any type of objective. Important here would be the various word perception abilities, vocabulary, basic comprehension skills, and critical evaluation. To a large degree the comprehension skills are those growing out of the reading purpose we have already discussed—reading for the main idea, following direction, following a sequence of ideas, forming generalizations, and the like.

One can find almost as many lists of comprehension skills assumed to be important in reading and study as there are writers on the subject. Niles (9) contends, however, that at the heart of the ability to comprehend content of any kind there are three major skill areas. The first is the ability to find and understand thought relationships (comparison-contrast, chronological, cause-effect, etc.). The second is the ability to set specific study objectives and purposes. These we have already discussed at length. The third is the ability to make use of the backlog of real and vicarious experiences that relate to and serve to amplify the new materials. Without a doubt these are essential competencies that would serve well the purpose of reading or study in any area.

The common study skills are those to which frequent reference is made in the literature. They are skills and abilities used in study rather than casual reading and used similarly regardless of the area or subject. Usually these are referred to as location of information with reference to a particular reading task or objective; selecting and evaluating information in the light of the objective; and organizing information (facts, principles, generalizations) in a form or manner demanded by the situation. This task may be in the form of an outline for an oral report, notes for a discussion, an investigative paper, a dramatization, or a cartoon or drawing to illustrate a synthesis of ideas.

Frequently, recall or retention is listed as one of the common study skills. I am omitting it here for it has always seemed to me that recall is inherent to the act of organization. Recall is a by-product of the organization process rather than a separate competency to be developed. In the second place it carries the connotation of memorization for later rote recall or recitation of such things as lists, isolated facts, and statements. These we would hardly accept as the end toward which the study process should be directed.

I am omitting from our discussion anything having to do with the actual teaching procedures for the development of the common study skills, chiefly because the monograph on study skills in the Perspectives in Reading series, prepared under the sponsorship of IRA and compiled and edited by Harold Herber (6), covers this area so completely. This is a monograph that should be in the hands of every classroom teacher, particularly those on the secondary level. Well-written and extremely helpful chapters cover the development of word study skills, the use of book parts, sources of information, and visual aids. I recommend it highly as a source of practical help. Suffice it to say here that there is ample evidence that study abilities can be taught (2) and that the teaching of them contributes to improved learning.

Within the past twenty-five years or so we have become increasingly aware of the fact that efficient reading in the content areas calls for more than the general or common study skills referred to above. A considerable body of research evidence is available that competent reading in one area, literature for example, does not necessarily insure competent reading in science or mathematics. Though there may be skills that overlap one area with another, there are others quite unique to a given area. This is so because each content has its own specialized vocabulary, its method of treating ideas, its pattern of writing, and its own particular objectives which structure the kind of approach required (1).

Further evidence of this is in a study by Smith (17) who made an analysis of 52 tests in science, 60 in social studies, 49 in mathematics, and 45 in literature and arrived at a set of writing patterns used by authors in the development of content in each of these areas. From these writing patterns she derived the various response types demanded of the reader in dealing with the content. For example, social studies requires the reading of pictures, maps, and atlases; the analyzing of content for cause-effect relations, comparisons, sequence of events; and the critical analysis of content where different viewpoints are expressed, where facts are mixed with opinions, and where propaganda is used. This analysis is extremely helpful to teachers in aiding their students to read the subject matter in each of their teaching areas.

Other lists of skills and abilities assumed to be necessary for interpreting content in the various subject areas are found in any text in reading methods. I would want to call particular attention to another monograph in the Perspectives in Reading series titled *Reading Instruction in Secondary Schools* and edited by Margaret J. Early (3). Chapters by Bamman on reading in the science and mathematics areas, Herber in history, and Burton in literature are very comprehensive.

But in the final analysis, as helpful as these sources may be, it is quite difficult to tell Mr. Harris, teaching history in P.S. 46, precisely what study competencies *he* will need to develop. In the first place, the curricular design he follows will determine to a great extent the skills he will need to teach. If he follows a single text, the skills will be quite different from those he would need to develop were he using a problem centered approach. They will depend on the level of students in his class and to a large extent on their prior instruction. Consequently, Mr. Harris' best guide will come from the answer to a question he asks of himself: "What competencies do my students need in order to study my subject as I teach it?" Following this is the second question: "In which skills and abilities are my students sufficiently competent to deal with in my area?" These remaining skills then become the teaching responsibility of that teacher as they are required, keeping in mind of course that there may be students who will require individual help apart from that given to the group.

STUDY SKILLS PROGRAMS

The literature contains a number of action studies and a few pieces of well-controlled research attesting to the value of school programs devoted to the development of study skills and abilities. Many of these are described by Catterson (2). She points out that some programs are carried out under the aegis of English classes and others in special reading classes. She notes, however, a trend toward programs handled by classroom teachers in the regular content areas. If content area teachers are involved with content that students use for study purposes and if study competencies are to a substantial degree specific to each content area, then it must follow, as night the day, that the major responsibility for developing study competencies will be within the context of subject content on all grade levels.

But content area teachers have not been overwhelmingly responsive to this idea. One reason is, they say, that they lack the knowledge to conduct instruction. This, I think, is a rationalization; for if the doing of it is important, as evidence and sheer logic shows, then there are ample resource materials available for help. The two IRA Perspectives monographs to which we have frequently referred, to say nothing about the treatment of study in any reading test, would provide ample help. Moreover, reports of most of the successful reading and study programs on the secondary level have indicated that in-service training of teachers was an essential part of the program. Frequently such instruction was provided by the reading supervisor or coordinator.

Another reason, implied if not actually stated, for letting the task go by default is that the subject matter teacher feels that he hasn't time to develop study procedures along with the teaching of his subject content. The task is assumed to be something extra added to an already overextended course outline. Like selling football tickets on Saturday afternoon, it goes over and beyond the call of duty. But Catterson makes a statement that I think takes away the potency of this as an argument. She says, "The authors of these papers have made it obvious that they think of study skills not as *something* to teach, but as a *way* to teach—a way of teaching which advances not only the student's knowledge of subject matter but his ability to learn other subject matter independently and at will." In other words she was not talking about a unit on study to be added to an already overloaded course outline but something that should be a part of just good teaching.

But if we need to clinch the argument that the teaching of subject content cannot be divorced from the development of study competencies, the following question is offered as the *coup de grace*. What is the teaching of a particular subject such as social studies, science, literature, or home economics other than that of teaching the pupil or student to recognize and face issues, questions, or problems inherent to that body of content; to locate appropriate informative content; and to derive from that content ideas, generalizations, and principles that will help him answer his questions, resolve the issues, or form valid bases for opinions or judgments? It would seem, then, we are saying only in another way that *the teaching of a particular subject is the teaching of the study of that subject*; and that makes inescapable the fact that every teacher is a teacher of reading and study.

References

1. Artley, A. Sterl. "Influence of the Field Studied on the Reading Attitudes and Skills Needed," in W. S. Gray (Ed.), *Improving Reading in Content Fields*. Proceedings of the Annual Conference on Reading. Chicago: University of Chicago Press, 1947.
2. Catterson, Jane. "Successful Study Skills Programs," in H. L. Herber (Ed.), *Developing Study Skills in Secondary Schools*, Perspectives in Reading No. 4. Newark, Delaware: International Reading Association, 1965.
3. Early, Margaret J. (Ed.) *Reading Instruction in Secondary Schools*, Perspectives in Reading No. 2. Newark, Delaware: The International Reading Association, 1964.
4. Fay, Leo. "How Can We Develop Reading-Study Skills for the Different Curriculum Areas?" *The Reading Teacher*, 6 (March 1953), 12–18.
5. Henderson, E. H. "A Study of Individually Formulated Purposes for Reading" *Journal of Educational Research*, 58 (July-August 1965), 438–441.
6. Herber, Harold (Ed.), *Developing Study Skills in Secondary Schools*, Perspectives in Reading No. 4. Newark, Delaware: International Reading Association, 1965.
7. Herber, Harold. "Developing Study Skills in Secondary Schools: An Overview." In H. L. Herber (Ed.), *Developing Study Skills in Secondary Schools*, Perspectives in Reading No. 4. Newark, Delaware: International Reading Association, 1965.
8. Karlin, Robert. "Nature and Scope of Developmental Reading in Secondary Schools." In J. A. Figurel (Ed.), *Reading as an Intellectual Activity*, Proceedings of the International Reading Association, 8 (1963), 52–56.
9. Niles, Olive. "Comprehension Skills," *The Reading Teacher*, 17 (September 1963), 2–7.
10. Preston, Ralph. "Reading for What?" in J. A. Figurel (Ed.), *Reading as an Intellectual Activity*, Proceedings of the International Reading Association, 8 (1963), 13–20.

11. Robinson, H. Alan. "Reading Skills Employed in Solving Social Studies Problems," *The Reading Teacher*, 18 (Jan. 1965), 263–69.
12. Romano, M. J. "Reading and Science: A Symbiotic Relationship," *Education*, 81 (Jan. 1961), 273–76.
13. Schlesser, G. E., and C. W. Young. "Study and Work Habits," *The School Review*, 53 (Feb. 1945), 85–89.
14. Smith, Helen K. *Instruction of High School Students in Reading for Different Purposes* (Cooperative Research Project No. 1714), Office of Education, United States Department of Health, Education, and Welfare, 1966.
15. Smith, Nila Banton. *Reading Instruction for Today's Children.* Englewood Cliffs: Prentice-Hall, 1963, 307.
16. Ibid. p. 312.
17. Smith, Nila Banton. "Patterns of Writing in Different Subject Areas," *Journal of Reading*, 8 (Oct. 1964) 31–37; 8 (Nov. 1964), 97–108.
18. Spache, George. *Toward Better Reading*, Champaign: Garrard, 1963, 77.
19. Tyler, Ralph W. "Permanence of Learning," *Journal of Higher Education*, 4 (April 1933), 203–204.

(54) PATTERNS OF WRITING IN DIFFERENT SUBJECT AREAS*

Nila Banton Smith

PART I

The need for making adjustments when reading subject-matter in the different content fields is a fairly recent concept insofar as the history of reading is concerned. It was about 1940 when the first investigations began to come through in regard to reading in the content fields. Since that time such investigations have continued in ever-increasing volume. Still we are in the midst of a period of discovery.

The present article reports one additional attempt to obtain information concerning special reading needs in different subject areas. Part I in this issue of THE JOURNAL OF READING deals especially with literature

*Reprinted from the *Journal of Reading* 8 (October 1964), pp. 31–36, and (November 1964), pp. 97–102, by permission of the author and the International Reading Association.

and science. Part II, which will appear in the ensuing issue, deals with social studies and mathematics.

An Analysis of Textbook Content

The cue for an analysis of textbook content in science, social studies, and mathematics arose from an awareness of different patterns of writing in literature. It was hypothesized that there might also be special patterns of writing in the content of other subject fields. It was thought that if this were true and these specialized patterns could be detected and labelled, this information would be helpful to teachers in aiding their students to read subject matter in their respective teaching areas.

As analysis of text proceeded, an analysis also was made of questions, directions, explanations, and the various types of exercises that the books contained. All these aids and exercises in which the students are asked to make a response appear to be significant because they are indicative of the ways in which the subject specialist wants students to think and work with material in his particular field.

The materials analyzed embraced widely-used textbooks covering Grades 7 through 12: 52 science texts, 60 social studies texts (social studies and history), and history texts, 49 mathematics texts (advanced or commercial arithmetic, algebra, and geometry) and 45 literature texts.

In the two parts of this article only two aspects of the analysis will be reported: briefly, the one having to do with common study skills; primarily, and in greater detail, the one having to do with patterns of writing.

Common Reading Skills

It requires no special analysis to reveal that regardless of whether a student is reading in literature, science, social studies, or mathematics, he must be able to pronounce the words to get meaning from printed symbols, and to use appropriate reading rates. Breaking these general skills down somewhat we have (1) word recognition, utilizing sight words, picture clues, context clues, phonics, analysis of word structure and dictionary techniques; (2) understanding meanings involving literal comprehension, interpretation, critical reading, specific word meaning; and (3) rate—making use of different speeds according to intent for reading and nature of subject matter. These skill areas are drawn upon in all kinds of reading. Since these basic skills are used in all kinds of reading, they will be referred to throughout this article as the *common reading skills*.

COMMON STUDY SKILLS

The writer considers the study skills to be those specialized skills used in study situations over, above, and in addition to the *common reading skills* employed in non-study situations. She finds it helpful to think of the reading study skills as those skills used especially in situations in which it is desired to make applications of content covered. Thus conceived, the study skills in reading may be broadly defined as those skills used when we intend to do something with content while reading it or after finishing the reading.

In high school a boy may read a sports column to find who won the game; he may read a detective story to find who stole the black diamond; he may read an article on space travel because he is intrigued with this subject. He doesn't do anything with the content in any of these cases. He isn't using study skills.

But he is using study skills when he studies his textbooks for the purpose of gathering facts or generalizations to use in class discussion, in experimentation, in making a report, in preparing a summary, in solving a problem, in getting ready to take a test.

The analysis of questions, exercises, explanations, and directions stated in the various textbooks studied, revealed that there were multiple instances in which the student was confronted with specialized situations calling for the use of study skills. Space does not permit a report of these many specialized situations. There were certain study skills, however, which occurred with high frequency in all subject fields. Hence, these will be referred to as the *common study skills*.

These *common study skills* are (1) selections and evaluation—selecting an idea, paragraph, or section of text and evaluating it in terms of its relevance, importance, contribution, or relationship to other factors; (2) organization—putting items together in a list, outline, summary or report; (3) recall—fixing in mind certain items for recall purposes; (4) location of information in textbooks, reference books and periodicals; (5) following directions for doing something with text read. Because these study skills are used with such high frequency in all subject areas, it is particularly important that secondary school teachers provide special practice for students who are deficient in the use of any one of them.

PATTERNS OF WRITING IN LITERATURE

In opening the discussion of patterns of writing, it is probably obvious but perhaps advisable to state that no special analysis is necessary in discerning patterns of writing in literature. Patterns in this field have been established for years. There are the *story* (short story or novel); *essay*; *drama*; *biography*; *fable*; and *poetry* of many kinds (ballad, lyric, elegiac, epic, sonnet), some written in rhymed verse, some in free verse, some in blank verse and of many different meters.

Each of these patterns requires a different approach. A student should not read a story, an essay, and a drama in the same way. His purpose is different. He reads a story to enjoy plot, character, and setting, an essay to get the slant of the author as he discusses some aspect of life, a drama to interpret the conversations of the characters involved. Drama is further differentiated in reading in that it is cast in an entirely different format. Biography and autobiography should be read not merely to follow separate chronological facts but to get a conclusive impression of the person writing it or being written about. Sometimes within the essay or biography the detailed statement-of-facts pattern appears, but this is very light as compared with this pattern which is characteristically used in science. Cause-and-effect relationships appear sometimes within typical literature patterns, but these are not prominent and usually remain for the teacher or exercises in the book to reveal.

Poetry varies widely in the purposes for which it should be read and the form in which it is written. A student certainly should not read a ballad for the same purpose and in the same way that he reads a sonnet.

As the student reads different patterns in literature for different purposes and in different forms, he must adjust his reading skills, using different combinations of skills in different situations. In general, different combinations of the *common reading skills*, with heavy emphasis upon interpretations, serve a student well in reading literature itself. However, in answering questions and carrying out assignments stated in the textbook exercises, he will have to use the *common study skills*. Thus it is that the teacher of literature has a fourfold task in reading: (1) to teach his students to identify different patterns of writing; (2) to give them help in sensing the purpose for reading each pattern and adjusting their reading skills to this pattern; (3) to give practice on any of the *common reading skills* to students who need improvement in any one of these skill areas; (4) to give special practice on any of the *common study skills* in which some students may be deficient.

PATTERNS OF WRITING IN SCIENCE

An analysis of science textbooks reveals that they, too, contain specialized patterns of writing. The science text, like all other kinds of texts, calls for the use of the *common reading skills*, and the exercises call for the use of *common study skills*. Sometimes science writers make use of cause-and-effect text. However, it is in the social studies that this kind of text is most highly characteristic. But science does have unique science patterns which call for different approaches and different combinations of skills.

THE CLASSIFICATION PATTERN

One type of science text falls into the *classification pattern* in which living things, objects, materials, elements, gases, liquids, forces, etc., are classified under a common heading which in turn deals with sub-divisions, each of which has an element or elements in common with the other sub-classes but which vary in certain respects from one another. For example, in a chapter on "Hormones—Chemical Messengers of the Body," there is an introduction telling in general what hormones are; then follow sections of text each of which discusses a particular hormone, giving its location, name of its secretion or secretions, and their functions in the body. Under the general class known as hormones the following sub-classes are discussed: the thyroid gland, the adrenal glands, the parathyroid glands, the pancreas, the gonads, and the pituitary gland.

In reading this pattern, the student who identifies it as a classification pattern will concentrate on grasping the subdivisions and the chief characteristics of each one. In other words he will gear his reading procedure to obtaining the kind of information which is important in this particular pattern of writing.

EXPLANATION OF A TECHNICAL PROCESS

Another pattern of writing which is particularly characteristic of science, and perhaps the most difficult one to read, is the explanation of a technical process, which usually is accompanied with diagrams necessitating very careful reading of text with continuous reference to diagrams. The diagrams in themselves require special reading skills in addition to grasping the text explanations. As an example of this pattern, consider a section of text describing "How the Telephone Works." The entire process is explained and accompanied with numerous diagrams. This kind of reading requires a doubling of techniques: reading the text and reading the diagram alternately as one feeds into the other.

INSTRUCTIONS FOR AN EXPERIMENT

A third unique pattern in science is the one in which instructions are given for carrying out an experiment. This pattern consists of explicit directions that must be carried out exactly and which call for careful observations of what happens, an explanation of what happens, and the drawing of a conclusion.

a. Obtain several strips of different metals. b. Place several different liquid solutions in glasses or jars. These might include such things as salt water, soda water, sulfuric acid, vinegar, sugar water, or other chemical materials. c. Use the voltmeter to test your different electric cells. Try all the possible combinations of metals and liquid solutions. In the same way try other materials that are not metal. d. Make a list of the different electric cells which you have tested, and write down the volage discovered for each cell. e. What kinds of materials do you think are most useful in making electric cells? What types of materials seem to be unsuited for making electric cells?

The common study skill of following directions is used in this science pattern, but this skill isn't enough in itself. Experiments call for the plus mental activities of discriminating observation, careful explanation, and considered conclusion.

DETAILED STATEMENT-OF-FACTS PATTERN

Another pattern frequently encountered in science textbooks but not entirely unique to science is the *detailed statement-of-facts pattern.* This pattern in science differs from fact-giving text in other subjects in these respects: the facts are more dense, and they frequently embody a definition or a statement of a principle.

The atoms of some elements exist in different forms, called *isotopes.* The nuclei of isotopes of the same element all have the same number of protons. The nuclei differ, however, in the number of neutrons they contain. Ordinary hydrogen has one proton in the nucleus. *Heavy hydrogen, or deuterium, has a nucleus containing one proton and one neutron.* This nucleus is called a *deuteron.*

In reading this pattern the student can use the usual skill of finding, first of all, the most important thought or main idea in each section of content, then proceed to find details that reinforce this statement noting particularly any definitions or principles embodied in them.

The Descriptive Problem-Solving Pattern

A science pattern which is less difficult to read is the description of a problem-solving situation which has been met through a series of experiments usually conducted by several different people. For example, a chapter on "Releasing the Atom" discusses the successive steps in discovering atomic energy and in learning how to release it. In reading this pattern, the student should approach it with the idea of finding out what each successive problem was and how it was met.

Abbreviations and Equations

Another science pattern which requires a special kind of reading is that in which abbreviations are liberally used.

The temperature at which water freezes is called 0°C or 32°F and fixes the ice point on the thermometer scale. The boiling point of water under a pressure of 760 mm of mercury is called 100°C or 212°F and determines the steam-point on the thermometer scale.

Grasping the meaning of the symbol^0, and the abbreviations C, F and mm as these are integrated with words in text calls for recognition skills in addition to the usual recognition of word symbols. This pattern is still further complicated when the abbreviations are involved in equations.

PART II

Part I of this article dealt with patterns of writing revealed in an analysis of secondary school textbooks in literature and science. Part II discusses patterns resulting from an analysis of secondary texts in social studies and mathematics.

Patterns in Social Studies

Picture and Map Patterns. The text in social studies books at the junior high level usually contains narrative accounts which are easy to read, and which do not represent specialized patterns as a whole. There are, however, embodied in these narrative accounts, features which call for skills peculiar to social studies content at all levels.

For one thing, a student reading social studies material of any level often encounters a direction within a paragraph or text. This direction requires him to leave the text, refer elsewhere in the textbook to gather information, then to return to the point at which he was reading in the paragraph, and to integrate the information gathered from the reference into the content of the paragraph as a whole. This reference is usually made either to a picture or a map, each of which in turn calls for the use of special reading skills.

The ability to read pictures is a skill needed in this field. At the secondary level often the text of a paragraph may be interrupted by a direction such as "Look at the picture of the Aztec temple. How do you think it was made? What transportation was Cortes using?"

In the above example, students were guided in making an interpretation and in noting a detail. In many cases the picture is presented without calling attention to details and implications. A wealth of information can be obtained from reading pictures in this subject field. Teachers might well increase their efforts to sensitize their students to the usefulness of pictures and give them practice in *reading* pictures as a valuable supplemental aid in obtaining information from the printed pages of their textbooks.

The reading of maps is a highly specialized kind of reading in the social studies area. Maps, atlases and globes require the use of such skills as recognizing and interpreting symbols for rivers, mountains, lakes, towns and cities, boundary lines, scale of miles, color keys, meridians, and symbols needed in interpreting special maps of population, products, topography, etc. The efficient use of all these symbols requires *reading* activities, and if secondary school students are deficient in any of them, no time should be lost in teaching them these skills.

The Cause and Effect Pattern. While this pattern occurs to some extent in other subject fields, it occurs with the highest frequency in social studies and history. Every major event in history comes about as the result of some cause or set of causes, and when the event happens its effect or effects are felt. Sometimes the effect of one event becomes the cause of another event. Thus it is that history is made up of a chain of causes and effects. The student who is adept in identifying the cause-and-effect pattern and who gears his reading specifically to ascertaining causes and effects will find this to be one of his most valuable assets in studying social studies and history.

Sequential Events with Dates. Another pattern specialized in history is one that presents events in specific time sequence accompanied with dates. The student should read this pattern for two purposes: (1) to grasp the larger periods or whole blocks of events in their chronological order, and (2) to fix in mind the important dates of happenings within each period or block, stopping to associate events with dates, and thinking how each event led to the next one.

There are several kinds of pencil work that students find helpful in studying this pattern. They may make a brief summary of dates and events as they read; they may fill in an outline map of the locale, marking dates and events in their appropriate locations; they may make a chart of events and dates; or they may prepare a conventional "Time Line."

The Comparison Pattern. A pattern calling for comparison of likenesses and/or differences is a common one in history in the social studies. This pattern is most frequently encountered in a discussion of such coordinate and similar topics as differences in the theories of government, policies of different leaders, platforms of different political parties, the past and present functions of certain government agencies, and so on.

If the student is aware that he is about to read a comparison chapter or section of text he can approach it with the foremost purpose of noting likenesses and differences. Undoubtedly, such an approach will cause comparisons and contrasts to stand out in such sharp relief that both interpretation and recall will be facilitated.

Detailed Statement-of-Fact Pattern. There are sections of text in social studies and history which contain detailed facts. These sections, however, are usually included within one of the more characteristic patterns discussed above. The facts in such sections are not as dense as in this pattern in science, nor are they as technical. Too, these facts in history are more easily grasped because of their association with sequential events or with causes and effects.

The Propaganda Pattern. This pattern is one with which every student should be acquainted and one he should know how to read. Propaganda has been in existence throughout history. The astute reader can detect it in quotations from and actions of men as reported in history books, and by signs and cartoons sometimes depicted in history or social studies texts.

It is not the propaganda of the past, however, which should be our major concern. Students and teachers of the present are living in the midst of a communication network which is teeming with propaganda, and there is evidence that it will increase in volume in the years ahead. Some of this propaganda is used for good causes. More often it is misused for personal motives.

Every medium containing printed sentences or even phrases is used as a tool by the propagandist: billboards, handbills, leaflets, pamphlets as well as newspapers, magazines, and books. All these may serve this purpose. The important thing for the reader to know is how to detect the propaganda pattern so he will be aware of the intent of reading materials in which someone is trying to influence his thinking or behavior.

One of the most important things that the history teacher can do is to teach his students to recognize the propaganda pattern. It is true that propaganda can be intricate and subtle and not always easily detectable. There are, however, seven techniques which are generally considered to be basic among the tricks used by the propagandist. These tricks make use of "Glad Words" or "Glittering Generalities," "Unpleasant Words," "Transfer," "Testimonials," "Plain Folks Implications," "Band Wagon Techniques," and "Stacking the Cards."

Students should be made aware of these basic tricks, and given opportunities to detect and discuss them in various types of printed materials, encouraged to search for motives, and then to make decisions as to whether or not they care to be influenced by them.

PATTERNS IN MATHEMATICS

One of the special characteristics of mathematical text is compactness. Every word and every symbol is important. Skipping an unfamiliar word or filling it in from context has no place in reading mathematics.

Another characteristic of mathematics texts is that they are composed of two or sometimes three kinds of symbols all mixed together in the same paragraph. There are word symbols, number symbols, and in algebra and geometry there are letter symbols and various other kinds of symbols. The interpretation of so many different kinds of symbols makes for difficult reading.

The Problem Pattern. The most highly specialized pattern of text in mathematics is the short paragraph setting forth a problem situation. Regardless of whether the text is in arithmetic, algebra, or geometry, problems are usually stated in this format: at the beginning the situation is given, or the condition under which the problem took place is stated; then follows a series of numbers or other mathematical values, and finally the reader is asked or told what to find. Example: When a piece of brass is weighed in water, it weighs 1.977 lb. If it is weighed in gylcerin, its weight is 1.971 lb. The specific gravity of gylcerin is 1.26. How much does the brass weigh in air?

In geometry and physics, problems sometimes consist of only a single direction or a single question. The characteristic problem pattern, however, is as indicated above.

The *reading* of such problems involves four different processes: (1) reading the entire problem to grasp the situation as a whole; (2) concentrating on the question or statement at the end that asks or tells what to find; (3) deciding what processes or formulas to use in finding the answer; (4) pulling out the number facts or symbols presented for us in working the problem. After these *reading* activities accompanied with a high degree of reasoning have been completed, then the student is ready to compute the problem mentally or on paper. If a student is having difficulty in mathematics, it would be helpful to explain to him the importance of the *reading* activities which precede computation, and to provide him with special practice in the reading procedures involved.

Another adjustment which the student has to make to the *reading* of problems is a change from the basic eye-movement habits to which he has been accustomed. In reading problems he often uses vertical or left-directed movements to reread portions for better understanding or to pick out certain numbers or symbols. While some students read problems more rapidly than others, the problem pattern is most certainly not one that is appropriate for speed reading.

The Explanatory Pattern. The explanatory pattern in mathematics texts constitutes difficult reading. This pattern is similar to the explanation-of-a-process pattern appearing in science textbooks except that in this case the explanations expound a mathematical process rather than a technical scientific process, they are comparatively short in length rather than spreading over long sections of text, and usually they are accompanied with an example of a problem "worked out."

Students should be urged to read this pattern with the greatest of care. It is advisable in some cases for them to check their comprehension of the explanation by trying to repeat it to themselves in their own words. If an example is given to apply the explanation, they should of course follow through this step by step, referring to the explanation if necessary to find out why the step was taken. The success with which they are able to solve the problems that follow often hinges upon the thoroughness with which the explanation has been *read* and *comprehended*.

Graph and Chart Patterns. Other distinctive patterns in mathematics are found in graphs and charts. While these visual aids are used in science, social studies and other subjects, they represent mathematical concepts.

Reading a graph or a table is a different kind of reading than reading a paragraph. In order to get the most of a graph or table, students should be taught to: (1) read the title to determine exactly what is being compared; (2) read the figures or labels to make sure they grasp what it is that they stand for; (3) study the graph or chart to make comparisons in regard to the different items illustrated, (4) and finally, they should interpret the significance of the chart or graph as a whole. Due to the prevalence of graphs and charts, many secondary students might well profit from some additional practice in *reading* these types of pictured relationships.

Special Symbols, Signs and Formulas. Mathematics text carries with it a unique terminology: signs of various kinds, abbreviations, exponents, subscripts, formulas, equations, geometrical figures, and so on. For students, learning to recognize these symbols and their meanings is like learning to *read* all over again. It is, indeed, an astute teacher of mathematics who recognizes these characteristic symbols as *reading* content and who makes a special effort to teach his students to *read* them.

(55) READING INSTRUMENT USAGE*

Stanford E. Taylor

During the last decade, and particularly the past five years, there has been a rapid increase in the use of many audio-visual techniques, published devices, and reading instruments.

In early 1960, a survey was made of 7,616 members of the IRA. Of the 777 who responded, 417 of 59 per cent used one or more types of reading instruments at one level or another. *See Table I.*

Among the responses, there was evident a great deal of confusion as to trade names and types of instrumentation, most likely stemming from confusion as to the functions and purposes of the various reading instrument techniques.

*Reprinted from *The Reading Teacher* 15 (May 1962), pp. 449–54, by permission of the author and the International Reading Association.

TABLE 1

FREQUENCY OF MENTION OF USAGE OF INSTRUMENT
TECHNIQUES BY GRADE LEVELS

	1-3	4-6	Jr.H.	H.S.	Col.	Ad.
A. Tachistoscopes						
1. Group Projection Instruments						
a. EDL Tach-X	40	61	66	47	31	19
b. Keystone Flashmeter	10	26	23	17	16	9
c. SVE Speedioscope	2	5	6	2	3	4
d. Unspecified	10	24	27	24	16	10
2. Individual Devices						
a. Stereo-Optical Tachitron						
(Renshaw)	1	5	3	2	4	2
b. AVR Eye-Span Trainer	—	—	1	1	—	—
c. Tachisto-Flasher	—	—	—	1	1	—
B. Directional Attach Control Techniques						
1. Instruments						
a. EDL Controlled Reader	76	102	107	90	48	—
b. PDL Perceptoscope	—	—	2	3	4	3
c. Unspecified	2	2	2	1	—	1
2. 16mm Films						
a. Harvard University Films	—	—	3	11	15	7
b. Iowa University Films						
(college level)	—	—	—	—	15	13
c. Purdue University Films	—	—	2	3	4	2
d. C-B Educational Films	—	—	2	2	1	1
e. Iowa University Films						
(high school level)	—	—	4	12	—	—
f. Unspecified	—	—	—	—	1	1
C. Accelerators						
1. SRA Accelerator	3	9	18	24	10	7
2. AVR Rateometer	2	7	9	7	2	2
3. Psychotechnics Shadowscope	—	2	2	4	2	—
4. Stereo-Optical Reading						
Rate Controller	—	1	3	3	3	3
5. Unspecified	1	4	7	10	8	3
TOTAL INSTRUMENT USAGE						
BY GRADE LEVELS	147	248	287	264	184	84

The responses prompted this article which will briefly delineate some
of the differences in types and purposes of reading instruments. It is
hoped that such clarification will aid teachers of reading in better

understanding the place of reading instruments in a balanced program, as well as in making better use of specific instrument techniques at their disposal.

TYPES OF READING INSTRUMENTS

The primary distinction should be made on the basis of training approach and purpose, rather than size, shape or type of film used.

Until recently, there were three categories: those using tachistoscopic exposures, those with directional attack control, and those employing acceleration principles. A fourth and new category is represented by devices used to train selective reading skills of skimming and scanning.

All instrument techniques have proved to be highly motivating and successful in encouraging students to apply themselves. They vary, however, in the skills they attempt to develop. They also vary in their success in achieving their purposes, according to the soundness of their training principles, the adequacy of their accompanying materials, and the manner in which they are used. In discussing each instrument category, therefore, mention will be made not only of what it is intended to accomplish, but also of what it should not be expected to accomplish.

In evaluating these techniques, teachers should bear in mind that there can be as much difference between two instrument techniques as between a textbook on nuclear physics and a first-grade reader.

TACHISTOSCOPES

Whether projection devices for group work or individual devices using printed material, tachistoscopes present numbers, letters, words, etc., for brief timed exposures, usually ranging from 1/100 to 1½ seconds, with most training given at the higher speeds. The tachistoscope is primarily a means of developing the "intake" or initial impression stage of the perceptual process, but is of limited value in developing the "processing" or assimilation stage.

The importance of tachistoscopic exposures 1/10 of a second or faster is that the student can gain only one visual impression of the exposed material, for he does not have time to make more than one fixation or move his eyes over the material. As a result, he learns to approach seeing aggressively, to see more rapidly and with less possible wandering visually, and by working with progressively more difficult material, he grows in his ability to retain visual material in a more organized fashion.

For a time, some producers of tachistoscopic techniques proposed programs of "eye span" development, building up to longer and longer phrases, in the hope that students would develop the ability to take in a phrase at each eye stop and that this would result in more rapid reading. We now know that the span during tachistoscopic exposures is quite different from the span employed in reading. After a tachistoscopic exposure, there is a prolonged, undisturbed processing period which allows the assimilation of a greater amount of material; while during reading, the perceptual activity is continuous, complicated by overlapping images, and the processing time is comparatively very brief. The tachistoscopic span, even without training, can be three to four times greater than the span maintained during actual reading. Thus it is easy to see why an increase in "tachistoscopic span" cannot be directly transferred to the reading situation. While some students will tend to show rate gains after tachistoscopic training, this can usually be attributed to improvements in the *intake* stage of perception—in greater speed and accuracy, a more orderly approach to seeing, and greater mental alertness—rather than to span improvement (1, 2). Explained simply, the tachistoscope improves "seeing" skills as a foundation for better reading, rather than improving reading skills *per se*, especially rate (3).

Tachistoscopic procedures have been used effectively on all educational levels, with all ability groups. Ideally, however, this type of training should be stressed during the first eight grades: first, to initiate efficient perceptual skills, and second, to increase recognition ability in the areas of reading, spelling, arithemetic, etc.

DIRECTIONAL ATTACK CONTROL TECHNIQUES

All of these techniques, whether employing 16mm motion picture films or 35mm filmstrips in a specially designed projector, present continuous reading material in a timed, left-to-right fashion. Directional control techniques are conducive to improvement of the intake stage because of the higher attention level maintained during timed reading and because of the encouragement of more orderly apprehension; however, they have far more effect on the processing stage than do tachistoscopic techniques.

These techniques encourage the student to perceive and organize material in a more orderly fashion. While he is reading a story, the left-to-right visual control improves the student's coordination and mobility, conditions a more efficient directional attack, and eliminates excessive fixations, regressions and visual wandering. With no chance to reread, the student learns to concentrate. Because of the controlled rate of presentation, he learns to think rapidly and to organize his thoughts well. At the same time, he develops the ability to counteract certain subtractive influences which operate during the processing stage: the disturbance of overlapping images, image deterioration caused by the kinesthetic activity of saccadic movement, the restriction and alteration caused by purpose or set, and the inevitable environmental distractions.

There is more variation within directional attack control techniques than in any other category of reading instruments. Some present material in "blocks" or segments of a line; some attempt to divide material into phrases; and some cover and uncover material in a continuous uninterrupted manner. Some techniques have more flexibility in terms of speed control than others. Some have more extensive libraries of material—in terms of number, level and types of selections. All of these factors naturally determine the effectiveness of the method and the type and permanence of gains achieved through its use.

The techniques that provide a wide and flexible range of rates of presentation and a sufficient range of material, so that the teacher can start students well below their instructional levels, are the most successful in developing *coordination and mobility*. In order to develop in these visual-functional skills, the student must encounter an "uncomplicated" reading situation and be stimulated to move quickly over the reading material in an orderly fashion.

Those techniques that exert the most persistent conditioning influence on directional attack without inhibiting the perceptual or thinking process will cause the greatest change in *performance characteristics*: more consistent left-to-right movement (indicated by a reduction of the proportion of regressions to fixations), reduction of fixations and regressions, decrease in duration of fixation, and increase in span of recognition, resulting in increased rate of comprehension.

The best gains in *comprehension and interpretation* will be produced by those techniques which effect the greatest improvement in directional attack, orderly perception, and organized assimilation, and those with a sufficient library of material to enable the student to progress in small sequential steps in learning to organize and retain content.

Thus permanence of improvement achieved through the use of directional control techniques is directly dependent on the *degree* of change in functional, perceptual and organizational abilities; and this, in turn, is a function of the amount and type of training given, and the steps taken to stabilize gain (4).

In summary, directional attack control techniques are primarily concerned with building fluency, or decreasing the time needed for perceptual processing, and improving the accuracy with which content is assimilated and understood. The end result is the building of basic skills that underlie recall, comprehension, and interpretation. (Such techniques in and of themselves do not lend themselves to developing advanced interpretive skills of critical and evaluative reading.)

Directional attack control techniques are successfully used at all levels of instruction. Ideally, however, such techniques should be introduced within the first three grades to insure maximum success in reading throughout a student's school career.

ACCELERATING DEVICES

The effect of accelerating devices, whether they employ a falling shutter, moving band of light, descending rod, audible timing click or moving second hand, is to provide individual rate practice for the already competent reader. These devices offer no directional attack control but do have provisions for timing and a visual or audible "prompt" which urges the reader to maintain a higher attention level, dissuades him from rereading and encourages him to read at increasingly higher rates.

Acceleration practice techniques were designed for use by competent readers who can read grade level material comfortably and efficiently at rates in excess of 350 words per minute, and who have indicated by their good comprehension that they have mastered the skill of careful and inclusive reading. Since these devices have no directional attack control, they should not be used in an effort to improve the performance skills of functionally inefficient readers. Rate motivation without modification of basic habits can cause tension and discomfort, and may result in actual increase in fixations and regressions as the inefficient reader strives to cope with reading material under pressure (5). Teachers should also be cautioned against using such techniques with superficial readers; for them, rate motivation does not serve to stimulate greater accuracy and thoroughness, but can, in many cases, create less accuracy. Care must be taken not to stimulate the student beyond the limits of his competence.

The success of acceleration techniques depends to a large extent on the type and range of training material used and the type of comprehension required. The student should always be started on material several grades below his instructional level and should eventually be returned to material at his grade level.

In summary, acceleration devices are usually employed at the junior high school level. and above, with readers whose functional and interpretive skills are well developed.

SKIMMING AND SCANNING INSTRUMENTS

A fourth and new instrument category is represented by constant-speed devices used to aid the already competent reader cross the threshold from inclusive reading, in which every line of print is read, to selective reading (skimming and scanning). Selective reading can best be described as a process of "looking and reading" in that the reader looks for the more significant parts or important facts and stops to read them inclusively. Techniques for training selective reading should neither exercise control nor direct the reader down the page; rather, they should provide a reminder of elapsed time, helping the reader to maintain a rate within the selective reading range, avoiding the tendency to slip back into inclusive reading and the opposite tendency of racing over material so rapidly that comprehension is negligible. One device used to develop these selective reading skills employs a single bead of light that moves at a constant speed down the center fold of the text.

Training in selective reading should develop in the reader the ability to attend perceptually and organizationally at the highest possible level. Instruments designed to offer effective techniques for selective reading training are not intended and should not be expected to improve visual-functional reading skills, to aid in building basic comprehension or interpretation, or to serve as accelerating devices for use in increasing rate.

SUMMARY

In discussing reading instruments and procedures, every producer acknowledges that such techniques were conceived as aids to the teacher, not replacements; as part of a total program, not a complete approach; as developing certain specific skills and abilities, not as a panacea. There is a conviction, however, on the part of all who understand the function of instrument techniques, that they play an indispensable role in the balanced reading program of today and will play an increasingly important part in the schools of tomorrow, as the need is felt to teach more content in less time and to develop each student to his fullest potential.

REFERENCES

1. Spache, George D. "Evaluation of Eye-Movement Photography in Reading Diagnosis and Reading Training," *Research and Evaluation in College Reading—The Ninth Yearbook, National Reading Conference for College and Adults.* Fort Worth, Texas: Texas Christian University Press, 98–106.
2. Taylor, Stanford E., Helen Frackenpohl and James Pettee. "Grade Level Norms for the Components of the Fundamental Reading Skill," *EDL Research and Information Bulletin No. 3.* Huntington, N.Y.: Educational Developmental Laboratories, 1960, 12.
3. Bormuth, John R., and Cleatus C. Aker, "Is the Tachistoscope a Worthwhile Teaching Tool?" *The Reading Teacher* 14 (January, 1961), 172–76.
4. Bottomly, Forbes, "An Experiment with the Controlled Reader," *Journal of Educational Research*, 54 (March, 1961), 265–69.
5. "A Concentrated Junior High School Reading Program," *EDL Newsletter No. 14*, Huntington, New York: Educational Developmental Laboratories, Inc.

(56) DEVICES TO IMPROVE SPEED OF READING*

Miles A. Tinker

Examination of the book and materials exhibits at the national meetings of the International Reading Association reveals a bewildering array of gadgets promoted to improve the speed of reading. In addition are the advertisements in both scientific and popular magazines, plus the visits of persuasive salesmen. The claims made for these devices are enticing and more often than not appear valid to the teachers and others who want to improve the reading speed of pupils or of themselves. It is high time to

*Reprinted from *The Reading Teacher* 20 (April 1967), pp. 605–609, by permission of the author and the International Reading Association.

make an objective evaluation of the usefulness of these devices or machines or gadgets.

All or most of these devices have their origins in attempts to improve reading speed by training (i.e., pacing) eye movements. In these attempts stress was placed upon the difference between the eye movements during reading of poor and good readers. The good readers tended to make few fixations and regressions per line of print, while poor readers usually made many fixations and regressions in their reading. This observation eventually led to the practice of attempting to improve rate of reading by training eye movements. Early procedures "trained" a reader to fixate three times on vertical marks equally spaced across lines of the length of ordinary printed lines. Presumably, after this habit was perfected, the reader would use only three fixations for each line of print in reading. Another variation was to print or type phrases separated by extra spaces and to encourage the reader to make one fixation on each phrase. But individuals vary greatly in the number of fixations employed in reading a line of print even after training such as described above. Any statements that superior readers make only three or four fixations per line are misleading generalizations of the facts. When a line of twenty-four to twenty-six picas (commonly used in printing books) is used, six to eight fixations per line are employed by good readers, according to data cited by Anderson and Dearborn (1). In fact, it has been shown that after the training described above readers continue to make more than three fixations per line. Buswell (3) also notes that few subjects ever achieve three fixations per line.

Soon gadgets or devices appeared on the market designed to pace eye movements so that only three fixations would be employed to read a line of print. One of these machines is the metron-o-scope, a triple-action electrically operated tachistoscope (short exposure apparatus) which exposes successive thirds of a line of printed matter. (Although this apparatus is no longer on the market, hundreds of them are owned by schools and clinics.) After the first line of a selection has been exposed in this manner, the second line is exposed similarly. This continues with successive lines until the whole selection has been read.

Using the metron-o-scope gives rather uniform results in promoting faster reading. The question arises as to whether the use of the apparatus is necessary to achieve speedier reading. Whether dealing with children or adults, the answer is no. Cason (4), working with third grade children, found significant gains: (a) by use of the metron-o-scope, (b) by well motivated reading in the library, and (c) by use of special phrases marked up into phrase units. The gains proved to be just as good by one method as by any other. Her analysis indicated no special benefit from use of the machine. And Westover (10) found that college students who used ordinary materials and methods in a well-motivated speedup program made just as good gains in speed of reading as students using a modified metron-o-scope.

Another device which has found wide usage is the Harvard Reading Films or modification of the principle such as the High School Reading Training Films (State University of Iowa). These are motion picture techniques in which phrases, grouped in thought units, appear on a screen in boldface type on a faint printing of the whole page of connected material. The rate at which the phrases succeed one another can be varied by adjusting the speed control of the projector. The alleged values of the films are that they (a) give a mechanical stimulus which focuses attention and aids concentration and the rapid association of meanings without verbalization, (b) provide practice in reading by thought units, and (c) give students objective evidence that improvement is possible.

Glock (5) evaluated the film technique by studying the effect upon eye movements and reading rate of three methods of training: (a) using the Harvard films, (b) employing a new film which exposed two successive lines simultaneously, and (c) reading printed material while motivated to read fast and comprehend. Four weeks of training was given to six sections of college students. The students made significant improvements in eye movements and thus in rate of reading under all three methods of training. But there were no significant differences between results of the three methods, i.e., the technique that paced eye movements (Harvard Films) was no more effective than either of the others in increasing speed of reading.

Other pacing machines are in common use. Some devices pace the reader by moving a shutter, line by line, over the material being read. The reader is expected to keep ahead of the shutter. The rate of moving the shutter may be varied from slow to fast. In one variety of this type of machine, a shadow from a wire moves down the page of printed material. The reader tries to keep ahead of the shadow. The trade names of some of these machines are: Controlled Reader, Reading Accelerator, Reading Rate Controller, Rate Reader, and the Reading Board. The same end may be accomplished by a push-card method. The teacher pushes a large card from top to bottom of a page while the reader is supposed to keep ahead of the card. The rate of moving the card can be varied to suit the needs of the particular pupil.

Reading speed is increased for many but not for all pupils by use of pacers just described. But there is no assurance that the gains are lasting after the pacing is stopped. Also, the improved rate is not transferred to other types of reading material without special training. Proponents argue that the machines improve rate of reading because of the increased motivation of the reader while using the gadget. Spache (8) states: "The answer that research gives to this question is that gains in reading rate or speed of word recognition can be achieved equally as well by ordinary motivated practice or carefully planned classroom activities." He also states that the use of these pacers when other methods fail to provide sufficient motivation or impetus will help some students to read faster. And he notes that the pacers are not successful with all students and cannot be used indiscriminately.

Should the teacher use the reading accelerator type of pacer to improve the speed of reading? One argument usually advanced for use of pacers is that pupils are tremendously interested in the use of the device and thus highly motivated. This is true. But even so, such children make no greater gains than do those taught by regular methods. Any skilled teacher should be able to provide the incentives that promote good motivation. There is always a possibility that some child will improve with machine training but not by good classroom methods. However, no investigation has shown this to be so.

Another difficulty is that, when speed per se is taught by machine, the pupil may be prevented from becoming a versatile user of rates of reading, i.e., from becoming flexible in the use of different rates according to the kind and difficulty of the material to be read and the purpose for which the reading is done. Too frequently, a teacher may consider that a machine will solve all her problems, and will use it not as a supplement but to the exclusion of proper emphasis on more fundamental aspects of reading instruction.

The Flashmeter, the Tach-X, and other short exposure devices known by the general name tachistoscopes are employed to flash number series and words upon a screen for a brief interval. The aim of this technique is to develop quick perception and increase the span of recognition, and hence speed of reading. Flash cards may be used instead of a tachistoscope. However, Anderson and Dearborn (1) are doubtful that tachistoscopic training has value in increasing speed of reading. They conclude that the time might be better spent on promoting growth in comprehension. But Brown (3), on the other hand, describes and supports the alleged advantages of using the tachistoscope to improve reading, including rate. His report, and others like it, apparently fail to take into account the role played by other factors in an experimental program, such as motivation to improve vocabulary, comprehension training, etc. In a carefully controlled experiment Manolakes (7) checked the influence of tachistoscopic training on improvement of eye movements and hence on speed of reading. When the effects of other factors were isolated, he found that the use of the tachistoscope had no effect upon reading performance. In a more recent study Bormuth and Aker (2), using sixth grade pupils, investigated the influence of tachistoscopic training on reading performance. All other factors in the experiment were carefully controlled. They found that the tachistoscopic training over a period of twenty weeks was ineffective in improving rate of reading, comprehension, or vocabulary. Jones and Van Why (6) also found that tachistoscopic training over a period of three months had no effect on reading rate and comprehension with fourth and fifth grade pupils. An evaluation of the entire body of relevant literature by Tinker (9) suggests that tachistoscopic training to improve rate of reading is of no, or at least of questionable, value.

A summary for the evaluation of machines, gadgets, and devices used to improve speed of reading follows:

1. Many so-called procedures for training eye movements or for controlled reading result in improved speed.

2. The improvement obtained by eye-movement training, with or without elaborate apparatus, is no greater than that resulting from motivated reading alone.

3. Experiments concerned with pacing eye movements and controlled reading usually involve other techniques and are never divorced from increased motivation. Buswell (3) flatly states that "training eye movements does not increase reading ability."

4. The use of pacing devices too often becomes a ritual tending toward an over-emphasis upon the mechanics of reading to the sacrifice of adequate attention to the more important processes of perception, apprehension, and assimilation. This mechanical training may result in a decrease in the flexibility and adaptability of reading habits that characterize good readers. According to Buswell (3), "The exploiting of

machines and gadgets" to control reading "by persons who do not understand the psychology of reading seems at present to be adding greatly to this mechanistic folly."

5. The tachistoscope is without value for increasing speed of reading. And the tachistoscope and rate controller devices are relatively expensive equipment. The money might be better used for books and other more worthwhile supplies.

6. It is the view of this writer that as long as gadgets and comparable devices are used by those with an inadequate understanding of the psychology of reading we shall continue to have the undesirable emphasis upon oculomotor mechanics.

REFERENCES

1. Anderson, I. H., and Dearborn, W. F. *The Psychology and Teaching of Reading*. New York: Ronald Press, 1952.
2. Bormuth, J. R., and Aker, C. C. "Is the Tachistoscope a Worthwhile Teaching Tool," *Reading Teacher*, 14 (1961), 172–176.
3. Brown, J. I. "Teaching Reading with the Tachistoscope," *Journal of Developmental Psychology*, 1, No. 2 (1958), 8–18.
4. Buswell, G. T. *Remedial Reading at the College and Adult Levels*. Supplementary Educational Monographs, No. 50, 1939.
5. Cason, E. B. *Mechanical Methods for Increasing the Speed of Reading*. New York: Bureau of Publications, Teachers College, Columbia University, 1943. No. 878.
6. Glock, M. D. "Effect Upon Eye Movements and Reading Rate at the College Level of Three Methods of Training," *Journal of Educational Psychology*, 40 (1949), 93–106.
7. Jones, R., and Van Why, E. "Tachistoscopic Training in the Fourth and Fifth Grades," *Journal of Developmental Reading*, 6 (1963), 177–185.
8. Manolakes, G. "The Effects of Tachistoscopic Training in an Adult Reading Program," *Journal of Applied Psychology*, 36 (1952), 410–412.
9. Spache, G. D. *Toward Better Reading*. Champaign, Ill.: Garrard Publishing Company, 1963.
10. Tinker, M. A. "The Study of Eye-Movements in Reading," *Psychological Bulletin*, 43 (1946), 93–120.
11. Westover, F. L. *Controlled Eye Movements versus Practice Exercises in Reading*. New York: Bureau of Publications, Teachers College, Columbia University, 1946. No. 917.

(57) FLEXIBILITY IN READING*

Arthur S. McDonald

For more than a quarter century reading flexibility has been considered one of the most important characteristics of effective reading. Reading flexibility has been so universally accepted that it has become an axiom, often stated as: "The hallmark of effective reading is flexibility."

The continually increasing pace of discovery in every field of learning (called by some the "information explosion") has brought a corresponding flood of printed material. This deluge has brought reading flexibility into new prominence because of the obvious need for effective extraction of information and the efficient processing of meaning from the never-ending stream of books, journals, monographs, and newspapers.

This increased stress on reading flexibility as a prime characteristic of reading evoked the following questions: What is it? How can it be taught? How can it be measured? What is the relationship of flexibility to other factors involved in reading?

A widely prevalent misconception about reading flexibility concerns the ability of the reader to deliberately and consciously vary his reading *rate*. Such ability has been greatly overestimated. From the beginning of discussion of reading flexibility, it was asserted, on the basis of *a priori* (if seemingly logical) reasoning, that a flexible reader could and would select the *rate* which was best suited to his purpose and the reading material. So, reading flexibility was said (and often is still so defined) to be the ability to vary the rate of reading at will to meet different kinds of reading situations.

Yet, it is also recognized that reading rate is only *one* of the processes involved in reading performance. In defining the efficiency of the reading performance, numerous interpretations of the terms "reading rate" and "comprehension" have been proposed. Conflicting methods of computing reading efficiency based on various mixes of rate and comprehension scores have been devised. Some reading instructors have despaired of validly assessing reading efficiency with standardized tests. A few have

---

*Reprinted from *Reading As An Intellectual Activity* 8 (1963 Convention Proceedings), pp. 81–85, by permission of the author and the International Reading Association.

even advocated the use of the reader's subjective evaluation of his reading performance. (As shown elsewhere, this type of assessment is especially likely to lead to "placebo" responses.)[1]

Thus it may be said that the nature of reading flexibility is misunderstood because of disagreement and confusion about:

1. relationship of speed and comprehension
2. differences between reading and skimming
3. ability of the reader to *consciously* change his reading pace while performing the complete reading act
4. methods of measuring reading efficiency

We suggest that much of this disagreement is the consequence of dealing with "rate" (i.e. the number of words over which a reader moves his eyes in a set time) and "comprehension" (the number of questions about a given reading selection answered correctly) as independent or coequal entities. They are neither. Both rate and comprehension are, of course, interdependent "constructs." The concept of reading rate as an independent factor in reading is patently illogical. We are never concerned with pure speed—that is, with just the rapidity with which a person can move his eyes over a given number of words without understanding. Similarly, treating comprehension as an independent factor introduces a host of complex variables (one of which, of course, would be intelligence). Many of these variables are only distantly related to the reading process itself, however much a part of the reader's behavioral processes they may be.

Important pioneering work carried on by Leston,[2] Sheldon,[3] and Spache[4,5] revealed the great complexity of the reading characteristic known as flexibility. Further research has shown that readers possess very limited ability to vary their reading rate in accordance with explicit instructions (under circumstances involving comprehension also). For

[1] Arthur S. McDonald, "The Placebo Response and Reading Research," *Twelfth Yearbook of the National Reading Conference*, 1963.

[2] Charles T. Letson, *The Construction and Evaluation of a Test to Measure the Flexibility of Reading Rate*. Unpublished doctoral thesis. Boston University, 1956.

[3] William D. Sheldon and L. W. Carillo, "The Flexibility of Reading Rate," *Journal of Educational Psychology*, 43 (1952), pp. 299–305.

[4] George D. Spache, "Diagnostic Tools" in *Fifth Yearbook of the Southwest Reading Conference*, 1955.

[5] George D. Spache and Paul Berg, *Faster Reading for Business*. New York: Thomas Y. Crowell Co., 1958.

instance, Spache found that only five per cent of his college and adult subjects could do this. Research has lead to the conclusion that reading flexibility involves many specific factors rather than being one inclusive ability.

Our study of more than 6,000 elementary, secondary, college, and adult readers has shown that most persons are not efficient readers. More than 90 per cent tend to maintain a characteristic approach to nearly all types of reading, despite instructions for differentiation of purpose and in spite of variations in difficulty of style, text, and content. A majority even maintain this reading approach in spite of the spur of periodic timing pressures.[6]

Continued research has led us to conclude that reading flexibility consists of the ability to utilize those reading processes and techniques which are particularly appropriate for the style, difficulty level, and theme of the reading material while, at the same time, being consonant with achieving the reader's purpose at the optimum level of performance. Thus, the flexible reader possesses those reading skills, techniques, and methods of attack which enable him to achieve as complete an understanding of the author's meaning as is dictated by the reader's purpose. The flexible reader also has a psychological set toward the reading process which leads him to differentiate his reading approach to suit the difficulty of the article's content and style, the amount of background knowledge he possesses as well as the urgency of his need to satisfy his purpose through reading the article. The flexible reader, as the result of his attention to purpose, difficulty of material, complexity of theme, and background knowledge, makes many adjustments of reading approaches and specific techniques. These adjustments may occur within a single section or even a single paragraph of an article. Such adjustments are, of course, reflected in measurement of rate. Variability in rate, however, is *not* the *cause* of flexible reading. Rather, rate variability is the *result* of flexible reading approaches. Work with standardized paper-and-pencil instruments as well as eye-movement photography has clearly confirmed this conclusion.

It will thus be appreciated that reading flexibility is truly a high-level reading ability. It rests on mastery of basic reading factors such as functional skills, perceptual skills, reading experience in general, a definite appreciation for different approaches in reading, etc. Therefore, it is

---

[6]Arthur S. McDonald, "Factors Affecting Reading Test Performance," *Ninth Yearbook of the National Reading Conference*, 1960, pp. 29–35.

futile to attempt to develop reading flexibility without insuring a sound reading foundation.

Reading as an intellectual activity requires, then, a certain indispensable basic level of instruction, intellectual aptitude, and experience. As a human activity, however, reading may be efficiently or inefficiently performed. The person who is efficient in reading is he who puts forth effort commensurate with the task.

It has been found that *mere* ability to talk about the importance and desirability of varying reading performance does not produce efficiency.

Investigations by Shores[7] and Sister Theophemia[8] clearly reveal that the majority of students do not alter their reading approach regardless of the instructions presented them, the type of material given them or the preliminary teaching they receive (in the form of being told the principles and purposes of varying "rate").

An issue which has complicated the teaching of reading flexibility—as well as its measurement—has been the disagreement about whether skimming and scanning are just faster reading or whether they belong in a separate category as a reading approach *sui generis*.

Discussing this issue, Spache[9] points out that skimming "cannot be confused with the normal act of reading and its physiological limits." Similarly, as a conclusion of his studies of skimming, Moore[10] asserted that "there are significant differences in skimming processes which place this type of reading in a category apart from slow, normal, and rapid reading."

Moore then warns that:

Not all skimmers are good readers, as judged by scores they are able to make on comprehension tests of the materials used or on reading tests of a standardized nature. Some individuals are not able to answer any questions following their skimming—striking evidence of the price paid for

[7]J. Harlan Shores, "Reading of Science for Two Separate Purposes as Perceived by Sixth Grade Students and Able Adult Readers," *Elementary English,* 37 (1960), pp. 461–468.

[8]Sr. Mary Theophemia, CSSF, "Testing Flexibility in Reading," *Challenge and Experiment in Reading* (J. Allen Figurel, ed.), International Association Conference Proceedings 7, 1962, pp. 138–139.

[9]George D. Spache, *Toward Better Reading.* Champaign, Ill.: Garrard Publishing Company, 1963, p. 266.

[10]Walter J. Moore, "The Skimming Process in Silent Reading," *Challenge and Experiment in Reading* (J. Allen Figurel, ed.), International Reading Association Proceedings 7, 1962, p. 204.

speed. Some individuals who have mediocre or poor reading scores on standardized tests, are able to skim, perhaps defying logic as well as their own expectation of their abilities to successfully engage in skimming.

Many investigations have shown that flexible readers possess certain common characteristics. The flexible reader reads with a definite purpose in mind. It may be said, in fact, that most ineffective reading is the result of the lack of an operationally defined purpose on the part of the student. Flexibility in reading is also related to the reader's ability to perceive and adapt his reading approaches (*not rate*) to variations in style, content, difficulty of vocabulary, distance from his own background knowledge, and density of ideation. Further, the flexible reader, as Stone[11] suggests, varies his techniques to match the kind of "idea collecting" which his reading task demands.

Reading flexibility also requires certain emotional freedoms. The flexible reader feels free to look beyond the lines of words on the page to the meaning behind them. He dares to reshape the ideas and even to reorganize the structure of the passage in his idea-synthesis.

In contrast, as Laycock has pointed out:[12]

. . . a rigid reader habitually uses a single approach that he has come to rely on. In fact, he uses it so regularly that he seldom, if ever, asks himself beforehand how he is going to read. But where a passage is such that he clearly should change, he may persist, nonetheless. It may be because his constitutional equipment permits little alteration, or because he does not recognize the appropriateness of change, or because he cannot permit himself the risk of trying something strange.

To attain reading efficiency, the student needs flexibility of attack rather than speed alone. He must read his text with the methods and techniques which will most effectively achieve his purpose rather than just getting through it rapidly or attaining near perfect comprehension.

A number of investigations have shown that most readers who possess reading flexibility (and, as previously noted, their proportion is small) have attained this efficiency on their own rather than as the result of

---

[11]David R. Stone, "Speed of Idea Collecting," *Journal of Developmental Reading*, 5 (1962), pp. 149–156.

[12]Frank Laycock, "The Flexibility Hypothesis in Reading and the Work of Piaget," *Challenge and Experiment in Reading* (J. Allen Figurel, ed.), International Reading Association Conference Proceedings 7, 1962, p. 242.

formal instruction. But, since efficient reading is planned purposeful reading utilizing the most effective techniques for the material, purpose, and the reader's situation, the need is clearly indicated for assessment and *planned* development of reading flexibility. Teaching for this objective should begin as early as the fifth grade with those students who have attained basic reading adequacy.

In working to develop flexibility, teachers should present their students with a varied "reading diet": light, easy fiction; nonfiction of easy readability level; nonfiction of moderate readability difficulty; fiction of moderate readability difficulty; complex nonfiction written in a rather easy style, etc. The teacher should also insure that her students read for a variety of purposes: to learn the central idea of a selection with a few essential supporting facts; to find a single fact answering a specific question; to appreciate beauty of literary style; to understand and assess the thesis of the selection, evaluating the author's support of his main points with details and illustrations, etc. Discussions accompanying these reading tasks will help the students to realize that reading approach and choice of reading techniques are influenced by a few vital factors: difficulty of the material, amount of the reader's background information on the topic, vocabulary, style and theme of the author, and the student's purpose for reading.

The kind of instruction, the choice of reading material and the number, type, and frequency of reading assignments should be governed by the deficiencies and needs revealed by standardized assessment of the student's reading flexibility.[13] Weekly informal teacher-made tests can be used to provide both teacher and students with indications of progress in developing reading flexibility. Leston[14] has described two types of such tests and suggests methods of developing and using them.

Reading flexibility is no longer a "nice" goal to strive for if time permits. It is essential. The steadily increasing store of knowledge in

[13]Standardized tests measuring reading flexibility which are currently available are:
George D. Spache, *Reading Flexibility Test.* University of Florida, Gainesville, Fla., 1956 (for college students and adults).
Arthur S. McDonald and Sr. M. Alodia, *Reading Versatility Test* (Basic). Huntington, N.Y.: Educational Developmental Laboratories, Inc., 1961 (for 5th-9th grades; available in two equivalent forms).
Arthur S. McDonald, George Zimny, and James Byrne, *Reading Versatility Test* (Advanced). Huntington, N.Y.: Educational Developmental Laboratories, Inc., 1962 (available in two equivalent forms for high school seniors, college students and adults).
[14]Charles T. Letson, "Building an Informal Flexibility Test," *Education*, May, 1960.

every field of learning makes reading efficiency indispensable if teachers and students are to keep their learning current. The touchstone of reading efficiency, however, is reading flexibility. Research has shown and continues to underscore the great need for systematic instructional programs aimed at developing and maintaining this indispensable reading characteristic. Thus, reading instruction and assessment must be reshaped to include the attainment of reading flexibility as a prime objective.

Part Five
Programs in Today's Schools

◆◇◆◇◆◇◆◇◆◇◆◇◆◇◆◇◆◇◆◇◆◇◆◇

Chapter 12. Administrative Organization for Reading

Chapter 13. Reading for Disadvantaged and Urban Children

Chapter 14. Measurement and Evaluation of Reading Achievement

Chapter 12

ADMINISTRATIVE ORGANIZATION FOR READING

INTRODUCTION

Most educators will agree that individuals differ greatly in abilities, interests, achievements, and other characteristics. Yet the question of how to cope with these differences in school organization has not produced any single, clear-cut solution. Current grouping practices tend to give more emphasis to differences of an inter-individual nature and tend to slight the known differences that occur within an individual.

The purpose of the selections in this chapter is to attempt to explore certain concepts about the nature of individual differences and the types of provisions generated by the school through organizational devices to meet those differences. Powell attempts to identify and discuss a few of the important dimensions of individual differences which can affect reading instruction. Cautions and problems in devising administrative schemes to solve differences in reading performance are presented by McHugh. His seven factors which influence the administrative structure of school reading programs deserve thoughtful consideration.

How reading might be organized for instructional purposes, how it has been so organized, and some of the rationale, problems, and research evidence concerning different plans is dealt with in the presentation offered by Ramsey. He discusses six administrative provisions for differences in reading: in-class grouping, the Joplin plan, individualizing instruction, team teaching, departmentalization, and the non-graded concept. An additional way to serve the needs of pupils is pupil-team learning, an approach endorsed by Durrell.

(58) THE NATURE OF
INDIVIDUAL DIFFERENCES*

William R. Powell

Differences between and within individuals are the primary focus of this chapter. Many factors affecting individual differences obviously could be identified and explored at length; only those traits, however, which have a presumed effect on reading achievement will be given particular attention here.

CHARACTERISTICS OF INDIVIDUAL DIFFERENCES

Although the literature concerned with individual differences is highly fragmented, four basic concepts tend to implicitly characterize this diverse area. Any programic attempt to improve reading instruction is confronted with the situation of having to deal with these latent characteristics. The four characteristics which typically affect individual differences are normality, variation, covariation, and velocity.

Virtually all measures of traits and abilities, whether they be physiological or psychological or any combination of traits, show the characteristic of *normality*. In any measurement of large groups of individuals the results tend to be distributed according to the normal probability or bell-shaped curve. The distribution is bilaterally symmetrical on each side of the mean with just as many persons above the average as below it. In Figure 1, the normality is indicated by the shape of the curve and the even numbers represented on each side of the mean.

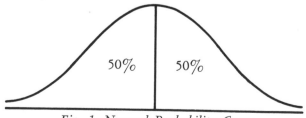

Fig. 1. Normal Probability Curve

*Adapted from *Organizing for Individual Differences*, Perspectives 9, 1967, pp. 1–17, by permission of the author and the International Reading Association.

Everyone knows that living things vary. Two trees are never exactly alike. Not all puppies born to the same dog in the same litter are exactly alike. Individuals are not different in this attribute (except identical twins, and environment soon modifies even their sameness). *Variations* are the deviations among the members of any species of living organisms. On any given measure, individual scores tend to disperse or spread themselves out on a continuum. This range or distribution is illustrated in Figure 1 by the line XY. If a heterogeneously grouped classroom is measured on the same selected factor, such as average reading ability, the range of average reading ability (the spread from the best reader to the poorest) is usually two thirds of the chronological age of the usual child in that classroom (7). Teachers with heterogeneous classes have to find a way to meet the wide range of differences to provide instruction.

The difficulty in reducing this range of differences is closely related to the problems of assessment. When one moves from the original separating criterion (in this illustration, average reading ability), the scores tend to disperse again on any other criteria, such as vocabulary, comprehension, or the more specific skills of syllabication or summarizing. The fact that persons have intra-individual as well as inter-individual variation causes the reduction of heterogeneous groups to be possible by only 20 to 25 percent. We can reduce the range of scores, except on the original factor, only by one fourth to one fifth of the initial spread (6, 1). This fact means that if we were to make a profile analysis of the specific reading skills of a group of youngsters, after grouping initially on average reading ability, the intra-individual test patterns would reveal wide discrepancies (up to 75–80 percent) between areas and types of competence. The phenomenon of intra-individual variation in reading abilities is, in fact, so common that it is surprising how little it has been utilized or even investigated.

Not only do traits and abilities vary but they *covary*. Separate reading abilities do not develop along a discrete parallel continuum; they interact and are interrelated to the other reading skills. In the development of reading behavior, a child's word perception skills normally grow in a close relationship with his comprehension skills. This nature is undoubtedly true of the highly specific skills within an area such as word perception. Covariation is a positive sign, and it is only when selected reading skills do not covary in their usual relationship that difficulty is encountered. It is when normally covarying abilities become discrepant that difficulty arises. When such cases occur, a differential diagnosis is necessary.

Within normal development, abilities are not stationary, although admittedly they can enter into an abeyant state. Children grow, develop, mature, and learn, but at an individual rate or *velocity*. The term velocity implies direction. Pupils' rates of change in a given direction not only differ but fluctuate. Each child has his own built-in velocity system; and even with youngsters who apparently have the same rate, their cycling process (rate of fluctuation) often operates on a different calibrated scale. One child's learning rate *plateaus* for a period of time, while the other child's learning ascent moves forward, only to level off at a different stage. Both children could have the same generic learning ratio, but the teacher perceives a notably different style of learning.

DIMENSIONS OF INDIVIDUAL DIFFERENCES

"Difference" implies a comparison with a criterion or standard. Typically, two types of standards are considered for comparison purposes. One type lies outside the individual. Often this type of difference is expressed in terms of some previously defined, hypothetically average person. These differences are *inter-individual.* The second type of difference is considered in terms of the individual himself and thus is an *intra-individual* difference. One teacher expressed this type of difference well when she told the writer that "the child is a whiz at calling words, but he cannot tell me a thing about what he has read."

Intra-individual differences often deal with constructs which may also be described in both inter- and intra-individual terms: "The child has the word pronunciation ability of a seventh grader, but he comprehends at the second grade level."

Whether to compare a skill internally or externally can best be decided in terms of the type of educational decision to be made. Perhaps too often the classroom teacher has the tendency to limit his observations and concern to the inter-individual differences. Typically, the focus on intra-individual differences is attended to only when a child has been singled out for more intensive evaluation. Far too frequently, plans for instruction are based on the differences between individuals and neglect to account for the differences within individuals. Ideally, both types of differences should be given equal consideration in planning for more efficient and effective educational programs for children.

Dimensions of individual differences which have direct influence on reading growth are many. What follows are dimensions which represent the major variables investigated in this relationship: chronological age, growth age, sex differences, intelligence, cognitive abilities, cognitive style, interests, and cultural background. Some of these dimensions are distinctly inter-individual differences; others represent both types of differences.

CHRONOLOGICAL AGE

Chronological age is considered to be a unitary inter-individual difference. This dimension of individual differences has been traditionally (and basically still is) the standard basis for school admission and promotion policies. The implications from such policies have applied, unfortunately, even to the level of instructional materials to which children are exposed during the school year.

As our knowledge from research has accumulated about rates of growth, maturation, and learning, it has become more widely recognized that chronological age is insufficient as a single criterion for school admission. Regrettably, the legal structure has not yet acknowledged this fact completely. However, Vernon (25) implies that at present this is the only stable and accurate assessment which is acceptable to society as all other arrangements tend to arouse intense controversy.

Comments are frequently made using age as the referent, when in reality what is implicitly meant is ability, interest, aptitudes, etc., of the average child of a specific age. In spite of all the inherent difficulty in the use of the criterion of age as calculated from the calendar, it has the strong practical appeal of simplicity. Chronological age can be easily and accurately determined, is readily understood by all, and is subject to a very stable rate of change (25). In our culture, the greatest asset in the use of chronological age is probably that it is extolled with the popular virtue of being democratic, non-prejudicial, and equalitarian.

GROWTH AGES

In evaluating the total growth of a child, many different ages can be determined—not just chronological age. Relying principally upon physiological and anatomical growth factors, Olson (19) developed the concept of organismic age. He averaged the seven qualities of weight, height, dentition, carpal development (measurement of wrist bones), grip, mental age, and reading age into a composite score which he contended represented the central age of the organism. It is readily apparent that this procedure of Olson's is heavily weighted in favor of the physical characteristics of an individual's growth pattern. Five of his seven factors are physical measurements. Whether just adding a few psychological measures to several aspects of physical growth raises our predictability of educational achievement is severely open to question. In fact, other investigations (5) have challenged this concept. The adding of physical factors to mental age alone will raise a multiple correlation coefficient a negligible amount. The difficulties in obtaining and integrating such data would hardly be worth the effort, that is, if prediction is of primary concern.

A similar type of approach of combining various factors, only this time with the emphasis being more on the psychological factors, is now being experimented with in various parts of the country. This approach produces an emotional age or behavior age and may indicate whether a child is under- or over-placed in his school setting (15). Such an approach, and any others like it, challenges the use of chronological age as the major determinant of individual differences in school placement.

SEX DIFFERENCES

Sex is distinctly an inter-individual difference. Differential performance between the sexes, especially in reading, have been reported with consistent regularity. Three hypotheses have been offered to explain this phenomenon—a maturational based theory, an identification hypothesis, and a conjecture based on the evolutionary character of man.

The classic explanation for the sex differences in reading is based on the fact that boys have slower maturation rates than do girls. By inference, it is suggested that this difference affects the reading achievement of boys. While this differential growth rate does exist between the species' gender, this theory does not account for the existence of the greater differences within a particular sex in achievement than the differences between the sexes in reading performance.

The second hypothesis offered to explain the sex differential in reading achievement is expressed in terms of sex-typed behavior and sex-role identification. Boys in our society are taught to view feminine pursuits with disdain as indicated by a youngster's remark when told to do some of the housework, "Aw, gee, Mom—that's sissy work." If boys perceive reading in a similar manner, then reading becomes inappropriate for them. Cultural patterns encourage certain types of sex-linked activity. Our culture encourages boys to seek out roles which exemplify that mythical "All-American Boy"—and that role does not emphasize reading in the idealized model. Further complications arise when a culture does not provide ample opportunities for identification with appropriate models at home and at school. It is suggested that our culture suffers in providing such models. The cultural limits of such a view are supported by the Preston (20) study which indicated that in Germany the boys typically are better readers than girls. As added injury, one recent investigation indicates that the teachers' marks (grades) are biased in favor of girls over boys (2). Should a male youngster select a sex role rationale for his difficulty, he likely will find much corroborative evidence in the classroom.

Bannatyne (3) suggests a third hypothesis for the differential achievement between the sexes. He explains these deviations as a function of an evolutionary difference based on survival value. Bannatyne speculates that men of greater visuo-spatial ability (the ability to manipulate objects and their inter-relationships intelligently in three dimensional space) tended to survive and reproduce. Those that did not have this ability risked the possibility of extinction. The strong visuo-spatial male was more adroit at throwing spears, shooting arrows, and avoiding his adversaries than were those of low ability in this area. In contrast, the female, in order to be successful in family rearing, needed to be able to manipulate the members of the family group. This manipulation required excellence in communication or verbal skills. The spatially able tend to utilize both visual fields and both hemispheres of the brain. The verbally able, in western languages particularly, utilize the right half of the body, especially the right visual field which is controlled by the left hemisphere. Thus, Bannatyne suggests the evolutionary changes in man have biased the male toward greater interhemispheric integration and females to left hemispheric dominance with a resultant advantage in verbal skills.

While the first and the third hypotheses explaining the sex differences in reading may be tenable (they have not been proved or disproved), it is the second theory which provides some possibility of giving the educator clues as to variables he can change. Social determinants are far more malleable than genetic determinants.

INTELLIGENCE

This dimension of individual differences has variously been labeled as intelligence, capacity, potential, and expectancy. It is often invoked to indicate the differences *between* children in terms of their maximum expectancies—both in rate of learning and in level of achievement at a point in time. While there is, and can be, some theoretical discussion as to the degree of "thingness" the term should be given, it is nonetheless of practical value in aiding in the determination of realistic goals or expectancies for children.

Two methods are commonly used in expressing intelligence. The first method utilizes a quotient or ratio figure to obtain what is commonly called an "IQ score." This procedure provides a measure of differences between persons of the same chronological age. Chronological age is treated as a constant. While this method does identify the broad concepts like "superior" or "retarded" rather well, this type of information may not be the most propitious for the day-to-day decision-making process necessary in the classroom. A second method of expressing differences in potential is through the concept of mental age. The use of this approach provides a comparison of differences without chronological age being fixed. By this method, the standard becomes the typical performance of an "average" child with a given chronological age and gives some indication of level of functioning. This approach provides the teacher with a technique for judging the appropriateness of instruction for a given child. While this second method has the advantage of setting theoretical expectancies for achievement, it ignores several other important traits of the individual.

A distinct disadvantage of describing this dimension of individual differences by either method outlined above is that it tends to lead to a false assumption that intelligence is a singular trait; and thereby, the concern should be with inter-individual deviations. Actually, intelligence is composed of many components or cognitive abilities and is subject to inter- and intra-individual differences.

COGNITIVE ABILITIES

One of the more persistent sources of confusion in the field of psychological measurement has resulted from the failure to define the relation between specific mental abilities and general intelligence. Scores on separate components of intelligence tests are usually substantially correlated; yet the existence of persons who show much greater competence in one area than another has long been noted. Earlier in the century, Thurstone (22) declared that IQ was not a homogeneous trait. He thought intelligence could better be defined as a cluster of primary abilities, and an individual's intellectual assessment could better be illustrated by a profile of scores rather than by the designation of a single score. Guilford's (13) more recent work supports and expands Thurstone's original conception. Guilford believes there are many underlying dimensions which contribute in varying degrees to a wide variety of intellectual skills, and that these factors can be identified and classified. Such identification and classification would lead to notable intra-individual differences in intelligence.

Teachers in the course of their classroom experience come across many children with discrepant abilities. When these discrepancies within a person become extreme, the individual may be termed "an idiot savant," meaning persons who are well known for their phenomenal calculating feats or the ability to remember total musical scores while being unable to learn to read. Though it is more typical to find the cognitive abilities of children developing at a fairly even rate, it is not unusual to discover youngsters with a high mathematical ability or a very favorable artistic aptitude who are afflicted with an apparent "block" when it comes to printed verbal material. Other discrepancies could easily be identified. Any person who has ever administered an individual intelligence test like the Wechsler or Stanford-Binet to children can easily identify cases where pupils achieve a highly similar total score, but yet an analysis of the items passed and failed reveals that the similar score was achieved through markedly different abilities. Seemingly different intellectual abilities were functioning to achieve the global summary score.

COGNITIVE STYLES

Recent investigations by students of cognitive style have been concerned with the problem of determining what type of orientation toward the environment facilitates the cognitive processes and what type does not. To avoid misunderstanding between the areas of cognitive abilities and cognitive style, one distinction will be offered. Researchers in the area of cognitive abilities are attempting to discover a minimum number of functions to account for the covariation of mental abilities, while the students of cognitive style are attempting to study the processes underlying the primary mental abilities.

Witkin, *et al.* (27), found individuals are of two types in their orientation to the environment. One approach is field-independent; the other is field-dependent. The field-independent oriented persons are basically free from irrelevant and distracted perception. The field-dependent oriented individuals are impulsive and cannot separate an item from its context; thus, they have a low ability to discriminate. Kagan (17), using different terms for the same categories (field-independent—analytical;

field-dependent—relational), found essentially the same type of behavior. An analytically-styled person is objective and more able to control his environment, but a relational-styled individual is impulsive and subjective. He sees his environment in a global way. Kagan (16) found a positive relationship between the reading behavior and the relational style of learning, and this finding was verified by another investigator among children with a reading disability (21). Teachers of reading most likely could produce better readers if they would train children to be less impulsive in responding.

Enough evidence is available to support the contention that children differ in their approach to learning experiences and that a learner may be one of several different types. Each type of individual will learn most effectively when taught by methods which take his type into account. This dimension of cognitive preference is another variable that needs to be accounted for in making provisions for individual differences.

INTERESTS

A brief conversation with the children in virtually any classroom will quickly reveal a variety of interests in both range and kind. Normally, the older the children are, the greater the range of interest is, because interests can develop commensurate only with the quantity and quality of experience. Without experience, there cannot be interests. Tyler (23) makes a major point of encouraging the use of interests as one of the features in planning for individual differences.

Too often in the reading situation all of the children are exposed continuously to the same diet of material. Olson (19) declares that the solution to the diversity of interests is through "self-selection." In this approach the teacher permits the children to seek and select their own reading materials. Olson and other advocates of this system contend this approach will also result in children reading at their instructional level. However, Fleming's (10) recent study casts doubt on the efficacy of a system of self-selection. Using a fifth grade population, Fleming explored the relationship between pupils' reading levels and their choices. Low positive correlations were found, but they hardly give strong practical support to a system of attending to individual differences on the basis of self-selection.

CULTURAL BACKGROUND

It is no secret that the educational system is built around middle class values and is usually run by middle class teachers and administrators; nor do we need to apologize for this fact. Perhaps what we do need to do, though, is follow Plato's admonition to "examine thyself." An *a priori* assumption of many teachers is that the classrooms are composed of persons being socialized into the society of which he, the teacher, is a member. He anticipates among the youngsters a similarity of extra- and preschool experience and a comparability of these experiences with a rather amorphous national norm. In many instances these assumptions may be justified, but there are many significant exceptions. Sometimes the entire class is quite consistently different in background from that of the teacher and the "average class"; other times only specific individuals differ markedly.

Among the many factors influencing the development of the child, one must recognize the effect of the child's environment, the people with whom he associates, the sounds and words that he hears, and the places he has been and seen. The extent to which the child experiences these things will be primarily determined by the home and family of which he is a member. The home environment in turn is greatly influenced by the social class status, economic level, and cultural background of its members. Not only will socioeconomic class often determine the child's aggressions, motivations, and interests but "studies repeatedly show that the home is the single most important influence on the intellectual and emotional development of children" (4). Other studies have quite clearly indicated that the relationship between socioeconomic class and achievement is higher than the correlation between intelligence and achievement (11).

Vilscek (26), in 1964, replicated the early mental age studies of the 1930's (12, 18) but added the dimension of socioeconomic class. Her findings reinforced the previous studies but indicated the functional relationship between socioeconomic and mental age: the lower the mental age, the higher the socioeconomic level must be for children initially learning to read: and conversely, the lower the socioeconomic level, the higher the mental age needs to be. The concept of "cumulative deficit" could have been a corollary from findings such as these.

Other critical areas which may be affected by cultural variations are the following: amount of language experience; dialect; multilingualism; proportions of verbal to nonverbal expression of ideas; experience with abstractions; interests; and factors involved in motivation, such as, types of reinforcement, values and attitudes to school, and the effectiveness of immediate and deferred reinforcement. The implications of studies in these areas for instruction remain to be developed in practical environments.

READING ACHIEVEMENT

Differences in reading behavior are affected by all the characteristics of individual differences: normality, variation, covariation, and velocity. Typical reading differences in a heterogeneous classroom could be similar to the diagram represented in Figure 2. If we assume Figure 2 represents a typical third grade classroom, we see that only 12 of the 30 pupils read "at grade level" and nine pupils read above and below grade level. This figure describes only the normality and variation of the class members; still each pupil has reading skills which covary and an individual velocity system which must be considered. It is precisely situations like this one that necessitate a discussion of the practical administration matters considered in this volume. Decisions must be made constantly by school administrators and teachers as to how to cope with these variables.

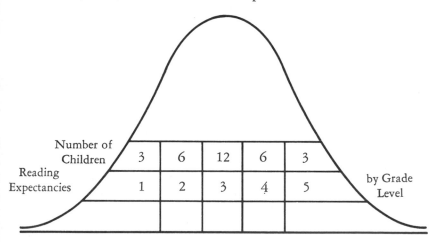

Fig. 2. Example of the range and grade level expectancies in a typical third grade classroom.

If the professional literature is any indication, the principal concern in reading and its related areas has been with factors of how one child differs from another. A more significant, and less explored, area is the way an individual reader differs within himself. The most generally used concept of intra-individual differences in reading is the "expectancy level discrepancy." This discrepancy is closely related to the common comment that a person is not "reading up to his capacity." More formally, it is a measure of the difference between the current level of reading achievement and the inferred potential (with corrections for measurement errors). Many important instructional decisions can and should be based on an analysis of this type of discrepancy. For example, if a youngster's performance level is much below his class, though quite in keeping with his potential level, the teacher may seek simply to maintain the potential-achievement relationship while modifying the surroundings. If the potential-achievement discrepancy is significantly large, the teacher must plan for decreasing this difference by bringing achievement more in harmony with potential. This type of analysis concerning level and potential is of general classroom importance.

Empirical data are not abundant on the variation of intra-individual differences in specific reading skills. Yet the downfall of many a grouping plan in reading rests on the disregard of deviations in skill within the readers themselves. When divisions are made on the basis of a generic score, the variations between and among pupils on specific reading skills redistribute themselves after the initial grouping. Any grouping pattern is subject to the covariation of skills, and the instruction within a given pattern should attend to those differences.

REFERENCES

1. Anastasi, Anne. *Differential Psychology*. New York: The Macmillan Company, 1958, 68, 320.
2. Arnold, Richard D. "The Relationship of Teachers' Sex to Assigned Marks and Tested Achievement Among Upper Elementary Grade Boys and Girls." Unpublished doctoral thesis, University of Minnesota, 1966.
3. Bannatyne, Alex. "Psychological Bases of Reading in the United Kingdom," in Marion D. Jenkinson (Ed.), *Reading Instruction: An International Forum*, IRA Proceedings of the First World Congress on Reading, Paris, 1966, 327–366.
4. Bloom, Benjamin, Allison Davis, and Robert Hess. *Compensatory Education for Cultural Deprivation*. Chicago: Holt, Rinehart, and Winston, Inc., 1965, 69.
5. Bloomers, Paul, Lotus M. Knief, and J. B. Stroud. "The Organismic Age Concept," *Journal of Educational Psychology*, XLVI (1955), 142–150.
6. Cook, Walter W. *Grouping and Promotion in the Elementary School*. Minneapolis: University of Minnesota Press, 1941, 33.
7. Clymer, Theodore. "Criteria for Grouping for Reading Instruction," in *Reading Instruction in Various Patterns of Grouping*, Helen M. Robinson (Ed.), Supplementary Educational Monographs, No. 89. Chicago: University of Chicago Press, 1959, 43.
8. DuBois, Philip H. "Individual Differences," *Annual Review of Psychology*, XI (1960), 225–253.

9. Ferguson, George A. "Human Abilities," *Annual Review of Psychology,* XVI, (1965), 39–62.

10. Fleming, James T. "Children's Perception of Difficulty in Reading Materials." Paper read at the American Educational Research Association, New York City, February 1967.

11. Frierson, Edward C. "Determining Needs," *Education,* LXXXV (April 1965), 462.

12. Gates, Arthur I. "The Necessary Mental Age for Beginning Reading," *Elementary School Journal,* XXXVII (1937), 497–508.

13. Guilford, J. P. "The Structure of Intellect," *Psychological Bulletin,* LIII (1956), 267–293.

14. Hunt, J. McVickers. *Intelligence and Education.* New York: The Ronald Press Company, 1961.

15. Ilg, Frances L., and Louise Bates Ames. *School Readiness: Behavior Tests Used at the Gesell Institute.* New York: Harper and Row, 1965.

16. Kagan, Jerome. "Reflection-impulsivity and Reading Ability in Primary Grade Children," *Child Development,* XXXVI (1965), 609–628.

17. Kagan, Jerome, Howard A. Moss, and Irving E. Sigel. "Psychological Significance of Styles of Conceptualization," in Basic Cognitive Processes in Children, *Monograph of the Society for Research in Child Development,* XXVIII (1963), 73–114.

18. Morphett, Mabel V., and Carleton Washburne. "When Should Children Begin to Read," *Elementary School Journal,* XXIX (1931), 496–503.

19. Olson, Willard C., *Child Development.* Boston: D. C. Heath Company, 1959, 3–7.

20. Preston, Ralph C. "A Comparative Study of the Reading Achievement of German and American Children," in *Changing Concepts of Reading Instruction,* J. A. Figurel (Ed.). New York: Scholastic Magazines, 1961, 109–112.

21. Santostefano, Sebastiano, Louis Rutledge, and David Randall. "Cognitive Styles and Reading Disability," *Psychology in the Schools,* II (1965), 57–62.

22. Thurstone, L. L. "Primary Mental Abilities," *Psychometric Monograph,* I (1938).

23. Tyler, Leona E. "Toward a Workable Psychology of Individuality," *The American Psychologist,* XIV (1959), 75–81.

24. Vandenberg, Steven G. "Innate Abilities: One or Many?" Paper read at the American Educational Research Association, New York City, February 1967.

25. Vernon, Philip E. "Education and the Psychology of Individual Differences," *Harvard Educational Review*, XXVIII (1958), 91–104.

26. Vilscek, Elaine C. "An Analysis of the Effect of Mental Age Levels and Socio-Economic Levels on Reading Achievement in First Grade." Unpublished doctoral thesis, University of Pittsburgh, 1964.

27. Witkin, Herman A., *et al. Psychological Differentiation.* New York: John Wiley and Sons, Inc., 1962.

(59) FACTORS AFFECTING THE ORGANIZATION OF ELEMENTARY SCHOOL READING PROGRAMS*

Walter J. McHugh

Over the years, proponents of the improvement of the quality of instruction in the elementary school have devised no less than forty *bona fide* patterns of organization. Among educators, forty patterns soon take on local adaptations, modifications, and combinations. The single most outstanding piece of originality is usually the local or provincial name given to a particular plan or grouping pattern.

In recent years, there has been a definite trend among well-meaning administrators to "try something new." What really is new? How old is the so-called nongraded school? The Joplin plan? Even the first attempt at team teaching in the United States dates back to Batavia, New York in 1855!

There are certain factors which have had little influence on the continued search to improve school practice. Although these factors are well documented in the research literature, they are of sufficient importance to restate them here.

1. No one organizational plan or pattern of grouping pupils has been so clearly superior to another design that it should be widely adopted or practiced.

2. There is a greater variety among ways in which individual teachers treat an organizational pattern than the pattern itself.

3. The initial high teacher-principal-pupil interest in a new method

*Reprinted from *Organizing for Reading in the Elementary School*, Highlights 1967, pp. 15–17, by permission of the author and the International Reading Association.

of school or class grouping is short lived. Usually, after a three year period, interest is low and initial promising results diminish. The search and interest for a different program to better meet pupil learning needs is instigated.

4. The need and demand for specialized teaching mushrooms as attempts at individualizing instruction are initiated. The more the grouping pattern highlights individual needs, the greater the challenge to the teacher's inventiveness and competency.

5. Each grouping pattern envisaged has one or more distinct advantages over other groupings. Conversely, each plan has its distinct short-comings.

Perhaps the most important factors governing the type of school or class organization are local needs and particular interests. Several well-known grouping patterns have their origin around such factors as teacher and/or pupil shortages, lack of adequate cafeterias, gymnasiums or transportation facilities. The sparsity of employment for potential school dropouts during the depression led to mass departmentalization of junior high schools so that slow learners could be kept in school and the instruction better fitted to their capacity.

Although we continue to seek improved methods of grouping children and initiating and changing school and class organizations, there is one highly important variable that changes very little—*the individual child.* Regardless of the grouping pattern, he still needs to be taught. Teaching the individual child would be a simple task if we had one teacher for every child. When we multiply the diverse needs of one child by his somewhat complicated and more diverse needs in each school subject, we have many problems. Now multiply one child's needs by thirty or more and your product is one of the most fascinating and difficult challenges of modern classroom teaching.

Some of my teacher friends who have had extensive classroom experience look with little or no enthusiasm upon the new principal's or curriculum director's plan for reorganizing the school. Long, devoted careers have taught teachers that regardless of the method or pattern of grouping utilized over the years, none is revolutionary. Many of the new grouping patterns are actually quite old, but are cloaked in a newfound name.

It may well be that we have placed entirely too much emphasis on the method of grouping and far too little on the method of teaching.

Many curriculum innovators, and particularly reading specialists, are more concerned with the principal tasks to be solved. Regardless of the grouping pattern, first priority must be given to the learning needs of children.

Any innovation which will increase the economy and efficiency of pupil learning bears study and possible adoption.

Before examining so-called new or innovative grouping patterns, particularly in reading, the following ever-present factors must be seriously considered.

Regardless of the grouping pattern, there is a vast difference in the instructional needs of children of similar reading achievement. A wide difference may exist between a child's vocabulary and comprehension scores. When these scores are combined the child may well appear to be "average." With any group of children whose reading average scores fall within the range of the same grade level, vast differences in achievement exist in all other component skills. A typical example of this phenomenon is the specially grouped fourth grade class whose average reading (vocabulary and comprehension) scores range from 3.5 to 4.5. In all other component reading skills, the range of ability differs from 1.5 to 7.5. This wide range is particularly apparent in word analysis, speed, sequence of events, spelling, use of reference and thinking skills, and reading in the content areas.

The learning needs of children of similar reading achievement cannot be met by uniform instruction. We open Pandora's box when we examine supplementary skills instruction needs as illustrated above. Diversification of the teaching of reading must be based on pupil needs rather than on the next lesson appearing in the box or package. Working with particular weaknesses necessitates the temporary or partial grouping of children according to the skill weakness observed. This leads to groups within groups or subgrouping. Teaching to the subgroups, to a particular weakness not apparent on a standardized reading achievement test, may be necessary until the skill is mastered.

Children within any reading group will progress at vastly different rates, even when the instruction is uniform. One of the great problems in being a high achiever in reading is waiting for the rest to finish their work. The great trial and trauma of the low achiever is that he never finishes anything.

Until we design reading programs that adapt the instruction, first for levels of ability and then for differing rates of progress, even the most exotic of grouping designs can go afoul.

The learning problems of the bottom third of any group of children are vastly different and oftentimes complex and compound. For these children, great care and attention need to be directed to each individual case, for each is unique. Instructional planning often requires small group or individual teaching. Confusions in previous learning need to be resolved. High motivation needs to be present. Each child, regardless of his level, is entitled to know the extent of his individual progress every day, no matter how small it may be. Otherwise, he has no incentive to continue.

The intensity of needed instruction varies from group to group and from child to child. The number of repetitions, practices, or drills needed for a child to acquire a certain concept, idea, skill, or ability varies widely. This highlights the need for self-help type activities that require a minimum of teacher direction. The ideal high-intensity multiple practice activities are self-correctional so that a child can pace himself.

The enrichment of reading instruction is needed by all children regardless of level, weakness, or rate of progress. Little learning takes place unless the instruction is meaningful, possesses significance, and has usefulness to the child as an individual. The more the child is required to think about what he is reading and learning, perceive relationships with previous learning, and relate this with his personal world, the more permanent the learning becomes. Although this precept is not new, it is probably more necessary today, with the increasing knowledge explosion, than it has ever been before.

It may well be possible to solve the grouping maze by a single type of school or class organization. The method of grouping may be totally unimportant. What is being taught and how it is being learned might someday replace the groping for the right grouping. When this occurs, the focus will be on adapting the instruction to the learning needs of the child.

(60) A CONCLUSIVE LOOK AT THE CARING FOR INDIVIDUAL DIFFERENCES IN READING*

Wallace Ramsey

In a real sense it is not possible to take a conclusive look at the subject dealt with in this volume. More research is needed on every phase of the topic; but children, schools, school administrators, and teachers cannot

*Abridged from *Organizing for Individual Differences*, Perspectives 9, 1967, pp. 115–133, by permission of the author and the International Reading Association.

wait for more research. Schools must be built; staffs must be recruited and given in-service training for whatever administrative organization is to be used; children must be grouped in some way; and instruction begun.

All that can be done is to review some important facts as they relate to this topic and make some recommendations that may prove helpful.

IN-CLASS GROUPING

In-class grouping makes it possible to keep children together in a family-like arrangement where a teacher can become well acquainted with twenty-five or thirty children and care for their needs. The value of such a situation for the shy and withdrawn child is substantial, especially in the primary grades. The number of first graders who are overwhelmed by the rush and hustle of school, and the bone-tiring requirements to sit reasonably still and attend to what is said and done, is legion.

The need for a mother surrogate, in such a situation, is great. To be with a child enough to find out which demands of school he can or cannot meet, and why he is that way, can result in a degree of understanding that will enable a teacher to make the learning situation successful and secure for every child. All of this depends, of course, on having a teacher who is curious, alert, perceptive, and discerning—and all teachers do not fit the description.

It is easier, nevertheless, for a teacher to really understand a group of children if she doesn't have so many to learn about and remember.

In the teaching of reading, since reading is probably the most useful learning tool in today's schools and is involved in every subject, one teacher who is teaching all subjects can use her knowledge about the child (and his idiosyncracies of learning to read) to good advantage. Lohman (15) has shown that reading skills can be taught as well at fourth grade level in connection with social studies and science as in reading class. The writer would not conclude that all reading should, therefore, be taught in content classes. *Some* reading skills, however, can probably be taught better in content classes than in reading class. Robinson (26) has pointed out, for example, that outlining can better be taught using expository rather than narrative material. Many other examples could be cited.

The above paragraph would suggest, therefore, that the process of having one teacher teaching all subjects to a small group would have some advantages in teaching reading over that of the teacher who teaches many more children and fewer subjects.

When teachers who utilize in-class grouping fail to do a good job, it is frequently due to insufficient materials, an uninspiring routine which lacks a variety of activities and approaches, insensitivity to pupils' needs, or having too many children to teach. Insufficient materials are certainly not a function of the administration provision used to care for individual differences—neither are too many children. Use of uninspiring routine and lack of a variety of activities may be a characteristic of a teacher at any level and in a school organized in any one of a dozen ways. Insensitivity to pupils' needs frequently stems from an innate lack of perceptiveness, an unsuitable mind-set, or poor training.

Teachers get in ruts (quite a different situation from being "in the groove") and can be lifted out of ruts by any measure which alters the teaching situation enough to demand some thinking, preparation, and changes in behavior of the teacher. Children and parents are sensitive to changes in teacher behavior. A teacher's excitement is caught by the children and results in greater interest and effort on their part. In the past, changes generating this kind of excitement have frequently been administrative changes of the team teaching, Joplin Plan, or non-graded school variety with accompanying new problems, sometimes vastly more complicated than those in the previous situation. Wouldn't it make sense to find ways of generating this excitement while preserving the advantages of in-class grouping?

American schools have been notoriously under financed—in view of their appointed task of universal education. Our belief in the leavening and enriching effects of having children of disparate backgrounds and levels of intelligence in the same classroom has not been accompanied by the finances to cope with a situation so complicated. Classrooms have simply not been equipped with the mass and diversity of materials necessary to care for individual differences. State supplied textbooks constitute poor equipment to accomplish the task set for the schools.

There are evidences of the dawning of a new day in supplying classrooms with materials. People who have been unwilling to vote taxes to support schools at the local and state level have grudgingly agreed to permit the remote power, the federal government, to use tax money for schools. In many communities we have, in 1967, the strange phenomenon of disadvantaged children being taught in small groups and with a diversity and quality of materials denied to the "advantaged" children. How long it will be until *all* children are given the educational advantages that the "disadvantaged" children are now being given, no one can say—but the sooner the better! It is unfortunate, in a sense, that this result must come from Washington where, nevertheless, the most likely solution to the problem of under-equipped and under-supplied classrooms appears to come.

The writer would contend that in-class ability grouping has not outlived its usefulness. On the contrary, conditions are now such that the time is right for it to come into its own and pay the kind of dividends it has the potential to pay. Certainly the child in the culture of today needs the security of one teacher, one group, and one room to which he feels a sense of belonging, being anchored, and being able to draw from such a situation the kind of strength and understanding that will enable him to cope with the world's buffetings. There is no reason or need to discard the idea of the self-contained classroom; there is little evidence that its failures are due to intrinsic weaknesses. Energy might well be devoted to its improvement rather than to its grave-digging.

THE JOPLIN PLAN

The Joplin Plan has been pointed to as being "one of the most provocative reading plans ever to be developed" (6). This remark can safely be branded as one of the grossest educational overstatements of the century. At best, the plan can be described as a promising practice for experimentation; at worst, it may be a way for some teachers to escape teaching the poor readers. Its greatest danger lies in the possibility that the use of the plan will be an excuse for not having a well-planned program of reading *instruction* or that it will be heralded as an end to the need to adapt instruction to individuals. The writer has observed too many systems that describe their reading *program* as being "the Joplin Plan."

While its proponents do not even imply that a Joplin Plan group of twenty-five to thirty children is a homogeneous group, such groups are often taught as if they were homogeneous. Anyone possessing knowledge of the true nature of inter- and intra-individual differences would know that the diversity of need in a Joplin Plan group would be almost as great as in a classroom group and demands the same degree of adjustment of instructional practices to care for individual differences. In other words, in-class grouping or individualization are a vitally necessary part of the teaching of reading in the Joplin Plan situation.

The drawbacks that come when the child's content area teacher does not have intimate knowledge of the child's reading development are present in the Joplin Plan. Even if a teacher is vitally interested in every child she works with, the sheer weight of numbers prevents the teacher from having adequate knowledge about each one's reading.

That the Joplin Plan works well in Joplin is no surprise when one reviews all of the information pertinent to its operation (although it may be well to note the absence of carefully controlled studies to indicate its superiority in Joplin). A substantial part of its success is undoubtedly due to the skilled leadership exerted in its direction. The in-service training and supervisory leadership provided would make a profound difference no matter what plan was used. The existence of the recreatory reading period and the presence of substantial numbers of high-interest low-vocabulary books are powerful features of the program. There are many signs that the quality of instruction is quite high.

The superior achievement shown by many of the Joplin Plan experimental groups can be attributed to the Hawthorne Effect—the influence of "newness" on the energy exerted by teachers and pupils. In very few of the studies was the inauguration of the Joplin Plan the *only* change made when spectacular gains were obtained.

The Powell study (21) is one of the few in which most of the important variables were measured and controlled—and it did not show any superiority for either plan.

The chief advantage of the Joplin Plan lies in the possibility that by inaugurating its use certain other changes will take place that will have a very favorable effect on reading achievement. If teachers are thereby made more perceptive to individual differences and more determined to do something about them, then it serves as a highly useful device. If the adoption of the Joplin Plan can change a situation from one in which the poor reader has *little* chance to succeed to one in which he feels he has a *good* chance for success, then the step taken is a good one.

INDIVIDUALIZED INSTRUCTION

The promise of individualized instruction is almost without limitation. To be able to suit instruction to the specific needs of every child is an objective worthy of striving for even if attainment is not possible. It is a pity that too frequently teachers and schools are unable to achieve the objective. The writer views individualized instruction as a goal that will one day be achieved in most American schools. Several changes are needed before this goal comes to pass, however.

Reduction of class load is a first-order necessity for individualization. The statement that research has shown no clear-cut advantage for smaller classes is an excuse, not an explanation, for not reducing class size. As long as teachers teach classes of fifteen in the same way they teach classes of thirty-five, there will be no advantage in reducing enrollments.

Actually, successful individualization involves the basic way that teachers *think* about children and teaching. To perceive them as individuals, to be alert to their needs, to view learning as something which children structure for themselves—these are the changes that must be brought about in teaching.

An intimate knowledge of how reading skills are taught is most helpful in individualizing reading. One excellent supervisor whose teachers were signally successful in individualized reading gave the writer an eight-word description of the best kind of skills preparation for such teaching: "Five years of experience in teaching basal readers." What the teacher does in the absence of this experience was not made clear.

The writer can see problems in teacher education for individualized reading—problems that cannot be solved in the present framework of undergraduate teacher preparation. Opportunities to observe *how* such teaching is done are sadly lacking on most campuses where teachers are trained. Such observation is highly desirable if a program is to produce teachers possessing the attitudes and abilities to succeed in individualization.

The reading fraternity is deeply indebted to the zealots of individualized reading. This latter group of highly vocal but dedicated people helped us refocus our attention on what is important in teaching reading. Some professionals, in their eagerness to find and perfect the best method of teaching word perception or to most perfectly control the introduction of sight vocabulary, forgot the role of the library in helping children to *learn* to read. *Reading books* has always been a good way to perfect one's basic reading skills. The size and availability of the library collection are probably more important than which basal series is used—or whether a basal series is used at all. Few individualizers would dispute the need for skills instruction, but they stress the overpowering need for follow-up practice in books which lure the child on to get the meaning.

The economy of educational plenty may be the final change that will usher in the era of individualization. Large quantities of materials *are* needed to make individualization work, and increased educational expenditures will make the purchase of such materials possible. It is all right to say that we can equip classrooms with books from attics and children's personal libraries, but in our saner moments we know that such measures are only stop-gap and won't work in every school.

There is little more to be said about individualization. It is a procedure that needs to be used no matter what administrative provision is made for individual differences. It seems to this writer that its use would be less complicated in the self-contained classroom, where the total number of children to be kept in mind is fewer. However, its use in any situation is desirable and should, therefore, be promoted in whatever way possible.

TEAM TEACHING AND DEPARTMENTALIZATION

The rationale used to support team teaching and departmentalization is logically simple and sound. By permitting a teacher to teach only (or mostly) in an area where his training and interests have given him special strengths, he exposes more children to better instruction in his specialty. By combining two or more classroom-size groups, homogeneous groups can be set up and mass teaching can be done. (Mass teaching is not an intrinsic part of these approaches but often is used.) In content areas, the teacher who has had several more courses in science, history, etc., has a greater background and thus (it is reasoned) will make a better teacher *in the field* than the other team members who have specialized in other areas. Specialization may be in *how* to teach in a certain area (reading, for example) rather than in subject matter.

Team teaching and departmentalization in reading have frequently come about because one or two teachers have had advanced training in teaching reading and are chosen to teach reading (usually corrective or remedial) to two or more groups of children. Because of the great shortage of well-trained reading teachers the use of special teachers in the field is booming. Quite frankly, many of the Title I ESEA projects could not function if this specializing were not done. As a measure of expediency, then, teaming and departmentalization are filling an important void. Whether the situation created by an emergency will develop into a long-term plan is not possible to say. Research illustrating the long term superiority of the two innovations is certainly lacking.

The barriers to getting funds for evaluating long term effectiveness of several innovations discussed in this volume have been cited by Heathers (28): "The unwillingness of granting agencies to provide sufficient funds for applied research and development on new organizational plans has been a stumbling block. Ordinarily, funds have been granted for demonstration-tests of plans rather than for bringing plans to the level of development where they are ready to be tested or demonstrated. This has been true with *team teaching plans, nongraded plans*, and the dual progress plans" (Italics are this writer's).

Research on the long term advantages of such plans is further complicated by the fact that, frequently, when teaming and departmentalization are instituted, certain other changes are made which make the new situation different in several respects from the old. (School administrators have not hesitated to publicize achievement test results from old and new groups, labeling them "control" or "experimental" and attributing differences to teaming or departmentalization or whatever innovation has been instituted.)

An example of multiple changes when teaming is introduced is revealed in a description of the Norwalk, Connecticut, Plan (26): "A report on the Norwalk Plan after two years summarizes attitudes of the fourteen volunteer team teachers without giving specific findings. The most attractive feature of team teaching, in the views of these teachers, *was escaping from clerical and other routine duties that were being performed by nonprofessional aides*." (Italics are the present writer's.) Even in the Norwalk Plan there are undoubtedly *other* important changes that occurred when team teaching was begun.

It is hoped that despite the problems present definitive research can be done to properly evaluate the plans. If studies can be designed (and financed) that will meet the criteria for good research studies in reading (10), some helpful answers should be forthcoming. Not until we get the results can a firm decision be made about the value of any of the innovations described in this volume.

NONGRADED SCHOOL

Nongradedness is one of the most exciting of the innovations now being tried in education. This conclusion is due, in part, to the rationale so succinctly outlined by Goodlad and Anderson (12). Visiting and working in new schools specially constructed for nongraded instruction (like the Sherwood Elementary School in Greeley, Colorado, or the Dixie and Lansdowne Elementary Schools in Lexington, Kentucky) with their carpeted classrooms and movable walls are exciting experiences.

Buildings, however, do not make a program. The writer has observed rigid, unimaginative programs in buildings built on specifications suited to a far more flexible and imaginative program. Some curricular crimes being committed in the name of nongradedness would chill the blood of Anderson, Goodlad, and their disciples. (The writer is *not* referring to programs in the three schools mentioned above!)

The great amount of movement and noise extant in nongraded schools would seem to the writer to be unsettling to a child who lacks emotional stability or who is high strung, easily distracted, or insecure. (The writer would certainly be interested in finding out how brain-damaged and perceptually handicapped children would fare in the hustle and bustle of the nongraded school—especially in those rooms full of colorful bulletin boards, with near and far movements of large numbers of children, and with a wide variety of noises.) The relatively large numbers of adults that a child must meet with, and relate to, in a nongraded school call for more maturity and stability than many children possess.

There are indications that teachers and administrators in nongraded schools recognize the problems referred to above. One group of four teachers working with 120 first graders in a carpeted, gymnasium-size area told the writer that they had requested the installation of sliding doors to cordon off small "room-sized" areas for instruction because of the high noise level and the distracting movements of teachers and children in all parts of the area. (It is significant that in an evaluation of a team teaching experiment in Oceano, California, almost half of the teachers who were interviewed in the course of evaluation of the project favored continuing the experiment *if* soundproof movable walls were provided.)

Nongraded school teachers are frank in saying that some children simply cannot adjust satisfactorily to the nongraded school. The creation of "satellite" classrooms (essentially self-contained) in the laboratory school at U.C.L.A. is a tacit acknowledgement of this fact, in the judgment of the writer.

In a sense the commitment of nongraded education is a lot like the commitment to individualized instruction—it is a drastic step for teachers who have had certain stereotyped ideas about the nature of differences (especially intra-individual) and the ways children learn. Unevenness in the rates of development within an individual (or even unevenness of development in a single trait) make the need for flexibility in grouping particularly acute in the nongraded school—if the Goodlad philosophy of education is to be carried out. Children do not settle into a group and stay there. They frequently are on different group levels in different subjects. The need for moving children from one group to another is demoralizing to teachers who want things to "settle down" so learning may proceed. In the nongraded school things almost never "settle down." In a real sense the nongraded school is for the young or the young in heart.

Personnel of school systems jumping into nongradedness without making sure the total situation is ripe for it often live to regret their move. In recent communications with officials of over 130 nongraded schools in the nation, the writer found over twenty that had abandoned the plan in the last three years. This percentage does not necessarily indicate innate weaknesses in the nongraded philosophy, but it does very probably indicate difficulties in implementing it.

Final judgment on the ultimate value of the nongraded school awaits definitive research. On a dollar-for-dollar basis it may be as supportive of children's social and emotional growth while stimulating optimum academic achievement as is a graded school. We cannot, at this point, say. Factors unrelated to school organization will probably determine this matter.

REFERENCES

1. Allen, Roach Van. Address before the Fall Reading Conference, University of Kentucky, October, 1965.
2. Axline, Virginia. "Non-directive Therapy for Poor Readers," *Journal of Consulting Psychology*, XI (1947), 61–69.
3. Bell, John. "Emotional Factors in the Treatment of Reading Difficulties," *Journal of Consulting Psychology*, IX (1945), 3–125.
4. Bormuth, John. "Cloze as a Measure of Readability," *Reading As An Intellectual Activity*. Report of the Proceedings of the Annual Conference of the International Reading Association. New York: Scholastic Magazines, 1963, 131–134.
5. Botel, Morton. "Newer Techniques in the Supervision of Reading Instruction," *Frontiers of Elementary Education*. Syracuse, New York: Syracuse University Press, 1957, 25–39.
6. Brown, B. Frank. *The Appropriate Placement School*. West Nyack, New York: Parker Publishing Co. Inc., 1965, 56.
7. Chall, Jeanne, and Shirley Feldman. "First Grade Reading: An Analysis of the Interactions of Professed Methods, Teacher Implementation and Child Background," *The Reading Teacher*, XIX (1966), 569–575.
8. Clark, William T. "A Study of Factors Related to the Effectiveness of Educational Programs," unpublished doctoral dissertation, University of Kentucky, 1967.

9. Davis, Sister M. Catherine. "The Relative Effectiveness of Certain Evaluation Criteria for Determining Reading Levels," unpublished doctoral dissertation, University of Iowa, 1964.

10. Dolch, Edward. "School Research in Reading," *Elementary English*, XXXIII (1956), 76–80.

11. Furst, Norma, and Edmund Amidon. "Teacher-Pupil Interaction Patterns in the Teaching of Reading in the Elementary School," *The Reading Teacher*, XVIII (1965), 283–287.

12. Goodlad, John, and Robert Anderson. *The Non-Graded Elementary School.* New York: Harcourt, Brace and World, 1959.

13. Julitta, Sister Mary. "Selection and Use of Standardized Reading Tests," in *Evaluation in Reading.* Supplementary Educational Monographs, No. 88 Chicago: University of Chicago Press, 1959.

14. Kilgallon, Pat A. "A Study of Relationships Among Certain Pupil Adjustments in Reading Situations," unpublished doctoral dissertation, Pennsylvania State College, 1942.

15. Lohman, Idella Duff. "A Comparative Study of the Improvement of Reading Skills of Pupils During Fourth Grade in Two Types of Curriculum Organization," unpublished doctoral dissertation, University of Tulsa, 1964.

16. Mann, M. "What does Ability Grouping do to the Self-Concept?" *Childhood Education.* VIII (1960), 351–360.

17. McCracken, Robert. *Standard Reading Inventory.* Bellingham, Washington, Pioneer Printing Co., 1966.

18. McCracken, Robert. "Standardized Reading Tests and Informal Reading Inventories" *Education*, LXXXII (1962), 368.

19. McGinley, Patsy. "Reading Groups as Psychological Groups," unpublished doctoral dissertation, University of Kentucky, 1967.

20. Plessas, Gus. "Another Look at the Reading Score," *Education*, LXXXIII (1963), 344–347.

21. Powell, William. "An Evaluation of the Joplin Plan," *Elementary School Journal*, LXIV (1964), 387–392.

22. Project Talent Office. "The Story of Project Talent," *Bulletin No. 1*, Pittsburgh: University of Pittsburgh, Project Talent Office, November, 1959.

23. Ramsey, Wallace Z. *Learning to Read in Kentucky.* Lexington, Kentucky: The Bureau of School Service, University of Kentucky, 1966.

24. Ramsey, Wallace Z. "The Value and Limitations of Diagnostic Reading Tests for Evaluation in the Classroom," in Thomas Barrett, (Ed.). *Evaluation of Children's Reading Potential and Achievement.* Perspectives in Reading No. 8. Newark, Delaware: The International Reading Association, 1967.

25. Ransom, Peggy E. "A Study to Determine Reading Levels of Elementary School Children by Cloze Testing," unpublished doctoral dissertation, Ball State University, 1965.

26. H. Alan Robinson. "Reading in the Total School Curriculum," address before Kentucky Reading Association, April 14, 1967.

27. Rosenthal, M. *Experimenter Effects in Behavioral Research.* New York: Appleton-Century-Crofts, 1966.

28. Shaplin, Judson T., and Henry F. Olds, Jr. *Team Teaching.* Evanston, Illinois: Harper and Row, 1964.

(61) PUPIL-TEAM LEARNING:
OBJECTIVES, PRINCIPLES, TECHNIQUES*

Donald D. Durrell

Pupil team learning has many possibilities for differentiating and enriching instruction. It consists of combining pupils in pairs or groups of three to five for mutual aid in learning.

The fact that children prefer to work and play together in small groups has long been known. Gregariousness has always been included in lists of "natural tendencies" of children. Any study of children's preferences for different types of classroom activities will show that they desire to work in pairs or small groups rather than alone. This desire offers a motivating force which can be utilized in the classroom. Grouping in small teams provides an administrative technique for providing for individual differences. It has possibilities for reinforcing and enriching instruction, as well as for increasing the amount of pupil practice per hour.

The basic objective of pupil team learning is the same as for all educational practices: to increase the amount and quality of learning. Any school procedure should stand this test: if it produces a greater amount and quality of learning in a particular situation, it should be continued. If it tends to diminish either the amount or quality of learning, or if it is less economical in the use of classroom time than other methods, it should be discontinued. We are not concerned here with

*Reprinted from *Changing Concepts of Reading Instruction* 6 (1961 Convention Proceedings), pp. 75–78, by permission of the author and the International Reading Association.

group dynamics, decision-making, leadership roles, or power structure in the classroom; we leave these to our psychological and sociological friends who enjoy dealing with nebulous learning outcomes. We expect pupil team learning to be evaluated in terms of learning power and economy.

Pupil team learning is not proposed as a panacea to replace all other types of classroom activities. We still have too much of the "cultist" mind in professional education which considers every proposal in an all-or-none situation. We must be "for" or "against" each proposed method or type of organization. Yet almost every proposal for education may have some place in the educational process, for some child at some stage of development, for some learning objectives. Our task is to discover the place and proportions of each proposal. Let us look at pupil team learning, not as a method to be used with every pupil, in every subject, every hour in the school day, but as a technique which may prove suitable for certain learning tasks.

In our extensive tryouts of pupil team learning, we have found several types of activities which are immediately acceptable to both teachers and pupils. The major ones are the following: team progress methods in skills instruction; team discussion techniques following individual study or mass presentation; team use of study guides; team practice in oral activities and remedial drills; team work in pupil specialties.

Team progress methods combine the motivating power of individual progress with that of the security of having partners in learning. Since children are stimulated by seeing their progress and by being members of a team, the combination is especially suitable for learning that can be neatly "packaged," such as arithmetic, spelling, language-grammar skills, phonics, map and globe skills, outlining, and recall practice. We have always found spelling and arithmetic to work well in pupil team learning; consequently these are the first subjects in which team learning is introduced in most classrooms.

It should be said at once that the success of team progress instruction rests heavily upon the suitability of the "learning package" to the needs of the group. There must be close adjustment to the varying levels of achievement; if the task is too advanced for the group, frustration results; if the task is not challenging, interest will be low. The gradations of the task must be suitable for pupil requirements of progress; slow learners must have more practice at each stage, while rapid learners may skip many steps. The task must be definite, clear, and specific; indefiniteness invites confusion. Obviously, the task must be meaningful and important to the group; enrichment and meaning activities should be built in as an integral part of the package. Provision for scoring the results as soon as the task is finished adds to learning incentive and increases effectiveness. The neatness of the package is also important; tasks which are messy in appearance will seem less important to the learner.

These qualities of the team learning package are much the same as are required for "programs" in teaching machines. Team learning packages, however, have several advantages over teaching machines: they require no expensive "hardware," they may be built by teachers, their "density" is more easily managed, and they may employ mutual aid in learning. A speller or an arithmetic book is easily "packaged." A typical adaptation for pupil team learning is "*Arithmetic Job Sheets* to accompany *Growth in Arithmetic*, published by Harcourt, Brace and World. The same publisher has produced phonics packages for intermediate grades, *Word Analysis Practice. Fun with the Globe,* published by A. J. Nystrom Company, and the reading and spelling laboratories of Science Research Associates, are learning packages which may be used with pairs as well as with individuals.

Team discussions following individual study or mass presentations seem much preferred by pupils and teachers as compared to the typical recitation in which each pupil recites when called upon. When all members of the class have read the same text, seen the same television program or motion picture, heard the same oral presentation, observed the same demonstration, taken part in the same field trip, or are faced with a problem in planning, a group attack on the review or study questions posed by the teacher always yields good results. A study recently completed by Culliton[1] indicates that the optimum size of groups in discussion following mass presentation is three. He found retention of learning by groups of pupils to be in the following order of desirable size: three, two, five, and one, regardless of the types of questions used to evoke discussion.

Again, in team discussion, there are several conditions which contribute to successful results. The tasks set must call for a specific written response, usually the listing of answers by the group secretary; to ask a group to "discuss" without requiring a written product is to invite aimless verbal activity. The quality of the questions also contributes to the success of the discussion; selective recall or listing of ideas by categories

[1]Thomas Culliton. *Team Size in Discussion Tasks*, Unpublished doctoral study, Boston University, 1961.

calls for more thinking than does answering multiple-choice or short-answer questions, although these latter are preferred by pupils. Elaborative thinking questions which require applications, uses, illustrations, or relationships are harder than simple recall questions. Critical thinking questions, in which evaluations are required, are also suitable for team discussion. In all types of group discussion, pupils want an immediate evaluation of the product. This is usually provided by having one group read its answers while others check their lists to find additional or varying answers. It is desirable, too, that the group product be collected and checked by the teacher, although it is not usually marked and returned. We find that "planned heterogenity" is desirable in team discussion, grouping children with different levels of ability together. This practice is supported by research findings which show low correlations of all types of thinking with mental ability and scholastic achievement.

Team discussion methods are used also in classroom planning and are advantageous in improving the flow of ideas in written composition. They are also used in spelling methods which emphasize varied word usage techniques to increase the transfer to writing.

In team use of study guides, children generally work in pairs. These guides are designed to aid the pupils in comprehension; they may contain a glossary in addition to key questions to be answered during study. Questions on the study guide may vary in types and number, depending upon the level of ability of the pupils and the nature of the recall task being emphasized. Answers to the questions in the guide may be printed on the back or on separate answer sheets. At the very easiest level, the questions on the study guide may be presented orally by a pupil-teacher, with a pair of slower pupils finding the answers and reporting orally. A more difficult recall task requires the pupil to read part of the selection, then uncover the questions over that portion of the lesson and write answers. Still more difficult is the requirement that the pupil give an unaided oral summary while his partner checks against a listing of major ideas in the selection.

Team practice in oral activities permits a marked increase in opportunities for pupil practice. In a class of thirty pupils, if one pupil reads at a time while all others are listening, the amount of practice is greatly multiplied by having fifteen pairs of pupils read to each other. In "show and tell" activities in primary grades, small group audiences permit more practice than a single presentation to a whole class. Pairs of pupils may assist each other in flash-card drill on arithmetic combinations or in the dictation of lists in spelling. Oral activities are often un-economical, in that there are far more listeners than talkers. Only in rare situations does the listener learn as much as the performer. It would be helpful to education if the inventors of teaching machines could design a "sympathetic listener," with a built-in corrector and a self-adjusting praise and caution dispenser. This would relieve the teacher who feels that only she is an adequate audience for all oral presentation of pupils.

Pupil specialties, either curriculum-related or long-term personal interests, may be done either in teams or individually. In the curriculum-related specialty, special topics are assigned a month or six weeks in advance of their presentation to the class. They are supplemented by pictures and exhibits to be unveiled at the time when the subject appears in the curriculum. After the report is given, questions are asked by the pupils; then teams of pupils are given questions, usually of the elaborative thinking type, which require them to make relationships of the report to previous knowledge.

What are the psychological factors involved in pupil team learning? One should always be wary of psychological rationalizing, since either side of any question may be supported by psychological principles. However, here are some of the psychological potentials for team learning. With partners there is the stimulus of group activity; mutual support provides security; a team is much more likely to reveal a difficulty in understanding. In the more complex skills, such as problem-solving in arithmetic or word analysis practice, there is an exchange of systems, techniques, and information. Where elaborative thinking is involved, the contributions of one member spark additional ideas from others. Critical thinking is involved in the evaluation of answers; wrong or weak answers are rejected by the group. There is usually a greater number of pupil responses per minute; in team learning, it is always one's turn. It is possible, also, to adjust learning tasks much more closely to pupil needs, providing many levels and types of practice at the same time.

The place of the teacher is still paramount in team learning. The teacher sets the tasks; she reacts to every team product, although she does not mark the group product, but only the interspersed individual tasks which test growth in abilities. She disciplines when the noise of a group indicates non-working noise, usually by having the team members work alone for a period. She is still the "authority figure" but much less so, since much of the recitation is to one's peers. Since superior learners require little teacher attention in team-progress subjects, the teacher has much more time for remedial work with slow learners. Superior learners are guided in library research tasks which reach far beyond the textbook. The teacher decides the balancing of classroom activities: when there will be whole-class presentations, when whole-class discussions will be profitable, when multi-sensory aids will be used, when enrichment activities are necessary, when individual tasks are to be set, when tests are to be given. She generally decides the membership of teams, although the more "democratic" minded teachers may allow more pupil choice.

The usual fears of team learning expressed by teachers before they try it are the following: the amount of classroom noise, the possible loss of discipline, poorer pupils loafing and leaning on the more capable, the possibility of cheating when answers are readily available. There are sensible ways around these presumed difficulties. Few of them arise if the assignments are important and the classroom climate is good. The teacher can readily control the noise level by insisting on lower voices; she can readily detect non-working voices.

Team learning is probably as old as the human race. One can readily imagine a cave man asking a neighbor for advice on skinning a buffalo or for getting a badger out of a hole. Certainly the male graduate student in professional schools has used team learning since the earliest days on the university; the bull session is highly regarded as an effective learning activity. If it had not been invented earlier, it would have been discovered by telephone teams of junior high school girls doing homework. Individual teachers have used pupil teams for many years, especially in rural schools where the multiple grades prevent individual attention to pupils. One wonders, however, why it has not become an established technique in all classrooms, since it seems to fit the nature of the child so well. Certainly, it has much to offer that is not present in lonely, insecure individual study.

Chapter 13

READING FOR DISADVANTAGED AND URBAN PUPILS

INTRODUCTION

The task of teaching reading to disadvantaged pupils, especially those residing in the inner city of metropolitan areas, is of deep concern to the teachers involved. Often such children live in substandard housing, located in decaying neighborhoods. Because of home conditions and other circumstances, many of them enter first grade lacking the enriching experiences, sufficient language skills, pleasant exposure to the printed word, and types of manipulative and play activities which build readiness for a successful start in reading. If their strengths and weaknesses are not realistically appraised and a program planned to meet their needs, they lag increasingly behind as they continue in school.

All conscientious teachers wish to provide the learning conditions and the guidance that will insure growth in reading for every child. The articles in this chapter have been selected to aid teachers of disadvantaged pupils in this task. Too often the teacher is frustrated as she frequently faces overcrowded classes in obsolete buildings without appropriate materials and sufficient help in understanding these pupils.

Edwards identifies the deficiencies many disadvantaged pupils exhibit in comparison with more advantaged pupils and explains the crucial role of the teacher as a mediator between the child and his environment. Cohen states two hunches and twelve conclusions based on data; these offer guidance to teachers who work with the disadvantaged.

Not all disadvantaged children live in urban centers. As another situation, a study of Mexican-American children in Texas is reported by Arnold. In this study oral skills were taught as a second language. Science materials were used in classroom activities as a basis for instruction in both oral language and reading.

How should the problem of pupils who speak a nonstandard dialect be handled in the reading class? Roger Shuy presents a comprehensive picture of present findings in work with urban dialects and suggests some of the modifications in approaches to reading instruction for speakers of a subgroup dialect.

Helene Lloyd offers six benchmarks of progress being made in large cities in teaching developmental reading to children in the inner city. Finally, the chapter closes with a description of a nursery school project, since early intervention is both promising and imperative.

(62) LEARNING PROBLEMS IN CULTURAL DEPRIVATION

Thomas J. Edwards*

The recent shift of educational concern to the problems of the culturally disadvantaged requires a precise analysis of the specific deficiencies manifested by the disadvantaged learner. If he is deprived early of certain experiences or learnings which are normally and routinely enjoyed by more advantaged learners, exactly what deficiencies result? And how do these deficiencies manifest themselves and militate against later school learning or general life adjustment?

Of equal cogency is the problem of the psycho-social adjustment of the culturally deprived learner: How has his minority status affected his self-image? Is he saddled with attitudinal problems which have deleterious effects upon his learning and overall life adjustment?

To these problems this paper is addressed within the context of the vital role which the teacher or mediator must play in reversing the debilitating effects of cultural deprivation, almost irrespective of age. This is true because at every level—pre-school, primary, intermediate, pre-dropout, dropout or adult functionally illiterate—we must see the syndrome of cultural deprivation as a mobile monolith that tends to move essentially unchanged up the chronological age scale. Thus we find at practically every age level the manifestations of virtually the the same symptoms.

BASIC LEARNING DEFICIENCIES

There are a number of important learnings which are prerequisite to successful school achievement. The normally advantaged child receives sensory and intellectual stimulation from birth which provides these prerequisite learnings. The culturally disadvantaged child, on the other hand, is either deprived of these learnings or must revise markedly many earlier learnings that interfere later with successful school achievement. The following points must therefore be considered in programs designed to reverse the effects of this disadvantage.

*Reprinted from *Reading and Inquiry* 10 (1965 Convention Proceedings), pp. 256–61, by permission of the author and the International Reading Association.

1. *Restricted Experiential-Conceptual-Informational Background.* Characteristically, the disadvantaged child moves within a very small geographical area near his home. This tends, of course, to limit quite severely his contact with the "outside world" and, thereby, robs him of vital first-hand experiences necessary to expand his fund of concepts and general information. In addition, he generally does not have anyone at hand to provide the mediation essential to help him carve meaningful concepts even from those experiences which he has had.

Much of the curricular content to which children are exposed is based on the assumption that most of them have seen and understood certain objects and processes prior to their entry into first grade. *The disadvantaged child from a severely restricted experiential background, however, will not have the conceptual foundation upon which to build this superstructure of new concepts which are imposed on him in school.* He, therefore, experiences confusion and fails to learn while other children are easily and happily expanding their repertoire of information. And thus the achievement gap between him and more advantaged children widens.

Reading ability is also affected by a meagre background of experience, concepts, and general information. One very fundamental aspect of the reading process is translating printed words into their spoken counterparts and knowing what they mean; that is, what *concepts* they represent. As the conceptually poverty-stricken reader moves down the printed page, he may unlock word *sounds* successfully, but ultimately reaps a harvest of meaningless nonsense. Also in the reading process the deciphering of unfamiliar or irregular word forms frequently depends upon the use of context clues to suggest what a printed word probably "says." The effective use of context for this purpose, in turn, depends upon one's having previous relevant experience to bring to bear in interpreting the context. This, of course, the culturally deprived student is not likely to have. And this experiential deficit will also militate against his grasping more complex global concepts contained in sentences and longer selections.

It is, therefore, absolutely imperative that anyone responsible for a good educational program for culturally disadvantaged learners first understand that these learners have severely debilitating experiential-conceptual-information deficits, that they know that these deficits are *not* a reflection of any innate mental deficiency, and then that they take measures *constantly* throughout the learning program to literally pump in meaningful experiences and mediate effectively to help permanent, well understood concepts evolve from these experiences.

2. *Auditory Discrimination.* Auditory discrimination is a learned ability that develops very early during the pre-school experiences of the normally advantaged child. He has adequate speech models and, in addition, conscientious parents mediate constantly to correct his misperceptions of speech sounds and his pronunciation errors. In a majority of disdavantaged communities, however, language precision is not given much attention and dialectical pronunciations are given to many speech sounds which are at considerable variance with the standard speech of their regions.

Auditory discrimination ability correlates significantly with success in beginning reading. The probable reason for this is that a child must be familiar with speech *sounds* before he can master the *symbols* that are used to represent these speech sounds on the printed page. Hence, inadequately developed auditory discrimination undoubtedly accounts for much of the difficulty that culturally disadvantaged children experience with phonics in beginning reading.

Lack of adequate auditory discrimination ability also penalizes the child in listening situations. Much learning takes place through listening and if words are misperceived or confused with similar sounding words, there is likely to be inaccurate listening comprehension.

In order to provide the culturally disadvantaged learner with this essential prerequisite to success in both reading and listening in the classroom, it is important that he be helped to develop careful auditory discrimination ability. He must be literally *immersed* in the speech sounds that he is to acquire. He needs to imitate adequate speech models and be assisted when speech sounds are not perceived or reproduced correctly.

3. *Vocabulary Expansion.* The importance of precision in the knowledge of word meanings is rather apparent as it relates both to school success and to effective communication in general. In the *receptive* areas of communication—listening and reading—a person is severely handicapped if he is confronted with many unfamiliar words that are crucial in conveying meaning. Similarly, in the *expressive* areas—speaking and writing—meaning may not be communicated with clarity and precision if the communicator has a meagre vocabulary.

The vocabulary of the culturally disadvantaged learner is likely to be restricted because he is encapsuled in an environment that is linguistically isolated. If he is to operate effectively in the linguistic world beyond his narrow environment, he must experience intensive immersion in words in a variety of meaningful contexts. And it is one of the very important mediating functions in the disadvantaged student's program to supply new words and insure precise perception of the sounds and knowledge of their meanings as more and more experiences and concepts are being provided.

4. *Oral Language Fluency.* The oral language of the culturally disadvantaged student is likely to be fluent when he is speaking his *own* native dialect. However, his attempts at fluency in "middle-class" English are likely to be abortive as he struggles for correct constructions or for precise words. Yet, he needs fluency in this somewhat alien tongue if he is to move comfortably outside of his ghetto.

Assistance provided to help him make this transition from his native dialect must be given with extreme care. Initially, he should be encouraged to speak freely and spontaneously in familiar topical areas *in his own dialect.* Attempts to change his patterns of speech will stultify his spontaneity if imposed too soon or with any derision or rejection of his former language. Eventually, however, he will begin to make this transition as he tries to imitate the language of his instructor, as he memorizes poems or lines from plays, as he listens to stories, or as he learns songs. Often, too, the instructor can listen to his comments and then paraphrase them back in more standard form without drawing special attention to the differences. Specially designed exercises should be created for memorization that have high interest value and which purport to teach those syntactical patterns or sentence constructions which the culturally disadvantaged student tends to say differently.

5. *Reasoning Ability.* The normal mediation provided by the parents of advantaged students and the fairly constant verbal interaction which they experience with their peers and siblings stimulates logical thinking and reasoning ability. Problems are often contrived for them to solve, either situational or verbal. This is not true, however, in the case of the disadvantaged student. He is, therefore, quite likely to flounder in the numerous kinds of problem-solving situations constantly presented by school and life in general.

Every opportunity should be seized in the disadvantaged learner's program to stimulate enthusiastic and effective attacks on a variety of problems. Formal logic (induction, deduction, etc.) of various types should be woven into the program at every appropriate juncture.

PSYCHO-SOCIAL ADJUSTMENT NEEDS

The conditions which deny the disadvantaged learner the prerequisites important to school success tend also to present other problems involving his general psychological and social adjustment. The following are significant areas for consideration in planning the psycho-social movement of the disadvantaged learner in attempting to forestall or reverse the negative effects of this disadvantage.

1. *Achievement Expectancy.* It is crucial that any learner view the probability of his success with optimism, since a defeatist attitude frequently accounts for failure. Because this assumption of probable success is generally born of *experience with success*, it is essential to provide the disadvantaged learner with success-yielding challenges. Such a balanced diet of challenges and successes should carry over to many learning situations so that learning *per se* will carry its own intrinsic motivations.

2. *Attitude of Inquiry.* The earlier natural attitude of inquiry is likely to diminish later for a student who has had a long history of failure; yet, it can be rekindled if the learning situation is stimulating enough. This involves, among other techniques, the very skillful use of questions to generate and direct the learner's pursuit of understandings. Such questioning should be challenging, but should also be within the conceptual and reasoning grasp of the student. In addition, spontaneous questioning on the part of the learner himself should be encouraged and should be satisfied by explanations or by his being helped to discover the answers himself.

3. *Sense of Personal Worth.* Neglect of a child's personal, social, and intellectual needs is often characteristic of the depressed environment that spawns generalized deprivation. An effective program for a student who comes from this type of environment should provide the kind of peer-group interaction that will enable the learner to develop the healthy self-image that comes from acceptance. Also, the mediator working with such students should recognize his own role in assisting the development of ego strength by encouragement and praise and also by creating a learning environment in which there is adequate challenge coupled with success and recognition of achievement.

4. *Level of Aspiration.* Progress in learning specific school oriented tasks and in achieving general life-adjustment aspirations is contingent upon goal setting which is simultaneously challenging and realistic. This goal-setting orientation is not characteristic of the culturally disadvantaged child who has had little experience with success, who has a vague sense of futurity, and who has come to feel essentially powerless to command any control over his destiny.

It is important, therefore, that the mediator in a special program for this kind of child help him to learn to set goals that are within his grasp, but which carry with them the rewards of effortful achievement. He should be conscious of this goal-setting behavior and should even verbalize his intended achievement. Encouragement at points of failure and generous rewarding praise should, of course, be forthcoming from the mediator.

5. *Socialization.* The culturally disadvantaged child is not likely to have come from a home in which he has been given experience in the very practical social amenities necessary for harmonious interaction with others or for appropriate behavior when he enters school. These social skills must, therefore, be taught. Sharing, taking turns, respect for the classroom authority figure, and various forms of self-control are fundamental to socialization. The mediator needs to be alerted to signs of lack of social skills and should employ many of the principles discussed previously in regard to the specific role of the mediator in the learning situation.

6. *Value Orientation.* Certain of the fairly standard values that are held by the general society are not likely to have been assimilated by the disadvantaged child. Lacking them, he may at best encounter derision and rejection and, more seriously, he may run counter to the laws in which many of these values are embodied. Examples of such values include: respect for the personal and property rights of others, common courtesy, citizenship responsibilities, intra-familial duties, appropriate regard for authority, etc. These and other values can be woven into many of the activities of the disadvantaged learner as effective means of reversing certain of the deleterious effects of cultural deprivation.

THE MEDIATOR IN THE LEARNING SITUATION

In many of the special programs that are currently being created for the culturally disadvantaged learner, instruction is provided by someone other than a traditionally trained teacher. In certain instances, peers, parents, or a variety of types of volunteers are responsible for the implementation of the curriculum. In any case, however, a vital aspect of the learning experience is the presence of an effective person to *mediate* between the learner and his environment. Mere exposure is not enough, particularly for the culturally disadvantaged student who has had severely limited experience in learning independently.

The purpose of mediation is *to direct the attention, the perception, and the interpretation of the student in the learning situation.* In addition, the mediator *provides encouragement in attacking a learning task, correction and encouragement when incorrect responses are made and confirmation and praise when correct responses are made.* Each of these functions is particularly crucial in the case of the culturally disadvantaged learner whose anticipation of failure is likely to be extreme, emotionally laden, and therefore, debilitating.

Despite the value of his developing independent work habits and the value of exploration and the inquiry, there are times when the learner requires *information or explanations* and these must be provided by the mediator. In addition, the mediator must play the important role of a *model* whom the learner imitates in establishing language proficiency, patterns of general behavior, or values. A very significant problem in the case of the culturally disadvantaged learner is the absence of *someone to mediate between him and his environment in order to make his experiences meaningful and to provide new ones*. And he also lacks adequate models to emulate.

Diagnosis en route is another important function of the mediator and this will have to be done in both the cognitive learning and the psychosocial adjustment areas. As learning progresses, the mediator must be alert to special problem areas and provide the necessary follow-up or "branching" activities by which to remedy errors in learning. When there is evidence of personal or social adjustment difficulties, the mediator should be alert to them and either provide assistance in solving them or make referrals when appropriate.

Some assessment must also be made by the mediator of the learner's ability in terms of *the size of the learning increments* which he can manage and also *the degree of complexity of material* which he can handle. Furthermore, and of special importance in the case of the student from a depressed environment, the mediator must *recognize when prerequisite skills or concepts are non-existent* and, therefore, the desired learning cannot take place. In such instances, of course, the mediator must be perceptive and resourceful enough to move back and provide these prerequisite learnings.

Lack of early and continuous guidance in the life of the disadvantaged student quite frequently results in anti-social behavior and a general disregard for authority figures and regulations. In attempting to *handle the inappropriate behavioral deviations prevalent among neglected learners*, the mediator must strike a healthy balance between firmness and freedom. Limits must be clearly established beyond which the learner is not permitted to transgress if he is to accept the regulations which any organized society must realistically impose. And practically any learner— advantaged or disadvantaged—will test these limits to determine how far he can go. He will continue this testing behavior until he has adequately assimilated these limits as internalized regulators.

The range of permissible behavior within the limits set for the learner should permit enough latitude to provide for a healthy amount of self-expression, creativity, and exploration. He must be given opportunities to demonstrate that he is developing internalized controls and a sense of responsibility and initiative. And he should be consciously aware of the fact that he is himself attempting to achieve maturity in this area of self-control.

When limits are being set with firmness or even with punitive measures, the learner should be helped to understand that his personal worth is not under question, but only that his behavior is unacceptable. This approach will permit the mediator to modify behavior without doing essential damage to the learner's self-concept.

What may seem here to be excessive emphasis on the role of the mediator—the teacher, the parent, the volunteer in a program—is in actuality extremely crucial in the case of the chronically neglected, culturally deprived learner. It is crucial because this vital ingredient of mediation has been essentially absent or, at best, slipshod, and its absence accounts for most of his psycho-social and educational problems. *The mediator must, therefore, make very conscious use of himself*, understanding exactly what his role must be and fulfilling it conscientiously; otherwise, attempts to impart specific knowledge and skills will be reduced to a futile exercise in absurdity.

It is indeed encouraging that our society is at last focusing concern, allocating funds, and training manpower to retrieve its heretofore forgotten citizens. And it is my very firm personal conviction that the rewards to the people directly involved in this massive endeavor and to our society in general will be vast, immeasurable and permanent.

(63) SOME CONCLUSIONS ABOUT
TEACHING READING TO
DISADVANTAGED CHILDREN*

S. Alan Cohen

Here are two hunches and twelve conclusions about teaching socially disadvantaged children to read and write. Cold data back the conclusions. The hunches are on thinner ice.

*Reprinted from *The Reading Teacher* 20 (February 1967), pp. 433-35, by permission of the author and the International Reading Association.

Hunch One: Most of the characteristics listed in the literature on socially disadvantaged youth echo textbooks on the adolescent. Certain language patterns are peculiar to slum children. But many psychosocial characteristics associated with socially disadvantaged youth are, in fact, characteristics of adolescents in general, disadvantaged or not.

Hunch Two: Suburban kids sit still, read "Look, Jane! Look!" get in line in a hurry, and do their homework no matter how meaningless the task. Slum kids are not as acquiescent; unless it is really meaningful, they are less likely to play according to school rules.

Now, to safer grounds—conclusions based on data.

Conclusion One: Compensatory programs for socially disadvantaged children have not proved successful. The reasons appear to be that the persons involved have not specified goals; they have not delimited goals (they usually bite off more than they can chew); they have not controlled relevant variables; they have not measured outcomes accurately.

Conclusion Two: Most Puerto Rican, Negro, Mexican-American, and Appalachian white children are retarded in reading. Not *many*, but *most*. Many educational administrators that I have talked with are not just kidding visitors to their schools; this is understandable if not defensible. More seriously, they are kidding *themselves* by not recognizing and accepting the magnitude of the problem. When they kid themselves, there is little chance of effecting significant change in reading instruction for these unfortunate children. For example, one superintendent of a city slum school system conceded that four or five children at the end of grade one in a particular school might be below grade level in reading in June. When we administered the entire Durrell Analysis of Reading Difficulty battery individually to all first graders in this school, we found only two or three children per classroom reading on grade level. Every other child was already retarded in reading.

Conclusion Three: Most children learn to read, write, and do arithmetic in spite of psychosocial problems. Psycho- or sociotherapy does not need to precede reading instruction.

Conclusion Four: Culturally deprived children learn to read *before* their emotional problems are solved. Many learn to read while they continue to live in slums with prostitutes for mothers and narcotics addicts for fathers. If we wait until we win the War on Poverty before we teach disadvantaged children to read, we might as well close down slum schools for the rest of this century. On the other hand, if we could teach reading thoroughly to 90 per cent of the Negro children in Bedford Stuyvesant we would do more for social change in the War on Poverty than any brainstorm of Sargent Shriver's.

A comment on Conclusions Three and Four: The best elementary school I have seen this year is in the heart of Harlem serving severely socially disadvantaged children. More children are reading on or above grade level and are enjoying an exciting full curriculum than in most suburban schools I have seen. Two blocks away a principal whose school services the same type of population keeps telling me how impossible it is to teach anything to these disturbed children from such deprived backgrounds.

Conclusion Five: Phonics in any form by any name will not win the War on Poverty. Nor will it solve the reading problems of culturally deprived children. However, we do know that retarded readers, socially disadvantaged or not, lack word attack skills, including phonics skills. We do know that training in these word attack skills is one necessary component in a remedial program.

Specifically we know that most disadvantaged retarded readers in seventh grade do not know the alphabet. We know, further, that most do not discriminate sounds in words accurately. Most Negro and Puerto Rican children who are retarded in reading in the early grades do not discriminate letters accurately. We know that auditory discrimination of sounds in words and visual discrimination of letters are two prerequisites to successful reading for all children regardless of ethnic background or socioeconomic level.

Conclusion Six: Most socially disadvantaged retarded readers tend to be visual rather than auditory or phonic readers. This is probably true of middle-class retarded readers as well. Their visual memory scores are low, but they are significantly higher than their scores for auditory discrimination of sounds in words. We also know from abundant experience that once hooked on a sight approach to reading, these children are extremely difficult to move to a phonic and structural approach to word attack. This suggests that a linguistic-phonic skill should be built into the beginning reading program early in formal and informal reading instruction—as early, perhaps, as kindergarten. This explains partially why blending sounds is so difficult to teach to retarded readers and leads this author to suggest that sounds in words or digraphs be taught without blending.

Conclusion Seven: The perceptual development of culturally deprived children at the beginning reading grades (K through three) is severely impaired. Since these children have so little going for them in other areas, these perceptual dysfunctions preclude the possibility that most of them will learn to read well. One major component of a Head Start or kindergarten program should be perceptual training.

Conclusion Eight: Compensatory programs for culturally deprived children are usually more of the same. Most ESEA Title I projects attack quantity rather than quality. More services, longer hours devoted to reading instruction, more basal readers, more time with the teacher will not solve the problem of reading retardation in socially disadvantaged children. New programs utilizing new methods and materials geared to changing quality rather than quantity are needed.

Conclusion Nine: One particular approach to teaching reading to all culturally deprived children is not the answer to their reading retardation. Culturally deprived children are human beings. They are members of a species made up of individuals with different learning styles. That means they must be taught as individuals.

Conclusion Ten: Thorough, continuous, quality instruction will teach culturally deprived children to read. A high intensity learning program in which content, level, and rate are adjusted to individual needs has worked every time this author has tried it with socially disadvantaged children and youth.

Conclusion Eleven: Most teachers do not know what materials and methods are available for teaching socially disadvantaged children. In addition, they do not read journals and are unaware of research and programs conducted in many sections of the country. Like lawyers and physicians, teachers blame (with good reason) their poor professional training for their deficiencies. But unlike most lawyers and physicians, teachers often do not make up these deficiencies once they enter the field.

Conclusion Twelve: The culturally deprived child depends more upon the school for language development and general verbal intelligence than does the middle-class child. In fact, the latter learns most of his verbal behavior, including reading, informally through his home environment. Thus the school has never really had to teach reading and language development. A sort of quick and dirty glossing over has been enough to get middle-class children "on grade level." Now the culturally deprived child has been discovered and we educators are on the spot.

I hope we can deliver. Right now I have my doubts. If we do not deliver, we will be replaced, and by "we" I mean the public schools. Perhaps the gradual replacement has already started under the aegis of the War on Poverty. Look closely and you will see what I mean.

(64) AN EXPERIMENTAL READING PROGRAM FOR DISADVANTAGED CHILDREN LEARNING ENGLISH AS A SECOND LANGUAGE*

Richard D. Arnold

INTRODUCTION

Of major concern to many educators is the large number of Mexican-American children who are disadvantaged. In Texas the problem is statewide. Past records indicate that up to 80 per cent of these children repeat the first grade, probably because of their inability to read (Texas Education Agency, 1962). Mass failure and deficient reading appear symptomatic of a more fundamental problem. Many of these children have little knowledge of English, the language of instruction in the schools.

In an effort to accelerate growth in English language skills through direct instruction, the San Antonio Language Research Project under the direction of Thomas D. Horn was inaugurated in 1964 as one of twenty-seven first grade reading projects sponsored by the U.S. Office of Education Cooperative Research Project number 2648 (Horn, 1966a). What appears to be a highly successful method of teaching English to children using science as the content vehicle has resulted. Up to this time the highly structured Developmental Oral Language (DOL) program has been taught in first, second, and third grade classrooms.

Though they may have learned to speak English more effectively, data from standardized reading tests indicate that the children receiving the Developmental Oral Language program have not made significant gains in reading. Indeed, the transfer effects from the DOL program in science to the reading content may have been less for the experimental groups than the transfer effects from incidental language development to the reading content for the control groups. What appears to have happened is that the language patterns, vocabulary, and content of the basal

*Reprinted from *The Reading Teacher* 21 (April 1968), pp. 634–39, by permission of the author and the International Reading Association.

reading materials, have not been particularly related to the oral language patterns, vocabulary, and content of the DOL program.

It became apparent that it was necessary to establish a closer relationship between oral language and reading. It seemed imprudent to discard the language program specifically designed to teach English to these children and replace it with a language program centered around basal readers designed for an essentially different pupil population. This action appears even more imprudent when one considers the inappropriateness of the middle class orientation of basal readers for an atypical, disadvantaged population. Another and seemingly more reasonable alternative was selected. A decision was made to develop reading materials centered around the DOL program with its structured experiences in the "culture fair" science content.

The Southwest Educational Development Laboratory, Austin, Texas, sponsored a summer writing seminar in 1967 to develop reading methods and materials that would be complementary to the existing oral language and science programs.

UNDERLYING ASSUMPTIONS

Several assumptions were made in considering the most appropriate way to teach reading to disadvantaged children who are learning English as a second language or dialect. The assumptions are based in part on observation of an experience with the population under study and in part on inferences drawn from reported research on similar children. To date, insufficient empirical data have been gathered to validate these assumptions on the particular population being studied. However, the assumptions seem reasonable and applicable.

First, the disadvantaged Mexican-American children begin school with a highly different experiential background from the more typical Anglo children. Many have never been out of the city limits or have "seen" the country mainly from the rear of a migrant truck, the rate of broken homes is extremely high, and have other environmental deficits associated with the disadvantagedness.

Second, these children in general are underdeveloped in visual-perceptual abilities associated with success in learning to read. Relative to other factors, however, this subset of skills is more highly developed than those discussed below. Visual-perceptual factors then are considered a strength in this population.

Third, the children's knowledge of English is highly inadequate, and their expressive abilities are even more depressed than their level of understanding.

Fourth, the auditory perception-discrimination abilities associated with success in beginning reading are grossly underdeveloped in the children. Not only can they not understand what is being said, they cannot discriminate between the differences in many of the sounds being uttered by their teachers. Indeed, some sounds used regularly in English are not even present in Spanish.

EMPHASES IN THE EXPERIMENTAL PROGRAM

With the above assumptions in mind, the writing team devised a method of teaching reading that emphasizes the following:

1. The content of the reading material follows the content of the existent DOL program, science.
2. The experimental reading program utilizes the experiences which are universal to all children in the DOL program.
3. The experimental reading program primarily utilizes the English language patterns which have been learned by all children.
4. The experimental reading program capitalizes on the relative strengths of visual-perceptual skills of these children while strengthening the relative weakness of the language associated skills outside of the reading lesson.
5. The experimental reading program emphasizes reading for meaning and understanding.
6. The experimental reading program assures systematic evaluation of reading progress.

The reading content emerges in expository form rather than literary form. The children learn to read about what they have seen and described in their science lessons. With the heavy emphasis on physical rather than life sciences in the AAAS Science program, the resultant reading materials remain primarily at the descriptive level.

Since it is assumed that these children come to school with meager experiences, it was decided to use experiences obtained directly in the classroom through the science curricula. Science lessons commence early in the school year, and reading is delayed until some oral facility is established. Thus, the children have learned the concepts they are to read about before they face the reading task. In this manner, control is exerted over the background of meaning the children bring to the reading task.

The Developmental Oral Language (DOL) program provides for the direct teaching of English language patterns associated with the science materials developed by the American Association for the Advancement of Science (AAAS). That is, the AAAS content is the vehicle around which natural English language patterns are taught. These patterns or sentences which are largely of a descriptive nature are taught using techniques developed in the field of teaching English as a second language. Thus, the children learn the language of science through teacher modeling and child response procedures. The children receive extensive and intensive practice in English language patterns which ultimately are habituated. It should be noted that the science-based language appears to be unique in the sense that these first grade children who are noticeably deficient in their general English language development are quite proficient in describing science materials. It is not unusual to observe a first grade child walk up to a table containing science materials, and accurately describe an object by saying, "This is a rectangular prism. It is a three dimensional shape. It has length and width and thickness."

A major thesis of the experimental reading program is that the teaching method emphasizes the relative strengths of the population being taught. Their weaknesses should be "remediated" outside of the reading program. This means that the visual modality is used extensively and that word recognition is initially taught primarily through visual analysis skills. Children learn to look carefully at words and word parts, as well as morpheme-grapheme correspondences. Phonetic analysis skills are developed as the child's speech improves, thereby eliminating problems which would be confusing to these children if usual phonics instruction is utilized.

The de-emphasis on training in phonics in the beginning reading program should not be construed as a lack of concern for the development of the more phonological oral-aural skills. The point here is that it is deemed very important that special curricular provision should be made to develop these skills. The DOL program and the broader language arts program *do* contain highly structured lessons to remediate these deficits. With this provision, the teacher during reading lesson is relieved of trying to teach children how to hear and say unfamilar sounds while she also tries to teach them unfamilar graphic symbols— that is, words.

Many authorities in the field of reading emphasize the need to make reading a meaningful experience. Yet, the research on children's vocabularies upon entering school suggests that the typical first grade child comes to the reading materials with listening and speaking vocabularies sufficient to cope adequately with the meanings. The disadvantaged Mexican-American population of concern here clearly does not. Therefore, meaningful referents and understanding become a critical focus for the reading program.

Several factors are involved. *First,* the science content, preceding the reading program as it does, insures the presence of experiences and concepts needed to understand the printed page. *Second,* all reading occurs within previously learned and habituated oral language patterns. Thus, the reading content becomes a visual representation of the children's language. *Third,* the children learn to read a full sentence at a time. The sentence represents the habituated language pattern and is a full meaning bearing unit. *Fourth,* the teaching method always proceeds from the known to the unknown, from larger units to smaller units. That is, first the children learn several sentences of a similar linguistic structure which is then followed by learning to recognize the language pattern itself, learning individual words which substitute into the slot of that language pattern, and finally learning the individual elements which make the words graphically unique. *Fifth,* word recognition skills are taught from meaningful references, *i.e.,* known words.

The last emphasis for the experimental reading program is that careful evaluation of the children's reading progress is made. It is considered essential to determine whether or not each child has successfully learned the vocabulary and language patterns taught. Specially constructed evaluation activity sheets based on behavioral objectives for each lesson have been diagnostically designed to determine success or failure. These evaluation sheets accompany every reading lesson. The tests have been designed so that the teacher can see which children have learned the lesson and which have not. For those who have not, it can further be determined exactly which word or language pattern has not been learned. With proper use of these evaluations, the teacher will be able to structure carefully lessons for reteaching to eliminate specific weaknesses of the children.

THE READING METHOD

The experimental reading program utilizes some of the teaching procedures developed in the field of teaching English as a second language. At the beginning of every reading lesson, the teacher reviews orally with the class the language patterns and concepts previously developed in the DOL program. In this procedure a teacher-children dialogue occurs. At this point the teacher typically does not have to model the language patterns except when they emerge incorrectly from the children. Hand gestures indicating "listen" and "talk" accompany the structured dialogue.

Once the language pattern is elicited, the teacher then writes the pattern on the chalkboard. A key procedure for the teacher in the reading method is to say, "Watch me while I write." She then writes the language pattern. When completed, the teacher using one hand signal to tell the children to listen, models the language pattern orally as she simultaneously uses a sweeping left to right gesture under the written language pattern with the other hand. The teacher repeats this procedure an appropriate number of times. She then gives the response hand signal and uses the sweeping gesture as the children respond orally as a group.

The preplanning phase of the lesson is critically important. The teacher must plan carefully the specific questions to ask the children in order to elicit the proper language patterns as responses. Another critical element is the teacher's awareness of the composition of certain language patterns. Different types of language patterns require different types of class participation.

The experimental reading method is similar in many respects to the sentence method of past years. This method, of course, has as its strength the development of the sense of meaning in a sentence. It brings to the child's attention that thoughts are expressed in sentences. The sentence method, however, is only one aspect of the experimental program. Word recognition skills are also stressed. Focus on individual words occurs in the same lesson but within the context of the language patterns. Activities such as matching words with word cards and framing individual words are stressed.

The experimental reading method is somewhat related to the language experience approach to teaching reading. The difference, however, is that the experimental program is highly structured and utilizes preplanned concepts, language patterns, and experience charts.

A final important characteristic of the experimental reading method is the evaluation activities. For every lesson involving new material to be learned, child behavioral objectives are established. Specific terminal behaviors, usually the reading of certain words or language patterns, are written down in the lesson plan objectives for the teacher. Upon completion of the lesson, evaluation activities are presented to them. Each behavior specified in the objectives is then "tested" with a cluster of items on the activity sheet.

This method, based on a set of assumptions different from what is typically used for the general population in developing reading methods and materials, will be field tested on a limited scale this year. It is hoped that some progress will be made toward developing a method to improve the reading of disadvantaged children learning English as a second language.

REFERENCES

Horn, T. D. *A Study of the Effects of Intensive Oral-Aural Spanish Language Instruction, Oral-Aural English Language Instruction, and Non-Oral-Aural Instruction on Reading Readiness in Grade One.* Austin, Texas: The University of Texas, 1966.

Horn, T. D. "Three Methods of Developing Reading Readiness in Spanish Speaking Children in First Grade," *The Reading Teacher*, 1966, 20, 38–42.

Ott, Elizabeth H. *A Study of Levels of Fluency and Proficiency in Oral English of Spanish-Speaking School Beginners.* Austin, Texas: The University of Texas, 1966.

Texas Education Agency. *The Preschool Instructional Program for Non-English Speaking Children.* Austin, Texas: Texas Education Agency, 1962.

(65) STARTING A READING PROGRAM FOR SPEAKERS OF SUB-GROUP DIALECTS*

Roger W. Shuy

When a person quotes from a best-seller of several years ago, he automatically runs the risk of being typed as so cheap that he waits for the book to come out in paperback or so culturally deprived that he is slow in catching on to the current literary scene. But, risk or no risk, I cite a passage from Harper Lee's *To Kill a Mockingbird* because it suits so well the position I would like to present. I have in mind the passage where Jem and Jean Louise conclude that Calpurnia, the Negro servant,

*Reprinted from *Linguistics and Reading*, Highlights, 1965, pp. 51–58, by permission of the author and the International Reading Association.

uses one form of English to them and quite a different form of English to her own circle of friends. The two children ask her why she speaks to her own ingroup the way she does, especially when it is obvious that she knows better. Calpurnia answers:

> It's not necessary to tell all you know. It's not lady-like—in the second place, folks don't like to have somebody around knowin' more than they do. It aggravates 'em. You're not gonna change any of them by talkin right, they've got to want to learn themselves, and when they don't want to learn there's nothing you can do but keep your mouth shut or talk their language.[1]

Calpurnia's sensitivity to linguistic behavior is not only mature and perceptive but it is articulated in a way which is relevant to our problem. In an article in *School Review* several years ago, Werner Cohn stated the usefulness of lower-class English in a somewhat different manner: "Intimate and satisfying personal communication among lower-class parents, children, and friends is carried on almost exclusively by means of lower-class speech" (2). Calpurnia, of course, was ill-equipped to handle phrases like "satisfying personal communication," but she had the basic idea clearly in mind. She knew that it was sociologically and psychologically important to shift gears linguistically. She showed penetration and understanding in a bidialectal situation.

TEACHER ATTITUDES TOWARD DIALECTS

Similarly, teachers must show penetration and understanding in bidialectal classroom situations. Such attitudes are characteristic of dialectologists. Tolerance and objectivity are basic to the science of their scholarship. As they work with dialects, teachers will want to share in these attitudes.

The application of dialectology to the classroom, as far as the teacher's attitudes are concerned, may be summarized as follows:

1. The teacher must understand language well enough to know that speakers of one dialect are not inherently superior to speakers of another dialect.

2. However much the teacher wishes to change certain features in the sub-group dialect, he must not ridicule it, privately or publicly.

3. The teacher must learn that both standard and sub-group dialects have a systematic structure.

4. Many teachers must understand that their own social status, par-

ticularly if they have recently arisen from lower strata, may cause problems in their attitudes toward the sub-group dialect from which they have just emerged.

The attitudes of the scholar-dialectologist and the dialect-teacher have been stressed because the term *dialect* to many people connotes some of the same unfortunate side effects which made the designation, *colloquial*, unusable to the editors of Webster's *Third New International Dictionary*. That is, just as the generally understood meaning of *colloquial* carried the prejorative notion of *slang*, so the generally understood meaning of *dialect*, to many people, connotes what Raven I. McDavid, Jr., refers to as the Wordsworthian snydrome.

I suspect that people achieve three levels of understanding of dialects. At first, they believe that dialects are spoken by funny little old men who hail from various areas of cultural deprivation. The field workers for *The Linguistic Atlas* frequently note that their informants believe that dialects characterize *other* parts of the country but not their own. Once a person realizes that we all speak a regional dialect of some sort, he has reached the second level of understanding. The third, and frequently overlooked, level of understanding comes when we realize that dialect differences exist socially within regional patterns. McDavid gives this definition of *dialect* in a recent issue of *The Reading Teacher*: ". . . a variety of a language, generally mutually intelligible with other varieties of that language, but set off from them by a unique complex of features of pronunciation, grammar, and vocabulary" (3). *Sub-group* dialects are simply the next layer of dialect taxonomy—the sub-categories of the dialect, whether defined regionally, socially, or by a combination of both. We must be careful to note, however, that *sub* does not mean below par in any sense. I conceive of a *sub-group* as any somewhat unified and identifiable body of people, whether wealthy or poor, educated or ignorant, who operate within the somewhat unified and identifiable larger group.

THE CHANGING AND ENLARGING FIELD OF DIALECTOLOGY

Scholarly investigations of dialects started with rural and regional studies and have recently been extended to urban areas. Linguists interested in dialectology began their scholarship in this country by describing the features of pronunciation, grammar, and vocabulary which characterized regional, rural subgroups. *The Linguistic Atlas of the United States and Canada* has made a great deal of the information on this segment of dialectology available. It appears in various books, monographs, articles, and dissertations as well as in the Atlas files. Atlas field work has been carried on for about 35 years now and the United States has had first-layer coverage in most states. The first-layer research, however, concerned itself largely with rural areas and the speech of older persons because, as McDavid pointed out, the aim of the American Atlas project was . . . "to trace the affiliations of American dialects with each other, and with other dialects—standard and folk and intermediate—of the British Isles" (4). In the past few years, however, many American dialectologists have turned their attention to the urban areas, with their complex intermingling of in-migrants and native born.

Of immediate significance is the recent work of Lee A. Pederson in his dissertation, the *Pronunciation of English in Metropolitan Chicago: Vowels and Consonants* (1964) and in his subsequent articles. Pederson relied heavily on the questionnaire used by field workers for the Linguistic Atlas, changing it only to elicit items to which an urban Chicago resident might naturally respond. He extended the Atlas technique somewhat, however, by doing many additional shorter interviews, a technique which enabled him to examine more thoroughly some of the items which the regular interview revealed to be significant. Furthermore, Pederson utilized a more elaborate scale for classifying the informants socially than any previous Atlas materials had used. This enabled him to note finer socio-linguistic details than the more traditional equivalent to upper-, middle-and lower-class distributions permitted.

A somewhat different approach is being used in New York City by William Labov. In his interviews he tried to elicit data which would reveal various styles of linguistic behavior such as careful speech, the reading style, casual or spontaneous speech, and the pronunciation of words in lists. The traditional Atlas approach has been geared primarily to casual speech. The dimensions added by Labov may greatly augment the application of linguistics to the reading program.

It should be clear, therefore, that contemporary dialectologists do not feel bound to a particular method of gathering data on English. New ideas have modified Atlas techniques to serve the needs of the more complex urban situation.

DIALECTOLOGY AND THE PHONEME-GRAPHEME APPROACH TO READING

Although techniques of linguistic data-gathering may, on the surface, seem unrelated to the development of a reading program, this is not the case at all. The recent focus on the various social dialects of American English has pointed out some of the problems which beginning readers face. Labov's recent study, "Stages in the Acquisition of Standard English," (5) for example, points out six stages of the acquisition of mature spoken English. This information, based on interviews with young people in New York, should prove valuable to anyone interested in gearing a reading program to the child's facility without various ranges of English. Labov's study reveals, for example, that New York children between 5 and 12 tend to replace the influence of parents' speech with that of the peer group. Thus, neighborhood dialect patterns become automatic. In early adolescence, a child becomes aware of the social significance of the speech of his peer group even before he is able to do anything about it. In later stages of acquisition the speaker develops stylistic variation, a consistent standard, and finally, a full range.

One implication of the work of such recent dialect study seems particularly relevant to the classroom. When the in-migrant reaches first grade and begins to read, he usually brings with him the dialect of his parents. When placed in daily school contact with a peer group, however, the child tends to shift to local dialect patterns. Any reading materials which attempt to present the phoneme-to-grapheme relationships consistently will have to consider not only the accurate presentation of the phoneme-grapheme relationships of one dialect but also those of the other. In other words, the spelling-pattern approach developed by Fries and used in the Philadelphia schools might find itself with dialectal impositions of inconsistency.

If we assume, as many linguists do, that the child's initial reading experience should be geared to the form of language which is as close to his speech as possible, then the obvious thing to do is to first find out what's the child's dialect, his pattern of speech. This suggests strongly that different reading materials be prepared for different dialects, whether defined by region, by social standing, or by a combination of both. If the child does not distinguish between the pronunciations of *pin* and *pen* and is told by his textbook that *pin* fits a pattern with *fit* and *tip* while *pen* fits a pattern with *pep* and *pet*, the advantage which the spelling-pattern approach offers is nullified. The alternative, forcing the child to change his pronunciation *before* he learns to read, violates the advantage the young reader gains by learning to read in that form of language which is as close to his spoken language as possible.

A further complication, that of the in-migrant child's switch to the local vernacular of his peer group, poses still another problem. If spelling-pattern oriented reading materials are prepared for different regional and social dialects, how can the teacher determine when to substitute materials of the local dialect for the materials of the in-migrant dialect?

What the dialectologist is asking for, in essence, is thoroughness and consistency. He admits the usefulness and desirability of the spelling-pattern approach; but he wants to see it operate consistently in a typical urban situation where over-all dialect patterns are not simply generalized and where the penalties of being an outsider are great enough without adding problems to the initial reading experiences.

DIALECTOLOGY AND GRAMMATICAL INTERFERENCE IN READING

We have indicated thus far that a dialectologist offers help to the reading teacher primarily in the matters of identifying sub-group dialects, developing a pedagogically and psychologically satisfactory attitude toward them, and in pointing out structural interference on the phonological level. Very recent research, particularly by William Stewart in Washington, D.C., and Juanita Williamson in Memphis, has pointed out that structural interference may also exist on the grammatical level. (6)

Stewart carefully describes some of the changes which take place in the dialect of Washington, D.C., boys. He describes Washington, D.C., as a city, in which a formerly widespread dialect of the bottom socio-linguistic hierarchy, under pressure from an encroaching linguistic system, has been replaced as the usual communication channel by the general community but has been generally preserved by children. He points out, furthermore, that adults in such communities assume that it is natural for children to speak this dialect. By the age of seven or eight, Stewart observes, certain shifting begins to occur in the child's dialect. Whereas he had not formerly indicated a distinction between present and preterit tenses ("I see it" could mean *I see it* or *I saw it*), he now begins to add /-t/ and /-It/ to form such preterits as /kliynt/ and /rentit/ (*cleaned* and *rented*). What is particularly interesting in Stewart's research is the fact that this linguistic shifting coincides with a change in a boy's social position within the peer group. Like adults, big boys regard the lower-echelon dialect as small boy talk.

Miss Williamson's research on the speech of Memphis Negroes, like the work of all the dialectologists mentioned thus far, began with a thorough description of the current linguistic situation. One of the more interesting grammatical aspects of her study is the systematic reversal of the third person singular verb inflection with the other persons and numbers. That is, Negro high school students of a particular sub-group in Memphis convert the standard

I walk	we walk
you walk	you walk
he walks	they walk

into

I walks	we walks
you walks	you walks
he walk	they walks

Thus the Stewart and Williamson studies have shown that the almost universal approach to grammar followed by English teachers, that of the eradication of individual offensive *items*, is less productive than an approach to what the systematic sub-group *patterns* of that dialect might be. For the reading program in particular, these studies suggest that the superimposition of the sub-group dialect on the standard dialect may be the real cause of what may appear to be phoneme-grapheme misreadings. That is, the student who, in reading, pronounces the words *he walks* as "he walk" may not really be forgetting to pronounce the grapheme *s* but may be suffering from the interference of the sub-group grammatical pattern on the standard grammatical pattern. Of this substitution, Stewart observes ". . . this would indicate more success than failure on the teacher's part; that the child understood the meaning of the printed material so well that he began to supply his own linguistic expression for the situation described" (7).

The advancing study of dialectology will inevitably modify along the lines I have suggested, and along other lines as well, the approaches and expectations in the reading program for sub-group dialect speakers.

NOTES

1. Harper Lee. *To Kill a Mockingbird*. New York: Lippincott, p. 36.
2. Werner Cohn. "On The Language of Lower-Class Children," *School Review*, 67, Winter 1959, p. 437.
3. Raven I. McDavid, Jr. "Dialectology and the Teaching of Reading," *The Reading Teacher*, December 1964, p. 207.
4. McDavid. "The Dialectology of an Urban Society," *Communications et Rapports du Premier Congrés International de Dialectologie Générale.* Louvain: 1964, p. 73.
5. Labov's article will appear in the forthcoming National Council of Teachers of English publication, *Urban School Dialects and Language Learning.*

6. Stewart's article, "Urban Negro Speech: Sociolinguistic Factors Affecting English Teaching," and Williamson's research, "Report on a Proposed Study of the Speech of Negro High School Students in Memphis," will appear in the forthcoming NCTE publication, *Urban School Dialects and Language Learning.*
7. *Idem.*

(66) PROGRESS IN DEVELOPMENTAL READING FOR TODAY'S DISADVANTAGED*

Helene M. Lloyd

In today's world, the reading needs of the disadvantaged child have come to the foreground. The nationwide Project Head Start program, the increased number of Title I projects, the accelerated movement of the disadvantaged to urban centers, the drive by publishers to develop new reading materials, and the justifiable pressures from the disadvantaged themselves that they be taught to read—all these have demanded that educators and lay personnel pool their time, talent, and resources to develop a reading program that will meet the needs of today's disadvantaged.

Progress—definite progress—*is* being made in several basic areas in which tremendous needs exist. The progress made, however, represents only the "plug in the hole in the dike;" a long-range action program *must* be developed to insure steadier progress in meeting the needs of nonreaders both in and out of schools throughout our country.

What are benchmarks that indicate progress *is* being made in developmental reading for today's disadvantaged?

UNDERSTANDING CHILDREN'S NEEDS

The first benchmark is the fact that *much progress has been made in understanding the needs of the disadvantaged child in* relation to reading. At least three of these needs are becoming recognized.

(1) It is necessary that the child have confidence in his ability to learn to read. It is clear that teachers, parents, and the disadvantaged child himself must recognize that the child *can* learn to read and—given instruction suitable to his needs—*will* learn to read as well as his more

*Reprinted from *Vistas in Reading*, 11, Part I, (1966 Convention Proceedings), pp. 35–39, by permission of the author and the International Reading Association.

advantaged classmates. The progress in reading being made by disadvantaged children who *do* develop confidence in the worth of their own ability testifies to the importance of a positive self-image. Creating and extending a positive self-image is now recognized as a component of the process of teaching reading. Giving the Negro child, and others, specific instruction in the history and culture of their ethnic backgrounds is an example of a way of brightening their self-image and thereby increasing the likelihood of their progress in reading.

(2) It is necessary that we recognize the factors, the handicaps, that have been responsible for curtailing progress in reading by the disadvantaged. For example, we must recognize and act upon the lack of auditory perception among the disadvantaged. The child coming from a disadvantaged home is not familiar with the sound and structure of formal English; he does not recognize the sounds, the accents, the language patterns. Both the Puerto Rican and the Negro child have difficulty with the rhythm of English; it is much too fast for these learners; they hear only an unperceived mass of sounds.

Another factor we must recognize and act upon is the weakness in the disadvantaged child's experiential background. He lacks the ability to recognize English words and language patterns as symbols or sound-pictures of things and ideas. Because of his weakness in experiential background, we now know that he has difficulty in understanding the language of textbooks and of his teacher.

(3) It is necessary that there be an extended, sequential developmental program in which corrective-clinical services are an integer.

This need implies that reading must, for the disadvantaged child, be taught throughout his entire school life, pre-kindergarten through grade 12, with a carefully planned network of services to meet the needs not only of the in-school child but also of out-of-school poor readers and non-readers. The needs of this latter group should and can be met through the establishment of a network of reading centers in libraries, schools, community centers—even vacant stores, if necessary—under the supervision of expert teachers of reading.

This need for comprehensiveness implies also that all special reading services, whether for the advanced or the retarded reader, must be regarded as a basic part of the developmental reading program.

This need for a long-span system implies, in addition, that a sequential skill program for the full gambit from pre-kindergarten to grade 12 must be carefully developed. In New York City, the schools recognize this aspect and are revising our skill-development program, for publication next fall.

So our first benchmark of progress is the feeling that we are beginning at least to define the problem in terms of the child's need for a positive self-image, in terms of the handicapping factors, and in terms of the long-range service-aligned reading design.

NO SINGLE "OPEN SESAME!"

The second benchmark of progress is the growing recognition that *no single reading approach, no lone combination of approaches will guarantee that the disadvantaged child will learn to read.* His needs are not met by a formula that fits all his brethren.

Rather, the classroom teacher must become master of all approaches and master of all procedures that will enable her to analyze the child's needs and to prescribe the approach best suited to his present needs. The classroom teacher must know that needs change as they are remedied or met, and therefore the reading approach must change, too. Today a child may benefit from an audio-lingual approach; tomorrow, from a language-experience approach; next week, from a basal-reader approach; and next month, from an individualized-reading approach or from a unique combination of approaches.

This benchmark asks much of the classroom teacher, for she is not likely to be master of all these matters. In a pilot study with teachers of disadvantaged children who were beginning readers, Albert J. Harris found that the teachers *thought* that the children made better progress the initial months of the school year by using basal readers than they did by using the language-experience approach; by the close of the year, however, they found that children with whom they *did* use the language-experience approach were gaining faster than did the basal-reader children. Teachers will need much help in fulfilling the responsibility that we have come to recognize: the need for varying approaches to fit the circumstances of children's learning needs.

The ability to bring together the right reading approach and the right child requires superior skill in the teaching of reading. It also requires recognition of the fact that learning to read is a highly individualized matter: instruction of a class as one reading group in day-to-day practice has no place in today's program for teaching the disadvantaged to read.

NO MAGIC ELIXIR

Our third benchmark of progress grows from the second. Just as there is no single approach for teaching reading to the disadvantaged, so is there

*no single type of material whose use will insure the reading progress of
the disadvantaged.* But there are basic characteristics that materials used
successfully with the disadvantaged must possess:

(1) The materials must be based on experiences to which the disadvantaged child can relate. The Bank Street Readers, the revisions of
popular basal series, and new supplementary materials are moving in this
direction. Much more needs to be done, however, to develop materials
for use by pupils at all grade levels (and especially at the intermediate
and upper grades), based on children's experiences. Commercial use
should be made of the experience charts developed by capable teachers
as they work with the disadvantaged. Harris' pilot study, to which I
referred, underscored the advantages of using language-experience charts
as a basis for beginning reading for the disadvantaged.

(2) Materials for the disadvantaged should have an audio-visual
emphasis. Pilot studies, such as one being financed by Astor funds in ten
elementary schools in disadvantaged areas in New York City, show the
value of stress on audio-visual aspects. All the work done to date by
Martin Deutsch with the disadvantaged further confirms the need for
intensive audio-visual work as a basis for beginning formal reading.

(3) Materials for the disadvantaged should involve the learner in
their use so that he gains a feeling of responsibility for his own reading
progress. Materials such as the SRA kits, the Reader's Digest skill texts,
Macmillan's skill builders, as well as the programed materials in reading skills being developed by the New York City school system for the
use of the disadvantaged, use the basic idea of involving the learner in
responsibility for progress. There is well-defined need for materials that
include (a) a simple inventory test to determine reading-skill needs; (b)
material a pupil can use, to a large extent independently, to meet these
needs; and (c) a simple method by which the child can keep a proud
record of his own reading progress.

TRAINING, THEN RETRAINING

A fourth benchmark in our progress in developmental reading has been
*the universal recognition of a need for a new, extensive, imaginative
program of preservice and in-service training and retraining for both
teachers and supervisors.*

That program should not focus on reading instruction alone, as
though it could be isolated into a tight specialization. As John B. King,
executive deputy superintendent of the New York City schools, pointed

out in a recent address, the training and retraining should concern itself not only with reading *per se* but also with "urban anthropology, linguistics, psychology and pedagogy of teaching English as a second or third language. . . . The various NDEA institutes and fellowship programs should be expanded as rapidly as state, federal, and foundation funds can be made available."

As we expand these programs, however, we must make certain that their caliber of instruction remains high. As one who had the privilege of evaluating several NDEA institutes, I should like to stress that it cannot be emphasized too often or too loudly that such institutes *must* be tailored to prepare teachers for working with today's *dis*advantaged children. The content of the institutes, the approaches suggested, the methods demonstrated, the reading materials reviewed or suggested, should not be "old wine in new bottles" but new potions brewed to meet the complex reading needs of the countless thousands of disadvantaged children who pass through our schools children who, in the words again of John King, "will find in reading mastery the prime means of breaking the poverty cycle and of acquiring economic, cultural, social, and personal fulfillment."

It is not enough for teachers and supervisors to learn more about reading instruction *in general*; they must learn more about—*all* about—reading instruction for the disadvantaged *in particular*.

There is evidence that big strides are being taken in this regard, quite beyond the institutes and workshops that have been mentioned. In our city alone we are using television, team teaching, films, the buddy system, creative programed instruction, expanded in-service increment courses, expanded preservice orientation of teacher trainees, and many other means of helping teachers learn to work with the reading problems of the disadvantaged. We are not alone in this battle; other cities are making similar assaults. Certainly all of us must make wider and more effective use of every type of preservice and in-service training and re-training that we can imagine. Much *is* being done in this regard—a benchmark of progress.

SQUARER EVALUATION

A fifth benchmark of our progress in teaching reading to today's disadvantaged children is *the nearly universal clamor for new tools of evaluation*. The hue and cry is for several new instruments:

(1) There is need for simple types of evaluation in which the child

can be involved and for which he can be responsible. This evaluation can concern itself with skills, materials, reactions to stories, and many other aspects of reading experience.

(2) There is need for easily-available materials for teachers to use in evaluating needs and points of progress, in relation to specific skills at various sequential levels.

(3) There is need for tools that teachers can use in their work with disadvantaged children at all levels to evaluate the children's ability in auditory and visual perception. *Much* more material, many more tools, are needed in this area, especially for older children.

(4) There is need for extensive revision of standardized reading tests so that teachers of the disadvantaged can gain more accurate and deeper insight into their pupils' reading progress and their status in terms of standardized norms.

The point here is not only that there is a need for squarer yardsticks but also that the need is recognized—and *that* is progress!

COMMUNITY ORIENTED

A sixth benchmark of our progress is the general recognition that *a program to help the disadvantaged to read better must involve the parents*.

One of the exciting advances that we may attribute to Project Head Start is how much we have learned about the effectiveness of including parents, and indeed the whole community, in the children's "head start."

In the work done by Martin Deutsch with the parents of disadvantaged pre-kindergarten children in New York City—a project that was the forerunner of Project Head Start on a national level—he found that the effectiveness of the work with the children *was directly related* to the extent of parent involvement.

In New York City we have used many means to involve parents in our programs for helping our disadvantaged children, including special films on the learning-to-read process, brochures to guide parents in helping their children, reading exhibits to which parents are invited, and many pilot projects—our Astor study, for example—which include specifically planned roles for parents who are drawn into the projects.

We have only scratched the surface in regard to parent participation, of course; but it is a benchmark of progress to note that the scratch is deep and the interest in it is nearly universal.

GETTING SOMEWHERE

We cannot point to test scores as evidence of our progress in meeting the reading needs of the disadvantaged; for this juncture in educational history, America's Education is tooling up for this newly accepted responsibility and is still working with its pilot models. The assembly line is not yet in full gear. Indeed, the flood of in-migrants to the urban centers is so great that a school system may well congratulate itself in maintaining reading test scores on the plane that they have in recent years.

The evidence lies in the fact that education's responsibility to the disadvantaged *has been recognized and accepted*, the fact that education is directing its enormous talent to the solution of the problems involved in the responsibility. This is why I have been able to point so proudly to what education and educators have accomplished—

1. have come to understand the needs of these children;
2. have come to understand that there is no single formula of uniform application but rather a need for diversified approaches to reading instruction;
3. have ascertained that there is no single kind of material that will meet the needs of so many different kinds of handicapped learners;
4. have seen that the immediate key lies in training and retraining teachers (and have taken much action here);
5. have defined the need for new kinds of tools of measurement and evaluation;
6. have pinpointed the critical role of the parents of the disadvantaged.

True, we have only defined the dimensions of our problem and made brush contact—by pilot studies—with elements of the problem. But we have established principles, we are loading the guns. I believe that most of us now have a reasonable sense of direction in what we are doing.

True, the task ahead is greater than the task behind us; but the floodlights have been turned on and we can "see" what we are doing. And among the stirring things we are doing is buckling on the armor of determination and dedication. Our disadvantaged *are* going to master the basic requisite to their future success as American citizens—*they are going to learn to read!*

(67) THE PRESCHOOL-DISADVANTAGED CHILD*

Queenie B. Mills

The truly disadvantaged-preschool child is on a collision course with reading failure in first grade unless something intervenes to prevent this academic disaster. Reading inability among all children is estimated as 15 to 20 percent. Among the disadvantaged children as a group the disability estimate is as high as 50 percent (8), and it is even higher in the case of children from severely impoverished backgrounds.

We are only now beginning to understand the full impact of severe deprivation on the preschool child. We still have much to learn about him and about ways of working with him to compensate for his learning handicaps. A number of well-designed experimental programs is in progress, but to date results from these are either incomplete or inconclusive. We still do not know enough to prescribe with confidence the type of program or programs that will ensure optimum learning opportunities for these young children. At this stage of our knowledge what kind of compensatory educational experiences should we provide for severely disadvantaged preschoolers to improve their chances for success in learning to read?

In this paper I shall attempt to identify the truly disadvantaged child and his specific disadvantages in relation to beginning reading, to describe some of his developmental and learning deficits, and to suggest some guidelines for teachers. Some of what I have to say is based on my experiences as an educational consultant with Project Headstart; some of my observations and suggestions are directly related to experiences I have gained from an exploratory project involving severely disadvantaged pre-schoolers at the University of Illinois.

THE SEVERELY DISADVANTAGED-PRESCHOOL CHILD

Who is the severely disadvantaged-preschool child? He is roughly between the ages of three and five, and he has not yet entered first grade. If he is enrolled in an educational unit other than a day-care center, it is

*Reprinted from *Vistas in Reading*, 11, Part 1, (1966 Convention Proceedings), pp. 345–49, by permission of the author and the International Reading Association.

either a nursery school, a pre-kindergarten, or a kindergarten. Chances are, however, that he does not yet attend a school of any kind. He is not merely a poor child; rather, he is a child whose improverished-family environment has had such an impact upon his early development that he is ill-prepared for either the behavior requirements of the classroom or the demands of the learning process.

There is a good deal of confusion about the descriptive label *disadvantaged* and quite some disagreement about its appropriateness. We seem to have run the gamut in short order from *underprivileged* through *culturally deprived* and *culturally disadvantaged* to just plain *disadvantaged*. This term, too, has its drawbacks; for it is easy to build a case for certain "disadvantaged" middle-class children as well as for those from lower-class families.

The fact is that there are many degrees of disadvantage. It should also be recognized that not all poor children are necessarily disadvantaged. A colleague of mine was born in an oil camp in Texas. His family moved constantly from one oil camp to another. He was fourteen before he and his five younger brothers and sisters first entered school. But he wasn't disadvantaged! According to him he was merely poor at that particular time.

The truly disadvantaged child in my frame of reference comes from a bottom-of-the-range, lower-class poor, multiple-problem family. His deprivations have been many and the impact has been severe. He has inherited poverty. And the enormous significance of his deprivation is that he is being socialized in a "culture of poverty" (7) which has already started to retard his cognitive development.

Research has demonstrated that such children have many developmental and learning deficits in common. They score well below their middle-class peers on standardized measures of intelligence; their language development is retarded and of poor quality; auditory and visual-discrimination skills are not well developed; and skills for coping with the expectancies of a teaching-learning situation are almost nonexistent (2, 6).

It would be incorrect, however, to say that there is a disadvantaged preschooler per se. A decided range of differences with respect to the degree of disadvantage exists even at the lower end of the deprivation scale. Moreover, these disadvantaged American children come from different ethnic backgrounds and live in different sections of the country. The Oriental child in California and the Hawaiian child in rural Oahu, the Mexican-American or the Indian child in the Southwest, the Puerto-

Rican child in Spanish Harlem, the Negro child in a Chicago slum, and
the Caucasian child in Appalachia have different needs and backgrounds.
The great challenge is still the challenge of individual differences.

LEARNING DEFICITS RELATED TO PRE-READING SKILLS

There are a number of basic learnings related to reading which middle-
class children acquire during the preschool period and which disadvantaged children fail to acquire. For example, Durkin (4) reported that
books and "being-read-to" were experienced regularly and with pleasure
by the early readers in her research project. Books and being-read-to are
unknown quantities in the life of a young disadvantaged child. Because
of this fact, he builds neither an understanding of what it means to read
nor the desire to learn how.

It is pretty well agreed that we must have a child under attention if we
are to teach him to read. Yet, one of the prime characteristics of the
disadvantaged child at the preschool level is his notoriously short attention span. Related to this characteristic is the difficulty he has in following
the teacher's directions. This child's predominantly physical approach to
learning (3) may further complicate the problem of getting him involved in reading which, after all, is a fairly sedentary and abstract task.

I do not need to remind teachers that a high level of auditory
discrimination is required of the child in the beginning stages of learning
to read. Disadvantaged youngsters, however, appear to be surprisingly
insensitive to subtle differences in sound. It may be that, living in
unadulterated noise, they have learned how *not* to listen (3). The
resultant learning deficit is a serious one. It is important that the child be
able to distinguish "p" from "b." It is equally important that he be able
to listen to and benefit from the language spoken by the teacher.

The young disadvantaged child is a language cripple. He is not, strictly
speaking, a non-verbal child; but his verbal inadequacies are such that
they present a grave threat to his success in learning to read. This child
has not had many experiences with objects and ideas which are familiar
to middle-class children. As a result he does not know what these things
are or that they have names. Even the simplest pre-primer may present
concepts and vocabulary that are altogether unfamiliar. Add to this the
fact that his language is crude and limited, and the prognosis is not too
bright.

Basil Bernstein (1), the British sociologist has suggested that the language a child learns shapes and limits the *what* and *how* of his future learning. He describes two modes of verbal communication: *restricted* and *elaborated*. Restricted language is characteristic of the disadvantaged. Sentences are short, simple, often incomplete. It is used primarily for social interchange and is understood easily with a minimum of verbal cues. A kind of "disadvantaged pidgin," this type of communication affords little need for reflection. Elaborated language is more precise. The range of concepts, vocabulary, structural elements, and information is greater. It permits reflection and encourages the cognitive use of language as tools of thought.

Imagine a disadvantaged mother who wants to sweep the floor. Her young son is playing in the exact spot where she wishes to use the broom. She points toward the door and says, "Get out!" He obeys without responding verbally. This is restricted language. Now imagine a middle-class mother in the same situation. She might say, "Darling, Mother wants to sweep here. Would you please play in the other room for a few minutes until I have finished?" Something more must be done about this sentence than just listening to it. According to Hess and Shipman (5), the verbal categoric command, "Get out," cuts off thought; whereas the more elaborated message gives the child a reason for his mother's request. Given a rationale, it may encourage him to *ask* why in another situation. This type of verbal interchange may also encourage the child to learn to look for action sequences in his own behavior and in that of others. This more cognitive use of language is essential to interpretation in reading.

THE ILLINOIS NURSERY-SCHOOL PROJECT

Disadvantaged children have much to teach us about themselves. A two-group nursery-school project was initiated at the University of Illinois by Celia B. Stendler and myself on March 1, 1965, BHS—"Before Head Start"—that is, before the maiden summer voyage of the national effort in behalf of deprived four- and five-year-olds. The major purpose of the Illinois project was to gather descriptive data on severely disadvantaged preschoolers at two different age levels and under two different programs and to explore various approaches to parent education at this depressed level.

Both groups were housed in the Child Development Laboratory at the university and met for two and one-half hours five afternoons a week. Both were used as demonstration projects in the training of Head Start personnel.

The major criterion for selection was severe disadvantage. Public welfare officials and principals of schools in the most deprived areas of Champaign-Urbana were contacted for recommendations. It would be difficult to assemble a more bottom-of-the-barrel group of families than the ones we finally recruited. These were truly hard-core poverty cases. Moreover, the principals had nominated those families where there had been other children who had given the school real trouble over the years. To let the university take off some of the rough edges of behavior before this next child arrived on the kindergarten or first-grade doorstep was an obviously inviting temptation. Prayerfully principals made their recommendations, and we selected the most disadvantaged.

The children ranged in age from two and one-half to five years. They were divided into two age groups. Approximately one fourth of the sixteen children in each group was Caucasian, and the rest were Negroes. The older group was subjected to a highly structured situation using Piaget-inspired materials. The younger group was exposed to a more conventional and informal type of nursery-school program. Concrete experiences, concept development, and oral language were emphasized in both groups—individually and informally with the threes, and in small structured groups with the fours. The three-year-olds stayed at the laboratory for almost five months; but the four-year-olds were available to us for only three months.

The first thing we noticed about these children was that they were unable to manage space. Our playrooms are enormous. Unaccustomed to such freedom of movement indoors, they simply used the square footage as they would outdoor space—to exhibit open-field running. We learned shortly to break up this space, to limit the time for "free play" to twenty minutes at first, and to organize for "structured freedom." In this highly structured program for the four-year-olds, attention span was noticeably short and the activity level was very high. These two factors together necessitated a shifting program, versatile teachers, and small-group activities for short periods of time.

Next we learned that more teachers were needed in the four-year group than in the three-year group. A ratio of one teacher to four children appeared to be the most effective arrangement for small-group, direct-teaching activities. In contrast, the less structured, more traditional nursery school functioned well with only three teachers for sixteen children. Teacher personality undoubtedly had some effect on the situation, but it is a difficult variable to assess. Both head teachers were fine, intelligent, dedicated people. From observation, however, the younger children's teacher appeared to be somewhat warmer, more relaxed in her teaching style; and she was better trained to work with young children.

One of our most startling discoveries was the way these children used equipment. They threw everything they could pick up! A hole is to dig; a stick is to throw. A book isn't much different from a stick if you have never seen a book and you don't know what it is for or how to use it. Slowly, step by step we had to model how these concrete objects could be used. We were building concepts along the way. The old admonition not to make models for children to copy is still good advice but it needs some modifications. Children who have no built-in schemes for looking at picture books, listening to stories, or using paints and crayons need someone to model these activities for them.

One rather curious reaction was noted repeatedly in connection with the plastic toy animals. The children were afraid of them. They seemed unable to accept the fact that these toys were not real animals. When the gray rat-sized elephant was presented to one child, he ran away screaming, "He bi me! Bi me!"

These severely disadvantaged youngsters were capable of as much as ten to fifteen minutes of sustained play, but we learned early that it is important to guide or direct them before they reach some commitment to an undesirable activity. How to set limits and how to reinforce desirable behavior were perhaps our most challenging control problems. When we failed to use physical punishment, the children thought we weren't serious about the limits. On the other hand, praising a child for a task well done was no guarantee that it would be repeated.

The language deficits were severe in both groups, and much time was spent in the manipulation of concrete objects, naming, classifying, and helping the children to extend their spoken language. Even among these severely disadvantaged children, however, the range of language ability was surprising. For example, on the Templin fifty-item articulation scale, the scores ranged from 1 to 49 correct responses.

Both groups changed in language behavior. Test-retest gains on the Stanford-Binet over a three-month period were positive but not statistically significant. The average increase for the three-year-olds was 5 points; for the four-year-olds, 5.69 points. Shifts in scores on the Peabody Picture Vocabulary Test (PPVT) gave us better information. Initial testing on the PPVT was done after approximately two months in nursery school. The interval between testing was approximately two and one-half months. Average increase for the three-year-olds was 13.8 significant beyond the .025 level. Teacher ratings and structured parent interviews also indicated the improvement in language use.

GUIDELINES FOR TEACHERS

The following points are offered in summary as guidelines for teachers:

1. Not all young disadvantaged children are alike. They have different backgrounds, different needs, and may present different degrees of deprivation. Moreover, the range of individual differences within a group may be as great as it is among groups.

2. Learning deficits related to prereading skills are associated with auditory discrimination, concept formation, and language development. Compensatory educational programs should emphasize learning activities which will eliminate the existing handicaps.

3. Young disadvantaged children have to learn to be taught; therefore, at the preschool level, teachers should emphasize the "learning to learn" rather than the "learning to read" skills.

4. Teachers planning activities to help children "learn to learn" should give attention to helping children find pleasure in books and stories.

5. Always the teacher is the master key to the motivation problem with preschool-disadvantaged children. When there is mutual respect between teacher and child, the teacher can and must serve as a secondary reinforcer for the learning behavior she expects from him.

6. Since there is no one-best educational model for all disadvantaged preschoolers, compensatory educational experiences should be integrated with the best of traditional preschool practices (9, 10, 11).

REFERENCES

1. Bernstein, B. "Social Class and Linguistic Development: A Theory of Social Learning." In A. H. Halsey, Jean Floud, and C. A. Anderson, Eds., *Education, Economy, and Society*. Glencoe, Illinois: Free Press, 1961.

2. Bloom, Benjamin S.; Davis, A.; Hess, Robert. *Compensatory Education for Cultural Deprivation.* Working papers by participants in the Research Conference on Education and Cultural Deprivation. Chicago: Holt, Rinehart and Winston, Inc., 1965.
3. Deutsch, M. "The Disadvantaged Child and the Learning Process." In A. H. Passow, Ed., *Education in Depressed Areas.* New York: Columbia University Teachers' College, 1963, 163–180.
4. Durkin, Dolores. "Children Who Read Before Grade One," *The Reading Teacher,* January, 1961.
5. Hess, Robert D. and Shipman, Virginia C. "Early Experience and the Socialization of Cognitive Modes in Children," *Child Development,* 36 (December, 1965), 869–885.
6. Hunt, J. McV. *Intelligence and Experience.* New York: Ronald Press, 1961.
7. Lewis, Oscar. *The Children of Sanchez.* New York: Random House, Inc., 1961.
8. Riessman, Frank. *The Culturally Deprived Child.* New York: Harper and Brothers, 1962.
9. Sears, Pauline S. and Dowley, Edith M. "Research on Teaching in the Nursery School." In N. L. Gage, Ed., *Handbook of Research on Teaching.* Chicago: Rand McNally and Co., 1963.
10. Strodtbeck, Fred L. *Progress Report: The Reading Readiness Nursery: Short Term Social Intervention.* Chicago: University of Chicago, August 1963. Mimeographed.
11. Swift, Joan W. "Effects of Early Group Experience: The Nursery School and Day Nursery." In Martin L. Hoffman and Lois W. Hoffman, Eds., *Review of Child Development Research.* New York: Russell Sage Foundation, 1964.

Chapter 14

MEASUREMENT AND EVALUATION OF READING ACHIEVEMENT

INTRODUCTION

Over the years more tests have been made available to measure reading performance than to measure performance in any other area of the curriculum. Yet, it appears that teachers of reading know less about reading tests and about their use than almost any other "tool of the trade." This shortcoming may be due to the lack of emphasis on measurement and evaluation in teacher education programs or the lack of articles published in professional periodicals on this topic. Whatever the reason, the teaching profession must institute an "operation bootstraps" to become knowledgeable in the measurement and evaluation of reading behaviors and reading related behaviors.

Although the present chapter does not provide a complete course in the measurement and evaluation of reading, it will provide the reader with a short course on this topic. To begin, Davis provides some very practical suggestions about the use of standardized reading tests. His article is followed by Hayward's discussion of criteria for assessing and selecting diagnostic reading tests. These two articles should provide some initial anwers to such questions as: What types of reading tests are available? On what bases should reading tests be selected? How should reading test results be used? Next, as indicated by the title of his article, Lennon deals with the question, "What can be measured?" In attempting to answer this difficult question he focuses attention on the problems inherent in attempting to measure comprehension abilities. Finally, King discusses the complexities of dealing with some of the problems of test development noted by Lennon. In so doing, she provides insight into the possible avenues that may be followed in the assessment of critical reading.

(68) FUNCTIONAL USE OF STANDARDIZED READING TESTS*

William Q. Davis

It has been established that at least 37 million standardized achievement tests are administered to school-age children every year. (2) This usually involves a consequent commitment by thousands of teachers to administer (and in many cases score!) these tests. Ultimately, each score is recorded into each pupil's cumulative record folder. And there it will probably sit, unused, until the next testing go-round when another batch of test scores will be inserted alongside the previous year's—a mute testimony to each child's having invested yet another hour of classroom time—into a one-way activity: a test about which most pupils will not get any feedback, and rarely any clear explanation of the scores gained.

This afternoon, I would like to discuss some possible uses to which you might consider putting these test results—some practical, fundamental, in some cases well-known, ways in which you might apply standardized test data.

First, like anything you do in the classroom, you must know why the test is being given. You must have something to *evaluate*. You must test for some need—not just because reading tests are always given in May, because June is too hot.

There are two major purposes for evaluation: one is to assess the progress of the total reading program in order to assure that the adopted objectives of the program are being met. A second purpose is, of course, to ascertain the progress of students in reading. To repeat, then: there must be a test purpose; in turn, the purpose for evaluation should be firmly rooted in basic reading program objectives. If program objectives and the methods of evaluation are not in some way closely related, then this whole business of testing is just a big waste of time all around. For example, one broad functional use of a standardized reading test such as the new Gates-MacGinitie Survey D Reading Test might be to evaluate the general reading achievement level, in vocabulary, of a total class

---

*Reprinted from *Methods of Evaluating Reading* 13, Part 4 (1968 Convention Proceedings), in press, by permission of the author and the International Reading Association.

group in terms of national expectations as reflected by the test normative data. Or, the test might be legitimately used to screen each grade for exceptionally low achievement scores. Or, more specifically, a single child might be tested so that his *general* strengths and weaknesses of reading achievement might be estimated.

Everyone must have clearly in mind the objectives of such test results. Evaluation of the reading program (which in effect such test results in sum total many times are) is the process of determining the extent to which objectives sought have been achieved. It is essential that reading teachers and supervisors, working with various school personnel, clearly formulate objectives of the reading program before choosing tools for evaluation purposes. Such objectives should be concerned with the over-all program (for example, "a wholesome attitude toward reading result-ing from a multitude of satisfying experiences with reading") and specific objectives of the program (such as, "the ability to grasp the main idea of a poem").

Any functional use of a test result, then, will depend on these two things: reading program objectives and each test's purpose.

Second, once you know why, how, and when to use the tests, it is equally important that you *use* the results. This is the function of testing!

What, then, are some of the functional uses of test results?

1st, they are commonly used to aid in classroom grouping when initial fall reading instruction is to begin. For those of you who are looking for a sound approach to this particular problem, you might look at the 1968 C.R.A. conference Proceedings where, at Knoxville Dr. Rita Sawyer from Memphis State University presented an excellent approach to grouping by test scores, using an estimated reading capacity score (3). Basically, this approach is based on using a child's potential capacity for growth, rather than his present reading achievement level, to determine his true reading status. Estimated reading ability is calculated by multi-plying the number of years in school times I.Q. plus 1 (1). Let's take Jake, for example, who is in the fifth month of the fifth grade with an I.Q. of 150. Since he has been in school 4½ years, we find that the for-mula (4.5 x 1.50 + 1.0) shows Jake to have an E.R.A. of almost 7.8. As you can see, even though Jake may score 6.0 on a standardized reading survey test, he is actually almost two years retarded in his reading achieve-ment.

2nd, test scores help us to compare groups both locally and nation-wide. In a local school district where several schools are rumored to be less desirable because children's reading achievement levels within these schools generally appear to be lower than those of other schools in the district, a comparison might be made between selected groups from various schools over a few years' span of time. Where significant differences do exist, a closer examination might be in order by curriculum coordinator to try to determine what methods and materials have contributed to such reading success. Similarly, at the secondary level, national comparisons are also desirable where, for example, students competing for college entrance must be able to meet the reading challenge—and this they can do better when they are given some indications of just what present proficiency levels are.

3rd, standardized reading survey test scores help not only to screen but to make tentative semi-diagnostic "guesstimates"—for example, Vicky in the 4th grade who has an average capacity to learn to read, earns a total score on the California Reading Test of 4.0. She has scored as she would be expected to score—on grade level.

However, this does not give much information about Vicky's reading. And the picture changes drastically when further analysis reveals this total grade level score of 4.0 to be comprised of a very high vocabulary score (6.0) balanced by an extremely low comprehension score (2.0). Most manuals accompanying standardized reading tests give considerable help to the teacher in using the test for a diagnosis of the individual's or the group's reading abilities. When studied carefully, such manuals will give hints on the use of scores and their possible classroom applications.

4th, standardized test scores can be diagnostic. A machine score will only yield a total raw score which can be converted in turn to another more meaningful score such as a grade level score, a percentile rank, or a stanine. Machines do not generally yield an error analysis for diagnostic purposes. That is, we are not able to get any feedback as to which elements of comprehension a student is consistently unable to use. We have no idea from this low score in comprehension whether Vicky should have emphasis in any or all of such reading skill areas as paragraph patterns, critical or creative comprehension skills, finding the main idea stated or implied, drawing conclusions, making inferences, and the like. But, if we return to Vicky and handscore her California Reading Test, we can itemize answers omitted or incorrectly answered and, by use of the Diagnostic Analysis of Learning Difficulties, which is printed on the back cover of each test booklet, even more accurately detail her more specific reading needs. There, for example, we find that each question is coded, that each test item was deliberately included to evaluate certain comprehension sub-skill areas. For example, if our fictitious Vicky had correctly answered items 1 and 2 on the California Upper Primary Reading Test, but not items 3 or 4 in the Reference Skill section, we might then speculate that she had some knowledge about Parts of a Book but knew little about the latter area—Use of Dictionary. In this same vein, a survey test can be used to show other testing needs, as, for example, we might wish to use the Durrell Analysis Test selectively to probe certain reading skill areas in more depth.

A fifth use of test scores is to reveal a child's reading level, usually taken to be their "frustration level." One of the weaknesses of standardized test scores is that they are comprised of an undeterminable ratio of reading knowledge and sheer guesses. What is more, this knowledge is of an "aided recall" variety, not pure recall. In general, studies have revealed that, to make a standardized test score realistic in terms of what a child might be able to do on an informal reading inventory, we subtract at least a year from the total score (3). That is, we assume that most children will exert every power, including their powers to guess well, to score as high as possible on every standardized test involving objective items. Obviously, such effort could not be sustained, in a typical reading situation, for any extended period of time without much frustration resulting. The child, then, is generally revealing by his standardized test score, what his frustration level is. He would not normally attempt such difficult reading as he did on the test. If we are to more reasonably estimate at what level he can comfortably read, we would begin by giving him materials to read at a lower level of difficulty; that is, we would place him in reading materials written at a lower grade level where the vocabulary load and sentence arrangement are somewhat less involved.

To return again to Vicky, then, I would probably be more accurate if I said that her total score of 4.0 more realistically reveals a functional reading level of approximately third grade level!

A sixth functional use of standardized reading test scores should be to reveal instructional objectives. For example, a survey test should reveal gross reading strengths and weaknesses, such as general achievement level of comprehension and vocabulary. In general, a teacher should be able to make an initial decision as to which students might need special emphasis on one of these several skill areas.

A seventh use of such test scores should be to guide parents. No parent-teacher conference should be scheduled without the teacher first assembling a file of pertinent samples of the student's work related to reading activities. In addition to anecdotal data and information from the cumulative folder, she must also evaluate recent test results in the light of student performance and ability. A well-explained standardized test rating, backed by samples of classroom work in reading, such as a recently tape-recorded oral reading session, will many times induce a hesitant, somewhat hostile parent, to offer help and encouragement at home.

Another functional use of a standardized test result is to give a student insight—first, that he has a problem, and then more specifically what the nature of his reading problem is. An excellent example of such "self-diagnosis" was given at the 1968 College Reading Association Conference at Knoxville, Tennessee. Wark (4), at the University of Minnesota, has devised, as part of AID (Automated Individual Diagnosis) a self-analysis worksheet. While this example is at the college level, it seems to me that much of what has been done at the University of Minnesota could be converted for use at the upper elementary and secondary levels. Like other test profiles, the student plots his own test profile, using a tape recording that explains what the scores mean, what the tests measure, and in general how to do the profile. The unique part of this, however, is that the *student* uses the profile. Wark provides the rules for making decisions, and the student then decides which area he needs work in, such as spelling, study skills, written comprehension, or vocabulary, and indicates this choice. In a very real sense the student is channelled into a contract situation—a contract which *he* makes with the Reading and Study Skills Center. He then goes through an individualized treatment sequence which is overseen by a trained counselor.

There is more to this, of course, such as provision for personal problems, research, and feedback, and I would encourage you to write to Dr. Wark at the University of Minnesota for a more comprehensive explanation. What I want to do here is point out that what he has done with his test results is two-fold: 1st, he has made the student feel a real need for help; 2nd, he has further involved the student by nudging *him* to select, on the basis of rules he is given, his own particular treatment area.

Finally, I would invite you to begin to look at the functional use of standardized reading test scores in a more innovative way—in a different context, so to speak.

One such approach was used in Herrin, Illinois where, throughout the month of March, I was administering standardized reading tests. Each third and each fifth grade classroom was given five of the more widely used standardized reading survey tests. In all eight schools, the teachers generally experienced a gradual shift in attitude—from one of indifferent cooperation to an attitude of interest and curiosity regarding test content and possible outcomes of the study. A reading specialist in one of the schools picked up this growing interest and very quickly designed an attitudinal study. Following the last test session, all 19 teachers involved in the testing were given a set of directions which, basically, asked each of them to rank each student in their class on the basis of general reading achievement. This was to be done only on the basis of what they, as teachers, had observed by way of reading achievement in their regular classroom situations. Then, they were asked to further refine these rankings by making some judgment as to what each ranked child's achievement level was, in terms of a total grade level score, in years and months.

And, when examined, the rationale for such a follow-up study becomes quite clear. You see, one of the biggest problems in this technological, published and programmed era is to get teachers to continue to exercise and use their own knowledge and experience. But this will not happen with any teacher who basically has a weak self-concept. What we must do, as test users, is not undermine this confidence, by contradiction through isolated test score examples, but support daily classroom "analysis-through-observation," the closest thing yet we have to continuous evaluation.

Obviously, this study provided data that well supported already proven theses concerning the high validity of teacher perception, observation and judgment. The data were valuable, as were the 13 test scores I collected on each child. But the subtle result of the secondary study this teacher thought of on the spur-of-the-moment is far more enlightening perhaps. Here, the teachers were not asked to accept administrative edict concerning perennial spring testing. They were involved, first by indirect exposure, then by invitation to participate in a study of their own where each teacher had to actually look closely at her whole class, and at each student's position within that class. They were asked to grossly evaluate each child's standing within that class, and then to very finely describe, in terms of years and months, each child's grade placement achievement level. All this was done before any reading test scores were released back to the schools.

Action research of this kind will do more, even had it stopped right here, than perhaps a month of exposure to annual reading convocations.

But imagine, after all this, when each teacher receives a copy of the scores from each of the five standardized reading tests and compares it with his estimate of each child's reading performance!

While all the data are not in at this moment, from just "eye-balling" the results so far, I can assure you that the correlation between teacher judgment, and expert opinion as reflected by a widely published standardized test, was high as ever. The end result was increased teacher self-respect—and a consequent greater respect for otherwise nondescript standardized measures of reading achievement. The function of a test result in this case can only be to take the false halo from a published test, since it corresponds well with a teacher's judgment, yet simultaneously increases respect for a published test—simply because in general it will yield an objective result that will be similar to that of a well-informed teacher after months of observation.

CONCLUSION

It has occurred to me that the success of a clinic approach in the remediation of most reading problems may be due to any number of factors such as a 1-to-1 relationship, greater abundance of materials, diversity of method, an environment conducive to learning without routine interruption, and the like. However, perhaps the biggest success factor lies in the diagnosis. Testing is done in depth and the results of all these tests are put to use. They do not sit on a clinical file card, forgotten; they are not closed to the clinician because they are confidential records. What I have tried to point out to you here today is that without additional data, teacher judgment, and just a little teacher intuition and innovation, a test result is just a test result.

I'll leave you with this challenge, then: when all the standardized test results are in next month, what will you do? Breathe a sigh of relief that total pupil absence was less than 1%? Or that grade 3 didn't repeat last year's confusion by attempting to take the sixth grader's test by mistake?

Or does this instead spell the beginning of several months of parent-teacher conferences, inservice workshops, curriculum meditation; a re-examination of remedial reading group selection; and, perhaps a greater burst of enthusiastic effort from the school reading committee because general classroom achievement has risen substantially over the year . . . I challenge you. What will *you* do?

REFERENCES

1. Bond, Guy L., and Tinker, Miles A. *Reading Difficulties: Their Diagnosis and Correction.* New York: Appleton-Century-Crofts, Inc., 1957, 78–80.
2. Hawes, Gene R. *Educational Testing for the Millions—What Tests Really Mean For Your Child.* New York: McGraw-Hill Book Co., 1964, 54–55.
3. Sawyer, Rita. "Classroom Diagnosis," *Proceedings of College Reading Association*, 9 (Fall 1968).
4. Wark, David M. "Automated Self Diagnosis in a College Reading Center," *Proceedings of College Reading Association*, 9 (Fall, 1968).

(69) EVALUATING DIAGNOSTIC READING TESTS*

Priscilla Hayward

INTRODUCTION

Most teachers are familiar with survey reading tests which they regularly administer to the entire class. From such tests they learn where the class as a whole and individual students within the class stand relative to some outside criterion. The outside criterion, a set of norms, is most commonly expressed as percentile ranks or grade-equivalents based on a national sample of pupils who took the same test. In some cases the survey test may provide several subscores, which give the teacher further insight into the class's strengths and weaknesses. For those pupils who score low on the survey test, another instrument is needed to pinpoint with greater precision the nature of the problems that are contributing to the overall low score so that remedial instruction can be appropriately planned and carried forth. The diagnostic reading test is designed to fill this need.

HOW DO SURVEY TESTS DIFFER FROM DIAGNOSTIC TESTS?

For the purpose of this article, a distinction between survey and diagnostic tests was made on the basis of the number of subscores each test yielded. Survey tests may provide only a total score, or they may provide

*Reprinted from *The Reading Teacher* 21 (March 1968), pp. 523–29, by permission of the author and the International Reading Association.

up to three subscores and a composite—for a total of four scores. Typically, the three survey subscores may be vocabulary, word meaning, or word recognition; comprehension or sentence and paragraph meaning; and speed or rate. Some survey tests may tap these skills by requiring the pupil to read words and paragraphs orally, while others may require silent reading of the test content.

Diagnostic tests are usually intended only for those pupils who have been screened first by a survey measure and identified as poor readers. By breaking down reading comprehension into its component skills and measuring each skill separately, the diagnostic test enables the teacher to concentrate remedial efforts on the skills that show greater weakness in a particular child or group of children.

Diagnostic tests may yield four or more subscores. Subscores are not to be confused with item classifications provided by some survey tests. Such item classifications are based on the grouping of test questions which measure a common component. These groupings, when combined with other groups, yield a meaningful total score, but taken by themselves they are too small (frequently being based on only three to ten items) to yield reliable subscores. Reliability is a function, at least partially, of test length and therefore most diagnostic tests having real utility are necessarily time-consuming.

WHAT TYPES OF DIAGNOSTIC READING TESTS ARE AVAILABLE?

Two major types of multi-score reading tests have been identified. In this article the term "diagnostic" has been kept for those tests which yield scores on such reading components as word attack, auditory and visual discrimination, blending, vowel and consonant sounds, reversals, and other objectives usually found in reading instruction emphasizing the acquisition of phonics skills.

The term "work-study" has been applied to a second category of tests. These tests yield scores on such components as skimming ability, use of an index, and ability to read for main ideas or for factual information. The work-study or critical reading tests emphasize the ability to adjust one's reading approach and speed according to the type of material (fiction, science, social studies, index, dictionary, etc.), the length of the material (words, sentences, paragraphs, extended passages, etc.), and the purpose (to get the main idea, retain details, make inferences, etc.).

The sets of skill groups represented by these two types of tests may need to be diagnosed at different periods in the pupil's school career. The teacher in the primary grades may be concerned more with phonics skills which emphasize word recognition and word attack abilities, whereas the teacher of pupils who have already mastered word skills may wish to concentrate on developing critical reading skills of the word-study type.

HOW ARE DIAGNOSTIC TESTS SELECTED?

Three criteria are suggested as guidelines for reviewing diagnostic tests:

1. How does the test measure the component skills, and do the subscores represent meaningful areas for providing remedial instruction?
2. Are the subscore reliabilities sufficiently high (above .90) for individual use?
3. Are the intercorrelations among subtests sufficiently low (below .65) to warrant differential diagnosis?

MEANINGFUL SUBSCORES

The meaningfulness of subscores can only be determined by examining the test content directly. Some subscores, for instance, may be so global in nature that they do not provide much more information than the subscores available from a survey test.

In addition, several publishers may use the same subtest label and yet refer to entirely different abilities. For example, syllabication to some means identifying the precise point at which a word divides itself into syllables, whereas to others it may mean to count the number of syllables or to read aloud a polysyllabic word. Vocabulary may be measured by selecting a word that matches a picture, by selecting a word that fits a definition given orally or in writing, or by placing a word that best fits the context. Paragraph comprehension may be measured with simple factual questions or with complex questions at or above the readability level of the paragraph on which the questions are based. It is therefore wise to look closely at the test and decide what skills the pupil is expected to demonstrate. Furthermore, the teacher will want to determine which components should be diagnosed for children at different reading levels. For some, the phonics skills will be of importance, and for others the word-study skills will be more meaningful in the particular situation.

SUBSCORE RELIABILITY

Reliability of a score indicates the consistency or stability of that score. No test has perfect reliability, since it is only a sample of all possible questions that could be asked. If the test contained a different sample of questions, different results might be obtained. The more questions included, the more likely one can place confidence in the results. Thus, the longer the test or subtest the more likely the reliability is to increase. Higher reliability is required when interpreting subscore patterns of individuals than when dealing with mean differences in a larger group.

As a rule of thumb, a test is expected to yield reliability coefficients in the .80's to be satisfactory for group decisions and in the .90's for individual decisions. If the coefficient is lower, the scores might fluctuate by chance and an observed difference might not be a true difference at all. Diagnostic tests, because they are usually not used with an entire classroom, but are for individualizing instruction for a single pupil, should meet the higher level of reliability in the .90's.

A correlation coefficient may be squared to indicate the percentage of common score variation that exists on the two sets of scores that are correlated, i.e. the scores on two halves of a test, the scores on two alternate forms, etc. Thus, a coefficient of .90 indicates consistent performance in 81 percent of the scores. The percentage of common variance or the consistency with which a test yields reliable scores decreases rapidly as the correlation coefficient decreases.

SUBSCORE INTERCORRELATIONS

It is generally considered that, if scores on the component parts of a test are to be differentially useful, each should possess some unique significance and should be relatively independent of other components.

When the correlation coefficient is used in studying the subscores, it should be low to indicate that the components are independent and unique. The higher the correlation between subscores the more likely it is that they are measuring the same thing. The lower the correlation between subscores the more likely it is that they are measuring different things.

When the subscore intercorrelation coefficient is squared, the percentage of interdependence or shared variance on the two subtests is obtained. On a reading test, it may be expected that vocabulary and comprehension scores will be highly correlated. A hypothetical correlation of .70 indicates that almost half (49 percent) of the correlation may be accounted for by some type of overlapping in what is being measured. The remainder, (51 percent) is unaccounted for and apparently unique to each subtest.

In diagnostic tests, if feasible, more than half of each subscore should be pure and independent of other subscores. If the intercorrelation between two subtests is .65, there is a 45 percent overlap (.65 squared) and 58 percent that does not overlap. A correlation coefficient of .65 or lower is considered a desirable criterion when differential treatment is indicated by subtests supposedly measuring independent skills.

However, in the case of diagnostic tests, which are intended for pupils of low achievement rather than for a larger population of widely varying ability, the desirability of low subscore intercorrelations may be of less importance than the other criteria of meaningful and reliable subscores. Reading abilities of the student population as a whole may be intercorrelated above the .65 level, because good readers are generally good in all reading components and poor readers are generally poor. In diagnostic testing there is less concern with inter-individual differences than with intra-individual differences. Within one individual, one component skill may be mastered well and another not mastered at all. In the individual case, then, the correlation may be negative or low, even though the intercorrelations for a larger population were too high to meet the generally accepted criterion of .65.

WHAT OTHER FACTORS SHOULD BE CONSIDERED IN SELECTING DIAGNOSTIC TESTS?

Other criteria for judging diagnostic tests are the same that apply to all tests, such as ease of administration and scoring, time, cost, and adequacy of interpretative information. Here, the ease of administration and scoring may depend upon the type of school staff that is available. If the school has a psychologist or a reading specialist with clinical training, a test that is difficult to administer may present no obstacles. If classroom teachers are expected to conduct the testing, the tests chosen must necessarily be easier to administer and should yield subscores that lend themselves to direct interpretation in terms of concrete teaching objectives.

WHAT ABOUT NORMS?

Ideally, the publishers of standardized tests describe the norm sample carefully in terms of grade levels, geographic distribution, number of cases, socioeconomic status, community type, and general ability level. If norms are provided with a test, such information should be available. Unfortunately, these criteria are not universally met.

Some diagnostic tests do not provide norms on the premise that remedial efforts should be directed toward all pupils who show less than complete mastery of a component skill. Nevertheless, such tests do provide interpretative information. Instead of norms based on number right, they supply error analysis scores or check-lists. The tests look at the number wrong rather than the number right. These tests then classify errors within meaningful categories. The goal becomes a perfect score or complete mastery rather than obtaining a relative rank. This approach seems justified, although there should be evidence that the component scores are useful and that the test content has been pretested on a sample of students similar to the group for which it is intended.

As mentioned previously, the intra-individual pattern of scores is of prime importance in diagnostic testing. The differences between subscores for a single individual are inspected to find what areas should be stressed in remedial instruction. Since intra-individual profiles do not depend so heavily on outside criteria, there is another reason for accepting tests which lack norms. Here there may be less concern with how the individual pupil deviates from the total population. It is already known that his reading performance is low, and the major concern is with how his own skills deviate among themselves.

DO DIAGNOSTIC TEST RESULTS GIVE THE WHOLE PICTURE?

While diagnostic reading tests may provide clues to the content and level of remedial instruction, the competent reading specialist will take other factors into consideration. Classroom observation of oral and silent reading skills and habits will contribute to a better understanding of each child.

Information from other types of tests may also yield useful data. Specifically, tests of intelligence or scholastic ability, listening comprehension, and arithmetic computation are tools which can play an important part. If the scores on a survey reading test are on a par with those from a test in any one of these areas, the pupil may be reading at his optimum level for the time being. Remedial efforts may help him retain his relative standing. His progress will be slow as his reading component skills (perhaps also on a par with each other) improve at a steady pace.

If, on the other hand, the intelligence, listening, or arithmetic scores are considerably above a reading score, the child may be expected to benefit more quickly from a remedial program designed to correct his deficiencies. The score discrepancy often indicates that the pupil has potential to increase his reading skills to the level indicated by the higher scores on the other test or tests. The usual expectation is that a child who can deal with abstract figures and reasoning problems in an intelligence test, understand the spoken language in a listening test, or manipulate numerical symbols on an arithmetic computation test without word problems, can also handle letter symbols and words in their written form. This expectation is confirmed for the general school population by the high correlation that exists among intelligence, listening, reading, and arithmetic tests. Individual exceptions will, of course, occur. Some diagnostic reading tests include listening measures on the very premise that listening ability serves as a frame of reference with which reading ability can be compared.

This article is intended only as a guide in evaluating diagnostic reading tests. The final judgment must come from the teacher, for only he knows what will work best with his children.

(70) WHAT CAN BE MEASURED?*

Roger T. Lennon

We can look back today upon virtually a half-century of experience in the development of objective, standardized tests of a wide variety of reading skills and abilities. Such tests, numbering well into the hundreds have been making their appearance year after year since about 1910;

*Reprinted from *The Reading Teacher* 15 (March 1962), pp. 326–37, by permission of the author and the International Reading Association.

some have enjoyed decades of apparently satisfactory use, others have lapsed into disuse after relatively brief careers. The period since 1910 has witnessed prodigious research activity in the reading field; for the past several decades, an average of a hundred or more publications per year have swelled the literature devoted to this endlessly fascinating topic. Much of this research literature has been concerned with analysis of reading skills, speculation and experimentation concerning the nature and organization of reading abilities, and development and utilization of appropriate instruments. To undertake even the most cursory review of the reading tests that have appeared, or of the implications of the voluminous research with respect to reading measures, is far too ambitious a task, and yet an answer to the proposed question requires at least passing cognizance of some of the history and research.

THE PROBLEM

What can be measured? An unsuspecting student who sought to answer this question from an examination of test catalogs, or of the instruments which they describe, might say, "We can measure paragraph comprehension, word meaning, word discrimination, word recognition, word analysis skills, ability to draw inferences from what is read, retention of details, ability to locate specific information, rate of reading, speed of comprehension, visual perception of words and letters, ability to determine the intent of a writer, ability to grasp the general idea, ability to deduce the meaning of words from context, ability to read with understanding in the natural sciences, in the social sciences, in the humanities, ability to perceive relationships in written material, ability to sense an author's mood, or intent, ability to appreciate poetry, ability to grasp the organization of ideas, ability to read maps, charts, and tables"—The list may be extended, if not *ad infinitum*, at least *ad* some seventy or eighty alleged reading skills and abilities. And this, mind you, from an inspection only of tests that are labeled as reading tests, without any consideration of other tests which look very much indeed like blood brothers to the reading tests, but which mask their familial ties under such beguiling aliases as tests of "critical thinking," of "educational developments," or even—most artful deceivers of all—as tests of "mental ability," "intelligence," or "scholastic aptitude."

Surely, no reader is so naive as to suppose that there really corresponds a separate, identifiable skill or ability to each of the test names.

What then may we assume we are actually measuring with the scores and scores of differently named tests?

It is one thing—and a necessary thing—to make a careful analysis of reading ability, to spell out its various supposed components in detail, and to prepare extensive lists or charts of the specific skills or abilities to serve as statements of desired goals or outcomes of the reading program. It is quite another thing to demonstrate that these manifold skills or abilities do, in fact, exist as differentiable characteristics of students; and still a third thing to build tests which are in truth measures of one or another of these skills, and not of some more general, pervasive reading ability.

But if the number of abilities or dimensions of reading is not the seventy or eighty indicated, what is it? And how can we tell? Can we reduce this vast complexity to a single, global measure of reading ability, as some have concluded—or three, or five, or ten? Twenty years ago Dr. Arthur Traxler (14) addressing a conference on problems in measurement of reading, adverted to this same issue, and remarked that "What is apparently needed is a mathematical resolution of the difficulty by means of a thorough-going factor analysis of the abilities which enter into silent reading." Even as Dr. Traxler made his plea, such empirical attacks on the problem were under way, and during the decade or so following, there appeared a series of excellent studies of this kind that shed much light on our topic.

REVIEW OF RESEARCH

Traxler himself in 1941 (15) reported an analysis of the Van Wagenen-Dvorak Diagnostic Examination of Silent Reading Abilities, one of the most impressive tests of this kind that had appeared up to that time. He sought to ascertain whether the several parts of the test yielded "measures which are independent enough to warrant their separate measurement and use as a basis for diagnostic and remedial work." Studying the results of these tests for a group of 116 tenth-grade students, Traxler concluded that the "measures of Central Thought, Clearly Stated Details, Interpretation, Integration of Dispersed Ideas, and Ability to Draw Inferences appear to be measuring closely related reading abilities. There is at least reasonable doubt concerning whether or not the separate scores contribute anything greatly different from the reading level score." He found most of the parts so highly correlated that diagnosis based on the scores had little real meaning. In fact, when the intercorrelations were corrected for attenuation, most approached unity.

Even before Traxler's call for research, Gans in a 1940 study (5) had analyzed the relation between a specially built measure of "the critical types of reading required in the selection-rejection of content for use in solving a problem," and a reading composite based upon two stand-ardized reading tests, Thorndike-McCall and Gates Silent Reading, and four sections of the California Test of Mental Maturity. (Worthy of note is the fact that Gans justified the composite as a general measure of reading comprehension on the basis that the intercorrelations among the components approached their respective reliabilities—even though the components were as superficially varied as the Thorndike-McCall score, Gates' scores on Appreciating General Significance, Predicting Outcome, and Noting Details, and California Delayed Recall, Numerical Quantity, Inference, and Vocabulary.) Analysis of the results of a group of 417 intermediate-grade pupils led Gans to conclude that "the abilities [i.e., the reference-reading abilities] are not closely enough related to those in the reading criterion to be measured by tests designed for discovering the criterion abilities," and "the composite which functions in reference reading is made up of a number of variables, with *reading ability*, as measured by the reading criterion one factor, and the selection-rejection pattern another." ". . . another factor operates which possibly includes some function of delayed recall."

A trail-blazing study, and probably still the best known of all the investigations of this type, was that reported by Davis, originally in 1941 (3). Davis sought to identify some of the fundamental factors in reading comprehension and to provide a means of measuring them. On the basis of a comprehensive survey of the literature, he listed nine supposed cate-gories of basic skills of reading comprehension. He proceeded to develop test questions to measure each of these skills, administered the tests to a group of subjects, and computed the intercorrelations among the nine tests. He interpreted a factor analysis of the results as indicating the presence of nine factors, six of them clearly significant. These latter included word knowledge; ability to manipulate ideas and concepts in relation to one another—"reasoning in reading"; ability to grasp the author's expressed ideas; ability to identify the writer's intent or purpose; ability to follow the organization of a passage; and knowledge of literary devices and tech-niques. Of Davis' nine factors, word knowledge accounted for by far the greatest part of the variance, followed by the so-called "reasoning in reading" and the literal meaning factors.

Davis concluded that at least two factors, the word knowledge and the reasoning factor, were measured in his tests with sufficient reliability for practical use, and that adequately reliable measures of three other factors—literal meanings, inference, and ability to follow the organization of a selection—could be developed as a practical matter.

A re-analysis of Davis's data by Thurstone (13), employing a somewhat different factor analysis technique, led Thurstone to conclude that a single factor was sufficient to account for the obtained correlations. The apparent conflict in interpretation reflects different purposes served by the respective types of factor analysis employed in the two investigations. Davis, reacting to Thurstone's re-analysis of his data, continued to maintain that his first six factors, at least, represented significant dimensions of reading comprehension, though admittedly, several of them accounted for very little variance in reading scores (4).

Langsam in 1941 (9) reported a factor analysis of results of six reading tests, yielding fourteen scores, and one intelligence test yielding seven scores. She identified five factors, labeled respectively a *verbal* factor, concerned with word meaning, a *perceptual* factor, a *word* factor denoting fluency in dealing with words, a *seeing relationships* factor, perhaps concerned with logical organization, and a *numerical* factor. The factors were found to overlap to a considerable degree, beclouding their interpretation.

Conant in 1942 (2) undertook to answer the questions: "Is there a general reading comprehension, or does reading proficiency depend upon skills using a number of different reading techniques? If there are different reading abilities, how are they interrelated?" She developed an outline of a test to measure the following skills: (1) Reading to get in detail the pattern of the author's thought, including comprehension of the main points, comprehension of specific facts which support main points, comprehension of cause-and-effect relations, and comprehension of words in context. (2) Ability to interpret and make a critical evaluation of material read, including selection and organization of facts relevant to a more general idea, and ability to draw inferences.

Conant developed tests designed to measure these skills and administered them, together with the Nelson-Denny Reading Test and American Council Psychological Examination. Intercorrelations among all the measures except five were above .50, leading Conant to state that there was no evidence "that students in general employed relatively independent abilities in this study-type reading." She concluded that the results were largely accountable for in terms of a single factor, tentatively defined as general comprehension. Three other factors appeared, but accounted for extremely small parts of the variance. Conant pointed out that her results by no means precluded the possibility that some individuals may show marked differences in their relative abilities to use different reading techniques.

A doctoral dissertation by Artley in 1942 (1) explored the relationship between general comprehension ability, as measured by the Cooperative C-1 Level of Comprehension test, and hypothesized special reading abilities in the social studies area, measured by the Cooperative Tests of Social Studies Ability, Proficiency in the Field of Social Studies, and Survey Tests in the Social Studies, including ability to obtain facts, to organize, to interpret, to generalize, to perceive logical relations and to evaluate arguments. For a group of two hundred eleventh-grade students, Artley found the correlation between the general comprehension measure and the composite of the specific measures to be .79 (.86 corrected for attenuation). He found also that the correlations of the several specific measures with total reading comprehension all fell within a fairly narrow range, from .6 to .8 and he concluded that one could not "dismiss the possibility that there are a great number of pupils who might profit from a specific type of instruction." Artley interpreted his findings as "evidence that there exists a significant degree of specificity in the measures relating to reading comprehension of the social studies."

Hall and Robinson reported in 1945 (6) an attempt to develop independent measures of various aspects of reading. After analyzing the research and the available tests produced up until the time of their study, and concluding that these tests left very much to be desired from the standpoint of diagnostic potentiality, they develop a battery that included twenty-five measures, many of which were tests of reading of non-prose material. Factor analysis of the results of administration of this battery of tests to one hundred college students yielded six factors, which Hall and Robinson defined as "attitude of comprehension accuracy"; an "inductive" factor; a verbal or word meaning factor; a "rate for unrelated facts" factor; a chart-reading factor; and a sixth undefined factor. In other words, six factors, one of which was quite nebulous, were sufficient to account for the variance in the twenty-five separate reading measures.

Harris in a 1948 study (7) identified seven skills or behaviors called for in comprehension of various types of literature, as follows: recognition of synonyms for uncommon words and groups of words; recognition of words or groups of words that are used figuratively; recognition of antecedents of pronouns, of subjects and predicates in loosely organized statements; recognition of summary of ideas expressed or implied; recognition of summaries and characteristics of persons or characters; recognition of author's attitude toward his characters, of his mood or emotion and of his intent; recognition of relationship between technique and meaning.

After administering a battery of tests designed to yield measures on each of these seven skills to two groups of adults, and factor-analyzing the results, Harris concluded that "(1) one and only one ability is common to the comprehension of these literary passages of different types; and (2) that one general factor is adequate to account for the intercorrelations of the seven variables."

Maney and Sochor in 1952 studies (10, 11) sought to develop tests to measure specific factors in comprehension of science and social studies material. Their tests yielded measures of "literal comprehension" and of "critical interpretation" in these two areas. Administering these tests together with the Gates Survey Test and the Pintner General Ability Tests (Verbal Type) to some five hundred fifth-grade pupils, they found correlations from .61 to .67 between the literal and the critical reading scores; from .60 to .76 between these scores and scores on the Gates test; and from .67 to .75 between these scores and scores on the Pintner tests. The "critical" scores correlated slightly lower with the general reading ability or the intelligence test scores than did the "literal" reading scores. Maney and Sochor interpreted the findings as showing considerable independence between literal and critical reading skills, and between the specific abilities required for critical reading and "general" reading comprehension. In other words, they saw a high degree of specificity in the types of processes involved in different reading situations.

Another 1952 study, the doctoral dissertation of Lyman Hunt (8), represents one of the most competent studies in this area. Hunt sought to determine whether the six factors identified by Davis would reappear in an independent investigation, or, more generally, whether reading comprehension is made up of aspects sufficiently specific to be measurable as independent variables. Hunt developed tests to measure each of the six factors, taking great pains to insure that every item included as part of the test for a given factor was judged with very high consistency by competent consultants to be measuring the ability in question. For a group of 585 college students he first compared item-discrimination values for every item with respect to each of the six postulated factors. Despite the fact that the items had been constructed specifically to measure a carefully defined aspect of reading ability, and had been judged by qualified consultants to be measuring that particular ability, Hunt found that in general the items classified in any given area—as, for example, vocabulary items, or items intended to measure reasoning—correlated no higher with the total score on the ability they were supposed to measure than with the score on any of the other abilities. That is to say, there was no evidence in the item-discrimination statistics that the items possessed any differential validity as measures of one aspect of reading comprehension rather than another. Factor analysis of the scores led to the same general conclusion—that, except for the vocabulary test, the other measures "may be measuring much the same function of reading comprehension." Comparing the factor structure revealed in his study with that reported by Davis, Hunt reports emergence of a first factor somewhat resembling Davis' reasoning factor, a second factor similar to Davis' word knowledge factor, though appearing much less important than it did in the Davis study. He found a third factor like Davis' organizing ability, but it accounted for only 8 per cent of the total variance. He also found three other factors, all probably not significant.

A later study by Stoker and Kropp (12) reported a factor analysis of results of Iowa Tests of Educational Development administered in 1959 to a sample of ninth-grade students. Three sub-tests of the Iowa are concerned respectively with ability to interpret reading materials in the social studies, in natural science, and literary materials. Stoker and Kropp found intercorrelations (uncorrected for attenuation) among these three parts from .67 to .76. A first factor, identified by them as "general mental ability," had extremely high loadings on these three sections and on the Verbal section of the Scholastic Aptitude Test; no other factor contributed significantly to the variance on these parts of ITED. They concluded, therefore, that there were no differentiable reading abilities in the three areas, at least as measured by ITED.

Most of the references cited above have to do with the state of affairs that exist at the secondary or college level. We may very well ask whether reading ability has not become so highly organized at this stage that an individual's performance on all kinds of reading tasks is pretty much of a piece, defying diagnosis or differentiation. It is certainly conceivable that at lower grade levels reading ability is much less highly organized than it is at the high school, college, and adult levels. We may readily suppose that in the beginning stages of reading, emphasis is on the perceptual and mechanical aspects of the task to a greater extent than on central thought processes; and that, since the requisite perceptual skills are being acquired at varying rates by children, there may exist among pupils more readily differentiable degrees of proficiency in various components of reading ability. Such a conclusion seems probable, but it should be said, too, that this belief is buttressed by no such amount of experimental data as are available concerning the nature and organization of reading abilities at the higher levels—and, indeed, there is some contrary evidence, as in the intercorrelations among the subtests of the Gates Primary Batteries, or the several reading tests of the Metropolitan Achievement Tests. Virtually all of the tests of lower-level reading abilities that purport to be diagnostic are based upon *a priori* identifications of the various reading skills; and however expert one may consider the analysis and the identification, it nevertheless remains true that we still have little experimental evidence about the reality of the distinctions that are made among the various reading abilities and about the validity of supposed diagnostic profiles of reading skills. In the realm of vocabulary, for example, we have measures that are labeled tests of "word recognition," or of "word discrimination," or of "phonetic analysis skill," all of which characteristically yield quite substantial intercorrelations relative to their reliabilities.

IMPLICATIONS

The studies cited above are not the only ones bearing upon the organization of reading comprehension ability, but together they comprise a representative sample of the research in this area. Even from brief recapitulations, one can sense a lack of consistency in the findings with respect to the generality or specificity of comprehension abilities. What are we to make of it all? Shall we conclude that the reading experts, with their lengthy lists of objectives, of finely differentiated, ever more specific skills, have simply been spinning a fanciful web that bears no relation to the realities of the nature of reading ability? Or shall we charge the test makers with a lack of ingenuity in devising test exercises to provide reliably differentiable measures of the several skills, with a failure to provide instruments that will match in their comprehensiveness and sensitivity the goals elaborated by the reading experts? The truth, it seems to me, is to be found between the two extremes. The following discussion is an attempt to make sense of the research findings, and to suggest their implications for the question, "What can be measured in reading?"

One generalization seems to emerge with very considerable support. With distressing sameness, or with gratifying consistency, depending upon one's point of view, the studies agree that most of the measurable variance in tests of reading competence, however varied the tests entering into the determination, can be accounted for in terms of a fairly small number of factors, certainly not more than six being required to account for better than 90 per cent of the variance. One investigator after another has launched his battery of tests, with all segments neatly labeled, carefully segregated and packaged in separate if not watertight compartments, only to have the vessels founder on the shoals of hard data, with the cargo jumbled together in a single heap, or in a few mixed-up collections. It seems entirely clear that numerous superficially discrete reading skills to which separate names or titles have been attached are, in fact, so closely related, as far as any test results reveal, that we must consider them virtually identical.

It would seem that we may recognize and hope to measure reliably the following components of reading ability: (1) a general verbal factor, (2) comprehension of explicitly stated material, (3) comprehension of implicit or latent meaning, and (4) an element that might be termed "appreciation."

The "verbal factor" in this context is intended to connote word knowledge: breadth, depth, and scope of vocabulary. Every investigation shows vocabulary to be substantially related to other measures of reading ability. Extensive word mastery, or fluency in handling words, is almost a prerequisite to attainment of high competence in any type of reading skill. We are well equipped for reliable measurement of this factor at virtually every level.

Under "comprehension of explicitly stated material" is included such skills as the location of specifically stated information, comprehension of the literal meaning of what is written, and ability to follow specific directions set forth in what is read. Many reading tests are available that measure these skills acceptably; probably the most widely used tests measure this type of reading ability to a greater extent than any other.

The third component, "comprehension of implicit meanings," embraces all of those outcomes that we tend to label as "reasoning in reading." Included here would be the ability to draw inferences from what is read; to predict outcomes; to derive the meaning of words from context; to perceive the structure of what is read—the main idea or central thought, and the hierarchical arrangement of ideas within a selection; to interpret what is read, as manifested either by applying the information to the solution of a problem or by deriving some generalizations or principles from it; in a word, all those abilities that demand active, productive, intellectual response and activity on the part of the reader. The research, in my opinion, does support the belief that this type of reading ability can be differentiated from the ability to comprehend what is explicitly stated, though we should always expect to find the two correlated because the ability to get at the implicit meaning of what is read presupposes the ability to understand the explicit or literal meaning.

Test makers have been, and are, devoting more effort to the measurement of the inferential, interpretive abilities, and such abilities are well represented in the reading tests produced in recent years. It is perhaps not inappropriate to comment in passing on what seems to be a false issue that has sometimes been raised by those who object that reading tests which stress this factor are too much like intelligence tests. My view is that the intellectual operations or processes that it is common now to include in the notion of reading as a thinking process are indistinguishable from at least some of the operations and processes that we define as comprising "intelligence." In other words, it is inconceivable that a good test of reading as reasoning should not also be a valid measure of some aspects of the complex we term intelligence.

Finally, we have the factor termed "appreciation." By this is meant such things as sensing the intent or purpose of an author, judging the mood or tone of a selection, perceiving the literary devices by which the author accomplishes his purposes, etc. Existence of these types of outcome as distinct from the ones enumerated above seems less clearly established by the research findings, but here some of the blame may perhaps be laid at the feet of the test makers, who have, by and large, been less concerned with the development of suitable instruments in this area than in the three general areas suggested above. We may reasonably hope that more satisfactory measures of outcomes of this kind will be produced.

SPEED

Thus far the measurement of our old friend, rate or speed, has been neglected. That speed of reading is an important and desired outcome of reading instruction goes without saying. Evidence concerning the extent to which a pupil is improving in rate of reading is highly desirable in any evaluation of a reading program. Our assessment of rate, however, leaves much to be desired, though paradoxically enough, we are better off today because we have a keener appreciation of the limitations of our speed measures than we were twenty-five or thirty years ago, when it was not uncommon to encounter the belief that measurement of rate was a fairly simple, straightforward operation.

Our problems in the measurement of rate stem from the fact that we are never really concerned with pure speed—that is, with just the rapidity with which the subject can move over a given number of words or lines of written material. Rate is only meaningful as it defines the rapidity with which the reader covers material at a particular level of comprehension. We are all now well aware that an individual's rate is a function of the level of difficulty of the material being read; and some would say also of the type of material, though the experimental data on this question are inconsistent. Indeed, this ability to change rate of reading is accepted as one of the desired outcomes of reading instruction; we want the student to adapt his reading to the demands of the particular material, to move as rapidly or as slowly as the requirements of the material and his own purposes in reading dictate. The question of the relation of speed and comprehension is a perplexing one, to which the experimental data give no single clear-cut answer.

We are troubled also in the measurement of rate by the fact that the test situation poses quite a different motivation for the reader than does the normal, unsupervised reading situation. Unfortunately, from the standpoint of validity the difference between the test situation and the normal reading situation, as far as motivating property is concerned, varies from one subject to another, and our interpretation of rate of reading scores derived in test situations must, therefore, always be subject to some reservation—at least in the case of rate measures obtained when the subject is aware that his speed of reading is being appraised.

Nevertheless, our measures of rate are not without usefulness. For the estimation of change or development, rate measures derived from the same test are quite serviceable. Research, moreover, suggests that while rate measures are not perfectly correlated by any means, there is an appreciable community among the various measures. We thus may identify with a good deal of confidence those readers who are excessively slow; and this is perhaps the most important use of rate measures.

CONCLUSION

As important as what *can* be measured in reading, perhaps, is what *cannot*. There remains the uneasy feeling that no matter how excellent our measure of comprehension, whether of explicit or latent meanings, no matter how clever our techniques for assessing "critical" reading skills may become, our evaluation still leaves much to be desired. Whence this dissatisfaction? Is it sensible to anticipate that we can develop wholly adequate objective measures for "reading ability"? Consider what reading is, or should be. Not only do we read what we read; in the layman's peculiarly apt term, we read *into* what we read—that is, we read something of ourselves into the written word. We bring to bear on the material we are reading our total experience, background, interests, understandings, purposes, and so on. The response that each person makes to a given piece of reading matter, therefore, is necessarily and desirably a unique, personal kind of response. When we set before a student an exercise in arithmetic, or a word to be spelled, or a problem in algebra, there is only one response that is desired and that is to be considered correct. When we are concerned with appraisal of a person's ability to read insightfully and meaningfully, we almost assume that there will be many different but equally acceptable responses to the stimulus material. Under these circumstances it looms as a very difficult task to conceive a completely objective test that will permit us to assess the quality or richness or correctness of each person's interpretation of a given selection.

"Reading," in the words of Francis Bacon, "maketh the full man"— and this neatly epitomizes the goal of reading instruction. It is important for people to learn to read because reading can enrich their lives so enormously. We want people to be able to read the sign that says "Stop," so that they will not endanger themselves and others at crossings. We want people to be able to read the directions, simple or complicated, that enable them to comply and cooperate with the practices necessary for getting along with others. We want them to read because in no other manner can they so readily share in the experiences of the rest of mankind that will inform and ennoble them. For these purposes, surely *what* a person reads is as important as how well he reads it; but I am afraid that we have no measures of the wisdom with which persons make their choices of reading matter, nor have we any measures of the extent to which they profit from their reading in the manner suggested above; and I for one am dubious that we shall ever have such measures.

Like many other students who have considered reading tests, I have suggested that the labels on the tests are perhaps poor indicators of the jobs the tests actually perform. I am less dismayed by this fact than some critics have been, for I feel that it does not preclude the possibility of considerable usefulness and value in these measures. Insofar as uncritical acceptance of test names as representative of their contents leads to erroneous descriptions and improper diagnosis, such names are, of course, harmful. But, in a fortunate way, the very difficulty that surrounds our efforts to develop differentiating measures of various reading skills becomes our salvation in the instructional program. If these abilities are substantially related and overlap to the extent that the various studies make it appear, then it is entirely likely that efforts devoted to improving one or another of the types of skill will carry over to improvements in the other types of skill. There is nothing in the research reports which would lead us to believe that it is fruitless to attempt to set up varied types of goals or outcomes, to prepare exercises calculated to develop power in these several skills, and even to use these analyses as bases for developing tests. Indeed, in no other way can we sensibly plan or conduct the instructional program.

References

1. Artley, A. S. "A Study of Certain Relationships Existing between General Comprehension and Reading Comprehension in a Specific Subject Matter Area." Unpublished doctoral dissertation, The Pennsylvania State College, 1942; and in *Journal of Educational Research*, 37 (1944), 464–473.

2. Conant, Margaret M. *The Construction of a Diagnostic Reading Test.* New York: Teachers College, Columbia University. Contributions to Education No. 861 (1942).

3. Davis, Frederick B. "Fundamental Factors of Comprehension in Reading." Unpublished doctoral dissertation, Graduate School of Education, Harvard University, 1941; and in *Psychometrika* 9 (1944), 185–197.

4. Davis, Frederick B. "A Brief Comment on Thurstone's Note on a Reanalysis of Davis' Reading Tests." *Psychometrika*, 11 (1946), 249–255.

5. Gans, Roma A. *A Study of Critical Reading Comprehension in the Intermediate Grades.* New York: Teachers College, Columbia University. Contribution to Education No. 811 (1940).

6. Hall, W. E., and Robinson, F. P. "An Analytical Approach to the Study of Reading Skills." *Journal of Educational Psychology*, 36 (1945), 429–442.

7. Harris, C. W. "Measurement of Comprehension of Literature: II Studies of Measures of Comprehension." *School Review*, 56 (1948), 332–342.

8. Hunt, Lyman C. "A Further Study of Certain Factors Associated with Reading Comprehension." Unpublished doctoral dissertation, School of Education, Syracuse University, 1952.

9. Langsam, Rosalind. "A Factorial Analysis of Reading Ability." Unpublished doctoral dissertation, New York University, 1941. Abstract in *Journal of Experimental Education*, 10 (1941), 57–63.

10. Maney, Ethel Swain. "Literal and Critical Reading in Science." Unpublished doctoral dissertation, Temple University, 1952.

11. Sochor, E. Elona. "Literal and Critical Reading in Social Studies." Unpublished doctoral dissertation, Temple University, 1952.

12. Stoker, Howard W., and Kropp, Russell P. "The Predictive Validities and Factorial Content of the Florida State-Wide Ninth-Grade Testing Program Battery." *Florida Journal of Educational Research*, 1960, 105–114.

13. Thurstone, L. L. "Note on a Reanalysis of Davis' Reading Tests." *Psychometrika*, 11 (1946), 185–188.

14. Traxler, Arthur E. "Problems of Measurement in Reading." *Proceedings of the 1941 Invitational Conference on Testing Problems* (mimeo.). American Council on Education, pp. 65–73.

15. Traxler, Arthur E. "A Study of the Van Wagenen-Dvorak Diagnostic Examination of Silent Reading Abilities." *Educational Records Bulletin* No. 31. New York: Educational Records Bureau, January, 1941. Pp. 33–41.

(71) NEW DEVELOPMENTS IN THE EVALUATION OF CRITICAL READING*

Martha L. King

Developing a nation of critical readers appears to be an educational aim more lauded than comprehended, more sought-after than accomplished. For despite the improvement in general literacy statistics of the nation, teachers and other thoughtful citizens are showing increasing alarm over the inability of Americans to read critically. Much has been written about the probable causes of this special reading deficiency. Vague and ambiguous concepts of the nature of critical reading, inadequate definition of the specific skills involved, insufficient instructional materials and techniques, and the limited abilities of teachers to instruct pupils in these higher level reading skills are commonly identified as inhibiting factors.

*Reprinted from *Forging Ahead in Reading* 12, Part I, (1967 Convention Proceedings), pp. 179–85, by permission of the author and the International Reading Association.

A fifth deterrent has undoubtedly been the lack of procedures and instruments to use in evaluating the achievement of pupils in this area.

Teachers tend to teach best those subjects and skills that are regularly and directly evaluated in the schools' organized testing programs. In reading this means, then, that word recognition skills, literal comprehension skills, knowledge of vocabulary, and some interpretation and study skills are the facets of reading best taught because these are the skills that are covered in the standardized tests most frequently used in elementary schools. Only rarely do such tests include items that require pupils to identify the author's opinion, detect hidden meanings, interpret figurative language or tone, or make generalizations from the facts given. Items which require the examinee to identify omission of important facts, irrelevant data, discrepancies in information, inappropriate analogies, and persuasive use of words are completely missing from elementary school reading tests. Yet, through newspapers, magazines, and television, youngsters daily confront reading materials in which such reading skills are needed.

It is the purpose of this paper to describe two types of evaluation instruments that were developed at Ohio State University as a necessary part of a research study of the feasibility of teaching critical reading at the elementary school level. When the researchers began designing procedures for teaching critical reading skills to pupils in grades one through six, it soon became apparent that new instruments for measuring effectiveness of instruction were needed. Recognizing that critical reading is a complex dynamic process involving various types of thinking, two very different kinds of evaluation instruments were devised. One was a battery of three tests, which were constructed for grades one through six, to measure the growth in achievement of the identified critical reading skills. The second technique was developed to measure the quality and kind of thinking that occurred when children were engaged in critical reading and discussion activities in the classroom. This second instrument also enabled the teacher to assess to a limited degree the effectiveness of her verbal behavior in stimulating the critical reading-thinking habits of her pupils.

DEVELOPING A TEST OF CRITICAL READING

Developing a test of critical reading skills for elementary school pupils was an arduous task because the skills of critical reading had not been identified and precisely clarified. Moreover, finding reading matter or writing new materials that would test critical reading ability and still be within the readability competence of the examinees was extremely difficult. The first step in test construction was that of clarifying that aspect of reading ability commonly referred to as critical reading. What knowledge and skills were essential for the critical reader? From a search of the literature a long list of reading skills, thought to be basic to critical reading, was compiled. This list was sent for validation to a panel of reading experts across the nation. They were asked to critically analyze the list, to rate the importance of each skill, to suggest other skills that should be added, and to indicate those that should be omitted. The revised group of critical reading skills was further validated by classroom observations of critical reading lessons, in which the completeness of the list of skills was checked. Despite the care that was used in developing the list of skills, duplication and overlapping were evident in the resulting list. Some skills, moreover, were very similar; others were quite distinct. To assure both balance and preciseness in the definition, the skills were categorized into three major groups. All of the items that concerned the validity (reasonableness) and reliability (trustworthiness) of reading materials were classified as *logic* skills. Included were drawing conclusions from stated premises, identifying unstated premises, identifying fallacies in reasoning, and recognizing persuasive devices in writing. The language skills were classified either under logic or the second major classification, *literary analysis* skills. Skills that involved recognizing and judging persuasive use of words, vague and imprecise words, and the multiple meanings conveyed by a single word were included with the logic skills. The literary analysis category contained such language-related skills as interpreting and evaluating metaphor, symbolism, personification, alliteration, and authentic speech. Other skills included under literary analysis were related to identification, analysis, and evaluation of 1) forms of writing; 2) the components of literature such as characterization, plot structure, setting, and theme; and 3) the literary devices that make up the author's style.

Those skills that involved going beyond a single piece of writing and comparing or evaluating it according to external factors were designated *general skills*. This group consisted of such abilities as identifying, comparing, and evaluating sources; judging the author's viewpoint and competence; determining the publisher's (or sponsor's) commitments; and comparing multiple sources in order to verify information.

CONSTRUCTING TEST ITEMS

Critical reading *ability* results from the readers not only knowing about and identifying such features of writing as logical fallacies, literary form, or the point-of-view of the author but also from their skill in analyzing, comparing, and judging various aspects of the written material. Constructing a useful evaluation instrument, then, called for devising test items that required the reader not only *to recognize* faulty reasoning, discrepant information, and elements of the author's style but also *to judge* the trustworthiness, truthfulness, and quality of materials. An example of a question which requires the reader *to recognize* and judge a statement—in this case a false analogy—is the following:

> A boy is like a tree. He must stand straight and tall.
> What is wrong with these sentences?
> 1. Trees are always straight, but boys are not.
> 2. Trees are always straighter than boys.
> 3. Boys are not as tall as trees.
> 4. Boys are not like trees in most ways.

The next question expects the reader to *analyze* statements and *apply* knowledge to reach a valid conclusion from a series of statements:

> Anyone who is on a TV show is rich. Captain Kangaroo is on a TV show.
> If the above statements are true, what else must be true?
> 1. Captain Kangaroo is rich.
> 2. People who are not on a TV show are poor.
> 3. Captain Kangaroo may be rich.
> 4. Anyone on a TV show may be rich.

In the example that follows the children are expected to make a *judgment* about the kind of question John's mother asked:

> John told his mother about his new friend, Bill. His mother said, "Is your friend a good boy or a bad boy?"
> What is wrong with this question?
> 1. Bill may be good one time and not so good at another time.
> 2. Bill might be better than John.

3. John's mother knew Bill was a good boy.
4. Bill was John's friend, so he was good.

Other questions in the test asked the examinee to compare two sources for likenesses and differences in content, form, author's purpose, and facts provided. The following illustrations from the primary form of the test show that students also were expected to go beyond the text provided in making judgments about the material.

LET'S READ ABOUT SEA SHELLS

What are sea shells? Sea shells are the hard coverings of many kinds of sea animals that belong to the mollusk family. Mollusks are animals with soft bodies. They are animals without backbones. The shell is the house that the mollusk lives in. There are many things that you can learn by looking at sea shells. One sea animal, the nautilus, grows a new room each time he gets bigger. When he adds a new room, he closes up the old one. Some shells have 30 rooms in them.

HOUSES FROM THE SEA

My sister and I walked along the beach with our empty pails. The ocean waves rolled in and out. The waves surprised us by leaving many shells lying on the wet sand. Many of the shells reminded us of butterflies, angel wings, Chinese hats, staircases, fans, tops, castles, and boats. We filled our pails with all kinds of shells. We found one large beautiful shell. When we held it up to our ears, we could hear the sound of the ocean. We want our friends to see our shells. We will tell you the funny names we made up.

Pretend you want to share a shell collection with your class. Which story would you read to find out more about sea shells?
1. The first story because it tells more about the sea shells.
2. The second story because there are funny names we can use.
3. The first story because mollusks are funny animals.
4. The second story because it talks about the ocean waves.
In what way do you think the two stories are different?
1. One is about a girl and a boy, and one is about backbones.
2. One is about a family, and one is about a house.
3. One has information about sea shells, and one is a story about collecting shells.
4. One has facts about angel wings, butterflies, Chinese hats, fans, and castles; and the other story has facts about houses.
What should the person who wrote the *first story* have done?
1. Gone deep sea fishing.

2. Studied about sea animals.
3. Studied about the nautilus.
4. Made a collection of sea shells.

Due to the practical necessity of constructing a testing instrument that could be administered to elementary school pupils within reasonable time limits, only a sampling of the extensive lists of critical reading abilities could be included. Selection of items for the initial forms of the tests was based upon criteria of appropriateness for the grade levels tested and the uniqueness of the skill. For example, if two abilities were judged to be very similar, such as recognizing the propaganda devices of namecalling and plain folk technique, only one item was included. Parallel items were written for each of the skills selected for both primary and intermediate grades. These were then organized into four trial forms of the test—two for pupils in grades one through three, and two for pupils in grades four through six. The tests were then administered to a population of 3,017 pupils in ten elementary schools in a four-state area. Results of this administration furnished data for both item analysis and coefficients of reliability of the two forms at each grade level. Following the item analysis, final forms of the primary test and intermediate test were constructed on the basis of two additional criteria: the discriminating power and the difficulty of the test items. The reliability of coefficients for the two trial forms ranged from .72 to .86 for the different grade levels. Although these were not exceptionally high, they were considered adequate for the purpose of this test, which was to assess growth of pupils in specific skills.

NORMING THE FINAL FORMS

Three forms of the Critical Reading Test were finally constructed. There were two primary forms, which differed primarily in the readability of the items, and one intermediate form. Both of the primary forms contained 10 questions pertaining to "general" skills category; 17 questions in the *logic* classification, which included propaganda devices and semantics questions; and 15 in the *literary analysis* category, which included literary form, plot structure, theme, characterization, and literary devices. The intermediate test was longer than the primary and was divided as follows: 15 items tested the general skills of comparing sources, determining author's competence and purpose, and selecting relevant sources; 21 questions were focused on logic skills; and 18 items pertained to literary analysis. The revised tests were administered to a second national sample for purposes of norming. Forty-six school systems in eight states in four geographical regions provided norming data from 3,527 pupils. Detailed data pertaining to grade level norms, coefficients of reliability of the final forms, and factor analysis are not given here but are available in a paper written by Bernice Ellinger (2).

HOW ADEQUATE IS THE TEST?

Comparison of the mean scores across grade levels shows that the level 2 primary test was very difficult for grade two in both spring and fall administrations and that the intermediate test was difficult for fourth graders in the fall testing, especially. Further investigation will show whether the forms of the test should be further revised for readability or moved up one grade level each.

The main criterion for judging the adequacy of a test is the degree to which it measures what it professes to measure. The skills that are included in the Ohio State Critical Reading Test were submitted to a group of recognized reading authorities for validation before items were written. In other words, the skills included in the test were judged by these authorities to be essential to critical reading. How successful the item writers were in devising questions that actually test the skills identified is yet to be determined. Factor analysis of the test, which is still in progress, will provide better data regarding the internal validity of the instruments.

Ralph Tyler has said that evaluation of learning should be considered a dynamic process that continues to change according to changing educational concepts, conditions, and purposes of evaluation. The developers of this test of critical reading view it as an embryonic effort that will change and improve as it continues to be used, researched, and revised.

CLASSROOM OBSERVATIONS AS AN EVALUATIVE TECHNIQUE

Paper and pencil tests provide one kind of evaluation data about pupils— that is, an indication of their level of accomplishment in selected skills or learning tasks at a given time. Such instruments do not provide appraisal data about the learning conditions that foster a specific type of behavior, nor do they furnish information about the thinking processes that pupils use as they are engaged in such cognitive tasks as critical reading.

Inasmuch as critical reading is a thinking act in response to written communication, it is highly important that teachers have tools for analyzing and evaluating children's thinking processes as revealed, not only by written responses, but by verbal responses, also. Research in the areas of teacher behavior and children's thinking has emphasized the importance of the teacher's language in fostering intellectual growth in children. From her studies of teaching strategies and the development of cognitive processes, Taba concluded that a teacher's questions play a crucial role in the development of pupil's thinking skills because her questions circumscribe the mental operations which pupils can perform and determine which modes of thought they learn (3).

It follows reasonably, then, that evaluation procedures, designed to give the teacher feedback about the kind and quality of thinking that was observable in the verbal interaction between herself and the students, should provide clues to ways of improving the instructional process. Such evaluation techniques should not only reveal the pupil's growth but should furnish data about the effectiveness of the teacher's language.

The second type of evaluation instrument that was developed and used in the Ohio State University Research Study of Children's Critical Reading was an observation scale. This tool enabled the researchers to analyze the relationship between the teacher's verbalizations and the pupils' responses and to assess the changes (or improvements) in both teacher and pupil utterances that occurred during the eight months of study. To fulfill the purposes of the research study an observation instrument, which would permit the classification of both qualitative and quantitative verbal behaviors, was devised. The scale consisted of two related category systems: one for recording the teachers' utterances and the other for noting the pupils' responses. The eight categories for classifying the teachers' talk show some influence of Bloom's *Taxonomy* (1); the definitions of the terms, however, have been altered and limited as is shown in the following definitions:

Specific facts: All talk that is intended to bring specific information to the learners.

Clarifying: Statements or questions used to refine previously discussed ideas or those misinterpreted by individuals; included are definitions, illustrations, rephrasing, or emphasis on a prior point.

Interpreting or Inferring: Providing meanings that go beyond the literal ones given in the written material. Included are the possible meanings which the reader associates with the text and his interpretation of the author's hidden meanings.

Analyzing: The statements or questions that require an identification and examination of component parts of a piece of writing, a situation, or a phrase; the nature of the relationship of the parts; and the internal consistency of the whole piece.

Applying: The statements or questions that require a direct application of information or criteria to another situation or piece of information.

Summarizing: A synthesis of preceding information and ideas, often showing relationship between parts, is the object of such questions and statements.

Evaluation: Statements or questions in which a judgment based upon criteria is made or expected. Both personal values and public criteria are bases for making judgments.

The main criterion for determining the five pupil categories was the differentiation of levels of thinking that were observable in their responses. Here the mental operations as identified by Guilford in the structure of the intellect proved useful in defining the separate types of thinking. The five different types of thinking—cognition, memory, convergent and divergent production, and evaluation—were arranged in a continuum horizontally across the top of the observation scale. *Cognition and memory*, which were grouped together and defined as literally understanding and relating what had been read or previously stated, were classified as level 2; *convergent responses*, those that indicated interpretation, illustrations, or reorganization of the content, were designated as level 3; *divergent responses*, those that revealed theorizing, hypothesizing, or making new and unique applications of information and ideas, were classified at level 4. Level 5 was reserved for responses that showed that pupils had made an *evaluative judgment* based upon personal or public criteria. Responses were classified at level 1 when there was evidence of guessing or random thoughts. Both level 3 and 4 responses were considered essential prerequisites to critical reading, but level 5 responses were judged to be the most desirable because of the evaluative nature of critical reading.

During the experimental year of the critical reading research study, 24 classroom teachers, four at each of the first six grade levels, were regularly observed while teaching reading. One half of the teachers (the experimental group) were given special materials and instruction in critical reading while the remaining twelve (the control group) had no special instruction in critical reading but were provided an equal amount of instruction and materials in selected areas of children's literature.

The purpose of the observations was to collect data pertaining to the similarities and differences in the verbal behavior of both teachers and pupils in the two groups and to ascertain what kinds of changes, if any, occurred during the time of the study. Each teacher was observed six times, providing a total of 144 observations for analysis. Two trained observers at each session made on-the-spot categorization of the teachers' statements or questions and the pupils' responses. Teachers' statements and questions were classified according to the seven types designated above. Pupils' responses were recorded in the same horizontal rows as the preceding statement or question made by the teacher; the responses, however, were classified within the rows according to the level of thinking exhibited. The observation instrument provided a graphic representation of the type of utterances the teacher made, the quality of responses given by the pupils, and the reciprocal relationship between the two.

The analysis of the 144 observations produced some ints ng and encouraging data, which have implications for the ׳s ition of critical reading. First of all, the study revealed that t groups of teachers improved their questioning behavior. They dec their use of specific fact questions and increased their use of e thought-stimulating questions. Experimental teachers changed i direction of asking more interpreting, analyzing, and evaluating ions; control teachers moved toward asking more applying qu . Apparently, knowing how to ask different kinds of questions rious purposes leads to greater improvement than does intuition ire. The control teachers wanted to teach increasingly better lessons did improve; the experimental teachers who had some training he art of asking questions asked significantly more questions, however, that demanded analytical and evaluative responses.

The findings further revealed a significant relationship between the teachers' questions and the intellectual effort exhibited in the pupils' responses. Those teachers who asked more interpreting, analyzing, and evaluating questions elicited from their pupils higher levels of thinking which could be classified as inferring, illustrating, hypothesizing, theorizing, and evaluating. Improvement in pupils' ability to engage in higher levels of thinking was noted during the time of the study, also. The experimental pupils, especially, were observed to give significantly more responses at the highest evaluative level. It appears that pupils may become increasingly aware of the goals of reading instruction through the questions the teacher asks; and that when they clearly understand the expectation to think more deeply or in a variety of ways, they are motivated to meet the expectation.

The observation procedures just described involved several outside observers because they were used to collect research data; the techniques, however, are adaptable to regular classroom situations. By recording reading instructional sessions on audio or video tape, the individual teacher can replay, listen to the recordings, and analyze the verbal exchange between herself and the children. If she samples instructional sessions regularly over a period of time, the teacher will be able to evaluate changes in her language and that of the children. One first grade teacher who regularly sampled the discussion in one reading group for a period of two months observed that when she asked better questions, the children responded with more independent and thoughtful contributions. She noted further that the parroting of answers, which was common among the first graders, decreased; children who seldom spoke at the beginning of the observations made worthwhile contributions after six weeks; children increased the length and number of sentences used; and pupils moved in the direction of responding to one another rather than to the teacher. Also, growth of individual pupils in analyzing, comparing, and evaluating reading materials was revealed through the comparison of recordings. After listening to more than a dozen tapes, this teacher concluded that the pupils became more highly motivated and interested in reading when they were challenged to interpret, apply, and evaluate and that success in these thinking processes brought the children more satisfaction and confidence in their reading.

Experimentations with two procedures in the evaluation of critical reading have been described. Although different, both of the two devices will provide the teacher with feedback essential to the improvement of the teaching learning environment. Together, the two instruments measure both knowledge and process objectives of critical reading.

References

1. Bloom, Benjamin, *et al. Taxonomy of Educational Objectives: Cognitive Domain.* New York: David McKay (Longmans, Green), 1954.
2. Ellinger, Bernice. "Development and Refinement of a Test of Critical Reading Ability of Elementary School Children," Occasional Paper 67–102. Columbus Ohio: Ohio State University, School of Education, 1967.
3. Taba, Hilda; Samuel Levine; and Freeman F. Elzey. *Thinking in Elementary School Children*, Cooperative Research Project No. 1574 (Mimeographed). San Francisco, California; San Francisco State College, 1964.

INDEX

Able readers, 23–24, 56, 174, 454, 485, 498

Accent generalizations, 217–225

Achievement, 12, 24, 27–35, 329–334, 397, 480, 509, 545–552

Affective dimensions of reading, 7, 30, 32–33, 283, 284–285, 302, 303–310, 424 (*see also* Attitudes, Curiosity, Interests, Literary appreciation, Problem solving)

Attitudes, 11, 269, 486, 509

Auditory discrimination, 9, 11, 125, 325–326, 331, 416, 417, 507, 514, 538

Automation (*see* Teaching machines)

Basal reading instruction, 97, 118, 132–136, 346, 368, 531

Beginning reading, 52, 73, 74, 135, 320, 337, 343, 346, 351–352, 361–368

Beginning reading, approaches to instruction:
computer instruction, 405–407
eclectic, 48, 50, 413–420
individualized reading, 368–372
Joplin plan, 489–490

language experience, 361–368, 419

linguistic, 52–61, 372–382, 419

machines, 94, 405–407, 419, 498

phonics, 383–399, 400–413, 419

programed reading, 400–403, 404, 407–410

talking typewriter, 403–404

Beginning reading problems, 113–118

Behavioral factors, 7, 15–24, 37–40, 75, 269

Behavioral values from reading, 303–310 (*see also* Affective dimensions of reading)

Books:
children's, sources of, 176–180
created by children, 120, 122–123, 140, 362, 363, 364
reports, 278–279
selection, 97, 130, 139, 149–153, 176–180, 288–289, 290, 292–297, 301, 366, 367, 370
sources of, 121, 131, 139, 140, 149

Case study approach, 6, 17, 23, 25–26, 333

Clinics 91–92, 114, 115

Cognition, 29–30, 33, 229–230, 231

Comprehension, 7, 11, 12, 16, 71, 72, 93, 105–106, 184–187,

Comprehension (*cont.*)
227–235, 264–274, 344–345,
450, 457, 460, 562, 563
(*see also* Teacher questioning,
Word comprehension)
extending, 130, 193, 242–251,
251–258, 258–264, 450
skills, 9, 12, 39, 130, 264–274,
430, 436, 500, 501, 507, 567
(*see also* Critical reading
skills, Language arts skills)
Concepts, 8, 15, 187–197, 345, 506
(*see also* Conceptualization,
Thinking)
defined, 188
formation of, 189–191
research on, 187–197
Conceptualization, 11, 14–15, 17, 25,
33, 71–72, 73, 79, 189–197,
307, 419
Content areas (*see* Subject areas)
Context clues, 7, 21, 39, 93, 186,
189, 191, 197–207, 398, 436
(*see also* Language analysis
skills)
Controversial issues in reading, 11,
36–37, 86, 160, 316, 339,
383–385, 397
Corrective procedures, 11, 86–94,
94–100, 101–107, 108–113,
113–118, 118–127, 149–150,
390, 498, 501
Corrective reading in the classroom,
118–127
Corrective reading methods:
blind writing, 126–127
child's own book, 122–123
color cues, 124–125
kinesthetic, 125–126, 416, 417
labeling, 119–120
phonics, 123–124
vocabulary control, 120–122
Creativity, 120, 122–123, 131, 140,
278, 362, 363, 364, 370

Critical reading, evaluation of,
572–583
Critical reading skills:
general, 152, 153, 256, 258–264,
268–269, 270–271, 430, 436,
501, 553, 574, 576, 579, 580
literary analysis, 20–24, 39, 245,
270–271, 279, 294, 438, 573,
574, 577, 580
logical, 7, 193, 281, 573, 574, 575,
577, 580
Cultural deprivation, learning
problems in, 505–512 (*see
also* Disadvantaged children)
Cultural factors in reading, 478–479
Curiosity, 283–284

Deficiencies in reading, 8, 113–118,
127
classroom methods in correcting,
94–100
Departmentalization in instruction
(*see* Team teaching)
Developmental reading, 96, 149,
529–535
Diagnostic procedures, 8, 15–23,
86–94, 115–116, 253–255,
547–548, 552–558
Dialects, reading program for
speakers of, 522–529
Dictionary (*see* Reference skills)
Differentiating instruction, 95–100
(*see also* Grouping pupils,
Individualized reading
instruction)
Difficulties in reading (*see*
Deficiencies in reading)
Directed reading lesson, 115, 117
368, 369 (*see also* Basal
reading instruction)
Disadvantaged children:
auditory perception, 507, 530, 532,
538

culturally, 9, 74, 192, 416,
    478–479, 505–512, 512–515
educationally, 9, 516–522
experientially, 506, 517, 518, 530
linguistically, in English, 516–522,
    522–529
materials for teaching, 532
preschool child, 536–543
progress in teaching, 529–535
teacher training for teaching,
    532–533
teaching of, 530–531
Dramatization, 131, 136, 140, 278
Dyslexia, 70, 76, 78, 79, 120

Early reading, 300, 314, 339–347,
    347–353, 353–358
Eclectic approach, 48, 50, 413–420
Emotional forces, 303–310, 342
Emotional problems, 114, 118, 127,
    513
Enjoyment, reading for, 140–141,
    177, 230, 285 (*see also*
    Extensive reading, Literary
    appreciation)
Environmental influences, 283, 297,
    300–301, 340–341, 346, 352,
    362, 479, 538
Evaluating instruments, 100–107,
    533–534, 572–582
Evaluating material read, 7, 266,
    268–269, 431, 437 (*see also*
    Organizational skills, Oral
    reading, Study skills)
Evaluating progress, 32, 101–107,
    371–372, 521–522, 533–534
    (*see also* Measurement,
    Teacher questioning, Tests)
Experience approach to reading
    readiness, 336–337 (*see also*
    Language experience
    approach)
Experience charts, 122–123,
    140–141, 521, 532

Experiences influencing reading, 9,
    11, 190, 192, 199, 345, 355,
    430, 506, 517, 518 (*see also*
    Affective dimensions of
    reading)
Extensive reading, 289–299, 306,
    363, 368–372
Eye movements, 15–16, 70, 127,
    454–455

Flexibility in reading, 137–138,
    459–465 (*see also* Rate of
    reading)

Generalizations, forming, 7, 14, 38,
    193, 242 (*see also* Critical
    reading skills, Literary
    analysis skills)
Gestalt concepts, 69–82
Goals of reading program, 7, 31–34
Grade levels, publishers and,
    164–168
Group learning, 65–66, 193, 500
Grouping pupils:
    ability, 96, 117, 138, 365, 366,
        371, 485, 489, 500
    flexible, 137–138, 365, 367, 369,
        459–465, 485, 494–495
    instruction, 88, 96–97, 129–132,
        137–138, 365, 483–484,
        485–486, 497–502
    interest, 97, 138, 371
    research, 138, 302
    team, 96, 138, 367, 497–500
    test scores, 546
    tutorial, 138
    whole class, 138, 365, 487–489,
        492
Groups, other when teaching one,
    129–132

Head Start, project, 9, 529, 534, 536,
    539

Independent activities, 129–132
Independent reading, 139, 152, 267, 281, 287, 289–291, 301–303 (*see also* Extensive reading)
Individual differences, 23–24, 81, 107, 186, 191, 341–342, 413–420, 484, 485, 486–497, 542
 nature of, 470–483
Individualized reading instruction, 89–94, 96, 118, 389, 420, 486, 490–492
Individualized reading, philosophy of, 368–372
Individualized reading program, lifetime reading habits, 299–303
Inferences, 7, 191, 199, 200, 245, 579
Informal appraisals, 18, 100–107
Informal reading inventories:
 group, 18, 102–104
 individual, 104–106
 limitations of, 108–113
 sources of, 106–107
i.t.a., 318, 394–397, 419
Inquiry, reading as, 251–258, 271, 509
Instruction in reading (*see also* Beginning reading)
 developing objectives, 35–42
 questions for instruction, 252–258 (*see also* Teacher questioning)
 time allotments for, 132–136
 unit teaching, 99–100
Intelligence, 9–11, 75, 190, 330, 475–476, 568
Intellect, components of, 227–229
Interests, reading, 26, 101, 136–141, 150–151, 152, 276–282, 282–289, 292, 344, 351, 352, 478 (*see also* Affective dimensions of reading)

Interpretation skills, 16–24, 436 (*see also* Reading skills)
Interviews:
 teacher parent, 145, 348
 teacher pupil, 20, 369, 371

Kindergartens, 9, 119, 317–321, 335–336, 342–343, 345, 346, 347, 349, 350–352, 514

Language ability, 44–51, 52–54, 56–59, 127, 300–365, 362–366, 498, 507, 508, 515, 538–539 (*see also* Oral language)
Language analysis skills (*see also* Context clues, Word analysis)
 Paragraphs and story, 11, 47–48, 173, 201
 Sentence, 11, 12, 47–48, 54–55, 172, 175, 194, 201, 204, 508, 521, 527–528
Language arts skills (*see also* Comprehension skills, Organizational skills):
 listening, 11, 12, 355–357, 507 (*see also* Oral language development)
 speaking (*see* Oral language development, Pupil interaction, Pupil sharing, Teacher questioning)
 spelling, 78, 79, 99, 351–352, 361, 366, 367, 379, 498, 500
 writing, 53–54, 123, 131, 136, 271, 296, 351, 361, 362, 364, 367, 370, 499, 500, 507, 532
Language experience approach, 118, 122–123, 140–141, 361–368, 531, 532
Language patterns: a linguistic view, 44–51
Learning theory, 13, 36–41, 231, 419, 478, 498, 505–512, 578

Levels of instruction:
   frustration, 548
   independent, 92, 102, 106
   instructional, 92, 96, 101, 102, 106,
      109, 111, 450, 478, 548
Libraries, 98, 100, 136, 151, 267,
   277, 297–298, 300–301
Linguistic factors in reading, 11–12,
   372–382, 419, 516–522,
   522–529, 532
Linguistically disadvantaged, 9,
   516–522, 522–529
Linguistics, structural:
   teaching suggestions, 52–61
   theory of, 44–51
Listening (*see* Language arts skills)
Literary analysis skills (*see* Critical
   reading skills)
Literary appreciation, 138–140,
   270–271, 282–289, 289–299,
   299–303, 362
   poetry, 131, 139, 279, 288, 296,
      438
Literature:
   a comprehensive program,
      289–299
   developing interest and taste in,
      282–289

Machines in teaching (*see* Teaching
   machines)
Materials for teaching:
   basal readers, 97, 164–168, 366,
      368
   controlled vocabulary in, 60,
      120–122, 153–157
   criteria for selection, 149–153, 281
   newspapers, 258–264, 366
   phonics, 158–163
   sources, 97, 131, 139–140,
      149–153, 295–297, 364, 431,
      491, 492
   textbooks, 151, 280, 499
   workbooks, 97–98, 115–117, 130,
      335–337, 346, 349

Meaning, reading for, 379 (*see also*
   Purposes for reading)
Measurement (*see also* Diagnostic
   procedures, Evaluating,
   Informal appraisals, Informal
   reading inventories):
   critical reading, 572–583
   diagnostic reading tests, 552–558
   reading readiness, 329–334
   standardized reading tests,
      545–552, 558–572
   survey tests, 552–553
Mental abilities (*see* Intellect,
   Intelligence)
   age, 476–479
Motivation, 12, 192, (*see also*
   Concepts formation,
   Purposes for reading, Teacher
   questioning)

Neurological dysfunction, 8, 13–14,
   70–71, 113, 118, 119–120,
   419–420
Nongraded school, 493–494

Objectives for reading instruction,
   35–42
Oral language development, 131, 136,
   267, 361, 362, 365, 397, 485,
   499–502, 507–508, 520, 567
   (*see also* Pupil interaction,
   Pupil sharing, Teacher
   questioning)
Oral reading, 12, 16, 39, 93, 96, 136,
   138, 186, 288, 340, 346, 363,
   365, 366, 381
   evaluating, 103, 104–106, 115
Oral responses, interpreting, 16–24
Organization of elementary school
   reading programs, 483–486,
   486–497
Organizational skills, 130, 131, 266,
   268, 364, 369, 370, 431, 437
   (*see also* Study skills)

Parents and:
the disadvantaged, 508, 534
phonics, 160–161
reading to children, 340, 351
report cards, 141–146
Perception, 14, 15, 17, 25, 29, 30,
33, 44, 76–77, 125, 449–450,
514 (*see also* Word
comprehension, Word
meanings)
whole word, 14, 72–74, 81, 124
Phonics, 81, 123–124, 140, 208–217,
345, 346, 367, 383–399, 436,
553
materials, 158–163, 385–397
Physiological factors:
laterality, 77–78, 419
motor ability, 11, 75–76, 77–78,
127, 331
sex differences, 191, 336, 474–475
speech, 71, 78–79, 191, 507
visual, 11, 70, 78, 331
Picture clues, 11, 205–206, 436
Poetry (*see* Literary appreciation)
Problem solving, teaching, 7, 65–66,
90–91, 264–274, 284, 425,
429, 437, 501, 508
Programed instruction, 94, 388–389,
400–413, 419, 499
Progress reports (*see* Reporting
pupil progress)
Psychological processes, 14–15, 25,
29, 30, 36–37, 69–82, 419,
501, 509–510, 580
Publishers, 158–163, 164–168
Pupil:
affective behavior, 302, 303–310,
494, 500, 501
identification with story characters,
293–294, 295–296, 302
independence, 130, 367, 369, 370,
372, 478, 486
interaction, 97, 117, 138, 365, 500
questions and purposes, 252–258,
271, 501, 509

research, 130, 131
responses, 18–23
sharing, 99, 138, 292, 298, 364,
365, 371
tutoring, 96, 138, 500
Purposes for reading, 8, 21, 74,
252–258, 271, 370, 426–430,
438, 441, 460, 461, 463, 464
(*see also* Study skills)

Questions, instructional, 242–251,
251–258 (*see also* Pupil
questions and purposes,
Teacher questioning)

Rate of reading, 8, 11, 12, 38, 39,
130, 268, 270, 345, 369, 436,
449, 450, 451–453, 453–458,
553, 568–569 (*see also*
Flexibility in reading)
scanning, 452, 462
skimming, 74, 452, 460, 462–463,
553
Readability, 164–168, 168–176, 190
Readiness for reading, 9, 52–53,
74–75, 300, 314–322,
322–329, 329–334, 334–339,
342, 344, 354–355
achievement, 329–334
current literature, 316–318
chronological, 343
developmental age, 74
developmentalists, 315–321
environmental factors, 74,
340–341, 346–347
experiences, prereading, 9
historical background, 314–315
intelligence, 74, 230, 330
kindergarten, 317, 318–319
letter name knowledge, 324–335
mental age, 335
research needed, 322–329, 333
social learning, 315–321, 332
spatial organization, 77
studies in, 334–339

Readiness for reading (*cont.*)
tests, 330–333, 334–337
visuo-motor, 78, 79, 331
word recognition, 336
Reading concepts, philosophical
differences in, 314–322
Reading defined, 28–30, 70, 243,
252, 325
Reading process and:
its ramifications, 6–27
psychological correlates, 69–82
Reading skills, 7, 18–21, 39–40,
50–51, 54–59, 96, 115–116,
130–131, 138, 151–152,
231–232, 365, 436–437, 498,
530, 566, 574 (*see also*
Context clues, Critical
reading, Language arts skills,
Phonics, Rate of reading,
Vocabulary, Word analysis,
Word recognition)
Reading specialists, 95, 98, 114, 484,
557
Reasoning, 200, 508 (*see also*
Thinking)
Recall, 106, 426, 431, 437, 498,
499–500 (*see also* Oral
language development,
Organizational skills, Teacher
questioning)
Records:
pupil, 369, 370
teacher, 369, 371
Reference skills:
dictionary, 7, 194, 205, 266, 267,
436
encyclopedia, 266, 267
library, 98, 136, 267, 491
locating materials, 267, 437 (*see
also* Self selection of reading
materials)
Remedial procedures (*see* Corrective
procedures)
Reporting pupil progress, 141–146,
437

Research:
needed, 337, 493
reported, 132–135, 208–217,
217–225, 242–251, 347–353,
435–446, 516–522, 572–583
Retarded readers, 9, 11, 13, 21,
25–26, 68, 94–100, 113–114,
174, 454

Selection of reading materials,
criteria for, 149–153
Self concept, pupil, 8, 9, 12, 26,
67–68, 99, 364, 486, 505,
507, 509, 510–512, 530, 549
Self selection of reading materials,
153, 267, 301–302, 305, 369,
478
Sight vocabulary, 7, 184–187, 206,
366, 367, 391, 392, 398, 436,
491
Silent reading, 16, 39, 105, 115, 136,
368, 370 (*see also* Extensive
reading)
Skills (*see* Auditory discrimination,
Comprehension, Context
clues, Critical reading skills,
Interpretation skills,
Language analysis skills,
Language arts skills,
Organizational skills, Reading
skills, Reference skills, Study,
Word recognition skills)
Social:
growth through reading, 295, 510
interaction, 66–67
problems, 114, 127, 510, 512–515
psychology of reading, 61–69
Speed of reading (*see* Rate of
reading)
Study:
effective, 422–435
skills, 432–435, 437, 440, 500
(*see also* Organizational
skills)

Subject areas, 19, 26, 99–100, 102, 104, 270, 280–281, 295, 296, 423–424, 430, 431–432, 433, 487, 498
   patterns of writing in, 435–446
   science, 516–522

Teacher:
   aides, 367
   abilities, 95, 98, 415, 418, 488, 510–512, 531
   as diagnostician, 16–24, 86–94, 100–107, 115, 415–416, 418, 549–550
   enthusiasm for reading, 287, 291–292, 297, 420, 491
   observations, 15–16, 92–93, 370, 501, 550 (*see also* Silent reading)
   personal qualities, 63, 64, 420
   or mediator, 510–512
   training, 45, 276, 304, 433, 487, 491, 532–533
   understanding, 523–524
Teacher questioning, 16–24, 105–106, 192–193, 231, 239–240, 242–251, 251–258, 279, 306–308, 351, 499, 509, 579
Teachers' manuals, 116–117
Teaching machines, 94, 400–413, 419, 446–453, 453–458
   accelerating devices, 451–452
   computers, 405–407
   directional control techniques, 449–450
   films, 455
   metron-o-scope, 454–455
   pacing machines, 455–456
   skimming and scanning, 452
   tachistoscopes, 14, 102, 186, 448–449, 456–457, 458
   talking typewriters, 318, 403–404

Teaching procedures, 6, 7, 11, 15–25, 24–25, 52–61, 86–88, 91–93, 94–100, 116–118, 129–132, 136–141, 186–187, 191–195, 346, 351, 362, 431 (*see also* Instruction in reading)
Team learning, pupil, 497–500
Team teaching and departmentalization, 492–493
Tests:
   auditory, 417
   diagnostic, 7, 9, 10, 16–17, 116, 169–170, 520, 552–558
   informal, 8, 19–20, 100–107, 108–113, 464
   intelligence, 9, 10, 330, 568
   oral, 7
   rate of reading, 568–569
   readiness, 7, 329–334
   reading capacity, 7, 10, 417
   standardized 16–17, 92, 242, 397, 417, 534, 545–552, 558–572
   study habits and skills, 7
   survey, 552–553
   teacher-made, 8, 101–102
   visual perception, 417
Textbooks, 164–168, 279–280, 436
Thinking, 20–21, 227–235, 235–242, 243, 258–264, 500, 501, 579
   frontiers in, 227–235
   teacher's task in development of, 235–242

Variety in the reading program, 136–141
Visual aids in teaching, 98, 100, 192, 363, 366
Visual discrimination, 11, 331, 514 (*see also* Word recognition)
Visual perception, 124, 126, 331, 417, 517
Vocabulary, 6, 106, 430, 507 (*see also* Oral language development,

Vocabulary *(cont.)*
Sight vocabulary, Word
comprehension, Word
meanings)
control, in materials, 60, 120–122,
153–157
Vowel rules, 208–217, 399

Word analysis, 46–47, 59–60, 72–73,
130, 171, 174, 184–187, 193,
199, 201, 335, 351, 357, 389,
393, 436, 501
Word comprehension, 71, 72, 73,
100, 125, 184–187, 187–197,
345, 358, 430, 491

Word meanings, extending, 7, 193,
344–345, 436
Word recognition skills, 7, 11, 17,
26, 39, 59–60, 73, 76, 93, 96,
130, 136, 184–187, 198–207,
344–345, 361, 366, 369, 371,
431, 436, 520, 521
accent generalizations, 217–225
grapheme-phoneme
generalizations, 7, 59–60, 124,
378
phonemes, 7, 47, 59–60, 124, 378
phonetic analysis, 92, 186, 199,
519
structural analysis, 7, 48, 186
Writing (see Language arts skills)